Percussion Instruments
and their History

by the same author

ORCHESTRAL PERCUSSION TECHNIQUE
Oxford: 1969: 1963: 1973
(Also in Japanese)

EARLY PERCUSSION INSTRUMENTS (with Jeremy Montagu)
(Oxford)

HOW TO PLAY DRUMS (with Johnny Dean)
(Elm Tree Books: 1985)
(St. Martins Press: 1992)
(Also in Spanish)

Contributor to The New Grove Dictionary of Music and Musicians
(ed. Stanley Sadie) (Macmillan, 1990)

Percussion Instruments and their History

JAMES BLADES O.B.E.

Former Professor of Timpani and Percussion
at The Royal Academy of Music, London, Hon. R.A.M.
and The University of Surrey, Hon M. Mus.

Revised Edition 1992

THE BOLD STRUMMER, LTD.

20 Turkey Hill Circle
P.O. Box 2037
Westport, Connecticut 06880

First published in 1970 by Faber and Faber Ltd.
This edition published by The Bold Strummer Ltd.
All rights reserved.
© 1970, 1974, 1984, 1992 by James Blades

Distributed in the /UK by
Kahn & Avrill
9 Harrington Road
London SW 7
ISBN 1-871082-36-6

Distributed to book wholesalers
and institutes of learning by:
Pro/AM Music Resources
63 Prospect St.
White Plains, New York 10616

ISBN 0-933224-61-3 paper
ISBN 0-933224-71-0 hard

To my wife Joan
and my friend Arthur Langford

A BOLD DRUMMER BOOK

Contents

Contents

Contents

Metric Conversion Table

INCHES	CENTIMETRES	INCHES	CENTIMETRES
½	1.27	11	27.94
1	2.54	12	30.48
2	5.08	15	38.10
3	7.62	20	50.80
4	10.16	25	63.50
5	12.70	30	76.20
6	15.24	35	88.90
7	17.78	40	101.60
8	20.32	45	114.30
9	22.86	50	127.00
10	25.40		

FEET	CENTIMETRES	FEET	CENTIMETRES
2	60.96	9	274.32
5	152.40	10	304.80
6	182.88	20	609.60
7	213.36	30	914.40
8	243.84	40	1219.20

Staff Notation Chart

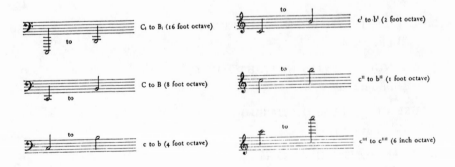

C₁ to B₁ (16 foot octave)

C to B (8 foot octave)

c to b (4 foot octave)

c¹ to b¹ (2 foot octave)

c¹¹ to b¹¹ (1 foot octave)

c¹¹¹ to c¹¹¹¹ (6 inch octave)

Illustrations

Plates

14. *Atumpan*, Ghana. From *Drumming in Akan Communities*. J. H. Nketia. Thomas Nelson & Sons Ltd.
15. *Balafo*, Central Africa. From *Nouvelle rélation de l'Afrique occidentale*. F. B. Labat, vol. II. By courtesy of the Trustees of the British Museum
16. Xylophone, *pandingbwa*, Central Africa. By permission of Musée Royal de l'Afrique Centrale, Tervuren, Belgium
17. Marimba, South Africa. By permission of Andrew and Paul Tracey
17*a*. **The Till Family Rock Band in the 1880'.**
18. Rock harmonica. By permission of G. P. Abraham, Keswick
19. Rock harmonica. (Richardson Bros.). By permission of the Fitz Park Museum Trustees, Keswick
20. *Mbira*, S. Africa. By permission of Andrew and Paul Tracey
20*a*. *Mbira* (bamboo slivers), Central Africa. Author's collection.
21. Ethiopian temple bell. By courtesy of E. Parsons. Photograph by M. Lindon
22. *Pien-ch'ing*. By courtesy of the Brussels Conservatoire. Photograph by A. C. L., Brussels
23. Gong-making (*a*) Semarang. From *De Gong-Fabricatie te Semarang*. By permission of E. J. Brill, Leiden, Holland
24. Gong-making (*b*) Semarang. From *De Gong-Fabricatie te Semarang*. By permission of E. J. Brill, Leiden, Holland
25. Gong-making (modern). By courtesy of the manufacturers M. M. Paiste & Sohn, Rendsburg. Foto-Gaspar, Rendsburg
26. Tam-tams, China. Author's collection. Photograph by Henry Ramage
27. Burmese gong chime. By permission of the Pitt Rivers Museum, Oxford
28. Bronze kettledrum, Karen people, S.E. Asia. By permission of The Horniman Museum, London
29. Raffles gamelan. British Museum. Crown Copyright
30. *Kemanak*. By courtesy of the Tropen Museum, Amsterdam
31. Music and Acrobatics – 'The Hundred Children'. Ming dynasty. By courtesy of the Trustees of the British Museum
32. *Tang-ku* (Hall drum). Author's collection. Photograph by Henry Ramage
33. *Bien-ta-ku*. Author's collection. Photograph by Henry Ramage
34. Braced drum, Sumatra. By courtesy of the Tropen Museum, Amsterdam
35. Wooden fish, *mu yü*. Author's collection. Behr Photography, London
36. Fish drum (wood), mid-Sumatra. By courtesy of the Tropen Museum, Amsterdam
37. Tiger, *yü*. By courtesy of the Brussels Conservatoire. Photograph by A. C. L., Brussels

Plates

Plates

57. Pair of ivory clappers. Egyptian, c. 2000 BC. By courtesy of the Trustees of the British Museum
58. Bronze sistrum. Egyptian, late period, after 850 BC. By courtesy of the Trustees of the British Museum
59. Bronze sistrum. Egyptian, late period, after 850 BC. (The discs and rods are modern.) By courtesy of the Trustees of the British Museum
60. Bronze cymbals. Egyptian, late period, after 850 BC. Connected by the original cord. By courtesy of the Trustees of the British Museum
61. Egyptian cymbals (bronze) 100 BC. (Mummy Ankhape – a musician). By courtesy of the Trustees of the British Museum
62. Bronze crotale discs. Thebes, c. 200 BC. By courtesy of the Trustees of the British Museum
63. Bronze crotales as clappers. Coptic period AD 400. By courtesy of the Trustees of the British Museum
64. Cymbal making – pouring (modern). By courtesy of Messrs A. Zildjian
65. Cymbal making (modern) – shaping and skimming. By courtesy of Messrs A. Zildjian
66. Crotales (modern). By courtesy of Messrs A. Zildjian
67. Finger cymbals (modern). By courtesy of Messrs A. Zildjian
68. Tympanon, Greece, fourth century BC. By courtesy of the Trustees of the British Museum
69. Clappers (*krotala*). Greece, c. mid fifth century BC. By courtesy of the Trustees of the British Museum
70. Scabellum and cymbals. Hellenic period, third century BC. Included in group of Grecian statues 'Invitation to the Dance' at Uffizi Gallery, Florence. Photograph by courtesy of Mansell Collection
71. Bronze cymbals (Greece) inscribed 'OATA', c. 500 BC. By courtesy of the Trustees of the British Museum
72. Cup-shaped cymbals. Roman, fourth century AD. Detail from the Silver Dish (Mildenhall Treasure). By courtesy of the Trustees of the British Museum
73. Tambourine, Roman relief, second century AD. By permission of Walters Art Gallery, Baltimore
74. Laced kettledrum, pottery (*tbilat*). By courtesy of the Tropen Museum, Amsterdam
75. Tympanon (Roman), c. second century AD. (Mosaic at Brading Villa, Isle of Wight.) By permission of Major Denys Oglander
76. Trapezoidal triangle with rings. (Richard III Bible, late fourteenth century.) By courtesy of the Trustees of the British Museum

Plates

77. Bronze cymbals. Marble bas relief (Luca della Robbia) *c.* 1430. Cathedral Museum, Florence. By permission of Mansell Collection
78. Cymbals, tambourine and nakers. 'The Assumption of the Virgin' Matteo di' Giovanni, late fifteenth century. By courtesy of the National Gallery, London
79. *Triccaballacca* (Neapolitan). By kind permission of Mrs. P. Troise
80. *Crécelle* (rattle). French fifteenth–sixteenth century. By courtesy of the Metropolitan Museum of Art, New York
81. Rommelpot (Dutch), after Hals 1580–1666. By permission of Mansell Collection
82. Tambourines. Marble bas relief (Luca della Robbia) *c.* 1430. Cathedral Museum, Florence. By permission of Mansell Collection
83. Timbrel (with snare). From an early fourteenth-century manuscript (English). By courtesy of the Trustees of the British Museum
84. Chime bells, handbells and dulcimer, etc. Hunterian Psalter. By permission of the University Library, Glasgow
85. Chime bells. Fourteenth-century Psalter. By permission of His Grace the Archbishop of Canterbury and the Trustees of Lambeth Palace Library
86. Chime bells. Luttrell Psalter, late eleventh or early twelfth century. By courtesy of the Trustees of the British Museum
87. Jingle ring and sistrum. P. Baudry (n.d.). By permission of Mansell Collection
88. Experiments in acoustics. Woodcut from *Practica Musicae*, F. Gaforus, 1492
89. Quadrangular psaltery, mid-twelfth century. Byzantine book cover (carved ivory). Said to have been made for Queen Melissenda. By courtesy of the Trustees of the British Museum
90. Pipe, tabor and dulcimer, etc. English, early sixteenth century. By courtesy of the Trustees of the British Museum
91. Béarnais strung drum and three-hole pipe. By permission of the Pitt Rivers Museum, Oxford

between pages 208 and 209

92. Turkish drum. Vittore Carpaccio, early sixteenth century. Accademia, Venice. By permission of Mansell Collection
93. Pipe and tabor. Richard Tarleton (Queen Elizabeth's jester) 1530–88. Portrait in ornamental letter T, published soon after Tarleton's death. By permission of Mansell Collection

Plates

Plates

147. Gusikow's xylophone (the player Mendelssohn so admired). By permission of the Austrian National Library, Vienna

148. Cimbalom. By permission of the performer, John Leach. Photograph by C. Brunel

149. *Tumir*, Southern Russia. By courtesy of the Museum of the Leningrad Institute of Music. Photograph by Micha Vofski

150. Devil's violin. By permission of the Horniman Museum, London

151. *Zilia massá.* (Thrace). From the Fivos Anoyanakis' (Athens) collection of Greek musical instruments

152. Mahir Karayïlan ('Black Snake') of Kastamonu, performing on the davul. Photograph by permission of B. C. Cawte

153. *The Soldier's Tale* ensemble. Newcastle, 1924. First performance in England conducted by the late Edward Clark. From the collection of Mrs. Edward Clark

154. Stravinsky in his Paris studio (1929). Photograph by Lipnitzki, Paris. Reproduced by permission

155. Hand-screw timpani (modern) by Boosey & Hawkes, London. Photograph by V. Hipgrave

156. Modern rotary-tuned timpano by Murbach, Lucerne

157. Machine timpani (modern) by Günther Ringer, Berlin. By courtesy of Messrs Ringer and Kurt Goedicke (London)

158. Leedy pedal timpani, *c.* 1935. Pawl system clutch. Photograph by G. Macdomnic. London

159. W. F. Ludwig 'Dresden' model timpani ('sawtooth' clutch)

160. Modern 'Dresden' timpani by Günther Ringer, Berlin. By courtesy of Messrs Ringer and Kurt Goedicke (London)

161. Pedal timpani by Premier Drum Co. Ltd., England. Balanced pedal action and rotary (foot) fine tuning. Neville Chadwick Photography, Leicester

162. Pedal timpani by Slingerland Drum Co., U.S.A.

163. Accu-sonic pedal timpani by Rogers Drums, U.S.A. Photograph by courtesy of Boosey & Hawkes, London, and Harrow Commercial Photos, London

164. Tuning gauges for pedal timpani. Ludwig and Premier. Photograph by courtesy of Percussion Services, London

165. Lapping drumheads (calf). L. W. ('Doc') Hunt, of the L. W. Hunt Drum Co. Ltd., London

166. Orchestral gong drum. L. W. Hunt Drum Co. Ltd., London

167. Orchestral bass drum (40″ by 20″) L. W. Hunt Drum Co. Ltd., London

168. Orchestral side drum. Premier Drum Co., Ltd., England

169. Deep orchestral side drum, showing snares. (Author's collection.) Boosey & Hawkes, London. Photograph by permission of the Galpin Society

Plates

TEXT FIGURES

Text Figures

Text Figures

Foreword

Everyone knows that James Blades is one of our great percussionists. He plays all the various instruments with accuracy and an infectious sense of rhythm, and his timpani playing is noted for its impeccable intonation and beautiful tone. I have been a lucky composer because, under my direction, he has played in ten of my operas, and also in those two difficult percussive nuts to crack – the *Nocturne* and *Cello Symphony*.

Not so many know that Blades is a brilliant and resourceful craftsman, experimenting with skill and ingenuity in the making and assembling of many of the instruments he plays, and in the creation of new ones. Some of the instruments he has made for me – often from the slenderest hints – are described in Chapter 16.

All his colleagues, and I am proud to consider myself as one, know what a generous friend Jimmy Blades is; how he will help an inexperienced player; how he will hurry to this or that school to advise the young in their percussion problems, or turn up at a recording session to give them confidence; and he will lend out his instruments, often at serious inconvenience to himself. We, who have toured abroad with him, have seen excited groups gathering around him after rehearsals and performances, commenting or questioning. Goodness knows what language he uses, but no matter, since he has a Slav-like ease of communication with everyone.

Now, on the publication of this great book, a large public will realise what a scholar Professor James Blades is. Of course many will have heard his enchanting lectures, or read his informative guides to Percussion Instruments, but now the vast range of his learning must come as a surprise.

Man, thousands of years ago, discovered that hitting something in a rhythmic way excited his friends or terrified his enemies, and through the successive years, in every part of the world, man has experimented with hitting something different in a new way. The results of these experiments are described and catalogued here, and are shown to us in exciting illustrations. For all its exhaustive information, James Blades' great tome is never exhausting, but is endlessly fascinating and entertaining.

BENJAMIN BRITTEN

Aldeburgh,
January, 1970

Author's Preface

The text of this volume is a record of the use of percussion instruments through the ages, and their purpose and mode of employment in the orchestra from the time of Bach to the present avant-garde. The technical aspect of these instruments I have discussed as a professional player without, I trust, becoming over didactic; an unnecessary emphasis in any case, in view of the high quality of the literature now available devoted to percussion technique. My endeavour has been to submit a balanced picture in chronological sequence of the development of the instruments of percussion. In assembling the known facts it has been necessary for me to profit from the research of others. In this to some extent I follow in the path of those who have been obliged both to burrow and borrow. I express my gratitude to those responsible for the information from which I have culled many facts, realizing that in many cases their information has been revealed only after long and tedious spade work. To begin a work that deals with a past shrouded in mystery, and to close it at a period of unparalleled activity and experiment has been no light task. It has, however, been to me a profitable endeavour, having brought to my notice many interesting facts of which I was previously unaware. I have said little of the frequent abuses to which percussion instruments are subjected – these are too well known.

Errors and omissions (on my part) I fear there must be. I can only ask for pardon with the same excuse as Dr. Johnson when a lady asked the reason for a mistake in his Lexicon: 'Ignorance, Madam, sheer ignorance.' In the final chapters outstanding examples by composers, some of whom have shown me great kindness, may have escaped me. I ask their indulgence, and at the same time tender my gratitude to the numerous composers past and present who have inspired the content of many of these pages. This leads me to say that without the assistance of a host of friendly people this book would never have been completed – quite possibly never started. This is particularly applicable to my wife, who, in addition to typing every word (at least thrice) has supported me physically and morally from the outset. I cannot speak too highly of the assistance and encouragement received from Arthur Langford, who as well as reading the typescript has given me unstintingly the benefit of his experience. Similarly my gratitude is due to my publishers for their constant sympathy and support.

The lack of space forbids me to acknowledge in detail my thanks to all who have given their assistance. Included are A. Hyatt King, Edward Croft-Murray and the staff of the British Museum. I am especially grateful to the Trustees of the British Museum for their permission to reproduce the numerous plates and MSS; Mrs. Jean Jenkins and staff of the Horniman Museum; the staff of the Victoria and Albert Museum; the Royal Manchester

College of Music; the Warburg Institute; the Royal Scottish Museum, Edinburgh; Pitt Rivers Museum, Oxford; Kneller Hall Museum; the Rotunda Museum, Woolwich; J. Wright Oxberry, the Fitz Park Museum, Keswick; J. D. Jones, Carisbrooke Castle Museum, Isle of Wight; the Historisches Museum, Basle; the Pushkin State Museum of Fine Arts, Moscow; the Museum of the Leningrad Institute of Music; the Rheinisches Landesmuseum, Bonn; Señor J. Ricart Matas, Museum of Musical Instruments, Barcelona; Dr. Olga Boone and staff of the Tervuren Museum, Brussels; René de Maeyer and Dr. F. J. de Hen of the Brussels Conservatoire; Dr. Gun Adler, Armé Museum, Stockholm; The Gemeente Museum, The Hague; the Tropen Museum, Amsterdam; the Paris Conservatoire; the Musée du Louvre, and the Institut National de la Propriété Industrielle, Paris; Sir Thomas Armstrong and staff of the Royal Academy of Music, London; Oliver Taylor; John Meloy and staff of the BBC Music Library; the Patent Office, London; The Metropolitan Museum of Art, New York; the New York Public Library; The National Library of Scotland; the Reid Music Library of the University of Edinburgh; the City of Edinburgh Central Library; the University of Glasgow Library; The Bodleian Library, and the Ashmolean Museum, Oxford; the Fitzwilliam Museum and the University Library, Cambridge; the Liverpool City Libraries; the Galpin Society; Messrs Mickleburgh, Bristol, and Messrs H. Potter.

Those concerned with the manufacture of percussion instruments have greatly helped me, e.g. Messrs Leedy, Messrs Ludwig and Messrs Zildjian of the U.S.A.; Günter Ringer, Berlin; Messrs Paiste of Rendsburg and Nottwil (Switzerland); and in Britain, the L. W. Hunt Drum Co, Messrs Boosey & Hawkes, the Premier Drum Co, and Messrs H. Band and Tuned Percussion. Helpful replies to enquiries have been received from such organizations as Deutsche Grammophon, and the Wagner Festival Theatre, Bayreuth. La Scala, Milan, and the Royal Opera House, Covent Garden, permitted me a study of their special percussion equipment, as did Messrs Ricordi of Milan. Publishers the world over have been extremely helpful. Among the composers who have assisted my enquiries are Stravinsky and Britten. I am also indebted to H. C. Robbins Landon, Charles Mackerras, Norman Del Mar, Professor R. Thurston Dart, Professor P. Kirby, Dr. R. Smith Brindle, Dr. Nigel Fortune, Dr. L. Picken, Professor H. V. Petrokovits (Bonn), Fivos Anoyanakis (Athens). Imogen Holst, Joan Rimmer, Dr. Grace Simpson, Dr. William Cole, Anthony Baines, John Wilson, A. A. Cumming, Noel Mander, Dr. Edmund Bowles, Ernest Borneman, John Levy, Walter Emery, Basil Ramsey, Raymond Raikes, Ubaldo Bardini, Barry Eaden, Andrew Ross, Lyndesay Langwill, Eric Halfpenny, Charles Cudworth, Dr. Hugh Tracey, Andrew and Paul Tracey, Guy Oldham, Ira Gale, G. P. Abraham, Captain Trevor Sharpe, John Hood Lingard, Lt. Col. Sir Vivian Dunn, Raymond Leppard, Dr. Paul Steinitz, Peter Reeve, David Charlton and the late Dr. F. Hiller.

Among my colleagues in Britain who have continually fed me with information are our most eminent players, and abroad, such household names as Gerassimos Avgerinos (Berlin Philharmonic Orchestra), Jan Labordus (Concertgebouw, Amsterdam), Saul Goodman (New York Philharmonic Orchestra), Tele Lesbines (U.S.A.), Professor Luigi

Author's Preface

Torrebruno (La Scala, Milan), Professor Richard Hochrainer (Vienna Philharmonic Orchestra), Micha Vofski (Leningrad) and Karel Černicky (Prague).

I have been constantly assisted in my research by Wendy Wills, Graham Melville-Mason, Jeremy Montagu, and my former students Eric Allen and Nigel Shipway. To all those mentioned and to those whose kindness may have temporarily escaped me, I tender my sincere gratitude.

London, 1970   James Blades

Author's Notes to the Revised Edition, 1992

It is surely fair to say that from the beginning of this century, and particularly from 1950 to 1975, no section of the orchestra has seen greater changes in instruments, orchestration, and techniques, than the percussion section. From 1975, however, the upsurge has perhaps been concentrated rather on techniques and their application than on the creation of the new and bizarre. The last sixteen years have seen far fewer innovations in percussion instruments than in the previous twenty. In the main, what new sounds have been employed by established composers have tended to rely upon extant instruments or the electronic variation of sounds produced by those instruments. Yet there have been commendable innovations, resulting in additional Bibliography, Recommended Literature, Techniques, Recital Works and Discography.

York University (G.B.) has recently acquired a remarkable collection of gamelan percussion instruments. Other recent collections of historic percussion include those of The Percussive Arts Society of America, the University of Edinburgh Collection of Historic Musical Instruments, and that of the Brithish Historical Drum Society, c/o Supreme Drum Co. of London, whose collection includes their mammoth bass drum measuring 13 feet in diameter and 4 feet in width.

The Zildjian family following the death of Avedis Zildjian in 1979, his sons Robert and Armand inherited and controlled the Norwell Cymbal factory in the U.S.A. In 1981 this partnership was dissolved and Armand, the elder son, took over the Avedis Company in Norwell, while Robert took over Azco Ltd. in Canada. As is his heritage and right, Robert continues to make cymbals under the 350-year-old traditional Zildjian process. These cymbals are known as Sabian cymbals, from the firm of Sabian Ltd. Meductic, New Burnswick, Canada.

In view of the prevailing reference (in English) to the *snare* drum as *side* drum in the standard repertoise and literature, *side* drum is used throughout these pages. Strictly speaking snare drum is currently correct, due to the popular use of the 'matched grip' and the declining use of the 'leg drum' angle in marching bands -thought by many to be a distinct loss of manly deportment.

The general interest in the art of percussion is reflected in an American Music Conference report which stated that in 1978 it was estimated there were 2,600,000 amateur percussionists in the U.S.A.

Many of the compositions etc. mentioned in the concluding chapters are no longer available and have been superseded, technically and otherwise by more advanced works, but as this is a historic survey, reference to them is included.

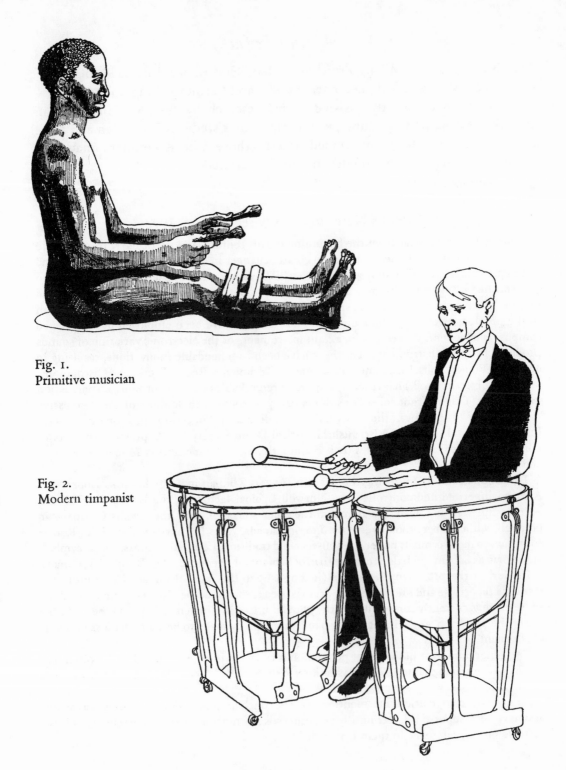

Fig. 1.
Primitive musician

Fig. 2.
Modern timpanist

I

Origins of Percussion

The story of the rise and development of percussion instruments is closely linked with the history of mankind and may justly claim to have exercised a tremendous influence on the human race.

The timpanist in full evening dress, performing with aplomb upon a group of foot-tuned kettledrums of burnished copper, reminds us of instruments much simpler, yet vital to the throb of life when the world was in its infancy. Forsyth[1] says: 'The first and lowest type of music is the purely rhythmical. So far as we can tell from records and from the study of savage races it underlies and precedes every other sort of music. It needs no instrument beyond the two knuckles of a man and a square of black mother earth.' Granet[2] believes however that 'The first crocodile created the harmony of the world when it drummed on its hollow belly with its tail.' (Why not the spider drumming on its web to attract its mate – or the male cicada, the drummer of the insect orchestra?). Yet other authorities say that the first musical impulses felt by any creatures of earth were those experienced by insects and birds. Forsyth[3] disagrees: 'The so-called "songs" of the birds have been cited in this connection. But they are really outside the circle of our argument. . . . One thing is indeed certain. No animals – not even the highest type of ape – have ever been observed to combine the sounds produced by their own muscular efforts into a series of beats at regular intervals; to combine them for the sake of their own pleasure; and to vary them when so combined. . . . These things, we know, cannot be; and the differences which they imply divide man at his lowest from the rest of creation at its highest'. Sachs[4] has his own view; discussing the

[1] Forsyth, Cecil and Stanford, C. V. *A History of Music*, Macmillan, New York, 1917, p. 3.
[2] Granet, Marcel. *Danses et Légendes de la Chine ancienne*, 1, Paris, 1926, pp. 263 and 326.
[3] Forsyth. ibid. p. 3.
[4] Sachs, Curt. *Rhythm and Tempo*, Norton, New York, 1953, p. 35.

33

remark of Hans von Bülow: 'In the beginning was rhythm. Organisation of rhythm came long after men – like the birds – had given melodic shape to mirth, and to mourning'.

Despite these conflicting opinions, the march of events in the history of music from prehistoric times to our own day offers no more fascinating study than that of the rise and development of the instruments of percussion. Much substantial evidence of their evolution is now at our disposal, and history has lately replaced myth. Modern knowledge of prehistoric and primitive instruments, the history of which may be traced back 30,000 years, is based on three substantial sources:

(1) Archaeological evidence (excavations, ice, sand and peat bog deposits etc.)
(2) Pictorial representations.
(3) Literary references, including studies of the numerous types of instruments preserved among primitive peoples.

Archaeological excavations supply the earliest substantive evidence of prehistoric instruments. In assessing their relative antiquity, however, it must be borne in mind that the existing specimens – mainly of bone, stone, pottery and metal – have survived either because of the durability of the materials used in their manufacture, or because they were preserved in some specially secure setting.

It would be interesting to be certain about the total range of materials available to early man and to know how many of them, in his struggle for existence, he was able to adapt as musical instruments, and to what purpose. History teaches us that Stone Age man was possessed of only one aim; to keep himself and his dependants alive. He had no set tribal laws, though families lived in small groups which gave them the advantage of extra protection from wild animals and extra man-power for hunting. Their religion was purely one of nature worship, with the greatest concentration on the animals they hoped to hunt on the following day. It seems doubtful if music was used to any extent at these ceremonies, which are believed to have consisted mainly of a pantomime of the proposed hunt and capture. (European cave paintings are devoted almost entirely to hunting scenes.) Since the Stone Age people were nomadic, having to seek where the game was most plentiful, they would have few possessions, and musical instruments of any size would prove too bulky and cumbersome to carry about; but their motor impulse was undoubtedly obeyed with a form of pre-instrumental music.

The seeds of the first instrument were sown unconsciously by an early man as he stamped upon the ground, beat upon his throat, clapped his hands, or slapped his body. He produced contrasting sounds with hollowed hands, flat palms, heels or toes, or by striking either bony or fleshy parts of the body. An early reference to the body slap can be found in the *Third Book of America*[1] which deals with the ancient Brazilian ceremony *tupinamba* (ritual fire dance) accompanied by *hochets* (*maracas*) and leg slapping. We are also reminded in Old Testament history of man's earliest rhythmic efforts: 'because thou hast clapped thine hands, and stamped with the feet, and rejoiced in heart . . .' (Ezekiel xxv. 6.).

Percussion – the act of striking – was an art in which primitive man was well skilled. He survived in every sense by the dexterity of his blow; from which it is fair to assume that the first instruments to augment the hand clap and stamp of the foot may have been the implements or weapons upon which he relied for food or survival. The striking of objects such as stones, the hide (or wood) shield, the hunting bow or the use of cudgels as clappers and so on, further suggests that implements used percussively were among the first instruments.

The practice of the warrior striking his shield or hunting bow to emphasize the rhythm of his battle songs has been described by many writers. Percival Kirby says: 'Undoubtedly the shield was formerly one of the principal drums of the Zulu.'[2] In a description by Rose (1829)[3] of a Kaffir ceremony, a reference is made to the women ranged in a semicircle beating upon the larger shields of the warriors as an accompaniment to their chanting.

Two rock paintings reproduced by Miss Helen Tongue[4] depict South African bushmen drumming upon shields. Stow[5] says: 'The Kaffirs proper had no musical instruments of their own; instead of drums they beat upon their shields.'

In describing a rock painting Stow discovered in Basutoland, he says: 'It is the representation of a dance in which a great number of Bushmen are engaged; the musician sits opposite to the centre of the line of dancers, whose bows have been collected and fixed in the ground before him, so that the strings are all on a level and inclined towards him, upon which he is playing by striking with a bow-stick; thus we are unexpectedly presented with the idea of a primitive dulcimer, composed of a combination of bows.'

The most important functions of the early percussion instruments were to assist the dance and to serve primitive magic and ritual. They were symbolic and possessed

[1] *Historia Americae*, part III, edited and illustrated by Theodor de Bry, Frankfurt, 1592, p. 228.

[2] Kirby, P. R. *The Musical Instruments of the Native Races of South Africa*, Witwatersrand University Press, Johannesburg, 1953, p. 23.

[3] Rose, Cowper. *Four Years in South Africa*, Colburn & Bentley, London, 1829, p. 141.

[4] Tongue, M. H. *Bushmen Painting*, Clarendon Press, Oxford, 1909, plates 14 & 15.

[5] Stow, G. W. *The Races of South Africa*, ed. G. M. Theal, Swan Sonnenschen, London, 1905, p. 107.

the power of magic. Few instruments were engaged in so many ritual tasks, or were held more sacred.

Despite the technical improvement in the construction and manipulation of these early instruments, they have never been freed from the supernatural power with which they were originally attributed. They remain indispensible in existing primitive life, in which is surely found an echo of the instruments of a bygone age.

EARLY INSTRUMENTS

Among the earliest instruments are found the percussion idiophones. These are instruments made of naturally sonorous materials, from which a sound can be produced without the addition of a stretched skin, string or vibrating column of air. They can be divided into several types:

(1) Shaken idiophones – sounding parts that strike together when the instrument is shaken.

(2) Stamped and stamping idiophones – pits, boards, hollow tubes.

(3) Scraped idiophones – rasps or notched sticks on which collision is created by scraping, resulting in a series of beats.

(4) Concussion idiophones – pairs of similar instruments, such as boomerangs or clappers.

(5) Struck idiophones – consisting of one or more pieces of sonorous material, struck with a stick or bone.

From a chronological point of view, it is interesting to observe that one of the first nursery toys with which we become acquainted is directly descended from what is considered to be one of the first instruments known to prehistoric man: Palaeolithic excavations have revealed a child's rattle made of clay.

RATTLES

In its earliest form the strung rattle (an instrument requiring little manufacture) consisted of a number of small hard objects such as teeth, hooves, shells or seeds laced or bunched together. It was used to stress dancing, the instrument being shaken, or hung from the ankle, leg, arm or neck of the dancer.

Rattles are found among the Bushmen of South Africa. The instruments (ankle rattles and bushman bells) are fashioned from the ears of the springbok, or dry hide. The ears – which are sewn together – are partly filled with small pieces of ostrich egg shell, or dried berries which act as rattling pieces. The bushman bells consist of large hollow balls made of dry hide, which contain a number of small pebbles. The 'bells' are fastened to the shoulders or upper arms, and shaken with a sudden jerk to the tempo of the refrain accompanying the dance. One of the commonest of South African rattles is made from woven palm leaves or a number of dried cocoons, in which are placed a few pebbles or hard seeds.

The use of a human skull as a rattle is described by Richard Wallaschek in 1893:[1] 'Even the human skull is used as a musical instrument – as a rattle. . . Its construction is as follows – the cleansed skull is covered with a wax mask stained with the red juice of *Arbus precatorius* and rattan stripes. The eyes are replaced by cowrie shells, and to the temples are fastened pendants as the natives wear them. The lower jaw is bound to the upper, and the whole skull, tied up with a thong and filled with stones, hard kernels of fruit, and pumice-stone, occasionally serves for a sort of rattle during a dance.'

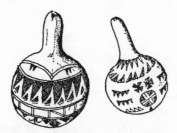

Fig. 3. Gourd rattles, Africa

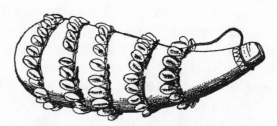

Fig. 4. Cowrie shell gourd rattle, Africa

The gourd rattle, in its simplest form a seed pod in which the dried seeds remain, or a calabash filled with small hard pellets (or seeds because of their magic potency), remains an important instrument of the North American shaman. These priests, traditionally men of extraordinary talents, are well-trained in poetry, medicine, philosophy, languages, athletics, conjuring and the art of music. When supplicating their gods, they have often moved men to teras with the magic of their poetry and music, accompanied in most cases with rattles.

The rattle is an important item of the equipment used by the African witch doctor. During the operation of ejecting an evil spirit, the 'medicine' man and his assistant shake their rattles and growl throughout the whole performance, in order to terrify the spirit and render the patient more susceptible to the uncanny influence of the ceremony. On occasions of this nature the illusion is often intensified by the use of rattles adorned with fetishes or the carved head of a supernatural being, while the various complaints are treated with separate rhythms.

[1] Wallaschek, Richard. *Primitive Music*, Longmans, London, 1893, p. 83.

Further afield we find the rattle in use at shrines in Korea, when a chanting priest invokes his god's attention by striking – with a small stick – a rattle held in his left hand. To the Brazilian who indulged in rattle worship, the rattle was the dwelling place of the devil (a custom observed also in Lapland).

Among the extensive and interesting collection of rattles in the Horniman Museum, London, is a fine Nigerian specimen from Benin. The instrument is in the form of a long ivory cylinder. The top, carved to imitate the joints of bamboo, is surmounted by a carved head and is hollow. It is deeply incised with geometric patterns. There are three long slits in the upper part, and a rattling piece of hard wood is enclosed. The rattle was used by a king of Benin to point out the animal to be sacrificed.

John Frederick Rowbotham[1] tells how, in a Guinea legend, a goddess gave a rattle to Arawoniti:

'As Arawoniti was walking by the river-side brooding over the troubles and miseries of humanity, a female form, the Crehu, arose from the stream, bearing in her hand a small branch which she presented to him, desiring him to plant it, and afterwards gather the fruit. He did so, and the fruit of the tree was the calabash. A second time did she arise from the stream, this time with some white stones in her hand, which she told him to enclose in the gourd. He did so, and this made the maraca.' It is under this ancient name that the gourd rattle survives in the modern Latin-American orchestra.

Certain rattles have seeds, shells or other rattling pieces outside as well as inside the gourd. The beaded calabash is of this type. It is a bottle-shaped gourd with seeds inside, whilst the exterior is covered with a network of beads or cotton mesh into which seeds are woven. Sound is produced from a beaded calabash in several ways.

A twisting movement in the air, or with the bowl of the instrument lying on the open palm, produces a swishing sound. An up and down movement combines the sound of a gourd rattle with the movement of the beaded framework, whilst a distinct click (acting as a timekeeper) is produced if the open palm strikes or is struck with the mesh.

Although little is known about the beaded calabash in early times, it is at present a widely used instrument. Its penetrating sound is a feature of the Latin-American dance orchestra, where it resides under the name of *cabaça* (see Latin-American Orchestra).

The shells of gourd rattles, the beaded calabash and similar instruments are provided in the main by the natural fruit. A handle and bowl are often fashioned, however, by the simple means of tying the calabash fruit near its stalk. The magical

[1] Rowbotham, J. F. *The History of Music*, Trübner, London, 1893, p. 19.

38

purpose of certain rattles is intensified by carvings on the shell, in the form of birds, crocodiles and animals.

A subsidiary rattle is added to certain instruments, as in the case of the reed-dulcimer – a common instrument in Africa, known as a corn stalk zither. This instrument is constructed from a number of corn stalks bound together with plaited grass. The 'strings' are raised over narrow wooden bridges in the manner of the

 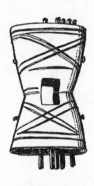

Fig. 5. Cabaça, Latin-American orchestra   Fig. 6. Wood rattle, Africa

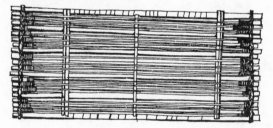

Fig. 7. Reed dulcimer, Central Africa

dulcimer or cimbalom. The seeds or pebbles which are inserted into the base of the instrument give a subdued rattle when the 'strings' are plucked.

The stamped pit, stampers, scrapers and clappers are contemporaries of the rattle.

STAMPERS

The stamped pit is a hole dug in the ground and covered with a rough wooden lid. In certain instances a board is fixed in the pit halfway down, so that the dull hollow sounds produced from the top of the pit and the mid-way board differ in pitch.

A variation of the stamped pit is a stamped curved board, positioned with the resounding cavity beneath. Stampers are still used by many primitive tribes. The

Royal Scottish Museum possesses a sounding board from the Andaman Islands in the shape of a shield. The narrow end of the board is embedded in the earth, whilst a stone supports the board at an angle. The performer strikes the board with his heel.

Among the implements used for stamping are sticks, gourds and tubes. Stamping tubes of suitable wood (such as bamboo) with both ends open or one end closed, are pounded against the ground, or against the player's bare flesh (thigh or knee). Tubes of varying length and diameter producing notes of different pitch are occasionally used in association with each other to produce a melody. Stamping tubes have a wide distribution. They remain a woman's instrument and are usually connected with fertility rites, particularly at sowing or harvest time. Mercedes Mackay says:[1] 'I think that the shantu of the Hausa harim are among the most fascinating and graceful of the Nigerian instruments. They are simply elongated gourds with a hole each end, and beautifully decorated with hot poker designs. They are used exclusively by the women in the harim and are played by stamping one end sharply against the bare flesh inside the knee with the left hand, while the right hand cups the hole of the other end.'[2]

The stamped mortar consists of a trough of stone or a wooden log. In the latter, holes of different shapes are fashioned. Rice is poured into the several cavities and stamped with pestles. The polytonic sound thus produced is used in connection with the rice ceremonials of Western Malaya and Siam.

SCRAPERS

This instrument is found as far back as the early Stone Age, when it almost certainly had the magical significance it still retains for primitive peoples. In its simplest form it consists of a notched stone, bone, shell or gourd, which is rasped with a stick or other rigid object, the sound being increased in certain instances by placing the instrument over a hole in the ground, or by fashioning the wooden instrument in the form of a box with a corrugated lid.

Evidence of the existence of the scraper in Central Europe in the early Stone Age is furnished by the palaeolithic bone scraper, with saw-like teeth, found in the Pekarna cave in Moravia. The instrument is exhibited in the Moravian Museum, Brno, Czechoslovakia. A few specimens have been found in archaeological excavations in America and Africa.

The bone scraper has been closely associated with the hunt, erotic rituals and

[1] Mackay, Mercedes. 'The Traditional Musical Instruments of Nigeria', *The Nigerian Field*, vol. XV no. 3. July 1950, p. 115. Arthurs Press Ltd. Woodchester, Stroud, Gloucestershire.

[2] Robert Farnon scored for stamping tubes (and *mbira*, q.v.) in his score for the film *H.M. O'Keefe* (1953).

funeral ceremonies. In ancient Mexico slaves scraped the bones of men and deer at the funeral of the king, and then they themselves were put to death. In erotic rituals the bone scraper possessed the power to arouse love. Sachs quotes the Cheyenne Indians:[1]

'Once there was a very beautiful girl in the camp, and all the young men wanted to marry her, but she would have none of them. The Dog Soldiers and the Kit Fox Soldiers had a dance, and each young man tried to do his best, but the girl would look at none of them. Then it came the turn of the Himoweyuhkis, and they felt discouraged, because they thought they could do no better than the other societies had done. But a man who possessed spiritual power spoke to them, saying, "That girl will be here to see you dance, and she will fall in love with one of you, and he will get her. Now go and bring me the horn of an elk – a yearling – one that has no

Fig. 8. Bamboo scraper, reso-reso, Mexico

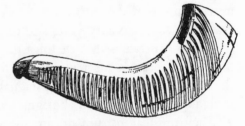

Fig. 9. Horn scraper, Mexico

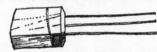

prongs on it, and the shank-bone of an antelope." The young men brought him what he asked for. He carved the elk-horn in the shape of a snake, and on it cut forty-five notches. Then he made from the shank-bone of the antelope an implement to rub over the horns; and this device was used in the dance. The girl was there to see the dance, and fell in love with and married one of the young men.'

Scrapers are found among the North and Central American Indian tribes, and among the South American tribes. The scraper is also widespread in Africa. A simple form of rasp is found in Portugal where two pine cones are rubbed against each other to mark time for dancing. In Central Europe use is made of a notched stick (*scadavaisse*) to which jingles are attached. In addition to its use as a provider of rhythmic accompaniment, the scadavaisse is used as a 'waker'. It is placed near to the ear of a sleeping person, and the 'alarm', a light tinkling sound, sounded by means of a gentle scrape. Instruments similar to the scadavaisse are found in Asia, some

[1] Sachs, Curt. ibid. p. 43.

equipped with small bells in place of the jingles. In some cases a number of bamboo rasps tuned to different notes are used as a melodic instrument.

The lore and magic of the scraper has been experienced in every continent and has survived into modern times.[1] As an instrument, the scraper in the form of a musical rasp cannot be seriously omitted from the percussion section of the modern orchestra. The stridulating sound is produced by the collision (striking) of the rigid object with the serrated edges or parallel grooves and not, (as may be reasonably argued) by friction (rubbing).

CLAPPERS

If the stamp of the foot, the slap of the body and the hand clap is accepted as a form of pre-instrumental music, the early use of clappers and concussion sticks as musical instruments would seem a natural development. It is interesting to observe the reasoning some seventy years ago of John Frederick Rowbotham on this matter.[2]

'It is to Australia – that we must turn if we would find the living resemblances to the musical instruments used by primitive man. In that tranquil continent not only has the animal and vegetable world stagnated, but human life "set" early and was fossilized; and so in the present aborigines we may see very well what we were ages ago.

'Their musical instruments are all extemporized for the occasion – thrown away as soon as used, most of them. Sometimes they beat two pieces of stick together, or two green branches, or, as the Moorunde natives, shake bunches of boughs. . . A considerable advance on the boughs and sticks was made when spears were used in the same way, or when the women rolled their skin-cloaks tightly together into a hard ball, and beat them upon their laps with the palms of their hands. For spears and cloaks are not things that would be thrown away the moment the performance was over, but once used and found effective would be employed over and over again; and thus by localising the production of sound to specific generators, the first idea of such a thing as a musical instrument would gradually dawn on the human mind.'

Archaeological and pictorial evidence in support of the universal use of the clapper is substantial, especially in Egypt and the Far East.

Two circular wooden discs (*kartal*) held in each hand and the faces struck are still used by Indian mendicants. Similar clappers are used by the Thonga natives to augment the sound of hand clapping. These clappers are made from flat slabs of wood, held securely to the palms of the hands by means of leather straps. They are occasionally used in various sizes to produce high and low sounds. A clapper is

---

[1] Cf. The *güiro* in the Latin-American Orchestra.
[2] Rowbotham, J. F. *History of Music*, London, 1893, pp. 17-18.

combined with an implement in the lime spatula used in south-east New Guinea. The handle of the spatula – used to convey lime to be chewed with betel nut – is split and forms a clapper. In the Society Islands (Central Pacific) pieces of pearl are used as clappers.

There is an endless fascination in the musical results of simple sounds from simple sources. The attractive click-click of the bamboo concussion sticks, for instance, in the hands of the Chow-chow man, plying his way and his wares through the streets of the busy Chinese city. Like the itinerant knife-grinder who was permitted by ancient privilege the use of a trumpet and, nearer to home, our own muffin man with his bell, the Chow-chow man with long bamboo pole balanced on shoulder, bowl of choice rice and meat on one end, portable charcoal fire on the other, calls attention to the excellence of his wares with a percussion recital, as insistent and intriguing as that of the maestro of the *claves* in the rumba band.

Simple sounds from simple sources – in fact, what appears to be more simple than a hollow tree trunk with one end covered with hide? Yet it is perhaps not so simple when we start to investigate the primitive drum and its development.

Bibliography: Chapter 1

ORIGINS OF PERCUSSION

DE BRY, Theodor. *Historia Americae*, part III, Frankfurt, 1592.

FORSYTH, Cecil and STANFORD, C. V. *A History of Music*, Macmillan, New York, 1917.

GRANET, Marcel. *Danses et Légendes de la Chine ancienne*, vol. I, Alcan, Paris, 1926.

KIRBY, P. R. *The Musical Instruments of the Native Races of South Africa*, Witwatersrand University Press, Johannesburg, 1953.

MACKAY, Mercedes. 'The Traditional Musical Instruments of Nigeria', *The Nigerian Field*, vol. XV, no. 3, July 1950, Arthurs Press, Stroud, Gloucestershire.

ROSE, Cowper. *Four Years in South Africa*, Colburn and Bentley, London, 1829.

ROWBOTHAM, J. F. *The History of Music*, Trübner, London, 1893.

SACHS, Curt. *The History of Musical Instruments*, Norton, New York, 1940.

—*Rhythm and Tempo*, Norton, New York, 1953.

SCHAEFFNER, André. *Origine des Instruments de Musique*, Payot, Paris, 1936.

STOW, G. W. *The Races of South Africa*, ed. G. M. Theal, Swan Sonnenschein, London, 1905.

TONGUE, M. H. *Bushmen Paintings*, Clarendon Press, Oxford, 1909.

WACHSMANN, Klaus. 'Some speculations concerning a drum chime in Buganda', *Man*, Jan–Feb, 1965.

WALLASCHEK, Richard. *Primitive Music*, Longmans, London, 1893.

2

The Drum

In our quest to trace man's earliest efforts to form for himself a drum, we are inevitably drawn to an instrument requiring little but the use of the crudest tools or weapons – the 'drum of the earth'. From the first travels of Marcel Griaule in Abyssinia we learn of the existence of a 'drum of the earth' – *wollogallu* – two holes of different depths in the shape of cones let into the ground. The orifices are beaten with the flat of the hands, the cavities vibrating in consequence. Dr. Paul Wirz[1] speaks of a similar instrument — a *sand-trommel*. He says that among the pigmies of New Guinea is found the 'drum of sand', a pit in the form of a small tunnel with two uncovered openings. The bridge between the two openings is beaten by the hand. In India, the Vedic Literature cites a 'drum of the earth' which is beaten by the priest at the winter festival.

Resonance from the 'drum of the earth' may well have suggested the log drum. In the form of the slit drum this instrument occurred chronologically with the stamped pit. It consisted of a hollowed tree trunk. Early man had discovered that hollowness is the first condition of resonance. The original instrument was placed over a pit in the ground and stamped upon, or (later) rammed with long sticks or struck with cudgels (as with the earth drum of the Catuquinarú Indians of Central Brazil).

Logs up to 40 feet in length were hollowed out through a long slit, the finished shell resembling a canoe, and possessing a resonant sound with considerable carrying power.

As with many instruments, the size of the slit drum diminished with its development. The types in use to-day vary from the small (portable) slit drums carried by Malayan watchmen, to the lengthy log which, to assist resonance, is placed on a framework of beams or four legs. The instrument is often expertly carved with head and tail, and decorated to resemble an animal, in much the same way as the food

[1] Wirz, Paul. *Die Marind-anim*, vol. 1, Hamburg, 1922, p. 80.

44

trough which, with its marked resemblance to a slit drum, suggests the early influence of food vessels on instruments of music.

The longitudinal cavity in the slit drum is fashioned with lips of different thicknesses, or large and small bores, to allow the instrument two distinct tones, one on each side of the aperture. The two notes are distinguished as male and female, the higher and stronger note usually being designated the masculine. On the Solomon Islands, however, the deeper sounding lip or end is called male and the higher sounding lip or end female. The double note of the early log drums was probably one of man's first steps in instrumental melody. In some instances the hollow interior of the slit drum is considered the home of the deity and the home of dead or still unborn sons. The tree drum is said to beat itself to create primeval waters. Apart from its magical significance, the large slit drum has been, and remains, important as a means of communication in primitive tribes. As a message drum it continues to 'speak' to a great number of people in the way it has spoken to their forefathers for centuries past.

In remote parts of Central Africa, the signals transmitted by means of a drum language (Bush Telegraph) consist of a form of Morse code. Strokes of differing strength and pitch provide a form of 'telephonic' conversation, by which news travels at considerable speed. The drum languages are as numerous as the almost innumerable languages and dialects of Africa itself. The early explorers were confounded by the obvious advanced knowledge of their movements over large areas. Stanley made constant references in his accounts of his expedition across Africa during 1875–77 to the sonorous war drums. Speaking of the tribe living on the banks of the Congo at the cataracts which now bear his name (Stanley Falls) he said: 'The islanders have not yet adopted electric signals but possess, however, a system of communication quite as effective. Their huge drums being struck in different parts convey language as clear to the initiated as vocal speech.'

The drum messages also play their mysterious part, it seems, in the transmission of a visible picture by telepathic means. This subject is far beyond the scope of this book (and its author), but there are those who speak of personal experience of this phenomenon. In *Africa Drums*, Richard St Barbe Baker, late Assistant Conservator of Forests in Kenya Colony and the Southern Provinces of Nigeria, remarks:[1]

'Sometimes my friends accuse me of being absent-minded when in my conversation; but at such times I am often feeling the pull of Africa: the drums may be calling – a picture is being mirrored in my mind. It is difficult for me to explain that in thought I am travelling thousands of miles and associating with my friends of the forests. As a blood brother of the tribe and an Initiate of the Kiama, I enter into their

[1] Baker, Richard St. Barbe. *Africa Drums*, George Roland, Wheatley, Oxford, 1953, p. 45.

secret meetings and share their councils round the camp fires. The rhythmic drums are ever talking, in mystic language more subtle than speech.'

The uncanny power of the drum is almost certainly an extension of that mystery – the phenomenon of sympathetic resonance. To the untutored savage, the roaring sound experienced when he placed his ear to the slit of the drum (as one places the ear to a suitably shaped sea shell) was a message from the supernatural; the voice of the gods. Sympathetic vibrations causing one drum to respond to the sound of its fellow, or to the human voice, (well known to the witch doctor), led to a further belief in the power of the drum and its magic powers, and to the reverence in which the instrument was, and continues to be held.

Certain slit drums are used solely for the purpose of transmitting messages from one kraal, village or tribe to another. The telegraphists frequently beat their drums from a hill top, or from a floating raft. The resonance and carrying power of some of these instruments is remarkable. This type of drum is sometimes in the form of a wooden gong, shaped like a cowbell, and is often suspended like a gong. The slightest flick of a finger produces a low boom. A blow with a beater so intensifies the volume that the sound is audible – to the trained ear, and under reasonable conditions – for a distance ranging from five to seven miles at night, and a mile or so less during the day. These distances constitute a normal working range, though it is claimed that given specially favourable conditions certain drums are audible over a distance of twenty miles.

Instruments of this kind feature prominently as museum pieces. Interesting slit drums are to be seen in the British Museum. The largest specimen is from Eastern Sudan. It measures nine feet in length and three feet in height, and is carved in the form of an animal with head, tail and four feet. The details on display read: 'Eastern Sudan Slit Gong used as the Khalifus war drum in the battle of Khartoum 1898 – given by H.M. George VI.' The reference to the slit drum as a gong here and elsewhere, raises an interesting point. Authorities disagree on the interpretation of the word gong. In his *History of Musical Instruments*, Sachs is emphatic in condemning its misuse in these words:[1] 'Many travellers, and even some anthropologists, call the slit-drum a "gong". This is an intolerable abuse; the word "gong" cannot designate anything but the bronze disk with turned-down rim which is made in India and the Far East.' Encyclopaedias and dictionaries generally support the metal disc; but it must be remembered that they normally refer to the instrument used in the orchestra.

Slit drums are common to many parts of Africa, Central and South America and the Far East (see China and Japan). Huge slit drums are used as a call to prayer in Burma; they are suspended vertically at the entrance to the temple. Slit drums are to

[1] Sachs, Curt. ibid. p. 30.

be found in the New Hebrides. These instruments – the Priest Drums – consist of a hollowed tree trunk, reaching to a height of 12 feet, which is carved to represent a monster with sinister face and body. The drum is played in an erect position. Its demoniac appearance is intensified by the light of the moon, for it is at the full moon that the natives gather to perform their special rites, the priest drummer casting a spell upon his audience with his performance upon instruments considered sacred, from which emerge voices also considered to be sacred.

Fig. 10. Khalifus war drum, Eastern Sudan
(British Museum)

A slit drum of pre-Aztec origin is found in the Mexican *teponaztli*. The slit in this instance is in the shape of the letter H carved horizontally in the wood shell. The tongues are chiselled on the underside to different thicknesses (or the section between the longitudinal slits divided unequally) to produce two distinct tones. The teponaztli is normally played (as it originally was) on a tripod, to increase its resonance. In some of these drums the quality of tone is sufficiently musical for a combination of several instruments to be used in melodic arrangements and, according to some scholars, this may have been their original purpose. The teponaztli is still used in Mexico on special occasions; it continues to be regarded with awe, and is preserved with great care and some secrecy. Museum exhibits included specimens of the teponaztli carved with lotus designs and ancient symbols, and shapes resembling animals, alligators, or grotesque humans.

Artistry is expressed in the carving and inlaying on many of the smaller slit drums of Africa and Central America. The ends are often in the form of people or animals – living and imaginary. The workmanship embodied in these instruments is all the more admired in view of the simplicity of many of the primitive tools used in the carving; superb pieces often being finished simply by burning and the use of stone chisels.[1]

A variation of the slit drum is the rubbed wood drum of New Ireland in Melanesia

---

[1] Slit drums are occasionally prescribed in modern works, e.g. Stockhausen's *Zyklus* and Berio's *Circles*.

known as the *livika*. This has three incisions of varying depth which form four teeth of different sizes. Four distinct tones are produced from this instrument by rubbing the teeth with the hand, which is smeared with resin or moistened with palm juice. There is an example of this instrument about 15 inches in length in the British Museum, where we are told: 'The livika is gripped between the legs and is played by smearing the hands with resin and drawing them across the keys. Its form represents a bird. It is played during certain ceremonies by a man concealed in a special hut, and its sound is believed by the women (who must never see it) to be made by ancestral spirits'. The tone of the livika is resonant and resembles that produced from a good violin when the bow is drawn over the open strings. The fourth (and highest) note of the livika tails off into a weird and peculiar whistle, well suited to the secret character of the instrument, and its use in death rites.

A STEP FORWARD

Of the numerous instruments of percussion, the membrane drum remains supreme. Its development provides a study of ingenuity and achievement. The covering of the hollowed log or clay vessel with a skin was a mighty step forward in the history of music. The discovery of such a form seems simple to us, but the savage with his rude reasoning refused to believe that a being like himself was capable of such an effort of intellect. Such intelligence was possible only in a deity, so the greatest instrument of savage legend shared the sanctity attached to its reputed inventor.

The instrument clearly existed before any historic record, but the claim of certain authorities that the drum was found earlier than any other instrument remains controversial and is unsupported by archaeological evidence. Such a claim must therefore be regarded as purely speculative. Although existing evidence suggests that the membrane drum was a late arrival in musical history, the possibility of an early use of fish, reptile and animal skin to cover a vessel, cannot be entirely disregarded. The durability of the materials used in the manufacture of the existing archaeological specimens (stone and bone scrapers etc. which have defied the destructive hand of time) and the perishable nature of skin and wood, must be taken into account before the drum's claim to be one of the most ancient instruments is dismissed. Its wide distribution further suggests its antiquity and, though in comparison with the gourd rattle, for instance, the membrane drum is a highly developed instrument, the surprising antiquity of many comparatively complicated instruments has been generally accepted.

The clay drums found in Germany and Moravia supply reasonable evidence of their existence in 3000 BC. Mesopotamian art depicts several types of drum around 3000 BC. The popularity of the membrane drum in the most ancient civilizations is established by the numerous representations of the instrument on monuments and in paintings of Egypt, Assyria, India and Persia.

The drum became indispensable in primitive life. It remains so. With few exceptions the most primitive tribes have drums even when they possess no other musical instrument. (The Vedda of Ceylon, perhaps the only race to possess no musical instruments at all, provide a 'percussion' accompaniment to their songs by slapping their naked bodies with their hands.)

The importance of the membrane drum and its influence on mankind through the ages is universally recognized. It is a vital instrument and the most compelling and significant of the instruments of percussion. Its use and development, if only because of its numerous forms and varying modes of manufacture – subtle or otherwise – is a story in itself. From its inception the drum had numerous ritual functions. It was credited with magical powers and was held more sacred than any other instrument.

How the first skin drum came into being must remain a matter of conjecture. The 'invention' of the instrument may have been the result of experiment or of pure accident; but if we are to judge from studies of primitive peoples, a reasonable conjecture would seem to be that the first skin drum was in the nature of a 'skin drum of the earth.' Who will deny the possibility of a new sound being discovered at the testing of the condition of a hide, which for drying purposes had been placed accidentally over a hole in the ground?

At an early stage a skin may have been dried and stretched by pegging on poles driven into the earth, as is observed in the *ingqongqo*, the most rudimentary type of drum found among the Bantu. The instrument consists merely of a dried ox-hide or bullock's skin suspended on poles, or held by the players who strike the skin with a stick.

The possibility of the early use of a skin held in a taut position over a receptacle is evident in certain primitive instruments of South Africa, particularly in the Swazi *intambula*. According to Professor Kirby, the name intambula is in all probability derived from the Portuguese *tambor*. Describing the instrument Kirby says:[1] 'It consists of a clay beer-pot or imbiza, over which a goatskin, not trimmed into circular form, is stretched temporarily. The hair of the skin is first removed, and the skin itself wetted. The player places the imbiza before him, and an assistant holds the goatskin tightly over the opening of the pot. The player then beats the intambula with a reed or stick held in his right hand. The intambula may be played by a single

[1] Kirby, P. R. *The Musical Instruments of the Native Races of South Africa*, Johannesburg, 1953, pp. 25 & 26.

individual. In this case he places the skin upon the ground with two of the leg-pieces towards him. He then kneels upon these to keep the skin in position, and, raising the skin, he puts the pot upon the ground beneath it. Then drawing the far edge of the skin tightly over the pot with his left hand and holding it in that position, he beats the "drum" with the stick held in his right hand.'

The next logical step was to find some means of securing the vellum permanently and this in all probability led early man in the direction of necklacing, by means of a circular cord near the end of a vessel; a desire to improve the resonance by a more secure method of tightening the skin may well have suggested the process of 'pegging', or 'buttoning'.

A study of the instruments used by primitive drummers of to-day shows a widespread use of pegging the skin to the vessel. That the method is age-old is proved by the form of the clay drum from the Stone Age (*c.* 3000–2500 BC) found in Germany, and those from Krapulay and Brozany (Bohemia), exhibited in the National Museum, Prague. The shells are fashioned with protruding 'studs' on which the vellum makes a firm grip. (The heads of many of the drums with wood shells, at present used in primitive Africa and elsewhere, are pegged or 'buttoned'. Similar protuberances are seen on a falconer's kettledrum (in metal) from 15th-century Egypt in the Livrustkammaren, Stockholm.)

The earliest drums were of wood, and were headed with the skins of water animals, lizards, fish and snakes. The shape of the 'shell' was gradually elaborated from the naturally hollowed tree trunk, to the vessel hollowed by fire or primitive tools.

Archaeological discoveries indicate that the original instrument was struck with the bare hands. All authorities agree the use of sticks occurred in later times and roughly coincided with the general use of the skins of cattle and hunted game, and in all probability with the invention of the *double-headed* drum, (one of our ingenious ancestors reasoning that two heads might be better than one). The classification of the double-skinned drum is difficult. Sachs places it in the Metal Age strata of his sequence. He says:[1]

'The purpose of the second skin could not have been for tuning, as the oldest drums were not tuned. These widespread examples of two-skinned drums filled with grain indicate that the second skin may have been originally necessitated by the filling.'

The change from the wood shell to a clay vessel presumably occurred with the advent of pottery; but if we are to study the earlier instruments in more detail and look for a typical example of the membrane drum in its original developed form,

[1] Sachs, Curt. ibid. p. 172.

we can hardly do better than to investigate the instrument's position in the culture of the remaining primitives of Africa and what is known of their predecessors.

AFRICAN DRUMS, DRUMMING AND DRUMMERS

Extracts from Portuguese books of 400 years ago refer to the existence and importance of the drum in South Africa. An extract from records of that period in the South African Public Library, Capetown, reads:[1] '. . . The king (Monomotopa) has another class of Kaffirs who are called Marombe, which means the same as "jester". These also go round and round the royal dwelling shouting in very harsh voices many songs and discourses in praise of the king . . . When the king goes out he is surrounded and encircled by these Marombe, who recite these praises to him with loud cries, to the sound of small drums, irons (m'bira) and bells, which help them to make a louder noise and clamour.'

The popularity of the drum throughout the continent of Africa has long been realized. Every race inhabiting this vast territory has, or has had a drum of some description during its history. No indigenous musical instrument remains as widespread or as greatly used. It has survived the influence of Western music and retains its dignified and unique position in contemporary life. It also retains much of its original purpose and form in multifarious shapes and sizes; these fall into two main classes (i) open drums; single-headed with an opening at one end; (ii) closed drums; single or double-headed with no open end.

Commencing historically with sections of tree trunk, we find the large tubular drum, still extant in primitive form in many parts of Africa, (and also in Oceania, South America and elsewhere). One end only of the tree trunk is covered with skin, whilst the opposite end is carved to form a foot, increasing the resonance of the drum by providing an outlet for the column of air. Drums not provided with this outlet are inclined whilst being played. Smaller footed drums are sectioned or fashioned with three or more teeth. The teeth also assist the instrument to be firmly fixed in soft ground, while the fashioned foot gives a grip and foothold on hard ground.

As with the log drum, the size of the skin drum diminished in the course of its development; the shapes varying from that of a hobby horse (ridden by the player with the skin between the thighs) to the slender *kalengo* (hour-glass) drum.

Large and small drums found among the Venda of the Northern Transvaal include the *ngoma*[2] and the *murumbu*. The ngoma is a single-headed drum with a hemispherical shell carved out of solid wood. The head, which is of cowhide, is pegged to the

---

[1] Theal, G. M. *Records of South Eastern Africa*, Capetown, 1901, vol. VII, p. 202.
[2] Ngoma is applied to various types of drums in other territories.

shell, which is carved and ornamented with handles. The murumbu is a smaller drum of similar design. The drums are used on many occasions in pairs – a style observed throughout the continent (and typical of the forerunner of the cavalry kettledrums, the Arabic *naqqarah*). As message drums the use of two instruments, of different pitch, (frequently considered male and female) permits a vast number of variations, corresponding to the mode of the slit drum. In some areas a piece of iron is occasionally fixed to the shell of the large drum of a pair. R. S. Rattray[1] was allowed to record the drum language of an Ashanti tribe, played by the master drummer on a pair of message drums (*atumpan*). Rattray says Lord Baden Powell became interested in drum language and that experiments in morse code with the dot and dash represented on the high and low sounding drums were carried out with fair success.

A single beater of hard wood is used to sound the ngoma of the Venda. Its uses are numerous. They vary from that of an accompaniment to song and dance, to use as a message or war drum, or its voice employed to invoke rain during a period of drought.

The use of drumsticks is common throughout Africa, though the instrument's highest expression is strongly associated with a characteristic style of playing by hand and stick. An indirect but interesting reference to drumsticks occurs in Fr. João dos Santos' description of his visit to eastern Ethiopia in 1586.[2] In a detailed description of the *ambira* (see xylophone) the instrument is described as being played with rubber-tipped sticks after the fashion of drumsticks. The drumsticks vary in construction from the heavy cudgel for sounding the ngoma and the more slender beater, tipped with rubber, to the elegantly curved sticks used with the Kalengo drum, and the thin bent sticks used in the *entenga* drum chime. To conform to ritual requirement, certain royal drums are struck with sticks made from human tibias.

To describe in detail the almost countless number of drums used throughout a large area of Africa is beyond the scope of this volume. The multitude of shapes and sizes of the instruments in existence in Central Africa, the majority of them primitive in origin, is discussed by Olga Boone (Doctor of Geography, attached to the Musée Royal de l'Afrique Centrale, Tervuren, Belgium)[3] in an exhaustive and informative volume dealing with the 'tambours' of Central Africa. Dr. Boone describes the magnificent collection which is the property of the Musée Royal. The collection comprises no less than 585 membrane drums.

[1] Rattray, R. S. *Ashanti*, Clarendon Press, Oxford, 1923, pp. 241–86.
[2] Theal, G. M. ibid., vol. VII, pp. 202–3.
[3] Boone, O. *Les Tambours du Congo Belge*, Tervuren, 1951.

Of the numerous shaped drums distributed throughout the continent, the most common are cylindrical or bowl-shaped. This type of drum – a kettledrum – is particularly associated with East Africa and the North (Sudan).

The design of the African kettledrum is an important feature in the story of the development of the instruments of percussion. The instrument consists of a bowl-shaped resonator, closed at the base entirely, or partially, with the top covered by a membrane. As a rule the skin is held taut with gut cords, which are directly attached to it, and secured to a smaller piece of hide which covers the lower part of the vessel. The smaller piece of skin is for securing the upper vellum, and is rarely used as a 'drum head'. The position of the loops for suspending the drum is at the top of the bowl, thus governing the playing position, which is usually upright.

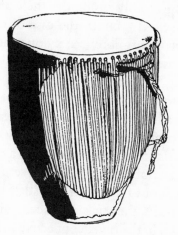

Fig. 11
Kettledrum,
Central Africa

The bowl-shaped resonator of the African kettledrum is made of wood. Authorities seem agreed that this shape is derived from an earlier clay form, and quote the similarity between drums and household pots, and with certain types of jars excavated from late Neolithic strata in Africa, Central and East Europe. To quote an early reference, Schreyer in 1681[1] says 'They take a pot and bind a skin over it, and on this pot the women beat with their hands and fingers, for these are their drums (trummeln) and kettledrums (paucken).'

G. W. Stow[2] describes similar instruments: 'Some of them were formed of a portion of shell of the great bush tortoise, the bottom being cut away and its place supplied with a skin stretched over it. This was probably the most ancient invention, and when such shells were not procurable, they were driven to the necessity of

[1] Schreyer, J. *Neue ost-Indianische Reisebeschreibung* etc. Leipzig, reprinted in *Reisebeschreibungen von Deutschen Beamten & Kriegsleuten* etc., Haag, 1931, p. 31.
[2] Stow, G. W. *The Races of South Africa*, p. 110.

substituting earthen pots, and these again from their liability of being easily broken in the excitement of the dance were displaced by a hollow block of wood or even a large calabash.'

Bamboo tubes used as water containers by certain tribes are often made into kettledrums. The gourd used as a receptacle for holding liquid is sometimes covered with membrane to form a drum. The Horniman Museum collection includes an instrument of this type. In Venezuela there is the *culo-en-tierra*, consisting of a coconut shell covered with skin and placed in a small hole in the ground.

Gourds and bamboo tubes are used extensively in the manufacture of primitive musical instruments, one of their most important functions being to give additional resonance; but though their function in this respect is primarily associated with the native xylophone, they are used ingeniously inside the shell of certain membrane drums, not only to strengthen the sound – but in the case of the tube to which a 'buzzer' is connected – to give a peculiar timbre (see xylophone and timpani).

Mercedes Mackay[1] refers to the use by the Hausa of calabash drinking bowls as percussion instruments, by reversing them on the ground and tapping them with fingers ringed with metal near the top joint.

In connection with gourds and additions to membrane instruments, reference must also be made to the friction drum, the shell of which in its original form consisted of a gourd or clay pot. Most friction drums have either a cord or stick passing through a hole in the centre of the membrane. The skin is set into vibration when the cord or stick is rubbed with resinous fingers, or the stick twirled between the palms of the hand. In some specimens the stick is placed within the resonating chamber and vibrated from below (as in the *cuíca*, connected with the modern Latin American dance orchestra). A primitive rubbed drum consisting of a small pit covered with a skin is used by the Bantu negroes. In Africa, the friction drum is the characteristic instrument at the initiation ceremony of boys and girls (see Rommel pot).

(Friction is employed on the vellum of a normal drum to produce glissandi, the player rubbing the skin with the moistened thumb or finger. When the drum is played in a squatting position, a similar effect is obtained with the heel. A sound like the roar of a lion is produced by these means from a large drum.)

In the majority of cases the drums so far described are single-skinned. They range from covered gourds and the roughly hewn and rudely covered log, to the more detailed kettledrum. Double-headed drums are less common, but similarly widespread. In some cases the membranes are pegged to the cylindrical shell, but much more frequently the skins are laced to each other.

[1] Mackay, Mercedes. *The Traditional Musical Instruments of Nigeria*, p. 114.

There is little evidence to verify an early appearance of the double-membrane drum in the musical culture of the natives of Africa. Professor Kirby[1] in referring to a cylindrical drum with two heads called *isigubu* as the last type of drum found in South Africa, says: 'The fact that no mention of the isigubu is made by the early writers, together with the fact that it is a double-headed drum, with the heads laced together, and beaten by two padded sticks, caused me to suspect long ago that it was not an original Zulu instrument, but had been deliberately copied from the European military drum, in all probability from the bass drum.' Double-headed drums resembling the European military bass drum and played in a corresponding position, are now fairly common in South Africa. In certain respects, however, there is a lack of European influence, as in many cases the heads on the African drum are braced to give different tones, and for certain purposes the instrument is played with either hands or sticks.

The most interesting double skinned drum found in Africa, however, is one that has little connection with Europe – it is the *kalengo*. This instrument is chiefly associated with Nigeria and the Guinea forest, where it bears dialect names such as '*fungu*' and '*popo*'. It has been quoted as the drum most heard in these territories. It is used by the Yoruba for their *sakara* dances, and as a means of signalling. The kalengo is a waisted drum, narrower in the middle than at the ends, taking the shape of an hour-glass. The skins are 'lapped' on cane hoops and laced together with gut strings or thongs of leather (see also the Japanese *tsuzumi*).

The drum is held under the arm (or in the hand) and, by squeezing the cords, the drummer puts pressure on the membranes and thereby alters the pitch. Only one skin of the kalengo is used for performance, the player, however, having the choice of either vellum, as they function similarly. The vellum is struck with the fingers or a short curved flat-ended stick.

The kalengo (or talking drum as it is often called) gives an example of an ingenious method of altering the pitch of a drum by pressure. The instrument is approximately 15 inches in height with the ends of seven inches in width. The body of the drum is of soft wood, so that the instrument is extremely light, its weight averaging little more than 16 ounces, except when small bells or similar jingles are added, or the shell partly filled with seeds to provide a subsidiary rattle.

Pressure on the cords gives a glissando and a range of several tones to the extent of an octave. Expert players (the Yoruba in particular) are able to imitate the rise and fall of the human voice, simulating the rhythms and inflections of their own dialect, and thus send signals or hold conversation with other players, or speak to those with the ability to interpret the drum language.

[1] Kirby, P. R. ibid. p. 45.

The Drum

Arthur Langford, who from 1951–5, was chief producer in the Nigerian Broadcasting Service, (now a Corporation) tells an amusing story of the possible misinterpretation of the kalengo's message in a country where the talking drum is in general use to translate a wide range of tonal languages and dialects. In the early days of radio in Nigeria, the kalengo's exciting tones made it an obvious choice as a tuning-signal, cutting cleanly through tropical atmospherics. The drummer copied faithfully the inflections of the English station identification: 'This is the Nigerian Broadcasting Service.' During the first week of its introduction between programmes the N.B.S. was inundated with complaints from various parts of the country, some of them accusing the radio of repeating vicious lies, others protesting at the obscenity of the message being transmitted; many explanations had to be made before the kalengo's notes were accepted simply as a tuning-signal.

Nowadays we are not compelled to visit Nigeria in order to experience the thrill of drum conversation. From time to time, recitals of African music are given in London and elsewhere, at which the beauty of the kalengo is demonstrated. (This remarkable instrument, with yet another dialect name '*bitin obonu*', has now entered the portals of modern jazz.)

The kalengo is but one of the many varieties of drums to be found in Nigeria. To quote a champion of the folk music of Nigeria, Mrs. Mercedes Mackay:[1] 'They range from the large *babba ganga* of the Hausa, to the beautiful "mother drum" of the Yoruba . . . Every size, every shape and every skin makes a significant difference to the meaning and rhythm . . . there is a substantial alteration of type and use for almost every tribe, of which there are two hundred odd in the territory.'

To the African, the drum can and does speak, therefore the 'talking drum' is not confined to any particular region. It is not necessarily an instrument in the shape of an hour-glass. In the hands of an expert what may appear to us an insignificant looking instrument will speak a drum language. Little wonder the drum remains supreme, and it is no surprise to find the drum sticks similarly respected, and that the wood for them is as carefully chosen as that for the shell of the drum.

Though the tree trunk is usually associated with the bodies of African drums, there are several interesting specimens with clay shells. The *sakara* drum of the Yoruba has an earthenware resonator with a vellum mounted in a manner so far not described. The shell is 10 inches in diameter and 1½ inches deep, and slopes funnel-wise for half its depth. (In appearance, the drum is not unlike a French sailor's hat.) The vellum is stretched over the larger rim to the full depth of the shell and secured halfway down with cord, or similar material (necklaced). The lower portion of vellum is then 'doubled back' and the membrane further secured by two or more short sticks.

[1] Mackay, M. ibid. p. 116.

The sticks are inserted close to each other into both vellums in the form of wedges, which lie an inch apart and surround the entire rim, thereby gripping the shell and stretching the skin outwards and taut.

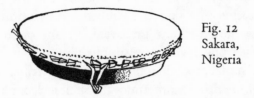

Fig. 12
Sakara,
Nigeria

DRUM MAKING AND RITUAL

The manufacture of an important drum is no light matter in primitive societies. The process is steeped in tradition. Certain rites must be observed during an instrument's construction.

The tree from which the body of the drum is to be fashioned is chosen with care. The wood must be hard and durable, and not easily spoiled by boring insects. The tree must be cut at an appropriate season. Before felling, homage is paid to the tree and various offerings are made to it. According to R. S. Rattray,[1] the custom in West Africa includes: 'First of all an egg is broken by being thrown against the tree, and the following words are spoken: "I am coming to cut you down and carve you, receive the egg and eat, let me be able to cut and carve you, do not let the iron cut me, and do not let me suffer in health" '. It is also believed that the drum-maker must shun water, which must not be touched with his hands, feet or lips before the drum is hollowed out, and on certain days he is obliged to fast. (Similar restrictions are imposed on the gong makers of the Far East). With the Lappons the fibres of the tree must grow in a certain direction; with other groups, the tree must not fall facing the direction from which the ancestors came. If the tree falls as intended, the body of the drum is fashioned on the spot. The finished shell is then taken back to the village to be covered; there the natives, suitably dressed for the occasion, await the final ceremony. In Melanesia (according to Sachs) the drum-maker climbs the tree that is to furnish the wood, and remains there until the drum is finished. In carving the shell, the drum-m aker is as concerned with the interior as with the outer shape. He constantly tests the pitch of the shell, usually with a thin stick, and carves the inside accordingly.

Fetishes are sometimes suspended from the sides of the shell; but more often they are placed inside the body of a drum before the skin is stretched across the opening

[1] Rattray, R. S. *Ashanti*, Clarendon Press, Oxford, 1923, p. 259.

These embellishments vary as they conform to the prevailing belief and include skulls, bones, shells, sacred stones, or part of an organ from the animal previously slain to supply the covering for the drum. In such a case the instrument is subject to various taboos, sometimes so severe that no-one dares to look into the drum before it is covered. On occasions the skins are rubbed with sacrificial foods.

With the Venda of the Northern Transvaal, a stone or stones called *mbwedi* are placed in the shell. The stones, which are supplied by the witch doctor, are supposed to be from the stomach of a crocodile, the totem of the tribe. Sometimes the fetishes hang from the side of the drum; sometimes the shell is decorated with a covering of leopard skin or coloured material, or again, the shell is carved with line designs.

In warfare the decorating of a drum with the skull or other remains of a defeated enemy was considered a symbol of the utter degradation of the victim. Nketia[1] says: 'Although it was disgraceful to lose one's state drums in war, it was even more humiliating for one to be beheaded, and one's skull or jaw bone or leg bone used for decorating drums. To have one's head hung on a drum symbolized a state of serfdom . . . The only consolation says the Akan maxim, was that the head enjoyed the music the better.'

The drum-maker is a man of importance and a skilled worker with the adze, axe and iron chisel. He is so revered in certain communities that only he is permitted to perform upon the finished instrument, which is sometimes made under conditions of secrecy. (In Oceania, a drum is considered useless if any female sees it before it is completed.) When the drum is completed, the maker prays to the god of thunder asking that the drum may sound well every day. At the inauguration of a new drum a dance is held, during which the instrument is beaten throughout the night. As a rule, drums are owned corporately, possessed by chiefs, or a shrine, or a social group.

The skins used in 'heading' African drums are as diverse as the shapes of the shells they cover: they include the hide of oxen and water animals, and the skins of sheep, goat, deer, buck, antelope, giraffe, zebra, monkey, leopard, gazelle, springbok, etc. The skins of reptiles and serpents, such as python and lizard are not uncommon. Among the more unusual membranes are skins from bats' wings, or elephants' ears, or the skin of a captured enemy. The skin from the ear of a female elephant is considered to give an especially rich tone. Varying powers are attributed to certain skins: cow hides, for instance, bring rain, while the dry, hard sound of a goat skin attracts thunder.

The thickness of the required vellum is normally determined by the size of the resonator. The source of supply is at times a governing factor, though in the case of royal drums or instruments for a ceremonial purpose, the ritual governing the

[1] Nketia, J. H. *Drumming in Akan Communities of Ghana*, Nelson, London, 1963, p. 122.

occasion must be observed. The skins may be dressed or undressed, depending on the type and purpose of the drum.

In the normal preparation of the hide the inner layer of fat is removed, during which process the vellum is 'evened' in thickness and such hair removed from the outer side as the purpose demands, usually from the centre. The skin may first be buried in the ground for several days to loosen the hair and flesh. In the final process the skin is moistened or greased, and then pegged out on the ground or fence, to be stretched and further evened before drying out in the sun. In mounting a vellum to a shell the skin is moistened. Moisture renders the skin pliable, so that it takes the shape of the shell easily and, in the case of necklacing, the sinew or cord bites securely on the vellum. Where the skins are pegged, buttoned, or braced, the required holes can be fashioned with reasonable ease in a moistened hide. In all cases a secured vellum shrinks and tightens in 'drying out'.

Skins are fastened directly or indirectly to shells, by one or more processes. They may be: (i) Necklaced; (ii) Pegged; (iii) Buttoned; (iv) Braced; (v) Glued.

(i) Necklacing is to tie with a circular cord near the head. The vellum is held secure by this simple operation which can be applied to shells of wood, clay or metal, often shaped or grooved to ensure a firm grip. Necklacing is normally used with drums of small circumference. A moderate adjustment can be made to a vellum so secured, all that is required to tighten the 'head' being to pull down the edge below the cord.

(ii) Pegging (Nailing) is applied to wood shells of all diameters, but in particular to single-headed drums with deep shells. Here the hide is secured to the shell directly by means of wooden pegs, or occasionally iron nails.

(iii) Buttoning secures a 'head' by means of looping. The skin is trimmed to form loops which are hooked to pegs in the shell, one or more loops frequently twisted to each peg. It is usual for the pegs to be driven at an angle into holes made in the shell – the further the peg is driven into the shell, the greater the tension on the skin. There are areas in which it is traditional for an elephant's tusk to be used for driving in the pegs. On occasions, the skin is pegged to a natural protrusion in the wood, or the shell is carved to form such.

(iv) Braced (or laced) skins exist in numerous varieties. The braces are made from thin strips of hide, or material twisted or woven into cord. The braces are directly attached, being laced through the holes in the skin. The cord that connects the two vellums of the double-headed drum is stretched along the body of the cylinder in a continuous series of V turns, or criss-crossed in the form of a net. A mixed tension in which the skin is both laced and pegged is not uncommon. Occasionally the cords are further tensioned with wooden dowels.

The woven designs employed in certain methods of lacing, are further proof of the considerable skill of the drum-maker.

Fig. 13
Pegged drum,
Central Africa

Fig. 14. Carved drum with lizard skins, E. Africa

Indirect bracing by means of circular hoops, over which the skins are rolled, (as in the majority of European side and kettledrums) is little used; the kalengo drum of Nigeria being a notable exception.

The method of mounting the vellum supplies the initial tension, some of which is lost in due course through constant use, bad storage and adverse weather conditions. The instrument is reconditioned by straining the head to the required degree of tautness by the application of heat, natural or artificial, (the sun's rays or the warmth from a fire) so that the drum is again tensioned to the desired pitch. If it is necessary to lower the pitch, it is customary with instruments of suitable design to moisten the tensioning cords, thus lengthening them fractionally.[1]

Quite often the head is weighted in the centre with a patch of paste (in the manner of the drums of South and North India – the *mridanga* and the *tablā*). In Africa, the paste is normally a mixture of bees' wax and roasted pea-nut powder. The tone of the drum is considerably deeper on or near the patch.

The Bible Society Centre in Edinburgh possesses an African drum with weighted head. The instrument is a tubular drum, twelve inches in diameter, and four feet in depth, with a skin (ox skin) pegged with bamboo pegs. The drum – from the territory of Livingstone – was originally used as a call to heathen dances and later

[1] In the cool of the night the drums are frequently 'tuned' during performance, cf. *bambus* and Japanese *o-tsuzumi*.

employed to announce Christian worship. A cross formed from strips of leather is pegged to the shell.

Some of the finest specimens of African workmanship are to be found in the drums of the Akan communities and Uganda. The *atumpan* are the principal talking drums of the Akan. They are a pair of bottle-shaped drums with the skins looped to pegs. This shape and style of head mounting is a feature of many Akan drums, including the *apentemma* and the *aburukuwa*. (The latter is encased in ornamental brass.) The atumpan, apentemma and aburukuwa are open drums, played in most cases with curved sticks.

Speaking of the atumpan and the drummers of Akan, J. H. Nketia says:[1] 'Of these the most important is the drummer of the talking drums, who alone may drum certain portions of the Akan drum language. He is considered the greatest of all drummers because of the breadth of his knowledge, the skill which his work demands and the role he plays as a leading musician in all ensembles in which the *atumpan* drums are used.'

Closed drums include an hour-glass drum – *douno* – resembling the kalengo. There is also the *etwie*, or leopard drum. This is 'headed' with the skin of a leopard, shaved to paper thickness. From this is emitted the sound of a snarling leopard when a bent stick is rubbed backwards and forwards on the vellum. Instruments resembling the ancient Sumerian hand drums are used in the popular bands.

The drums of Uganda can be classified in families: (i) Royal drums; (ii) the common drum; (iii) the *entenga*. The classification of royal and common can be applied to the majority of the instruments spread over the entire continent. The royal drums of Uganda vary in style and have many names, the largest instrument bearing the arresting title of *mujaguzo* (Jubilation). The most important of the common drums are the *embutu*, the *engalabi* and the *omubala*, of which the embutu is the standard drum and the most common in everyday life. The embutu is a kettle-drum. (Each tribe or district will have its particular name or names for a drum that is common to many territories.)

The engalabi is a long cylindrical drum with a single skin. It is usually coupled with the embutu in ensemble performances. The largest of the common drums, the *omubala* (counter) derives its name from its purpose, which is to count the thirty or more Ganda clans – reciting to the public during social functions, telling aloud the name of the clan. It is played with weighty sticks and the performer is often equipped with the leopard skin apron, similar to the bass drummer in the British regimental band. The embutu and the engalabi are played with the palms, the longer drum (the engalabi) playing counter rhythms to the rhythm of the embutu.

[1] Nketia, J. H. ibid. p. 153.

The Drum

The entenga (a drum chime) has the reputation of being the king of Ganda instruments, and until recently was reserved for royal occasions. It consists of a series of twelve drums tuned scale-wise, divided between four players, (the higher sounding drums to the left). An instrument of the entenga class is used as a carillon and a call to worship at the Nomebrembe Cathedral, East Africa, while the use of drums to accompany hymn singing in African churches is spreading rapidly.

One is reminded of the respect accorded to the standard drum (embutu) and its performer by the remarks of Joseph Kyagambiddwa[1] who says:

'Though the embutu's fundamental function is to support rhythm, yet its greatest service is that of rendering deeper effects to the music. Great drummers, such as Levi Nnyamayalwo of Masaka, play the embutu in a hundred styles – each style with its own name. For the embutu does not merely sound but speaks.'

Joseph Kyagambiddwa speaks for Uganda. He voices the feeling of reverence with which the drum has been held for many centuries throughout the entire continent.

Captain St. Barbe Baker[2] speaks similarly '. . . across the morning stillness of the valleys a man's voice called. It was answered from the distant hills like a faint echo. Again the silence. Suddenly the voice of a different drum, the lively N'goma with quick rhythmic beats, started in the valley. Then another along the winding trail among the small farms; then another from the crest of the escarpment. From all around the rhythm was taken up with ever-quickening time. Nearer and nearer they came, the chiefs with their drumming escorts, till the place of meeting was reached and the drums were silent.'

The experiences of people with first-hand knowledge of certain tribal customs, supply positive information regarding the ritual functions – actual and legendary. The stories they tell are startling, but by no means incredible. (In any case who are we to deny a race their beliefs, when there are many of us who will not walk under a ladder, particularly on a Friday?)[3]

The drum is credited with uncanny power. In addition to terrifying the enemy, its sound is believed to frighten the spirits of death and disease, and those of tempest and drought. It is credited with the power of speaking of its own accord in a moment

---

[1] Kyagambiddwa, Joseph. *African Music from the Source of the Nile*, Atlantic Press, London, 1956, p. 113.

[2] Baker, Richard St. Barbe. ibid., p. 9.

[3] The author's bass drum is possessed of a strange power according to the smallest member of his family. Whilst a repair was being executed to the cover of the instrument, the drum – due to the heads contracting in a changed atmosphere – creaked sharply, at which the child, quite startled, exclaimed 'Magic!'

of danger. In contrast, the drum is used to invoke good weather and a good harvest and, in the hands of the witch doctor, it has the supposed power to alleviate pain, the physician claiming to drive the headache from a patient by beating a drum near to the sufferer's ear.

The African medicine man is not alone in using the sound of a drum to assist his professional activities. In Europe it was the practice of the travelling dentists (tooth pullers) to conduct their business at fairs and similar functions. The platform would be assembled and a short entertainment given to attract and impress the customer. The subsequent operation of pulling the teeth was executed to the accompaniment of a lusty tattoo played on a drum, rendering the cries of the patient inaudible. An English painting on wood *c.* 1620 representing a football match, shows each side accompanied by a drummer who in addition to rallying his team is endeavouring to drown the cries of the injured, who are being attended by doctors. An earlier instance of such suppression could be quoted from the Old Testament, in which it is recorded that the sound of tabrets was used to drown the cries of human victims sacrificed in the fire.

For centuries the drum has been associated with royalty and affairs of state. The custom is world-wide; the instruments at times being considered so highly that none but a reigning monarch would possess them. In many parts of Africa, drums – particularly large kettle-shaped drums – have been thus revered and are symbolic of royalty. They are a safeguard, and a talisman for luck and victory. Their possession substantiates the claim to the throne, and on the reigning king's retirement the sacred instruments must be handed down to his successor to prove in turn his legitimate royalty. On the day of coronation the drums are the feature of the parade to the palace. They signify imperial authority: the king himself tapping a few beats on them before declaring himself to be the eldest son and the legal heir.

The royal drum is all powerful. In certain circumstances even the ruler is unable to silence its defiant note, neither is he able to order the state drums to be played for his own pleasure. After his death the drums are played at his shrine – to release his spirit from their power – beating the words 'I am now free'.

When not in use, the royal drums are stored in a drum-yard or hut, which is guarded by persons of the highest integrity. In East Africa, the drum-yard is considered holy. It becomes a sanctuary in which animals entering it become taboo and fugitives and fleeing slaves are afforded temporary immunity. If a condemned man succeeds in escaping to the drums, he is safe and becomes their perpetual servant. The performer on certain royal drums is granted notable concessions; as for instance the player of the 'golden akukua', encased in gold leaf, who may not be killed for any offence whatsoever.

The Drum

When a drum of importance is considered to be too old for further use, it is not discarded in a thoughtless manner. It is usual for it to be deposited in a sacred place and offerings are made to it. (Offerings of food to drums is referred to in an ancient Sumerian text.)

The ritual surrounding the drum and its manufacture is extended in some form or other to the drummer. Though a privileged person he is bound to observe tradition. He is invariabily humble towards his instrument and the legion of drummers who have preceded him. A master drummer will often precede a performance with a brief libation to his drummer ancestors who bequeathed to him their craft – or he may pray that witches will not seize his wrists and cause him to make mistakes.

In general it is customary for father to teach son, and drumming as elsewhere is a family tradition, though in the past in Ashanti '. . . a drummer should not teach his own son his art – should a father teach his son it is thought the former would die as soon as the latter had become proficient'.[1]

MODUS OPERANDI

Constant reference is made to drumming in the narratives of early travellers. Thunberg (1796)[2] describes a drum made from a pot covered with sheepskin well-moistened and secured by a thong. He states '. . . the players pressed the four fingers of the left hand upon the edge of the drum with the thumb in the middle, and struck upon the other edge with the first two fingers of the right hand'.

Twenty-eight years later, Burchell[3] refers to a drum used by Bushmen performers, which he calls a 'water drum' and describes as follows: 'This drum was nothing more than a bambus or wooden jug having a piece of wet parchment strained over the top, and containing a little water. This instrument was occasionally inverted for the purpose of wetting the parchment, as often as it became dry. It was beaten with the right forefinger, by one of the women; while she regulated the pitch or quality of the sound by placing the forefinger and thumb of her left hand, upon the parchment. It seemed to be accurately in tune with the voices of the assembly; a concordance which could hardly be accidental.'

Burchell refers to the method of striking the drum with the forefinger of the right hand, and controlling the pitch and quality of sound with the forefinger and thumb of the left hand. In 1838 J. E. Alexander[4] in describing his first impression of

[1] Rattray, R. S. ibid. p. 263.

[2] Thunberg, E. P. *Les Voyages de Thunberg*, Paris, 1796, vol. I, p. 233.

[3] Burchell, W. H. *Travels in the Interior of South Africa*, London, 1824, vol. II, pp. 65-7.

[4] Alexander J. E. *Expedition of Discovery into the Interior of Africa*, Colburn, London, 1838, vol. II, pp. 182-3.

a pot-dance, refers also to this style of execution in the following manner: '. . . one of these held before her a bambus, in which was a little water, and over the top of it was stretched a piece of sheepskin. This was occasionally wetted with the water inside, and was beaten with the forefinger of the right hand, whilst the pitch was regulated by the forefinger and thumb of the left.' This technique remains a feature of African drumming, which at its most complex may involve the full use of the hands, extending beyond the employment of finger and thumb to the use of the four fingers, thumb and palm of one or both hands.

Much of the technical aspect observed by the early explorers remains evident. Generally speaking, the technique of striking the drumhead varies according to the type of instrument and mode of drumming. Three different methods are employed; 'hand technique', 'hand and stick technique', and 'stick technique', all common throughout Africa, and governing broadly speaking the degrees of intensity, duration and tone differences.

'Hand technique', which enables the player to vary the tone quality and pitch, is normally adopted for drums of the sonorous type. The pitch and timbre are adjusted by the positions at which the drumhead is struck (generally: edge – high, centre – low) and by controlling the weight and release of the blow, as well as by using various shapes and parts of the hand, such as the base of the palm, and/or fingers spread or otherwise.

In 'hand and stick technique', the stick – straight or curved – is normally held in the right hand, whilst the left hand mutes or strikes a note as required. 'Stick technique' involves the use of a stick in each hand. This method is applied particularly to message drums, where a great weight of sound is necessary. With sticks, a slight variation in pitch and tone quality is produced by the timing and release of the blow, and in the depression of the drumhead by forceful strokes, and muting. A similar technique is included in the playing of certain Asian drums. (It is used to little extent in the West). The various styles of African drumming call for a specialized approach. Nketia[1] says: 'As a rule no drummer changes from one technique to the other while playing on the same drum at one and the same performance. His choice of technique for the particular drum is guided by tradition, for there is a prescribed technique for each drum, and the drummer is expected to make the most of the possibilities which it offers. Many drummers, therefore, specialise in one or more of the four techniques. A good player for the hour-glass drum (requiring armpit control) may be a poor exponent of the "hand technique", while an expert at the "stick technique" may not be found to be as good at the "stick-and-hand technique".'

---

[1] Nketia, J. H. ibid. p. 20.

(Similarly in the West, where the expert timpanist is not always a first-class side drummer, and so on.)

The constantly repeated basic rhythm (strictly adhered to) supports the master drummer whose exotic rhythms, calculated and improvised, cast a spell on all within earshot. As much to be admired as the skill of these musicians are their powers of endurance: a frenzied performance often lasts for several hours, or in the case of notable ceremonial celebrations, throughout the night.[1]

In a drum ensemble, especially when accompanying xylophones or other tuned instruments, the drums are often tuned scale-wise, or in such a way as to conform to the harmony of the 'orchestra'. The sound of the drums 'tuning up', together with the preparation of the xylophonists before a performance by a typical group of Chopi musicians expresses Africa, and equals in charm the delightful preamble of the Western orchestra which precedes the entry of the conductor.

Films, broadcast talks and television programmes, have made the man in the street aware of the superb artistry of these native musicians. Certain commercial recordings and the 'tapes' of private enthusiasts allow an impression of the excitement of the drum rhythms, but permit only a moderate analysis. In the words of the late Professor E. M. Hornbostel: '... it is syncopated past comprehension'. Admittedly so, but though a combination of various African rhythms is almost unanalysable, the results of some areas of enquiry must be accepted. For some time Western musicians have been interested, and influenced, by the seemingly basic principles governing African rhythm. Many of the separate units have long been recognized.

The Occident is by no means unacquainted with the intricacies governing the pulse of African music, and its challenge has stimulated enthusiasts to make exhaustive enquiry and experiment, providing in some instances a descriptive analysis of African technique. The Rev. A. M. Jones analyses it with confidence.[2] 'The writer makes two bold but sober claims: first; that the musical examples are valid for the points they illustrate; they are by no means a setting down of what he *thought* the Africans were doing; they have been tested by every objective means that he could devise. The more elaborate ones are transcribed from the markings made by an electric tape machine on a strip of paper. Such a machine is essential for complicated examples, for though the separate rhythms played by each performer may

---

[1] Perhaps not so remarkable a feat as that of the taborer who accompanied Will Kemp in his sensational nine days' dance from London to Norwich in 1600. Kemp, in addition to winning a bet, was awarded a life pension by the Mayor of Norwich. We trust the taborer was suitably recompensed.

[2] Jones, A. M. *African Rhythm*, Oxford, 1961, p. 26.

be simple, the method of their combination results in a sound so baffling as to be quite unanalysable without mechanical aid. The second claim is that the description of African technique is not an hypothesis; what is set down is what the African actually does. Any person who puts the matter to test with a party of Central Africans will find this to be so.'

'Drumming,' says A. M. Jones,[1] 'is the very heart of African music,' further adding that it is not syncopated, nor is it complicated, except for the master drummer. From his remarks and printed examples, it is clear that the main beats of the drums supporting the master drummer seem never to coincide, the main beat of the measure of the second player falling on the second beat of the measure of the first player, and so forth.

A. M. Jones is of the opinion that normally in African drumming 'there is never any beating of 2 against 3 or 3 against 4 in the European sense'. Hornbostel,[2] however, says: 'The combination of binary and ternary time is characteristic of African metre in general.' (Stravinsky uses this rhythm in *The Rite of Spring* [Cortège du Sage].)

By permission of Boosey & Hawkes Music Publishers Ltd., London.

The markings made by an electric tape machine on a strip of paper, and similar research, have in a sense laid bare a few of the African players' secrets, so that some would claim that any competent Western musician could reproduce African rhythms. Yet Professor Hornbostel[3] says: 'African rhythm springs from the drummer's motions and has far outstripped European rhythm, which does not depend on

[1] Jones, A. M. ibid. pp. 39 & 43.
[2] Hornbostel, E. M. von. *African Negro Music*, Oxford, 1929, p. 25.
[3] Hornbostel, E. M. von. ibid. p. 34.

motion but on the ear. A white man, even if he is the most capable of musicians, finds it hard enough to get hold of a negro melody or rhythm accurately.'

Dr. Tracey[1] says: 'When a drummer has to repeat his performance in exactly the same way each time to fit in with the set steps of the dancers or the set music of the musicians it will be easy to write. But on the other hand, where the drummer plays to his own fancy we shall not be able to write it down.'

The opinion of Western musicians may differ: some will support Professor Hornbostel, while others feel that the formula has made it possible to approach the root of African rhythm on a Western basis. Many, however, may have serious misgivings regarding a European interpretation of the original, reasoning (soundly) that a knowledge of the recipe does not make the cake and that, though the ingredients with complete instructions can be found in the cookery book, the finished article usually seems to taste better when 'Mother makes it'.

The drum continues to speak. During a dark period in our national history its defiant note carried a message in a manner worthy of the instrument's tradition.

We leave Africa for London, for Bush House, in the Aldwych; the time, late 1940. Towards the end of this eventful year, the European service of the BBC was considering a campaign to impress upon its listeners in the occupied countries the significance of the term 'V' for victory as a symbol of resistance. Attempts were made to put the morse code pattern of the letter V (. . . -) to music in the form of a short signature tune. The experiments tried with woodwind, brass and stringed instruments proved unsatisfactory. Finally, the author was requested to make tests upon various percussion instruments. Among the numerous instruments assembled none equalled the arresting note obtained from an African drum. (Similar, it is possible, to the note emitted from Drake's drum some 350 years earlier.)

After numerous experiments, the required four strokes were timed to occupy four seconds and were executed in this manner – the first three strokes occupying one second, the fourth stroke one second, with two seconds silence between the recurring patterns :

The studio clock was used as a metronome and the short and long notes of the morse code letter 'V' (and coincidentally the opening bars of Beethoven's Fifth

[1] Tracey, Hugh. ibid. p. 85.

Symphony, provided the quaver rest is mentally omitted) were faithfully imitated by 'shortening' the notes of the triplet and allowing the crotchet to 'ring'[1] (see *Timpani* technique).

The result was approved by the 'panel' and the signal adopted as an interval signal to precede the news broadcast to the occupied countries and elsewhere. (For technical reasons the African drum was subsequently replaced by two drums with screw tension.)

The recorded signal took a new form at the close of the war when a pair of kettledrums reinforced by the bells of St. Margaret's, Westminster, announced victory. The kettledrums were tuned to an interval of a fourth, with the notes sounding B flat and E flat to suit the pitch of the chimes.

The sound of the kettledrums (without the bells) is still used as an interval signal (or 'spacer') in the BBC European Service. It is possible that this, and the original signal, are among the most frequently heard sounds in the history of world radio. (Recorded with the assistance of my brother Thomas who controlled the vibrations.)

[1] The opening two bars of Beethoven's Fifth Symphony (with which the V-signal was so strongly associated) was used by several generations of orchestral musicians as a hailing signal.

Bibliography: Chapter 2

THE DRUM

ALEXANDER, J. E. *Expedition of Discovery into the Interior of Africa*, vol. II, Colburn, London, 1838.

BAKER, R. ST. BARBE. *Africa Drums*, George Roland, Wheatley, Oxford, 1953.

BALFOUR, Henry. 'The Friction-Drum', *Journal of the Royal Anthropological Institute*, London, 1907, vol. XXXVII.

BOONE, Olga. *Les Tambours du Congo Belge*, Tervuren, 1951.

BURCHELL, W. H. *Travels in the Interior of South Africa*, London, 1824, vol. II.

CHAUVET, Stephen. *Musique Nègre*, Société d'Editions, Geographiques, Maritimes et Coloniales, Paris, 1929.

HORNBOSTEL, E. M. von. 'African Negro Music', O.U.P. 1929 reprint from *Africa* vol. I, no. 1.

JONES, A. M. 'African Rhythm', Oxford, 1961, reprint from *Africa* vol. XXIV, 1.

KIRBY, P. R. *The Musical Instruments of the Native Races of South Africa*, Witwatersrand University Press, Johannesburg, 1953.

KYAGAMBIDDWA, Joseph. *African Music from the Source of the Nile*, Atlantic Press, London, 1956.

MACKAY, Mercedes. 'The Traditional Musical Instruments of Nigeria', *The Nigerian Field*, vol. XV, no. 3, July 1950, Arthurs Press, Stroud, Gloucestershire.

NKETIA, J. H. *Drumming in Akan Communities of Ghana*, Nelson, London, 1963.

RATTRAY, R. S. *Ashanti*, Clarendon Press, Oxford, 1923.

SACHS, Curt. *The History of Musical Instruments*, Norton, New York, 1940.

SCHREYER, J. *Neue ost-Indianische Reisebeschreibung*, etc; Leipzig, 1681, reprinted in *Reisebeschreibungen von Deutschen Beamten & Kriegsleuten*. Haag, 1931.

STOW, G. W. *The Races of South Africa*, ed. G. M. Theal, Swan Sonnenschen, London, 1905.

THEAL, G. M. *Records of S. E. Africa*, Capetown, 1901.

THUNBERG, E. P. *Les Voyages de Thunberg*, Paris, 1796, vol. I.

TRACEY, Hugh. *Ngoma*, Longmans, London, 1948.

WIRZ, Paul. *Die Marind-anim*, Hamburg, 1922, vol. I.

RECOMMENDED READING

NKETIA, J. H. *Our Drums and Drummers*, Ghana Publishing House, 1968.

WACHSMANN, K. P. 'Some speculation concerning a drum chime in Uganda', *Man*, Jan.-Feb., 1965.

3

The Primitive Xylophone

The xylophone in its simplest form originated among primitive men. It was one of the earliest melodic instruments. The earliest historical references suggest that it was widespread throughout Asia and Africa. The instrument consists of a number of wooden bars of varying pitch, the pitch being determined by the length, width and depth of the bar.

The original instrument, a leg xylophone, comprised one, two, or three rough slabs of wood, disconnected and of different pitch. These were laid across the legs of a player seated on the ground, in a manner observed in the prehistoric-type lithophone of similar proportions, discovered in use in Indo-China as recently as 1958.

It can safely be assumed that in experiments to produce a fuller sound, the bars would be supported on the shins of the player at the two points corresponding to the nodes of vibration, and that early use was made of a pit dug between the legs to form a resonance chamber, as with the stamped pit. Sticks or clubs were used to strike the bars. The playing of two slabs, with their differing notes, constituted an early effort at instrumental melody. This simple instrument developed into the log xylophone, with the bars loosely laid on two parallel logs. Later, the bars were made fast to a structure resembling a table, or a frame which hung at the player's waist.

Owing to the perishable nature of the material used in the construction of the xylophone, archaeological excavations are not helpful, and no early specimens have been preserved.

Pictorial representations take us to Asia – to the reliefs at the temple of Panataran in Java, carved in the fourteenth century. Literary references concerning Asia point to the metallophone of AD. 900 as an extension of the already highly developed trough xylophone. (The first mention of the xylophone in Europe appears in 1511.)

The invention of the xylophone is lost in antiquity, and it is to Africa that we must turn to make acquaintance with the instrument in its near original form, and to observe its development, for it is here – in remaining primitive cultures – that some of the earliest types of xylophones are still to be found. In the middle of the sixteenth century early explorers found the instrument in an already elaborate form, fully resonated and very similar to instruments in present-day use. Fr. João dos Santos describes such an instrument in a record of his visit to eastern Ethiopia in 1586[1]: 'The best and most musical of their instruments is called the ambira, which greatly resembles our organs; it is composed of long gourds, some very wide and some very narrow, held close together and arranged in order. The narrowest, which form the treble, are placed on the left, contrary to that of our organs, and after the treble come the other gourds with their different sounds of contralto, tenor, and bass, being eighteen gourds in all. Each gourd has a small opening at the side near the end, and at the bottom a small hole the size of a dollar, covered with a certain kind of spider's web, very fine, closely woven, and strong, which does not break. Upon all the mouths of these gourds, which are of the same size and placed in a row, keys of thin wood are suspended by cords so that each key is held in the air above the hollow of its gourd, not reaching the edges of the mouth. The instrument being thus constructed, the Kaffirs play upon the keys with sticks after the fashion of drum-sticks, at the points of which are buttons made of sinews rolled into a light ball of the size of a nut, so that striking the notes with these two sticks, the blows resound in the mouths of the gourds, producing a sweet and rhythmical harmony, which can be heard as far as the sound of a good harpsichord. There are many of these instruments, and many musicians play upon them very well.'

Professor Kirby, an authority on African musical instruments, remarks[2] '. . . This is an extraordinarily interesting description. Its date clearly shows that the instrument was developed entirely without European influence. It will be noted that the performers upon it were specialists, and that its name ambira is the same as mbila, by which it is known to-day. Further, that the beaters had heads made of balls of sinew, not of rubber, which is invariably used at the present time . . . João dos Santos' statement that the slabs of wood of higher pitch are placed to the left of the instrument does not hold nowadays; but his account is so wonderfully accurate that one hesitates in suggesting that he was mistaken in this solitary particular.'

The xylophone in Africa 400 years ago, then, was already highly developed, and from Fr. Santos' observation – he noted many instruments and many players – firmly established as a popular instrument, and one demanding great skill, differing little in essentials from the native xylophones of to-day.

The placing of the higher sounding bars to the left of the instrument, which

[1] Theal, G. M. *Records of South Eastern Africa*, vol. VII, pp. 202–3.
[2] Kirby, P. R. *The Musical Instruments of the Native Races of South Africa*, p. 48.

surprised the European explorer, is puzzling. Possibly the arrangement of the bars corresponded to the style employed by the drummers (if any) of this tribe. Certainly no influence from Asia, where, for centuries, the lowest note on primitive instruments – such as panpipes – is said to have been on the left side.

About the time of Fr. Santos' discovery, there is evidence of the xylophone in Uganda, found by the legendary leader Kato Kintu (c. 1550–1610). Joseph Kyagambiddwa[1] in *African Music from the Source of the Nile* says: 'There are two kinds of Ganda xylophone — the *Akadinda* and the *Amadinda* . . . the Akadinda was the original type of xylophone that Kintu (ancient hero of the Baganda) and his men found in Muwawa (Uganda). He entrusted its care and improvement to the *Envubu* (Hippopotamus) Clan – one of the Egyptic indigenous clans. The Baganda developed the Akadinda from seventeen to twenty-two keys.'

F. B. Labat[2] in a work published in 1728 refers to a similar instrument to that discovered 150 years earlier by Fr. Santos: 'The native folk have an instrument on which they play to amuse themselves, called the balafo. It consists of 16 hard wooden strips, as broad as the thumb . . . of which the longest is 18 thumbs' length and the shortest seven to eight thumbs' length. They are arranged on a small frame about one foot high, on the edges of which they have fixed with nails this strong leather . . . which keeps the blocks spaced regulary. Under the keys, they attach calabashes, from trees, round, and of unequal sizes, that is to say that they put the largest ones under the longest keys, and this in descending order of size. This instrument bears a resemblance to our organs, and emits an agreeable sound, varied by the manner of touching the keys with two sticks, almost the same as drumsticks. They cover the head of the sticks with leather so that the sounds are softer.'

The arrangement of the wooden slabs shows a similar method of insulation to the Asian trough xylophone (and the modern orchestral xylophone). Note the care taken in spacing the blocks regularly and the covering on the beaters, a constant effort to produce a fine musical sound from simple materials.[3]

Literary reference to the xylophone from the sixteenth to the nineteenth century and the more recent works dealing with the progress of this instrument provide a wide range of information, leaving little unanswered except the link responsible for the similarities between the advanced xylophones of Africa and those of Indonesia.

On this point the opinions of the musicologists differ. Ankermann denied any

---

[1] Kyagambiddwa, Joseph. *African Music from the Source of the Nile*, p. 115.

[2] Labat, F. B. *Nouvelle relation de l'Afrique occidentale*, Paris, Cavelier, 1728. pp. 332, 333.

[3] The references to the beaters being covered with leather are significant and will be considered in the context of the unending controversy as to the possibility of some form of covering of the sticks used on the kettledrums during the classical period, or earlier.

contact; Hornbostel believed there was a contact and found analogies between the scales of Java and Africa. Nadel disagreed with Hornbostel; Kunst was convinced of the contact, believing that the Javanese *slendro* and *pelog* scales were exactly reproduced in Africa. Although some doubt has been placed on the accuracy of his measurements, the comparison is still valid. Sachs states firmly that the advanced xylophone of the African primitives was borrowed from the higher civilizations of the Malays. Professor Kirby's opinion is that Indonesia has played a not inconsiderable part in the development of Central African culture.[1] The Belgian scholar Dr. Boone feels that more research along ethnological lines is needed before any decision is reached.

One thing is certain – with the exception of the means of resonating the bars (the Asiatic trough and the African gourd) the *gambang* of the Far East and the gourd and xylophone of Africa, have undoubtedly much in common. These similarities suggest a personal contact through migration or commerce, as in the case of Central America, to which the xylophone travelled westward, crossing the Atlantic with the slave trade.

To treat the numerous aspects of the xylophone exhaustively is not the purpose of this volume, nor is it possible to cover such a vast subject in a single chapter. We can only note its development and use, past and present, and observe its influence on a familiar and active member of the 'tuned percussion' group in our modern orchestra.

Those who desire a better acquaintance with the historical details, disposition, manufacture and employment of the xylophone, are recommended to the extensive and well-documented research of such authorities as Ankermann, Hornbostel, Nadel, Schaeffner, Kunst, Sachs, Kirby, Jones and Boone.

Professor Kirby has dealt as thoroughly with the African xylophone as with any of the instruments he describes in his admirable work on the musical instruments of South Africa, whilst Dr. Boone[2] gives us an exhaustive survey of the xylophones of Central Africa, together with a detailed description (including over 50 plates) of the instruments domiciled in the Musée Royal de l'Afrique Centrale, Tervuren, Belgium.

In observing the xylophones of Africa, present and past, one becomes aware of two features. First, that the instrument is essentially an instrument of music, and apart from its use on occasions for the purpose of 'signalling' in the manner of a drum, it is connected entirely with entertainment and pleasure. It has little connection with ritual performance. Secondly, unlike the primitive xylophones of the

[1] See Kirby's 'The Indonesian Origin of Certain African Musical Instruments', *African Studies*, vol. XXV, no. 1.66. Witwatersrand University Press, Johannesburg. 1966.
[2] Boone, O. *Les xylophones de Congo Belge*, Van Campenhout, Brussels, 1936.

Pacific and Far East which were played in many instances by women, the African xylophone seems essentially an instrument concerned with the male sex.

The constant reference by early travellers to the musical quality of the instrument, and to the high standard of performance on it, is echoed in present-day experience. Together with the drum and the *mbira* (a plucked instrument consisting of a series of thin iron tongues, or slivers of bamboo cane clamped to a soundboard, whose invention is credited to Africa) the xylophone remains one of the most expressive instruments of this most musical continent.

As with the drum, the manufacture of a xylophone – often with the crudest of tools – is a work of considerable skill and importance. For an instrument of superior quality the slabs are cut from durable, resinous wood. Settala, mutondo, takula and mwendze are typical. Pine and deal are also used, though the softer woods, particularly if unseasoned, suffer considerable alteration in pitch as they dry out, sharpening with the consequent shrinkage.[1]

The pitch of each wooden bar is governed by several factors – the nature of the material, the length and width of the bar and its depth. If the bar is thinned in the centre in the form of an arch ⬚ the pitch is lowered considerably. In some cases the bars are tuned by tapering the ends. (There seems no evidence of the tuning of the bars of the African xylophone by means of weighting with wax, etc., observed on some xylophones of the Far East.)

The bars are mounted in a single row in various ways, depending on the style of the instrument and local customs. With the primitive log xylophone (which is not resonated), the bars are quite free, merely resting, with no form of insulation, on the supporting logs which lie on the ground. In more elaborate xylophones of this kind the bars are 'spaced' by means of bamboo strips or lengths of other wood, which are driven into the supporting log at the required points. These methods apply in the main to sizeable instruments, with bars ranging from a foot to three feet in length. On occasions the lighter bars tend to 'wander' during performance. It is amusing to watch the player (or an assistant – usually a boy) juggling them into position with a lightning stroke of hand or foot. Occasionally the bars are left free on smaller instruments, offering the advantage of easy transportation. The player removes the bars from the frame and rolls them into a bundle which he places under the arm. With the other hand he grasps the framework and the 'deck is cleared'. With such instruments the player will at times juxtapose the bars to suit his convenience – a recourse by no means unfamiliar to the chimes player in the Western orchestra. Where the instruments have fixed bars, the slabs are secured by lacing, pegging, or

[1] For the bars of the orchestral xylophone and marimba, it is customary to use Honduras rosewood, or a plastic material. See Orchestral Xylophone p. 403.

75

both. They rest on a cushion of fibres, beaten bark or similar substance fixed to the upper edge of the framework – made of banana stems or wooden poles, which are sometimes long enough to form handles for carrying the instrument.

The various means of securing the bars to the frame have a common feature. The holes bored for the pegs or lacing material, if so secured, occur at the nodal points. If the bars are laced to the frame, the cord is laced round the bar at this same particular point, thus ensuring the utmost resonance. (It is possible to place considerable pressure at the points mentioned, without reducing the resonance to any degree; a detail further discussed in a later chapter.) Normally the bars are drilled vertically for pegging at one end only, the other end being held in position with lacing or spacing pegs.

Fig. 15
Xylophone bars, pegged and laced,
Congo

Other methods include both ends laced with the lacing round the bar, or passing through two holes bored at the nodal points, or one hole bored horizontally through the bar. The two latter arrangements enable the bars to be suspended in the framework; both being particularly applicable to the xylophone with gourd resonators.

It is in the resonating of the bars of the African xylophone that a distinct feature is observed: it is usual for each bar to have its own resonator, in contrast to the Asian trough xylophone where the bars are suspended over a wooden cradle, a style of resonating infrequent in Africa.

The separate resonators are spherical or tubular, consisting of gourds, cucumber-shaped calabashes, or similar receptacles, with an opening at the top. The Horniman Museum collection includes a xylophone with cow horns serving as resonators. Nadel refers to a pumpkin-shaped vessel as a resonator.

Xylophones used in the Rand mining area are equipped with resonators made from empty tins.

In all cases the resonators hang at a given distance directly beneath the wooden bar, strung to cross members of cane or wood, or secured by wax to a piece of wood pierced with holes to correspond with the number of bars, the resonator with the greatest air content being placed below the lowest sounding bar, and so forth.

The function of the resonator is to amplify the sound of the bar. Each gourd or calabash is chosen or cut, so that the frequency of the air column contained in it corresponds to the frequency of the bar above it. The fundamental note of the bar is thus considerably strengthened, particularly in the shallow bars of the deep sounding instrument which, frequently thinned for half their length to a depth of quarter of an inch, have an indistinct note of little volume unless aided by the resonator.[1] A feature of the resonator is the ingenious buzzing contrivance which forms a vibrator and amplifier. This mirliton device consists of a tube or ring which is inserted into the gourd or calabash. The opening at the face of the tube is covered either with a skin formed from the substance covering spiders' eggs, or a portion of bat's wing, or wafer-thin membrane. (Cf. Mexican marimba and Deagan 'Nabimba').

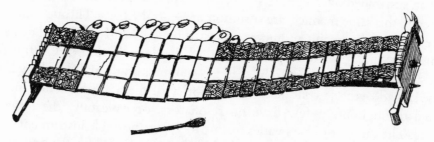

Fig. 16. Gourd-resonated xylophone, Central Africa, (British Museum)

Individual differences are observed in the various African territories, mainly in the design of the framework, the materials used in construction, the tuning of the scales and the method of performance. In most cases the instrument bears a tribal name. Dr. Boone, Stephen Chauvet, and Professor Kirby, designate the instrument in their works dealing (all in detail) with African musical instruments. Briefly, the profusion of local names can be thus summarized: marimba; malimba; jimba; madjimba; akadinda; amadinda; balinga; mandjanga; balafon; manza; mbila and timbila. Of these numerous appellations, the western world (Mexico, Central and South America in particular), has adopted the native name marimba and applied it, as far as the orchestra is concerned, to the deep sounding resonated xylophone, distinguishing an orchestral instrument so named from the higher sounding xylophone (resonated or otherwise).

In Africa, generally, Nadel says:[2] '. . . if we use the name marimba for this instrument we signify the gourd xylophone.' It must be borne in mind, however, that there are territories where the unresonated xylophone is called a marimba, and that

[1] Cf. Orchestral marimba (*Marimba a Basse*).
[2] Nadel, S. F. *Marimba Musik*, Holder–Pickler–Tempsky, Vienna, 1931, p. 5.

the name marimba is also applied in some cases to instruments of the *sansa* type (mbira).

Percival Kirby says:[1] 'The most elaborate musical instrument found in South Africa is the resonated xylophone, commonly called marimba. Two varieties are met with, the first among the Venda and the second among the Tshopi. Both are called by the same name, mbila, and both are constructed on the same principle; but the two types are made from different materials, and the two races have each their own manner of performance.'

Such similarities and differences occur throughout Africa. Similar methods of construction are used on instruments ranging from a single bar to those with twenty or more keys – such as *Venda mbila* and the *Ganda akadinda*. Instruments with a single bar, suspended over a gourd resonator, and those with two bars, mounted and resonated in this same manner, are common in Central Africa. Throughout this vast area the xylophone remains an important instrument. The Musée Royal de l'Afrique Centrale, Tervuren, Belgium, possesses a remarkable collection of Central African musical instruments. Here are to be seen xylophones, crude and developed, typical of those spread over the continent. The majority of them are moderate in size and resonated throughout. A few have no resonators, or have only the lower notes resonated. The number of bars varies from 5 to 17, the portable instruments seeming to average from 8–12 bars. In her analytical notes dealing with the collection Dr. Boone describes more than 100 of these instruments.

Large instruments built in the form of a table, with slabs three feet in length are used in the Rand mining area; here are found the *timbila* bands, in which up to 30 instruments are employed, many of the players being Tshopi people from East Africa, a race of xylophonists. In such an ensemble, the instruments are placed in three rows. The players upon the large instruments perform in a standing position, behind the instrumentalists performing upon smaller instruments. These performers are seated, with the instruments laid on the ground. The xylophones are treble, alto, tenor, bass, and double bass, each with appropriate native names. The double bass xylophone in the timbila band (*gubu*) is often confined to three or four slabs.

In other circles it is not unusual for players to be placed on each side of the instrument, normally a sizeable log xylophone. In this case the bars are struck on the extreme edges instead of the centre. Smaller xylophones are frequently played at an angle, with the ends of the bars farthest from the player tilted upwards. The manner of supporting the instrument in this position varies – sometimes it is propped up with stones or spare gourds, or held in place with a cord from the player's shoulders, or

[1] Kirby, P. R. ibid. p. 47.

strung to stakes in the ground. For marching purposes, a small xylophone is suspended in front of the player at waist height.

Little change is observed in the general construction of the African xylophone of to-day, and those discovered by the early explorers.

Since the discovery of the instrument, the concern of the African xylophonist (and maker) has been for the production of a mellow sound; a quality of tone, together with the covered beaters, referred to by successive explorers. The characteristic tone of the African xylophone is also rendered individual by the tuning, which to western ears has an intriguing quaintness.

Musicologists have undertaken a vast amount of research in an attempt to define the scales to which African xylophones are tuned. Briefly it may be said that no apparent standard pitch is observed, that a lack of detailed accuracy in tuning is noticeable, that the foundation or tonic note of the scales, whilst normally tuned to one pitch in a given territory, varies from area to area. By a comparison of numerous specimens, it has been found that the scales tend to fall roughly into seven or five notes.

Hornbostel,[1] in comparing the scale to the white notes of our keyboard, says: 'The scale of the instrument in itself mostly precludes an *organum* in its strict sense; the fourths and fifths are not exact, and the neighbouring steps are not always equal in size.'

Monochord measurements of a number of museum exhibits of the xylophone type, taken in this country and elsewhere, reveal similar differences. Deductions from such sources are naturally somewhat 'sketchy' due to 'weathering' and similar prevailing conditions, and should be taken with due reservation.

In general, the compass of the African xylophones appears to cover a range of little more than four octaves (with the bars arranged in a single row in all cases). Joseph Kyagambiddwa[2] shows the range on the Ganda akadinda as:

Percival Kirby[3] quotes from his collection, an mbila with 21 notes sounding thus:

[1] Hornbostel, E. M. von. *African Negro Music*, Oxford, 1928, p. 21.
[2] Kyagambiddwa, Joseph. ibid. p. 115.
[3] Kirby, P. R. ibid. p. 52.

The Primitive Xylophone

An instrument in the author's possession with similar intervals spread over 17 notes has a range (sounding 8 va.):

Native xylophonists use a similar and comparable technique to the drummers. (According to Hornbostel, African rhythm is ultimately founded on drumming.) The methods are taught systematically, in most cases skilled players imparting their art to their descendants.

Sachs says:[1] 'Though xylophone music is melodic, a strong motor impulse still shapes its melodic style. Obeying the hands rather than the mind, the player indulges in shakes, graces, rolls and flourishes, mostly in a giddy tempo; the music, improvisatory in early stages, has slowly grown to highly accomplished and often intricate structures, which call to mind European toccatas.'

Generally the player's right hand is employed with the melody, whilst the left hand assists in octaves, or supplies a counter melody, or a rhythm similar to a drum rhythm. Where a number of xylophones are used, accompanied by drums, the rhythm played on the lower sounding xylophones matches the drum patterns. The manner of holding the sticks reveals similarities with centuries-old Asiatic methods (and present-day orchestral practice). The shaft of the beater is gripped between the thumb and forefinger. When two beaters are held in one hand (usually the left hand) the additional beater is held between the first and second fingers (see orchestral xylophone). A comparison of styles a over period of years is interesting. Fourteenth-century reliefs at the temple of Panataran in Java depict xylophonists with a pair of beaters in each hand (see Asian trough xylophone).

An additional aspect of technical approach is disclosed in Professor Kirby's description of the South African mbila. The Professor, an eminent authority and a practical instrumentalist says:[2] 'The necessity for two left-hand beaters arises from the fact that the deepest notes are produced by wide slabs of wood, and the distance to be covered in jumping, say, an octave, would be too great for a single beater to accomplish in the required time, left-hand beaters are used alternately never together.'

The following examples are from Professor Kirby's numerous illustrations. The orchestral xylophonist will no doubt term these 'a real piece of knitting'.[3]

[1] Sachs, Curt. *The History of Musical Instruments*, p. 54.

[2] Kirby, P. ibid. p. 53.

[3] The author is reminded of an occasion when he received an urgent request from a London film studio to play a short tune on a xylophone. It transpired that the work in hand was to 'cover'

3. Sounding board, Andaman Islands. Wood with clay ornament. The pointed end is fixed in the ground, convex side uppermost with a stone underneath and the board is then kicked with the heel of the foot. By courtesy of the Royal Scottish Museum, Edinburgh

4. Sticks for beating at dances, Australia. By courtesy of the Royal Scottish Museum, Edinburgh

1. Ancient Brazilian ceremony *tupinamba* from *Historia Americae*, Part III, Theodor de Bry, 1592. By courtesy of the Trustees of the British Museum

2. 'Drumming' on shields *Kuba sithlangu*. The end of each movement and many of the actions are punctuated by the hitting of their shields with their sticks, making a loud report. From *African Dances of the Witwatersrand Gold Mines*. Hugh Tracey

6. *Teponaztli,* Puebla Mexico. Collection of Dr. and Mrs. F. Ll. Harrison, Oxford. Photograph by courtesy of the owners

5. Double slit drum (signalling gong), Duallas Tribe, Cameroon River. By courtesy of the Royal Scottish Museum, Edinburgh

9. Footed drum, Central Africa. Author's collection

7. Xhosa women playing upon the *ingqongqo*. From *The Musical Instruments of the Native Races of South Africa.* Percival R. Kirby

8. Swazi men playing upon the *intambula*. From *The Musical Instruments of the Native Races of South Africa.* Percival R. Kirby

10. Venda *ngoma* and *murumbu*. From *The Musical Instruments of the Native Races of South Africa.* Percival R. Kirby

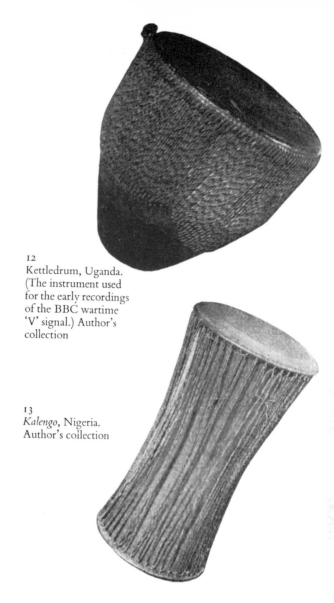

12
Kettledrum, Uganda.
(The instrument used
for the early recordings
of the BBC wartime
'V' signal.) Author's
collection

13
Kalengo, Nigeria.
Author's collection

11. Banana drum, Congo. By courtesy of the Royal
Scottish Museum, Edinburgh

14. *Atumpan*, Ghana. From *Drumming in Akan Communities.*
J. H. Nketia

16. Xylophone, *pandingbwa*, Central Africa. By permission of Musée Royal
de l'Afrique Centrale, Tervuren, Belgium

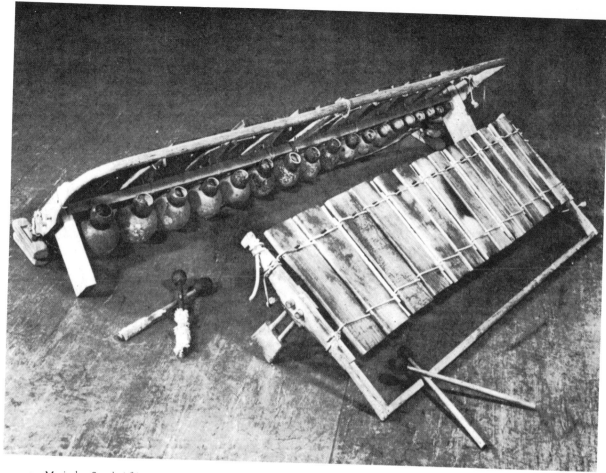

17. Marimba, South Africa. By permission of Andrew and Paul Tracey

17A. The Till family rock band in the 1880's. Photograph by permission of Dr. M. Till.

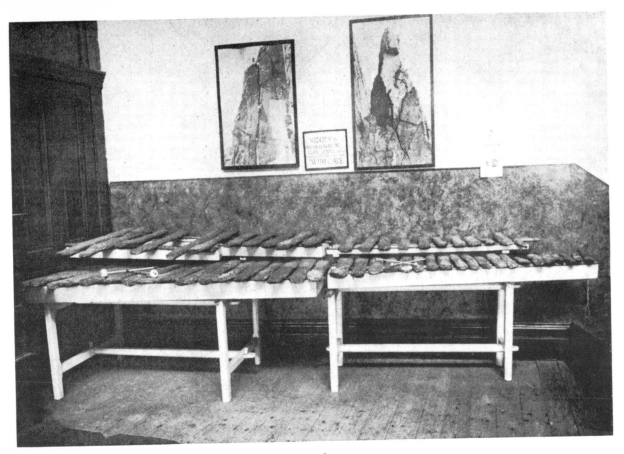

18. Rock harmonica. By permission of G. P. Abraham, Keswick

19
Rock harmonica.
(Richardson Bros.)
By permission of the
Fitz Park Museum Trustees,
Keswick

20
Mbira, South Africa. By
permission of Andrew
and Paul Tracey

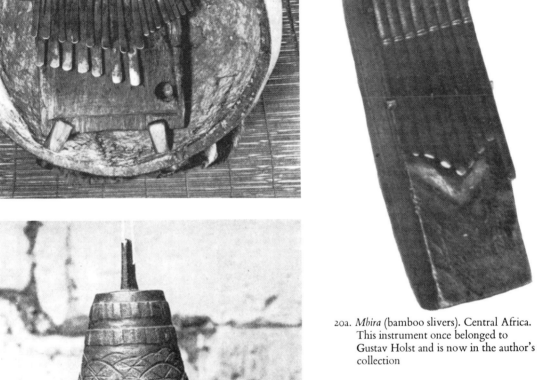

20a. *Mbira* (bamboo slivers). Central Africa.
This instrument once belonged to
Gustav Holst and is now in the author's
collection

21
Ethiopian temple bell. By
courtesy of E. Parsons

22. *Pien-ch'ing*. By courtesy of the Brussels
Conservatoire

23. Gong-making (*a*) Semarang. From *De Gong-Fabricatie te
Semarang*. By permission of E. J. Brill, Leiden, Holland

24. Gong-making (*b*) Semarang. From *De Gong-
Fabricatie te Semarang*. By permission of E. J.
Brill, Leiden, Holland

25. Gong-making (modern). By courtesy of the manufacturers
M. M. Paiste & Sohn, Rendsburg

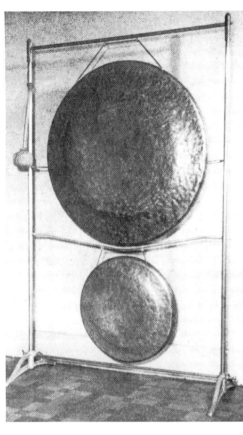

26
Tam-tams, China.
Author's collection

27. Burmese gong chime. By permission of the Pitt Rivers Museum, Oxford

28
Bronze kettledrum, Karen
people, S. E. Asia. By
permission of The
Horniman Museum,
London

29. Raffles gamelan. British Museum.
Crown Copyright

30. *Kemanak*. By courtesy of the Tropen Museum,
Amsterdam

31
Music and Acrobatics – 'The Hundred Children'. Ming
dynasty. By courtesy of the Trustees of the British Museum

33. *Bien-ta-ku*. Author's collection

32. *Tang ku* (Hall drum). Author's collection

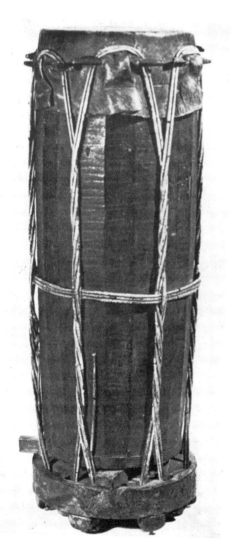

35. Wooden fish, *mu yü*. Author's collection

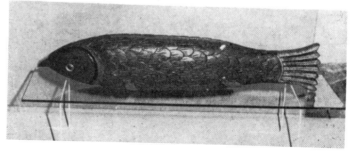

36. Fish drum (wood), mid-Sumatra. By courtesy of the Tropen Museum, Amsterdam

34. Braced drum, Sumatra. By courtesy of the Tropen Museum, Amsterdam

37. Tiger, *yü*. By courtesy of the Brussels Conservatoire

39. Chinese bell, *po-chung* (fifth century B C). By courtesy of the Trustees of the British Museum

40. Wooden bell (*gegroemboengan*), Bali. By courtesy of the Tropen Museum, Amsterdam

38. *P'ai-pan*. By courtesy of the Royal Scottish Museum, Edinburgh

41. *Taiko*, Japan. By permission of the Royal Manchester College of Music

42

Temple bell (*furin*), Burma. By courtesy of the Royal Scottish Museum, Edinburgh

43a, b. Two cabinets of Indian percussion instruments. Victoria and Albert Museum, Crown copyright

1. Drum of black earthenware. *Ghutru*
2. Drum of wood. 'Tom-tom'
3. Drum of glazed pottery
4. Tambourine of wood and brass. *Khanjari*
5. Double drum (wood and earthenware). *Jaraghayi*
6. Tabor. *Dampha*
7. Kettledrum of iron
8. Drum of wood. *Mridanga (mrdanga)*
9. Small drum of wood. 'Darjeeling'
10. Drum of wood. *Janul* or *Dhol*
11. Drum of wood. *Huruk*
12. Drum of wood. 'Tom-tom'
13. Drum of brass. 'Tom-tom'
14. Small kettledrum of wood
15. Kettledrum of iron. *Nagara*, Madras
16. Kettledrum of wood
17. Drum of wood

(*V & A classification*)

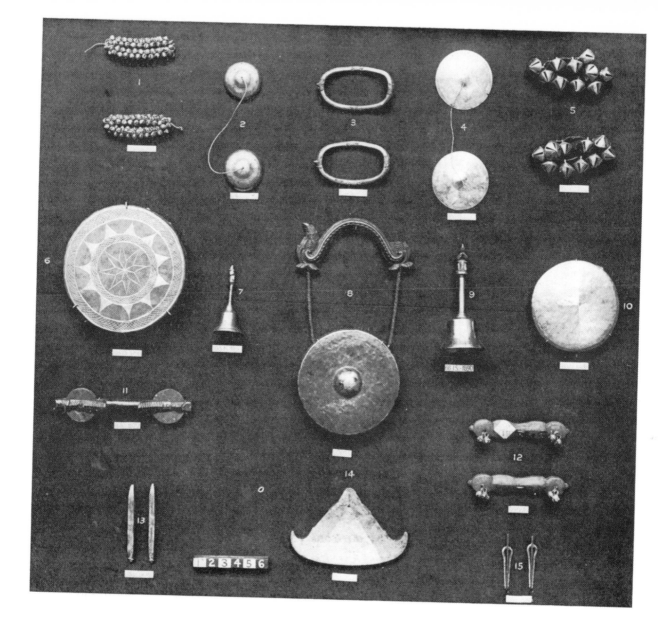

1. Anklets of bronze. *Ghungara*
2. Cymbals of bell metal. *Mandira*
3. Anklets of bronze. *Napura*
4. Cymbals of bronze. *Kharatala*
5. Anklets of bell metal. *Ghanara*
6. Gong of bell metal. *Khansara*
7. Handbell of bronze. *Kshudra*
8. Gong of bronze.
9. Handbell of bronze. *Kshudra Ghanta*
10. Gong of bronze. *Khansi*
11. Castanets of wood with brass discs. *Chiplya.*
   Bombay
12. Castanets of wood with bells. *Chiplya*
13. Castanets of steel. *Khat-Tali*
14. Gong. 'Kyeezee'
15. Jews' Harps of tinned iron. *Murchang.* Kashmir
          (*V & A classification*)

45. Cylindrical and barrel drums. 'Marriage of Siva', ninth–tenth century A D. By courtesy of the Trustees of the British Museum

44. Cylindrical drums eleventh–twelfth century A D. Mysore. By courtesy of the Trustees of the British Museum

46. Laced-kettledrums and hooked sticks. Eighteenth-century Ethiopic manuscript. By courtesy of the Trustees of the British Museum

The possible influence of Asia in the advanced xylophones of African primitives is not extended to metallophones. No instruments of the *saron* and *gender* type occur in Africa. With the exception of single or double toned iron gongs, the remaining percussion instruments with any form of scale are of the most elementary nature. They are water pots containing varying quantities of water to sound different notes and multiple rock gongs which vibrate with a ringing tone when struck with a heavy object.

The first recorded discovery of ringing rocks used for the production of musical notes was made in Nigeria in June 1955. Hammered depressions provide evidence of their having been used as percussion instruments. Subsequent discoveries have revealed rock gongs in current use, their purpose varying from use in religious ceremonies, to providing an accompaniment for singing and dancing. They are also

a section in a documentary film dealing with African life, in which a number of natives were marching down a village street, headed by a youth playing a gourd resonated xylophone. The original 'track' had suffered severe damage, leaving no guide but the tempo of the marchers. The musical director confessed to no great knowledge of African music, but felt certain that between 'us' something could be 'cooked' to cover the sequence (a situation not altogether unprecedented . in the film industry). With the aid of the pentatonic scale, a little 'double stopping' and a few crushed notes, a somewhat unauthentic but jaunty epic evolved, which, to do it justice, fitted the action of the player on the screen. Some few months later the author was shown a letter received by the musical director concerned, advising him, if he had not already done so, to see the film – as here was an opportunity to hear what the native instrumentalists actually play on their xylophones.

used as anvils by African smiths; possibly the earliest blacksmith discovered their musical qualities, as Stone Age man may have recognised the pitch of stalactites, etc.

Anthony King[1] describes rock gongs in the west region of Nigeria, thus: 'A rock gong is any slab or rock which, when beaten with stones at a number of definite points, is used to produce a rhythmical background to traditional songs. The beating produces a ringing sound from the rock, and this may or may not have definite pitch.'

Bernard Fagg[2] says: 'It is somewhat surprising that these rock gongs have escaped serious notice for so long. It is still premature to speculate on their origin, but it is possible they came into current use with the introduction of blacksmithing, for most African smiths use anvils of solid rock. It is equally possible that they may eventually prove to stretch back into the remotest antiquity and to have been among men's earliest musical instruments, for the men who depended for life itself on their ability to fashion implements by flaking must have been conscious of the musical quality of stone.'

Further investigation may reveal a freak of nature to be the reason for these particular rocks in Nigeria possessing musical properties. There is evidence of this phenomenon in the Far East, South America and Europe, a sufficiently uncommon occurrence to warrant our leaving Africa for the moment to consider one of the most striking instances of the discovery of musical stones and their use as musical instruments. It is to be found in the 'rock harmonicas' connected with the English Lake District. Exhibits in the Keswick Museum and originally in the museum of G.P. Abraham Ltd., Keswick, are probably unique throughout the world.

One instrument (in the town museum) dates back to 1785. It consists of 16 stones embracing two diatonic octaves plus one note. Each stone is lettered (by chipping) ascending according to the lettering from B to C. The pitch of the instrument does not conform to the present-day A – 440. The stone marked A sounds D, and so forth. It is possible the instrument was tuned from, or to comply with, an organ or other keyboard instrument in the district. (There was no accepted standard of pitch at the time this lithophone was conceived – organs varying between one third above or below modern pitch; the dampness of the Keswick area could well account for a further difference).

According to local history this set of musical stones – the first to be discovered in England – was found by Peter Crosthwaite, a local publisher of maps. Eight stones were found in the bed of the river Greta, and eight on the nearby mountain of

---

[1] King, Anthony. *African Music*, vol. II, no. 4, African Music Society, Johannesburg.

[2] Fagg, Bernard. 'The Discovery of Multiple Rock Gongs in Nigeria', reprinted from *Man*, 1956, no. 23, London.

Skiddaw. Here indeed is a link with the past, if we accept the Chinese tradition (and why not?) that about 2,000 years ago a complete stone chime was found in a pool, from which by Imperial decree future instruments were modelled.

A later instrument to be seen in the museum is of similar proportions and rock formation to the original model by Crosthwaite. It is comprised of eighteen stones and sounds F sharp to B in the key of A major. In this case the notes are identified by pencilled lettering. The instrument is one third away from our normal pitch, the note sounding C sharp being marked A, and so forth. Both instruments are well in tune with themselves – chipping or flaking is apparent.[1]

The *pièce de résistance* of the Keswick exhibits is a rock harmonica 12 feet in length, comprising five chromatic octaves of rock slabs. The largest slab measures 37 inches in length and four inches in width. It sounds identical with the lowest note on the normal orchestral marimba, one octave below middle C. The smallest slab measures a little over six inches in length.

A handbill advertising a public performance on the instrument supplies this information:

RICHARDSONS'

ORIGINAL MONSTRE

ROCK BAND

Invented and manufactured by
Messrs Richardson and Sons
after 13 years' incessant labour and application
from rocks dug out of the mighty Skiddaw in Cumberland (1827–40)[2]

In construction the instrument bears certain resemblance to Asiatic and African xylophones. The slabs lie over a sound box, insulated at the appropriate points, on ropes of straw. The slabs are not secured in any way.

The instrument bears a remarkable history. The Richardson family became expert performers upon this unique construction, reputed at this time to have embraced a compass of seven octaves. The family met with tremendous success as concert artists, touring Britain and the Continent. Their repertoire included works by Handel, Mozart, Donizetti and Rossini, press reports speaking highly of their great

[1] The Horniman Museum, London, has a lithophone with twenty stones of similar dimension collected from the Keswick region.

[2] Curt Sachs lists a *Lithokymbalon* built by Franz Weber and displayed in Vienna in 1837. Sachs, *Reallexicon*, p. 243.

artistry. The ensemble was honoured with two command performances at Buckingham Palace. During the period between these performances, various instruments of percussion, including steel bars, Swiss bells and drums were added to the instrument. It is interesting to note that at the second royal performance (1848) Her Majesty did not approve of the additional instruments.

Most of the instruments remain intact. They included several beaters, among them a 'T'-shaped double-ended beater evidently for the bass notes, some interesting foot pedals (for a bass drum), a cable-tensioned bass drum patented by Cornelius Ward, a few loose calabash gourds (obviously an attempt at resonating), and much of the original music. (The use at this period of a pedal-operated bass drum etc., is interesting, cf. nineteenth- and twentieth-century patents).

Within a short distance of Keswick museum was a further example of the musical properties of Lakeland stone. Here, in the museum above the shop of Messrs G.P. Abraham Ltd., was displayed a lithophone of similar properties to the Richardson Rock Harmonica, a fine specimen of workmanship, with a range or nearly five chromatic octaves. The instrument was built by Mr. Abraham's forbears and took twelve years to complete, commencing in the year 1886. The 58 stones which are similar in composition to the Richardson instrument are of igneous origin known as spotted schist (or hornblend). The stones were removed from the nearby mountain of Skiddaw. The material property of these stones is apparently unique to this small area of Cumberland. They are rendered musical because of a freak of nature, caused when the active volcano of Skiddaw overflowed. The lava, being unable to flow out evenly all round because of the other close mountains of Blencathra (Saddleback), being compressed over a small area.

The Abraham Rock Harmonica is now owned by Mr. W. Chamberlain of Reading, a hammer dulcimer enthusiast who has reconstructed the stones and featured them in his tours of G.B. and the U.S.A.

In 1881 another Lakeland family (Mr. Daniel Till and his two sons and two daughters) exhibited and performed upon a similar instrument at the Crystal Palace, London. Later the group toured extensively in the United States of America. Due to the recent research of Dr. A. M. Till of Gloucester (G.B.) and Professor Meier of Zurich, a Till instrument comprised of one row of twenty-two stones has been located (though not on display) in the Metropolitan Museum of Art, New York, (Ref. No. 89/4/2931. Catalogue 1904).

Today the stones are extremely rare, particularly those with a deep tone. It seems improbable that Skiddaw could provide a further instrument of any size.

METAL INSTRUMENTS

The metal instruments of Africa include *sansas* (plucked idiophones), small bells, jingles, and gongs. The sansa or mbira is well known in almost every part of Negro Africa. Though not strictly a percussion instrument it is of such significance that we have included it here. In the majority of instances it is crudely made, but it is highly expressive. It plays a prominent part in religious and secular music and quite often constitutes the principal part of an orchestra.

The instrument comprises a set (variable in number) of narrow tongues of metal (or slivers of hard bamboo) mounted on a resonator consisting of a soundboard made from a slab of wood hollowed on one side, or a soundbox in the form of a hollowed block, or two or three hollowed-out lengths of bamboo joined together. It is usual for rattling pieces such as small shells, beads, or metal plates to be fixed to the soundbox, or on the tongues. The tongues are rigidly braced by means of a metal bar over two bridges a short distance apart in the upper part of the soundbox. The bar is secured between the bridges by bindings of thin iron wire. The bridges consist of two metal strips, or one metal strip (the lower bridge) with the top of the soundboard forming the upper bridge. The tongues are broad at one end, often lessening to a point at the other end; they are bent into a shallow curve. Mounted to the soundboard in the manner described, each can vibrate freely. The free ends of the tongues are plucked downwards by the thumbs, and downwards and upwards by the forefingers. (The Afro-Cuban *marimbula* is similarly constructed).

The mbira is tuned to a definite scale, peculiar to the tribe, the pitch of each tongue being determined by its length from the bridges. It is possible to alter, quickly and easily, the length of the tongues, and thus rapidly adjust their tuning to suit immediate requirements. (In some cases the pitch of a tongue is flattened by adding the weight of a portion of bees' wax to the underneath of the tongue). In performance, the instrument is often placed inside a resonating gourd, to which is frequently added rattling pieces.

A recent development of the traditional instrument by Hugh Tracey is called *kalimba*. The 17 tongues progress diatonically from the centre, alternately from left to right.

Of the history of the sansa, Klaus Wachsmann says:[1] 'For its ancestry no pedigree has as yet been suggested. It appears in travellers' reports for the first time in 1586,[2] already with the hall-marks of a perfect tool. Its day is by no means over; it is the

---

[1] Wachsmann, Klaus. 'The Primitive Musical Instruments', *Musical Instruments through the Ages*, edited Anthony Baines, Faber, 1966, p. 34.

[2] Dos Santos – as *ambira* (author's note).

popular instrument of the common man, and will continue to be so unless the import of Western instruments puts an end to its use.

Returning to percussion, we find small bells or jingles used as rattles. They are also used as anklets, or worn on the waist or chest of dancers. Occasionally, jingling pieces are attached to drums. Small hand bells are also used – mainly as time keepers, to supply a steady rhythm in music for singing and dancing. Iron rings worn on the thumb and finger function similarly, in the manner of castanets or finger cymbals. For centuries, the tinkle of a small hand bell has been used by the leper to give warning of his approach, a sound happily becoming less frequent.

Circular gongs of bronze and so-called gongs of beaten iron are found in nearly all negro populations. In the majority of instances the latter instruments resemble pear-shaped bells. With few exceptions they are clapper-less, the player striking the instrument with a beater, consisting of a metal rod or stout wood shaft, with or without a covered end. A handle, also of iron and quite often of considerable length, is attached to the closed end of the bell. These iron gongs are in two forms – a single gong with handle, and a pair of gongs of different size and pitch joined by a metal bar, which also forms a handle. An instrument of the latter type, known among other names as *ogell*, *damuro*, or *gong-gong*, is the foundation instrument in many West African dances.

In the Congo they are used with the drums and xylophones, and in most areas are associated with ceremonial occasions, religious dances, ancestor worship, and to announce and convey information by means of a language resembling that used with the message drums. A West African instrument named *tabala*, resembling an orchestral cymbal, is employed similarly. It is frequently carried between two men who strike it like a bell, thus announcing events, or calling attention to the issuing of orders. Iron gongs are still associated with agriculture. For generations the labour of the workers in the African field has been lightened by rhythmic music in some form or another, particularly that provided by such simple percussion instruments as clappers or double gongs.

In Africa, the circular gong (like its Far Eastern counterpart) is credited with power to overcome certain evil spirits and to protect. It is connected with interesting ceremonies, at which it is regarded as a talisman. During the seven days' fattening period required by a prospective member of a certain secret society whose member-ship denotes high social status, the candidate, whilst on his daily round of visits, beats on a small circular gong to attract attention. Among the several strict rules which he must observe – such as sitting on nothing but a mat of the Society, taking no food unless it has first been tasted by an initiated member, and similar acts of discipline – he must under no circumstance hand over his gong to a non-member.

Bibliography

Historical references confirm the use of iron gongs over several centuries, and quote these instruments in elaborate forms in the sixteenth and seventeenth centuries as the work of the skilled craftsmen of Benin in Nigeria. Similar skill is observed in some of the implements used for striking the gongs, also in the exquisitely sculptured bells in metal, ivory and wood.

A bronze plaque in the British Museum, one of several hundred cast in the sixteenth and seventeenth centuries to ornament the wooden pillars of the palace of the King of Benin, portrays the Chief performing a dance accompanied by an attendant playing a pair of iron gongs. The instruments are held one in each hand, and appear to be shaken in the style of maracas.

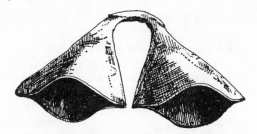

Fig. 17. Double gong-gong, Central Africa

Of the two types of gongs discussed, the pear-shaped gongs of iron are the more numerous. It is in the Far East that the circular bronze disc holds pride of place.

Bibliography: Chapter 3

THE PRIMITIVE XYLOPHONE

ANKERMANN, Bernhard. 'Die afrikanische Musikinstrumente', *Ethnologisches Notizblatt*, vol. III, Berlin, 1901.

BOONE, Olga. *Les Xylophones du Congo Belge*, Tervuren Museum Collection, Van Campenhout, Brussels, 1936.

FAGG, Bernard. 'The Discovery of Multiple Rock Gongs in Nigeria', reprinted from *Man*, 23, London, 1956.

HORNBOSTEL, E. M. von. African Negro Music, Oxford, 1928, reprint from *Africa*, vol. I, no. 1.

JONES, A. M. 'Experiments with a xylophone key', *African Music*, vol. III, no. 2, 1965, African Music Society, Roodepoort, Transvaal, South Africa.

KING, Anthony. *African Music*, vol. II, no. 4, African Music Society, Johannesburg.

KIRBY, P. R. 'The Indonesian Origin of Certain African Musical Instruments', *African Studies*, vol. XXV, no. 1.66. Witwatersrand University Press, Johannesburg, 1966.

—*The Musical Instruments of the Native Races of South Africa*, Witwatersrand University Press, Johannesburg, 1953.

KUBIK, Gerhard. 'Discovery of a trough xylophone in Northern Mozambique', *African Music*, vol. III, no. 2, 1965, African Music Society, Roodepoort, Transvaal, South Africa

KUNST Jaap. *Hindoe Javaansche Muziek-Instrumenten*, Wellevreden, Indonesia, 1927.

KYAGAMBIDDWA, Joseph. *African Music from the Source of the Nile*, Atlantic Press, London, 1956.

LABAT, F. B. *Nouvelle relation de l'Afrique occidentale*, Cavelier, Paris, 1728.

NADEL, S. F. *Marimba Musik*, Holder–Pickler–Tempsky, Vienna, 1931.

SACHS, Curt. *The History of Musical Instruments*, Norton, New York, 1940.

SCHAEFFNER, André. *Origine des Instruments de Musique*, Payot, Paris, 1936.

THEAL, G. M. *Records of S. E. Africa*, Capetown, 1901.

TRACEY, Hugh. *Chopi Musicians*, Oxford, London, 1948.

WACHSMANN, Klaus. *Musical Instruments through the Ages*, ed. Anthony Baines, Faber, London, 1966.

4

Percussion Instruments of
China and the Far East

The Chinese believe their music to be the first in the world. Whether or not this is true, they were certainly concerned with music as far back as 3,000 BC as can be proved from written records.

There existed in ancient China a close relationship between the constitution of the state and music: for generations the art was under state supervision, in order to guard against the introduction of any note contrary to the ordinance.

In turning our attention to the East, we find that – as in other territories – the origin of music is closely bound up with that of religion. The Chinese builds his world upon the harmonious action of the heavens and earth, co-ordinating his music with the movements of the stars and the change of seasons, with their accompanying phenomena. They ascribe the origin of their music to at least the third millennium BC, at which time the emperors were represented as having each founded a musical system and an empire.

By the period of the legendary Emperor Shun, (2255–2206 BC) bells and other percussion instruments were well established. This ruler is credited with being responsible for dividing musical instruments into eight classes in accordance with the natural philosophy of Fuh shi.

Van Aalst,[1] who gives the accompanying classification, says: 'The Chinese therefore put Nature under contribution for the production of eight kinds of instruments corresponding to the eight symbols – pa-kua – of Fuh shi, which, they believe, are the expression of all the changes and permutations which take place in the universe.'

1. Stone.	N.W.	Autumn	Winter	The Stone Chime.
2. Metal.	W.	Autumn		The Bell Chime.

[1] Aalst, J. A. Van. *Chinese Music*, King & Sons, London 1884, p. 47. (Reprint Paragon, N.Y., 1964.)

3. Silk.   S.   Summer   The Lute.
4. Bamboo. E.   Spring   The Flute.
5. Wood.   S.E.   Spring   Summer   The Tiger Box.
6. Skin.   N.   Winter   The Drum.
7. Gourd.   N.E.   Winter   Spring   The Reed Organ.
8. Earth.   S.W.   Summer   Autumn   The Porcelain Cone.

During the *Shang* Dynasty (1766–1122 BC) a Chinese ode written 1135 BC mentions the drum and bells.

> In what unison sounded the drums and bells!
> What joy was there in the hall with its circlet of water!
> The lizard-skin drums rolled harmonious,
> As the blind musicians performed their parts.

The earliest excavations of musical instruments in China date from the *Shang* Dynasty; they are a globular flute carved from bone, and a set of sonorous stones.

It is unfortunate that although drums and bells are mentioned, no specimens from this period have been preserved. Our knowledge of primitive Chinese culture is also greatly hindered by the destruction of all books, music and musical instruments in 212 BC by the command of the Emperor Che Huang-ti.

The proof of the exceptional interest taken in music by the Chinese people – and Eastern Asia generally – is the large number of musical instruments they possess. Confucius (551–479 BC) who with his pupils played a significant role in the development of Chinese music, in one of his works refers to over a hundred different instruments of music. There is little doubt that sonorous percussion instruments were numerous. These include idiophones of stone, wood and metal, and membrane drums.

Idiophones are more essential in the Far East than in other civilizations. Their importance in Chinese music is proved by their early development, in company with the majority of East Asiatic idiophones, into instruments capable of melody; a practice completely opposed to the general use of idiophones in Western civilizations, where they were restricted almost entirely to rhythm.

Among the most ancient and valued instruments of the Chinese people are instruments of percussion consisting of one or more tuned stones. The foremost of these is the *King* (*pien-ch'ing*) – reputed to have been invented by the Emperor Tschun and the Chinese Orpheus Kuei, and said to have existed as far back as 2300 BC. About this time a chant of Konei, the Emperor Yao's court musician, refers to a musical stone, the *Te-ch'ing*.

When I smite my musical stone – be it gently or strong,
Then do the fiercest hearts leap for joy, and the chiefs do
    agree among themselves,
When ye make to resound the stone melodious,
When ye touch the lyre that is called Ch'in,
Then do the ghosts of the ancestors come to hear.

Stone chimes were indispensable in Chinese antiquity on all formal occasions. According to the philosopher Mencius (372–289 BC) a concert was complete only when the large bell proclaimed the commencement of the music and the ringing stone proclaimed its close. Referring to the pien-ch'ing, Sachs[1] says: 'Each verse of the hymn to Confucius is ended by a single blow with a disconnected hammer in order "to receive the tone" and transmit it to the following word.'

Sonorous stones occur in scattered regions. In Ethiopia stone chimes are used as church bells in certain Christian places of worship. Equally remarkable is a stone chime in Africa immediately south of the Sahara, which responds to the wind. In South America, some have been found in Venezuela, and in Europe, on the islands of Chios and Sardinia. (Nearer home are the 'singing stones' preserved in Keswick Museum).

In Asia, ringing stones in the form of tuned stone slabs are found in Annam, China (particularly the province of Liangchou), Korea, Samoa, and in Southern India (the musical stone pillars at the Vaishnavite shrine in Tirunelvēlei).[2] It is possible that the oldest set of tuned stone slabs are those found in 1949 in Indo-China, in the region which nine years later three stone slabs were found to be in actual use. The playing position of these three slabs (undoubtedly prehistoric-type instruments) resembles one of the rarer positions for xylophone playing, the players being seated with the slabs across their thighs. Archaeologists are unable to state the age of the finds, though according to Klaus P. Wachsmann, the surfaces show the typical flaking technique of Stone Age man, and the edges apparently fashioned for tuning purposes.

Literary references and pictorial representations dealing with lithophones are unanimous in their references to the territory of Annam (Indo-China). The preserved specimens in the museums are mainly from this territory, where it seems evident that the geological formation, due to possible volcanic eruption or a freak of nature, has resulted in certain rocks possessing unique musical qualities.

---

[1] Sachs, Curt. *The History of Musical Instruments*, p. 169.

[2] The *Ye* stones from the Central Highlands of West New Guinea have a remarkable musical quality – almost the sound of a marimba. With the people of this remote territory the stones serve no musical purpose, though they are valued and used as a medium of exchange.

The sizes of ringing stones range from a few inches upwards. Though not always possessing a bell-like sound (certain primitives preferring slabs with a low and muffled note) the sonority of some of these instruments is remarkable, as with the Lakeland (Keswick) rock harmonicas. The largest tuned stone slabs are to be found in Annamese temples. These enormous stones are struck with small, though heavy, wooden clubs.

In contrast, the slabs comprising the Chinese King are smaller. This instrument consists of sixteen stones (of graduated size and thickness) cut in the shape of an L., but with the angle obtuse. This configuration – discovered early by the Chinese to be conducive to the production of musical sound – and its relative dimensions, are rigorously adhered to. (The *T'ê-ching* or 'single sonorous stone' is similarly shaped). The stones comprising the King are pierced in the angled corner. They are suspended in two rows in an ornamental wooden frame. The stones are struck on the long side with wooden mallets, or padded sticks. They are tuned to the twelve tones of the *Lu* octave and its four additional tones. The original lu, or 'standards', were fixed in ancient times by the Music Office of the Ministry of Norms and were the basis of the musical system of the Chinese. Six of the twelve tones (odd numbers) are attributed to the male, and six (even numbers) to the female. The scale of the lu, though not corresponding exactly to our tempered chromatic scale, can be considered from F sharp ascending in semitones to F natural, the male notes ascending in tones, F sharp, G sharp, A sharp, C, D, E, and the female G, A, B, C sharp, D sharp, F. Van Aalst[1] states of the pien-ch'ing (the King): 'It is exclusively used in court and religious ceremonies, and it would be a profanation to use it elsewhere.'

Certain of these instruments were richly ornamented, one such instrument called *Nio-King* being played only by the Emperor. An instrument resembling the Nio-King is among the specimens in the possession of the Brussels Conservatoire. The sixteen stones (from Annam) are exquisitely ornamented. (In a reference to the pien-ch'ing Hermann Smith[2] states: 'The number of stones has varied under different dynasties from fourteen to twenty-four'.)[3]

The *Musée de l'homme*, Paris, possesses a lithophone consisting of ten stone slabs from Annam. Two lithophones dating back to neolithic times, from Vietnam, Indo-China, are to be seen in the Horniman Museum, London (cf. Nigerian rock gongs and Cumberland lithophones already discussed).

GONGS

Whilst the lithophone plays an important part in the historical sequence of the

[1] Aalst, J. A., Van. ibid. p. 5.   [3] The *pien chung* (sixteen bronze bells) is similar in design.
[2] Smith, Hermann. *The World's Earliest Music*, Reeves, London, 1904, p. 160.

instruments of the East, it is the metal percussion instruments of the Orient that suggest to a greater degree the Far East corner of Asia.

Gongs are the most important metal instruments in the south east. All types and sizes are covered by the same definition. They are made of bronze in circular shape, with the surface flat or bulging and the rim bent down (the vibrations issuing from the centre).

The origin of the gong is uncertain, but there seems little reason to doubt the claim of the Chinese whose tradition ascribes it to the country Hsi Yu between Tibet and Burma, where it is mentioned early in the sixth century in the time of Emperor Hsüan Wu (AD 500–516). According to Sachs it is possible that this instrument was similar to two instruments existing to this day: the Korean *tjing*, from fifteen to sixteen inches wide and rather deep, and the *rang* of the Garo (an aboriginal tribe in Assam). The conclusion of Jaap Kunst is that the gong came in the beginning of the sixth century from the West to China.

Speaking of the gong in 1841, G. Tradescant Lay[1] writes: 'The *lo*, or what the Javanese in imitation of the sound call a *gong*, was at first nothing more than a platter for washing, or other similar purposes. There are two kinds: one large and flat, used chiefly on board the Chinese junks, where, at sunset and on setting out or returning home, it is sounded in the room of prayers or praise; for a Chinese thinks he shall be heard for a great noise than for much speaking. The smaller sort is rounded with a cylindrical edge. The sound emitted by it when struck by a stick is very loud, and far exceeds what the sight of so small an instrument would lead us to anticipate.'

The name 'gong' had its origin in Java. Scientific research has established four principal centres of manufacture – Burma, China, Annam and Java (where there are at least seven different types of gong – *gon*, *kempul*, *bende*, *beri*, *kenon*, *kempyan*, and *ketuk*).

The instrument is involved in every kind of human activity. As a musical instrument the gong serves the natives for their war, sword, joy and macabre dances, and as an accompaniment to songs and theatrical performances. It is used to transmit messages. In the army it gives the signal of retreat, and in the hunt it is used as a decoy.

In the lower civilizations it has been credited with a strong magic power: healing sickness, attracting the wind and chasing away evil spirits, a defence against ghosts, and with its help morbific demons were banished from the human body. It is even said that bathing from a gong gives health, and drinking from a gong enforces an oath.

In Asiatic families the gong was considered a token of prosperity and an object

[1] Lay, G. Tradescant, *The Chinese as they are*, W. Ball, London, 1841, p. 90.

of the highest value. As a badge of rank and property it served to represent the family, and among its numerous usages it acted as a form of currency.

Gongs were owned by princes and chiefs: the greater their riches the larger were the dimensions of the instrument. Certain individual gongs were so esteemed that names were given to them, such as 'Sir Tiger' or 'Sir Earthquake', and as is usual with exotic instruments they are frequently classified as masculine and feminine: gongs with deep bosses are called male, and those with shallower bosses, female.

The gong had considerable power as a talisman. To be touched by a gong created happiness and strength, part no doubt of the accepted belief of some Asiatics that by touching the body with metal the soul became strengthened. The spirits of the departed were invoked by the sounding of gongs and the souls of the ancestors were believed to share in the enjoyment of the music referred to in the chant of Konei (2300 BC) in praise of the musical stone.

The death of a male was announced with strokes on a gong in groups of threes. The alarm, calling the workers from the fields and woods to defend the village, was sounded on a gong in the following manner: first a number of quick accelerating beats on the dome, followed by one deep tone, then two short notes – repeated – on the body of the gong. Such messages and numerous other known rhythms were used as a language (and may still be) in a similar manner to the style of conveying information by drums, used in parts of Africa to this day.[1]

According to Sir James Frazer[2] '. . . the Sea Dyaks and Kayans of Borneo beat gongs when a tempest is raging; but the Dyaks, and perhaps the Kayans also, do this, not so much to frighten away the spirit of the storm, as to apprize him of their whereabouts, lest he should inadvertently knock their houses down.'

From the ninth century, gongs are reported in Java, and other islands of the Malay Archipelago, and New Guinea. The making of the best gongs was the speciality of a small number of old foundries at Semarang in Java. Only certain families were privileged to be gong makers, the process requiring great skill; the *modus operandi* (as with the manufacture of certain Turkish cymbals) being handed down from generation to generation.

The art of gong making is still surrounded by a good deal of romance and not a little secrecy. In the making of the best gongs, particularly those used in the gong chime associated with the Gamelan orchestra, the makers believe their work can only

[1] For many years a large Chinese gong was used as a fog signal on the Bar Flat lightship (The Wash). This instrument, now in King's Lynn Museum, produces a powerful and resonant note, sounding 'the first E below the bass' clef.

[2] Frazer, J. G. *The Golden Bough*, Macmillan, London, 1935, part I, vol. I, p. 328.

succeed with the special help of a higher power. They are considered to be more exposed than other mortals to attack from malicious spirits. They fast on certain days, and to protect themselves they adopt other names; and in consequence the work proceeds unhindered (cf. African drum maker).

The high standard of craftsmanship in metals maintained in past centuries, leads to a good deal of speculation on the quality of many instruments that have been lost to us through deterioration or vandalism, or are as yet undiscovered. Whilst a picture of Chinese art from the Shang Dynasty to modern times – a period of some 4,000 years – may be considered fairly complete, there is always a possibility of a 'find' that will reveal the workmanship embodied in ancient musical instruments. (A discovery similar to that of the cymbals found in the tomb of the Egyptian musician 100 BC would be of tremendous assistance in comparing the relative qualities of the percussion instruments of ancient peoples).

The geological and historical survey of the late nineteenth century, assisted by the cutting away of sepulchral mounds in the process of engineering railways, revealed vast hidden treasures of past ages and many unsuspected glories of Chinese culture. Hitherto, ignorance of these arts was largely due to the reverence in which the Chinese held their dead. The sanctity of the grave and tomb was of high importance. To disturb the burial place, no matter how remote the period, was sacrilege and punishable by death.

The art of the Shang period so far revealed (1600–1100 BC) has brought to light carved bone, ivory, and bronze vessels of a workmanship that has never since been rivalled in China, or any other country. Who is to say what may yet remain hidden in the way of instruments of metal, particularly in gongs?

From the works of Jacobson and Van Hasselt[1] and Simbriger[2] and other authors, we gain a clear picture of the methods originally employed in the gong forges of Semarang (on the north coast of Java), the home of the domed gong, and the similar craft employed in China where the flat gong predominates.

Such research has revealed many interesting facts concerning the making of gongs, and will permit, as far as this volume is concerned, a reasonable analysis from their references.

The formula of the metal varies with the quality and purpose of the instrument. Gongs of good quality are made of bronze; the approximate formula being 80 per cent copper, 20 per cent tin. In instruments of lesser quality the amount of copper is reduced to 70 per cent and 10 per cent lead (or tin) is added. Gongs of dark colour

[1] Jacobson, E. and Hasselt, J. H. Van. *De Gong-Fabricatie te Semarang*, Brill, Leiden, 1907.
[2] Simbriger. H. *Gong und Gongspiele*, Internationales Archiv für Ethnographie, Band XXXVI, Brill, Leyden, 1939.

are said to contain a quantity of iron. In Annam, special gongs contained a good deal of silver. These instruments had a far-reaching sound. They were light in colour and were costly, often five times the price of normal gongs. In olden times (as the occasion demanded) the mixture included a certain amount of gold.

There has been little change in the methods employed in forming the gongs. It would seem that five main processes are involved: 'pouring', 'hammering', 'smoothing', 'tuning', and 'polishing and ornamenting'.

Over a fire of charcoal, blown by primitive bellows, the copper is made fluid and the required quantity of other ingredients added. The molten metal is well mixed with an iron bar and the top 'scum' removed, resulting in a loss at times of up to 25 per cent of the mixture. After several testings by the chief smith, the metal is poured into wax or clay moulds of the required shape (process 1), or, as is more common with the better toned gongs, into cakes of metal which are shaped by constant hammering (process 2). The smith then shapes the hot metal from the centre. His helpers meanwhile turn the mould, and assist in some of the beating. The metal is constantly re-heated (each heating lasting 30 seconds). In the case of a large gong, the heating process is repeated up to 150 times. When the instrument has approached the finished shape, it is surrounded with an iron ring and whilst still at a high temperature suddenly immersed in cold water, rendering the metal elastic; if the disc were brittle it would crack under the final tuning process, which requires a considerable amount of hammering.

The third process is that of smoothing out any major unevenness, and filling in small holes. Such imperfections are filled with a resinous paste, which is heated with a glowing bar, and in cooling becomes stone hard. (In the West we have never mastered this process: to us the satisfactory repair of a chipped gong or cymbal remains impossible.)

The fourth process of tuning – when the gong is quite cold – is an effort of supreme skill. The requisite number of hammer strokes and the striking positions are known only to the expert. In the case of gongs of high quality, the instrument requires three separate tuning processes before the desired timbre is considered constant. It is also maintained that in certain instances the full beauty is not realized until the instrument is thirty-years-old.

The final process involves polishing and ornamenting. Many Chinese tam-tams – large flat gongs – include a further work of art by way of adornment. On the face of the instrument, in most cases to the extent of half its surface, is engraved a dragon, resplendent among storm clouds and other phenomena of nature. The dark surface of the gong is scraped until the final 'picture' appears. The noble beast, a typical image of the Chinese conception of the creature is, to the 'man in the street', an emblem of the Emperor, a bringer of rain, and in general an auspicious being, not by any means like its Western counterpart, a symbol of darkness and evil.

In Christian art the dragon is represented as symbolical of paganism, but with the Chinese the dragon plays an important part in every natural event; it is usually benevolent, occasionally capricious, and stern and vengeful only when its displeasure has been incurred by some wrongful act of man such as during an eclipse of the sun, when to prevent a celestial dragon from devouring the luminary, the Chinese resorted to making a tremendous noise on cymbals and drums.

The dragon is perhaps the commonest of all animal motifs in Chinese art. It lives in the swirling mists on the mountain tops, or in the great rivers and lakes of the plains. Its sinuous form is interwoven throughout the life fabric of the people. It is fitting that the creature should emblazon the large gong.

A few specimens of this type of tam-tam have entered this country. They serve a noble purpose in symphony orchestras, supplying their tremendous wealth of sound at the appointed time.

The J. Arthur Rank Film Corporation have agreed to the disclosure of the fact that the arresting notes apparently produced by the Herculean figure in their screen trade mark, consists of an expertly recorded super-imposition of strokes delivered (by the author) on a Chinese tam-tam.

The dragon engraved on these tam-tams is illustrated with four claws, thus permitting the public use of such an instrument. On instruments of this quality, had the dragon been depicted with five toes, it is doubtful whether the export of such gongs would have been permitted. On late Ming and Ch'ing objects, five-clawed dragons, scaly, with whiskers and horns, indicate a piece made for palace use.

Dragons and similar creatures are featured on smaller cast gongs, and are painted, with other suitable traditional emblems, on bossed gongs of different sizes. At times the ornaments are engraved into an oxydized surface, blackened with a mixture of copper sulphate and plant juice. The numerous shapes and sizes in these instruments show a variation in diameter from a few inches to over three feet, and the weight from a few ounces to upwards of two hundred pounds.

In recent years there has been a marked revival in the manufacture of gongs in the Far East. The Chinese are producing gongs (and cymbals) of fine quality, and in Java at Surakarta (Sala) the gamelan gong industry is flourishing. What of such industry in the West? The history of the Paiste family answers this question. Their concern for many years has been the making, in Europe, of gongs of high quality.

Instruments from the Paiste firm have found their way into many of the leading orchestras of the world and even to Buddhist monasteries in China and Japan. Since 1906 the present family (to quote their records) '. . . have been deeply devoted to their handicraft art . . . exercised by only a few men on earth . . . that is based on carefully guarded secrets handed down from their forefathers.' First, the simple workshop in (then) St. Petersburg. Later, the modern factories now situated in Schacht-Audorf (Germany) and Nottwil (Switzerland), each producing musical instruments of fine quality.

Fig. 18
Bronze gong, bossed,
Cambodia

To-day, the tam-tams of Messrs. Paiste are famous. Though lacking certain traditional Eastern features, the instruments possess the character of the Orient with their superb tone and attractive appearance. Gongs (tam-tams) measuring up to five feet in diameter with a voice of thunder, are manufactured by this ingenious family. In contrast, instruments diminishing to a diameter of a few inches, but retaining a tone of great sonority, are among their products. What is their secret? We may never know, so we must limit ourselves to comparing aspects of their methods (supplied by themselves) with the information at our disposal regarding the ancient craft of the Far East.

Firstly, the formula of the metal from which the Paiste gongs are manufactured. Here we find a bronze alloy which differs only by a few ingredients in its components from the compound used in the manufacture of the best quality gongs of the Far East; the formula of the Paiste metal being approximately 68 per cent copper, 24 per cent tin, and 8 per cent nickel. (Under modern conditions of analytical research, the composition of such a compound remains no secret).

Gongs

In contrast to the Asiatic method of pouring the molten metal into moulds, before forging it into a plate, the compound forming the Paiste gongs is cast and rolled under scientific conditions into sheet form, from which the circular discs are cut. From this second process to process number three, during which the round plate is heated 'red hot' and the edges and general form moulded by hammer strokes. The disc is reheated from time to time during the process of forming and tempering the metal disc. These latter processes and the consequent hand hammering employed in 'tuning' the gong, are surrounded by the same secrecy as were the methods employed by the ancient craftsmen.

The metal disc is now a musical instrument. It is rested for a period of three to four months, after which it is finally tuned and polished, and in most cases ornamented with Chinese characters signifying: 'Come the good; Go the evil'. Again we find an echo of the original craft in the resting period and re-tuning, to guarantee the disc an individual tone.

A further Oriental aspect is observed in a recent addition to the Paiste products – complete scales of cupola gongs. These instruments resemble in appearance and tone the Far Eastern gongs employed in the gong chime. The Paiste cupola gongs, which measure from 7–32 inches in diameter, have a compass of four octaves.

In addition to the manufacture of gongs, the Paiste family are responsible for the output, on a large scale, of a variety of cymbals, with as high a reputation in the musical profession as their gongs, so that they are truly a family of artificers in 'precious metal'.

Establishments with a similar tradition have existed in Italy since the middle of the last century. In Pistoia, Tuscany, a region associated with metal craftsmanship for generations, is situated the firm of 'Ufip' (*Unione Fabbricanti Italiani Piatti Musicali e Tam-Tams*) established in 1847. 'Ufip', in addition to the manufacture of cymbals, are responsible for the production of tuned gongs, covering a chromatic range of two octaves. Prominent among other Italian manufacturers of cymbals and gongs is the firm of Zanchi, also with a high reputation. In recent years, the experiments made by British firms have proved highly successful, in particular the 'Zyn' cymbal, a product of the Premier Drum Company.[1]

Returning to the East, we find tuned gongs in varying numbers and method of assembly. The pure and distinct tone of the deep gong renders this instrument, among all other gongs, of the greatest musical value. They are convexly embossed in

[1] Cf. Zildjian family.

the middle, with dropping rims round the edges. The tuned gong has an essential part in the *gamelan*, a native Indonesian instrumental ensemble, using string, wind, and numerous percussion instruments, among the latter being the most outstanding percussion instrument of South East Asia, the gong chime. A gong chime (*bonang*) consists of a number of deep gongs of definite pitch, which rest on, or hang from, cords suspended on a low horizontal frame or bed, the instrumentalist performing in a squatting position. Gong chimes are built in several sizes, an octave apart, with the frames built in various forms. The bed of the Javanese gong chime resembles a couch, whilst in other territories the bed is quadrant shaped, or reaches (at times in two rows) the full circle, as with the modern Cambodian chimes and those of Burma and Siam.

The rows of gongs are tuned to one of the several scales used in South-East Asia. In some cases final tuning is done by sticking a composition of lead and bees' wax to the inner surface of the concave boss. The composition is first softened by beating, and when applied lowers the pitch.

To deal with the differing systems of tuning would require a textbook. Briefly they include the pentatonic scales of China and Japan, the Siamese octave with its seven equal parts, the *slendro* octave, which is divided into five equal parts, and the *pelog* which has five unequal divisions. The bonang is made up of two rows of gongs, ten in the slendro system and fourteen in the pelog. (Gongs with actual pitch, similar to those used in the gong chime, are occasionally employed in the western orchestra. Puccini scored for a number of gongs with the pitch notated in *Madam Butterfly* and *Turandot*; Richard Strauss scores for five large Chinese gongs with definite notes in *Die Frau ohne Schatten* (1919); Carl Orff requests ten large Javanese gongs in his stage play *Antigonae* 1947-8 and, in *Oedipus der Tyrann* 1957-8, for two Javanese gongs and three to five tam-tams in different sizes.)

An instrument resembling the arrangement of the gong chime is found in the Burmese drum chime. Sachs refers to the unparalleled drum chime of Burma (*tshaing naing*) as an interesting fusion of Indian and East Asiatic elements. The instrument comprises a series of carefully tuned drums, normally twenty-four, suspended inside the walls of a circular pen. The player squats in the centre of the pen, and strikes the drums with his hands in a toccata-like melody. (The *kong-tham* of Madagascar consists of a circle of seventeen drums, cf. African drum chime.)

The largest type of Indonesian orchestra, called gamelan gong,[1] in addition to metallophones and drums, includes several gong chimes, two large gongs, a number of small gongs, and small high-pitched cymbals (mounted in pairs). The smaller gongs mark the end of short sections of the music, and the large gongs conclude the

[1] *Gamelan* is the general name for the orchestral ensemble of Java and Bali.

main parts. The largest gongs are suspended in upright frames; the smaller instruments rest on low stands. The gongs are struck with beaters called *tabuli*. On occasions the boss of the large suspended gong is struck with the clenched fist. (At the first reading of an involved part, the western percussionist is sometimes obliged to use a similar stroke, when he finds himself confronted with the nightmare situation of an important beat of the tam-tam and every style of striking implement within reach but the required heavy mallet.)

A further instrument of metal is the *rejong*, a gong chime employing a pair of tuned deep gongs which are secured to the ends of a dumb-bell-shaped piece of wood. Rejongs are played in pairs, in opposite rhythms. The instruments differ in size, the larger rejong producing the two lowest notes of the scale, and the smaller instrument the two highest notes. They are tuned a second or a minor third apart. The usual playing position is for the instrumentalist to be seated with the rejong across his lap, though the instrument is occasionally pictured with the gongs suspended in an elaborate frame. Bas-reliefs show that rejongs existed in Java as early as the fourteenth century.

METALLOPHONES

Metallophones have existed in the Far East for over 1,000 years. The Far Eastern metallophone is an instrument that has influenced certain of the present day orchestral instruments of percussion. Metallophones are bronze adaptations of the xylophone. An instrument of Turkish origin consisting of sixteen slabs of metal suspended in an upright frame, is said to have been introduced into China in the seventh century. This instrument would appear to be an imitation in iron of the ancient stone chime.

Bronze slabs came two or three centuries later, in two forms, the Javanese *saron* and the *gender*. Bronze metallophones differ from the earliest instruments inasmuch as the metal slabs are suspended horizontally over a cradle of wood, similar to the trough xylophone. The instruments are described as ranging from a single slab to those embracing twenty or more tuned bars, with the bars arranged in a single row.[1]

The body of the saron acts as a resonance box. The slabs rest crosswise on the upper edges of the box, the edges being padded for the purpose of insulation. The slabs are drilled at one end to receive a small pin which secures them to the edge of the box. Pins are inserted between the slabs at their opposite end to isolate them (a system adopted on many orchestral glockenspiels). The saron has a range of one octave, and is constructed in four main sizes one octave apart. There are seven slabs in the pelog system and six in the slendro.

[1] Carl Orff scores for metallophones in a number of his compositions.

The cradles of some models are curved in the shape of a crouching dragon, or otherwise fashioned, and occasionally inlaid with mother-of-pearl. Though the tone of the saron is rich, due to the quality of the metal constituting the bars and the assistance of the resonance box, the sound of this instrument is slightly inferior to that of the gender.[1]

At first sight certain genders resemble the saron, but a closer inspection of the method of mounting the metal slabs (usually 12) and their amplification reveals certain marked differences; namely, that the slabs are generally strung on two cords and suspended at a short distance over the edges of the frame, and that the tone of each bar is enriched by means of closed bamboo tubes which are placed in the frame in a vertical position under the slabs. Each tube is tuned by adjusting its length to sound in unison with its corresponding slab.

The gender and the saron have distinctive roles in the gamelan, supplying melody and variants in the large ensembles. The performers on either instrument display a marked agility and co-ordination of the hands in rapid passages, one hand acting as a damper, as the other strikes the following note.

In keeping with the arresting appearance of these instruments, the beaters are often similar works of art. The mallet completing the saron in the British Museum represents a fish with open mouth holding the striking piece.

In any survey of instruments of metal, and of gongs in particular, the *yün-lo* must be included because of its historical significance. It is an instrument associated with joyful occasions at the Chinese court. Musically it is unimportant. Sachs says of the yün-lo:[2] 'It has no relation with either the usual gong or the splendid chimes of the Malayan Islands, and is musically of little interest. Ten small, bronze disks shaped like small soup plates, about four inches in diameter, are suspended in a wooden stand to form three vertical rows. The arrangement within these rows is either:

		10	or			10
9	8	7		9	8	7
4	5	6		6	5	4
3	2	1		3	2	1

1 indicating the lowest and 10 the highest note of a more or less diatonic scale; number ten, added at a later time, is never played.'

Authorities are in complete agreement about the yün-lo. Hermann Smith says:[3]

[1] In remote areas iron or bamboo strips are used on the saron and gender. Until recently orchestras composed entirely of bamboo were not uncommon.

[2] Sachs, Curt. ibid. p. 208.

[3] Smith, Hermann. ibid. p. 162.

'Moreover, when the existing stone chimes – or, rather the Yün-lo, or gong chimes constructed to correspond in scale to the stone chimes upon the same twelve lüs principle – are submitted to examination of the necessary rigid enquiry by tests, they do not bear out the true semi-tonal character that has been asserted. Mr. Ellis tested two specimens in the South Kensington Museum, but both differed greatly, and he failed to find anything like the assumed scale; and such scale as he did find he was unable to give any theory for.'

Another instrument of little musical consequence, but which is nevertheless considered precious and important to ritual, is the *drum gong*, a bronze kettledrum. These drums are in two pieces – a hollow cylinder, one or two feet high with curving sides, with one end covered by a flat circular plate of thinly beaten bronze, in place of the customary head of hide. Normally the instrument is suspended, the centre of the plate being struck with a heavy stick and the side wall with a light bamboo, the plate emitting a lower sound than that produced from the cylinder. Ear-shaped handles are soldered to the cylinder for the suspending cords. The instrument is customarily decorated with small tree frogs, an engraved star and concentric circles, in which are birds, fishes, beasts and other symbols. A large number of frogs on the striking surface indicates a gong of high value.

History shows the bronze kettledrum in use as early as fourth century BC, though tradition credits General Ma Yuan (the conqueror of Northern Indo-China in AD 43) with its invention. It is said this resourceful soldier deceived the enemy by placing bronze drums under waterfalls, thus producing a roaring sound, mistaken by his opponents for the approach of a superior force.

It is not surprising to find these instruments considered as sacred objects. They were believed to contain spirits and that their roar of thunder could daunt the enemy. Some instruments have a hole in the side to allow the spirits to escape. As with certain other instruments, ownership of a drum gong indicated social status. The man or village owning such instruments was considered wealthy (worth more than 'he who owned seven elephants'). Wars were frequently waged to obtain possession of these precious instruments, which were often buried with their owners. (We find a similar custom amongst the Burmese and the ancient Egyptians.)

A bronze kettledrum in the Raffles Museum, Singapore, is reputed to be over 2,000 years old. This immense drum gong has a diameter of 34 inches and a height of 22 inches.

No less spectacular is the bronze kettledrum in the British Museum. The instrument, probably Han Dynasty, is 30 inches in diameter and 24 inches deep. Four handles are fixed to the cylinder. The metal head is engraved in the usual manner (star and circles) and completed with four lifesize frogs. The Indonesian bronze drum (*moko*) particularly associated with Alor, has a deep shell (with handles) in the form of an hour-glass drum.

Returning to the gamelan, we find that to the bell-like tones of the gender and saron is added the sound of an earlier instrument, the xylophone, and in some instances – as with the classical gamelan of certain parts of Bali – a further idiophone, the *angkloeng*.

The gamelan xylophone (*gambang*) is a trough xylophone. It consists of a series of slightly rounded wooden slabs of teak or some other hard wood, sixteen to twenty in number, carefully cut and tuned to cover a range from 3½ to 4 octaves. The slabs lie crosswise on the upper edges of a trough which acts as a resonance box and, like the saron, they are arranged in a single row and usually secured by small pins which pierce the bar at one end, and lie between them, as spacers, at the other end. At times, the exact tuning of the slabs is achieved by fixing under the fore-end of the bar (the end nearest the player) a composition of scraped lead and bees' wax, in the same way as employed in the final tuning of bossed gongs.

The gambang has a greater range of notes than the saron or the gender. In the example of music for the gamelan it is seen supporting the melody played by the *rebab* (spike fiddle). See below.

The trough xylophone used in the Indonesian gamelan is common to many parts of Asia, and is widely used in Japan and Burma.

Reliefs at the temple of Panataran in Java, carved in the fourteenth century, depict the xylophone and certain details of the instrument together with the style of

From the New Oxford History of Music, Vol. I. *Ancient and Oriental Music*, Ch. 2, 'Music of Far Eastern Asia', L. Picken. By permission of Oxford University Press, London, p. 169.

execution. Three of the reliefs show the playing of a duet by a male and female performer on separate instruments, each of which is enlarged on the right hand side with two longer slabs. What is also important (and possibly something of a surprise to some present-day orchestral percussionists) is the manner in which the players hold their beaters. Two beaters are held in each hand. Whether held separately or fixed at a 'Y' angle is not clear, but it is apparent that both performers beat upon two slabs simultaneously, in a manner observed by early explorers, anticipating by several centuries the style of 'four hammer playing' in Western culture (cf. African xylophone).

The Indonesian trough xylophones have much in common with those found in Africa. Certain structural and tuning details are in accordance, likewise a similarity in the form of music played on them. As yet, there remains the question as to what link is responsible for these similarities, though it is widely believed by musicologists that it is no coincidence, and that personal contact through commerce and migration can be assumed.

The 'Raffles Gamelan' – a spectacular collection of Javanese percussion instruments exhibited at the British Museum includes a number of the more important instruments already discussed.[1] The function of the ensemble is described as follows: 'The greatest range of notes (17 keys and about 3 octaves) is provided by the bird shaped *gambang kayu*, but the melody is normally led by the *bonang*, with 12 gongs mounted on the table framework. In larger assemblies, however, it is the instruments of the *saron* group which supply the melody. The larger drum (*kendang gending*) is used by the leader of the orchestra for timing and leading in musical phrases. The large gongs (*gong-ageng*) are used to end melody periods.'

Included in the xylophone category is the angkloeng (also known as the *angklung*): a rattle xylophone consisting of two or three bamboo tubes, tuned in octaves and arranged vertically and loosely in a slender wood frame, with the lower ends of the tubes shaped to move freely in slots cut in the bamboo pole forming the base of the frame. The base of the tube is closed, and the open end cut away to form a tongue tuned to the pitch of the tube. Each tube is slotted at the upper end and passes through a strip of the framework, the slots being sufficiently wide to allow the sides to strike the strip when the instrument is shaken, augmenting the sound produced from the lower end of the tubes as they strike the ends of the slots. The tone from this simple structure is most pleasing, a number of instruments of different size giving an impression of chimes. The angklung has a definite place in the classical gamelan of

[1] Similarly the gamelan instruments at the Tropen Museum, Amsterdam and the Gemeente Museum, The Hague. A remarkable specimen has been acquired by York University.

Bali (the ensemble is sometimes referred to as gamelan angkloeng). T. S. Raffles refers to the antiquity of the angkleong in the following terms:[1] '. . . the first music of which they (the Javanese) have any idea was produced by the accidental admission of air into a *bambu* tube, which was left hanging on a tree . . . the *angklung* was the first improvement upon this Aeolian music.'[2]

The use of bamboo in the making of musical instruments is age-old, as must be the suspended xylophone, which consists merely of a number of bamboo tubes or laths strung in a row. The *tjalung* of West Java is an instrument of this nature. In this case the bamboo tube is fashioned in half section.

The tjalung is normally suspended from a tree. If the player performs in a standing position, the instrument is secured to his waist; if played in a sitting position, the cords are secured to the knees. Spoon-shaped beaters (similar to those used on a cimbalom) are employed on the tjalung. The principal instruments of the Cambodia orchestra include two xylophones with bamboo keys – the *ronéat-ek* with 27 keys and the *ronéat-thum* with 17 keys.

The primitive tube zither is another example of the ingenious use of the bamboo tube. The strings – narrow strips of bamboo – are formed by lifting up outer edges of the tube. Small blocks of wood are inserted under the strings at each end, holding them away from the stem. The blocks also serve as tuning bridges, and the tube acts as a resonator, because of a hole cut in the side. Klaus P. Wachsmann[3] says: 'In the zither group exploration of melodic music continues. First there are zithers whose construction is integral, strings and all . . . Such "idiochord" strings are often used singly, and their percussion character is prominent even to the point of their being played with sticks or beaters like a dulcimer.'

The element of percussion is to be found in a number of primitive stringed instruments; the ground zither and the musical bow being two prominent examples. These two instruments are fully described in volumes dealing with cordophones and their development. The ground zither can claim to be an instrument of percussion since the vibrating string is normally struck with a stick. The string is stretched between two posts over a pit dug in the ground. A piece of bark acting as a sound-board covers the pit. From a horizontally stretched string runs a vertical string, which is secured to the centre of the bark lid. Two different notes are obtained if the upper string is divided into unequal lengths. Ground zithers are common to many parts of South-East Asia (and Africa). Sachs suggests that

[1] Raffles, T. S. *The History of Java*, Black, Parbury & Allen, London, 1817, vol. I, p. 472.

[2] Carl Orff writes for angklung: e.g. *Ludus de Nato Infante Mirificius*, 1960.

[3] Wachsmann, Klaus P. *Musical Instruments Through the Ages*, ed. Anthony Baines, Faber, London, 1966, p. 40.

the Annamese ground zither is the older instrument on account of its great size.

The difference of opinion concerning the origin of the musical bow is not our concern; but there is no disputing that this ancient instrument is associated with both plucking and striking. Musical bows are widely distributed – a proof of their great age. Stow says[1] '. . . the bow strings of the mammoth hunters gave out the first musical sounds derived from an artificial source that ever fell upon the human ear'. In a simple and primitive form such an instrument, in the shape of a hunting bow, is still used in Assam. The instrument is cradled against the shoulder, the string is tapped with a small stick held in the right hand. (A form of our orchestral *col legno*.) Pressure on the bow from the left hand tightens or loosens the string, varying the pitch of the note. (A musical bow with gourd resonator is common in S. Africa.) It is frequently argued that in Africa the struck bow or string preceded the plucked string, whilst in the East, according to the authorities, this development was reversed.

In speaking of a dulcimer, Wachsmann reminds us of an instrument that originated in the Middle East. It reached the Far East after a circuitous route, arriving in China about 1800, where it bears the name *yang-chyn* (foreign zither). The wire strings of the yang-chyn are stretched over two bridges, and struck with two very light sticks which end in broad blades. It is an attractive instrument, sweet in sound and often picturesque – it spread quickly, soon reaching Japan, Korea, India and Mongolia. (The method of tuning and performance is discussed later, in connection with an instrument which makes an occasional, though impressive, appearance in the Western orchestra – the *cimbalom*.)

A further tuned percussion instrument is the *Shui Chan*, an instrument consisting of nine bowls struck with sticks. According to Farmer[2] this instrument was known in China in AD 1300. He described this method of making music as 'hoary with antiquity'. A. C. Moule[3] says the nine cups of the *Shui Chan* probably contained different amounts of water.

CYMBALS

Metal discs have been essential to Chinese music for centuries. Their function as melodic instruments in the form of gongs and metallophones remains peculiar to the music of South East Asia, but the use of cymbals has been, and remains widespread. China is often credited with being the oldest cymbal-making country, but a study of the most authentic records suggests that cymbals entered China by means of

[1] Stow, G. W. *The Races of South Africa*, p. 107.

[2] Farmer, H. G. 'Armonica' in Grove, G. *Dictionary of Music and Musicians*, Fifth Edition, London, 1954, p. 204.

[3] Moule, A. C. A list of the musical and other sound producing instruments of the Chinese, vol. XXXIX, 1908. *Journal of the North China Branch of the Royal Asiatic Society*, p. 148.

foreign influence. Chinese history points to her being exposed to western influence during the Middle Ages; her numerous wars, and expanding commerce, resulted in a constant contact with neighbouring civilizations. According to the *Yo Shu*, the bible of Chinese musical instruments written in AD 1101 by Ch'en Yang, cymbals came originally to China from Tibet.

Two other sources are quoted as being responsible for introducing cymbals into China – India and Turkey. It is known that an Eastern Turkestani orchestra was established at the Chinese Imperial Court in AD 384. Cymbals are considered to have been among the instruments of this very early orchestra. A possible Turkish influence is suggested in the similarity of the Korean name for cymbal – *tyapara* – to that of the Turkish – *colpara* (Chinese – *po*, and/or *nao*). This influence has persisted through the ages, the manufacture of cymbals being associated almost as strongly with the Chinese as it is with the Turks.

It is generally supposed that the old sacred cymbals were composed of 81 per cent copper, with 19 per cent tin, a formula similar to that used traditionally in the manufacture of the 'Turkish' cymbal. To-day, however, there is a marked difference between 'Turkish' and Chinese cymbals now known as *nao po*, the latter being instantly recognized by their individual appearance and tone. Existing specimens of various sizes have a boss up to one inch in depth. The width of the boss is approximately three times its depth, and the overall dimension of the cymbal from edge to edge, is nearly seven times the diameter of the boss, the relative measurements seeming to be as rigidly observed as those governing the pien-ch'ing (stone chime). The bow, the curving section from the boss to the edge shows, in the majority of cases, a distinct curve upwards, commencing approximately two-thirds of the distance from the centre of the cymbal. Small cymbals usually have larger bosses.

The tone of these Chinese cymbals is as individual as their shape and content, the process of casting rendering the instruments brittle in sound and texture.

Gigantic cymbals nearly 40 inches in diameter are found in Mongolian temples. The Metropolitan Museum, New York, (Crosby Brown Collection) owns a pair of Chinese lama cymbals with a diameter of approximately 23 inches.[1] In contrast, there are the small cymbals used in the gamelan orchestra (*slentem*) and the finger cymbals used by female dancers and others. These instruments have a deep cup and small rim, with an overall measurement of three inches or thereabouts. The metal is thick, rendering the tones clear and bell-like, and of definite pitch. It is customary in the gamelan orchestra for a pair of cymbals to be mounted on a block, and struck with a pair of cymbals of similar size, which for convenience of performance are often secured to the end of short sticks.

[1] The writer's collection includes a Chinese cymbal 26 inches in diameter.

Cymbals

Small cymbals are used in a curious manner in the Chinese theatre. Before a speech to which special attention is to be drawn, a player strikes them several times in quick succession. The conductor of an orchestra sometimes uses a pair of finger cymbals as time keepers. Occasionally in the gamelan orchestra a similar timbre is produced from the clashing of a pair of *kemanak*, consisting of two metal objects resembling hollowed bananas with the addition of a curved handle. Kemanak are also used for ritual purposes.

Fig. 19
Chinese cymbal

For generations the Chinese have used cymbals in addition to drums, gongs and bells, as a means of directing troop movements on the field of battle, or to terrify the enemy. In the Chinese *Book of War*[1] written in the fifth century BC is found: 'The drum was used to beat the assembly, and in the advance, the bell as a signal to halt.' In a night attack innumerable pairs of cymbals were rubbed together.

Allied troops engaged in Korea in the early 50's testify to the unnerving experience of this age-old method of attack. A similar uncanny sound is experienced during the period of mourning for an important person, when pairs of cymbals of various sizes and with a wide range of sounds are played by the mourners, for the comfort of the soul of the departed. In Thailand the clashing of cymbals accompanies prayers for rain.

A further type of Indonesian, Burmese or Annamitic metal plate chime is the *kyeezee*. It is triangular in shape, with elaborate curved lines. A number of plates of differing size and pitch are suspended vertically. The instrument does not appear to be performed in concert. Sachs mentions that this triangular type of metal plate also

[1] *The Book of War*, translated by E. F. Calthrop, John Murray, London, 1908, p. 31.

occurs in Tibet, the fanciful, triangular outline being interpreted as a crescent or a mountain. These metal plates have clarity and exceptional resonance.

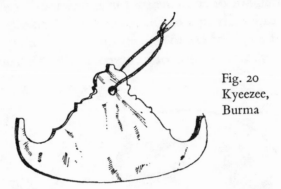

Fig. 20
Kyeezee,
Burma

THE SKIN DRUM

Early documents (*c.* 1300–1050 BC) are said to contain characters depicting such musical instruments as suspended triangular stones, bells, and drums struck by a drumstick. Legendary evidence suggests the drum was introduced into China from Central Asia as early as 3500 BC. Ancient records refer to them as barbarous instruments from Turkestan and Tibet.

Many types of drums (*ku*) are attributed to China. It is said that eight varieties existed to conform with the eight natural elements, and that the skins of cowhide, pigskin, or fish skin were tanned. (The Chinese tanned pigskin as early as 3000 BC.) The Rites of Chou Dynasty (1125–255 BC) refer to drums with various types of heads, including a fish skin.

Van Aalst[1] says: 'Drums made of baked clay, filled with bran, and covered with skin were the first in use.' Yetts[2] is of the same opinion. He says: 'According to the repository of ancient lore compiled in the third century BC . . . the most primitive of Chinese drums was an earthenware pot (*fou*) over which was stretched a deer skin.'

A giant drum called the *hiuen-kou*, was said to have been invented for the exclusive use of the Imperial Palace in 1122 BC during the dynasty of Chou. In 1886 Emil Naumann[3] described this instrument and concluded prophetically '. . . The size of this colossal drum is at once seen on comparing the height of the performer. . . It is placed on a specially-prepared stand: it oscillates, and has two smaller drums, one on each side. The Chinese ear finds special charm in the contrast of the deep-booming

---

[1] Aalst, J. A. Van. ibid. p. 75.
[2] Yetts, W. Percival. *The Eumorfopoulos Collection*, Benn, London, 1929, vol. II, p. 12.
[3] Naumann, Emil. *History of Music*, Cassell, London, 1886, p. 14.

thunder of the large drums and the more rattling of the two small drums, a charm for which our European ears are possibly being prepared, should the increase on instruments of percussion in the modern orchestra continue at the same rate as heretofore.' The smaller drum to which Naumann refers is an instrument with sloping sides and heads of different diameter – an unusual feature in Chinese drums.

In contrast to the great drum hiuen-kou, there is a reference in old records regarding a small drum named *kero* used in China about the period of the T'ang dynasty. This drum was used to symbolize the appearance of dawn, as in the Shinto temple the large drum is used to this day.

In addition to the hiuen-kou and the kero (and numerous other drums, too profuse to classify) China had an ancient grain-filled drum, *po-fu*, and a clapper drum *t'ao-ku*, the latter dating back to the Shang dynasty. (The modern po-fu is smaller than the ancient drum and is no longer grain-filled.) The t'ao-ku (unlike the clapper or pellet drum of India and Tibet) is mounted on a stick which passes through the body of the drum (in some cases two drums) and forms a handle. The beads suspended on the shell of the drum strike the skins when the instrument is twirled to and fro. Small clapper drums are used to-day by hawkers and beggars.

The instruments so far mentioned have two nailed heads. In contrast, there is the *pang-ku* (loaf drum), a hoop-drum with a single head of cowskin (nailed). This instrument is common in theatres, and is the leader of the orchestra. It is normally suspended on a tripod and played with sticks of thin bamboo.

A tambourine, *pa-fang-ku* is mentioned by Moule. It is described as octagonal with seven sets of jingles and a head of snake skin, and associated with the area of Peking.

The most common drums in China are barrel shaped. They include the *tou-ku* and the *ying-ku* (large temple drums), the *t'ang-ku* (hall drum), the *bien-ta-ku* or to-day *pieng-ku*, and the *shu-ku* (book, or reader's drum). At times, a drum resembling the bien-ta-ku is mounted on a pole, or a small handle is attached.

The body of a barrel drum is made of wood, frequently 'built up' in sections (like a cask). The length of the shell differs considerably, ranging from the short drum in which the length of the barrel is much shorter than the diameter of the heads, to the long drum where the depth of the barrel exceeds the diameter of the heads. The heads – usually thick cowskin or pigskin – are nailed to the shell at both ends with iron nails. With their barrel form, nailed heads and constant pitch, the majority of Chinese drums provide a contrast to the tunable heads of many important Asian cord tensioned drums.

The wood shell of the Chinese drum is invariably coloured, frequently red, and the skins varnished or covered with colourful paintings, featuring the phoenix and the dragon encompassed in jagged clouds. In addition to adorning the vellums, the skins thus treated remain reasonably taut under varying atmospheric conditions.[1]

In China the barrel drum is played in two positions – heads horizontal and heads vertical. Iron rings are inserted in the barrel, allowing the instrument to be suspended in a frame or attached to the body by a cord, as is the *ya-kou*, a small drum in the form of a tub. Sachs points out that the large Sumerian drums and the large barrel drums of the Far East were closely related, and probably had a common origin somewhere between Mesopotamia and China, and that the use of the two sticks striking the same drum could be interpreted as derived from the two drummers striking the same skin on Sumerian reliefs.

Similarly, we may find the influence of India in the *chang-ku*, which according to Moule is 'perhaps the only Chinese drum of which the heads can be tightened with cords'. Galpin contends this drum may have been introduced from India, where such methods of tuning are common. The fact that we find only rare instances of Chinese drums described as tuned to certain notes, and the absence (with the exception of the chang-ku) of braced drums with tunable heads, at least since mediaeval times, is surprising, bearing in mind that Southern China was the original home of the *kakko*, a laced drum of considerable importance, considered to have inspired the Japanese handdrums (*ko-tsuzumi* and *o-tsuzumi*).

The chang-ku is a spool-shaped drum with protruding vellums stretched on iron rings. The cords, which are in 'W' formation are drawn taut with iron rings, a decided Indian feature, as is the double skin at one end, in the case of the chang-ku a snake-skin sewn into a cow-hide.

A braced drum with an unusual method of tensioning is found in the region of

---

[1] The shallow drum (*pieng-ku*), common in the Chinese orchestra, entered the western dance band in the early 1920's. The instrument referred to somewhat loosely as a *tom-tom* kept company with its 'fellow countrymen' the Chinese cymbal and woodblock, forming an integral part of the percussion equipment used in this pioneering period of western dance music. These instruments varied approximately nine to fifteen inches in diameter and three or more inches in depth, and the majority were equipped with an appendage consisting of a spiral spring, a few inches in length, which was affixed to the inner wall of the shell. The spring vibrated when the head was struck, producing a sound which did not conform to the western instrumentalists' requirements. Many of these players, loathe to disturb the nailed vellums, cut a hole in the wood shell to allow the removal of the rattling piece. The outer surface of the shell was red lacquered, and the skins decorated with the customary features.

Copland writes for a Chinese drum in his Concerto for piano and orchestra (1929) and Roger Sessions for a small Chinese drum in his Symphony No. 3 (1962). Cf. Britten's parable operas *Curlew River, The Burning Fiery Furnace* and *The Prodigal Son*.

Samutra (Batak tribe). Wooden pegs are 'threaded' into the vellum. A rattan (palm) rope passes behind the protruding ends of each peg and passes underneath a circular block of wood on which the body of the drum rests. Tension is applied by forcing (with wedges) the shell upwards from the wooden base. This simple method of adding pressure to a vellum is incorporated in a Russian kettledrum.

The function of the Asiatic drum is as varied as its construction. Writers of the past constantly referred to the large part played by the drum in the life of the Far Eastern Asiatic ... drums with a marriage procession, at a funeral cortege, 'drum towers', where, every evening vast drums, six feet in diameter, were beaten against the powers of evil. They speak of the old stone drums at the Confucian temple in Peking, which were made for the Emperor Chu-Kung (669 BC) and supposed by many authorities to have been actually beaten in religious ceremonies. A new set of similar drums was added by Chien-Lung (AD 1700).

Speaking of the religious rites at the Lama temples, which include such music, necessitating a somewhat large orchestra of drums, trumpets and stringed instruments, G. P. Green says:[1] ... 'The drums are of two descriptions, one, about three feet in diameter, made with a long handle and carried by a priest, with another priest to beat a slow note of intonation, generally B. The other is a highly ornate drum of similar proportions.'

Like its European counterpart, the Chinese drum has long been an essential instrument in warfare. Its function is described in the following quotation from *The Book of War*.[2] 'At one beat of the drum the ranks are put in order; at two beats of the drum, formation will be made; at three beats of the drum, food will be issued; at four beats of the drum, the men will prepare to march; at five beats of the drum, ranks will be formed; when the drums beat together, then the standards will be raised.' Together with the flag, the drum was carried on the commanding chariot, its position in battle deciding the movement and the fate of the army. It was regarded as a talisman for luck and victory, and its magic character was strengthened by the belief in the power of protection attributed to the nails in securing the skins to the shell.

Giant drums, approaching six feet in diameter, were a feature at the head of battle formations. The drums and their performers, quite often madmen recruited from prisons, were secured to waggons drawn by oxen. The frenzied performers 'pounded' their instruments unceasingly with heavy clubs or whips. The din was undoubtedly terrifying, in fact it has been said that invariably the side which made the greatest noise won the battle, often before a blow was exchanged. (An experi-

[1] Green, G. P. *Aspects of Chinese Music*, William Reeves, London, 1901, p. 48.
[2] ibid. p. 98.

ment of this nature might well be tried in this present period of enlightenment).

Drums of various styles are used in the Confucian temple, each having a specially allotted function. It is only at a certain stage during the progress of the ceremony that the instruments of music are ordered to play, and then in their respective groups: strings, wind, and the percussion instruments which include chimes, gongs, cymbals, tiger box and drums. A small drum is struck six times at the end of each verse in answer to the three beats of the larger drum.

Forsyth says:[1] 'Besides the huge ceremonial drum which is placed in the eastern pagoda of the Hall to balance the principal bell in the western, three other smaller drums are used in the Ritual Music. One is a larger drum (*ying-ku*) . . . about three feet in diameter. It is beaten three times after each verse of the Hymn and each beat is answered by two beats of a slightly smaller double-headed drum known as *tsu-ku*. A smaller drum (*po-fu*, meaning right-left) whose use is forbidden except for religious purposes, answers the two beats of the middle-sized drum with three strokes – one right-handed, one left-handed, and one double-handed.'

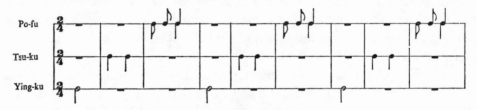

In describing the po-fu, Sachs says:[2] 'A temple musician held it horizontally on his knees and, at the end of each verse of the hymn to Confucius, beat it three times with the bare hands – once with the right hand on the right skin, *po*, once with the left hand on the left skin, *fu*, and a third time with both hands on both skins, *po-fu*.'

The Chinese have long been a nation of percussionists. A treatise on beating the drum scientifically dates from about AD 860. A further ancient writing, the *Li chi* states that: 'Though the drum has no special relation to any of the musical notes, without it the musical notes cannot be brought into harmony'. The drum remains an indispensable member of the Chinese orchestra, regulating the rhythm and divisions. It functions similarly when accompanying vocal music. In performance it is sounded with sticks, knobbed or otherwise, or in some circumstances it is played with the hands – governed by tradition and purpose. The technique involved is typically Asian. G. Tradescant Lay observed this style in 1841:[3] 'In the Chinese drummer we miss the roll, which depends on each stick giving its stroke in pairs,

[1] Forsyth, Cecil. *A History of Music*, p. 35.   [2] Sachs, Curt. ibid. p. 172.
[3] Lay, G. Tradescant. ibid. p. 90.

though it must be allowed he plies his sticks with dexterity.' There is no doubt that Chinese drumming reaches a high level, technically and stylistically, though we must confess to an agreement with Dr. Laurence Picken, who contends that Chinese drumming never approaches the rhythmic complexity of that of India.

WOOD DRUMS

One of the most arresting percussion instruments of China (and Japan) is the wooden fish (*mu-yü*) generally known to the western world as a Chinese temple block. In form it is a slit drum, carved from a piece of camphor wood to resemble a mythical fish. It is hollowed out through a shaped slit representing the creature's open mouth, the body is lacquered red and gold. Occasionally a small movable ball is skilfully carved inside a cavity, ornamenting the upper part of the instrument.[1] The wooden fish is symbolical of wakeful attention; its sound is believed to attract the notice of divinity. It is also connected with prayers for rain, and the rites of death and resurrection, while it may also signify wealth and abundance. At the funeral of a person of high rank, the mourners, often in their hundreds, march in procession each striking in slow tempo and perfect unison a small drum of this type. Similar instruments are used by pilgrims. In the temple it is used by the priests to mark certain intervals during the Confucian service. In the Buddhist service it is struck persistently whilst the name of Buddha is chanted.

On occasions huge 'temple blocks' are used by priests at temple ceremonies. The instrument rests on a large cushion. It is struck with a heavy beater in a remorseless rhythm to punctuate the prayer.

For musical purposes, a small wood block is held either in the hand of the player, suspended, or placed on a cushion. It is struck with a heavy pear-shaped beater, also coloured red.[2]

[1] The Javanese *kentongan* is a bronze gong which resembles the Chinese mu-yü.

[2] For some time 'temple blocks' have proved something of a boon to Occidental musicians, ranging in purpose from the 'clippidy-clop' of the hill-billy, to the fascinating automatic rhythm supplementing the mallet strokes during the process of building the ark in Benjamin Britten's *Noye's Fludde*. This reminds me of an occasion in the mid-thirties when I was performing in the dance band of a notable West End establishment. At the conclusion of a Western ballad ('Over the Prairie') in which wood blocks were a decided feature, an Oriental, who sat at a table adjoining the bandstand (no doubt for want of accommodation at a further distance) politely drew my attention to the solemn character of certain percussion instruments in the Far East, particularly the 'temple block'. Despite the sincerity of the informant and the impression made on the percussionist, to avoid horrifying the establishment, from manager to commis boy (apprentice waiter), the blocks remained an integral part of such masterpieces as the item mentioned.

In addition to the mu-yü there is the fish drum, an instrument carved in very detail to resemble an actual fish. An instrument of this nature measuring eight feet in length is used by Buddhist monks on the Isle of Puto. This fish drum is suspended from the ceiling of a temple. Its resonant sound announces the time for prayer and meditation. The Zen Buddhists use similar instruments, and wood plaques, for the same purpose.

A small wooden slit drum, oblong in shape, known as the *t'ak* (or *pang-tzu*), is used by night watchmen. The wood block used in the Chinese orchestra (mainly in opera ensembles, in combination with the big drum-*ganggu*) is the *kuan-tun-pa*. This type of instrument occurs frequently in western orchestral scores, where it is referred to as 'wood-block'.

A further type of wood drum, and one connected with the Confucian service is the trough (*chu*). This instrument, having the form of an ancient grain measure, may have originated in a farming civilization. According to Sachs, it was obviously connected with the music of certain agricultural rites similar to the Malayan rice pounding in tuned mortars, explaining why the Chinese strike the inside of the trough instead of the outside. The trough is mentioned in a poem as early as 1100 BC, though this instrument had a forerunner in the Korean *chuk*. The Chinese trough is constructed of boards, the base being a foot or more square, with the four side walls sloping upwards. A hole in one of the sides gives access to a hammer (*chih*) which is linked to a pivot on the base. In some cases the hammer is disconnected. The trough is struck at the beginning of the Confucian service. (A similar sound is experienced in many European theatres to announce the start of a performance). In the hymn to Confucius, the trough is struck three times before each verse. (A similar instrument, though of wood or metal, is found in Japan – the *shoku*.)

An instrument used to announce the end of the Confucian service is known as the Tiger (*yü*), or tiger box. It is carved to represent a crouching tiger, somewhat idealized, and with a facial expression embodying pain. The spine of the animal is notched, and is scraped with a split rod of bamboo. The Tiger rests on a resonant box, about three feet long and twenty inches wide. At the end of the grand Confucian hymn performed in the presence of the Emperor and all his Court, the chief officer assigned to this service delivered three blows on the head of the Tiger. The rod was then passed with a vigorous swish three times along the 27 serrations on the Tiger's back, thus announcing the end of the strophe.[1] (The Tiger, again in recumbent position, is found in the Japanese *gyo*.)

---

[1] 27 serrations, that is three times the significant number nine (see bells).

CLAPPERS AND BELLS

Clappers are important in Chinese music, both secular and sacred. The *tchoung-tou*, a hand clapper consisting of a number of flat bamboo strips joined at one end, is used by the Chinese temple singers, as is also a clapper (*shou-pan*) consisting of two pieces of hard wood, tapered and hinged at the base, with the addition at times of small jingles. Clappers resembling the western castanets are *p'ai-pan*.

In addition to the p'ai-pan and the tchoung-tou, concussion sticks (with a variety of names) are prominent in almost every form of national music. These instruments range from small pieces of cane to quite sizeable sticks (dancing sticks). In some parts of the Far East metal clappers resembling double castanets are used. Rarely does one hear the traditional music of China without the support of the simple and age-old instruments of percussion. They play their part in the classical and court orchestra, particularly the clapper which serves as a baton, being used by the conductor as a signal to start or conclude an item, or to indicate a change of tempo.

Naumann in a description of a Chinese orchestra says:[1] 'In the background, towards the south, in front of the portraits of the ancestors, stands the table of perfumes; on it is placed lighted candles, flowers and scent. To the right, towards the west, are the bell and time-beaters, pan-pipe and Cheng players; to the left, towards the east, are the players on the kettle-drum, rattle-drum (*Tao-kou*), and the flute-players.' In many representations Chinese musicians appear to be blind. Ancient tradition described Chinese musicians as blind. It is known that special encouragement was given to the blind to obtain proficiency in music, the members of the Imperial Household being empowered to confer on them ranks or degrees. On the other hand, it is suggested that this remarkable tradition arose through ancient musicians closing their eyes whilst performing, so that no external object should engage their attention. It is from this habit that people gave them the name of the blind.

To the Chinese, the bell (*chung*) is an important instrument. Its place in the orchestra is no small tribute to the skill attained by the Chinese in the making of bells; they are in fact credited with discovering the art of bell founding. In early songs, the references to bells suggest these instruments as the Bronze Age counterparts of sonorous stones.

The bell in the Chinese orchestra is struck from the outside with a disconnected hammer. Bells struck by an internal clapper are usually (as far as the East is concerned) hand bells, or, those suspended from the necks of animals, which are regarded, as elsewhere, as amulets to protect the wearers against evil spirits. Clapper

[1] Naumann, Emil. ibid. pp. 16–17.

117

bells (*ling*) do occur, in some instances in Oriental music. The military bands of the Chou dynasty included at least two hand bells. Van Aalst[1] speaks of the *to*, a tongued bell with a metal or wooden clapper, and handle at the apex. He says four different kinds of tongued bells were used in the army. In the dance, each military dancer had a bell with metal tongue, and each civil dancer one with a wooden tongue.

Generally speaking, the large bells of the Far East are not chimed or rung in the western manner; they are used singly, and struck as the bell in the Chinese orchestra. There are occasional exceptions. The 1856 *Synopsis of the Contents of the British Museum* describes a Chinese bell from a Buddhist temple near Ningpo in this manner: 'On the top is the Imperial dragon, the national emblem of China, crouching and forming the handle. Beneath this is the orifice where the clapper has been placed'. Engel[2] contends that if this really was the case it must be considered as quite exceptional.

Authorities agree that the empty bell preceded the clapper bell, but are hesitant as to its origin. Sachs[3] says: 'We do not know how the bell originated. Primitive peoples possess rough bells made of natural material, such as crab pincers, shells and wood. But it is not sure that non-metallic bells preceded the metal bell; most of them are clumsy imitations probably due to the lack of metal and foundries. It is not even certain that the riveted iron bells of African Negroes came earlier than the Chinese bells.'

A set of inscribed bells discovered in a tomb near Lo Yang confirms the existence of a series of bells some four to five centuries BC. Chinese and European scholars are divided in their interpretation of the inscription, as the date mentioned gives the year of the reign of the monarch, but not the king's name. A bell of the sixth century BC in the Victoria and Albert Museum, London, is inscribed (in archaic characters) '. . . this bell, Harmonious Spirit, made for use by the elder of Hing village in Ting District'.

The most ancient Chinese bells were quadrate in form, changing in shape through the ages. The characteristic beehive or harebell shape of Chinese bells is attributed to the Chan dynasty. At the temple of Confucius stood a great bell which the Chinese said was made to correspond with the big drum; the drum giving the signal to begin, and the bell to announce the end of the ceremonies. The smaller temple bell (*po-chung*) was placed on the moon terrace, and struck with a beater between the verses of the Confucian hymn, to give the note at the beginning of each verse in order to manifest the sound; bells of different pitch being used at each season of the

---

[1] Aalst, J. A. Van. ibid. p. 57.
[2] Engel, Carl. *The Music of the Most Ancient Nations*, pp. 69, 70.
[3] Sachs, Curt. ibid. pp. 169, 170.

year to conform with Chinese cosmology. Confucian bells are associated with ideas of fertility, as is proved by the decorations on many of them. The exterior of the bell is divided into two zones; the undecorated section representing the field concealing the seeds; the other section being studded with four squares of nine bosses each, signifying according to Chinese custom the nipples of the female breast.

Great importance was attached to the purity of the tone and note of the bells used in the ancient ceremonies of ancestor worship. It was not uncommon to mix with the molten metal (bronze) the blood of a sheep or an ox as a sacrifice to the bell. The legend of the casting of the great bell of Peking refers to the possibility of human sacrifice. The Great Bell, the largest in China, which stands 14 feet high, is 34 feet in circumference, with walls one inch in thickness, and weighing 20,000 lb, was cast in the fifteenth century AD by order of the Emperor Yung-lo. It was to be struck only when the monarch prayed for rain. The most skilled masters in the already ancient art of bell founding were employed in the construction of the instrument which was to be in the form of a memorial. The legend relates, that after two unsuccessful castings, the lovely young daughter of the mandarin responsible for the perfection of the instrument learned from an astrologer that success would only be secured if a maiden's blood were mixed with the ingredients. The metal was cast for the third time. Whilst the molten metal was poured into the mould, the girl threw herself into the boiling fluid. The bell was perfect. It remains in service and is still bright and sound, and is considered to be one of the finest works of art in the whole of Asia. It is without flaw of any kind, and is covered in relief both inside and out with myriads of Chinese characters, less than one inch in size, consisting of prayers from Buddhist classics. It could not be duplicated by any western foundry, whatever its resources or skilled man-power.

Many of the larger bells of China have fallen to the ground, their great weight having caused the collapse of the towers or frames in which they were suspended. The majority of these bells display excellent workmanship. There is no existing evidence of the bells referred to by the Chinese writer Chang Heng (AD 78–139) who speaks of 'enormous bells in the palaces weighing 300,000 lb', though the 'great bell of Canton' is described by Burrow as 20 feet in diameter and sixteen inches thick.

Bells of all sizes from those weighing fifty tons to the small instruments with clappers and the *Feng-ling* or 'Wind-bells', such as those which hang from the eaves of houses or pagodas, were to be found all over China.

Ten types of bronze bells named in Chinese literature are five large clapperless bells and five smaller bells with clappers. The entries concerning the smaller bell, deal with their use in warfare, the *d'ak* being carried by the leader of a file of mens and the *nan* (another small bell) being carried by the commander. A special banner, the dragon banner, was edged with small bells. A number of small bells on a handle in the form of a bell-tree is used in Java.

Wooden bells with clappers are hung from the necks of animals. Specimens up to three feet in length are hung from the necks of oxen.

It is true to say that with the Chinese a large and potent source of music was found in bells, drums and gongs, in instruments ranging from the giant bell to the humble *nyma*, a small pottery vessel used to mark time in singing.

The Chinese consider there is little music of account to compare with their own, and that the reputed 'Father of Music' was their own Emperor Fhu Hsi, who reigned little short of 5,000 years ago. Such a view is scarcely surprising when it is borne in mind that the Chinese were writing learned works on music and musical instruments, at the time when the Pharaohs were building the pyramids.

Bibliography: Chapter 4

CHINA AND THE FAR EAST

AALST, J. A. VAN. *Chinese Music*, King, London, 1884, reprint Paragon, New York, 1964.

The Book of War, translated by E. F. Calthrop, Murray, London, 1908.

ENGEL, Carl. *The Music of the Most Ancient Nations*, Reeves, London, 1864.

FARMER, H. G. 'Armonica,' Grove, G. *Dictionary of Music and Musicians*, Fifth Edition, London, 1954.

FRAZER, J. G. *The Golden Bough*, Macmillan, London, 1935.

GREEN, G. P. *Aspects of Chinese Music*, Reeves, London, 1901.

JACOBSON, E. and HASSELT, J. H. VAN. *De Gong-Fabricatie te Semarang*, E. J. Brill, Leiden, 1907.

LAY, G. Tradescant. *The Chinese as they are*, Ball, London, 1841.

MOULE, A. C. 'A list of the musical and other sound producing instruments of the Chinese', vol. XXXIX, *Journal of the North China Branch of the Royal Asiatic Society*, 1908.

NAUMANN, Emil. *History of Music*, translated Praeger, Cassel, London, 1886.

PICKEN, Laurence. *Ancient and Oriental Music*, vol. I, Oxford, London, 1960.

RAFFLES, T. S. *The History of Java*, Black, Parbury & Allen, London, 1817.

SACHS, Curt. *The History of Musical Instruments*, Norton, New York, 1940.

SIMBRIGER, Heinrich. *Gong und Gongspiele*, Internationales Archiv für Ethnographie, Band XXXVI, E. J. Brill, Leiden, 1939.

SMITH, Hermann. *The World's Earliest Music*, Reeves, London, 1904.

STANFORD, C. V. & FORSYTH, Cecil. *A History of Music*, Macmillan, New York, 1917.

STOW, G. W. *The Races of South Africa*, ed. Theal, Swan Sonnenschen, London, 1905.

Bibliography

WACHSMANN, Klaus. *Musical Instruments Through the Ages*, ed. Anthony Baines, Faber, London, 1966.
YETTS, Percival. *The Eumorfopoulos Collection*, Benn, London, 1929, vol. II.

RECOMMENDED READING

MONTAGU, Jeremy. 'What is a Gong?' *Man*, London, Jan.–Feb. 1965.
NEEDHAM, Joseph. 'Chinese Bell Technology', *Science and Civilisation in China*, vol. IV, no. 1, Cambridge, 1954.

5

Japan

Despite the tremendous changes in all aspects of Japanese national life which include a genuine acceptance of Western music, there remains a support of their traditional musical culture. It is fortunate that the majority of the musical instruments involved (especially the instruments of percussion) retain much of their original form and purpose.

The subject of Japanese music and musical instruments is so vast that one of the first westerners to write exhaustively on the subject, Sir Francis T. Piggott[1], says of his book '. . . it is only an introduction to the subject'. Over 50 years later William P. Malm, in his foreword to his *Japanese Music and Musical Instruments*, says:[2] 'Like Piggott's book, this too can be but an introduction to a most complex subject. I am fortunate, however, in having many more sources to draw upon than did Piggott.'

Despite the modesty of these eminent authors, their works are acknowledged text-books, and deal with Japanese music as a whole. We are here concerned only with percussion instruments, but this is no small matter, bearing in mind the extent of the Japanese 'batterie'.

Historical writings tell us that in the Soshun era (AD 588) the young men of Japan who were chosen for the musical profession, were sent to learn their art from the Koreans, and to study specially the *kakko* (Korean, *kol ko*), the drum of Southern China, an instrument still found in Japan, but no longer associated with China. The fact that Japan borrowed and appropriated from China follows the natural sequence of events, the Chinese being their nearest neighbours and related to them by blood. In music especially, the Japanese would find a source of inspiration in the Chinese, and their instruments. That the young men of Japan became adept in performing upon the kakko is obvious, for their skill is reflected in Japanese drumming, past and

[1] Piggott, F. T. *Music and Musical Instruments of Japan*, Batsford, London, 1909.
[2] Malm, W. P. *Japanese Music and Musical Instruments*, Tuttle, Rutland, Vermont, 1959, p. 15.

present; and here we must call attention to the individual approach, technical and otherwise, involved in the Japanese manipulation of the most prominent instrument of percussion. The African drums with his hands or sticks; the Hindu with fingers; the East Asian with fingers, hands and sticks, but his 'stick technique' is quite opposed to the manner in which the drum is struck (with sticks) in the west. In Japan, as elsewhere, the drums and the drumming are as individual as the executants.

The drums of Japan fall into two main classes: braced heads and nailed heads. The nailed drums have convex cylinders (wood). The vellums (two) and shell are frequently ornamented in the manner of many Chinese drums. The *o-daiko*, measuring $2\frac{1}{2}$ feet in diameter and a cylinder depth of 3 feet, is the largest of this group. It forms part of the *dai-dai kagura* orchestra and is used occasionally in temple services. The *ko-daiko*, a small form of o-daiko, is used in the orchestra, though its chief use is as a processional drum.

Fig. 21
O-daiko, Japan
(after Piggott)

The *tsuri-daiko* or 'Hanging Drum' is essentially an orchestral instrument, and connected chiefly with the *Bugaku* (dance) orchestra. This drum is suspended on a stand and struck on one side in the centre, with short sticks having leather covered knobs. Special instructions are given for playing this drum. Piggott says:[1] '. . . a loud drum point with the male stick (*obachi*) (R) is invariably preceded by a soft beat with the female stick (*mebachi*) (L)'. A similar grace note also played 'hand to hand', is a feature of our own rudimentary and orchestral drum technique, where it is known as the 'flam'.

The tsuri-daiko is frequently played by two performers. They face each other, one player striking the head in the normal manner, with the second performer playing – with sticks – on the barrel of the drum. A smaller drum with nailed heads – *guku-taiko* – resembles the shallow barrel drum common in China.

Barrel drums with nailed heads take many forms, the tsuri-daiko holding pride of

[1] Piggott. ibid. London, 1909, p. 162.

place. The tsuri-daiko at one time was generally called only *taiko*. Piggott gives taiko as the generic name for drum, any prefix turning the initial t – to d – e.g., *o–daiko*, large drum, etc. The ideograms, according to the Japanese dictionary, define taiko as denoting drums in various forms, braced and nailed, also to drum-beat, a drumhead and drumsticks. *Tsuzumi*, also meaning drum, is applied to braced drums, in particular to those in spool shape. It would seem that any drum might be called a taiko and also a tsuzumi, but that tsuzumi usually suggests an hour-glass drum, and taiko a braced or nailed drum, barrel or cylindrical. A possible analogy would be our bells and chimes; either can be used for the same thing, but we would usually use bells for the handbell shape, and chimes for the tubes.

Drums with braced heads are as numerous as those with the heads nailed. Braced drums include the *da-daiko*, the *ni-daiko*, the *kakko*, the *uta-daiko* and the tsuzumi. These drums possess a distinct feature, in that the skins have a much larger diameter than the cylinder. The two heads are connected by a cord which passes in 'W' form through holes in the protruding edge. The heads are secured to iron rings, normally by stitching. The skins are first tightened by pressure from the 'W' braces, and further tensioned by means of an encircling central belt. The leverage on the 'floating' head permits considerable pressure on the vellum with seemingly little effort. (This ancient method of mounting a drumhead was applied centuries later to the kettledrum. Its incorporation in the modern machine timpani and orchestral side drum as a floating head, was generally regarded as something of an innovation).

The largest of the braced drums is the da-daiko. This is Japan's largest, and (with the *ko-tsuzumi*) the most picturesque drum. The skins, which are more than six feet wide, stretch over a cylinder four feet in diameter and five feet in depth. Two skins comprise the striking head. The tensioning of the da-daiko is an important and strenuous business, a terrific pressure being placed on the heads by means of 'winding' the braces with stout wooden poles. Two heavy lacquered beaters are used to strike the da-daiko, which according to Malm is always struck in left to right sequence, in contrast to the Chinese drum called po-fu, meaning right-left, and struck in like manner.

In describing the da-daiko, Sir Francis Piggott says:[1] '... the large drum used only on the greatest occasions in the Bugaku orchestra instead of the tsuri-daiko. It is erected on a special platform, draped and tasselled, with a gold railing and steps. The drummer, who is specially selected for his skill, stands in front of the drum, the directions being that he should, for greater vigour in striking, place his left foot on the platform, and his right on the upper step. It (the drum) is surrounded with a broad rim ornamented with phoenix and dragon, and edged with red *kwayen* or

[1] Piggott, F. T. ibid. p. 163.

flames.' In addition to adding its tremendous weight of sound on the occasions described by Piggott, two of these elegant instruments are used as ornaments in the choreography of certain dances.[1]

In contrast to the mammoth da-daiko there is the *kakko*, a small drum of Chinese origin and leader of the Bugaku orchestra. This instrument is capable of high expression. It requires an individual technical approach. The kakko is played in a horizontal position mounted on a stand; both heads are used. Piggott tells us[2] '. . . It is struck in three different ways: *Katarai*: a number of quick strokes with the left stick, slightly increasing in speed. *Mororai*: a number of alternate strokes with both sticks, also increasing in speed making a slow roll. *Sei*: a single tap with the right stick. The stroke is a circular motion, figured in the "Records of Ancient Music" as a *"tomoyé"* ' :

Motion of left stick   Motion of right stick

The recent information from Malm concerning the strokes employed on the kakko suggests little change in technical approach since the last century. Sachs says:[3] '. . . Of the small varieties, the kakko, lying on a low stand, is the most important as counterpart of the tsuri daiko in the bugaku orchestra. Their rhythmic style is interesting as the accents differ from ours; indeed, they are the reverse:

```
            occidental accents ↓↓   ↑
beats                         1 2 3 4
        Japanese accents . . . ↑   ↓↓
```

We deduce from Sachs a strong 'off beat' in the Japanese rhythm section, with which we are perhaps too familiar in 'pop' music of the west.

The commonest of the Japanese drums is the *uta-daiko* – the Song Drum – uta meaning 'song'. This instrument is the king of the Geza theatre. Malm speaks of an instrument of this description as the taiko of the *Noh* orchestra. The uta-daiko, a shallow cylindrical drum with protruding heads, is normally played with plain sticks, resembling slender rolling pins or cylindrical rulers. The drum is placed in a special stand and played at an angle resembling the upward tilt favoured by many orchestral timpanists. Evidence points to the use of the uta-daiko from the sixteenth century onwards and to the high status of the players.

[1] In addition to such ornamentation, certain drums are surmounted by a small figure, a custom now almost peculiar to Japan.

[2] Piggott, F. T. ibid. p. 166.

[3] Sachs, Curt. ibid. pp. 214, 215.

Japan

Like his Chinese counterpart so admired by G. Tradescant Lay, the Japanese performer 'plies his sticks with dexterity'. In addition he produces a variety of sounds: normal drum tone with the tip of the sticks, a sharper sound with part of the shaft striking the skin, and an improvised snare effect by resting one stick on the skin whilst beating with the other.[1] The uta-daiko has three basic sounds: *sho, chu, dai,* which according to the numerous dictionary definitions signify *pp, mf, f.* In addition to these basic sounds there are numerous tones produced by the positioning of the sticks on the drumhead. A characteristic of the Japanese percussionist is his control of the duration of certain beats accomplished in the shortening of the note by leaving the stick on the drum after its impact, a style foreign to most Western percussionists, whose pride is in the immediate 'release' of the stick. Again we find, in contrast to our loose wrist action, the Japanese player using a stiff arm from elbow to fingers, and little or no drum rolling as we know it. He is, however, no mean showman with his various flourishes with arms and sticks, somewhat reminiscent of signals in semaphore.

The ni-daiko resembles in construction the da-daiko but is a much smaller drum. It is a processional drum which is suspended on a pole carried on the shoulders of two men, the performer walking alongside; the ko-daiko is also carried and played in this manner. (An instrument similarly supported, but struck by the bearers with a hooked stick is associated with India and is depicted on the reliefs of Amaravati.) A further processional drum is the *kerō,* a small drum, an import from China.

Hour-glass drums complete, as far as it is practical to complete such a galaxy, the Japanese drums with braced heads. Hour-glass drums, tsuzumi, include the ko-tsuzumi and the o-tsuzumi. Tsuzumi is defined in general as a hand drum, a tabor, or a long snare drum, the snare here possibly referring to the rope braces. The ko-tsuzumi is known as the 'younger' or shoulder drum. When played it is held over the right shoulder.

The body of the ko-tsuzumi is made of zelkana wood. As with many African drums, the wood comes from trees chosen to conform to certain standards, ritual and otherwise. The body is spool-shaped and lacquered black with gold decoration. The inside of the shell is hand carved, an operation demanding considerable skill as the quality of the drum is dependent to a great extent on the inner form of the body. The two skins of horse hide are stretched over iron rings and secured by stitching. For the purpose of tone control an additional patch of skin is fixed to the inside of the 'back' skin, referred to as such because of the playing position of this instrument. Further control is exercised by the application of small patches of paper to this skin. The papers are newly applied at each performance in a similar manner to the paste

[1] Cf. side drum.

126

(*soojee*) applied to the lower head of the mrdanga of South India. The two heads of the ko-tsuzumi are connected and tensioned by a length of cord in 'W' formation, and further tensioned by a separate cord forming a central belt, as on the kakko.

The colour of the cords has for centuries denoted the grade of the musician: orange red for the ordinary player, light blue for the next higher rank, and lilac for the highest rank. The colours of the cords, combined with the black and gold of the elegant body and ornamental heads, render the ko-tsuzumi a work of art.

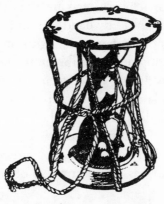

Fig. 22
Ko-tsuzumi,
Japan

The o-tsuzumi is less spectacular in some respects, though still a handsome instrument. This drum is known as the Elder or side drum. In performance it is supported on the left thigh. It is a larger drum than its partner the ko-tsuzumi. The shell, which is of cherry or Chinese quince, is in dumb-bell form. Rings are carved on the shell, though the inner carving is less elaborate than the interior of the ko-tsuzumi. The skins (cowhide) are unlacquered, and are often heated before a performance: a reminder of the heating by the sun or the fire of an African drum. Malm speaks of a freshly heated drum being brought on stage half-way through the performance of the Noh play.

The ko-tsuzumi, the o-tsuzumi and the uta-daiko (or taiko) with a flute, form the musical background of the long-established Noh drama. Emphasis falls on the ko-tsuzumi, from which is produced five basic sounds, as opposed to three on the o-tsuzumi. It is in these basic sounds and their production that Japanese percussionists, with the Hindu tablā player, differ from their western counterpart. Skilled as, for instance, may be the orchestral timpanist of the western orchestra, with his nuances, change of pitch by mechanical pressure, and change of tone by means of carefully graded beaters, the various timbres produced by his eastern rival, with deft positioning and pressure with hand or stick, could be considered the more subtle.[1]

[1] For a detailed description of the technicalities and purpose of many Japanese percussion instruments, see Malm.

Japan

The basic sounds of the ko-tsuzumi are produced by striking the head with the right hand in various positions at different dynamic levels, with one or more fingers, plus the change of pitch with glissandi produced by pressure on the tensioning cords. In performance the ko-tsuzumi is held on the left shoulder by the left hand which grips a portion of the cord to add pressure as required.

The basic sounds of the o-tsuzumi are produced by striking the head with one to three fingers of the right hand, while additional timbres are obtained by covering the finger-tips with thimbles of papier-mâché or deerskin. In contrast to the ko–tsuzumi, no control of pitch is exercised on the head by hand pressure on the tensioning rope.

There are various styles and schools of Japanese drumming; guilds have been in existence for many centuries, operating quite possibly in the manner of the illustrious guilds of European kettledrummers during the sixteenth and seventeenth centuries.

The Japanese percussionist assimilates his art mainly by rote. It is customary for the teacher to direct the pupils by demonstrating the strokes with two fans on a *hyoshiban* – a special box for instructional purposes.

The charts (from Malm) give typical examples of the figuration, basic sounds and style of Japanese drumming. The first is a transcription of *chirikara-byoshi* and the second is traditional notation.

chi ri ka ra   tsu ton   tsu ta tsu   ta   tsu ta   ton tsu ta   tsu   pu   pon

Traditional notation

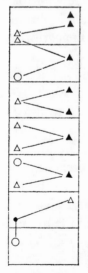

From: *Japanese Music and Musical Instruments*, (p. 269). William P. Malm.
Published by Charles E. Tuttle Company of Rutland, Vermont and Tokyo, Japan.
Copyright in Japan, 1959.

128

Japan

The drum in a simple form is found in the *uchiwa daiko* (uchiwa – a fan) a small frame drum consisting of a skin secured to a hoop and completed with a handle. This drum resembles the medicine man's drum of North America, and the frame drum of the Lapps. In Japan its gentle sound accompanies the voice of the itinerant street singer. How different from the tremendous clanging announcing the rise of the sun of which Goethe speaks! In the Shinto temple the giant drum (da-daiko) is struck to herald the day. The awe-inspiring strokes are delivered with an impressive accelerando, suggestive of the approaching activity of daylight. The increase in tempo of the strokes is so subtle that it could be likened to the bouncing of a celluloid ball on a hard topped table.[1] Various percussion instruments are combined in the percussion 'concerts' which announce dawn and dusk. In these, the relationship of light and sound is expressed.

The Shinto monk is certainly active as a percussionist. He is responsible for the rapid striking of the *Han* (a wood plaque) as a call to numerous duties, the ponderous strokes with heavy club on the massive *mo-kugyo* (wooden fish) to mark the intervals in prayer, and the striking of the huge clapperless bell. Numerous other instruments of percussion, including gongs (metal and porcelain), cymbals, clappers, etc. are concerned with the ritual service. Gongs are numerous.

The *shoko*, the gong of the Bugaku orchestra, is said to have been the first metal instrument introduced into Japan from all reports from China. It was used for a considerable period with the drums in the battle formation to give the words of command. There are numerous types of small gongs still in use in Japan, such as the *dora*, the *hi*, a teacup-shaped porcelain gong, and the *atari-gane*. The last instrument is played on the inside with a small bone hammer striking the rim. A more unusual instrument is the *kei* or *hoyko*, the temple gong which stands on a table to the right of the altar. In shape it resembles the stone chime; in tone it is pure and resonant, similar to that of the kyeezee.

The *waniguchi*, the shark's mouth gong, and the *furin*, are further instruments of the temple. The former hangs at some height from the ground at the entrance of shrines. It is struck by worshippers on entry and it is sounded in an unusual manner. Hanging in front of the gong is a rope. The worshipper grasps the lower end of the rope, and with a gentle flick, brings the bulk of the remaining portion into contact with the face of the gong. Thus announced he enters, sustained no doubt by the belief in the strengthening power of the instrument. A similar ritual is observed at the conclusion of a religious service, when a bell is struck with a deer's horn.

The furin is usually suspended at each corner of the temple. The furin is a wind bell and is typical of Asia, with its broad flat clapper (and streamers) coming below the

[1] Cf. Britten's parable opera *Curlew River*.

body of the bell to catch the wind. It is one of the few bells with clappers to be found in the Far East. Continuing, we find cymbals (*dō-byōshi*, *ennen*, etc.), and at least two rattles, the *zuzu*, a small bell rattle used in folk dances and by the dancing ladies of the temple, and the *furi-tsuzumi*, or shaking drum: an instrument used by the leader of the processional band in conjunction with the *kerō*. The furi-tsuzumi is a combination of two small drums, each with a number of rattling bells. The drums are fixed to a staff, highly ornamented and terminating in a gilt spear head, in style and purpose not unlike the Turkish crescent (which may well be a descendant of an Asian instrument: the shaman's staff capped with bells). As with many shaken instruments, in particular the sistrum of ancient Egypt, the furi-tsuzumi was for many centuries deemed sacred.

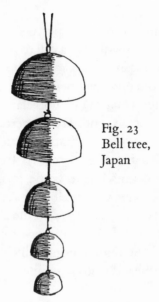

Fig. 23
Bell tree,
Japan

Wooden or bamboo clappers, and concussion sticks with a variety of names, *hyōshigi*, *byakushi*, etc., serve several purposes. As instruments of music they provide an accompaniment to the song, the singer himself marking certain intervals. In the theatre, the hyōshigi, consisting of two pieces of hard wood, are used to beat a tattoo on the floor to emphasize confusion in the stage action. These instruments also serve as a means of drawing attention to the performance of itinerant jugglers, athletes and similar entertainers. They are also used by night watchmen.

A further instrument in the nature of a clapper drum is the *shoku*, resembling the Chinese trough, its predecessor. The influence of China is apparent in many Japanese instruments. It is particularly obvious in the Japanese scraper: the *gyo*, a small edition of the Chinese tiger, and in the *mo-kugyo*, corresponding to the Chinese *mu-yü* (wooden fish). Occasionally the base of the mo-kugyo tapers to form a handle.

Cymbals (*ennen, do-byoshi, chyoppa*, etc.) large and small, serve other purposes than supplying rhythmic support, though in situations such as the classical Noh dance and similar scenes, their function as timekeepers is a prominent part of the musical accompaniment. In Japan, particularly in the temple service, cymbals are associated with a feeling of mystery and gloom. Consequently we find them an integral part of the funeral service, where they are combined with a suspended drum and a small bell.

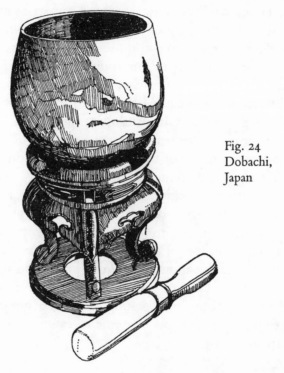

Fig. 24
Dobachi,
Japan

One of the most remarkable instruments found in Japan (and China) is in the form of a bell. It is the *dobachi* or *kin*, also called the copper cup or resting bell. It consists of a heavy basin of hammered bronze, with the upper edge overturned. The vessel is placed on a cushion or rests, insulated by means of a ring of soft material, on a decorated wood stand, with the customary red lacquering. The rim is struck, in an upward movement with a leather covered wooden stick. In some cases the rim is inscribed with messages of goodwill. These bowl-shaped gongs have a remarkably full and clear sound of incredible sustaining power. They vary in diameter from a matter of some inches, to a width of three feet. The largest existing specimen is believed to be the instrument in the Chao-Ch'ing Monastery at Hangchow.

The earliest dated resting bell is preserved in the Mission Inn Museum, Riverside, California. It is dated Japanese year 2, corresponding to the year AD 646.

In Japan, no great emphasis is placed on 'tuned percussion'. There is the *mokkin*, a xylophone with 16 keys, resembling the gamelan gambang, a 'gong chime' consisting of a series of mushroom bells suspended pyramid fashion, and sets of bells of varying sizes and pitches including the *oroguru*. Small bells have, as is observed universally, a long history.

Discoveries in tombs of high-ranking persons buried prior to the seventh century AD include earthen statuettes portraying dancers and musicians using tiny bells worn on the ankle or wrist, and in the form of a rattle. Similar instruments are used to this day by the shrine maidens to ward off evil spirits, and to purify the place of worship. Large Japanese bells, corresponding to our church bells, are clapperless. They are struck from without by a mallet, or a conveniently suspended log of wood. A large bronze bell in the British Museum dated late prehistoric period, *c.* fourth century BC, is a typical example of the metal craftsmanship of this period.

We find that these age old instruments convey a message of goodwill in addition to fulfilling their role in the music of the theatre, concert, court, and the magic of the temple rites. These magic elements survive in many Japanese shrines and temples, and in rural districts and cities where the ritual song, accompanied by percussion instruments, is used to drive away evil spirits, birds of prey, and molesting animals. The belief still remains, as with many primitive peoples, that the beating of drums and gongs during an eclipse of the sun forces the heavenly body to show his face again. Such musical sounds continue to invoke protection against the powers of darkness. In Japan the voice of Buddha is heard in the solemn sound of the temple bell, with its melancholy note reverberating like deep gongs and speaking of eternity. These instruments of the past continue to cast a spell in a country in the forefront of modern technology.

Bibliography: Chapter 5

JAPAN

MALM, W. P. *Japanese Music and Musical Instruments*, Charles E. Tuttle, Rutland, Vermont, 1959.
PIGGOTT, F. T. *Music and Musical Instruments of Japan*, Batsford, London, 1909.
SACHS, Curt. *The History of Musical Instruments*, Norton, New York, 1940.

RECOMMENDED READING

HARICH-SCHNEIDER, Eta. *The rhythmic patterns in Gagaku and Bugaku*, Brill, Leiden, 1954.

6

India and Tibet

INDIA

Nowhere in the world has drumming reached a higher degree of perfection than in India. Here is a country where the drum has long been, and remains, the characteristic instrument associated with all the acts of life.

The Hindus, like the Chinese, connect the origin of their music with their religion. Gosvami says:[1] 'The study of the evolution of religion reveals to us that the use of music in religious rites and ceremonies all over the world was not only common but necessary. The reason is obvious. By music alone could such rites, ceremonies and worships be amplified and prolonged; and by music alone could a certain feeling be aroused and sustained in a great crowd of people. Moreover, the early religious services were conducted in classical Sanskrit, and they were long . . . so, in order to keep their flock interested, the early priests sought to please both the eye and the ear by interesting singing and dancing.'

Music is regarded by the Hindus as an immediate gift from the gods. The Muria Ghonds of Bastar State sustain a legend that their great god Lingo, who had eighteen instruments which he played all at once, was the first musician. The eighteen instruments included all the basic instruments of the tribe: drums, fiddles, zithers, gongs, cymbals, jingles, rasps, horns and flutes.

At least five hundred varieties of musical instruments have evolved in the course of Indian history, each with a distinct name, shape, quality of tone and technique. Most of the early instruments remain in use. The instruments of percussion claim the longest pedigree with their origin in the stone chime and wooden castanets.

Ancient beliefs and legends refer to the drum in many aspects, in one instance almost as a lesser divinity. One supreme god of the Hindus, Brahma, keeping watch

[1] Gosvami, O. *The Story of Indian Music*, Asia Publishing House, Bombay, 1957, p. 5.

133

over music in heaven, is pictured with hands busily employed in beating a small drum. From an ancient Hindu book dating back to 200 BC comes the legend of a magical drum given to an aged hermit by Brahmadatta. The drum possessed great powers: when one side was beaten the hermit's aggressors were put to flight. What is more astonishing is the power attributed to the other side of the drum: when this was struck the enemies were turned into trustworthy friends.

In the *Rigveda*, the first of the four primordial books of the Brahmins, written in Sanskrit and known as the *Vedas*, there are hymns intended for music. Mention is made of four instruments in these ancient writings, which are supposed to date back to 1500 BC. One of these instruments, the *aghāti*, was a percussion instrument, in the form of either a clapper or a drum. A drum is quite definitely indicated in a later *Veda*, (the *Atharva Veda*). It is referred to as the *dundubhi* and is a wooden drum (kettle-shaped with cow skins) used as a thundering war instrument. Excavations provide evidence of the use of simple percussion instruments resembling rattles, cymbals and drums in 3000 BC. Drums are thus ascribed to the earliest known civilization in India. They are represented in several forms on Indian temple relics at Bharahat 200 BC and include an hour-glass drum being played with two sticks by an ape. The instrument is suspended from the animal's shoulder. The width of the drum is little less than its length. The skins are laced with cords and a central belt. The instrument depicted on this relief is larger than the modern Indian hour-glass drum, which is held in the hand.

For information regarding the chronology of Indian instruments there is no more important source than the temple of Borobudur in Java. On the outer walls of this edifice, which was erected by Indian settlers about AD 800, are numerous reliefs depicting Indian life before Islam, showing drums of several varieties, including cylindrical and barrel-shaped drums with laces and a conical drum. A stone relief from Pālā (ninth to tenth century AD – British Museum) depiciting the marriage of Siva and Parvati shows similar instruments.

The drum is well represented on art works of various kinds. An eleventh century temple relic from Western Rajasthan (Ashmolean Museum, Oxford) depicts three types of instruments and individual styles of performance: (i) played in the manner of a tambourine, (ii) played horizontally, (iii) played at an angle.

On an early twelfth-century bronze figure from Mysore (B.M.) three drummers are seen performing on cylindrical rope-tensioned drums. In each case the drum is suspended from the player's waist in a horizontal position and played with the hands. The left hand of the central figure (a lady) is placed between the shell and the tensioning cords, in a manner suggesting that the player may be varying the pitch of the instrument. This style of playing is frequently illustrated.

India

Kettle-shaped drums are seen on the famous Buddhist temple, at Borobudur and on ancient temples in India and Cambodia. A seventeenth-century picture shows an ensemble of kettledrums from Northern India. There are 12 small drums arranged in six pairs, together with larger drums played individually. The performers are illustrated with drumsticks, or playing with the hands, or with hand and stick.

Fig. 25. An ensemble of kettledrums, Northern India (after A. H. Fox Strangways)

To summarize, the percussion instruments of India, North and South, present and past, include drums (of which there are more than 300 varieties of each class). The membrane instruments, *avanaddha vādyas*, include frame drums (*tambattam, chakravādya,* etc.); kettledrums (*tablā, nāgarā, naqqāra,* etc.) and double-headed drums, (*mrdanga* etc.). Resonant solids – *Ghana vādyas* comprise cymbals, castanets, gongs and bells.

Foremost among the percussion instruments of India are the tablā and the mrdanga.[1] The mrdanga – a concert drum – is the classical drum of South India. It is an ancient instrument; Brahma is said to have invented it to serve as an accompaniment to the dance of Mahādeva, after his victory over Tripurasura. In South India the mrdanga is an indispensable accompaniment to vocal and instrumental music of all types and

[1] Also *mridangam, mridang,* etc.

is a solo instrument in chamber music. (In the north the mrdanga is used mainly as an accompaniment to the *vina*, and certain styles of singing; other instruments and types of vocal music being accompanied by the tablā.) Sambamoorthy says:[1] 'The concert-drum in Indian music plays a far more important part than in European music. It is played continuously and it also closely accompanies the singer. The pitch of the concert-drum is invariably the same as the key-note of the singer or the principal performer . . .'

The mrdanga is constructed as follows: the body is formed from a single block of well-seasoned jack-wood or red-wood (originally the shell may have been of clay, mrdanga literally meaning – clay body); the walls are curved in the form of two truncated cones combined at their larger bases, taking the shape of two bottomless flower pots joined at their rims; the depth of the shell is approximately 20 inches, and the diameter at the widest point, which is a little off-centre, is a matter of 11 inches (these measurements vary a little according to the model). The skins are fastened to leather hoops and secured by leather braces (strips of buffalo skin) in 'W' formation; wooden dowels are normally placed between the shell and the braces, adding pressure to the vellums and thus assisting in adjusting the pitch of the instrument, which is initially raised or lowered and 'trued-up' by downward or upward strokes with a small hammer (or at times a stone) on the hoop at the appropriate points.

The right-hand head (approximately seven inches in diameter) consists of three layers of skin, the innermost vellum (buffalo skin) being concealed by a second layer of sheepskin. The third layer of skin consists of a ring of calf skin which overlaps the outer edge of second vellum, thus forming an outer and an inner ring. In the centre of the inner ring is a permanent fixture of black paste, called the eye, giving the drum its characteristic tone. The patch is circular and thins out towards the edges. It is a composition of manganese dust, boiled rice and tamarind juice, or of iron filings and boiled rice.

The left-head is composed of two skins, an outer and an inner ring. The outer head is of buffalo hide, overlapping the inner ring of sheepskin, the diameter of the whole being little smaller than the right-hand head.

A paste mixture of coarse ground flour and water is applied temporarily to the left head. It is fixed to the centre of the inner ring at the start of a performance and removed at the close of the concert, as are the small pieces of paper on the Japanese ko-tsuzumi. This circle of paste, in addition to giving the drum harmonic overtones and its peculiar timbre, assists, by reason of its weight, in tuning the head. The

---

[1] Sambamoorthy, P. *Catalogue of Musical Instruments*, **Government** Museum, Madras, Madras Government Press, 1955, p. 19.

136

quantity of paste is normally adjusted to render the pitch one octave, or a fourth or fifth below the note given by the opposite head, which is tuned to the keynote of the instrument or voice.

The mrdanga is played with the two hands, wrists, fingertips, and the base of the thumbs. The expert player, in addition to his agile manipulation, displays his powers of creative skill by numerous permutations and combinations of rhythm.

A drum used in Northern India, a descendant of the mrdanga and resembling it, is called *pakhawaj*.

In Northern India, the instruments corresponding musically to the mrdanga are the tablā; a pair of instruments played by one performer (*Tabalchi*). Similarly to the mrdanga in South India, the tablā are the most outstanding, typically and artistically, of the percussion instruments of North India.

The tablā could be described musically as a mrdanga (or pakhawaj) in two pieces, high and low, with the faces turned upwards. The instruments are called tablā (or *daina*) and *bhaya* (*bāmyā*), the tablā giving its name to the combination of the two instruments (names differ according to territory).

The bhaya, the lower sounding instrument, is a small kettledrum with a deepish shell of clay, wood or metal. The shell of the present-day instrument is of metal, its diameter and depth being approximately nine inches. The 'head' resembles that on the left side of the mrdanga. It consists of two skins secured to the shell by a hoop consisting of twisted thongs which winds through the holes in the vellum at short intervals. A black patch three inches in diameter (of the same composition as the patch on the right head of the mrdanga and giving the drum the same harmonic overtones) is fixed to the lower skin, a little off centre, lying when the hand is in playing position under the tip of the forefinger.

The bhaya's partner, the tablā, has a wood body in the shape of two truncated cones, the lower cone being considerably shorter than the upper; this instrument, with its bright and high pitched tone, plays the treble. Sachs[1] says: 'The manner in which the bottom is carved shows clearly that this instrument originally had a second skin, such as with the *pakhavāja*, which was given up when the drum came to be used in a vertical position.' The depth of the shell varies, rising to 12 inches. This is often painted in various coloured stripes. The head, a little smaller than that on the bhaya, is six inches in diameter, and is comprised of three skins identical with the right head of the mrdanga, with the circular patch of black paste fixed centrally, and the skins secured and braced similarly with thongs in 'W' formation, and tightened by wooden dowels.

Different opinions are held respecting the history of the tablā. With some it is

[1] Sachs, Curt. *The History of Musical Instruments*, p. 230.

considered that the tablā, distinct from the bhaya, has been derived from the pakhawaj and mrdanga, because of their constructional similarity; to which is added, that the music suitable for performance on the pakhawaj may also be played on the tablā. It is also claimed that similar instruments occupied a prominent place among the instruments of Arabia before the birth of Islam. Gosvami, in his *Story of Indian Music* says:[1] 'In pagan Arabia it was a popular instrument but was somewhat different in structure. When we study the history of the tablā from that time to the present day, it becomes more difficult to attribute the origin of the tablā to pakhawaj. ... It seems that the Muslims must have brought with them their favourite tabl. But here in India they found the percussion instruments varied and well developed. So they improved their own tabl on the lines of Indian varieties, and laid the basis for a new type of instrument to which they added a smaller variety of the duff which, because of its similarity with the tabl, was known as tablā, and the latter bayan.'

Many Hindu scholars agree that the instruments have existed as tablā and bāmyā from the fourteenth century. Legend tells of a player of that period, who cut a mrdanga in half and formed the *tab-bo-la*. Various styles or schools of tablā playing exist, amongst them: Lucknow, Ajarda, Farrukhabad, Benares and Punjab. In some instances the skill has remained in families for generations, some of whom claim that the instruments originated with their forefathers.

In performance (as a pair) the bhaya (meaning left) is placed to the left of the player, and the tablā (or daina, meaning right) to his right. The drums are tuned and played in a similar manner to the two heads of the mrdanga and pakhawaj, the treble (tablā) being tuned to the tonic note of the singer or instrumentation. From the point of view of skill emphasis is placed on the bhaya. The left hand controls to a great extent the desired pitch (by pressure and other means, the compass of the bhaya extends to one and a half octaves) adding glissandi with the finger, at times moistened with resined water, and performing numerous complex rhythms, quite incalculable to all but the initiated.[2]

The styles of playing the tablā and the mrdanga are governed by the form of the music to be accompanied. The mrdanga follows the melodic line throughout the performance. The tablā accompaniment alternates between keeping time for the soloist and solo improvisations. It is usual at the start of a *gat* (an instrumental piece) for the tablā to make a dramatic entrance, and then keep time whilst the soloist improvises. The soloist in turn then repeats the main melodic line without embellishment whilst the tablā player improvises. This principle is repeated throughout the gat, the performers presenting each other with an occasional challenge.

[1] Gosvami, O. ibid. p. 311.
[2] For the science of Indian drumming see, e.g. Fox-Strangways, A. H. *The Music of Hindostan.*

India

Even with a tape recorder at speeds from $7\frac{1}{2}$ to $1\frac{7}{8}$ inches per second little light is thrown on the remarkable technique of the tablā and mrdanga players: the rhythms and timbre remain incalculable. (With due deference to the vina – generally considered to be the most perfect and the most national of Hindu instruments, its antiquity proved by the frequent mention made of it in a great number of Hindu poems – it is possible that no higher expression is experienced in Indian music, indeed in percussion playing anywhere, than in a skilled performance on the mrdanga or tablā.)[1]

The importance of the tablā player is emphasized by virtue of the prominent part played by the 'drum' in the small ensemble performing chamber music or accompanying a singer. (It is the small ensemble that is the fundamental unit in Indian music, not the orchestra.)

In his own country a skilled mrdanga or tablā player is revered. He is a musician of eminence and a soloist in his own right. His art is understood and appreciated by the whole community. (This esteem of the drummer is of long standing. Legend refers to him receiving fourteen *mattars*, whilst the horn blower received but two). Western musicians are no less appreciative of the consummate skill of these great players. Donington says:[2] 'In Eastern music, drum technique includes additional methods, in which the separate fingers and the palm of the hand are all employed to produce tone qualities and rhythmical patterns of the most extraordinary sublety, greatly surpassing our own use of drums.' According to Fox-Strangways[3] 'The drum is used not, as with us, to assert the accent at special moments or to reinforce a crisis, but to articulate the metre of the singers' melody, or to add variety to it by means of a cross metre.'

Imogen Holst confesses with disarming frankness:[4] 'The rhythms were more bewildering than anything else, and I never got much further than the beginners' class, where we clapped one-in-a-bar ... having learnt the tune the Indian way, by ear. The claps were silent, and, as in African music, they only existed in the background, without adding any rhythmical effect to the tune itself. The drum-rhythms in the classical music were far too difficult to follow. My teachers would sit round me while we were listening to a raga, and would mutter encouragingly: "Tala Tivra; seven matras. Count seven." But as soon as they stopped counting with me I lost the beginning of the sevens.'

[1] Berio scores for tablā in *Circles* (1960), and Henry Cowell for Indian tablas in his *Concerto for Percussion and Orchestra* (1961).

[2] Donington, Robert. *The Instruments of Music*, Methuen, London, 1949, p. 39.

[3] Fox-Strangways, A. H. ibid. p. 225.

[4] Holst, Imogen. *Tune*, Faber, London, 1962, p. 51.

Tala and matra are two of the three aspects of the division of rhythm in Hindu music, the full sequence being: tala, time measurement; matra, the smallest unit of the tala; laya, tempo – thrice-divided, slow, medium, slow.

Ancient Hindu literature quotes 120 talas; to-day about 40 are used. Each tala has a separate name and count: Tritala 16 counts, 4-4-4-4-; Chautala 12 counts, 4-4-2-2- and so on. Applied to the drum the different strokes of the right and left hand or both, are defined and named by the use of such syllables as Ta-Na-Ki-Ghi-Ga-Dha-Dhinn. It requires an expert to deal with the almost unlimited and lengthy phrases involved in these complicated systems; on the part of the drummer they require the rendering of the tala and florid improvisation within the bar, together with various beats and moves of the hand to give directions to the singer, and to indicate a return to the first beat of the bar, *sama*. To quote an expert, Shripada Bandoypadhyaya:[1] 'One should be very particular about the ending of the tala.' The vocalists, instrumentalist and dancers also complete or finish at the *sam* like the drummers, who keep time in the performance. The *khali* is the wave of the hand-beat that helps the artists to find out the place of sam in particular talas. It is an accepted rule that the khali must come just before the sam so that, however lost the singer may be in his improvization, the khali shows him the way back to the sam.[2]

Featured with the tablā and the mrdanga in the chamber percussion ensemble are the mud pot (*ghāta*), the tambourine (*k(h)anjari*), and on occasions a voice part representing percussion. The kanjari is typical of the Asiatic tambourine with deep shell, with fewer jingles than its western counterpart, and occasional small clusters of small ankle bells. It is usually played in an upright position, with the head, glued or nailed, facing outward. The fingers of the hand holding the tambourine strike the vellum near the rim. The fingers of the other hand strike the skin in various places. High sounds are produced near the rim and lower sounds towards the centre. The force behind the minimum of movement is considerable, as with tablā and mrdanga.

The ghāta is one of India's most ancient time-keeping instruments. The mouth of the pot, a somewhat narrow opening, is placed against the stomach of the player, giving the instrument a deep tone. The pots are designed to produce a given note, conforming to the tonic of the instrumentalist or singer. A ghāta player is thus equipped with a large number of pots in order to comply with the requirements of

[1] Bandoypadhyaya, Shripada. *The Music of India*, Taraporevala Sons & Co., Bombay, 1958. p. 63.

[2] The author is indebted to Ayana Deva Angadi, founder and director of the Asian Music Circle in London, and to V. K. Ramakrishnam of the Press Trust of India, for assistance in completing certain details regarding the tablā and other percussion instruments of India.

the soloists. In performance, the player constantly varies the timbre of the instrument by holding it away from the stomach, and by striking the pot in various places, the butt of the left hand produces low notes, and fingers and nails of the right hand, higher notes (a similar technique to that employed on the tablā).

The mud pot remains a feature of ordinary street music, where quite often the performance is concluded with the pot falling to the ground, and smashing to pieces at the exact conclusion of the measure (tala). There is a great demand for these instruments and, not surprisingly, their replenishment. The majority of pots for musical purposes are made in Southern India.

In addition to the small kettledrums associated with chamber music, there are the larger kettledrums, *nāgarā*, used in the temples and for ceremonial purposes. Whilst it may not be possible to attribute the origin of the kettledrums to India, they are freely quoted at an early stage in their history in Hindu historiography. Authorities agree the original home of the kettledrum to be the Orient, from whence it travelled slowly to the west. In India, these instruments are found in a great variety of shapes and sizes and serving numerous purposes.

The most spectacular of Indian kettledrums are those used in state ceremonies and processions, in an ensemble known as the *nahabat (naubat)*, of which Sachs gives this description:[1] 'The most impressive instrument of such a band is the *sahib-nahabat*, or "master drum", a pair of silver kettles, having the gigantic diameter of five feet and weighing about four hundred and fifty pounds. They are mounted on an elephant and draped with a hanging cloth ten feet long; each drum has its own player sitting on its rim and striking with a silver stick. The *sutri-nahabat* brings up the rear of the procession. It is a pair of small kettles, draped and mounted on a camel, and both struck by the same drummer.' This must have been an impressive sight and was evidently a custom extending over several centuries, as was the general use of kettle-drums and other percussion in ensembles of this nature. The instrumentation of the band of the Emperor Akbar in the sixteenth century included 42 drums and a pair of large cymbals (ten more drums than Berlioz demands in his *Grande Messe des Morts*).

The India of the past is no exception to the belief in the magic power of the kettledrum, seeing it as a talisman of good luck and victory in warfare.

Suidas, the Greek lexicographer of the tenth or eleventh century AD, speaks of kettle shaped drums (dundubhi) made of pine wood and covered with heads of bull hide, which were used by Indian tribes in battle. Bronze bells were fitted inside the shell of these ancient Hindu drums. The cacophony resulting from the jingling of the bells and sound of the drum – which was held aloft and beaten in a terrifying

[1] Sachs, Curt. ibid. p. 229.

141

manner – may have proved a deciding factor in the progress of the battle, as has been observed in the warfare of the Chinese. Plutarch, (AD 46–120) attributed a large drum of this character to the Persians. He said: 'The Persians have no horn or trumpet to give signal of battle, but they use a certain big basin covered with leather. They strike it on every side, and cause it to render a hollow and terrible sound similar to thunder.'

The nāgarā is a shallow kettledrum, varying in size, with a shell of copper, brass, or riveted sheet iron. Large drums of this description, with a head diameter from $2\frac{1}{2}$ to 3 feet, are used in temple services. The skin is tensioned by leather thongs which pass round the under side of the shell (nailed heads in India are normally restricted to certain tambourines). In the procession of the deity, the nāgarā is mounted on a two-wheeled hand drawn carriage. The performer who sits on the carriage, which is at the rear of the procession, beats the drum with curved sticks. At times, the instrument heads the procession, carried on the back of a decorated elephant, in a manner similar to the sahib-nahabat. In country districts the nāgarā is found in a simpler form, with wood shell covered with buffalo hide. Huge instruments with tremendous carrying power, frequently with six performers on one drum, are used in tribal dances, the drumming persisting, as in Africa, on some occasions throughout the night.

Deeper drums are observed in the *damarān*; a pair of conical drums with wood shells, laced together are placed on a bullock, which heads the temple procession. These drums are played with two sticks, one curved and the other straight. The origin of the curved or hooked stick (crozier stick) is symbolic. It is considered that Persia gave the hooked stick to India. Curved sticks still exist in parts of Far Eastern Asia and India, but are rarely found to-day in Europe and the Middle East. Crozier sticks are well-illustrated in an early thirteenth century Arabic manuscript and in an Ethiopic manuscript of the Revelation of St. John The Divine, before 1730 (see plate 46).

Whilst the kettledrums (minus the elephant) have spread to the four continents, certain instruments, not necessarily of Indian origin, remain peculiar to the East. One such instrument is a clapper drum (dāmaru – *darmu*, or *budbudika*), a small hour-glass or spool drum. This is a sacred instrument, one attribute of Siva, the destroyer (credited with the origin of music), who is depicted with the instrument.

The dāmaru is simple in construction and performance. One or two cords ending in a knot or small ball are attached to the centre of the shell. When the drum is moved rapidly to and fro with a twisting movement of the forearm, the ends of the cords strike the skins. (Small drums resembling the dāmaru, but with a rattling piece inside the body in place of the knotted cord are similarly operated.) This sacred instrument serves a secular purpose in the hands of the man with the dancing bear or monkey, the animal responding to the often considerable skill of his master with evident relish. The small clapper drum is frequently referred to as a 'monkey drum', since these engaging creatures find and give amusement with their prowess upon this fascinating instrument when accompanying the itinerant musician.

The drum most common in North India is the *dōlak* (*daulak*). It is a simple drum with a barrel-shaped wood shell and plain 'heads', braced by cord in the customary 'V' formation. The cord passes through metal rings which serve as tensioning lugs. The dōlak is played with the hand and stick, or with the hand and fingers, in the manner of the mrdanga, and with equal skill (by both male and female executants).

Among the other 'common' drums are found the *dhol*, the *dholkee* (a small *dhol*) and the *daff*. The daff, a frame drum, is often beaten with two long pieces of wood or with a twig held in the left hand and a short thick stick, held in the right hand. The dhol is played with the hands when accompanying the voice, and with a stick when playing in concert with pipes etc. This drum is little used by professionals. A small drum, *tavil*, is common in South India; it corresponds to the *duggi* of North India.

Drums resembling the Far Eastern da-daiko are encountered in Ceylon and South India. The faces of this type of drum consist of skins lapped round stout hempen rings, which are larger than the cylindrical wood shell. The heads are strained by interlaced leather thongs which stand away from the shell, permitting further tension by means of a central cord, which gathers in and tightens the thongs, in the same way as the hour-glass drum is tensioned.

Singhalese percussion instruments include various drums, such as the *udakki*, an hour-glass drum with variable pitch; the *berrigodea*, a large double-headed drum beaten with the hand; the *doula*, a drum similar to the berrigodea, but beaten at one end with a stick and at the other with the hand; a small kettledrum (*hewisi*), and a large frame drum, the *tammatam* (or *temmettama*) called *tambattam* by the Tamils. In addition to the drums are small cymbals (*talam*) and temple bells.

As well as the temple drums of India already described, there are hour-glass drums, the udakki and the *idakki* (corresponding to the Japanese tsuzumi), the *timila*, a double-headed drum suspended vertically near the waist and played by the hand; the *sūryapirai* and *chandrapirai*, and the *panchamukha vādyam*. The sūryapirai and the chandrapirai are frame drums consisting of parchments strained over iron rings, shaped to represent the sun (sūryapirai) and the moon (chandrapirai). Handles with a curved section to fit the forehead are fixed to the rings. The instruments are used in pairs, secured to the foreheads of separate players who strike the drums with sticks.

The panchamukha vādyam is a huge five-faced drum used in temple music. The faces are named after the five faces of Siva. The shell of the drum which is of bronze, embodies five hollow cylinders, each covered by a skin secured by cord. The central cylinder is the largest. The panchamukha vādyam is played solo and also in conjunction with other instruments, by a privileged class of people, the Pārasaivas.

India possesses many ingenious tribal instruments, the *villadi vādyam* and the *pullavan kudam*, for example. The villadi vādyam consists of a bow, seven or eight feet in length which rests on a pot. The cord of the bow is uppermost. A few bells are suspended from the bow. The cord is struck with small sticks by four or five players. The pullavan kudam is formed from a mud pot and a piece of twine. A vellum is stretched over the narrow mouth of the pot. The twine is struck with a stick, the pot serving as a resonator. This instrument is used by the Pullvans of Malabar, a tribe of serpent-worshippers.

Among other tribal instruments which include friction drums, steel tongs with the addition of small bells, are to be found two further pot drums, the *tantipānai* and the *gummati*. The latter resembles a drinking vessel with an open spout. A skin covers a hole in the bottom of the pot. The drum is held horizontally and played with the fingers of the right hand, whilst the palm of the left hand performs occasional covering strokes on the open spout end; the combination of the two sounds providing an attractive accompaniment to the ballad singer.

The tantipānai is one of the most captivating of the South Indian tribal instruments. It is a pot with a gut or metal string, threaded with jingles inside the vessel. The mouth of the pot is covered with a piece of goat skin through which the string is threaded and secured to a small disc, such as a coin or button. The jingles consist of seven metallic rings threaded on the string inside the pot. The drum is slightly inclined so as to allow the metallic rings to vibrate near the aperture at the back of the pot, when the coin or button in the centre of the drum head is struck. The performer taps the centre piece alternately with the middle fingers of the right and left hand, producing harmonious, rhythmic sequences. (In Switzerland, Canton of Appenzell, an instrument is similarly used. The sound is produced by coins spun round the inside edge of an earthenware pot.)

In addition to the membrane drums of India, there are many percussion instruments made of metal, including instruments that are more universal than the characteristic mrdanga and tablā, i.e., cymbals, gongs and bells.

Gongs (*Thalla*) are not frequent in India. They have little in common with the Indonesian gong, in that they are flat without a boss, and usually of small dimension and high sounding. Little is known of them before the seventh century AD. Gongs (*khansara* and *khansi*—Figs. 6 and 10, Plate 43b), and other metal discs are used for certain musical and ritual purposes. The thick circular bronze disc, *ghari*, is used to

47. *Tablā* (India). Author's collection

48
Skull-cap pellet drum,
Tibet. By permission of
the Horniman Museum,
London

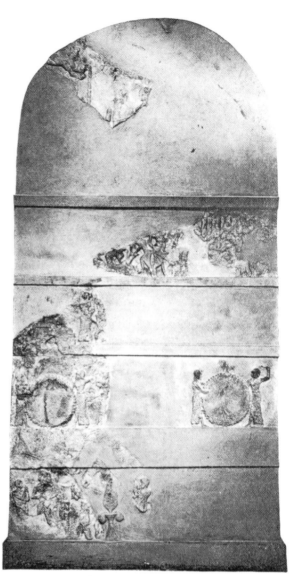

50. Sumerian drum *c.* 2500 B C, Ur. By permission of the University Museum, Philadelphia

49. Plaque from the Royal Cemetery *c.* 2700 B.C. Ur. Featuring harp, sistrum and timbrel. By permission of the University Museum, Philadelphia

51. Sumerian drum *c.* 2500 B C, with figure of Ea. By courtesy of Musée du Louvre, Paris

53. Drum and horn. Carchemish relief *c*. 1250 B C. By courtesy of the Trustees of the British Museum

54. Kettledrum and cymbals, Babylonian plaque *c*. 700 B C. By courtesy of the Trustees of the British Museum

52. Lyres, timbrels and cymbals. Assyrian bas relief *c*. 680 B C. By courtesy of Musée du Louvre, Paris

55
Timbrel, double pipe and psaltery. Ivory box, Nimrûd. *c*. 800 B C. By courtesy of the Trustees of the British Museum

56. The Royal Elamite Orchestra, Assyrian bas relief *c*. 660 B C. By courtesy of
the Trustees of the British Museum

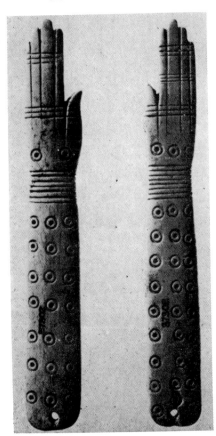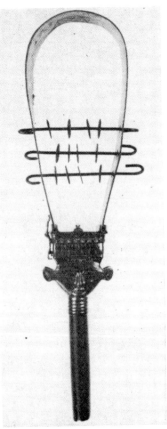

57. (*left*) Pair of ivory clappers. Egyptian, *c*. 2000 B C. 58. (*centre*) Bronze sistrum. Egyptian, late period, after 850 B C.
59. (*right*) Bronze sistrum. Egyptian, late period, after 850 B C. (The discs and rods are modern.)
By courtesy of the Trustees of the British Museum

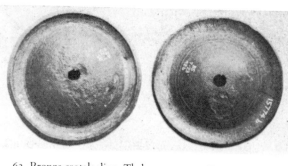

62. Bronze crotale discs. Thebes, *c.* 200 B C. By courtesy of the Trustees of the British Museum

60. Bronze cymbals. Egyptian, late period, after 850 B C. Connected by the original cord. By courtesy of the Trustees of the British Museum

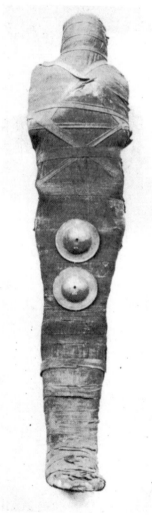

61. Egyptian cymbals (bronze) 100 B C. (Mummy Ankhape – a musician). By courtesy of the Trustees of the British Museum

63. Bronze crotales (as clappers). Coptic period A D 400. By courtesy of the Trustees of the British Museum

64. Cymbal making – pouring (modern). By courtesy of Messrs. A. Zildjian

66. Crotales (modern). By courtesy of Messrs. A. Zildjian

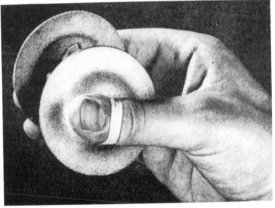

67. Finger cymbals (modern). By courtesy of Messrs. A. Zildjian

65. Cymbal making (modern) – shaping and skimming. By courtesy of Messrs. A. Zildjian

68. Tympanon, Greece, fourth century B C. By courtesy of the Trustees of the
British Museum

69
Clappers (*krotala*). Greece,
c. mid fifth century B C.
By courtesy of the
Trustees of the British
Museum

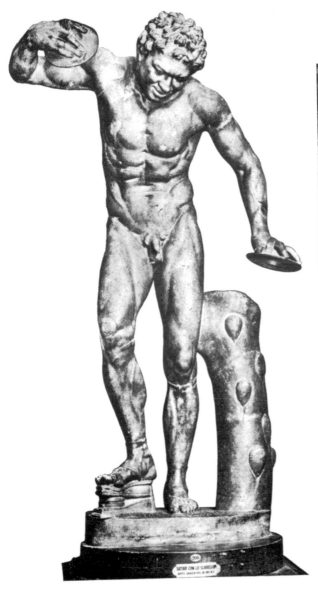

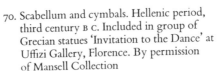

72. Cup-shaped cymbals. Roman, fourth century A D.
Detail from the Silver Dish (Mildenhall Treasure). By
courtesy of the Trustees of the British Museum

70. Scabellum and cymbals. Hellenic period,
third century B C. Included in group of
Grecian statues 'Invitation to the Dance' at
Uffizi Gallery, Florence. By permission
of Mansell Collection

71. Bronze cymbals (Greece) inscribed 'OATA', c. 500 B C.
By courtesy of the Trustees of the British Museum

73. Tambourine, Roman relief, second century A D. By permission of Walters
    Art Gallery, Baltimore

74. Laced kettledrum, pottery (*tbilat*). By courtesy of the Tropen Museum, Amsterdam

75. Tympanon (Roman) *c.* second century A D. (Mosaic at Brading Villa, Isle of Wight.) By permission of Major Denys Oglander

76. Trapezoidal triangle with rings. (Richard III Bible, late fourteenth century.) By courtesy of the Trustees of the British Museum

77
Bronze cymbals. Marble bas relief (Luca della Robbia) *c.* 1430. Cathedral Museum, Florence. By permission of Mansell Collection

78
Cymbals, tambourine and
nakers. 'The Assumption
of the Virgin' Matteo
di' Giovanni, late
fifteenth century. By
courtesy of the National
Gallery, London

79. *Triccaballacca* (Neapolitan). By kind permission of Mrs. P. Troise

81
Rommelpot (Dutch).
After Hals 1580–1666.
By permission of
Mansell Collection

80. *Crécelle* (rattle). French fifteenth–sixteenth century. By courtesy of the Metropolitan Museum of Art, New York

82
Tambourines. Marble bas relief (Luca della Robbia) *c.* 1430. Cathedral Museum, Florence. By permission of Mansell Collection

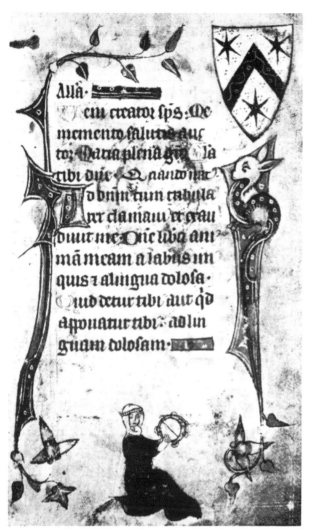

83. Timbrel (with snare). From an early fourteenth-century manuscript (English). By courtesy of the Trustees of the British Museum

84. Chime bells, handbells and dulcimer, etc. Hunterian Psalter. By permission of the University Library, Glasgow

87. Jingle ring and sistrum. P. Baudry (n.d.). By permission of Mansell Collection

85. Chime bells. Fourteenth century Psalter. By permission of His Grace the Archbishop of Canterbury and the Trustee of Lambeth Palace Library

86
Chime bells. Luttrell Psalter, late eleventh or early twelfth century. By courtesy of the Trustees of the British Museum

88. Experiments in acoustics. Woodcut from *Practica Musicae*,
F. Gaforus, 1492

89. Quadrangular psaltery, mid-twelfth century.
Byzantine book cover (carved ivory). Said
to have been made for Queen Melissenda.
By courtesy of the Trustees of the British
Museum

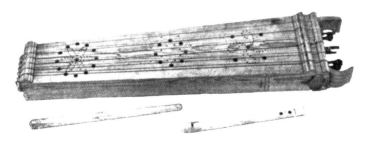

91. Béarnais strung drum and three-hole pipe. By permission of the
Pitt Rivers Museum, Oxford

90. Pipe, tabor and dulcimer, etc. English —
early sixteenth century. By courtesy of the
Trustees of the British Museum

mark certain periods in the Hindu service, or to announce the different hours of the day. With the Muslims, the gong is for the latter purpose only – struck as a clock.

In Southern India the Pandārams (mendicants) solicit alms by singing Tamil songs to which they provide an accompaniment by striking a small gong, the *sēmakkalam*, in conjunction with a small tambourine – the *dāsari tappattai*.

Cymbals (in company with other musical instruments in Hindu mythology) are attributed to the gods. Early Hindu-Javanese reliefs depict instruments resembling cup-shaped cymbals. They are more clearly established on a Garwha temple relief dating from the 5th century AD. Clashing and tinkling cymbals struck in the Indian manner, typically Asian, are depicted on Borobudur reliefs AD 800.

Cymbals, clashing and tinkling, are important as time keepers in the Indian orchestra and in Hindu music generally. The clashing cymbals (*jhānjha – brahma-tālam*, etc.) are those associated with the temple services and the court orchestra. They are the bronze discs with a flat rim and central boss, and connected by a loose cord. 'Tinkling' cymbals are smaller and heavier, with a broad central boss and sloping rim, with an outer circumference of a few inches. They are of brass or bell metal and include *mandira*, *tâla*, *jālrā*, etc. used in chamber music. When accompanying the voice, the player strikes the cymbals together, forming notes in accordance with the voice, or the other accompanying instruments. This cymbal accompaniment is performed with greater execution than may be conceived possible from the nature of the instrument. Professor Sambamoorthy says:[1] 'There are experts in *jālrā* who are able to cope with the most talented mridangam players.'

A hundred years ago Captain Meadows Taylor (in the Proceedings of the Royal Irish Academy) said:[2] 'Players on these cymbals are extremely dexterous, and produce a not unpleasant accompaniment to the voice, or to instrumental music, by striking the cups together in such a manner, outside, inside, and upon the edges as to form notes in accordance with the voice or the other instruments by which it may be accompanied. This cymbal accompaniment is played with more execution than may be conceived possible from the nature of the instrument. I have heard *professors* even play solos upon it, which if not very intelligible as to tune, were at least curious in execution and diversity of time, as suited to the various styles of music.'[3]

In the dance drama, a pair of small basin cymbals, *tālām*, are used. These cymbals

[1] Sambamoorthy, P. *Dictionary of South Indian Music*, Indian Music Publishing House, Madras, 1959, vol. II, p. 242.

[2] Taylor, Meadows. *Proceedings of the Royal Irish Academy*, Dublin, 1865, vol. IX, Part I pp. 107–8.

[3] A good last minute deputy for the cymbal part in the duel scene of Tchaikovsky's *Romeo and Juliet* Overture.

are of heavy metal and are unconnected. Usually only the edges of the tālām are struck, the high pitched sound thus produced being sweet and bell-like.

Bells appear in several forms and capacities, in particular the typical Asian clapper-less bell in a frame. Small tulip-shaped handbells with a thick clapper used by Hindu priests are mentioned in philosophical writings 200 BC. The clapper bell suspended from the neck of the elephant is an Indian feature, the prize bell being awarded for distinction in the field of labour. The winner displays the dignity also observed in the bearing of the Alpine champion milk yielder disporting the large cowbell and milkstool crown.

Bronze anklets and clusters of small bells forming anklets worn by dancers and singers (Hindu and Muslim) are considered professional symbols and to some extent are held sacred. The investing of a female dancer with these professional tokens, a ceremony of considerable significance, binds the recipient to a career from which she cannot escape.

Indian castanets, *chiplā*, *kurtar*, *chittaka*, etc., have distinct features. These instruments are composed of two pieces of hard wood (blackwood or rosewood) about six inches in length, provided with slits into which are inserted metal discs, or with ankle bells at each end. Occasionally both accoutrements are embodied and sometimes a brass ring is fixed on the back of each wooden piece for the fingers to pass through. (In some instances metal strips are used in place of the pieces of wood.)

An instrument providing rhythm in the manner of a gourd rattle, *pūjāri kaichi-lambu*, is used in the temple. It is a simple instrument consisting of a small metal container, oval in shape, containing metal pieces.

Melodic percussion instruments include a xylophone of primitive construction, *kāshta-tarang*, and the *jalatarang*. To-day the kāshta-tarang is little used in comparison to the jalatarang, which remains a prominent instrument in Indian music. It is spoken of in ancient Indian literature as *udaka vādyam*, and the art of playing it was included amongst the 64 arts (*Chatush-shashti Kalas*). Its name jalatarang means 'water waves', an appropriate name for a simple instrument consisting of porcelain bowls partly filled with water. The earthenware vessels, which possess a distinct sonority and pitch, are further tuned to sound the required note by adjusting the amount of liquid. The bowls are arranged in a semi-circle before the performer, who strikes them with thin bamboo sticks, sometimes felt covered or tipped with cork. It is used in the orchestra and as a solo instrument where, in the hands of a skilled performer, the crystal-clear tone of the instrument is distinctive in moods, languorous or agile. A shake or quiver (the *gamaka*) is produced by placing a small wooden spoon into the cup a number of times after the vessel has been struck (rendering the vibraphone a late arrival it seems).

In speaking of the construction of the jalatarang, Sambamoorthy says:[1] 'Metallic cups were originally used, and they were later substituted by porcelain cups.'[2] There is also the *septasvaral*, also called *septaghantika* or Indian glockenspiel, an instrument consisting of metal plates or small bells.

TIBET

The land of monasteries and temples possesses music equally mysterious. Tibetan monks connect certain sounds in their human body with their musical instruments, thudding (big drum), clashing (cymbals), ringing (bells), sharp tapping (hand drum). Hermits in their solitary retirement are sustained by pursuit of the art concerned with bell and drum (collectively) or cymbals. Little wonder that the music of Tibet is dominated by instruments of percussion. In many of these the influence of India and China is apparent, both in the style and manner in which they are employed in the orchestra and elsewhere. In the temple orchestras are found nailed drums, braced copper kettledrums, hour-glass drums, bells, cymbals, gongs and bronze discs, the latter two instruments so typical of Tibet. The majority function prominently in processional music, in conjunction with wind instruments, the percussion providing an incessant basic rhythmical pattern. In contrast, when used as an accompaniment to the voice, percussion instruments in the nature of bells, cymbals and drums are often the sole accompaniment. In this medium the mode of accompaniment varies, ranging from the use of a clapper, small drum, or metal disc, struck in a measured manner at lengthy intervals, to the more elaborate and decidedly interesting use of the percussion, observed in example (p. 148) about which Laurence Picken says:[3] 'Instruments and voices may be rhythmically independent of each other, or they may coincide and proceed together in an unstressed rhythm of equal pulses.'

Bells are important to the Tibetans who excel in their casting. In addition to the use of bells as orchestral instruments, they are used extensively in religious services, in particular a small handbell, the *dril-bu*. The bell is tulip shaped with clapper. The handle is fashioned with the head of *Pranjina Parainitā*, symbolical of wisdom. The dril-bu is held in the left hand of the lama, whilst in his right hand he holds the sceptre, or *dordje* (thunderbolt). Alexandra David-Neel says:[4] 'The dordje is method,

[1] Sambamoorthy, P. *Dictionary of South Indian Music*, p. 240.
[2] Henry Cowell requests eight graduated rice bowls in his *Ostinato Pianissimo* (1935), and five porcelain bowls of different tone heights in his *Concerto for Percussion*.
[3] Picken, Laurence. *The New Oxford History of Music*, Oxford, 1960, vol. I, p. 138.
[4] David-Neel, Alexandra. *Initiations and Initiates in Tibet*, Rider, London, 1958, fig. 22.

the handbell is knowledge, both are the true essence of the purified mind.' Small bells are worn on the ankles of dancers in the mystery plays and, as elsewhere, an interesting variety of clapper bells are used to useful and ornamental purpose suspended from the necks of animals. Bells are used also to ornament the exterior of the religious edifice, functioning as emblems, pendant from the lower jaw of a noble lion. Cymbals also have a dual significance. They are used by the Tibetans in the

From the New Oxford History of Music, vol. I. *Ancient and Oriental Music*, Ch. 2, 'Music of Far Eastern Asia', L. Picken. By permission of Oxford University Press.

worship of heavenly and earthly divinities. These instruments resemble in shape and sound the clashing and tinkling Hindu instruments. The gentle sound of the small cymbals is associated with the powers above, whilst in contrast, a curiously strident and resonant sound produced by the repeated clashing of the larger Tibetan death cymbals, is connected with the funeral service.

L. A. Waddell says[1] that in certain rites and celebrations, 'The pauses are marked by bells and cymbals. Although the instruments are wielded with great clamour, each is manipulated according to rule. Thus with the cymbals, at the word *argham*

[1] Waddell, L. A. *The Buddhism of Tibet*, Heffer, Cambridge, 1934, p. 432.

the cymbals are held horizontally and struck with middle finger erect. On *pragham* – held below waist and upper cymbal is made to revolve along the rim of the lowest etc., etc.'

Tinkling cymbals include the *rol-mo*. These small cymbals are connected with a cord, and struck by contact of the rims in the manner of the Hindu jālrā. The larger clashing cymbals *tsög-rol* etc., average 12 inches in diameter; they are disconnected and struck vertically and horizontally, in the style of the ancient cymbals of the Assyrians, Israelites and the Greeks.

Fig. 26
Dril-bu,
Tibet

Continuing, we find a pair of laced kettledrums, *idu-mān*, a shaking drum, similar to the Japanese *furi-tsuzumi*, and a large single head frame drum, *lāgna*. The lāgna has a diameter of three or more feet. It is struck with a heavy leather-covered drum stick, or bamboo cane.

In the Victoria and Albert Museum, London, there is a Lamaist drum with a surface of beaten metal in place of the usual parchment. The workmanship embodied in this Lamaist drum, with its wood shell overlaid with brass and set with turquoise and coral, is typical of many Tibetan musical instruments. In contrast, there is the *rna-ch'un*, an instrument of simpler construction. The rna-ch'un is an hour-glass drum, often made from human skulls. A smaller Tibetan clapper drum is similarly constructed to the hour-glass drum rna-ch'un, the two skull caps being joined at the sutures, with the open ends covered with a membrane. Like so many other of the percussion instruments of Tibet and India, these instruments are used in religious services.

Bibliography: Chapter 6

INDIA AND TIBET

BANDOYPADHYAYA, Shripada. *The Music of India*, Taraporevala, Bombay, 1958.

DAVID-NEEL, Alexandra. *Initiations and Initiates in Tibet*, Rider, London, 1958.

DONINGTON, Robert. *The Instruments of Music*, Methuen, London, 1949.

FOX-STRANGWAYS, A. H. *The Music of Hindostan*, Clarendon Press, Oxford, 1914.

GOSVAMI, O. *The Story of Indian Music*, Asia Publishing House, Bombay, 1957 and 1961.

HOLST, Imogen. *Tune*, Faber London, 1962.

PICKEN, Laurence. *The New Oxford History of Music*, vol. I, Oxford, London, 1960.

SACHS, Curt. *The History of Musical Instruments*, Norton, New York, 1940.

SAMBAMOORTHY, P. *Catalogue of Musical Instruments*, Government Museum, Madras, Madras Government Press, 1955.

Dictionary of South Indian Music, Indian Music Publishing House, Madras, 1959.

TAYLOR, Meadows. *Proceedings of the Royal Irish Academy*, vol. IX, Dublin, 1865.

WADDELL, L. A. *The Buddhism of Tibet*, Heffer, Cambridge, 1934.

RECOMMENDED READING

CROSSLEY-HOLLAND, P. C. 'Tibetan Music', in Grove, G. *Dictionary of Music and Musicians*, vol. VIII, Fifth Edition, London, 1954.

DAY, C. R. *The Music and Musical Instruments of Southern India and the Deccan*, Black, London, 1891.

KETTLE, Rupert. 'Thoughts on Table Notation', *Percussive Notes*, vol. XI, no. I, Fall, 1972.

MAYER, John. 'Indian Music', *Composer*, no. 32, 1969.

7

Mesopotamia and Egypt

Praise to the Lord upon instruments of percussion! Constant reference throughout the chapters of the *Old Testament* to 'that which is struck' leaves no doubt as to the prominent part played by percussion instruments in the music of the Israelites. It is here that we experience in a full sense an evolution from folk and ritual instruments, to instruments devoted to a definite musical purpose. Biblical references have much to tell of the use of 'percussion' 5,000 years ago, a story substantiated with the evidence from the three sources (excavatory, pictorial and literary) upon which we rely for early information.

The ancient people of Mesopotamia and Egypt have vanished, but they have left us authentic records of their culture, from which we find they were possessed of a flourishing music, highly developed and artistic. No other lands have produced more archaeological evidence, or more profuse literary references, from which we learn that music was practised on the banks of the Nile *c.* 4000 BC.

Research in musical instruments in these territories has been assisted by two important factors: the preservation of many instruments from decomposition and the Egyptian belief that pictorial representations of domestic life secured a happy existence in another life.

The aridity of the desert soil and the seclusion of the tomb have preserved and revealed the character of instruments dating from the third millennium BC. A fragment of vase found during the excavation of a south Babylonian temple in Bismya, portraying musicians performing upon the harp and drum, possibly the most ancient depiction of musical instruments in existence, is reputed to date from before 3000 BC.

Pre-historic contact between Egypt and Mesopotamia, and the consequent influence of Sumer on Egypt is agreed. Sachs says:[1] 'Their relation is particularly

[1] Sachs, Curt. *The History of Musical Instruments*, p. 86.

noticeable in music; the so-called Old Kingdom (2900–2475 BC) had not one instrument that did not exist in Sumer simultaneously, or even earlier.' With this fact in mind, our first call is to Sumer and Babylonia, before turning to the music of the Old Testament, (surely one of the most useful of the literary sources of information regarding early music). In Mesopotamia, excavations from early layers have revealed clay rattles, admittedly in the form of birds and animals, and according to Sachs, obviously toys, but of interest if only in proving the wide distribution of a simple instrument of percussion that has undoubtedly given pleasure to generations over an immense period of time. A red pottery rattle is included in the Egyptian musical instruments possessed by the British Museum. Regrettably the date and provenance are unknown. The imperishable nature of baked clay, and the resemblance of the material comprising this rattle to certain tablets that have provided us with the history of music in ancient times, together with the primitive appearance of the instrument, suggest it to be of great age. Rattles of clay have also been found in Palestine, in the excavations at Gezer (near Jerusalem), and Tell Beit Mirsim. It is possible that these objects were toys. On the other hand, they may confirm to some degree the opinion of certain authorities that instruments of this nature were used by Israelite musicians. The Cairo Museum collection of Egyptian antiquities contains prehistoric rattles and those of the eighteenth dynasty. Clay rattles dated early second millennium BC (in the form of toys) are at the British Museum.

DRUMS

Five thousand years ago, ancient Mesopotamia possessed instruments of music of an advanced degree of construction in great variety. Instruments of percussion date from that period. They include drums, clappers, sistra, bells and cymbals. The earliest record, the fragment of vase from Bismya *c.* 3000 BC, depicts an instrument, somewhat indistinct, but resembling a rectangular frame drum. The instrument is held under the arm of a man who is marching in procession behind two harpists. Other Mesopotamian art works depict, much more clearly, drums in at least four styles and in many sizes. Small rectangular frame drums (timbrels) with shallow frames and one, or possibly two heads, appear as early as 2700 BC. A seal of Queen Shubad portrays a banquet depicting a player performing on an instrument of this shape as an accompaniment to a bow shaped harp. The University Museum, Philadelphia, possesses a plaque (*c.* 2700 BC) from the Royal Cemetery, Ur, on which can be seen a figure of a jackal-headed creature with timbrel and sistrum. This animal is portrayed as a skilled percussionist. It appears to be tapping the drum (laid on its lap) with the left paw, whilst shaking the sistrum held in the right paw.

Drums

The largest instrument to be observed on these relics is a remarkable specimen. It is a monster drum appearing on a Sumerian art work; a sculptured upright slab over four thousand years old (again in the University Museum, Philadelphia). The drum, most likely a temple drum, is within a few inches of the height of the two men who stand at either side of it. The frontal position of the instrument shows only one face, rendering it difficult to determine whether the drum is a frame drum, shallow drum, or barrel drum. The two men appear to be striking the instrument on both sides, reasonable evidence of two skins, and a shell of no great depth, ruling out the possibility of a barrel drum, which is usually as wide as its diameter. One feature seems certain – the nailed head (in the manner of many of the drums of the Far East). The player to the right is striking the face of the drum with the palm of the left hand. The left arm of the opposite player, whose general position is identical to that of his partner, disappears behind the drum; from which it would be reasonable to infer that each side of the drum is being struck simultaneously.

An equally significant exhibit of near antiquity is the Sumerian vase (c. 2500 BC) in the Louvre Museum, Paris, on which is depicted a drum somewhat smaller than the instrument observed on the sculptured slab at Philadelphia. It is nevertheless of considerable size, reaching the shoulders of the players who stand at each side, suggesting a diameter of at least three feet. The players, a man and a woman, face each other, in a style similar to that adopted by players on the Philadelphian exhibit, and are portrayed as striking the drum with the left hand simultaneously. The right arm of each player is raised in what is clearly a position ready to strike with the palm on the opposite side, suggesting that the instrument is a shallow frame drum. This drum, which is in a frontal position, resembles a huge tambourine. Large pegs are projected round the circumference of the skin. Canon Galpin writes of it:[1] 'The skin head, probably varnished, like that of the Chinese drums, to resist the weather, was attached to the frame when wet by wooden pegs . . .' A detail, quite unusual, is the addition of a figure of Ea (God of Music and Wisdom) set on top of the drum. The figure appears to be some eighteen inches in height.

Continuing chronologically, we find from Sumerian texts that a grand-daughter of Maram-Sin (c. 2280 BC) was appointed the player of a drum in the temple of the Moon in Ur. Ten measures of meal were allotted to a temple drum, whilst only two measures were allotted to the great well. Smaller frame drums, played with the bare hands by women, are observed on clay statuettes dated about 2000 BC. A figure in the British Museum represents a performer striking with bare hands a small cylindrical drum on both sides. The drum is suspended from the waist in a horizontal

[1] Galpin, F. W. *Music of the Sumerians*, Cambridge, 1936. (Libraire Heitz, Strasbourg, reprint 1955, p. 6.)

position. According to British Museum information, the object comes from Ur, where it was found in the unstratified area known as Diqdiqqeh. It can be dated stylistically to the old Babylonian period.

It is at this period that drums appear with certainty in Egypt. Actual specimens and art representations are numerous. Bearing in mind the Egyptian tradition that their God Thot was the originator of the drum raises the question 'Did the drum exist in Egypt before the time we find it depicted on art works?'

Though there is evidence from delineations on archaic patterns and the walls of tombs of the popular use of clappers, hand clapping, and concussive instruments from the fourth millennium BC the drum, with the exception of a small tambourine, is absent. The measured movements of the arms and feet, pictured so frequently to the accompaniment of hand clapping, is a style that persisted through several centuries. A work written in 1774 remarks on the custom resorted to by Egyptian men and women of marking the rhythmical measure of the song by clapping hands in the absence of drums to serve this purpose. According to Sachs there is little to support a reasoning that drums may have existed in Egypt before 2000 BC. He says:[1] 'Drums might have existed before then without being depicted on art works. But even if we admit this vague possibility, the lack of any archaeological reference in a country so rich in realistic art documents would seem to prove that they did not exist.' (A drum seen on the fragment in the Munich Museum, from the temple near Abusir *c.* 2700 BC, is the solitary exception and by no means convincing. It is considered by Sachs to be an importation from Sumer.)

This seemingly late arrival of the drum among the numerous rhythm-providing instruments is nevertheless surprising for this reason: the earliest authentic references point to the instrument in a highly developed form.

Preserved in the Cairo Museum are the remains of a cylindrical double-headed drum considered to be nearly 4,000 years old. This remarkable relic is from a tomb of the Middle Kingdom (tomb of Dedŷt-Baqt). It is well described by Garstang:[2] 'The barrel is carved in a single piece of wood taken presumably from the trunk of a tree. Its length is 69 cms and its breadth 29 cms. The ends are of parchment, connected together by a network of leather thongs. There is to be seen the leather attachment for suspending the instrument; and there is also a coil of leather which was obviously used for tightening up the thongs, being twisted with a short stick, and thus enabling the requisite pitch of the instrument to be maintained.'

Hickmann's catalogue of the musical instruments in the Cairo Museum includes rectangular and circular frame drums, the latter with painted heads, and double-

[1] Sachs, Curt. ibid. p. 96.
[2] Garstang, John. *Burial Customs of Egypt*, Constable, London, 1907, p. 156.

headed drums with cylindrical bodies, with the heads braced with thongs in most instances. In other cases certain features suggest the heads were nailed. A bronze shell (cylindrical), attached to which are two rings, infers that this drum was suspended in a horizontal position and played on both sides in the manner of the English 'long drum' of the eighteenth and nineteenth centuries.

J. G. Wilkinson speaks of similar instruments:[1] '. . . the only drum represented in the early sculptures is a long drum'. This authority describes a drum 2 feet or 2½ feet in length, and braced by cords. It was beaten with the hand, like the Roman tympanum, and when played was slung by a band round the neck of the drummer, who during the march carried it in a vertical position at his back. Like the trumpet, the drum played an important part in military manoeuvres to give signals and assist the march. Clements of Alexandria states that the drum was used by the Egyptians in going to war. Wilkinson says the long drum was used not only in the army, but by buffoons who danced to its sound. This writer's description of a further type of Egyptian drum (written more than 125 years ago) deals with aspects of interest to the text of this volume, and must we feel be included, with only minor exceptions, in its full text. The reference to the covering on the drumsticks is significant.[2]

'Besides the long drum, the Egyptians had another, not very unlike our own, both in form and size, which was broader in proportion to its length . . . being two feet and a half high and two feet broad. It was beaten with two wooden sticks; but as there is no representation of the mode of using it, we are unable to decide whether it was suspended horizontally and struck at both ends, as is usual with a drum of the same kind still used at Cairo, or at one end only, like our own; though, from the curve of the sticks, I am inclined to think it was slung and beaten as the tambour of modern Egypt. Sometimes the sticks were straight and consisted of two parts, the handle and a thin round rod, at whose end a small knob projected for the purpose of fastening the leather pad with which the drum was struck: they were about a foot in length, and, judging from the form of the handle of one in the Berlin Museum,[3] we may conclude they belonged, like those above mentioned, to a drum beaten at both ends. Each extremity of the drum was covered with red leather braced with catgut strings, passing through small holes in its broad margin, and extending in direct lines over the copper body, which, from its convexity, was similar in shape to a cask. In order to tighten the skins and thereby brace the drum, a piece of catgut extended round each end, near the edge of the leather, crossing the strings at right

[1] Wilkinson, J. G. *The Manners and Customs of Ancient Egypt*, Murray, London, 1837, pp. 266.
[2] ibid. pp. 268–9.
[3] From Thebes.

angles, and being twisted round each separately, braced them all in proportion as it was drawn tight. This was only done when the leather had become released by constant use, and as this piece of catgut was applied to either end, they had the means of doubling the power of tension on every string. It is true that this kind of drum does not occur in any sculptures hitherto discovered, yet it is not less certain that it was among the instruments of the country, one of them having been found in the excavations made at Thebes by S. Joum d'Athanas in 1823.'

Throughout the Middle Kingdom elongated and barrel-shaped drums braced in various styles were numerous. In the New Kingdom, some four hundred years later, frame drums, circular and rectangular, (ordinarily called tambourines) elongated barrel drums, small kettledrums (*baz*) and vase-shaped drums are observed with indication of clay, wood and metal bodies. All records from this period show the performers as women; in fact the whole practice of the art of music appears to have been entirely entrusted to the fair sex, with one notable exception, the God Bes, who is frequently represented with a drum with cylindrical body. In all cases the instruments are struck with bare hands, an ancient and widespread custom. To return at this point, 1100 BC, to Sumer, this style is emphasized on a relief dated about the ninth century BC excavated at Carchemish by the British Museum expedition just prior to the first world war. A fragment of the slab, which was broken, is in the British Museum, the remainder is at the Hittite Museum, Ankara. A photograph of the entire slab as found is alongside the British Museum exhibit. The drum, seen accompanying a short horn, is about three feet in diameter with the head nailed. It is held in a frontal position by a third man, whilst the two players strike it with bare hands. Like the monster drum described on an earlier Sumerian art work, the players appear to be striking (with apparent care) the instrument on both sides, suggesting that the drum is double-headed. The relief depicts priests sounding a call to prayer and is from a carving of a scene of worshippers outside the temple of the goddess Kubaba.

Striking the drumhead with the palm of the hand, as depicted on this relief and other subjects, appears to be common practice. There seems no conclusive evidence of the use of drumsticks at this period. Possibly the stick was taboo, because the hide of the animal was considered sacred. Akkadian texts *c.* 300 BC taken from tablets found at Erech and now in the Brussels Museum support this contention; they deal with instructions for furnishing the bronze kettledrum (*Lilis* [*Lilissu*]) with a skin head. Canon Galpin[1] has made an English abstract of the French translation by Thureau-Dangin:

'A bull without defect, black in colour and untouched by stick or whip was

[1] Galpin, F. W. ibid. p. 65.

selected; if spotted with seven groups of white spots in star-form, it was unsuitable. The animal was brought to the "House of Knowledge" (the temple) on a propitious day and offerings were made to the great Gods and especially to Lumha (Ea), God of Music and Wisdom. A reed mat was placed on the ground and covered with sand: on it the animal was held. More offerings were made and perfumes burnt. A torch was then lighted and the bull was singed. Twelve linen cloths were laid on the ground and twelve bronze images of the Gods of Heaven, Earth and the Under-world placed upon them. Sacrifices were made and the body or bowl of the drum was set in its place. The animal's mouth was washed and, by means of a tube of aromatic reed, incantations were whispered into its ears explaining, in dialectical Sumerian, the honour which was about to be done to the bull by its divine use. A hymn was next chanted to the accompaniment of the double reed-pipe. The bull was then slain, its heart burnt, and the body, after it had been skinned, wrapped in red cloth. The skin was treated with fine flour, beer, wine, grease, Hittite alum and gall-nut. It was then stretched over the bowl of the drum and tied round with a cord. Pins or pegs of box, cedar, ebony and other woods were driven through the skin into holes previously made in the body of the drum and, to render all taut, the tendon of the bull's left shoulder was twisted round the edge of the drum-head, the twelve bronze images of the gods having been previously placed inside the bowl. The first cord was then undone and, at a later time, an ornamental binding was placed over the edges of the skin, the pin-heads being also wrapped round with coloured wool and varnished. The now edified bull was bidden to guard well the sacred images within. On the fifteenth day after, sacrifices were again offered and the drum was carried into the presence of the temple gods. Only the initiated were allowed to witness these rites, and the drum became "The Divine *Lilissu*".[1]

Here we have that boon to the investigator – literary and archaeological evidence in firm agreement. Despite the lack of the musical system of these ancient nations, such representations convince us of the importance of the drum, and suggest its use on great occasions. These ancient works of art yield pictures of performance upon musical instruments. The drummers are intent and give the impression of experts. Such discoveries are treasures from a musical point of view, adding a premium to their value as antiquities.

Continuing chronologically, we find a Babylonian plaque *c.* 700 BC representing a kettledrum said to be metal in the form of a deep drum shaped like a goblet. A fragment of an ivory box (Pl. 55) from the palace of Nimrud (second half of the eighth century BC) depicts a procession of musicians. The 'percussionist' performs upon a small frame drum. The drum is held in the player's left hand, in a position to

---

[1] Thureau-Dangin, F. *Rituels accadiens*, Paris, 1921, p. 12.

suggest that the four fingers apparently control, to some degree, the timbre, and (or) assist the strokes being delivered by the right hand. A barrel drum is seen on a relief of the late epoch from the tomb of Zanefer, *c.* 600 BC. This interesting relic (in the museum at Alexandria) portrays an elderly man playing a harp, accompanied by a young woman performing with bare hands on a cylindrical drum which is suspended almost vertically at her waist. The bulging body of the drum is reminiscent of the Hindu drums; suggesting a possible cultural contact with India.

A small hand drum appears on one of the most remarkable portrayals of musicians of ancient times discovered to date; the royal Elamite orchestra and choir delineated on an Assyrian bas relief (*c.* 660 BC) in the British Museum. Eleven instruments are seen, including upper and lower-chested harps, double reed pipes, and a drum. The drum is single-headed (nailed) and is suspended at the player's waist. The performer is striking the instrument in the customary manner, with bare hands.

Engel refers to a spherical drum, small in diameter, but about three feet in length. He compares this instrument to those seen on a drawing in a work by A. H. Layard, *Discoveries in the Ruins of Nineveh and Babylon* 1849. The scene depicts Assyrians cutting down the palm trees belonging to a captured city. Engel[1] says: 'It is worthy of notice that we find rhythmical sounds of the drum here employed apparently for the purpose of facilitating the execution of some menial labour.'

In Egypt we find a large tambourine over two feet in diameter being used at the time of Osorkon II (*c.* 800 BC). Specimens of circular frame drums, the majority of smaller dimensions, are conserved in many museums. The only known specimen of a rectangular frame drum, excavated at Thebes, is in the Cairo Museum. The period is given as eighteenth dynasty. These relics give no indication of jingling contrivances, nor are such confirmed on reliefs or pictorial evidence depicting small frame drums. Canon Galpin[2] in dealing with the Sumerian timbrel says: 'As the name is sometimes preceded by the determinative Urudu there must have been some "copper" about it, may be "jingles" or a metal covered frame.' The paucity of information concerning this matter has led to a good deal of speculation among musicologists. The answer is sufficiently elusive to warrant a constant enquiry. Having in mind the manner in which the instrument, in some cases, appears to be held aloft and shaken, it is possible that a jingling contrivance was not unknown. No mention is made of the structure of these instruments in priestly writings such as those describing the kettledrum. The numerous Old Testament references (from Genesis to Ezekiel) to the *toph*, translated as *tabret* and *timbrel*, are agreed to indicate small hand drums, already found in Mesopotamia and Egypt. There is little proof at

[1] Engel, Carl. *The Music of the Most Ancient Nations*, Reeves, London, 1864, reprint 1929, p. 101.
[2] Galpin, F. W. ibid. p. 9.

this period of the jingling contrivance. In these Biblical references the word tinkling or metal is used in connection with bells and cymbals, but not with tabret or timbrel. Artists over a period of time have drawn their own conclusions, by no means conclusive. Cf. *tympanon* of ancient Greece.

In one instance Miriam the prophetess, who we read (Exodus xv, 20) 'took a timbrel in her hand, and all the women went out after her with timbrels and with dances', is drawn with an instrument closely resembling a modern tambourine. Jingles, or spaces for them, are visible on the framework. The same situation, the Deliverance of Israel, is portrayed by another artist with Miriam performing on a small kettledrum with side drum sticks; a reminder at least of the value of present-day photographic equipment. We are better served with information regarding the use of the hand drum which, except that the instrument was invariably played by women, varied considerably with the nations we are discussing. In Sumerian and Babylonian art works, instruments of this type are portrayed in processions. On occasions the instrument is held on the left shoulder, whilst the player strikes it with the right hand. Drums of this description were of importance in the temple service. In Egypt it served in a similar capacity. It was one of the chief instruments used during the funeral lamentations. In contrast, the Israelites associated this instrument with processions, and with joy, feasting and mirth. There is one grim exception; when tabrets were used to drown the cries of human victims, sacrificed, or passed through the fire in the valley of Hinnom.

The nomenclature of the Mesopotamian, Egyptian and Hebrew membrano-phones etc, presents no small problem. To quote Dr. Farmer:[1] 'much perplexity lies in their names'. Text book references in few instances connect ancient texts and the arts. Only the Sumerian kettledrum is confirmed as lilis from its mention in literary sources and a carving above the figure of a drum. Otherwise literary sources do not describe these instruments in any detail. The Sumerian names and their Akkadian and Egyptian equivalents are dealt with in detail by authorities such as F. Thureau-Dangin, Canon Galpin, H. G. Farmer and Curt Sachs. Briefly, we find that the best known Sumerian name for drum is *balag*, from a verb – 'bal' – to beat. In the reign of Gudea, the priest king (*c.* 200 BC), two individual instruments so named are mentioned, *nin-an-da-gal-ki* and *ushumgal-kalam-ma*, the latter giving the name to a certain year in Gudea's time. The large shallow drum on the Carchemish relief is, according to Farmer's reference[2] 'believed to be the Sumerian *alal*'. The same authority submits *mesi* as a small frame drum. Canon Galpin gives *adapu* for the ancient Sumerian rectangular frame drum, and refers to a grain measure of similar

[1] Farmer, H. G. 'The Music of Ancient Mesopotamia', *Ancient & Oriental Music*, The New Oxford History of Music, London, vol. I, 1960, p. 239.   [2] ibid. p. 240.

shape with the same name. The generic name for drum in Egypt was *teben* ('teh' or 'tehen' – to beat, to play). The drum called *gem gem* was in all probability a cylindrical drum. The Hebrew toph (*tupim*) is translated as a small frame drum, already mentioned as tabret and timbrel, (corresponding to the Greek tympanon and Arabic *duff*). Sachs compares the position to–day regarding the confusing nomenclature with the position of a scholar five thousand years hence endeavouring to find out the difference between the French terms *tambour* and *caisse*.

CLAPPERS

The excitement of the drum has put us a step or two ahead chronologically. We must go back several paces, for in the clappers of ancient Egypt we find one of man's earliest instruments and, incidentally, the first instrument that Egyptian sources record. Archaic pottery of the fourth millennium BC depicts clappers with curved blades. These prehistoric Egyptian vases feature one-hand clappers consisting of two curved sticks both held in one hand and clapped one against each other, concussively. They are played by both female dancers and the musicians who accompany them. That they are an adaptation of the primitive boomerang and served a dual purpose as a missile and a musical instrument, there can be little doubt, since sticks similar in shape were common as missiles in hunting. Ancient Sumerian seals show curved clappers resembling those on the early Egyptian vases. The curved blades of copper found at Kish and Ur which were at first considered to be weapons, are now recognised as dancing sticks. On the archaic seal from Ur (*c.* 2800 BC), owned by the University Museum in Philadelphia, is seen a small animal playing a pair of short clappers. A seal from the same region, dated *c.* 2700 BC, shows a dancer accompanied by a performer on a lyre, with attendants clapping curved sticks. Sticks held in each hand and clapped together (a common custom of music making among primitive peoples) are represented on Egyptian reliefs as far back as the third millennium BC. They were associated with magic (assisting the harvest) and the lightening of labour. On an ancient Egyptian tomb (nearly 5,000 years old) is seen a group of rural workers clapping together short sticks held one in each hand, as they stride in the fashion associated with the rites of fertility. An instance of early 'music while you work' is experienced on a relief featuring a wine press. The labour of the vintagers, who press the grapes with their feet, is controlled, and thus rendered less arduous by the rhythmic support of two men who are clapping the rhythm with percussion sticks.[1]

[1] This engaging and age-old custom is widespread. It persists in areas as far apart as Central Africa and the Far East, where work in the field is still executed to the accompaniment of simple instruments of percussion.

Sistra

The popularity of clappers of all descriptions is established by the numerous specimens to be found in museums. In London for example, in the British Museum collection there are specimens of curved ivory clappers from Diospolis Parva, Middle Kingdom *c.* 2000 BC. Instruments of the same period and shape are seen from Abydos and elsewhere, some exquisitely carved in the form of hands and feet. A small bone clapper dated the fifth dynasty (2400 BC) is from Mostagedda. Wood clappers are dated 1100 BC and 850 BC the former inscribed 'made for the chantor of Hathor'. The Horniman Museum possesses two pairs of Egyptian clappers dating from the sixteenth century BC. One pair is of wood and the other of ivory, both in the shape of hands and arms. Elsewhere other decorations include the heads of animals or men and frequently the head of the goddess Hathor (Isis), with whose worship clappers are so strongly associated. Such instruments are found in the lavish collection of clappers in the Cairo Museum (described in detail in Hans Hickmann's *Catalogue of Egyptian Antiquities*). Clappers in the form of castanets are not recorded on Sumerian or Egyptian art works, nor are they mentioned in the Bible. Instruments resembling castanets existed in Egypt in two forms: one in the shape of a small wooden boat cut in half lengthwise and grooved, the other nearer the shape of Spanish castanets (Sachs considers they were not properly Egyptian). Castanets of this description are included in the Cairo Museum collection.

SISTRA

The *sistrum*,[1] an instrument of immemorial age, is characteristic of the land of the Nile. One dictionary definition that a 'sistrum' is 'an instrument consisting of a thin metal frame, through which is passed a number of metal rods, and furnished with a handle by which it is shaken and made to jingle' whilst substantially correct, does not complete the picture. The instrument is found in several forms, the earliest evidence of which may be found in the shark rattle preserved by Malayan and Melanesian fishermen, an implement consisting of a framework of rattan bent in the shape of a two-pronged fork or a tennis racket, strung with loose discs of coconut shell. The Sumerian and Babylonian instrument is portrayed as a U-shaped instrument with rings on crossbars. It is clearly represented in this shape on a seal dated about 2500 BC. Little is known of the use of the sistrum in Sumeria. Historians consider its employment was discontinued at an early date, or confined to certain temples. The remains of an instrument discovered at Ur reveal highly decorative features. The ends of the handle and points of the fork are tipped with ornamental knobs. The jingles are of cut shell. A spur-shaped sistrum in the Tiflis Museum, discovered in Caspia, points to Mesopotamian influence.

[1] From the Greek *seistron* meaning 'thing shaken'.

Galpin says Egypt was thought the pre-eminent home of the sistrum. This is supported by the fact that the majority of museum exhibits are of Egyptian origin, and that sistra of various kinds were known. Only one Egyptian specimen is reported in the Sumerian shape. This instrument (preserved in the Egyptian Museum, Berlin) is in the form of a wooden spur, the jingles consisting of metal bars. The most common sistrum is an instrument with a frame generally of metal – in the shape of a horseshoe. Holes in the side of the frame receive the jingle pieces consisting of two, three or four wires with bent ends, to secure them in the framework. The wires slip backwards and forwards in the loose holes and jingle as the bent end touches the frame.

Jingling discs were added to the wires during the Old and Middle Kingdoms. For some reason this increased sound seems to have found no favour in the New Kingdom; instruments preserved from this period are without discs. Numerous names are attributed to the Egyptian sistrum; *iba, sehem,* or *kemken* appearing to imply the instrument so far described. The superb craftsmanship in metals is emphasised in the rich symbolic decoration of the finer specimens, of which there are numerous examples in the Cairo Museum. Included in the British Museum collection are bronze sistra dating from 850 BC. In one instance, the handle in the form of the goddess Bes, the healing god, is surmounted by a frame covered with chased designs showing the goddesses of Upper Egypt carrying sistra, the goddess Bast and vultures. At the top of the frame is the head of Hathor, in other instances the figures of cats and birds, with the wires terminating in ducks' heads. Among the Lower Egyptian deities there is a bronze figure of the goddess Bast holding a Hathor-headed sistrum. The majority of these instruments give the impression of metal casting. The *naos* sistrum (*sešesĕt*) an instrument confined to Egypt, is among the British Museum collection. The frame, a glazed composition, is in the shape of a small temple or 'naos'. It is supported on a handle featuring Hathor's head. Jingling cross wires complete the instrument. The original implement had no cross wires; according to Sachs it was a mute emblem. Many of the earthenware sistra discovered in a broken condition in tombs, are now known to have been interred in this condition as a sign of mourning. The Egyptian sistrum was an instrument primarily associated with the worship of the goddess Hathor-Isis. It was carried by women of exalted rank, and by priests and priestesses. It marked special parts in the temple service, similar to certain percussion instruments in the Confucian service, and the bell in the Catholic mass. In contrast, the instrument is reported as an accompaniment to rites of wanton and lascivious character. In a finer sense, it was credited with power over evil spirits, and remained an instrument of importance for many centuries. At the battle of Actium (31 BC) it is said that Queen Cleopatra used numerous sistra, played by women, to intimidate the enemy, giving rise to the appellation 'Cleopatra's war trumpet'. It is no surprise to find disagreement among historians regarding the use of the instrument for such a purpose. Virgil's description of Cleopatra leading her forces to battle to the sound of the sistrum: 'Regina in mediis patrio vocat agmina sistro'[1] is considered by Stainer to be intensely sarcastic, in the light of the customary use of the instrument during rites of a very wanton and lascivious character. It is difficult to appreciate the value of such a gentle-sounding instrument as a form of clarion call, or to believe that the sound produced by a large body of women shaking such instruments could terrify a powerful foe. The opinion of one writer who considers the use of the sistra as an emblem to signify the power of the Egyptian Queen, seems feasible.

There is little evidence of the use of the sistrum in the Egyptian orchestra. It is possible that its absence from music with an emphasis on rhythm was due to its important function in the worship of the gods, and its supposed magic character. In the 'jingle ring' the intriguing sound of this age-old instrument has found a place in the modern orchestra, as indeed has the lady percussionist.[2]

Biblical references concerning the sistrum are scant, occurring with certainty on only one occasion, 2 Samuel, vi. 5 where the Hebrew text, though variously described, is generally agreed to refer to sistrum. In 1 Samuel xviii. 6 mention is made of Shalisham interpreted as 'instruments of music': 'And it came to pass as they came, when David was returned from the slaughter of the Philistine, that the women came out of all cities of Israel, singing and dancing, to meet king Saul, with tabrets, with joy, and with instruments of musick.' As the word 'shalisham' has been disputed more than any musical term in the Hebrew language, we face something of an impasse in attempting to classify this doubtful quantity. Sir John Stainer says:[3] 'A triangle it might have been, but it is more probable that it was a sistrum.' Biblical translators have suggested triangular harps, three stringed lutes, fiddles and triangles. An instrument bearing the name *shalisham* has been illustrated as a stirrup shaped steel rod, threaded with jingling metal rings, resembling the instrument which made its appearance in Europe in the fifteenth century. Sachs is convinced that the term cannot mean an instrument for reason that the *Talmud* does not mention it, and that the Holy Script separates the precarious word from the one musica instrument mentioned in the same verse.

The use of the sistrum was continued by the Greeks and Romans; it spread to the

[1] Virgil. *Aeneid* viii, 696: 'In the centre the queen calls up her forces with the Egyptian sistrum.'
[2] In modern scores the sistrum occurs in Carl Orff's *Oedipus der Tyrann*, 1957-8, and sistra in *Double Music*, 1963 by John Cage and Lou Harrison.
[3] Stainer, John. *The Music of the Bible*, Novello-Ewer, London, 1879, p. 149.

outposts of the latter Empire. Because of its connection with the worship of Isis, it was known as the Isis clapper. Instruments with a marked resemblance to the ancient sistrum are in use to-day over a large area especially North and South America and Spain. The Egyptian bronze sistrum *c.* 1600 BC, and the Ethiopian sistrum (used in church services) displayed in the Horniman Museum possess striking similarities. In the same collection are specimens from Japan, India and Northern Nigeria. The latter is of wood with discs of gourd and is used for dancing. The Indian instrument is used similarly. In Japan, the sistrum is employed in Shinto worship. In parts of Abyssinia, the sistrum under the name of *tsanatsel* is still used by priests. A fork-shaped rattle resembling the implement preserved by Malayan fishermen is used by the Eskimos to entice seals.

BELLS

The remaining instruments of percussion prominent in the musical life of the nations of the Old Testament were (if we exclude, from lack of clear evidence, the dulcimer,[1]) cymbals, and to some extent bells.

In Sumer, Babylonia and Assyria, small bells and similar tinkling pieces were commonly suspended from the trappings of horses, mules or camels. Small bells were common in ancient Egypt, many of them resembling those of Assyria. There are at least fifteen examples in the British Museum, all of bronze, many with a hole at the top, and some with iron tongues. They include several of the large number discovered by A. H. Layard in a chamber at Nimraud. They vary in size from $3\frac{1}{2}$ inches high and $2\frac{1}{2}$ inches in diameter, suggesting their use arranged in regular order to conform to a succession of intervals. In a description of these bells, Engel[2] speaks of an Assyrian bell with a slit from the rim upwards 'which was most likely filed after its discovery for the purpose of ascertaining the exact composition of the metal'. This may well have been the case. On the other hand, there is also the possibility that the instrument may have had a fine crack in the wall, and the tone restored by widening the split (a policy adopted to-day with cymbals so damaged). A repair of this nature was administered quite early in life to one of the most distinguished bells in history – our own Big Ben. The popularity of bells is emphasized by their appearance as small ornaments on ancient Egyptian necklaces

---

[1] The references by many writers to the use of a dulcimer in the Assyrian Kingdom are based on the evidence of a British Museum bas relief known as the 'Procession of King Assurbanipal'. Canon Galpin contends that this instrument is a Trigon or triangular harp, and that the supposition of dulcimer is due to faulty restoration.

[2] Engel, Carl. ibid. p. 65.

of gold and silver, probably as charms, as there is evidence of the use of bells, obtained from the priest, to ward off pests and evil spirits. The ceremonial bell from Babylonia *c.* 600 BC (Berlin Museum) which is decorated with the symbols of Ea was, according to Galpin, probably hung from the high priest's neck and used for incantations for avoiding evils and calamities. The numerous bells, with and without clappers, in the Cairo Museum, described by Hickmann, include instruments of superb craftsmanship. Jingles or small bells are mentioned on three occasions in the Old Testament. In Exodus xxviii. 33–34 and xxxix. 25–26, we are told of the bells of pure gold upon the robe of Aaron the high priest, placed there according to God's orders 'and his sound shall be heard when he goeth in unto the holy place before the Lord, and when he cometh out, and that he die not' – bells to adorn his garment, to announce his presence, and to protect him. The bells were arranged beneath the hem of the garment '. . . A golden bell and a pomegranate, a golden bell and a pomegranate, upon the hem of the robe round about.' A short reference is made to bells on horses in Zechariah, xiv. 20. Wilkinson[1] speaks of a species of fan, to which was probably attached small bells, or pieces of metal.

CYMBALS

It is evident that cymbals have been used over a scattered area for at least 3,000 years. Historians refer to the use of cymbals in Central Asia Minor 1200 BC, in the worship of the goddess Cybele. The use of metal clappers may well go back even further into antiquity. Considering that instruments of the clapper type were among man's most ancient inventions, and have persisted through the generations, it would seem reasonable to deduce that cymbals in some form may have occurred when man began working in metal, a craft existing in Chaldea as early as 3000 BC.

Cymbals closely resembling those in use to-day are portrayed serving various musical purposes from the turn of the first millennium BC. A Babylonian plaque dated *c.* 700–600 BC (British Museum) shows a lady cymbalist accompanying a male performer on a kettledrum. The cymbals are held vertically (a style maintained in the modern orchestra). They are plate type and appear to measure between eight to ten inches in diameter. An Assyrian bas relief *c.* 680 BC depicts cymbals held horizontally. These instruments are funnel-shaped with the necks of the funnels serving as handles. Galpin says such instruments or their simple predecessors were used for temple worship. In some instances, funnel and similarly shaped cymbals are shown with the rims meeting slightly off centre: for reason of tone production, it is considered.

[1] Wilkinson, J. G. ibid. vol. II, p. 237.

A Babylonian statuette of the Hellenistic period shows a player performing upon a pair of cymbals as an accompaniment to a harp. The cymbals, which are cup-shaped, and approximately five inches in diameter, are held in a vertical position. They seem to be strapped to the hands or fingers, or held by a strap. Instruments

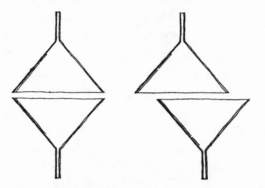

Figs. 27, 28. Assyrian cymbals

of this pattern played in the same way are observed on Greek sculpture. They are described by Mersenne in his *Harmonie Universelle* published in 1636.[1] His illustrations include a pair of cymbals in the shape of dishes, held by means of straps which are secured to the bowl. The instruments are portrayed in a horizontal

Fig. 29
Cup cymbals
(from Mersenne)

position, giving the impression that they are intended to be struck with a vertical movement. A further illustration is of a pair of cup cymbals with bossed rims and rigid handles fixed to the bowl, which Mersenne[2] describes as: 'a picture of antique cymbals which were clashed together, holding them in both hands by the handles'.

[1] Mersenne, Marin. *Harmonie Universelle*, Paris 1636.
[2] Mersenne wrote several books on musical theory, and the information conveyed on contemporary and early instruments in his *Harmonie Universelle* is held in high regard by musicologists to-day.

Cymbals

Egyptian cymbals, of which many interesting specimens survive, were of various patterns. The plate type had a flat brim with a raised central boss giving additional resonance.

The Egyptian cymbals in the collection of the British Museum are regarded as treasures. A pair of beaten bronze cymbals dated after 850 BC measure $6\frac{3}{4}$ inches in diameter and are approximately $\frac{1}{16}$ inch in thickness; the weight of each cymbal is $5\frac{3}{4}$ ozs. They are secured by the original linen cord. The cymbals found by the mummified body of Ankhape, a priestly musician of the temple of Amun (Thebes) first century BC, are $5\frac{1}{3}$ inches in diameter and $\frac{1}{16}$ inch in thickness, again of beaten bronze. The circumstances concerning the discovery of the cymbals with the body of Ankhape, confirm the use of such instruments for religious purposes in ancient Egypt, it being a common custom to place objects with which the deceased was familiar in the tomb, and thus enable the spirit to participate in former activities in after life.

In contrast to the cymbals of beaten metal, the British Museum collection includes several pairs of cast *crotales*. Strictly speaking, crotales are metal castanets, resembling cymbals. A pair of bronze crotales (from Thebes *c.* 200 BC) with large central boss and upturned rim, measure $2\frac{7}{16}$ inches in diameter, a thickness of approximately $\frac{1}{8}$ inch, and a weight of $1\frac{3}{4}$ ozs. These instruments produce well-defined notes, sounding a tone apart. The difference in pitch is due to the slight variation in thickness and weight of the discs. Such instruments were in all probability used by girl dancers in the manner of castanets. A pair of larger crotales (*c.* 200 BC) from Thebes, with a diameter of $3\frac{3}{8}$ inches, are approximately $\frac{1}{8}$ inch thick. They weigh $4\frac{3}{4}$ ozs, suggesting their use as a pair of cymbals. Cymbals on clappers are represented in relics from the Coptic period and comprise small crotales attached to the ends of wood or metal frames.

Instruments of similar construction are included in the collection of Egyptian cymbals and crotales in the Cairo Museum. One instrument consists of four crotales mounted on a four-pronged fork. (An instrument of this nature, the *zilli maşa*, survives in Turkey and Greece ('maşa' – pinchers). It is made with two, three, or more branches.) Gr. *zilia massá*.

Several pairs of crotales of the Coptic period appear in this collection; they measure from two to four inches in diameter. The British Museum crotales are identical, as are the cymbals. The Museum authorities confirm that the crotales are cast, and that the process of beating is particularly obvious in the case of the cymbals.

Historical evidence concerning the cymbals of the Israelites is mainly literary. Discoveries in Palestine, in the excavations at Tell Abu Hawan and elsewhere, resemble so closely the instruments of Egypt that it is difficult to confirm that they are of Hebrew origin. Pictorial representations offer little assistance, so it is upon literature, our third source of information, that we rely.

In many respects the Bible can be regarded as a history of music, particularly the Old Testament which records a great deal about the musical instruments of the Hebrews and their purpose. These ancient records have stood the test of time, often under the keenest scrutiny given to any historical document. They prove the aptitude of the Jews for music, an aptitude maintained to the present day. So it is to the Israelites that we turn for evidence relating to the early use of cymbals (*tseltslim, metsilayim,* etc.). The first reference to these instruments occurs in 2 Samuel vi. 5. *c.* 1050 BC where they appear among the numerous instruments that David and the house of Israel played before the Lord during the journey of the Ark. (Here we find evidence of the use of cymbals in Israel prior to their positive appearance in Babylonia and Egypt.) Throughout the Old Testament we are informed of the content, the purpose, and the exalted position of cymbals among a nation of consummate musicians.

Cymbals are mentioned in Samuel, Chronicles, Ezra, Nehemia and the Psalms, their use being confined to religious ceremonies giving praise to the Lord, and to the accompanying of sacred dances. These instruments were not merely timekeepers; they had a voice in the praise of God, expressed in the performance of musicians of proficiency and high degree.

At the dedication of the Ark, David commanded the chief of the Levites '. . . to appoint their brethren to be the singers with instruments of music, psalteries and harps and cymbals, sounding, by lifting up the voice with joy'. Three singers, Heman, Asaph (the chief) and Ethan, were appointed to sound with cymbals of brass. In company with the trumpets, cymbals were used at the laying of the foundation and the final consecration of Solomon's temple. Again, at the dedication of the wall of Jerusalem, the Levites were sought out of all their places to keep the dedication with thankfulness, with singing, with cymbals, psalteries and harps.

Though cymbals are not mentioned specifically in the instrumentation comprising Nebuchadnezzar's orchestra (Daniel iii) of cornett, flute, harp, sackbut, psaltery, dulcimer[1], and 'all kinds of musick', musicologists are agreed on the inclusion of some rhythmical instruments in this commanding ensemble, at the sound of which, all who heard were to fall down and worship the golden image, or be cast into the midst of a burning fiery furnace. The grim purpose of an orchestra of this calibre could well have been dominated by the clashing of cymbals.

'Praise Him upon the loud cymbals; Praise Him upon the high sounding cymbals,'

---

[1] The word 'dulcimer' in the Authorized Version of the scriptures is now considered a mistranslation for 'bagpipe'. The opinion is also held that 'psaltery' is a mistranslation for 'dulcimer'. It is therefore a possibility that the struck dulcimer existed as well as the plucked psaltery.

says David in Psalm cl. The Biblical translation determines the two species from the adjectives, noisy and clear, applied to the generic Hebrew terms defining cymbals, tseltslim and metsilayim. Here is evidence of clashing and tinkling, with the possibility in the first instance of sizeable instruments, shaped like a soup plate with a wide flat rim, and played by bringing the hands sharply together at right angles with the body. The instruments may have been connected with a cord in the Egyptian style, or strapped to the hands in the manner suggested by Mersenne. High sounding cymbals were probably conical cup-like instruments played by bringing down the one sharply on the other, or smaller thicker plates with broad rims and central bosses. (The existence of a species of gong cannot be dismissed. St. Paul's 'sounding brass or tinkling cymbal' is translated in the *New English Bible* 'sounding gong or clanging cymbal', 1 Corinthians XIII. I.)

In an endeavour to determine the quality of these instruments we are faced with no small difficulty. Archaeological evidence is scant; the spade has revealed little to date regarding the percussion instruments of the Biblical period. In another direction we are more fortunate. The excavator has unearthed metal objects of superb craftsmanship. It is surely fair to say that this high standard of workmanship would be extended to instruments of music. This generation excelled in the art of metal refining. W. F. Albright says:[1] '... nothing remotely comparable to the copper refineries of Ezion-geber has yet been found anywhere else in the ancient world.... Earthenware crucibles with a capacity of 14 cubic feet were numerous. Since the refinery site was chosen at a point where the wind blowing down through the 'Aqabah from the north is strongest, it is clear that intense heat could be generated by use of proper fuel. There can be no doubt whatever that Tell el-Kheleifeh was a great smelting plant, but just how the reduction of copper was accomplished remains a mystery to specialists in metallurgy who have studied the problem.'

The quality and profusion of objects cast in metal at this period points to considerable skill in moulding and metal pouring. Pots, shovels, flesh-hooks and 'all their musical instruments of bright brass were cast by Solomon in the plain of Jordan in the clay ground between Succoth and Zeredathah'. All their musical instruments would surely include the cymbals of brass of the Levite musicians, possibly the two species, the loud and the high sounding. The manufacture of the 'loud' cymbals leads to this speculation: were they cast or beaten, or cast and beaten? There is ample evidence of the two forms of craftsmanship. In the account of the building of the temple, we are told of the work in fine gold and brass. Solomon overlaid the fir tree with fine gold; the doors of the court he overlaid with brass. If this metal were in sheet form, there seems no reason why circular metal discs of this

[1] Albright, W. F. *The Archaeology of Palestine*, Pelican, London, 1949, reprinted 1961, pp. 127-8.

material were not beaten into the shape of cymbals, rendering the instruments light and easily manipulated in comparison to cast metal plates of some inches in diameter, assuming of course that the 'loud' cymbals were of the latter dimension and with deep walls. The method (casting and beating) employed centuries later in the craft of cymbal making would no doubt be practised by the Hebrews, and the Egyptians, having in mind the quality of existing instruments and the skill of such artificers in metals as Hiram of Tyre. Hiram, the widow's son, was a man 'filled with wisdom and understanding, and cunning to work all works in brass' who came to Solomon and wrought all his work. The art of such dedicated experts, without doubt fully expressed in musical instruments, has inspired succeeding generations of craftsmen. Cymbal manufacturers of to-day employ methods that date back many centuries, confirming to a great extent that the operations of casting and beating were employed in producing the cymbals of the Israelites and the Egyptians. The view that this form of workmanship is apparent in Egyptian cymbals such as those in the possession of the British Museum, and others elsewhere, is held by several authorities, including Robert Zildjian of the illustrious family of cymbal manufacturers, whose instruments are to-day world famous for their individuality and perfection.

It seems an opportune moment to become acquainted with the history and craft of these present-day artists in metals, a family of Armenian extraction whose name in the world of music is synonymous with fine cymbals. This family (whose name implies cymbal maker, 'Zil' being the Turkish word for cymbal, 'ji' for maker and the Armenian suffix 'ian' 'son of') are descendants of a line who have been making cymbals for three and a half centuries. In 1623 a forbear of the present Zildjians, a Constantinople alchemist named Avedis, discovered a process for treating alloys. He applied the knowledge to the making of cymbals, an already flourishing craft in Turkey. His fame spread to the extent of the guildsmen associating the terms for cymbal with his name, thus establishing the family name of Zildjian.

It became the custom of the senior member of the family to impart the family secret to the oldest male Zildjian next in direct line of descent. This custom has continued to the present time, and the process discovered by the seventeenth-century alchemist, and subsequently so closely guarded, remains Zildjian property.

For three centuries, with the exception of a short period, due to the political exile of a member of the family, the cymbals continued to be manufactured in Turkey. Until the middle of the nineteenth century the Zildjian establishment remained a modest enterprise, catering in the main for the demand of the Eastern Mediterranean area, the territory in which such instruments were principally used, the chief sources of demand coming from the Turkish military during the 'spate' of Janissary music, and the Armenian churches where cymbals were, and remain, instruments of worship.

Cymbals

During the latter half of the nineteenth century, due to the opulent scores of composers of the calibre of Berlioz and Wagner, which were coloured by an abundant use of cymbals (in certain instances an innovation), the instruments achieved an important and permanent position in orchestras. The result was that coupled with the business mind of the family leader of that period, an Avedis Zildjian, the Zildjian cymbals became universally recognised. Avedis displayed his products at international exhibitions, making personal visits to London and Paris. Each cymbal, hitherto signed with pen and ink, was stamped with a special trade mark, an inscription consisting of the company's name in Turkish, and its French equivalent. Until his death in 1865, Avedis stimulated the firm's activities. Two sons survived him, neither of them of age. Consequently the business passed to a younger brother of Avedis, named Kèropé Zildjian, who managed the business less ambitiously, though effectively until 1910. Kèropé had no sons, so he trained as his successor his nephew Aram. Aram's zest for politics resulted in his flight to Bucharest where he established a cymbal factory. After a lengthy period in Bucharest, Aram eventually returned to his native country, and for a short time maintained foundries in both countries, exporting cymbals universally, and in particular to America, which was by now the largest consumer of musical instruments in the world.

In 1928 Aram contemplated retirement. Since he had no children, the title of the firm was due to pass to the eldest son of his brother, his nephew Avedis. Domiciled in the U.S.A. and with a successful business in confectionery, Avedis was reluctant to return to Constantinople, but he succeeded in convincing his uncle of the wisdom of manufacturing cymbals in America, and in 1929 Aram joined his nephew for this purpose. A foundary was established in North Quincey, Massachusetts, near to salt water as was the original foundry in Constantinople. Aram imparted the family secrets to Avedis, who immediately became enthused, and within a year made the decision to give his full time to the craft of cymbal making.

The path of the new enterprise was by no means a smooth one. The tradition of the Turkish-made cymbal was so firmly established that players were slow to accept instruments made in the U.S.A. This fact, and the advent of the 'talkies' with resultant loss of employment for thousands of professional musicians the world over, subjected the firm to severe difficulties. Added to this, complications existed with regard to the continued manufacture of a 'Zildjian' named product in Turkey, resulting in litigation and embarrassment over a long period. Due to the sagacity of Avedis who now decided the firm's policy, the lull in the activities of the enterprise proved to be short, for the reason that a great variety of cymbals were made, catering for the requirements of percussionists engaged in every sphere of musical activity, professional and amateur.

Soon after the end of World War II the sons of Avedis, Armand and Robert, were initiated into the craft. Father and sons continue the Zildjian tradition, and with Armand and Robert having presented Avedis with male grandchildren, the family tree seems firmly rooted.

What is the secret this family holds, and what may they have in common with their fellow craftsmen of antiquity? One thing is certain; the formula is no secret. How could it remain such in the present period of advanced metallic analysis? The compound is an alloy of copper and tin, approximately 80 per cent copper and 20 per cent tin (similar to bell metal), to which is added, according to information supplied by the makers, a trifle of silver. An alloy containing such a high proportion of tin would, unless scientifically treated, render the compound extremely brittle. Plates of such a compound would most certainly tend to crack if clashed with considerable force. A good deal of the Zildjian secret is acknowledged to be in the mixing and the subsequent toughening of the metal which ensures its brilliance. Many interesting processes are involved from the cauldron onwards. The author is indebted to the Zildjian family for information which permits an insight into the manufacture of their remarkable instruments, also for much of the historical details so far related.

It is interesting to note the proximity to the sea of the North Quincey foundry. In discussing the site for the American factory, both Aram and his nephew Avedis left nothing to chance. Though neither was certain that salt air was a necessary ingredient of the Zildjian formula, it was decided that certain conditions surrounding the Constantinople establishment be maintained. Aram was emphatic that coal for the smelting furnaces be imported as originally from Cardiff (a procedure dispensed with when the elder retired). The all-important furnace room, a veritable 'holy of holies', is now equipped with electric furnaces, aglow with a white heat to cope with operation number one, that of melting ingots of metal prepared to the specified compound. The ingots are reduced to a seething fluid in iron crucibles, during which process the supreme and secret craft is exercised, under conditions which it is still not possible for the layman to experience, but which may well resemble those surrounding the refiner's fire of Old Testament history. The metal is next poured into moulds, and cools to produce silvery castings in the shape of saucer-like discs half an inch thick, which are taken to the workshop. Here the castings are re-heated in an oven to a temperature approaching 1500 degrees Fahrenheit, softening the discs for the operation of thinning in the rolling mill, a process involving a day's labour with repeated trips back and forth to the oven and mill, in certain cases as many as 25 times. During the process of thinning, the colour of the discs changes from silver to a deep purple. When the latter colour is reached, the discs, (by this time strange looking objects resembling an over-cooked pancake) are subjected to two further temperings, first in a chemical solution (a Zildjian formula) containing herbs and oils, and secondly in water.

After the temperings the discs are hammered to straighten them. The edges are then trimmed and the cups formed. These two operations involve the use of a machine which, with the rolling mill, is the only departure from the old alchemist's methods. With the exception of a few blemishes, the disc now a dull gold colour resembles a cymbal in appearance. After a week of cooling it is ready for the all important and age-old process of hand hammering.

The cymbal is hammered for at least three and sometimes four periods of ninety minutes each, during which process the upper and reverse curves (or bows) are formed. This process (which demands the utmost skill) gives the instrument its classic shape and brilliant tone. Finally it goes to the lathe for the drilling of the centre hole, and the shaving and cutting of the tone rings known as sound tracks. The finished article, an impressive object, brilliant in sound and colour, is stored for a period of several months, or in some cases for many years before it is considered in prime condition, and ready to add its lustre to the sound of music.

The several thousand cymbals manufactured yearly by the Zildjian Company include instruments measuring but a few inches in diameter (*crotales*) to giants with a diameter exceeding two feet. They cover a dynamic range from the 'tinkle' of finger cymbals, to the majestic clash of the 'Symphony' model, chosen and matched in many cases by the cream of American professional percussionists.

Whether it be the brilliance of the clash of cymbals delivered by the expert in the symphony orchestra, or the tremendous urge of the 'top cymbal' rhythm from the nimble wrist of the maestro in the swing group, the craftsmanship of the Zildjian family is evident. Their skill is recognized and admired by their competitors, who may well ask what secrets lie behind the Zildjian compound and its manipulation. But would the cymbals of antiquity compare with the first quality instruments of to-day? A good deal of the process discovered in 1623 by the Constantinople alchemist, Avedis (the forbear of the present Zildjian family), may have been known to the ancient craftsmen who, with furnace and hammer and consummate skill, fashioned the metal to give praise to the Lord.

The function and manufacture of cymbals has excited curiosity and interest over a long period of time. Frederick Adolf Lampe at the turn of the seventeenth century had sufficient to say about the construction and use of ancient cymbals to fill a book of 400 pages.[1] In 1700 he delivered a lecture on the subject to a distinguished gather-

[1] Lampe, F. A. *de Cymbalis Veterum*. The flyleaf of the British Museum copy bears the mark of ownership of Dr. Charles Burney.

ing in Bremen. The text of the lecture was committed to print. In the lecture, which appears to be a condensed version of the book, Lampe defines numerous Greek and Roman equivalents of cymbal and *acetabulum* to represent musical instruments half round in shape and hollow, some with handles, others with the convexity finishing in a point or a cross. According to this scholar the sound of the cymbal uttered various notes. He speaks of the acetabulum as a vessel like a cymbal (struck to give louder sound) made of a number of metals including bronze, silver and gold, invented by Diocles. *Acetabula* is interpreted 'composed of different metals, struck to produce mellow sound'. Lampe says Latin commentators of the Mosaic books spoke frequently of acetabula, which from ancient glosses are explained to be round vessels in which wine was kept near the altar. He adds: 'properly they were intended for vinegar, and were commonly used so'. Lampe also says that jugglers would set them up on a table tricking their audiences by transferring pebbles from one to the other. Reference is made to cymbals of brick (*testae*) imitating the noise of claps, and to *imbrices*, stone cymbals, whose sounds were imitated by people applauding with gutter or roof tiles, said by Suetonius to be a method of applause invented by Nero. Iron or wooden plates vibrated by stick or hammer among the Greeks or Saracens in place of bells are classified *naceriae*, a name given also to a rattle of the Middle Ages. According to Lampe the Phoenicians learnt the use of cymbals from the Phrygians and the Jews may have done likewise. He says Cadmus brought the worship of Cybele and cymbals to Thebes.

Numerous Old Testament references are quoted to support the use of cymbals in the worship of the true God. In contrast, we read of a wooden type of cymbal (*tabulae*) as used in Sardinia in human sacrifices to Saturn. The conclusion of this document deals with the secular use of cymbals. It is stated that the clashing of bronze bowls was considered a remedy for eclipses of the moon, commonly attributed by the ancients to the foul practice of witches. Cymbals were used to prevent a swarm of bees flying too far. Bees liked clapping and the sound of bronze, says Pliny (early second century AD). Lampe speaks of the introduction into the sick room of dancers with cymbals, and the power attributed to these instruments by the ancients to overcome certain diseases. He also states that dancing with cymbals was practised by beggars and vagabonds, and that they carried with them a statue of a deity, especially of the goddess Cybele, to assist them in obtaining charity.

In 1727 a further treatise on ancient cymbals appeared.[1] This work was by Richard Ellys, an Englishman of letters who described the use and properties of cymbals in ancient Greek and Jewish history. (Ellys' treatise was highly thought of by Fétis).

[1] Ellys, Richard. *Fortuita Sacra: quibus subjicitur commentarius de Cymbalis*, Hofhout, Rotterdam, 1727.

Cymbals

Many of the ancient percussion instruments of Egypt survived the test of ensuing centuries. The position during the early part of the nineteenth century is discussed in detail by E. W. Lane.[1] From this source we find a country drum (*tabl*) hung obliquely resembling our military side drum, and a bowl drum with a copper shell 16 inches in diameter, and four inches deep in the centre. The latter instrument, known also as a Syrian drum (*tab'l Sha'mee*) is suspended from the neck, and played with two slender sticks in the procession to the circumcision. The country drum has a good deal in common with the Arabian *atambor*, an instrument connected with processional and military music.

The small hand kettledrum (baz) is prominent, and pairs of kettledrums, two-thirds of a sphere with diameters of 4 inches and 18 inches attached to the fore part of a camel saddle, are included in religious processions. Lane refers to the large drum being on the player's right. (See timpani technique.)

Fig. 30. Darabukka,   Fig. 31. Goblet drum, clay,
North Africa   North Africa

Two types of tambourines (*tàr*) are common. One, a handsome instrument with a diameter of 11 inches and a deep hoop, covered (within and without) with mother-of-pearl, tortoise shell, white bone or ivory, has five sets of (two) jingles. The instrument is played near the hoop with the fingers of the hand holding the instrument, while the other hand strikes the centre for low sounds (*dum*) and near the rim for higher sounds (*tak*). A larger instrument, without jingles, is used by the low orders.

The most popular drum is the *dar'abook'keh* ('darabukka') a vase-shaped drum of wood or earthenware with, according to Lane, a head of fish skin. This instrument is

[1] Lane, E. W. *Manners and Customs of the Modern Egyptians*, Poule, London, 1860.

most often played with two hands, like the tàr, edge and centre.[1] (Bartok and Stravinsky, for example, request this procedure on the side drum.) A larger type of darabukka (18 inches to 24 inches in length) is used by Nile boatmen. The *derobuoka* of the Arabs is about 15 inches long with a shell of earthenware.[2] (Berlioz specifies *tarbourka* in the 'Slave Dance' of his *The Trojans*, 1869, Orff similarly in *Prometheus* (1967), and Jacques Ibert in *Mosquée de Paris* (symphonic suite, 1932).

Brass castanets *sa'gu't* (finger cymbals) are used by male and female dancers. There are also metal clappers – *karābib*. Larger cymbals are used in the processions. Happily, the majority of these instruments, including a psaltery, the *kanoon*, continue to play a part in the music of modern Egypt. To the north of this ancient country we find many of the instruments connected with the land of the Nile serving numerous purposes, with a decided focus on the cymbals. We therefore turn our attention to Greece and Rome.

[1] El-Dabh, Halim. *The Derabucca* (Edition Peters No. 6993) New York, 1965.
[2] Clay is much used to form the bodies of Egyptian and Arabic drums.

Bibliography: Chapter 7

MESOPOTAMIA AND EGYPT

ALBRIGHT, W. F. *The Archaeology of Palestine*, Pelican, London, 1961.

EL-DABH, Halim. *The Derabucca*, Peters, New York, 1965.

ELLYS, Richard. *Fortuita Saccra: quibus subjicitur commentarius de Cymbalis*. Hofhout, Rotterdam, 1727.

ENGEL, Carl. *The Music of the Most Ancient Nations*, Reeves, London, 1929.

FARMER, H. G. 'The Music of Ancient Mesopotamia', 'The Music of Ancient Egypt', *Ancient & Oriental Music*, The New Oxford History of Music, vol. I, London, 1960.

GALPIN, F. W. *Music of the Sumerians*, Cambridge, 1936, Librarie Heitz, Strasbourg, reprint 1955.

GARSTANG, John. *Burial Customs of Egypt*, Constable, London, 1907.

HARTMANN, Henrike. *Die Musik der Sumerischen Kultur*, Goethe Un, Frankfurt-am-Main, 1960.

HICKMANN, Hans. *Cairo Museum Catalogue*, 1949.

LAMPE, F. A. *de Cymbalis Veterum*, Trasect ad Rhenum, *c.* 1703.

LANE, E. W. *Manners and Customs of the Modern Egyptians*, Poule, London, 1860.

MERSENNE, Marin. *Harmonie Universelle*, Paris, 1636.

SACHS, Curt. *The History of Musical Instruments*, Norton, New York, 1940.

STAINER, John. *The Music of the Bible*, Novello–Ewer, London, 1879.

THUREAU-DANGIN, F. *Rituels accadiens*, Paris, 1921.

WILKINSON, J. G. *The Manners and Customs of Ancient Egypt*, Murray, London, 1837.

PHILLIPE VIGREUX, *La Derbouka, Edisud. La Calade, 13030 Aix-en-Provence.* (in French).

8

Greece and Rome

The music of the ancient Greeks received much from Asiatic and Egyptian sources. Similarly their musical instruments, which remained decidedly simple, had their origins in other lands. In fact, skilled as this nation was in numerous arts and pastimes, no instrument originated with them. A good deal is known of their music, culled from documentary evidence dating from the fifth century BC. From such information it would appear that the most important instruments with the Greeks were lyres, pipes and trumpets, with little emphasis on the use of percussion instruments, particularly the drum (tympanon), which seems to have had little place in any form of music, including, surprisingly, military music. The greater part of the rhythm of Greek music was, however, founded upon their poetry. Sung poetry was reinforced by means of the pitch of accompanying music, hence, presumably, the predominance of the lyres and pipes. Against this documentary evidence, thanks to the archaeologist, the popularity of certain percussion instruments is determined by their constant appearance on all works of art dating from 500 BC. There is little doubt that these artists would interpret in their work their impressions of everyday life, and from such can be gathered evidence regarding the use of castanets, clappers, cymbals, sistra and drums. The drum was associated with the worship of Cybele, and the god Dionysos. The instrument, usually a double headed frame drum struck with the hands, was played almost exclusively by women. The use of two skins, observed by Suidas, the Byzantine lexicographer of the ninth century AD, is supported by Sachs, who contends that the handles attached to some drums of the fourth century BC would have been unnecessary with single skins.

Greek vases of the first century AD show a form of bowl drum with a small opening covered by skin, which according to Sachs has only two parallels – the Chinese pang-ku, and the South Indian dāsari tappattai. Vases from the fourth century BC are unanimous in representations of the tympanon. The instrument is portrayed in various sizes, and is usually bowl-shaped with a central star or circle with an edging of dots, the artist may be indicating a nailed head or, keeping in mind the occasional wide spacing of the dots, possibly some form of pellet bells or jingles. Surrounding the circumference in some cases are hooks, most probably ornamental. In some instances Eros is seen performing upon such an instrument, though in the majority of cases the players are women, who are seen holding the drum in various positions: in the left hand, on the left knee, and on the left shoulder – the right hand striking in all cases.

Clappers (*krótala*)[1] and castanets are depicted in various forms over a period of several centuries. They appear on many Hellenic vases in the hands of Dionysian dancers, often supporting the flute. On a British Museum vase dated *c.* 500 BC Eros appears as an instrumentalist playing krótala, together with a lady performer on a drum. A Greek vase of the same period shows two lady instrumentalists, each with clappers. Certain South Italian vases show what appears to be a xylophone.

Fig. 32
Krótala
(from Bianchini)

The spread to the north into Asia Minor, Greece and Rome of the worship of the Egyptian goddess Isis involved the use of the sistrum. This ancient instrument was known to the early Greeks; it is well represented on numerous art works. It is also observed in an unusual setting on an early piece of Cretan art: 'The Harvester's Vase' 1600–1500 BC (in the possession of the Metropolitan Museum of Art, New York). On the vase are twenty-six men marching gaily to the rhythm of an Egyptian

[1] Francesco Bianchini in his *De Tribus Generibus Instrumentorum* (Rome, 1742) describes the crotala as a reed divided into two by a slit from the top.

sistrum. This artefact is all the more interesting in view of the fact that the sistrum is more frequently associated with women performers and religious worship.

A time-keeper is found in the Greek *kroupalon*, (Roman - *scabellum*) a loose wooden sole fixed to a sandal, or in a more elaborate form, a sandal made of two pieces of wood joined at the heel. To each board was fixed a castanet. This clapper-like instrument was worn on the right foot of the chorus leader and served to beat time. The Uffizi Gallery (Florence) collection includes a marble statue (Hellenic period third century BC) of a satyr wearing a foot clapper and playing cymbals. The Uffizi Gallery includes the sculpture in a group of Grecian statues and names the group *Invitation to the Dance*.

Cymbals appear on the earliest Grecian art representations. Historical references quote the instruments as imported from Western Asia, Egypt and Asia Minor. (It is from the Greek word *kymbos* that cymbal is derived). Art works and contemporary literary information indicate the use of instruments similar in structure to those employed in Mesopotamia, Israel and Egypt.

A pair of bronze cymbals from ancient Greece, *c.* 500 BC, at the British Museum, closely resemble *crotales* from ancient Egypt. They have a deep dome and a curved rim, and each measures 3½ inches diameter and weighs 7 ozs. Part of the original connecting chain remains, secured to the cymbals by means of a metal ring and form of split pin. Engraved on the rim in minute dots are the letters OATAS EIMI signifying 'of Oata' – 'I am.' Oata, a dancing girl, is thus considered to be the original owner. These instruments were obviously cast in a mould, though some form of lathe work is apparent in the grooving of the rings on each disc, which maybe was purely ornamental, or on the other hand was for tonal purposes. (Modern cymbals have tone rings.) Despite their antiquity, these cymbals are well preserved,

both in appearance and sound. Each produces a bell-like tone sounding

The antique cymbals (Grecian) in the Gemeente Museum, The Hague, and the pair in the National Museum, Copenhagen, resemble those in the British Museum and are in a similar excellent state of preservation. The instruments in the Gemeente Museum are half an inch larger in diameter than those in the British Museum. They are a little lower in pitch, sounding quite clearly: .[1] The Hague specimens are connected by a complete chain secured to each cymbal in exactly the manner described above. No name is inscribed on these instruments.

[1] The bronze crotales from Thebes (British Museum) are similar in pitch.

Tinkling cymbals, again the prerogative of the fair sex, appear in the finger cymbals (crotales or metal castanets) played in the manner of the Spanish castanets by dancing girls, or by musicians accompanying them. Small cymbals in the shape of a basin or vinegar cup (*acetabula*), held horizontally (similar to those described by Mersenne and Lampe), and somewhat larger instruments of the plate type with deepish cups, appear frequently.

An illustration from Herculaneum shows a pair of small cymbals connected by a strap. In contrast, cymbals unconnected and played in a unique manner are seen on an ancient Greek drawing of a female centaur and a Bacchante. The centaur strikes a lyre with her left hand. In her right hand she holds a cymbal which she strikes against an identical instrument held in the Bacchante's right hand.

Their combined actions are purported to be part of the musical activity assisting an orgy; a rite with which the Grecian cymbals were so closely associated. These cults were inspired by the ancient orgiastic rites of the goddess Cybele, at which Phrygian priests called Corybantes clashed cymbals to stir emotion in the breasts of Cybele's female supplicants. Similarly, the excitement of the raucous rites connected with the worship of Dionysos was stimulated by the tremendous clashing of cymbals, and further heightened by the beat of the tympanon. These instruments were later included in the music of the theatre, where they were permitted a somewhat more elevated purpose. In this situation they are seen (with a drum) on a mosaic found at Pompeii dated AD 73, depicting 'a comic scene in the antique theatre'.

A set of cymbals from the ruins of Pompeii, (to be seen in the City Museum) range from finger sets (crotales) to discs measuring sixteen inches in diameter. A pair of small cymbals from Pompeii (in the National Museum, Naples) are of exquisite workmanship. They are curved, and connected with an ornamental metal chain. The same collection includes an interesting sistrum. The cymbals are almost identical with their Greek counterparts in other museums. Size, shape, quality of metal, rings and connecting chain, have a remarkable resemblance, suggesting that the industry of cymbal making (and possibly that of the sistrum) was confined – as it may well have been in Egypt – to a small number of craftsmen, as is the case with the manufacture of high-quality cymbals to-day.

In addition to cymbals, the Romans used gongs and metal discs (*discus*). These discs were suspended from a central hole and used as signal instruments. Four bronze discs devised by Hipposos had the same diameters, but differed in thickness, and consequently produced notes of different pitch. A Roman gong in the Devizes Museum has been dated first or second century AD. The instrument, which has a deep lip, was discovered during mining operations in Wiltshire.

In the Mildenhall Treasure (British Museum) we find a further example of

Roman percussion instruments. On the Great Dish (fourth century AD), among the instrumentalists supporting a group of bacchanalian revellers is a female cymbalist. The cymbals are cup-shaped, and suggest a diameter of 6–7 inches. They are held horizontally and obviously struck vertically. The rim of each cymbal is ornamented with small studs. The base of the cup tapers to a stem.

In addition to the Great Dish are a pair of platters showing Pan holding a small bell, a tambourine – seemingly without jingles – and a pair of cymbals, in this case connected with cord. A tambourine with jingles (three sets) is seen on a second century AD Roman relief *The Triumph of Bacchus*.

The constant representation in detail of the instruments of percussion on many of the world's greatest art treasures leaves little doubt as to their widespread popularity.

There is no proof that the Romans themselves invented any percussion instrument. They most certainly borrowed instruments and music; they also adapted and developed what other nations had to offer. This is particularly evident in the emphasis on rhythm and percussion in their colourful popular music, including the music of the street musicians. In spite of a good deal of opposition, such as anti-luxury laws, the use of percussion instruments persisted, and we read of 'the thumping of brass and the rumbling leather'.

Rumbling leather surely indicates sizeable membrane drums, in addition to the tambourine species. Little information is available about the use of the drum in military music, where the emphasis was from all accounts on wind instruments. According to Sachs, the drum had no place in any form of Roman music, including military music. It was almost exclusively a woman's instrument, and served only the cults of Dionysos and Cybele. Forsyth holds a different opinion:[1] 'We need scarcely add that the Romans had all sorts of percussion instruments for military and other purposes. In particular they used the tambourine or "light drum" as they called it, and a "bronze drum", which was a military improvement on the small gourd-drums of the Arabians.' Marshal de Saxe, a very famous French soldier of the eighteenth century, stated that one reason why the Romans were generally victorious was that they were made to march in time. He says:[2] 'it is nothing more than to march in *cadence*, in which alone consists the whole mystery, and which answers to the military pace of the Romans. It was to preserve this, that martial sounds were first invented, and the drum introduced.'

The official adoption of Christianity by the Roman Empire brought a marked change in the use of certain musical instruments, due to the banning of music which

[1] Forsyth, Cecil. *A History of Music*, p. 72.
[2] Saxe, Count Maurice de. *Reveries or Memoirs concerning the Art of War*, translated by Sir William Fawcett. Nourse, London, 1757, p. 16.

was considered to be mischievous, licentious, and provocative of war. Among the instruments condemned were the trumpet, the old psaltery, the drum and the cymbals; the latter instruments being regarded by the reformers, particularly St. Clement, as the devil's pomposity. It was to be many centuries before a new Italy was to become a nation destined to provide the world with a musical heritage.

Bibliography: Chapter 8

GREECE AND ROME

BIANCHINI, Francesco. *De Tribus Generibus Instrumentorum*, Rome, 1742.

SAXE, Count Maurice De. *Reveries or Memoirs concerning the Art of War*, translated by Sir William Fawcett. Nourse, London, 1757.

STANFORD, C. V. and FORSYTH, Cecil. *A History of Music*, Macmillan, New York, 1917.

9

Arabia and Persia

To bridge the period between the close of our last chapter, (AD 300–600) and the time of the Crusades, AD 1100, (a significant period in the history of the orchestral instruments of percussion), we turn to Arabia and Persia. The origin of musical instruments among the Arabs must certainly have occurred in the misty past preceding the time from which it is possible to trace their civilization, that is to say, some 3000 BC. The influence of Mesopotamian, Indian and Semitic culture was evident in their ancient music and early instruments, which included lyres, pipes, and drums of the tambourine type. But our present concern is not with the Arabian and Persian music of so distant a past: it is with a later period, and the influence of these natural musicians over the other nations, that in turn were to provide the world with its most important orchestral instrument of percussion – the kettledrum. The period was one in which there was little activity and a complete lack of advance in the natural development of musical instruments in Europe. The stand that Christianity had taken in favour of vocal music, and the consequent exclusion of instrumental music, brought the development of the latter almost to a standstill. Percussion survived, and little change is noticed in the sequence of these instruments when compared with the order in which they are found in Assyria, Egypt and Israel.

Frame drums (tambourines) appear as early as pre-Islamic times in two forms, rectangular and round, with the generic name duff, related to the Hebrew toph. According to Sachs, duff in a narrower sense is given to a square or octagonal drum, round drums have the general name *da'ira* or 'circular'. From all accounts these instruments were hand drums of moderate dimensions. They served the normal purposes, accompanying the dance and song, and were associated with occasions of mirth and mourning. They were played chiefly by women; a situation by no means unusual. They remain in many respects in their original form, with the heads 'lapped' completely round the hoop, or nailed or glued to the rim of the shell.

The largest of the round drums was the *ghirbāl* an instrument resembling a sieve which, according to Dr. Farmer, had no jingles, but snares were stretched across the inside of the head. (The Arabs of Spain had a similar instrument, known as the *dof*.) This instrument had the approval of the Prophet in the seventh century. Here would seem the first direct reference of the appearance of the appendage we know to-day as snares, though it cannot be said with certainty that the modification of the tone of a drum by this simple method was not known at a considerably earlier date. With regard to the jingling contrivance on the tambourine, first let us quote Dr. Stainer[1]: '. . . had the ancient tambours little bells, plates of metal, or castanets inserted in the rim as we have in our tambourines? Possibly they had.' Speaking of an Arabian tambour, the *bendyr* (*bendaïr*), Dr. Stainer continues: 'There are holes in the rim which unmistakably suggest the probable insertion of some sort of pulsatile contrivance or other. Moreover, it is known that such appendages were not strange to the Greeks.' cf. Roman AD 200 Sarcophagus. The bendaïr (like the ghirbāl) has snares stretched across the inside of the head.

Fig. 33
Bendair,
Arabia

The approval of the Prophet was also given to a tambourine, though whether with or without jingles is in some doubt. Dr. Farmer says[2]: 'Some legists place the former among the forbidden instruments, whilst the latter was made "allowable", others said it was only the tambourine with "jingles" that was censured.' The reference by authorities to a tambourine with jingles is certainly interesting. An instrument of this type seems to be well established at this period (the early part of the seventh century). There is reason to believe that with the Arabians the instrument would be well developed, having in mind their claim to its invention. So it is in this period of musical austerity, enforced by the Prophet Mohammed, that we are provided with reliable information regarding 'rattling strings' and 'jingling pieces'. This period of enforced inactivity was short, as the Arabians (and the Persians) were intensely fond of musical instruments and wrote enthusiastically about them.

---

[1] Stainer, John. *The Music of the Bible*, Novello-Ewer, London, 1879, pp. 152, 153.
[2] Farmer, H. G. *Studies in Oriental Musical Instruments*, 1st Series, Reeves, London, 1931, p. 84.

Percussion instruments were numerous and popular with both nations, whose rhythmic expression also laid emphasis on one of the earliest forms of instrumental accompaniment – hand clapping. The earliest instruments of the Arabs included clappers and a percussion wand, the *qabīb*, a rhythmic wand, the tick-tick from which met with the disapproval of the Prophet (cf. switch). Cymbals (plate type), tinkling finger cymbals and kettledrums played an important part in their daily life. Persian texts about AD 600 speak of a drum called *tās*, possibly a small kettledrum similar to the instrument used by Persian noblemen to scare eagles and make them targets for the hunter. The later double-headed drum, the *atambor*, may well have been the precursor of the tabor and the military side drum.

The tambourine joined with a call to prayer and to herald the birth of a child. Its rhythm accompanied the singing in the household and paid a final token of respect at the funeral service. The more joyous occasion of marriage, with its display of more robust music, and the great religious festivals, called for the use of the drum. Military and processional music employed drums and cymbals, with the trumpets, horns and shawms. The evidence concerning the use of kettledrums in these ensembles and elsewhere during the period AD 600–900 is conflicting in certain details. All classical references to the use of the actual kettledrum describe the practices of Eastern people, or festivals of Eastern origin, and it is generally agreed that the original home of the kettledrum was the Middle East. To draw a conclusion from the available evidence regarding the existence of kettledrums in Arabia and elsewhere prior to the tenth century presents problems. From the latter period we tread on firmer ground.

Up to the time of the tenth century pictorial evidence provides little help. The Arabs had a strong aversion to portraits. They believed that on the Day of Judgment portraits would demand the souls of those who had delineated them. Sculptural evidence comes from Persia on a relief dated about AD 600 on which is represented a player with a small, shallow, bowl drum. The instrument stands on the ground and is struck with a stick. It is some centuries later that larger kettledrums appear with any certainty. Dr. Farmer says[1]: 'The martial instrument par excellence to the Arab is the kettledrum (*tabl*, *naqqāra*) . . .' In the tenth century we read of several types of kettledrums – the ordinary mounted kettledrum called the *tabl al-markab* (*naqqāra*, *dabdāb*), and the great kettledrum called the *kūs*, as well as an instrument with a shallow shell known as the *qasa*. Later, we find a monster kettledrum called the *kūrka*.'

Sachs says[2]: 'The first evidence of Arabian kettledrums is in the tenth-century

[1] Farmer, H. G. ibid. p. 87.
[2] Sachs, Curt. *The History of Musical Instruments*, pp. 249–50.

encyclopaedia of the *Ihwān al-Safa*. The book enumerates the bowl drum, *qasa* . . . and the deeper kettledrums tabl al-markab (the naqqāra) and kūs.' Sachs is not in agreement with Dr. Farmer's source which suggests the kūs as an earlier drum. He says: 'Farmer's source, however, is neither contemporary nor Arabian; the statement is taken from the narrative of a Turkish traveller who wrote in the seventeenth century, a thousand years after the Prophet's expeditions. It is likely that the Turk called the drum by the name which was familiar to him.'

It is in the twelfth century that we find the first firm evidence of a larger kettledrum, depicted on Mesopotamian miniatures of this period. In the earlier examples the bottom of the instrument is flat, pointing, as Sachs observes, to a primitive pot drum. Later, we find the drums rounded like an egg and in pairs with a difference in diameters, and finally with a hemispherical shaped kettle, e.g., the *atabal*, the kettledrums of the Arabs. The bowls of the instruments were made of metal, and the skins tightened with cords.[1] It is in this form that kettledrums of medium size or small shallow drums (*nakers*) were imported into Europe during the Crusades. At this stage, then, we have drums of different sizes, with consequent high and low notes, and probably a variable tension on the vellum, permitting some form of tuning to definite intervals; for we are not prepared to deny the kettledrummers of this period their 'tonic and dominant'.

The Islamic races were by no means without their 'tuned' percussion. According to Farmer[2] musical glasses called *tusūt*, (an instrument played with sticks) were known to Ibn Khaldūn (d. 1406). Similar Persian instruments included musical cups (*sāz-i tāsāt*), musical bowls (*sāz-i kāsāt*), and an instrument comprised of steel slabs, the *sāz-i alwāh-i fūlad*. The musical bowls may have resembled the earlier Chinese *shui-chan*. This method of making music has been described by Dr. Farmer as 'hoary with antiquity'.

There remains much of the past in the prevailing Persian and Arabian musical instruments. The Persian dulcimer and drum, the latter in some cases with a scale-wise rise and fall in pitch (e.g. the *tunbūk*), and the Arab drum *darbūka* with its *dum-tak-kah*, echo the musical style of an age that instrumental sounds well recapture.[3] This can be said of many percussion instruments, for instance the membrane drums of the Americas (see Appendix I) and particularly, the mediaeval drum.

---

[1] In some cases two drums are permanently coupled, as with the double drums of Morocco (*tbilat*) and certain African kettledrums.

[2] Farmer, H. G. 'Music of Islam', *Ancient and Oriental Music*, The New Oxford History of Music, vol. I, London, 1960, p. 442.

[3] Henry Cowell scores for Persian drum in his *Homage to Iran* (1956).

Bibliography: Chapter 9

ARABIA AND PERSIA

FARMER, H. G. *Studies in Oriental Musical Instruments*, Reeves, London, 1931.
—'Music of Islam', *Ancient and Oriental Music*, The New Oxford History of Music, vol. I, London, 1960.
SACHS, Curt. *The History of Musical Instruments*, Norton, New York, 1940.
STAINER, John. *The Music of the Bible*, Novello–Ewer, London, 1879.

RECOMMENDED READING

RIMMER, Joan. *Ancient Musical Instruments of Western Persia*, illustrated in the Dept. of Western Asiatic Antiquities, British Museum, London, 1968, published by the Trustees of the British Museum.

10

Mediaeval and Renaissance Europe

As yet, archaeologists have done little investigation of the Middle Ages, and as a result we have few surviving percussion instruments of that period. We have a number of instruments of all sorts of the eighteenth century, a few of the seventeenth, some mediaeval ivory horns (almost all of which on the Continent are said to be the horn that Roland blew at Roncevaux to recall Charlemagne), and a good many instruments from the Roman, Greek, Egyptian, Bronze and Stone ages. For the Middle Ages, and to some extent for the Renaissance, our main sources of information are a few treatises – at times inaccurate where percussion is concerned – and numerous paintings and sculptures, and a few stained glass windows.

Our main source of knowledge comes from the religious paintings of the period. It is fortunate that all the Annunciations, Weddings at Cana, King Davids, Souls Being Received into Heaven, and similar joyful occasions are in the modern dress of the artist's period, and the vast majority have either peasant or angel musicians in the background. A great many of these musicians carry, and play instruments that are obviously carefully and accurately painted, and it is on these that we depend for our information, not only for the appearance of the instruments, but also for how they were played and in what combinations. (When Stanley Spencer painted a religious scene in modern dress many were shocked beyond belief, but such a procedure seems to have been quite acceptable in the Middle Ages.)

An eye for the general accuracy of instruments of music is soon developed: if a flute has more holes than the player has fingers, or if a stringed instrument is held in a seemingly impossible playing position, then one is doubtful about the percussion instruments in the same picture, however tempting they may look. When wind and strings are accurately painted, and a few of those instruments have come to us to serve as a check, or when the instruments in a number of paintings by different artists correspond, we can take them to be accurate.

Mediaeval and Renaissance Europe

The information concerning percussion instruments derived from such works of art is doubly valuable, since until the end of the sixteenth century there was a decided reticence on the part of authoritative writers to include drums of any description in categories of musical instruments. Virdung (1511), who places as his third division of musical instruments 'those of metal or other resonant material', excludes the drum as *Rumpelfesser* ('rumbling tubs').[1] 'These are to the taste of such as cause much unrest to pious old people of the earth, to the sick and weakly, the devout in the cloisters, those who have to read, study and pray. And I verily believe that the Devil must have had the devising and making of them, for there is no pleasure or anything good about them. If hammering and raising a din be music, then coopers and those who make barrels must be musicians; but that is all nonsense.' In 1528, Martin Agricola, again excluding the drum, refers to cymbals, bells, xylophone (*strohfiedel*), and anvil.

By the end of the sixteenth century, however, there are a number of good sources. Arbeau[2] (1588) gives clear descriptions, and a French manuscript of about 1585 has some excellent drawings. The latter is an illustrated encyclopaedia made for Henry III of France, and a number of percussion instruments are very clearly shown, including a pipe and tabor, a deep side drum, a tambourine, a pair of German cavalry timpani with rope tensioning in the manner of their precursor, the Arabic kettledrums, and a trapezoidal triangle with rings strung on the lower bar.

By 1620 we have the incomparable Praetorius.[3] He heads his classification of percussion with drums (kettledrums and tabor) and includes triangle, bells, xylophone, tambourine, a pair of military kettledrums (German, with screw tension), two side drums (with snare) and an anvil.

He also includes a scale (the Brunswick foot) in all his drawings. Following Praetorius we have in 1636 the encyclopaedic *Harmonie Universelle* by Marin Mersenne in which the drawings are even better than in Praetorius; but there is no scale. Here we see a pair of castanets identical with those used by present-day Spanish dancers, a triangle with rings, two pairs of ancient cup cymbals, a pair of larger cymbals, a kettledrum (Egyptian), braced side drums showing snares, a pair of braced kettledrums, and a tambourine with jingles.

From early literature we know that the ships of William the Conqueror resounded with music when he sailed for Britain. Drums and cymbals are mentioned, though it is conceivable that percussion instruments were by no means a rarity in Britain centuries earlier, for when the Romans settled there they must surely have

[1] Virdung, Sebastian. *Musica Getutscht*, Basel, 1511.
[2] Arbeau, Thoinot. *Orchésographie*, Lengres, 1588.
[3] Praetorius, Michael. *Syntagma Musicum*, Wolfenbüttel, 1619.

brought with them the musical instruments associated with their recreations: cymbals, tambourine and drum. On a fine mosaic pavement in a Roman villa (*c.* second century AD) discovered near Brading, Isle of Wight in 1800, a scene of this description is preserved. On this mosaic is seen a dancing girl with a tympanon, accompanied by a male figure with a Pandean pipe. The drum held by the girl resembles those appearing on Roman and Greek vases. It is agreed that the use of percussion instruments, including the tabor, became common in Britain through Roman influence, though there is even earlier evidence of a tambourine according to Canon Galpin:[1] 'Its simple form was doubtless known to the Keltic tribes who in prehistoric days found their home in Britain. Suetonius, in his Life of Augustus, describes a Gaul who played upon it, and he tells us that it was circular and struck with the fingers.' Thus we find that Britain can claim little in the way of invention as far as percussion is concerned. Nor can Europe in general for a lengthy period of time; for we know that from the eleventh and twelfth centuries onwards the main source of instruments was the Middle East and that they came into Europe across the Pyrenees from Moorish Spain and as the souvenirs of the returning Crusaders. The Crusaders found many things to admire among their infidel enemies and adopted much from them, not only in the sciences, but also in the arts, particularly music.

The lute (*al'ud* – the wood), the rebec (*rebāb*), the shawm (*zamr*), the trumpet, the drum, the triangle (named for its shape but descended from the ancient Egyptian sistrum), the nakers (naqqāra), bagpipes and many others were among the instruments that were brought home by the Crusaders and were eventually adopted in Europe.

As in all places and times, percussion instruments were used for three main purposes: religious ceremonies, military signals and encouragement, and the dance.

Among the Arabs and their subject races percussion instruments were used for all these purposes. The bass drum and the large nakers were used by the armies; they danced to the small nakers, the drums and the cymbals; and, with the exception of the Muslims, they called to their gods with bells and sistra. All these uses survive in the Middle East to-day. The instruments which seem to have first attracted the attention of the Crusaders were those used for the dance. They were mainly the tabor – a small two-headed drum with a single snare on the struck surface, the nakers – a pair of small kettledrums hung from the belt, the tambourine, the castanets, the triangle and the cymbals. Some of these the Arabs invented, others, taken from the ancient Egyptians, Romans and Greeks they preserved while Europe sank into the Dark Ages. These, with the addition of small bells struck with one or two hammers, are the instruments which appear constantly on paintings and stained

[1] Galpin, F. W. *Old English Instruments of Music*, Methuen, London, 1932, p. 239.

glass throughout the early and late Middle Ages and the Renaissance. From this time on we have at our disposal more authoritative information from musicologists such as Praetorius and Mersenne, and later the quite definite and developed form and purpose of the majority of these instruments in the works of the masters from the classical period onwards.

TRIANGLE

The triangle, named for its shape, was closely allied in one of its mediaeval forms (with rings strung to the lower bar) to the ancient sistrum. Yet the first mention we find of a triangle in a tenth-century manuscript, is of an instrument without rings. A triangle without rings is depicted in the King Wenceslaus IV Bible (late fourteenth century) and again on a mid-fifteenth-century window in the Beauchamp Chapel, St. Mary's, Warwick. This latter triangle with its open corner has a curiously modern appearance, except that at the top angle the steel bar is twisted into a loop through which the thumb of the performer (an angel) passes. These examples would seem to be exceptional, as more often three or more small jingling rings are strung on the lower bar. The shape varied considerably, sometimes equilateral with open or closed end – as in Praetorius and Mersenne respectively – or trapezoidal in form similar in shape to a mediaeval stirrup, as in numerous fifteenth-century illustrations. In all cases the beater – a steel rod – is depicted; at times quite a formidable looking implement, frequently matching an instrument of large proportion, if compared to a modern triangle.

Like its ancestor the sistrum, the triangle was clearly used for religious ceremonies, quite widely in mediaeval churches judging from the frequency and virulence of the denunciations launched against them, and the necessity every few years to issue another edict prohibiting them. The triangle occurs more often than any other instrument except the cymbals in paintings of Bacchic processions and similar occasions, and angels will often be seen singing and playing a triangle at the same time. It had a place in secular music, and is seen occasionally (again with rings) as an accompaniment to the pipe.

Such was the triangle as it was known throughout the Middle Ages and the Renaissance, and indeed right down to Mozart (*Il Seraglio*) and possibly to Beethoven (Ninth Symphony). The rings did not finally vanish until the nineteenth century, until which time the sound of the triangle was not the 'ting' with its clear and penetrating sound that we know to-day, but a continuous jingle as the rings vibrated against the bar on which they hung – a reminder of the sistrum (and perhaps corroborating the opinion that this ancient instrument was struck as well as shaken).

CYMBALS

Cymbals remained unchanged throughout the Middle Ages. They resembled closely the instruments used by the Greeks and Romans, and in many respects were 'loud, high sounding and tinkling'. From pictorial representations the majority appear to be quite thick, perhaps $\frac{1}{8}$ inch or more and about six to ten inches in diameter. The dome, or raised part in the centre, was relatively larger than in modern cymbals so that the rim was not more than an inch or two wide. They were most likely cast rather than spun, and beaten to harden them. Instruments of this nature are frequently represented as played – by women and angels generally – in the manner of ancient cymbals in that they are held with one resting above one hand and the other hanging below the other hand so that they were horizontal and the hands came together vertically. Matteo di Giovanni (Assumption of the Virgin, fifteenth century) portrays cymbals played in this manner. From the way the performer is holding the instruments a rigid handle is evident. This style of performance and grip is corroborated by earlier and later artists. The later illustrations of Mersenne show the straps much as we use to-day. In Britain, cymbals both flat and hemispherical appear in thirteenth-century manuscripts. Cymbals in the shape of a ball – resembling those described by Lampe in an earlier chapter – appear in an English manuscript of the seventeenth century (British Museum Harl. 2034). The writer, Randle Holme III, defines the instrument crotala or cymball, a sounding ball.

There is some evidence for larger and thinner cymbals in many parts of Europe.[1] These seem to have been about 12 inches in diameter and would sound rather like the light cymbals used for dance music to-day. They were played in the modern style – vertically – and are to be found most often in the Bacchic processions referred to – although angels are sometimes to be seen with them also. There are so few of the larger cymbals that it is difficult to compare statistics, but from all accounts the larger light ones were used more often for pagan than for Christian rites and as instruments of war, and the small heavy ones were used more often by the angels. Cymbals were used also by dancers and were almost certainly used to some extent in ensemble music, for their rhythmic properties. The fact that the majority of cymbals used in the Middle Ages may have produced notes of definite pitch which might not have fitted the harmonic structure, seemed not to distract mediaeval musicians, who in any case, liked bell sounds of all sorts. It is, of course, always possible that a group of players would possess more than one pair so that a choice of pitches was available for music in different keys. Their somewhat restricted use in the mediaeval instrumental ensemble is admirably assessed by Sachs:[2] 'though they

[1] Known in England as clash-pans.
[2] Sachs, Curt. *The History of Musical Instruments*, p. 439.

were never regular implements of European art music, neither were they entirely absent.' (Cymbals were introduced into the orchestra in 1680 by Strungk in his opera *Esther*. They later became an important component of the Janissary orchestra en route, as it were, to their permanent position in the music of the romantics and moderns.)

CASTANETS

Castanets rarely appear in paintings, possibly because their use seems to be mostly confined to Spain, and comparatively few Spanish paintings of this period are available in reproduction; and possibly because most of the Spanish painters seem to be Italian trained and not greatly interested in the folk life of their own country. Also, castanets were very much peasant or gipsy instruments, and not until a later period was it fashionable to paint *genre* scenes of peasant merry-making. Since, however, castanets are known both in antiquity and to-day, we can assume that they were not spontaneously reinvented. This is particularly safe in Spain, where much survives from the Moors today in language, customs and culture generally. Little is known of their use in mediaeval music, though the interesting observations of Mersenne[1] point to their importance as musical instruments, particularly in Spain, where he says: 'They dance the Sarabande to the sound of this instrument.' He continues: 'Though the castagnettes have only one tone, it is possible to make music by using various sizes which keep the harmony proportion excellent for use in dances.' Describing the instrument, Mersenne says: 'They have the shape of small spoons. The cords which go through the holes should be tied to the thumb of the right and left hand in such away that the concavities of the two castagnettes fit together like two plates, but the borders should be slightly apart, so that they can be tapped with either the middle or fourth finger. They should be made of resonant wood such as plum tree or beech tree.' He continues: 'They sound well with all sorts of musical instruments, although they are mostly used with the guitar. The sound very much depends on the touch of the player, the movements of the fingers must be so quick that it is impossible to count the number of tappings . . . an agile player will produce quick trills like on a spinet, and these trills are quicker than one's imagination.' Mersenne connects the castanets with music for dancing.

We also have the *Cantigos de Santa Maria* by Alphonso X, 'The Wise', (1252–84) giving early evidence regarding the use of castanets in Spanish songs. He also refers to their use as an accompaniment in church music.

[1] Mersenne, Marin. *Harmonie Universelle*, Paris, 1636, pp. 47, 48.

Various other forms of clappers were also used. In the stave dances of the Morris men we find a relic of the concussion sticks of ancient Egypt, and the similarly ancient 'dancing sticks' of Western Asia. Sometimes they continued the ancient Egyptian pattern of the combination of small cymbals on the ends of flexible shafts which were joined together at the handle. Instruments of this type in a crude form are illustrated in the Bible of Charles the Bald, ninth century (National Library, Paris). Small discs, apparently jingling contrivances, are secured to the open ends of

Fig. 34
Castagnettes
(from Mersenne)

the strips forming the instrument in V shape. A psalter dated 1015 (Cambridge University Library) shows an identical instrument. The construction of the instrument and the position of the performer's hands, suggest that the jingling pieces are clashed by pressure towards the closed end near the handle. (An eleventh-century representation of Hebrew musical instruments shows a similar arrangement, cf. Egyptian cymbals and zilli maṣa.[1]) In the Anglo-Saxon Psalter of the eleventh century (Cambridge), Idithun is shown with a pair of clappers in his right hand. These instruments are without jingling pieces, as are clappers referred to in eleventh- and thirteenth-century Spanish manuscripts.

The clappers, flat pieces of bone or wood, were held one in each hand in the case of the large ones, a pair between the fingers of each hand in the case of the smaller ones. Mersenne speaks as appraisingly of the clappers as he does of the castanets. He says:[2] 'All the little bones and small wooden sticks, or anything that one holds between the fingers, and which one can manipulate in such a fast and agile way, and

[1] A contraption operated in a similar manner, known as 'sock' cymbals appeared in the paraphernalia of the trap drummer of the 1920's. Matyas Seiber writes for this effect in *Jazzolettes*, 1928, q.v.

[2] Mersenne, Marin. ibid. pp. 47, 48.

in such finely regulated cadences, that it is only possible to understand their movement if you are aware of the technique.' In mediaeval times, in addition to their use as instruments of music, clappers were used as bird scarers and by lepers as a warning. A painting in the Rijks Museum, Amsterdam, of the biblical leper Lazarus depicts the unfortunate man shaking a pair of small clappers. An instrument resembling the present-day orchestral castanets mounted on a handle, is seen in the hands of a leper in a picture by the Dutch artist Werner van den Walckert, *c.* 1565–1637 (Rijks Museum) and in English manuscripts of the same period.

Clappers in the form of marrow bones and cleavers were prominent in the traditional music of the butchers of England and Scotland. Both instruments are seen in Plate VI of Holbein's famous series (1538) 'The Wedding of the Industrious Apprentice to His Master's Daughter'. Shakespeare refers to such clappers in Bottom's remark in *A Midsummer Night's Dream*: 'I have a reasonable good ear in music: let us have the tongs and the bones.' The tongs in this case were almost certainly kitchen utensils. With other items from this important room of the household – such as the pot and stick, stick and salt-box (Merry Andrew's instrument), pan lids etc. – they were associated with burlesque music, though not on all occasions.[1] Such implements and utensils formed the 'orchestra' of the children and the elders of the poorer class who believed in the power of noise to keep away evil and add zest to rejoicing.

Simple instruments, among which are included the two pieces of a rib bone of an animal, known as 'knicky knackers' or nigger bones, were used by players in the nineteenth-century minstrel bands. These serve to remind us of man's early music, as indeed do the claves (two round sticks) used in the modern Latin-American orchestra, which recall their counterparts – concussion sticks of ancient Egypt.

Another form of clapper derives from the Greek and Roman custom of either building rattles into a thick sole of a shoe or making a double sole with the bottom part loose so that the parts clapped together at each step. Such instruments were not used in the 'best circles' and are seldom seen in the hands of angels, but all were common among peasants.

The Neapolitan *triccaballacca* (syn. of *tricca-vallacca*) consisting of three or more percussive clappers, falls into the clapper class, as does the Spanish *tric-trac*.[2] The Spanish *matraca*, (a rattle) is, according to Galpin, a rotary development of the more primitive tric-trac. The rattle (ratchet) was employed in the Roman churches

---

[1] Roberto Gerhard made use of pokers in his score of *The Plague* (1964).

[2] Or *click-clack*, in which a pivoted hammer oscillates on a wooden base. Originally used as a bird scarer and as a noise-maker during Holy Week, also as an alarm instrument by night watchmen.

especially during Holy Week when the bells were silent, when according to legend 'they fled to Rome'.

FRICTION DRUMS

Another peasant instrument (not strictly percussive perhaps, but still a member of the family), was the *rommelpot* (rumble-pot), a stick friction drum, the body consisting of a clay or wooden receptacle with a parchment head in which is affixed a short stick standing erect. The stick, rubbed with wet or rosined fingers, or in some cases placed through a central hole and pulled to and fro, produces from the membrane a roaring sound, pressure on the stick and/or head varying the pitch. The friction drum is known in many widely distributed primitive cultures. Its age-old connection with specific occasions is maintained in European traditions noticed from the sixteenth century onwards. In Flanders the rommelpot is particularly associated with Christmas. A clear illustration of this instrument is given by the Dutch artist Frans Hals (1580-1666). In Italy, where it is known onomatopoeically as *puttiputi* or *puttipu*, or alternatively as the *caccavella*, it is connected with vintage time. Neopolitan instruments used uniquely during the period of the Parish Festival of Piedigrotta, in September, include the caccavella. In Spain, a friction drum the *zambomba*, appears at festal rejoicings and on similar occasions in Germany, where it is now called *Reibtrommel*, though its old name was *Brummtopf*, or 'growling pot'.

In another form, the central stick of the friction drum is replaced by waxed or rosined cord, again affixed to the centre of the head. In England, this instrument was known as the 'jackdaw'. Instruments of this type and those resembling the rommelpot are still used in Hungarian folk music. To-day the orchestral percussionist knows it better as 'lion's roar'. As such it is included in Varèse's *Hyperprism* (1924) and *Ionisation* (1934) where it is defined *tambour à corde*.[1] In this class there is also the 'whirled' friction drum, the last descendant of the friction drum and according to Sachs possibly a descendant of the bull-roarer – a thin board whirled at the end of a string, still in use among primitive races. The instrument is best known under its German name *Waldteufel* – 'forest devil'. Despite its name it is associated with merry making, and exists as a child's toy. Carl Orff prescribed this instrument in his score for *A Midsummer Night's Dream* (1939, 1944, 1952). (The author produced for the BBC production the genuine article – purchased in a Munich toyshop.)

TAMBOURINE

The popularity of the tambourine was sustained throughout the Middle Ages in all parts of Europe. The use of a frame drum – a drum with a single head on a shallow

---

[1] Alexander Goehr scores for the lion's roar in his *Romanza for 'cello and orchestra* (1968).

body – is widespread in both time and place and the details vary almost as much, from the Lapp Shaman's drum to the large single-skinned orchestral bass drum of to-day. The commonest mediaeval type was very close to the tambourine we know to-day, and even closer to the Turkish instruments of the nineteenth century which are to be seen in many museums. These usually have four or more sets of jingles arranged equidistantly in groups of two pairs and the jingles are larger and thicker than the modern ones and are smoothly concave rather than domed. This is the form that appears more often in paintings and carvings in churches, and in illuminated manuscripts from the eleventh century and throughout the Middle Ages. Such instruments have numerous sets of jingles, as in the painting by Matteo di Giovanni, *The Assumption of the Virgin*, and some have small pellet bells as well as, or instead of, the ordinary jingles as illustrated by Praetorius.

A few instruments have no jingles of any description. (These resemble instruments used to-day in Spain, Central Europe and parts of Russia, and the tambour or hand drum – so called – in children's percussion bands.) In several instances the tambourine is depicted with a snare or snares running either above or below the head. Occasionally small bells or other rattling pieces surround the framework or are seen on the snare. There are several pictures in which it appears that the player is plucking the snare rather than striking the head, in which case the snare would rebound on to the head and so make the instrument sound. As it would not be practical to play quick rhythms by plucking the snare, such a method strikes one as being unlikely, though not impossible. Such evidence must occasionally be examined against the question: 'Does it feel right to do it this way?' In this case it does not; so it seems probable that the head is being tapped delicately by the fingers, a likelier explanation since this method of playing is characteristic of the Eastern style – generally adopted and so frequently illustrated – as against the flat hand or clenched fist stroke of later European styles. It is certain there was no lack of skill on the part of the instrumentalists (mainly women) whose dexterity is extolled in literature on numerous occasions. The tambourine is frequently illustrated in the hands of angels, but in many respects it was a rustic instrument, associated with wandering minstrels, showmen and jugglers. In the late Middle Ages it was given a part in concerted music (Henry VIII included four tambourines in his musical ensemble of 79 musicians.) It remained an integral ingredient of rhythmic music of many descriptions. Like certain other percussion instruments it has been given a variety of names.

In England the old English *tymbre*, later timbrel, was replaced by tambourine in the eighteenth century. On the continent we find *Tamburin* and *Schellentrommel* (Ger.), *tambourin de Basque, timbre*, and in modern times *tambour de Basque* and *tambourin* (Fr.), and *cembalo* – later *tamburello* or *tamburin* in Italian. Sachs says of the terms tambour de basque, tambourin and cembalo:[1] 'These three latter terms are incorrect or misleading and should be avoided. The instrument is not Basquish, a *tambourin* is correctly a long Provençal cylinder drum with one stick and the word *cembalo* connotes a non-existent relation to *clavicembalo*.' The argument is sound, particularly in view of the occasions on which the tambourine has taken the place incorrectly of the tambourin in the Farandole from Bizet's music for *L'Arlésienne*.

Closely resembling the tambourine without the skin head was the jingle-ring, consisting of a shallow wooden hoop or metal ring with jingles inserted in it. The instrument (already discussed) appearing on a Greek vase of 500 BC (National Museum, Prague), bears a close resemblance to the mediaeval jingle-ring. Raphael and Praetorius illustrated an instrument of this type (*Schellenreif*). Eugene O'Curry[2] refers to the use of a similar instrument in Ireland and says it seems to have been common enough in the Middle Ages. (He also mentions the clashing of spear handles and the use of a wooden gong as an accompaniment to song.)

CHIME BELLS

The continued popularity of small bells is apparent. Much of the dance music of the Middle Ages was permeated by the rhythmic susurration of small bells or jingles. These were not always thought of as separate instruments, but were attached to the clothing or to ribbons tied round the arms or legs so that they sounded as the dancers and players moved. As an ornament and tinkling pieces they were a feature of the jester's cap. They are used to this day by English Morris dancers, and by other folk dancers all over the world.

The most highly regarded percussion instruments of the Middle Ages were the true bells – chime bells or bell chime. Chime bells appear frequently in Continental and English illustrations from the tenth to fifteenth century, though Gregory of Tours mentions the use of such bells in churches in the sixth century, as does the manuscript of St. Blaise, presumed to be of the ninth century. King David is almost invariably shown with them; even when he is holding his harp, bells are illustrated. Chime bells are usually seen in small numbers, from 4 to 5 to 8 or 9 in a single set. They are struck with a single hammer or with two hammers, one in each hand. The bells, which are usually clapperless, are quite small – about the size and shape of

---

[1] Sachs, Curt. ibid. p. 289.

[2] O'Curry, Eugene. *On the Manners and Customs of the Ancient Irish*, vol. III, Williams and Norgate, London, 1873, see lectures 3-37, pp. 212 to 409.

modern handbells, or like hemispherical gongs – and are arranged in order suspended in a frame over the performer's head, or placed on a stand in front of him. The Bell Chime was the first instrument to attract the attention of the theorists after the monochord. Mersenne, in 1636, devotes many pages to the comparative pitches and weights of bells, and so do a number of other writers.

An eleventh-century treatise by Theophilus, a monk, (transcribed by Dr. Rimbault in his *History of the Pianoforte*) describes the casting and tuning of small bells, and gives the content of the metal as an alloy of copper and tin – one fifth or one sixth of the latter (the alloy used to-day is 13 to 4). As far back as the fourth century we find in the Viennese *Genesis*, the most important illustrated book of that time, a representation of an instrument consisting of four metal cups on a stand. A woman is striking the cups with two slender sticks as an accompaniment to an oboe player. (Some authorities give these vessels as small kettledrums.)

One of the clearest and most interesting representations of chime bells is in a Psalter of the twelfth century (Glasgow University Library), showing King David and musicians representative of the period. Here we see a row of fifteen bells. There are two performers, each with a hammer in each hand. Inscribed on the supporting beam are the names of the notes according to the Guido d'Arezzo system, *ut, re, mi, fa, sol, la, si, ut*, signifying two scales in reverse direction. Here the pitch of the bells would seem to depend on the thickness of the wall or the tuning by filing – described by Theophilus – as on sight there is no appreciable difference in the size of the bells. Also illustrated in the Psalter is a player with two hand bells, each with internal clapper. The Luttrell Psalter shows similar instruments. In a thirteenth-century manuscript of the Cantigas de Santa Maria, we see a further use of small clapper bells in an early form of chiming apparatus consisting of seven bells in a low frame with a cord bearing a label showing the name of each bell attached to the clappers. The bells are being rung by a seated musician who pulls the cords. The chime bells illustrated in Kelislaus' Bible (University Library, Prague) have internal clappers, though the lady musician is striking them with disconnected hammers. Chime bells were evidently popular in France, considered to be the leading musical nation of the Middle Ages. A thirteenth-century writer, Henri d'Andeli speaks of *Madame Musique aux clochettes*.

An instrument similar to that in the Viennese *Genesis* is seen on a window in the Beauchamp Chapel, Warwick (fifteenth century). Here the artist illustrates an angel playing on a set of eight bells with two sticks. The bells – rather crudely drawn – are hemispherical and rest mouth upwards in a row on a stand, with the largest bell **to** the player's right. A woodcut from Franchinus Gaforus's *Practica Musicae*, 1492, shows a series of 6 bells and 6 musical glasses being used to demonstrate harmonic intervals. The glasses (which are pictured filled with water) and the bells (which have clappers) are being struck with long sticks by individual performers.

Authentic music for these instruments is hard to find. It may be assumed that they were employed to distinguish the intervals in teaching music, mark the beginning of phrases, supplement the tenor as much as possible, provide a descant, or play the melody where practical.

A few modern composers have made a discreet use of hand bells and chime bells, and have recaptured a sound that has tended to escape us. Noah Greenberg's edition of *The Play of Daniel* (1959), Imogen Holst's realization (1960) of a twelfth-century work by Perotin (*Viderunt*), Michael Tippett's cantata *Crown of the Year* (1958), and Gordon Crosse's one-act opera *Purgatory* (1966) are noteworthy, as is the part for hand bells in Benjamin Britten's *Noye's Fludde* (1958), and the use of five chime bells in his opera *Curlew River* (1964).

The various names given over a period of time to small bells does not ease the constant difficulty with vocabulary. Where to-day we use the word cymbal for a metal disc with hollow centre, the old name for chime bells was cymbal. In mediaeval Latin a shallow cup-shaped bell was defined *cymbalum*. Mersenne in 1636 describes the carillon of bells provided with a keyboard as a *clavicymbalum*. Agricola's *Musica Instrumentalis* (1528) describes ten small bells on a frame as *glocklein oder zimbeln*. Canon Galpin says:[1] 'These Chimes were much used in churches, and with the organ, though they were not included in its mechanism, as in the present day at Westminster Abbey.' Thirteenth- and fourteenth-century writers speak of *chymme bells*, *cymballs* or little bells, and *chymes* also organs and *chymbes* are placed together. Doubtless because of its bell-like effect, the name cymbal applied to psaltery, and then to dulcimer, and later to the keyboard, in the English *clavicymbal* and the Italian *clavicembalo* which finally became harpsichord. Small wonder we find the cymbals misapplied to Bach and Handel, possibly due to a misinterpretation of the organ stop Cimbel or Zimbel, a mixture to produce a bell-like sound (still used). Praetorius referred to 'The Cimball' a compound stop or mixture intended to represent the sound of bells. Actual bells (small) fastened to star-like wheels, activated by wind pressure, were employed in the organ stop known as Zymbelstern. In some cases, instead of bells, small hammers on the wheel struck metal plates. Quite often the bells or metal plates were tuned, in which cases the register was also called Akkord.

This book cannot deal with the confusion in the vocabulary of early keyboard instruments, but it may be as well at this stage to take a glance at the dulcimer, an instrument whose name has been erroneously applied all too frequently over the years to the xylophone, glockenspiel, etc.

[1] Galpin, F. W. ibid. p. 263.

DULCIMER

In the mediaeval dulcimer we have a percussion instrument with a past shrouded in mystery, but one that can certainly be connected with ancient times. Musical sound produced by striking stretched strings has been traced as far back as the hunting bow of the cave man, tapped with plain sticks and with the handles of seed-shell rattles. Despite the inconclusive evidence (due to repair) of the seventh-century Assyrian representation of the striking of the strings of a ten-stringed harp and the fact that the dulcimer mentioned among the six instruments used by the Babylonians in their idol worship (Daniel iii. 5) may not have been the instrument we know to-day, we have the early evidence of striking the strings of the ancient form of dulcimer, hunting bow and ground zither (pp. 35, 106). As we are so in-debted to the past, would it be wise to rule out the possibility of striking the strings of the early psaltery as well as plucking them, or that an instrument in the form of a dulcimer (a struck psaltery) did not exist before the period which has furnished us with clear evidence of this instrument in Europe and elsewhere? Unfortunately, it is not easy to distinguish between plucked psalteries and struck dulcimers on early reliefs. Galpin says:[1] '. . . So alike, however, are the two instruments in every respect except in the manner of playing, and so easily could the long plectra employed by the performer on the horizontal form of Psaltery be used for *striking* the strings as well as for plucking them, that in all probability the earlier Dulcimers are included under the general name of Psaltery.' (Mersenne calls the dulcimer the *psalterium* and speaks of a small rod used for striking the strings as a plectrum).

Concerning Europe, it is said that St. Dunstan (tenth century) excelled in the psaltery, lyre and 'touching the cymbals' (chime bells presumably) and that when he was weary of his work he would play not only on his harp but 'in timphano'. It is known that an instrument called the *timpan* or *tiompan* was used in Ireland, Scotland and England. It is mentioned in Irish records of the eighth century. According to Professor O'Curry, the timpan – which belonged to the higher classes – was first of all a stringed instrument played with the finger nails or plectrum, and in later days the strings were struck with a rod or stick. This Irish authority says:[2] 'So that at length we may consider that we have arrived at a clear determination of the hitherto undecided difference between the Cruit, or harp, and the Timpan, as well as of the latter being a stringed instrument, and not a drum, such as the name would imply.' (The Irish timpan is sometimes known as *benn-crot*).

In the Middle Ages, with the exception of an ivory book cover of mid-twelfth-

[1] Galpin, F. W. ibid. p. 57.
[2] O'Curry, Eugene. ibid. vol. III, p. 363.

201

century Byzantine workmanship (in the British Museum) where the performer gives every indication of striking the strings of a quadrangular psaltery, we are compelled to rely on fifteenth-century representations and literature for the bulk of information regarding this instrument.

The fifteenth-century dulcimer seen on a carving in the roof of the nave of Manchester Cathedral shows the performer (an angel) striking the 15 strings with slender beaters with curled ends. (This style of beater and those with spoon-shaped ends apply to the majority of representations elsewhere.) The dulcimers illustrated in a fifteenth-century manuscript (City Library, Grenoble) have only three and four strings. Similar instruments are recorded in earlier manuscripts.

From the fifteenth century the dulcimer was well distributed. In the Middle East the *santir* the trapezoidal dulcimer of the Arabs, Georgians and the Persians; in Europe, the German *Hackbrett*, (Virdung gives an instrument with six strings, played with spoon-shaped beaters) the French *tympanon*, the Italian *salterio tedesco* or German psaltery, and in England the dulcimer. It remained a popular instrument for some considerable time. In 1662 Samuel Pepys wrote: 'Here among the fiddles, I first saw a dulcimer played on with sticks, knocking of the strings, and is very pretty.' Grassineau[1] describes an English dulcimer with about 50 single wire strings cast over a bridge at each end, the shortest string about 18 inches long, and the longest about 36 inches, with the bass strings doubled. In the German hackbrett, (or cimbal) two or three wire strings in unison for each tone were usual. Later, bridges were incorporated in the sound box of dulcimers generally, the wires passing over the bridges, permitting two notes from each string. According to Sachs, the stringing of these instruments never had fixed rules.

At the close of the seventeenth century, a German named Pantaleon Hebenstreit distinguished himself by his performance on an elaborate dulcimer – his own invention – which became known as the *pantaleon*. Hebenstreit composed overtures and concertos for his instrument, which was eleven feet in length, had two sound boards, and was strung with quadruple strings of gut and wire. The pantaleon, or similar instruments, are said to have suggested the invention of the pianoforte, and with good reason, for surely the piano is a keyboard dulcimer.[2] (This interesting instrument of percussion is further elaborated in the Hungarian *cimbalom*.) Mention should be made at this stage of a dulcimer or string drum, the companion of the pipe. This is the *tambourin de Béarn* of Southern France, an instrument consisting of six gut strings stretched over a wooden sound-box and tuned to the keynote and fifth of the pipe. The player strikes the strings with a stick as an accompaniment to the pipe

[1] Grassineau, James. *A Musical Dictionary*, London, 1740.

[2] A stringed keyboard instrument was known in the fifteenth century – the *dulce melos*.

Xylophone

(in the style of pipe and tabor). Altenburg[1] speaks of the *trombe* – a wooden chest about 1¾ yards long, with a hole in the centre of the top, and a gut string stretched over a bridge. The string, says Altenburg, can be tuned to C and G, and is beaten with wooden drumsticks, producing a sound similar to that of covered kettledrums. A two-string drum is among the numerous instruments depicted in the Angers Tapestry (1380).

XYLOPHONE

The xylophone (*strohfiedel*, Ger.) is first mentioned in 1511 by the organist Arnold Schlick as *hultze glechter* (wooden percussion). In 1528 Martin Agricola illustrates a series of 25 wooden bars as strohfiedel, and a century later we have such an instrument pictured by Praetorius, who shows a series of fifteen bars from six inches to twenty one inches in length, arranged diatonically in a single row pyramid fashion, (as is Agricola's). With his customary thoroughness Praetorius includes a pair of conveniently shaped hammers. Holbein left an excellent example of the xylophone of the sixteenth century in his cycle of woodcuts in *The Dance of Death* where he depicts a skeleton performing a death knell on a small xylophone. The instrument is suspended in front of the player much in the same way as the African portable xylophone. An unknown Czech painter of the second half of the seventeenth century, connects a xylophone with a violin, viola and flute. The xylophonist appears to be striking the bars with his finger-tips.

Mersenne illustrates and describes two instruments (given as *claquebois, patouilles* and *eschelletes*) on a grander scale. One is composed of 17 bars which are struck on the under side by individual beaters arranged as a keyboard. The other instruments consist of 12 bars struck with a small mallet. Mersenne deals with these xylophones scientifically. In the case of the instrument with 17 bars, he submits that it has a range of a 17th, and that the lowest sounding bar should be five times as long as the bar with the highest sound, since their two pitches follow a ratio of five to one. The instrument with 12 bars, says Mersenne, should follow a ratio of three to one, but he adds that makers diminish the bars so slightly that the first is only double the last, the length being compensated for by the thickness. He evidently considered the xylophone no mean instrument, having said that it gave as much pleasure as any other instrument, when played to its full effect.

Here could be mentioned a document entitled *Modo facile di suonare Il Sistro, nomato – il Timpanio* (Easy method for playing the 'Sistro', called the 'Timpanio'), published at Bologna in 1695, the author being one Giuseppe Paradossi. On the

---

[1] Altenburg, J. E. *Versuch einer Anleitung zur heroisch-musikalischen Trompeter und Paukerkunst*, Halle, 1795, reprint Bertling, Dresden, 1911, p. 126.

original title page is a black and white sketch of a xylophone with 12 bars and the book contains, in addition to an elaborate dedication, eight pages of melodies – chiefly folk dances – written in a numerical tablature.

To-day, sistro defines a series of small mushroom-shaped bells, in which case it is reasonable to conclude that Paradossi's method applied to the instrument he illustrated.[1]

A keyboard xylophone appears as early as 1650 in Kircher's *Tastenxylophon*. Here the wooden bars (17) are struck by under-hammers actuated from a finger keyboard. Galpin gives *régale de bois* (a similar instrument) in the same century. In the following century Heinrich Nicolaus Gerber (1702–75) invented (among other instruments) a keyboard xylophone, harpsichord-shape, with a compass of four octaves. The keys released wooden balls which struck the bars.

Fig. 35
Xylophone (from Holbein's
The Dance of Death)

In general, however, the xylophone of the Middle Ages was a simple instrument, the wooden slabs loosely strung together, or resting on ropes of straw, giving rise to the name 'straw fiddle', and sufficiently elemental to remind us of the bars of wood laid across the shins of primitive man. It was very much an instrument of the wandering musician until the nineteenth century when it rose to prominence as a solo instrument in the concert world and was given a part in the orchestral repertoire.

DRUMS

Amongst the drums used during the Middle Ages we find many instruments that

[1] The part for sistro in the original score of *The Barber of Seville* is written on a single line without key signature. Rossini may have had the triangle in mind (now generally used).

have bridged the gap between the skin-covered tree trunk of ancient man and the highly developed percussion instruments we associate with the modern orchestra. It is during the mediaeval period that we meet the nakers and the cavalry kettledrums which inspired the orchestral timpani, and in the tabor the forbear of the military side drum and our modern orchestral side drum. Surprisingly, perhaps, one of the most familiar of the drums of to-day and an instrument by no means unknown in ancient times, the 'bass drum', seems to have had little or no place in Europe in the Middle Ages or the Renaissance. The instrument has been known in the Middle East from the earliest times. It was used by the Sumerians, and it was probably used by the ancient Greeks (although Jaap Kunst, the famous ethnomusicologist, considered the Greek instrument was a large gong, unknown to Europe in the Middle Ages). A 'bass drum' was used in the Middle East all through the Middle Ages and is still used there to-day. The drum described by St. Isidore of Seville (*c.* AD 600) as *symphonia* 'a hollow wood, covered with skin on either end, that the musicians strike with sticks from both sides' may have been a drum of this nature.[1]

In Venice there is a painting by Carpaccio (early sixteenth century) which shows a Turkish musician playing a drum almost exactly the same shape and size of the military bass drum we know to-day, and supported in the same way – on the player's chest. Other instruments in the picture indicate that the drum forms part of an Eastern ensemble: the shawms have the large oriental type bells, rather than the smaller European type, and the trumpets also look more oriental than the few European ones that have survived. Though only one head of the drum is visible, the method of bracing suggests a double head. The straight sticks appear to be unpadded. With the exception of a mid-sixteenth-century German engraving, in which a large cylindrical drum is supported on the player's chest, there is no further evidence – pictorial or otherwise – of this type of drum until its appearance in the orchestra of the nineteenth century. (The instrument known to Mozart, Haydn, and Beethoven was possibly a long drum, deeper from head to head than its diameter, which was in the region of 20 inches.)

TABOR

The commonest form of drum in mediaeval Europe was the Tabor. Among a profusion of names we find *Taberett* (Eng.), *Taboret, Tambourin, Tambourin de Provence, Tambour de Provence* (Fr.), *Tambourin* (Ger.), *Tamburino* (It.), *Atambor* (Sp.) and *Timpanon* (Gr.). In German and Italian the same word is used for tabor and tambourine.

The mediaeval tabor had no definitive form; sometimes the diameter was greater

[1] St. Isidore. *Etymologiae, c.* AD. 600.

than the depth and sometimes less. It varied in size and shape from place to place and time to time. It was a double-headed drum with a single snare on the struck head. This accoutrement, already noticed on certain tambourines and the Arabic ghirbāl, is consistently represented, for in almost every case that the struck head of a tabor is clearly shown, (including wood and stone carvings) the snare is visible. Here we have an instrument that together with its successor, the military side drum, was the prototype of our orchestral snare drum.

Unfortunately we know little about some of the constructional details of the tabor: artists did not always paint-in such details. It is too much to expect that a painter should think of those who in four or five hundred years time would want to consult his work to find out how drumheads were attached and other details, so all too often we are reduced to conjecture. We are better off, however, than the musicologist of AD 2400 who looks at a Picasso to discover the details of twentieth-century guitars.

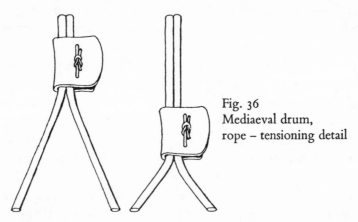

Fig. 36
Mediaeval drum,
rope – tensioning detail

The majority of mediaeval drums were rope-tensioned. On some instruments can be seen a network of cords, rather like some of the African and Asian systems. Occasionally the head is nailed to the shell. Many instruments depicted show no detail at all, but where they do the heads are usually tensioned with cord, much as the military side drum of a later period. The cord is shown going diagonally to and fro from one head to another. In some instances, buffs (or 'tug ears') are seen which serve to close the V-formation and add tension to the vellum. They are sometimes of leather and sometimes of cord and ribbon. In general the buffs are smaller than those used on roped drums to-day. (This system of bracing with cords was used by the ancient Egyptians.) There is some pictorial evidence of the use of a 'flesh hoop', but generally speaking artists portray the rope threaded directly into the vellum. (The combination of a flesh hoop and counter hoop came later; both appear with certainty on sixteenth-century side drums.)

The 'heads' were mounted in a number of ways. Mersenne speaks of the use of a circle of wood or metal, and there is a *Landsknecht* drum in Munich of the seventeenth century which has its head lapped round a ring of cane or withies; this is a system which has long been used in India and Africa, and it may well have been used in mediaeval Europe. Three or four cane or willow strips were twisted into a ring, rather as baskets are still made, and the head either forced between the strands, as in the Indian drum, or lapped over the whole as on the modern drum.[1]

Sheep- or calfskin was normally used for the heads of the tabor (and side drum), but there is evidence of occasional use of other skins, such as pig or goat, and possibly the skin of the ass or wolf. René Descartes, a French philosopher and mathematician, in his *Musicae Compendium* (1617) included some unusual particulars relating to the science of music. He refers in a curious manner to wolfskin: 'Thus also is the voice of a friend more grateful than that of an enemy . . . by the same reason, perhaps, that it is conceived that a drum headed with a sheep's skin yields no sound though strucken, if another drum headed with a wolf's skin be beaten upon in the same room.'[2] Mersenne, however, says that people should not believe that wolfskin is suitable for drums. The fact that the snare appears so frequently on the struck head of the smaller tabor suggests the use of 'thickish' vellums, since a snare will only respond freely to a light stroke on the opposite head if thin skins are used. It is not possible to say whether the heads were at times varnished to combat adverse atmospheric conditions. Such an expedient cannot be disregarded as the custom is age-old, and is continued to this day by a few Continental timpanists, who claim that the method has been 'handed-down'. On a particularly bad day resulting in a 'soggy' vellum, the mediaeval drummer would in all probability resort to the practice of his forbears (and contemporaries in other lands), and warm the instrument to tighten the skin.

As has already been said, there was considerable variation in the size of tabors, ranging from the shallow English drum, decorated with gaily coloured Morris ribbons, to the deep-shelled *tambourin* of Provence. Many mediaeval tabors (particularly in Spain) had a diameter equal to their depth.

Arbeau describes the tabor as a drum 2 feet (pieds) in length and 1 foot in diameter, which is struck with stick or fingers. He says that twisted threads are placed on the

---

[1] Mr. Jeremy Montagu has made reproductions of many mediaeval percussion instruments for use in performance; for flesh hoops he splices a rope ring the same size as the shell and stitches the head over it. This, he contends, would not work on modern orchestral drums, since the skins are too thin and are kept at too great a tension, so that the head would tear on the dotted line, but he has seldom had any trouble with tabors or nakers, using thick heads and low tension. (The heads on many seventeenth-century military kettledrums were stitched to the hoop.)

[2] Hawkins, John. *The History of Musick*, London, 1776, vol. II, p. 626.

skin extremities, whereas on the side drum there is a dual cord on one skin only. (From this we conclude that snares were, at times, employed on both heads, in France at least.) It is because of the twisted cords, says Arbeau, that the sound of the tabor is strident and throbbing.

The tabor was invariably played with one stick, slender in pictures where angels are performers, at other times rather clumsy in the hands of human players. An early fourteenth-century Serbian fresco *The Mocking of Christ* shows a tabor (rope-tensioned with two snares on the upper vellum) played with a hooked stick. In the Fra Angelico *Christ surrounded by Angels* of the mid-fifteenth century, the drumstick has the bead and taper of to-day. Very often the tabor player also plays a pipe. This combination of instruments is also known in the folk dance world as 'whittle and dub'. The pipe usually had three holes, two at the front for the fingers, and one at the back for the thumb. The ingenuity of a mediaeval musician (or the sculptor) is exhibited in a stone carving in Rosslyn Chapel (near Edinburgh). Here a player on pipe and tabor is equipped with wrist bells on the hand holding the drumstick. The tabor was usually strapped to the arm that held the pipe, or to the body. In some instances the drum is small, and hangs on the little finger. The tabor is portrayed at various angles, ranging from acute to vertical and horizontal. Among the stone carved figures of the thirteenth-century Angel Choir of Lincoln Cathedral can be seen the figure of an angel playing a pipe and tabor, with the drum in a vertical position. The superb workmanship embodied in this and other figures has been described as challenging 'the works of sculpture or painting of any country in the thirteenth century'. The tabor is suspended from the player's left arm. It is a shallow drum with two skins braced with cords. A single snare is visible. The stick, which is held in the player's right hand, is especially interesting, the end being covered with material to form a bulbous head. This rare instance of such a beater in a work of art of undisputed merit must be kept in mind at a later stage when we encounter the vexed question of the covering or non-covering of the early orchestral kettledrum sticks.

When the tabor was played without the pipe, it was often held in one hand and played with the other. It was rarely played with two sticks. The stone carving in Rosslyn Chapel where the performer is shown playing with two sticks on a small tabor – supported horizontally – is quite unusual. One occasionally sees the end of the pipe being used as an auxiliary beater to make odd flourishes, as can be seen in one of the Fra Angelico paintings of angels. A combination of pipe and drumstick is included in the collection of pipes and drums possessed by Andrew Ross (J. & R. Glen) of Edinburgh. The lower end of the pipe is fashioned to conform with the 'bead' on a normal side drum stick. A further unusual beater is seen in the English

93. Pipe and tabor. Richard Tarleton (Queen Elizabeth's jester) 1530–88. Portrait in ornamental letter T, published soon after Tarleton's death. By permission of Mansell Collection

92. Turkish drum. Vittore Carpaccio, early sixteenth century. Accademia, Venice. By permission of Mansell Collection

94
Tabor and cymbals, etc.
'Christ surrounded by Angels'
Fra Angelico, Florence
1386–7 to 1455. By permission of the
National Gallery, London

95. Pipe, tabor and wrist bells, fifteenth century. Rosslyn Chapel, Scotland. Crown Copyright: reproduced by permission of Ministry of Public Buildings and Works

96. Angel with pipe and tabor, thirteenth century. Lincoln Cathedral. Photograph by permission of J. W. Ruddock & Sons Ltd., Lincoln

97. Angel with tabor, fifteenth century. Rosslyn Chapel, Scotland. Crown Copyright: reproduced by permission of Ministry of Public Buildings and Works

98. Barrel drum and chime bells (*cymbala*). Twelfth-century psalter from the Abbey of St. Remigius, Reims. St. John's College, Cambridge. By courtesy of the Master and Fellows of St. John's College, Cambridge

99. *Tambour de Mousquetaires.* Parrochel, 1740. By courtesy of the Trustees of the British Museum

100. Swiss side drum, dated 1575. By permission of Historisches Museum, Basel

101. Side drum, 1581. Portrait by de Gillis Congnet of Pierson la Hues, city drummer of Antwerp. By courtesy of Musée Royal des Beaux-Arts, Antwerp

102. Wedding of Sir Henry Unton (painted by an unknown artist in 1596).
By permission of the National Portrait Gallery, London

103. 'The NightWatch' (1642).
Rembrandt. '(detail)'. By courtesy of
the Rijks Museum, Amsterdam

104. Drake's drum. By courtesy of the Trustees of
the late Robert Meyrick. Photograph by permission
of the City Museum and Art Gallery, Plymouth

105. Early seventeenth-century drum music. By
courtesy of the Trustees of the British
Museum

106. Early seventeenth-century drum music.
(Pistofilo, 1621.) By courtesy of the
Trustees of the British Museum

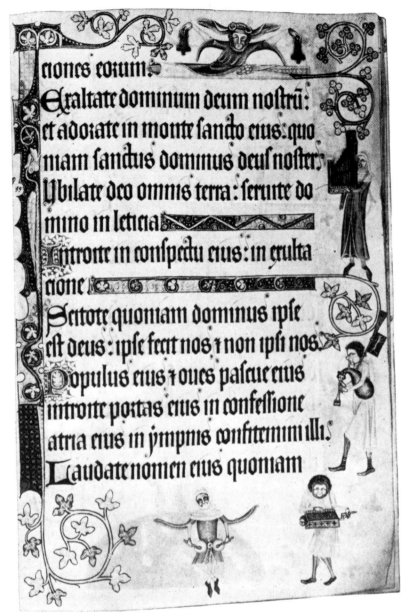

107. Nakers. Luttrell Psalter, fourteenth century. By courtesy of the
Trustees of the British Museum

108. Nakers. Luttrell
Psalter, fourteenth
century. By
courtesy of the
Trustees of the
British Museum

109. Nakers with snares. 'The Tournament', late fourteenth century. Worcester Cathedral. By permission of the Dean and Chapter of Worcester Cathedral.

110
Laced kettledrums and cymbals, late fourteenth century, by an unknown Genoese artist. By courtesy of the Trustees of the British Museum

111
Nakers with snares, triangle, pipe and tabor, etc., fifteenth century. By courtesy of the Trustees of the British Museum

112
Kettledrums and trumpets. 'The Triumph of Maximilian'. Burgkmair, 1526. By permission of Mansell Collection

113
Trumpets and draped kettledrums at the Funeral of Charles V. 1558. Joannes van Duetecum. By permission of Mansell Collection

113a
Kettledrums and trumpets at the Coronation of James II. Sandford. By permission of Mansell Collection

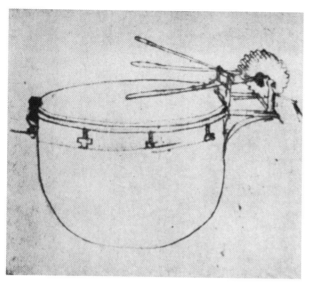

114. Study for mechanical kettledrum. Leonardo da Vinci. Cod. Atl., fol. 335r-c. By courtesy of the Trustees of the British Museum

116. Kettledrum with square top screws, c. eighteenth century. By courtesy of Mr. Stanley Vann

115. Artillery kettledrum, 1716. By permission of the Kungl Armémuseum, Stockholm

117
Tulumbaz, c. 1650.
By courtesy of the
Museum of the Leningrad Institute of Music.

118. *The Fairy Queen*. Purcell 1692. By courtesy of the Royal Academy of Music, London

119. Kettledrum sticks (wood), *c.* 1810. By courtesy of Edward Croft-Murray Esq.

121
Music for the Royal Fireworks.
From the original Handel manuscript.
By courtesy of the
Trustees of the British Museum

120. Negro kettledrummer. Rembrandt. *c.* 1638.
By courtesy of the Trustees of the British Museum

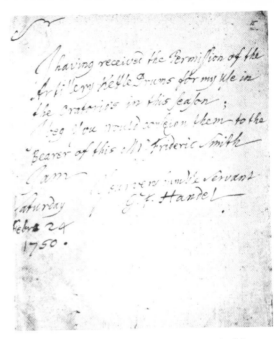

122. Handel's letter to the Master-General of the Ordnance; 1750. By courtesy of the Trustees of the British Museum

123. Artillery kettledrums. Detail from the Battle of Blenheim Tapestry, Blenheim Palace. Photograph by courtesy of His Grace the Duke of Marlborough and the Victoria and Albert Museum

Sinfonia
per
2 Clarini
5 Timpani
2 Flauti trav: cornett:
2 Violini
Violetta
Cembalo

124. (*Above*) Title page and (*right*) excerpt from score of Molter Symphony No. 99, *c.* 1750. Reproduced by permission of Baden National Library, Karlsruhe

125
Turkish musicians.
Agostino Tassi (1580–
1644). By courtesy of the
Trustees of the British
Museum

127. Portrait of a musician.
Horemans. By courtesy
of the Bavarian State
Gallery, Munich

126. Turkish percussion players.
Agostino Tassi (1580–
1644). By courtesy of the
Trustees of the British
Museum

128
Instruments of Music.
Pandean minstrels in
performance at Vauxhall.
By permission of
Mansell Collection

129. Relief of the Guard, St. James' Palace, *c.* 1790. By permission of Mansell Collection

130
Kettledrum, *c.* 1800. From the Guy Oldham Collection

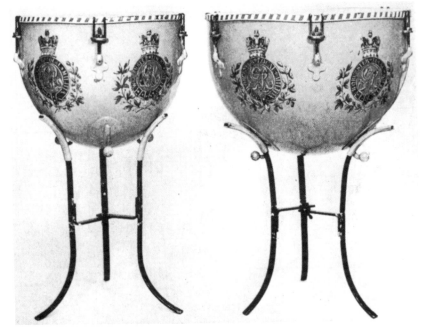

131
Early nineteenth–century kettledrums. By courtesy of Edward Croft–Murray Esq.

132. Mid nineteenth–century kettledrum (cable–tuned) by G. Potter. Author's collection

133. Kettledrum (cam–operated) by Kohler & Sons, London (1862). Author's collection

134. Late nineteenth–century kettledrum (rotary–tuning) by G. Potter. Author's collection

Tabor

St. Alban's Psalter of the twelfth century (in Hildesheim). Here a small bulb projects at right angles from an ordinary stick, suggesting that strokes were delivered by a twisting movement of the wrist.

When played with only one hand the rhythm on the tabor was fairly simple, since clearly it would not be practical to split the beat into a number of small units, particularly if the performer was playing two instruments at the same time and possibly dancing as well. The drum would best assist by playing an unvarying part, except when the pipe stopped for a moment, or held a long note. Except for a few extra strokes or an odd flourish to decorate cadential bars, or between the pipe's phrases, the drum rhythm was simple, in fact the instrument fulfilled its age-old purpose and acted as a time-keeper, though it would be foolish to deny virtuosity on the part of individual performers. Anthony Baines says:[1] '...it is usually beaten in fairly straightforward rhythms to guide the dance, as two-in-a-bar in six-eight time, or in dactylic rhythm in two-four'. Some simple rhythms which are obviously suited to the pipe and tabor have come down to us. A characteristic 2/4 rhythm is a crotchet followed by two quavers. According to Arbeau the music of the fife is improvised at the player's pleasure – the sound of the drum serves as a bass, and, because it has no definite pitch or tone, it accords with everything. It is clear that Arbeau was aware of the fact that the addition of snares (his 'twisted threads or cords') renders the tone of a drum indeterminate in pitch.

There is ample evidence of the widespread use of the tabor throughout Europe during the whole of the Middle Ages. According to Galpin it was introduced into England from Spain. A twelfth-century manuscript (St. John's College, Cambridge) associates the drum at this period with profane music. The instrument illustrated, however, is a barrel-shaped drum which is suspended horizontally in front of the performer (a juggler disguised as a bear) who is striking the drum with his hands. Sachs contends that a barrel-shaped drum was not familiar in Europe at that time and that its inclusion here was to give effect to the scene, though Galpin quotes a similar instrument in an English manuscript of the same century (British Museum Lans 383), and about a century later there is a literary reference to *bedons*, which may well have been drums shaped like a barrel.

During the thirteenth century the tabor – hitherto a smallish instrument and light in sound – appeared in a larger form, adopted with other customs by the armies of Western Europe from their oriental foes. Tabourers were present at the great feast made at Westminster in 1306. Edward III (1327–1377) included a tabor player in his household band. According to Froissart, when this monarch entered Calais he did so: 'à foison de trompettes, de tabours, de nacaires et de buccines'. Tabourers

[1] Baines, Anthony. *Woodwind Instruments and Their History*, Faber, London, 1957, p. 227.

are mentioned among the private musicians of the nobility of this period. By the fifteenth century the tabor, with a further increase in size, took as its companion the fife, forming the first organized style of military band in England, inspired by the Swiss fife and drum, a combination which provoked the same sort of envy and admiration among the crowned heads of Europe as did the kettledrummers of the Hungarian Cavalry at a later date.

The association of drum and fife is recorded in the Chronicles of the City of Basle for 1332. From that time there is evidence of the lustre of this historic combination, not only in Switzerland where these performers were incorporated in a guild and ranked as high officials, but throughout Europe, where they accompanied the Swiss Mercenary Regiments which served various foreign states from the sixteenth until the nineteenth centuries (a tradition still preserved in the Papal Guard). In their own country the Swiss drummers and fifers became an essential feature of all public festivals. The drum remains an integral part of Swiss communal life.

In England, an early notice of the larger tabor is contained in an entry in the Privy Purse expenses of Henry VII, who, in 1492, gave to '2 Sweches grete taborers' the sum of £2. This proves that foreign labour had been imported by either royalty or nobility, as was to happen in the case of kettledrummers in a later century. In France we find among the fifteenth-century stall carvings in Rouen Cathedral a large tabor, which is held by one man whilst another strikes it. This drum is unique in that small bells are shown on the snare (as in certain tambourines).[1] The small tabor continued its function as a folk dance instrument and, on the Continent at least, it became an important member of the Renaissance dance orchestra. The larger drum developed into an important military instrument. In England in the sixteenth century we find in military circles the name tabor or tabrett displaced by *drome*, *dromme*, *drume*, etc., a short step from its final form of side drum.

SIDE DRUM

The drome resembled the tabor in appearance, but differed in some respects stylistically. It was suspended at the side, (hence side drum) supported by a shoulder strap or body belt, as was the large tabor and, like this instrument, is seen at varying angles ranging from horizontal to vertical. In the majority of cases the side drum is represented at an angle of about forty-five degrees. On occasions it was strapped to the back of a man who marched in front of the performer (tabors were carried similarly). There are a few later instances of a side drum played by a performer on horseback. Here the instrument rests on the horse's neck.

[1] Galpin considers this instrument a Turkish-style bass drum.

Side Drum

Like the tabor, the size of the side drum varied considerably. Arbeau describes and illustrates a French side drum about 2½ feet in diameter and depth, closed at each end with parchment skins (secured by two hoops) bound with cords to keep them taut. Snares – a dual cord – are seen on one skin, and buffs for bracing the drum are shown at each end of the shell. The latter are common in pictures of this period. Michael Praetorius, whose numerous illustrations of musical instruments have been proved so true to scale, illustrates a side drum twenty-two inches in diameter and depth. This instrument has a single snare with what most certainly appears to be a threaded unit for the adjustment of the snare. A side drum dated 1575 in the Historisches Museum, Basle, has a shell a few inches deeper than its diameter (25 inches – 20 inches).

Mersenne illustrates a side drum – resembling those described by Arbeau and Praetorius – with a depth and diameter of equal proportion. This instrument has a double snare. Mersenne says the snare (he calls it *timbre*) can be adjusted to the required tone. With his characteristic thoroughness Mersenne shows clearly the function of the buffs to contract the V-formation of the rope, by illustrating the drum braced and unbraced. Arbeau says the skins were tightened when the player wished to beat the drum, and that the drum was loosened when not in use. A perfect example of the side drum and performer of this period is portrayed by Rembrandt in *The Night Watch* (1642). Here can be seen counter hoops, flesh hoops, a studded shell, snares and uniform rope-tensioning. The drum is suspended at the player's side at an angle of forty-five degrees. The sticks are perfectly poised and held in the traditional manner; and as an extension to such close observation Rembrandt has suggested the actual sound of the drum by the inclusion of a small dog who is clearly replying to the 'snap' from the snares.

Unlike the tabor, the side drum was normally played with two sticks and, certainly by the sixteenth century, the snare was below the lower head (where it is to-day), instead of above the upper head as on the tabor. In general, pictorial evidence indicates that the side drum sticks used at this period were heavier, and frequently shorter, than those used to-day. There are exceptions. Mersenne, for instance, illustrates a pair of slender and quite elegant side drum sticks with his drum. Large drums with stout heads would certainly require fairly heavy sticks (the reason no doubt why a number of the sticks illustrated in mediaeval pictures have heavy round heads). Heavy sticks and thick vellums must have created problems for the drummers of this period, particularly if the long roll were used. To perform the legitimate double-beat roll,[1] especially if the heads were at low tension, could not have been easy. It is feasible, therefore, that if a roll of any length was required,

[1] See 'Drum Technique'.

single strokes were used, a large drum producing a note of sufficient length to cover possible deficiencies in the roll. As has already been said, the lower tension was un-avoidable until the introduction of the counter hoop to safeguard the vellum.

With the increased tension on the drum head, made possible by the use of a flesh hoop on which the skin was lapped and a separate counter hoop for the ropes, the consequent rebound of the stick may well have led to the wider use of the long roll produced by a double beat from each hand, known to-day as Dad-dy, Mam-my. These strokes have formed the basis of rudimentary practice for the attainment of the long roll over a lengthy period. There seems no reason why the double beat, known quite early to Continental kettledrummers as double tonguing (*Doppel Zungen*), should not have been employed on the military side drum of the same period.[1]

Mersenne refers to the round beat (*baton rompu*) which is played two by two, also of *baton rond* (single-beating), *baton meslé* (single and double beatings) and of players who beat the drum at such a speed that it is impossible to follow each beat (a roll?). He also admires the strength of the drumskin which holds the beat coming down like hail, or with the sound of a cannon, though he adds that when the player required a clearer or less full sound he used the border. (To-day edge and centre are both used effectively in scores by Bartók, Stravinsky and others.) Though no clear instructions for a tremolo are given in the few specimens of music for the drum that have survived, it is clear that this characteristic feature of the instrument was included in the mediaeval drummer's curriculum.

The fact that little music was written for the drum during the Middle Ages and even later, is not surprising. A good deal of mediaeval music was unwritten, and it is not likely that the drum would be included among those instruments for which it was written. Music of the Middle Ages flourished as much by ear as by eye, and percussion playing was assimilated in the main by rote. Such drum music as we have is tied to military purposes, and consists mainly of instructions for the instrument's use in signalling and pace-making, little being said regarding the technical approach.

Arbeau's *Orchésographie*, 1588, is our earliest important source of information. In this treatise on the dance, which is in the form of a delightful dialogue with Capriol – an imaginary pupil – he deals with the side drum as a pace-making instrument, by which a body of soldiers could march in unison, or attack or retreat without confusion or disorder. Arbeau says:[2] '. . . our Frenchmen are instructed to make the rankers and bondsmen of the squadrons march to certain rhythms. In marching, if

[1] An anonymous printed instructor for the side drum published in Berlin, 1777 (the earliest of which we have knowledge) gives the double beat from hand to hand as the foundation of the roll. *Kurze Anweisung das Trommel-spielen*, Winters, Berlin, 1777.

[2] Arbeau, Thoinot. *Orchésographie*, Edition F. Viewig, Paris, 1888, pp. 6–17.

three men are walking together, and each one moves at a different speed, they will not be in step, because to be so they must all three march in unison, either quickly, moderately, or slowly . . . The French make use of the drum to beat the rhythm to which the soldiers must march. A drum rhythm contains minims, (called 'tans') of which the first five are beaten . . . the first four with one tap of the stick, and the fifth with two sticks together, and the other three beats are silent. The left foot must be put down on the first note, and the right on the fifth. . . . If all the eight notes were struck, a soldier could put down his feet on notes other than the first and the fifth, . . . but not when he hears distinctly the first and fifth notes.' Estimating the pace at four feet, Arbeau calculates that if the march continues for two thousand five hundred drum beats, the soldier will have covered a league.

Arbeau speaks of 'setting down the methods', by which it is assumed that he refers to certain rhythms used by French drummers of his period, who in their turn may well have been using rhythms 'handed down' for several generations. He lists the sounds he gave to the various units in his tabulations as follows: minim, one tap of the stick . . . *tan*; two crotchets, two taps of the stick . . . *tere*; four quavers, four taps of the stick . . . *fre*. Unfortunately he gives no clue as to the use of alternating single strokes, or double taps on the faster notes, though he mentions the drummer employing a succession of lighter and livelier crotchet beats, intermingled with loud blows of the sticks which sound like discharges of arquebus.

In the course of the dialogue, Capriol asks Arbeau for an example of the various rhythms. Arbeau's reply implies that if the drum rhythms are varied, they are more pleasing, and that two crotchets or four quavers could be substituted for the minim, with variation at the player's will. He insists, however, that the fifth note must always be a minim, unless the player wishes to repeat the rhythm a number of times, when the three rests occur at the end only. Arbeau speaks of the Swiss drummers, who put a rest after the third note, and three rests after the fifth. He also refers to triple time.

Colin tan plon

In triple time, Arbeau says the soldier brings down his left foot on the first note, and his right on the fourth, and so on (suggesting a feeling of 6/8). His description of a quick march is interesting. Here there is only one rest after the fifth note, the soldier bringing his left foot down on the first note, his right on the third, and again

213

his left on the fifth, while in the following measure the right foot is brought down on the first note, and so forth (in three-four time it seems). Here, reasons Arbeau,

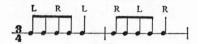

six feet are covered in each rhythm, and in this manner the soldiers cover a league in approximately one thousand, six hundred and sixty-six drum rhythms. He also emphasizes the value of a repetitive drum rhythm to the soldier, for he says 'should confusion occur through a change of step, the drummer beats a basic rhythm repeatedly, and the soldiers mend matters by getting back on the left foot when they hear the pause or the three rests'.

It is known from Mersenne and others that the French used a brisk march tempo, faster than the speed of the English march. When the French general, Marshal Brion, remarked to Sir Roger Williams – a soldier of Elizabeth's I's time – that the English march beaten on the drum was slow, heavy and sluggish, the gallant Sir Roger replied: 'It may be true, but slow as it is, it has traversed your master's country from one end to the other. [1] It is possible that this was the steady 'Pikeman's pace' later quickened by the Duke of Marlborough in forced marches.

It may well be asked: 'Why did Arbeau use such a seemingly long pattern to indicate one basic drum rhythm at a march tempo?' There may be several reasons. First, in speaking of the beats of time, Arbeau says: 'Some are double, others are triple, and either of these in their turn may be slow, moderate or quick.' Secondly the normal time unit has been represented at different times by different symbols. In the sixteenth century it was represented by the minim, whereas to-day the crotchet is used. Therefore, to us, where a group of eight minims implies a lengthy period, it is not unlikely that Arbeau's minims were beats of time in his quick tempo. (Prior to the sixteenth century, the value of a breve was short – in fact, a brief note.)

From Arbeau's 76 tabulations we select the following, adding a modern equivalent (*see facing page*).

Throughout the sixteenth century there are numerous references in English literature to the use of the side drum as a martial instrument and otherwise. The status of drummers at the time of Mary Tudor is well described in the Military Collections of a certain Ralph Smith. Smith says:[2] 'All captains must have drums and fifes and men to use the same, who shall be faithful, secret and ingenious, of

---

[1] Hawkins, John. ibid. vol. I, p. 229.
[2] Grose, Francis. *Military Antiquities*, S. Hooper, London, 1786–8, vol. II, p. 248.

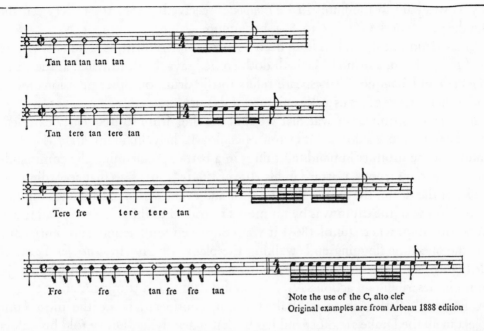

Tan tan tan tan tan

Tan tere tan tere tan

Tere fre   tere tere tan

Fre   fre   tan fre fre   tan

Note the use of the C, alto clef
Original examples are from Arbeau 1888 edition

able personage to use their instruments and office of sundry languages; for often-times they be sent to parley with their enemies, to summon their forts or towns, to redeem and conduct prisoners, and divers other messages, which of necessity requireth language. If such drums and fifes should fortune to fall into the hands of the enemies, no gift nor force should cause them to disclose any secrets that they know. They must oft practise their instruments, teach the company the sound of the march, alarm, approach, assault, battle, retreat, skirmish, or any other calling that of necessity should be known. They must be obedient to the commandment of their captain and ensign, when as they shall command them to come, go or stand, or sound their retreat or other calling.'

The ensemble providing Queen Elizabeth I's dinner music is said to have included side drums, kettledrums, trumpets, cornetts and fifes. The representation of the masque at the Wedding of Sir Henry Unton (painted in 1596) portrays a less robust style of performance provided by a 'broken consort' consisting of – treble lute, pandora, cittern, treble viol, flute and bass viol, to which is added a side drummer who may have performed with the ensemble or acted as a herald. In the royal Privy Purse expenses there are frequent entries of payments and gifts to drummers. Queen Elizabeth paid her three *Drumsleds*[1] £18. 5. 0. each per annum (the same shilling per

[1] *Drumsled* or *Drumslade*, Old English from the Dutch or Low-German meaning drum-beat, i.e. *Dromslades* – drum-beaters.

day as was paid to the flutes). 16 *Trumpettes* received £386. 16. 3. between them, and the player of the *Vyall* £30. 8. 4. per annum.

In Scotland, the drum had long been a national instrument, individually and with the fife. 'A drum, a drum! Macbeth doth come,' says the third witch at the entry of Macbeth and Banquo. Shakespeare refers to the drum on other occasions too, and with other writers gives us a clear picture of its purpose.

It is as an instrument of war that we find the side drum so frequently extolled. In warfare the drum is a dominant factor. Niccolo Machiavelli, in his *Art of War* (1521), states that the drum commands all things in a battle, proclaiming the commands of the officer to his troops. Garrard in his *Arte of Warre* (1591) says that according to the stroke of the drum, the soldier shall go, just and even, with a gallant and sumptuous pace. The use of the drum was by no means restricted to the soldier – it had much to do aboard ship, where (until 1865) it was concerned with action calls, burial at sea, and the one-time flogging and 'walking the plank'. In *An Accidence for Young Sea-Men* (1626) and later in *The Sea-Man's Grammar* (1627), the explorer Captain John Smith in describing an action says: '. . . sound drums and trumpets, and St. George for England'. Earlier there is Drake's drum, considered to be the most famous object in all the Drake saga. Legend has it, that when dying, Drake told his sailors to hang the drum at Plymouth, and if it was beaten in time of danger, he would return.[1] It was on this theme that Sir Henry Newbolt wrote his famous poem:

> Take my drum to England, hang et by the shore,
> Strike et when your powder's runnin' low,
> If the Dons sight Devon I'll quit the port o' Heaven,
> an' drum them up the Channel as we drummed them long ago.

Drake's drum is fortunately preserved.[2] The heads (possibly the original skins) are mounted on flesh hoops. Holes in the counter hoops signify rope tensioning (rope and snares are missing). In 1910 the drum – which hung in the Great Hall, Buckland Abbey, Devon – fell to the floor, and one of the counter hoops was damaged. Lady Drake instructed the local carpenter to repair it and at the same time to clean the drum. The removal of a considerable quantity of tallow and lampblack revealed Drake's coat of arms and crest painted on one side of the wood shell. The other side has a decorative pattern of studded nails. For many years this precious relic was

[1] It is said that the beat of a drum was heard in the Channel during the fateful month of August 1914, and again when the Kaiser's fleet came in to surrender in 1918. (See V-signal, 1940 in Chapter 2, 'The Drum'.)

[2] After considerable negotiation it is now a national heritage in the care of Plymouth Corporation. The instrument is on display at Drake's old home (Buckland Abbey).

exhibited during the summer months at Buckland Abbey. During the winter months the drum was returned – local history says under police escort – to the home of its owners, members of the Meyrick family, descendants of Drake's brother Thomas. In 1947, on the occasion of the visit of King George VI and Queen Elizabeth to Plymouth, the drum, with other Drake relics, was temporarily loaned to the City authorities and placed in the City Museum for Their Majesties' inspection. The relics travelled under police escort and a guard was mounted. The Museum Curator, Mr. A. A. Cumming, recounts that when shown the drum, His Majesty – to the horror of those concerned with the instrument's safety – promptly honoured the instrument with a powerful blow; evidently well executed for the drum stood the test well. The privilege of sounding Drake's drum has been given to few within living memory. On one occasion Mr. J. B. Lees, snr., for many years a principal in the percussion section of the BBC Symphony Orchestra was invited – with a few members of the BBC staff – to the Meyrick's home to inspect the drum. Mr. Lees was permitted the thrill of executing a few strokes on this famous instrument. He described the head as 'like a piece of leather'.

A seventeenth-century writer on military matters, Francis Markham, refers at some length to the purpose of the side drum. In his *Five Decades and Epistles of Warre* (1622) he says:[1] 'The Phiph is but only an instrument of pleasure, and not of necessity, and it is to the voice of the Drumme the soldier should wholly attend ... the Drumme being the very tongue and voice of the Commander, he is to have an exceeding careful and diligent ear. If he beat a retreat when commanded to Charge, or to beat a Charge when men are to retire, the army might perish by the action. The soldier must be diligent and learn all the beating of the Drumme and the drumme make plain the alterations of notes, and how they differ in their significations.' Markham refers to the duties of the drummer in sounding the discharge or breaking up of the Watch – The Summons – March – Retreat – Troups – and a Battalion or Battery, and states that when his duties in the field are finished, he retires with the fifer into the tent, 'wherewith to heal the minds and cares of his hearers' for, he says, he knew of 'no more sweet and solemn melody than that which the drum and flute afforded'.

Like Ralph Smith, Markham records the necessity of the drummer being a man of sundry accomplishments. He adds that no one strike or wound the drummer as he is rather a man of peace than of the sword, yet he is a man of valour and courage, his place is at the Captain's heels even in the middle of the battle, and that at funerals the drummer performing the last duty may for his fee challenge the sword of the deceased.

[1] Markham, Francis. *Five Decades and Epistles of Warre*, Matthewes, London, 1622, p. 63.

Markham mentions a document relating to instructions in drumming, though it seems he had little regard for it, for he speaks of one Hindar 'who took upon himself to write a book on this necessary subject'.

The fact that Markham made no further comment on this work is our loss, as the manual seems not to have been preserved, but there survives (among other literature) a royal document dealing with instructions to drummers. This is a warrant (*c.* 1632) of Charles the First directing the revival of an old English march, possibly the slow march described by Sir Roger Williams to the French general, Marshal Brion, as having 'traversed your master's country from one end to the other!' The warrant reads:[1] 'Whereas the ancient custome of nations hath ever bene to use one certaine and constant forme of March in the warres, whereby to be distinguished one from another. And the March of this our nation, so famous in all the honourable achievements and glorious warres of this our kingdom in forraigne parts (being by the approbation of strangers themselves confest and acknowledged the best of all marches) was through the negligence and carelessness of drummers, and by long discontinuance so altered and changed from the ancient gravity and majestie thereof, as it was in danger utterly to have bene lost and forgotten. It pleased our late deare brother prince Henry to revive and rectifie the same ordayning an establishment of one certaine measure, which was beaten in his presence at Greenwich, anno 1610.'

In a document dated 1643 entitled *Warlike Directions or the Soldier's Practice* by a practitioner in the art, the author, in referring to the march says:[2] 'I have thought meete for the benefit of each Drummer which is not yet perfect in the March, to prick downe the old English March newly revived in the plainest forme I could invent. Wishing that all Drummers would leave off other forms invented, either by themselves, or others herein unskilful, that there may be an uniformitie in this Kingdome, as in all other Nations.' A series of symbols give instructions for beating the drum with single strokes from the right and left hand, the spacing of the beats, and the use of the full and half ruff. (Dr. Farmer contends that the inattention to the fundamental drum beats prompting the issue of the royal warrant, was due to the addition of the pipe and fife. He says:[3] 'When pipe and fifes were made to accompany the drum, the precise beat of the latter fell into neglect.')

A copy of the royal warrant and reference to the march is included in a collection of notes in the handwriting of Randle Holme III for his *Academy of Armoury* written

---

[1] Walpole, Horace, (Earl of Oxford). *Catalogue of Royal and Noble Authors*, 2nd edition, London, 1759. pp. 200, 201 and 202.

[2] Anon. *Warlike Directions or the Soldier's Practice*, 2nd edition, Harper, London, 1643. pp. 4, 5, 6 and 7.

[3] Farmer, H. G. *The Rise and Development of Military Music*, Reeves, London, 1912, p. 22.

before 1688 (B.M. Harl 2034, f75–6), but it is to Walpole that we are indebted for the full musical notation of the march. The reproduction from Walpole's Catalogue is by permission of the British Museum authorities (Pl. 105).

It will be noticed that the notation of this march is similar to that of Arbeau's rhythms. The transposition into present-day figuration – as Arbeau's rhythms were treated – renders the 'Voluntary before the March' thus:

Any interpretation of pou – tou – R – poing and potang – must be, to some extent, hypothetical. The terms pou – rou are used for both the long and short notes (differing from Arbeau who makes use of tan – tere to some extent onomatopoeic, as are 'flam', 'drag' etc., in English).

'Poung' with its pause certainly suggests a held note – or perhaps a roll. Pou, tou, and R when compared with the symbols in the 1643 document, refer to right and left, and R to a ruff (full or half).[1]

Many of the rudimentary beats and ornaments we use to-day were already known to mediaeval drummers. Holme is helpful regarding such technical aspects. In his short history of the drum (*Academy of Armoury*) in which he remarks: 'A good drum beater can perform on his drum as well as any other can on his musical instrument', Holme sets down the 'flam', 'dragge', 'roofe', 'diddle' and the 'rowle', also the manner of beatings performed by singles and doubles, quick and slow, rights and lefts, and rowling blows. From these we can be fairly certain of the long roll, the 'paradiddle', and most certainly the 'flam', 'drag' and 'ruff' (see side drum technique). With this in mind, we offer the following versions of The Old English March (*see following page*).

Useful information regarding military drumming comes from an Italian source, Pistofilo's *Il Torneo* (written in 1621) devoted mainly to the law of tournament. Here the author devotes several pages to the art of drumming and includes examples of drum music. M. Cockle in his *Bibliography of English Military Works* says:[2] '*Il Torneo* is the earliest work in which I have seen military music written.' (Pl. 106.)

Pistofilo says of all the instruments used from ancient times to give the word of command, the trumpet and drum survive. This, he says, is due to their quality of sound, and that they appeal to the nature of men, also that they are suitable on horse

---

[1] Possibly drummers' jargon, and could have suggested: 'With a tow row row' – as in 'The British Grenadiers'.

[2] Cockle, M. J. *Bibliography of English Military Works*, Simpkins, Marshall, Hamilton Kent, London, 1900.

or foot. The drummer, he says must be a man of spirit, and an expert player, conversant with the style of every nation and every 'sonata' in war, corresponding to reveille; assembly; dismiss; march; halt; call to arms; disperse; open and close ranks; retreat; burial of the dead; the soldier in all cases to obey the beat of the drum.

The Voluntary before the March

The March

(J.B. interpretation)

In almost every respect Pistofilo agrees with Arbeau regarding the groups of notes with an accent on the last beat, followed by a rest. He speaks of orders of five or of seven (which might correspond to our three and five pace rolls) and beats on the drum before the soldier puts down his foot. Where Arbeau uses 'tan' 'tere' and 'fre' to define certain units, Pistofilo speaks of 'ta' 'pa' and 'ta ra ra'. In his examples of drum music (the lower line is for the soldier), tails down denote right hand strokes and tails up a stroke with the left hand. A dot above a note indicates a heavy stroke and the sign 3, according to Pistofilo, a trill. With regard to the latter, this writer informs us that Arbeau used a longer trill than the Spanish (presumably the long roll) (*see facing page*).

Shortly after Pistofilo there is a brief reference to music for the drum, coupled with what is considered to be the earliest music for the fife to be found in an English work. The work concerned, *Mars his Triumph* written in 1639 by William Barriffe, describes a military exercise performed at the Merchant Taylor's Hall in 1638. The author refers to the drums beating a preparative, a troop, a charge, and striking an alt, and at the conclusion of the exercise, the drummers, somewhat dramatically, directed to unbrace their drums: 'Unbrace your Drums, and let the warlike Phife no more distinguish twixt pale death and life.' (In general, this practice of slacking a rope drum when not in use remains.)

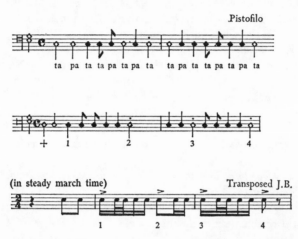

It is not until the Brothers Philidor (mid-seventeenth century) that we find anything comparable to Arbeau, Pistofilo and Holme, with reference to the technical aspects of the side drum, and its purpose in the foot regiments. It had, however, a rival in its companion in the field – the kettledrums of the cavalry, destined to become the aristocrat of the orchestral percussion. Kettledrums in Europe had their origin in the nakers.

Bibliography: Chapter 10

MEDIAEVAL AND RENAISSANCE EUROPE

AGRICOLA, Martin. *Musica Instrumentalis Deutsch*, Wittenburg, 1528, reprint Leipzig, 1896.
ALTENBURG, J. E. *Versuch einer Anleitung zur heroisch-musikalischen Trompeter und Paukerkunst*, Halle, 1795, reprint Bertling, Dresden, 1911

Mediaeval and Renaissance Europe

ANON. *Kurze Anweisung das Trommel-spielen*, Winters, Berlin, 1777.

ANON. *Warlike Directions or the Soldier's Practice*, 2nd edition, Harper, London, 1643.

ARBEAU, Thoinot. *Orchésographie*, Lengres, 1588, reprint by Fonta, Vieweg, Paris, 1888. English translations by C. W. Beaumont, London, 1925 and Mary Stewart Evans, Kamin, New York, 1948.

BAINES, Anthony. *Woodwind Instruments and Their History*, Faber, London, 1957.

BARRIFFE, William. *Mars his Triumph*, Leggatt, London, 1639.

COCKLE, M. J. *Bibliography of English Military Works*, Simpkins, Marshall, Hamilton Kent, London, 1900.

FARMER, H. G. *The Rise and Development of Military Music*, Reeves, London, 1932.

GALPIN, F. W. *Old English Instruments of Music*, Methuen, London, 1910.

GRASSINEAU, James. *A Musical Dictionary*, London, 1740.

GROSE, Francis. *Military Antiquities*, vol. II, Hooper, London, 1786–8.

HAWKINS, John. *The History of Musick*, vols. I & II, London, 1776, reprint Novello Ewer, London, 1853.

LAFONTAINE, H. C. de. *The King's Musick*, Novello, London, 1909.

MARKHAM, Francis. *Five Decades and Epistles of Warre*, Matthewes, London, 1622.

MERSENNE, Marin. *Harmonie Universelle*, Paris, 1636.

O'CURRY, Eugene. *On the Manners and Customs of the Ancient Irish*, Williams & Norgate, London, 1873.

PARADOSSI, Giuseppe. *Modo facile di suonare Il Sistro, nomato – il Timpanio*, Bologna, 1695.

PISTOFILO. *Il Torneo*, Italy, 1621.

PRAETORIUS, Michael. *Syntagma Musicum*, Wolfenbüttel, 1619, reprint, Kassel, 1929.

RANDLE HOLME III. British Museum manuscript, Harl. 2034, Folios 75 & 76.

SACHS, Curt. *The History of Musical Instruments*, Norton, New York, 1940.

SAINT ISIDORE. *Etymologiae, c.* 600.

VIRDUNG, Sebastian. *Musica Getutscht*, Basel, 1511, reprint, Kassel, 1931.

WALPOLE, Horace. *Catalogue of Royal and Noble Authors*, 2nd edition, London, 1759.

RECOMMENDED READING

CRANE, Frederick, *Extant Medieval Musical Instruments*, University of Iowa Press, 1972.

DART, Thurston. 'Music and Musical Instruments in Cotgrave's *Dictionarie* (1611)', *Galpin Society Journal, XXI*, 1968, pp. 70–80.

MONTAGU, Jeremy. 'On the Reconstruction of Mediaeval Instruments of Percussion', *Galpin Society Journal, XXIII*, 1970, pp. 104–114.

REESE, Gustave. *Music in the Middle Ages*, Norton, New York, 1940.

TITCOMB, Caldwell. 'Baroque Court and Military Trumpets and Kettledrums', *Galpin Society Journal, IX*, 1956, pp. 56–81.

11

Nakers and Kettledrums

Nakers, the English name by which small kettledrums of the mediaeval period were known, were of Arabic or Saracenic origin. Naker or *nacair* is derived from the Arabic naqqāra. Sachs says:[1] 'As early as about 1300, the French were using the Arabic term *nacaires*, the Italians *naccheroni*, and the English *nakers*.' Though kettledrums in pairs or otherwise must have been constantly employed in the East from early times, it is not until the period of the Crusades that there is direct evidence of their use in Europe. According to Dr. Farmer[2] 'One thing especially took the Crusaders' fancy, and that was the Saracen side drum and kettledrum, which were then unknown in European military music. They were introduced into our service as the tabor and naker, and are frequently mentioned in the accounts of the Crusaders.'

Percival Kirby considers it probable that the Moors were responsible for introducing the kettledrums into Spain, but Canon Galpin thinks otherwise:[3] 'As we do not find them at an early date in Spain, we may probably infer that their introduction into the West was due, not to the Moorish invaders, but to the Crusades, which brought also the Long Trumpet called the Buzine, with which they were closely associated.'

Literary references confirm the use of small kettledrums in Europe from the thirteenth century onwards. In a description of the crusade of Louis IX which took place between 1248 and 1254, Jean Sire de Joinville writes of tabours called nacaires : 'Lor il fist sonner les tabours que l'on appelle nacaires.' Marco Polo speaks of the armies of Alau and Berca (1261) and King Kaidu and the great Khan (1266) waiting for the sound of the *nacars* as a signal to commence battle.

[1] Sachs, Curt. *The History of Musical Instruments*, p. 251.
[2] Farmer, H. G. *The Rise and Development of Military Music*, p. 13.
[3] Galpin, F. W. *Old English Instruments of Music*, p. 250.

Nakers and Kettledrums

Nakers first appeared in England in the early fourteenth century, and soon became the symbol of aristocracy; used in musical entertainment, as an encouragement in the tournament, and to increase the sound and turmoil of battle. Janino le Nakerer is mentioned in the list of minstrels of Edward I. Edward III, in addition to a Tabrete among his musicians, had a Nakerer. According to Froissart, nacaires (and tabours) heralded this monarch into Calais. It will be noticed that, like de Joinville, Froissart distinguishes between tabours and nacaires.

The playing of these small kettledrums was an established art, the home of which was considered to be Germany. In 1384 the Duke of Burgundy sent one of his drummers to study the style of the German players.

Artists and sculptors have given us numerous representations of the instruments of this period. From these we see kettledrums (singly, but more often in pairs) from six to ten inches in diameter and with a common feature in the single skin, and in the resonator which is more or less hemispherical in shape.[1] Generally they are suspended in front of the player by a strap round the waist or from the shoulder. With isolated exceptions the player has a stick in each hand.

The Luttrell Psalter provides two excellent examples of the nakerer at work. One shows the player with a pair of small drums at his waist. In the other illustration he is seen with larger drums placed on the ground. In this instance the sticks are curved. A carving on the choir seats of Worcester Cathedral (late fourteenth century) portraying a tournament scene, shows a nakerer and a player on the 'clarion'. This carving is interesting, for here we observe an early association of trumpet and kettledrums, a combination that soon was to play a vital part in the history of the drum. The artist has portrayed snares on the nakers, a feature observed quite frequently at this period and later, both in England and on the Continent. In *The Dance of Death*, Holbein adds to the macabre situation by providing the nakerer, a skeleton, with a pair of thigh bones for drumsticks (a custom at one time connected with certain African tribes).

Until the seventeenth century there is widespread evidence, pictorial and otherwise, of small kettledrums. From this it can be seen that their purpose was twofold. Played by men, they were used mainly for martial purposes. Chaucer couples them with the 'clariounes', 'That in the bataille blowen bloody sownes'. In the hands of angels and women they appear as delicate instruments, and are associated with soft-toned instruments and chamber music. In an illustration in the Olomouc Bible 1417 they appear with fiddle, lute, horn, bagpipes, and a trapezoidal 'triangle'.

The nakers were used also for dance music, and were probably used for accom-

---

[1] A pair of small drums of Egyptian origin in the Victoria and Albert Museum is unusual. They are $6\frac{3}{4}$ inches and $4\frac{1}{8}$ inches wide, and 11 and $8\frac{1}{2}$ inches in depth.

panying songs, particularly where the song was in a dance rhythm. It is also likely that they were used in processional music in churches, such as the 'Conductus' and the 'Ductia'.

From the mediaeval paintings it is not always clear whether one drum is smaller than the other; in some cases there appears to be little difference in size.[1]

Fig. 37a. Nakerer
(from Holbein's *The Dance of Death*)

Fig. 37b. Kettledrums
(from Holbein's *The Dance of Death*)

The attachment of the heads is even more problematical with the nakers than with the tabor. One or two examples look as though they are rope-tensioned, others appear to have nailed heads, and some are 'necklaced'. Equally problematical is the material used for the shell. Prevailing conditions may have had an influence; if there was a good coppersmith the instruments could well have been in copper, if the local workers in wood were better they might be of wood, made in staves like a barrel, or they might be turned out of wood like a bowl. On the other hand, the shells might be made by the potter.

Little difficulty is experienced in deciding the material used for the drumsticks. Excluding the skeleton's bones mentioned above, the sticks were of wood, some light, some heavy, some fashioned, and others crude.

[1] An old pair of Arabic naqqāra in the Montagu collection are of the same diameter but one has a hole in the bottom and the other has not; this is not a detail that one could expect to be visible in a painting. (Drums of this size do not need a hole to prevent the heads splitting, as do larger kettledrums. In experimenting with copies of these instruments Mr. Montagu has found that if there is no hole in the bottom of the shell the higher harmonics seem stronger.)

Nakers and Kettledrums

More elaborate rhythms must have been used on the nakers than on the tabor, partly because two sticks were used, and partly because with two contrasting sounds possible, the player would not be restricted to using different note values to mark the strong beats, and so forth.

KETTLEDRUMS

Large kettledrums, the true cavalry kettledrums, precursors of the orchestral timpani, began to spread through Europe during the fifteenth century. They were already known in Egypt and Arabia. (The *naqqareh*, mounted on either side of the performer's camel, measured in the region of 24 inches and 18 inches in diameter.) Galpin says:[1] 'The introduction of the larger size, borne on either side of a ridden horse, for cavalry purposes, was due to the Hungarians, who, leaving Scythia about the ninth century, brought with them their military customs as well as their national dances and songs.'

In 1457, envoys representing the King of Hungary (sent to King Charles of France to treat for the hand in marriage of his Princess Madelaina) were accompanied by kettledrummers on horseback, with instruments the size of which prompted a Father Benôit to say that such drums had never been seen before. From this it is clear that though large kettledrums were unknown in Western Europe, they existed in the east of the continent. There is evidence of their use at this period in Poland and Russia. They were introduced into Germany about 1500, as we know from Virdung (in his *Musica getutscht*, 1511) who wrote disapprovingly of the big army kettledrums of copper, called *tympana*, which the princes had at court. It is clear that Virdung found little music in these enormous rumbling barrels, which he believed to be the invention of the devil. No doubt this authority on musical instruments, a man of the Church, was also disturbed by the display of pomp with which the kettledrums were associated and by the fact that they were primarily connected with war for, like the nakers, they were a symbol of aristocracy and occasions of state. It was expected of the kettledrummer to signify the high rank of his employers by a display of spectacular flourishes and affected elegance, which elsewhere would appear exaggerated and ridiculous. Jost Amman's (1584) famous woodcut of a mounted drummer no doubt portrays the current style, as with Hendrich Lubeck (1598) and subsequent artists. Virdung was not alone in his disapproval of the extravagance surrounding timpanists and their instruments. About the middle of the sixteenth century, it is recorded that the arrogance surrounding the entrance of a German baron, on his visit to a French nobleman, so annoyed the French that the

[1] Galpin, F. W. ibid. p. 251.

baron's kettledrums were ordered to be dashed to pieces, 'to his great abashment', it is said. Such instances, however, were rare; the popularity of the kettledrums increased and the fame of the German and Hungarian kettledrummers spread throughout Europe.

In 1542 Henry VIII sent to Vienna for kettledrums that could be played on horseback, together with men who could play them skilfully. In England, as elsewhere, possession of kettledrums remained for a considerable time the prerogative of royalty and nobility, taking their place, with trumpets, in a regular mounted ensemble; usually some twelve trumpets and one pair of drums. A combination of this description is mentioned in Hall's *Chronicales of Henry VIII* (1548) . . . 'Trompettes . . . twelve in nombre besyde two kettle dromes on horsebacke'. Similarly, we find in a description of an Elizabethan banquet in Hentzer's *Itinerarium*, this same combination, a pair of kettledrums with twelve trumpets, 'which together with fifes, cornets and side-drums, made the hall ring for half an hour together'. To quote Professor Kirby:[1] '. . . Royalty was evidently prepared to bear the infliction for the sake of glory . . .' to which it seems Edward VI was no exception. From the record of the entertainment provided for him at Christmastide 1551 we find among the instrumentalists one 'to plaie upon the Kettell Drom with his boye'.

Galpin says:[2] '. . . probably the "boye" was the unfortunate being who had to bear on his back the noisy burden'. It was not unusual for kettledrums to be supported in this way. In the engraving by Joannes van Duetecum of the Court Trumpeters at the Funeral of Charles V, 1558, a man with a pair of kettledrums suspended on his right shoulder walks by the side of the player. The heads of both drums are draped with cloth. In Sandford's *Coronation of James II* (Pl. 113a), a man bears a pair of larger drums on his back (preceding the performer). In this case the bodies of the drums are surrounded by an emblazoned banner, leaving the heads clear.

Kettledrums mounted on a carriage were known in England towards the close of the seventeenth century. Farmer says:[3] 'It is highly probable that the custom of our artillery chariot kettledrums came from the Continent.' This he supports with a reference to the great kettledrums of the Swedish army of 1655. He deals equally exhaustively with the kettledrums in 'Marlborough's train of 1702' (the great kettledrums of the Artillery) and other notable instruments.

Almost invariably kettledrums were played in company with trumpets, a combination associated with the cavalry regiments. In England, they were granted only

[1] Kirby, P. R. *The Kettledrums*, Oxford, London, 1930, p. 8.
[2] Galpin, F. W. ibid. p. 251.
[3] Farmer, H. G. *Handel's Kettledrums and other Papers on Military Music*, Hinrichsen, London, 1950, p. 85.

to the *corps d'élite*. Similar restrictions prevailed in Germany and elsewhere. Only if the instruments were captured on the field of battle was an ordinary regiment permitted the ownership of kettledrums. The loss in battle of the regimental kettledrums was considered so degrading (according to Altenburg)[1] that the regiment was not again permitted the use of drums unless the instruments were re-captured. The instruments and the accompanying armorial banners were quite often artistic in appearance. In some instances the drumsticks were decorated with costly jewels.

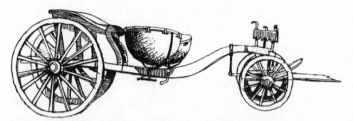

Fig. 38. Kettledrums: model of Marlborough's train of 1702.

The players were equally exalted. In Germany various Imperial decrees dating from 1528 led to the establishment in 1623 of an Imperial Guild of Trumpeters and Kettledrummers of which the regular members held the rank of officers and were privileged to wear the ostrich feather of nobility in their hats, in many cases three-cornered. The kettledrummer had further privileges, being allowed to ride on a gorgeously caparisoned horse, and to be near to his commander in the field. The secrets of the craft were closely guarded. To safeguard the craft, playing technique was handed down by rote from generation to generation, a fact largely responsible for the lack of written music over a long period. Initiates (carefully chosen from respectable families) were educated and then obliged to serve a term of apprenticeship to the Guild. Even so, they were not allowed to practise their vocation until attaining the distinction of a 'freeman', after which they enjoyed special privileges, including exemption from military law. It would seem that this Guild maintained a 'closed shop', and a rigid control upon its members, who, outside their military duties, could play only on permitted occasions and for agreed fees. (These rules were still in force in Bach's time, and it is thought that such instruments as the *corno da tirarsi*, for which he occasionally wrote, were disguised trumpets, which were played by blacklegs at performances where he was not permitted, or could not afford, to employ trumpeters from the Guild. Odd relics of such rules persist to this day: trumpets or timpani may not be included in an orchestra playing for a banquet in

[1] Altenburg, J. E. ibid. Halle, 1795.

London's Guildhall unless royalty is officially present). Only members of the Guild were permitted the use of kettledrums (and trumpets). Severe penalties were imposed on uninitiated persons who were discovered playing or possessing them. In England, the use of these instruments was similarly controlled: even with the King's troops kettledrums were granted only to the royal bodyguard, the Life Guards. Each troop was allowed one kettledrummer to four trumpeters. Later, when ordinary regiments of 'horse' were given the privilege of kettledrums, one pair was allowed for the colonel's troop, with two trumpeters. Other troops were allowed trumpets only.

There are numerous entries in the Lord Chamberlain's Records relating to music and musicians, and particularly to the status of kettledrummers and trumpeters.[1] Like their Continental counterparts, they were persons of consequence, in many cases with warrants of appointment signed by the King. In 1606 we find a William Peirson 'timpanist to Prince Henry'; in 1624 Richard Thorne, 'King's drummer', and from 1661 onwards various references to His Majesty's Kettledrummer.

The word kettledrummer appears for the first time in these records a year earlier (1660), in an entry dealing with the appointment of John Barteeske as Kettledrummer.

Despite the several references to the instruments as kettledrums, seventeenth century players often styled themselves timpanists. Of this temporary loss of the English term kettledrum, ('kettle' [cetel] is one of the oldest words in the English language) Professor Kirby says:[2] '... drummers had become infected with the disease imported by John Cooper the composer, who, on his return from Italy, styled himself Giovanni Coperario, thus setting a fashion that has still its devotees in England'.

The appellation 'timpanist' was not all that was imported. Such names appearing in the records as John Barteeske, Hans Bernghoski, William Goschen, Jean Noell Joose and Walter Vanbright[3] imply that Continental players were much in demand. (The popularity of foreign musicians is widespread and of long standing. There is evidence as early as AD 500 of Chinese musicians migrating to Japan. In the early part of the present century there was a marked entry in the U.S.A. of professional players from Germany, Italy and Great Britain.) It would seem that the Continental players exercised – for some time at least – the strictness of the German guilds, guarding well the secrets of their craft as, with few exceptions, the English players mentioned in the records are styled 'drummers' or 'drum-players'. Some of these

---

[1] Lafontaine, H. C. de. *The King's Musick*, Novello, London, 1909.

[2] Kirby, P. R. ibid. p. 8.

[3] Walter Vanbright was Charles II's kettledrummer. He, with a number of State trumpeters, was lost in the wreck of the frigate *Gloucester* off Yarmouth in 1682. In the early 'twenties the Original Dixieland Band were lost at sea in the same area.

men evidently graduated from the ranks – as is often the case to-day – to become kettledrummers. An entry in the Lord Chamberlain's Records dated 1680 reads: 'Certificate allowing Robert Mawgridge, his Majesty's drummer in ordinary, to continue the office of kettle-drummer to his Majesty's troop of Horse . . . he providing a sufficient man to perform the duty in his place of drummer.' (His Majesty's kettledrummers were highly paid men. There are several entries recording their receiving 5/- per day.)[1]

From all accounts there was by no means constant harmony in the musical circles of this period. Mr. Mawgridge, for instance, evidently used his words as forcibly as his drum sticks, for we find a petition of William Bull, trumpeter, to take his course at law against Robert Mawgridge, kettledrummer, for scandalous words (on account of faulty intonation, perhaps).

At this period 'service' musicians were under the control of the sergeant-trumpeter and the drum-major-general of the royal household, who had the power to conscript when necessary. (Farmer speaks of impressment as late as 1781.)

THE INSTRUMENTS

The earliest illustrations of kettledrums indicate various systems of laced tensioned vellums, similar to the bracing of nakers and the larger Arabic kettledrums and such Asiatic drums as the Indian nāgāra. This method of applying pressure to the head is observed throughout the sixteenth century (and later). Galpin refers to a Polish kettledrum with laced head and tuning wedges (in the manner of the Indian tablā and mrdanga). Mersenne depicts a laced kettledrum as late as 1636.

But in Germany, in the meantime, the kettledrums had undergone an essential change. From the start of the sixteenth century a major development is apparent – screw tensioning. Hans Burgkmair (*The Skill of Music, c.* 1550) illustrates a kettledrum equipped with this method of controlling pressure on the vellum. Here the instrument, a sizeable one, is associated with an orchestral ensemble. Subsequent illustrations by other artists point to the general adoption of this innovation.[2] Throughout the century and onwards, there are numerous representations of kettle-

---

[1] Over a century later (September 1818) the redoubtable Thomas P. Chipp (well known as the player of the 'Tower drums') received for his services on kettledrums and harp at the Theatre Royal, Covent Garden, the sum of 5/10 per night. A William Goodwin (bells, castanets, tambourine etc.,) was paid 20/- per week. (From the papers of the late F. Geoffrey Rendall, now in the collection of Graham Melville-Mason.)

[2] Leonardo da Vinci had already envisaged 'screw-tensioning' on the kettledrum relating to his scientific experiments in acoustics (Codex Atlantico f.355 r.c. c1487–90). A mechanical device for beating the drum is included. A similar device is attached to a side drum seen in his studies for percussion instruments (Codex Arundel f.175r) cf. Patents.

drums with 'side screws' varying in number, and applying pressure directly to a flesh hoop, or indirectly to it through the medium of a counter hoop. In the first instance the vellum is in the form of a 'floating head' (cf. Japanese tsuzumi etc.). It is lapped, or in some cases sewn, to a hoop complete with lugs for the tensioning screws. The skin is pierced at each lug to give the screw access to the threaded bracket attached to the shell of the drum. (This method of mounting a drumhead is still used on certain types of Continental timpani.) Where a counter hoop is employed, the vellum, which in this case fits closer to the shell, is lapped to a separate flesh hoop. Here the lugs for the tensioning screws are attached to the counter hoop. With these early kettledrums the screws in all cases were turned by means of a loose key. In the majority of cases the screws are 'square topped', though there are several instances in early models of the top of the screw being shaped to form a ring through which a short rod would have been passed. A kettledrum in the Kungl. Armémuseum, Stockholm, taken at the battle of Lutzen 1632, has fittings of this nature. In later German and other instruments the square-topped screw is general, though the ring top is retained on Russian and Danish kettledrums dated 1700 and 1716 in the Stockholm collection.

A pair of Swedish kettledrums (18 and 20 inches in diameter) in the Kremlin Armoury Moscow which were captured at the battle of Poltava (1709) have five and six square-topped side-tensioning screws. The heads are coarsely sewn to floating heads. An instrument (c. 1650) in the Leningrad Institute of Music Museum measures 34 inches in diameter. It has eight square-topped tensioning screws and a similar floating head.

The number of screws and the diameter and depth of the bowls vary in existing specimens and representations. In general, there are more tensioning screws on the earlier instruments (Virdung's illustration has 10). On later instruments between five and seven are seen on the smaller drum of the pair, and six to eight on the larger instrument. The shells were usually made of copper or brass.

The diameter of the bowl varies. Arbeau refers to a width of 2½ feet. Mersenne and Virdung say 2 feet. The instruments (*Heerpauken*) in the diagrams by Praetorius in his *Syntagma Musicum* (1615–20) are certainly smaller, measuring according to Praetorius's scale (Brunswick foot) 17½ inches and 20½ inches in diameter. The depth of each drum is in the region of 12 inches. Each drum has six threaded handles with square tops, and is complete with a strap for affixing to the saddle and feet for resting the instrument on the ground (observed on cavalry drums over a long period). With his usual thoroughness, Praetorius includes a loose tuning key in his illustration. The drum (1632) in the Stockholm Museum is approximately 26 inches wide and 14 inches deep. Preserved specimens of a little later period measure from 20–28 inches across, generally with a difference of approximately two inches between two of a pair, though in some cases rather less. (To-day the standard pair of orchestral timpani measure 28 inches and 25 inches across.)

The sticks used on early kettledrums are represented in numerous styles, sometimes with round ends, sometimes oval and quite often with narrow ends. There are literary references to wood and ivory ends. In the Vienna Museum there is a pair of solid ivory sticks dated seventeenth century. On the other hand, judging from the size of the ends of the sticks used in Persian miniatures, it is unlikely that these were of wood or ivory, as so heavy a ball would have proved disastrous to a drum skin, besides being too heavy for the handle and throwing the stick off balance. The heads of the beaters illustrated by Rembrandt, in his *Negro Commander and Kettle Drummer* c. 1638, are quite sizeable and suggest a lighter material than ivory or wood. In some instances kettledrum sticks are illustrated with straps for securing to the wrist.[1] Certain types are grooved to give a secure grip. Bessaraboff[2] refers to an unusual type of drumstick used on the *tulumbaz*, a Russian kettledrum used for hawking. This stick, known as a *voshaga*, consisted of a wooden ball affixed by a thick leather strap to a handle. Bessaraboff writes: 'A richly adorned tulumbaz was a proper present to send to Russian tsara by rulers of neighbouring countries. It seems that there is no counterpart of such a custom in western Europe, or at least the facts wait upon discovery.' He also speaks of cavalry kettledrums (*litavry*) of copper or silver, appearing in Russia in the sixteenth century.[3]

As already stated, the true cavalry kettledrums began to spread through Europe in the fifteenth century. From this period until the middle of the seventeenth century, where we meet the firm evidence of written music, we find their strictly musical purpose somewhat limited. In the early stages the drums functioned much as their Arabian and Egyptian forbears, the large and small drums (the large drum on the right of the player) giving a difference in pitch, with such differentiation used only to distinguish between the pair of drums for rhythmical purposes. The technique of the naqqareh was doubtless employed, such as that given by Villoteau in his work *De l'état actuel de l'art en Egypte* (*see facing page*).

Villoteau, Napoleon's musical surveyor, recorded the large Egyptian kettledrums as tuned to a fifth.

---

[1] In 1927 a patent was granted for drumsticks with straps for securing the sticks to the wrist. British Patent 815, 297–1927.

[2] Bessaraboff, Nicholas. *Ancient European Musical Instruments*, Harvard University Press, 1941, pp. 35 and 36.

[3] The kettledrums presented to the 'Blues' by George III and those given to the Life Guards by William IV are of solid silver.

The Instruments

More accurate tuning developed with the improvement in the construction of the drums and their constant association with the cavalry trumpets. In Europe, tuning in fourths was the general rule, a method derived from the technique of the trumpet (the part for the fourth trumpet is in fact so written in some old trumpet marches that it can also be played by the kettledrums).

Villoteau

The music they played would be, in notes, normally a simplification of the bottom trumpet part and, in rhythm, an elaboration of it. Altenburg says they sounded 'the fundamental bass of the trumpets heroic music'. (He composed a concerto for seven clarini and timpani shown in his Manual 1795.) Due to the size of the drums, and quite possibly to the coarse nature of the vellums used at this period, the compass of the instrument was restricted, the most likely tuning being D and A, or E flat and B flat, the tonic and dominant notes of the prevailing trumpet keys (D and E flat). For the most part the drums were treated as transposing instruments. In the majority of early drum music the following notes

are used. For some time the lower drum of a pair was styled the G drum. The smaller, higher sounding instrument was known as the C drum. Alternatively they were called 'bass' and 'tenor' respectively. The larger of the two was to the right hand, as with their forebears the naqqareh. This style, adopted by the cavalry kettledrummers, has been maintained in the horse regiments both abroad and in England. (In orchestral practice to-day, many Continental players retain the large drum to the right hand, elsewhere the instruments are (in most cases) reversed – see 'Orchestral Timpani'.)

Several reasons have been advanced for the original practice of the large drum being placed to the right hand: for example, that the animal bore the burden better with the extra weight to its right side. Again it has been agreed that it was primarily a matter of performance: with the majority of players the right hand is the stronger, so that with the pulse maintained on the less penetrating lower sounding drum, it would be natural to have that drum (the larger) to the right.[1]

With regard to tone production, it has been said that no great amount of musical quality was demanded from the early cavalry kettledrummer, though it is unlikely that 'one drum up and one drum down' was acceptable in every instance. Here we

[1] Professor Richard Hochrainer, timpanist of the Vienna Philharmonic Orchestra, is convinced that this is the reason.

will quote Mallet (1684)[1] who said the kettledrummer 'must have a stylish arm action, a good ear, and must take pleasure in regaling his master with agreeable airs on occasions of rejoicing'. The fact that such masters as Lully, Purcell and Bach accepted the kettledrums when former serious composers such as Byrd and Monteverdi had (with the possible exception of their use *ad libitum* in brass fanfares) been hesitant in putting these instruments to strict orchestral use, is proof enough of an improvement in intonation and tone production during the seventeenth century. This is the position of the kettledrums at this date in actual practice. In theory, much had already been said, including some foresighted reasoning by Leonardo da Vinci and Mersenne.

According to *The Notebooks of Leonardo da Vinci*[2] this fifteenth-century genius who said 'Tymbales should be played like the monochord, or the soft flute', conceived 'a drum with cogs working by wheels with springs'. He speaks of 'a square drum of which the parchment may be drawn tight or slackened by the lever. Just as one and the same drum makes a deep or acute sound according as the parchments are more or less tightened, so these parchments variously tightened on one and the same drum will make various sounds.' It is quite unlikely that such a scientific brain as that of Leonardo da Vinci would overlook the possibility of manipulating the 'lever' by hand and foot, so here, almost 500 years ago, we have, in theory, the machine drums of to-day.

Mersenne also had original ideas regarding the employment of percussion: 'The tune you want to obtain, depends, like the bells on the size of the drum.' He gives a chart showing the size of eight drums which make the notes of an octave together with the harmonic numbers. (Mersenne's reasoning may have inspired Reveroni Saint-Cyr who, in 1803 in an essay, proposed a timpani scale [*gamme timbalière*] of seven pipes covered by equal skins and supplied with air from an organ bellows through valves adjusted so that the pressures in them were in ascending sequence.) Unfortunately, the reasoning of Leonardo and Mersenne did little to help the composers of the latter half of the seventeenth and the early part of the eighteenth centuries. The instruments at the disposal of these pioneers were crude in comparison to those visualized by the earlier scholars. The best that can be said is that there was available in the majority of cases a pair of cavalry kettledrums, possibly with stout heads and hardish sticks, and a screw mechanism that permitted no rapid change of pitch. Even so, matters were improving and such composers as Philidor, Lully, Purcell and Bach made such excellent use of the kettledrums that from this period we find them firmly established as an orchestral instrument.

[1] Mallet, A. M. *Les travaux de Mars*, Paris, 1684, p. 98.
[2] Taylor, Pamela. *The Notebooks of Leonardo da Vinci*, p. 160, New American Library, 1960.

Bibliography: Chapter 11

NAKERS AND KETTLEDRUMS

ALTENBURG, J. E. *Versuch einer Anleitung zur heroisch-musikalischen Trompeter- und Paukerkunst,* Halle, 1795; reprint, Bertling, Dresden, 1911.

BESSARABOFF, Nicholas. *Ancient European Musical Instruments,* Harvard University Press, 1941.

FARMER, H. G. *The Rise and Development of Military Music,* Reeves, London, 1912.

   Handel's Kettledrums and other Papers on Military Music, Hinrichsen, London, 1950.

GALPIN, F. W. *Old English Instruments of Music,* Methuen, London, 1910.

KIRBY, P. R. *The Kettledrums,* Oxford, London, 1930.

LAFONTAINE, H. C. de *The King's Musick,* Novello, London, 1909.

MALLET, A. M. *Les Travaux de Mars,* Thierry, Paris, 1684.

SACHS, Curt. *The History of Musical Instruments,* Norton, New York, 1940.

TAYLOR, Pamela. *The Notebooks of Leonardo da Vinci,* New American Library, New York, 1960.

VILLOTEAU, G. A. *De l'état actual de l'art en Egypte,* Paris, 1812.

RECOMMENDED READING

EISEL, J. P. *Musicus autodidaktos,* Erfurt, 1738.

SPEER, Daniel. *Grundrichtiger Unterricht der musikalischen Kunst.* Ulm, 1687, 1697.

The Classical Orchestra

Though the introduction of kettledrums into the orchestra is generally credited to Lully in his opera *Thésée* (1675), there is evidence that the instrument was in use in musical ensembles in the early part of the century when, with trumpets, kettledrums figured in the stage directions concerned with masques.[1] In Jonson's *The Golden Age Restored* (1616) the Evils enter and dance to two drums, trumpets, and a confusion of martial music. Later, in Shirley's *The Triumph of Peace* a drummer is mentioned '... on horseback in a crimson taffeta coat, a white hat and feather tipt with crimson, beating two kettledrums . . .' The drums in these instances seem to have been employed as stage effects in addition to their function in the instrumental ensemble. The Festival Mass originally attributed to Orazio Benevoli for the dedication of Salzburg Cathedral in 1628 is now considered to be a late 17th century work by Andrea Hofer or Heinrich Biber. This work is for two combinations of trumpets and timpani. The drums are tuned to the same fourth (written C and G) each pair having original parts. Three works by Malachias Siebenhaarm consisting of sacred vocal music with instrumental accompaniment, published in the 1660's, specify on the title page *Heerpauken*. A Brithsh Museum manuscript (31438 f 53b), written in a mid-seventeenth century hand has the first trumpet part of an *Auffzug 2 Clarinde 2 Heerpauken,* by Nicholaus Hasse. (As with the works of Siebenhaarm the part for the drums is missing).

It is in the French military circles of this period that the first substantial written parts for the kettledrums *(timbales)* appear. The Brothers Philidor, musicians of the Court of Louis XIV, were responsible for the composition of a number of marches for trumpets and kettledrums (also several intricate pieces for the side drum, some to marches composed by their contemporary Lully). In 1685 Ballard published a volume of *Piéces de trompettes et timbales à 2, 3, et 4 parties* composed by the elder Philidor.

[1] Two drums (possibly kettledrums) are prescribed in the intermedia *Psyche ed Amore* (1565). This may be the earliest strict orchestral employment of kettledrums.

237

(André), who also compiled a large collection of marches and signals for trumpets and drums from almost every European country.

In France, where ensembles of brass and drums were a regular feature of court life, marches were occasionally performed on kettledrums alone. In 1665, according to the French historian Blaze, the Brothers Philidor described a military tournament at which a march was performed on two pairs of kettledrums. Later, in 1685, they composed and performed a march of this description in which an unusual tuning is recorded, one pair of drums tuned normally to C and G and the other to E and G (see pp. 237-240). This, and a march by the younger brother, Jacques, is included in a collection of seventeenth-century marches and other court music (*Partition de plusieurs marches*) published by the Philidor Brothers in 1705. This volume also contains *Marches de Timbales* composed by Bablon for the *Gardes du Roi* (Louis XIV). In Bablon's marches and that of Jacques Philidor the drums are tuned in fourths, indicated C and G.

These marches are ingeniously constructed, and typical of a high standard of execution on the part of the players. With their varied phrase lengths and intriguing couplets, the marches (on two drums only) employ rhythmic intricacies, whilst the work for two pairs of drums with its seventeen couplets, is indeed a masterpiece. In one of the *Marches de Timbales pour les Gardes du Roi* by Bablon, the group of

Marche de Timbales pour les Gardes du Roi

Faite par Bablon

From the original.

five semiquavers may indicate a flourish in the guise of a short roll. In the finale of this march the striking of two drums simultaneously to produce a chord, is the earliest known written instance of this device, which has been attributed (as far as the orchestra is concerned) to both Martini il Tedesco in his opera *Sappho* (1793) and to Beethoven in his Ninth Symphony. It is no surprise to find Bablon exploiting the timpani thus, for he was Louis XIV's *timbalier des plaisirs* (a highly-paid occupation demanding private service at the King's pleasure).

Whilst Bablon and the Brothers Philidor were engaged in composing for military ensembles, Lully, also active in this field, was concerned with the orchestra.[1] Although Lully's opera *Thésée* (1675) is generally cited as the first score in which the kettledrums appear, the honour of introducing the instrument into the orchestra should perhaps be divided between Jean-Baptiste Lully and Matthew Locke: for in the performance directions of Locke's opera *Psyche*, first performed in 1673, and published in 1675, the musical accompaniment includes wind instruments, violins and kettledrums. No parts for the drums appear in Locke's original score, whereas several of Lully's scores (*Thésée*, *Achille et Polixène*, *Bellérophon* and *Proserpine*) include written drum parts.

Lully, who refers to the drums as *Tymbales*,[2] gives them the customary interval of a fourth. In *Thésée*, where they play an important part in the prologue, and in the 'Entrée des combatons', the drums usually have the same rhythm as the trumpets and strings, though in other operas, *Bellérophon* for example, the drums have individual figures, frequently a series of semiquavers whilst the brass sustain a note, or vice versa. In the original manuscript of the 'Choeur de Peuple' (*Bellérophon*) the figuration in several places is to modern eyes perplexing:

There would seem to be two possible interpretations: either the crotchet and following quavers are misprints for a quaver followed by semiquavers (the dot being an error on the part of the movable type – a by-no-means uncommon error at this period), giving us:

or, if the dotted crotchet plus six joined quavers is authentic Lully, it could be that the notes joined by a curved line indicate a flourish, probably a short roll.

There is no clear instance of notation suggesting a longer roll in Lully's output. In *Thésée* there are demi-semiquavers written in small type (*see facing page*).

---

[1] Among Lully's occasional music written for the King is a march for kettledrums *March of the King's Musketeers*.

[2] Also given as *Tymballes*.

Thésée   Lully

In the 'Marche' in Act II of *Achille et Polixène* (completed by Pascal Colasse) both demi-semiquavers and semiquavers are given in small type.

Achille et Polixène   Lully-Colasse

Like Lully, Colasse writes the actual notes for the drums, (in this case D and A in the key of D).

Contemporary with Lully, we find a notable Moravian composer, Pavel Josef Vejvanovsky, giving a place to the timpani in his Serenades Nos. 23 and 27 composed *c.* 1680, for strings, cembalo, five trumpets and drums. In Serenada No. 23 (autographed) the drums (according to Vejvanovsky *tamburini*) are tuned in fifths, with the dominant (G) above the tonic (C), (the high note was practical on the small kettledrums of this period, the brothers Philidor employed it in their march for two pairs of kettledrums). Here the tamburini part is identical with that of the fifth trumpet (normal cavalry practice).

Serenada No. 23   Vejvanovsky

The dynamic marking is interesting, and in view of the prescribed part and the use of the drums in a quiet passage, suggests a composer with little interest in the 'rumbling barrels' and 'a noise like thunder' of the previous century, a sound which remained associated with the kettledrums, in literature at least, for some considerable time. In the Serenada No. 27 Vejvanovsky employs his tamburini in fourths. Here, the part (in small notes) resembles that of the fourth trumpet, the only difference being that the tamburini G is below the C, whereas the trumpet G is above the C.

Serenada No. 27   Vejvanovsky

Both examples by Vejvanovsky by permission of Artia Edition, Prague.

Vejvanovsky's use of the kettledrums in fourths and fifths, embracing the compass of an octave, and his request for the contrasting dynamics, *p* and *f*, are interesting features in a score of whose authenticity there seems to be no question. According to the notes in the recently printed edition[1] the revision was carried out on the basis of the manuscript material deposited in the Castle archives in Kroměříz, extant autographs and contemporary copies providing the material on which the volume was based.

The close of the seventeenth century found the kettledrums firmly established as orchestral instruments. Purcell, realising their musical significance, entrusted them in the Symphony to Act IV of his opera *The Fairy Queen* (1692) with what is considered to be their first orchestral solo passage.

The page of score (reproduced by permission of the Royal Academy of Music, London) is from the original holoscript as used in the production of the opera at the Dorset Gardens Theatre, London (the present site of Serjeant's Inn). The manuscript is partly Purcell's own, though the opening to Act IV is not in Purcell's handwriting. Zimmerman[2], who lists Purcell's forces, is of the opinion that the copyist appears to have worked under Purcell's supervision. (See pl. 118.)

Purcell used the English term kettledrums; apparently not influenced by the prevailing use of the term 'timpanist'. According to Zimmerman's catalogue, genuine Purcell kettledrum parts are included in *The Fairy Queen* (D and A), *The Indian Queen* (C and G), and the *Ode for St. Cecilia's Day* 1692 (D and A). In each case the drums occur with trumpets. In the *Ode for St. Cecilia's Day* the drums (with two trumpets) have an important role in the alto solo: 'The fife and all the harmony of war'; a situation echoed some years later in the alto solo in Bach's Cantata No. 71.

In editing Purcell's *March and Canzona for Queen Mary's Funeral*, Thurston Dart[3] has added a part for kettledrums (four in the March and three in the Canzona), remarking in the preface: 'The band of (flat) trumpets (slide trumpets) and sackbuts (tenor and or bass trombones) was certainly supported by kettledrums, and perhaps by other percussion instruments'. These may have been draped side drums.

Little is known about the use of the timpani in the orchestra between the music of Purcell and that of Bach and Handel. That kettledrums continued to be used in the orchestra is apparent from pictorial evidence concerning church and theatrical performances. A print from the Leipzig Hymnbook of 1710 shows Kuhnau (Bach's predecessor at St. Thomas's, Leipzig) conducting an ensemble (in St. Thomas's) consisting of organ, trumpet, strings, and a pair of kettledrums.

[1] *Musica Antiqua Bohemia*, Pavel Josef Vejvanovsky. Composiziono per orchestra, Praha, 1961. Státní Hudební Vydavatelví, Artia, Prague.

[2] Zimmerman, F. B. *Henry Purcell: an analytical catalogue of his Music*, Macmillan, London, 1963.

[3] Dart, Thurston. *An Introduction to March and Canzona for Queen Mary's Funeral*, Oxford, London, 1958.

An analysis of the manner in which Bach employed the kettledrums, connects the instrument almost entirely with the trumpets and chorus, and invariably with a mood of festivity or public ceremony. In all, the drums are found in 49 of Bach's compositions: (Church Music 39, Secular Cantatas 7, Orchestral Music 3). In 45 instances the tunings comply with the conventional interval of a fourth, the keys being – D (30), C (14) and B flat (1). With this last single exception the drums in these works are scored with trumpets, normally three. In the four remaining

works, all in the key of G, Bach employs the interval of a fifth.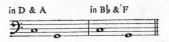

These are the only occasions on which he departs from his general observance of convention: i.e., the kettledrums sounding the fundamental or bass, with the dominant below the tonic.

Bach usually indicated the instrument under the name of *Tamburi*. The exceptions are Cantata 100 where he writes *Tympelles*, the Magnificat (D Major) in which the form *Tympali* is used, and the contraction *Tymp* in Cantata 191. Terry[1] says: 'Only in the memorandum addressed to the Leipzig Council in August 1730 he employs the German *Pauken*, probably reflecting that those he addressed would find another word unintelligible!'

In general Bach treated the drums as transposing instruments, scoring them in C in the bass clef with the actual notes indicated at the start of the work:

in D & A   in Bb & F

Transposition occurs in all cases where drums and trumpets are associated. In the key of G, (Cantatas No's. 79, 91, 100 and 195) where the drums are tuned in fifths and function with horns, Bach does not transpose, but gives the actual notes. His tuning of the drums in fifths could be attributed to the fact that the tonic, G, could not be sounded with any quality on the smaller drum (nor the lower D on the larger drum). It is possible, however, that here Bach desired the tonal placement of the dominant above the tonic. If so he differed both from his predecessors Lully and Purcell, and from his contemporary Handel, who, maybe on a point of tradition, rarely used the drums other than in fourths. In Cantata 143 in B flat Bach employs the drums (here with three horns) in their lowest register. Of this Terry says[2]: 'A tuning in fifths (dominant and tonic), though practicable, was obviously not preferable, since it diminished the resonance.' In contrast, in the

[1] Terry, C. S. *Bach's Orchestra*, Oxford, London, 1932, p. 50.
[2] Terry, C. S. ibid. p. 52.

Magnificat in E flat (subsequently revised in D major) Bach demanded high notes, according to Terry[1] 'tuning his drums in fourths, tonic, and (lower) dominant'. His use of a compass embracing little short of an octave,[2] and his employment of the unusual interval of a fifth, proves Bach co-responsible with the Moravian Vejvanovsky for developments frequently attributed to later composers.

Bach made no unusual demands upon the technical skill of his kettledrummer. Only on rare occasions does he employ demi-semiquavers, and then at a modest tempo. His beatings were straightforward, and chiefly rhythmical, and would present no problems in execution to the drummers of his generation, who were clearly well versed in single and double 'tonguing', and similar prevailing kettle-drum technicalities which Bach employed orchestrally.

The pitch of the drums (never more than a pair) remained unchanged throughout an entire work. Where there was a change of key the drums were silent, awaiting the return of the original key. Since the kettledrums normally supported the brass or full choir, it was only on rare occasions that Bach gave them a solo part or obbligato. In the opening chorus of the secular cantata of 1726 *Vereinigte Zwietracht der wechselnden Saiten*, the drum solo, a rhythmic figure:

Vereinigte Zwietracht der
Wechselnden Saiten
in D   J. S. Bach

is somewhat surprising, for the text 'Ye thundering drum-rolls exultant and clear' would seem to invite a roll, and there is ample evidence that Bach was by no means unaware of the tremolo. He was also fully conscious of the dramatic possibilities of the timpani. In the Michaelmas Cantata No. 130, drums, together with the blaze of trumpets, add to the battle as they accompany the bass aria: 'With rising fury Satan stands'. Bach considered the drums especially appropriate to the bass voice. In Cantata No. 119 and in *Preise dein' Glücke* they are added to the bass recitative. They also accompany the bass aria 'Zurücke, zurücke' in *Aeolus*, and in the bass recitative 'Ja! ja! die Stunden' the drums typify the thunder as Aeolus summons the Winds, in what Terry describes as 'one of the most vivid storm pieces in musical literature'. Their association with the alto voice (as with Purcell) is observed in Cantata No. 71 *Gott ist mein König*.

A further example of a drum obbligato occurs in the first chorus of the *Christmas*

[1] Terry, C. S. *Bach's Orchestra*, Oxford, London, 1932, p. 52.
[2] Obviously practical on the drums at this period.

Oratorio.[1] At the beginning of the oratorio, solo drums herald the choir's motif of rejoicing ('Christians be joyful') which is taken up by the full choir in unison, with the drums responding, again solo. In the accompanying example, taken from the facsimile of the autographed score, the notes in bar three are in one group and not divided as in some later editions.

Christmas Oratorio

in D & A

J. S. Bach

In bars 5–8 we have a clear indication of the roll.[2] Although Bach was the first serious composer to notate clearly a kettledrum roll, there is little doubt that the tremolo was no invention of his. Professor Kirby states that the roll was little used at this period; but although drum music up to the seventeenth century consisted mainly of 'open beating', we meet occasional groups of notes almost certainly indicating ornaments or a short roll, but written out in definite time (e.g. in Lully). Lengthy groups of semiquavers or demi-semiquavers, according to tempo, point to the use of what is termed a measured tremolo (to be discussed in drum technique). That at times the true roll was intended, though not clearly indicated, is generally accepted, but we can rarely be certain of the intention of early composers regarding either the roll or the exact length of notes. Bach rarely leaves us in doubt about either. He frequently indicates the rest following a quaver (♪𝄾 ♪𝄾) and the tied and dotted crotchet. (𝄞) In one or two instances he actually phrases, for instance the B minor Mass, Gloria. (𝄞) The timpani are prominent throughout this work, particularly the typical kettledrum figure in Sanctus: (𝄞) This rhythm is frequently played in triplet forms: (𝄞 or 𝄞) for many consider that Bach's intention was for the drums to correspond with the brass and choir: (𝄞).

In the *Christmas Oratorio* we have already seen the tremolo sign: *tr.*, plus the tying of the roll over four bars. In Suite No. 3 and the two Overtures in D for example, some of the long notes are sustained by means of a tremolo. There are cases where

---

[1] For a detailed comparison of this chorus with the opening chorus of *Tönet ihr Pauken* see C. S. Terry's *Bach's Orchestra*, pp. 54–5.

[2] With minor exceptions, e.g. the semitone shake in Schoenberg's *Five Pieces for Orchestra*, the *tr* sign in drum music indicates *tremolo* not *trill*.

the minims and semibreves are without a tremolo sign. Here Bach probably required the drum to be struck with a single stroke, the resonance of the instrument supplying the time value. Terry, who deals so scrupulously with Bach's instrumentation, says[1]: 'Indeed, since he used the instruments with fairly slack parchments, a held note without rolling would have ample resonance'. This is excellent reasoning on the part of Terry, since the drums at Bach's disposal were smaller than later instruments and were most frequently tuned to the notes C and G and D and A, thus concentrating on the lower part of their register.[2] At the same time long notes may have seemed uninteresting to timpanists of Bach's day, prompting them to sustain the note by means of a roll. Most kettledrummers were trained in the military school and accustomed to considerable freedom in performance.

It is not unlikely, therefore, that they would exercise a little latitude in the orchestra, at least to the extent of sustaining with a roll an occasional long note where the tremolo was omitted – particularly a closing note:　. To-day opinions are divided as to whether Bach intended a roll on such occasions. Some argue that it is not unreasonable to suppose that in this period of decoration, Bach was happy to leave such moments to the performer's initiative. Others contend that if Bach had required the tremolo on closing notes, he would have indicated this, quoting in support the last two bars of Cantata No. 19, where the roll is specified on the penultimate bar only:　.

In a musical document of 1732,[3] the author says that for the final cadence the timpanist should at all times make a good roll finishing with a strong beat. He also says that the timpanist must have a good knowledge of the music, relaxed hands and rhythmical sense, and not disturb the others by playing too early or too late. The document also contains interesting information regarding the drumhead. 'The covering skin should be only half cured; however, in order that they give a bright sound, the skins should be spread, when dry, with brandy wine and garlic, then dried in the sun or not too close to a low fire; then screw the skins around the frame in equal tension, the smaller timpanum tuned in C and the larger in G.' In an illustration of a pair of kettledrums, directions are given that the large drum should be to the left hand (then an exceptional placing of the instrument).

With regard to the quality of instruments at Bach's disposal it would seem that in general he was not well served in this respect, and we must conclude from all the

[1] Terry, C. S. ibid. p. 54.
[2] With the existing low pitch the skins would be sufficiently taut to yield musical notes.
[3] Majer, Joseph. *Museum Musicum*, reprint Kassel, 1954.

accounts available that, in Leipzig at least, only one pair of timpani was available to him, and that they were jointly owned by the two churches, St. Thomas's and St. Nicholas's. Records refer to the drums of St. Thomas's being renewed in 1686. These are probably the instruments seen in the print from the Leipzig Hymnbook (1710) and are those inherited by Bach. Regretably they are lost to us, and any attempt to assess their tonal quality must be governed by what we know of the instruments at this period, the type of sticks used and, by no means the smallest factor, the musicianship and adaptability of the performer.

The bulk of literary evidence refers to the 'dull thudding sound' or the 'harsh tone' of the orchestral drums at this period; and it must be granted that the limited dimensions of the bowls, the probable use of thick vellums and the frequent use of hard sticks support these contentions. Even so, while accepting that the drums of Bach's period were less resonant (and less powerful) than the scientifically designed orchestral drums of a later period, it seems inconceivable that Bach would have been satisfied with a 'dull thud' or 'harshness' from instruments which he consistently employed in some of his most important works throughout his life as a composer. Assuming some skill on the part of the player co-opted, it would be unwise to dismiss the possibility that Bach's timpanists produced a sufficiently musical tone to meet the demands of such a master. Furthermore, we are bound to ask whether Bach would have scored for the drums over such a long period had he considered them unworthy. Bach's orchestra was a permanent body, and as Terry says, 'schooled by frequent oral instructions in his requirements'. There can be little doubt that he demanded the best possible from every instrument, and that he accordingly expected the kettledrummer to produce as musical a sound as possible from instruments however indifferent.

This leads us to the matter of the drumsticks used at this period. Literary evidence points to the general use of sticks with hard ends, wood or ivory or a similar substance and the majority of preserved specimens support such information. Mallet[1] 1684, speaks of kettledrum sticks of boxwood having at one end a small rosette the size of a silver crown, the edge of which strikes the kettledrum, giving it a more pleasant sound than when struck with a side drum stick. Pictorial evidence (mostly concerned with military subjects) also points to a widespread use of sticks with uncovered ends. There is, however, evidence both literary and pictorial which points in another direction. Occasional illustrations of sixteenth-century kettledrummers show the players using sticks which appear to have material of some description wrapped round the ends. Charpentier (1709) illustrates drumsticks with ends encircled with a ring (possibly of leather). There are also the kettledrum sticks with

[1] Mallet, A. M. *Les travaux de Mars*, Thierry, Paris, 1684, p. 98.

bulbous ends portrayed by Rembrandt (this portrait is considered to be a life study made during a festival procession). Here we are reminded of the bulbous head on the drum stick held by the performer playing pipe and tabor in the thirteenth-century Angel Choir, Lincoln Cathedral, and of the evidence as early as 1586 of travellers who, in recounting their experiences, remarked on the nature of sticks used on African xylophones, 'sticks, at the point of which are buttons made of sinews' and others with the heads covered with leather, 'so that the sounds are softer'.[1] (In ancient times there was the padded stick used on the Chinese stone chime.) The covering of the drumhead was common enough as early as the sixteenth century, so to rule out the covering of the tip of the drumstick would be foolhardy. Eisel[2] (1738) says that by covering the skins with woollen cloth the drum tone could be muffled for funeral occasions; alternatively, he said, the sticks could be covered with chamois leather. Altenburg also refers to the custom of covering the drum and the stick for funeral purposes; the drum with a black cloth and the beaters with leather, or a cloth bound round the ends. In a Viennese collection of eighteenth-century kettledrum sticks, traces of a soft covering can be clearly seen in several instances.

H. C. Robbins Landon in a letter to the author says: 'I have examined in detail a whole collection of eighteenth-century sticks, and played the Mariazellermesse on eighteenth-century drums with various of these sticks, at the Piaristenkirche in Vienna. They were all very hard-tipped, but one could see that there were several types, and traces of a softer covering (now almost gone) could clearly be seen on several ends.' Berlioz in his *Instrumentation* states that there are three kinds of drum sticks. He complained, not of the lack of softer sticks, but of negligence on the part of earlier composers who failed to indicate in their scores the kind which they desired the performer to use. The reason why Bach and his immediate successors omitted this instruction may well be that these composers wrote not for posterity, but for specific occasions and with the players under their supervision, and that such matters would be given attention 'on the spot'. From a practical angle, many eminent present-day players consider that the orchestral timpanists of the eighteenth century (Bach's included) would not reject the aid afforded by covered sticks in the execution of certain tremolos and delicate passages at least, and that this possibly led to an extension of their use and to the term 'flannel it' – to play softly.

Bach's use of 'percussion' is confined to the kettledrums, if we exclude the obbligato for two bells (*campanella* B natural and E natural) in the cantata *Schlage doch: gewünschte Stunde*. (Some scholars consider this work is not by J. S. Bach.)

[1] See 'The Primitive Xylophone'.
[2] Eisel, J. P. *Musicus autodidaktos*, Erfurt, 1738, p. 66.

In the cantata the bells are notated ♪♪♪ considered either as a transposition, or a mistake of bass for treble clef.[1] These instruments (possibly true bells) would in all probability be operated from the organ manual. There is evidence of the inclusion of a series of chimes in at least one of Bach's organs. In a memorandum suggesting certain improvements in the organ of St. Blasius' Church, Mühlhausen, Bach requests[2]: 'The new chimes desired by the parishioners to be added to the Pedal, consisting of 26 bells of 4-foot tone; which bells the parishioners will acquire at their own expense, and the organ builder will then install them'. Possibly Bach shared with the parishioners a regard for the sound of bells, for many of his organ registrations are suggestive of these instruments. A similar taste is observed in several of the works of his contemporary and fellow-countryman Handel. These musical giants had also much in common regarding the use of the timpani.

Handel's employment of the drums was chiefly rhythmical, with no change of pitch throughout the entire work, and generally in company with trumpets and choir, and in most cases tuned in fourths. One exception occurs: in *Il Parnasso in Festa* (1743). In the key of B flat the drums are tuned in fifths: to G and D, and are marked *scord* – possibly employed as an effect. Elsewhere Handel confined the use of the drums to the keys of C and D (the former rarely) ♪♪♪ and except for a few early works in which he treated the timpani as transposing instruments, he wrote the actual notes for them. That he was fully aware of the dramatic possibilities of the kettledrums is obvious from the manner in which they function in many of his choral works. In *Semele* (Act V) there is an impressive solo announcing Jupiter's oath: 'Avert these omens!' There are similar passages for the timpani in the *Song for St. Cecilia's Day*.

Song for St. Cecilia's Day   Handel

. pia   for

In the first two bars the drums (marked down to *pia*) are completely solo. The figure occurs later on the lower drum (A). In *Solomon* there is an outburst to suggest the 'shaking of the dome'. When Timotheus (tenor) awakens the monarch in Part II of *Alexander's Feast* ('Break his bands of sleep asunder and rouse him like a peal of thunder') the drums, hitherto silent, add their voice in a sequence rendered the more effective by their being reserved for this particular moment.

Alexander's Feast   Handel

Similarly, the impact of the first entry of the drums in the 'Hallelujah Chorus'. Of this, Charles L. White says[1]: 'Few composers who have followed this great master have written more effectively for the kettledrums than did Handel. The 'Hallelujah Chorus' from his *Messiah* remains one of the most thrilling and effective parts ever written for the kettledrums, and it is one of the best examples of writing for the *character* of these instruments.' Handel was fully aware of the kettledrummer's craft. In *Semele* there occurs a series of semiquavers:

Semele   Handel

These were known to timpanists of his day as 'double tonguing', a technical term borrowed, with others, from the trumpeters a century or so earlier by German kettle-drummers, and fully described by Altenburg.

Lengthy periods of demi-semiquavers occur in *Ricardo I* matching figures in the strings etc. The dynamic markings are interesting; they surely disprove the comments by certain authorities that, at this period, the kettledrums were reserved for loud passages.

Ricardo I   Handel

In the 'Dead March' in *Saul* the drums (marked *p*) intensify the sombre character of the march. There is no instruction for the drums to be covered (muffled), suggesting that on this occasion at least, covered sticks may have been used. Handel frequently

[1] White, C. L. *Drums Through the Ages*, Sterling Press, Los Angeles, 1960, p. 147.

indicated the tremolo (usually ⎯⎯⎯⎯). An effective use of the roll is observed in *Israel in Egypt* ('He rebuked the Red Sea').

In the 'March Grave' from *Joshua* a tremolo sign is given beneath a series of demi-semiquavers. It is possible that a series of dots was intended, as indicated elsewhere. The addition of *tr* to the curved *tr⎯* sign in bar 5 in this march is the only occasion on which Handel indicates the roll in this way. There are frequent instances in manuscripts (not autographed, but published in Handel's lifetime) of a final bar being indicated so: ⊞⎯⎯⎯⎯⊞. (In several of these manuscripts the drums are referred to as *tympano*, probably in the hand of Handel's amanuensis, as the composer invariably used the contraction *tymp*. Only in a footnote to *La Réjouissance* (*Music for the Royal Fireworks*) do we find a reference to kettledrums in his scores).

On some occasions Handel's instructions are imprecise, as for instance, in the final chords in the 'Hallelujah Chorus' and 'Amen' (*Messiah*), where no roll is written. Also speculative is Handel's instruction for *Drum ad libitum wirbel* in the autographed score of *Joshua*. No part for the timpani is written for the chorus concerned – 'See the conquering Hero comes'. (This chorus was later transferred to *Judas Maccabaeus* as a tribute to the Duke of Cumberland). Chrysander in the Handel Society edition has noted *Timpani ad libituam tremolando per la seconda volta*, and applied the instruction to bars 1–16 and 25–32. Bars 17–24 are marked *senza*. Handel, it will be observed, says 'drum' not 'timpani' (or his more usual 'tymp'). Possibly he had in mind a continuous roll on a side drum, or the player to extemporise a rhythmic part to comply with the text, 'Sound the trumpet, beat the drum'. (The use of the kettledrum is arguable, for Handel never used the timpani in the key of the chorus in question – G major.) The side drum may have been used on occasions in the oratorio *Judas Maccabaeus*, in the chorus 'See the conquering Hero comes'. It was certainly specified in the instrumental version of this march.

Instructions for the use of side drums are given in the *Music for the Royal Fireworks*. In the Menuet Handel says: *La terza volta tutti insieme and the Side Drums*. In the Overture he prescribes *Tymp 3 per parte*. On the occasion of the first performance of this work (1749), tradition has it that no fewer than sixteen kettledrums and twelve side drums were used, anticipating to some extent Berlioz in his *Grande Messe des Morts*.

Handel could be credited with other originalities, e.g. the use of the effect of gunfire. After the first performance of *Judas Maccabaeus* (April 1st 1747), Miss Elizabeth

Carter in a letter to her friend Mrs. Catherine Talbot, said:[1] '. . . in this last oratorio he has literally introduced guns, and they have a good effect'. Of this, Winton Dean writes:[2] 'The guns were probably the outsize drums from the Tower of London in "Sound an alarm"'.

In addition to the works so far mentioned, the timpani are prominent in the *Dettingen Te Deum* and the *Occasional Oratorio*, to mention but two. It was for such moments as 'The Nations tremble at the dreadful sound, Heavens thunder, trumpets roar' and the battle between the Israelites and the Canaanites in *Joshua* that Handel may have first used the great kettledrums of the artillery.[3] He made frequent requests to the Master General for the use of these instruments which were known as the 'Tower Drums'. An entry in the Minute Book of the Board of Ordnance dated March 13th 1748 reads: 'That when Mr. Handel sends to the Tower for the Train Kettle Drums, they must be delivered to his Order, and his Indent taken to return them', An official indenture of the Board of Ordnance 26th February 1749 refers to Handel having received out of His Majesty's Store at the Tower, the Train Kettle Drums (a pair), and that they were directed to be lent to him for the use of his Oratorios, and to be returned when the same is ended. There seems little doubt that these notable instruments were used in the same year in the original performance of the *Music for the Royal Fireworks* for the Peace of Aix-la-Chapelle in Green Park. In February 1750, with another season of oratorios about to begin, Handel again begged the Master General for the use of the Artillery Kettle Drums. His original letter is in the British Museum.

Further entries in the Board of Ordnance records, dated 1753 and 1756 refer to requests on behalf of Handel for the use of His Majesty's Kettle Drums. That they were used after Handel's death, in 1759, is confirmed by an entry in the Official Records of 1762, and in a description by Dr. Charles Burney of the Handel Commemoration Festival of 1784.

From Handel's repeated requests for these instruments it is obvious that he considered their tone superior to the available orchestral timpani. According to Dr. Farmer[4] the measurements of the Artillery Drums (deduced from the comparative

[1] Carter, Elizabeth. *Letters*. F. C. & J. Rivington, London, 1808, vol. I, p. 134.

[2] Dean, Winton. *Handel's Dramatic Oratorios and Masques*, Oxford, London, 1959, p. 471.

[3] It is possible that it was in one of these choruses that the famous Jenkinson made his historic 'domino' of which Victor de Pontigny says: 'Even the late Mr. Jenkinson, the chief drummer of his day (the predecessor of Chipp), once came in a bar too soon in a chorus of "Joshua", and was so mortified that he inflicted summary punishment on himself by beating his own head with his sticks.' (From 'On Kettledrums', *Proceedings of the Musical Association*, vol. II, Spottiswoode, London, 1876, p. 54.)

[4] Farmer, H. G. *Handel's Kettledrums*, Hinrichsen, London, 1950, p. 94.

measurements of the model of the chariot in the Rotunda Museum, Woolwich) approximated to almost 36 and 38 inches respectively.[1] These measurements are mentioned in Burney's description of the 1784 Festival[2], where he speaks of 'two pairs of common kettle-drums, two pairs of double drums from the Tower, and a pair of double-base drums, made expressly for this Commemoration.'[3] The double-base drums to which Dr. Burney refers were instruments made from models designed by John Ashbridge, timpanist of Drury Lane Theatre Orchestra. According to Victor de Pontigny (considered as an authority on kettledrums in the latter half of the nineteenth century) they measured 35 and 39 inches in diameter, and yet he says they were 'much larger' than the Tower kettledrums. By 'larger' he almost certainly meant 'deeper', since Dr. Burney says the Tower drums were 'hemispherical . . . but those of Mr. Ashbridge are more cylindrical, being much longer as well as more capacious than the common kettle-drum', the latter factor according to the worthy Doctor, accounting for the superiority of their tone to that of all other drums (He also says that the drums were made in copper, it being impossible to procure plates of brass large enough, and that in the *Dettingen Te Deum* they had all the effect of the most powerful artillery.) In Dr. Burney's opinion, the three species of kettledrum, which he called 'tenor', 'base' and 'double-base', were an octave below each other. In this opinion he may have been mistaking the difference in the quality of sound for a difference in pitch, a not unpardonable error: many excellent musicians experience difficulty in defining the nominal note of a kettledrum. To quote Berlioz[4]: 'The sound of the kettledrums is not very low, it is played as it is written in the F clef in unison with the corresponding notes on the violon-cellos, and not an octave below as musicians have supposed'.

The common kettledrums which Burney calls the tenor, would sound

as the key demanded. Dr. Farmer says[5]: 'The "tenor" was, seemingly, the common *timpani* of the period, and they would certainly be larger than the ordinary kettledrum of the cavalry of those days which had a diameter of 19 inches and 21 inches, as we know from official sources.' (Furthermore, had the common kettledrums been small cavalry instruments with diameters of 19

---

[1] The original instruments are considered to have perished by fire in 1841.

[2] Burney, Charles *An Account of the Musical Performance in Westminster Abbey*, London, 1785, Part II, pp. 28–29.

[3] Dr. Farmer says: 'It is, of course, not improbable that *two* pairs of Tower kettledrums may have been a slip for *one* pair.' ibid. p. 93. This could well be, since Burney names four players; Burnet, Houghton, Nelson & Mr. As(h)bridge on the double kettledrum.

[4] Berlioz, Hector. *Instrumentation*, Lemoine, Paris, 1844, p. 267.

[5] Farmer, H. G. ibid. p. 95.

and 21 inches, an octave higher than [musical notation] would in any case have been impracticable, both mechanically and musically.) The Tower drums sounded (and here Burney was correct) one octave lower than the common kettledrums,[1] giving Handel an octave bass on the occasions when he employed these particular instruments, i.e., their parts were played an octave lower than written.

Handel's use of the *octave basso* could be claimed as an orchestral innovation. So was his use in the orchestra of an instrument which served the purpose of the present-day glockenspiel. Deutsch says[2]: 'The most exotic stroke in the dramatic oratorios is the introduction of a specially constructed carillon or glockenspiel, which transposed down a fourth, for the festivities in Act I of *Saul*.' Charles Jennens, with whom Handel collaborated, refers to this instrument in a letter written to his cousin Lord Guernsey. Jennens (who often criticised Handel) speaks of a visit to the composer whilst the libretto of *Saul* was in progress. He says[3]: 'Mr. Handel's head is more full of maggots than ever. I found yesterday in his room a very queer instrument which he calls carillon (*Anglice*, a bell) and says some call a *Tubalcain*, I suppose because it is both in the make and tone like a set of hammers striking upon anvils. 'Tis played upon with keys like a Harpsichord and with this Cyclopean instrument he designs to make poor Saul stark mad.' The instrument had a chromatic compass of

32 notes: [musical notation]. Opinions differ as to whether it was comprised of **true**

bells or metal plates. Percy Scholes in the *Oxford Companion to Music* says real bells, Sachs concludes metal plates, while Gevaert mentions an instrument resembling a toy imitation of the Flemish Church Carillons. Of this, he says[4]: 'Let us take, first of all, the carillon used by Handel in a passage of the oratorio *Saul*: when the Israelite women go to meet the young David, vanquisher of the Philistine giant, singing and dancing to the sound of the Tambourines and Triangles. The part written by the composer gives every evidence that it is a question of a *Jeu de timbres*[5] embracing the compass of two octaves and a fourth, and provided with a chromatic keyboard which can be played with two hands (although the music is written on a single stave). The notation is conceived as for a transposing instrument in G: the real sounds would be produced a fifth higher than written. On a carillon of real bells, the lowest (sounding C3) would have a weight of 2862 kg! One can imagine the

[1] The Tower drums could not be tensioned to [musical notation]
[2] Deutsch, O. E. *Handel*, Black, London, 1955, pp. 465-6.
[3] Deutsch, O. E. ibid. p. 466.
[4] Gevaert, F. ibid. p. 237.
[5] A keyboard glockenspiel.

construction of the instrument but can you imagine such a musical Leviathan installed in a concert hall or theatre!'

Thurston Dart, in conversation with the author, said: '... from Jennens' description, I'm inclined to think that Handel's instrument was a sort of very loud, damper-free, keyed dulcimer, with a very metallic bell-like tone.' Jennens' reference to hammers striking upon anvils certainly suggests a series of metal plates rather than small bells. Whatever the form, Handel was clearly impressed by this invention. He used the instrument in other works, including revivals of *Trionfo del Tempo*, *Acis and Galatea*, and in *L'Allegro ed il Penseroso*. In the latter work the part for the carillon occurs in 'Or let the merry bells ring round'. (Thurston Dart added: 'I feel the "old man" must have played this himself, it's a frightfully difficult part'.)

L'Allegro, il Penseroso   Handel

Carillon

Whether, in view of the present-day focus on 'tuned percussion', Jennens was entirely correct in attributing Handel's carillon to the maggots in his head, is a matter of opinion.[1]

Towards the middle of the eighteenth century a number of compositions appeared introducing a decided advance in the use of orchestral timpani. The first of these was a Concerto Grosso, published in Edinburgh in 1743, by Francesco Barsanti, an Italian from Lucca who came to England in 1714. Barsanti made demands on the timpanist not hitherto encountered. During the work, which is divided into two groups of five successive movements, the drums function in three keys: F, D, and C. In the first two movements – both in the key of F – the timpani are tuned in fifths, with the dominant above the tonic 𝄢. In Movements III, IV and V, which are in the key of D, the drums are tuned in fourths, with the dominant below the tonic. 𝄢 In Part II of the work, the first three movements are in C, followed by two movements in D, with the drums tuned respectively 𝄢 and 𝄢

---

[1] In recent performances of *Saul*, in England and abroad, the part for the carillon was played on two orchestral glockenspiels (mallet), the octaves divided.

Barsanti's use of the timpani in fourths and fifths and his use of the low F, though unusual in Britain, was no innovation as we have observed in works by such earlier composers as Vejvanovsky and Bach. It is the change of pitch during the work that qualifies Barsanti as a pioneer, for there is no previous record of such a procedure, the pitch of the drums hitherto remaining unchanged throughout an entire work. Barsanti's novel treatment of the kettledrums (frequently attributed to later composers) was probably the result of his familiarity with these instruments as a practising musician. He was a flautist and oboist of repute in London circles. After Hertel and Molter came the Italian composer Antonio Salieri, whose innovatory treatment of the timpani could well have influenced Beethoven (his pupil). In the opera *La grotta di Trofonio* (*c.* 1785) Salieri used the unusual interval of C and G♭ followed by a change to D and A to be effected during a tacet period of sixteen bars. In *Tarare* (1787) the drums are tuned to a major third (B♭ & D) and are heard in the chords of D, E♭, G minor and B♭. In an earlier work, *La Secchia rapita* (1772), three drums tuned to C, G and D are used in the key of C.

The second work was by the German composer Johann Melchior Molter (1695–1765), a prolific composer who was highly esteemed in his day. In his Sinfonia No. 99 (in F) for two clarini, two flutes, viola, cembalo, and timpani (*c.* 1750) he writes for five kettledrums tuned to F, G, A, B flat, and C. Molter possibly wrote the work for a reigning virtuoso. The writing is adventurous but entirely practical. This could also be said of a Sinfonia for eight obbligato timpani with orchestra attributed to J. W. Hertel (*c.* 1748). This work includes a complete cadenza for the drums.[1] (Kastner[2] refers to the performance by the premier Berlin timpanist, of a Concerto for ten timpani, accompanied by eight trumpets and full orchestra. The drums were situated in a raised gallery and the performer ran from one to the other, throwing the sticks in the air and executing other extraordinary feats. In contrast, Kastner refers to the lack of skill outside the main cities).[3]

Excluding Mozart's more subdued employment of two pairs of kettledrums, more than half a century was to elapse before the timpani were again exploited in the style of Molter, Hertel and Salieri, Barsanti's approach remained unique for a shorter period – until the time of Haydn.

[1] Outstanding writing for the timpani occurs in works by Christoph Graupner and Ferdinand Kauer. In a quartet for violino piccolo, zither, xylophone and bassoon, Kauer made florid use of the xylophone. (see later reference p. 309)

[2] Kastner, J. G. *Méthode de Timbales*, Schlesinger, Paris, 1845, p. 72.

[3] 'Kettledrum recitals were not unknown in England. In 1734 at Drury Lane Theatre the timpanist, Poitier (a player who could have collaborated with Barsanti) is reported as performing a preamble on the kettledrums. (Scouten, A. H. *The London Stage 1660–1806*, Part 3, 1729–49, Southern Illinois University Press, 1961, p. 391.)

Haydn became conversant with the timpani at an early age, whilst at school in Hainburg. Here, in return for his services as a chorister, he was educated in the rudiments of music. The Hainburg household boasted a small orchestra in which Haydn performed, his aptitude making it possible for him to fill many of the gaps that occurred from time to time in the ensemble. On the death of the timpanist the boy became the orchestra's kettledrummer. His early love of these instruments continued throughout his lifetime. In London in 1791, when he played the timpani in one of his symphonies, his skilful performance was applauded by the whole orchestra.

Speaking of Haydn conducting at the Salomon concerts in London in 1794, Sir George Smart says[1]: 'At a rehearsal for one of these concerts the kettledrummer was not in attendance. Haydn asked, "Can no one in the orchestra play the drums!" I replied immediately, "I can.' 'Do so," said he. I, foolishly, thought it was only necessary to beat in strict time, and that I could do so. Haydn came to me at the top of the orchestra, praised my beating in time, but observed upon my bringing the drumstick straight down, instead of giving an oblique stroke, and keeping it too long upon the drum, consequently stopping its vibration. "The drummers in Germany," he said, "have a way of using the drumsticks so as not to stop the vibration" – at the same time showing me how this was done. "Oh, very well," I replied, we "can do so in England, if you prefer it." It was Haydn, therefore, who first taught me to play the drums. . . .'

It is no surprise to find many of Haydn's symphonies and his choral works graced with finely written parts for the timpani. He employed the instruments rhythmically, harmoniously and dramatically, and with no problem of execution for the player. He did not transpose. H. C. Robbins Landon says[2]: 'Haydn was always very forward-looking in the matter of technical notation for his musicians, and he was writing timpani in real (as opposed to transposed) notation while Mozart was still writing C – G for tonic – dominant whatever the key.'

Haydn broke away from the convention of his Teutonic predecessors inasmuch as he scored for the drums in more than one key during a single work. In *The Creation* (1799), there are seven changes of tuning. Here, as in *The Seasons*, Haydn employs the low B flat and F (a common procedure from now on).[3] In Symphony No. 102 (1794) he uses covered kettledrums with muted trumpets (con sordini).[4]

---

[1] Smart, George. *Leaves from the Journals of Sir George Smart*, ed. Cox and Cox, Longmans, London, 1907, p. 3.

[2] Landon, H. C. Robbins. *Haydn Symphonies*, BBC Music Guides, London, 1966, p. 17.

[3] Changing pitch remained a slow and laborious business as the tuning screws were still operated by a loose tuning key.

[4] Cf. Mozart. *Idomeneo* and *The Magic Flute*.

The solo roll (on E flat) which opens Symphony No. 103 (1795) is an effect new to the orchestra and gives the work its name: *Paukenwirbel (Drum-roll)*. This symphony was written at a time of great national stress, and the roll itself may well have hinted at the current threat of war. If so, Haydn intended the roll to sound ominous; in which case it is not unlikely that he exploited the use of covered sticks. H. C. Robbins Landon in a conversation with the author said: 'Surely not hard sticks on this roll!'

In the autographed score of this Symphony, presented by the composer to Cherubini in 1800, the opening drum roll is given: . The autographed score of the *Missa in Angustiis* in D minor (*Nelson* Mass) gives a held note in the same manner: also a tremolo sign over a series of semiquavers: In the Breitkopf & Härtel 1803 edition of the Mass in C, (*Paukenmesse* 1796) occurs several times. In this work which Haydn himself calls *Missa in tempore bello*, the timpani are used throughout. The solo (ten bars in length) in 'Agnus Dei', with its crescendo spread over the final four bars is outstanding.

Equally arresting is the growl of thunder (from a series of demi-semiquavers) in *The Creation*. In Symphony No. 94, the *Surprise* (called in German *Paukenschlag* – 'Drumstroke'), Haydn's well-known joke engages the timpani, with the orchestra, in a brief moment of frivolity. (A sense of fun is apparent in the *Toy* Symphony: for so long attributed to Haydn, this work is now considered to be by Leopold Mozart. The toy instruments, possibly added by Michael Haydn, include a drum, triangle, rattle, quail and cuckoo.)

In the *Military* Symphony No. 100 (1794) Haydn added local colour by including 'percussion' from the forces of the Janissary military band – bass drum with stick and switch, cymbals and triangle. These instruments had appeared in earlier compositions, e.g. cymbals in Strungk's opera *Esther* (1680). Cymbals with other Turkish instruments were featured in Freschi's spectacular opera *Berenice* performed in

Padua in 1680. The triangle, according to Sachs, was employed in the Hamburg Opera as early as 1710. In 1717 two triangles were purchased for the Dresden Opera. Bass drum and cymbals occur in Gluck's *Le Cadi dupé* (1761), *The Pilgrims of Mecca* and *La Recontre imprévue* (1764). Gluck appears to have been the first composer to have given the bass drum a place in orchestral music. The earliest use of the tambourine could also be attributed to him: *Echo and Narcissus* (1779). Grétry wrote for the triangle in *La fausse Magie* (1775), and for the tambourine and triangle in *La Caravane du Caire* (1783), the parts to be improvised. Of Gluck's scoring for the cymbals in *Iphigenie en Tauride* (1779), Berlioz said that there had never been a finer effect of cymbals produced than that in the chorus of Scythians. In *Il Seraglio* (1782) Mozart represented the popular Janissary music with his use of bass drum, cymbals and triangle. The cymbals of this period are illustrated as smaller instruments than those used in the modern symphony orchestra, and the triangle would probably be equipped with jingling metal rings strung on the horizontal section, an accoutrement which persisted until the early part of the nineteenth century, when the instrument, relieved of its jingling contrivance, became a permanent member of the orchestra.

Towards the end of Haydn's life came the oratorios, *The Creation* and *The Seasons*, each with a rewarding timpani part. Haydn died on 31st May, 1809, and at the funeral was sung the immortal Requiem of Mozart. Like Haydn, Mozart made no unusual demands on the timpanist. On paper, in fact, his requirements appear to be slight, but in practice, his writing for the timpani (as for all instruments) calls for the highest degree of musicianship. With only one exception Mozart confined the tuning of the drums (a pair) to the interval of a fourth, with the tonic in its usual position above the dominant. This interval is so religiously observed, that the timpani are omitted from works in the keys of G and A for instance, where, because of the compass of the drums, the interval of a fifth with the dominant above the tonic would be necessary.[1] Professor Kirby says[2]: 'Mozart, however, must have recognised the value of tuning in fifths as well as in fourths, since in his curious Divertimenti for two flutes, three trumpets in C, two trumpets in D and four kettle-drums in G and C and A and D, composed about 1773, the fifth is used, though between one drum of one pair, and one of the other. The parts, however, would

---

[1] A pair of timpani at this period would doubtless cover an octave, so: ♪. Horemans' *Portrait of a Musician* (1762) shows a pair of drums which in perspective approach (in diameter) the standard pair of timpani used to-day, which cover the octave mentioned (allowing an upper or lower dominant in the keys of F and B flat).

[2] Kirby, P.R. *The Kettle-Drums*, Oxford, 1930, p. 14.

appear to have been written for one player upon *two pairs* of drums.' The author is inclined to share Professor Kirby's opinion, particularly as there seems no record of a separate part for each pair of timpani.

Divertimento K188   Mozart

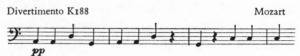

Mozart's reticence in employing the drums tuned in fifths may have sprung from one of several reasons. Due to the phenomenon of sympathetic resonance[1] tuning in fourths may have seemed to his super sensitive ear the interval par excellence on a pair of drums; or he may have been influenced by the tradition surrounding this mode of tuning. Since he gave the timpani no place in works where the keys would have required them to be tuned in fifths (compositions where trumpets are engaged included) it is clear that he had an aversion to placing the tonic below the dominant. For example in Symphony No. 32 where the drums are engaged in the key of G, they are not tuned in the usual manner, in fifths, but to an interval of a fourth, with the high G (the tonic) as the upper note.[2] Admittedly the drum part was added to the original score in a contemporary hand, but it is considered authentic. An identical part is included in a very early copy of the score in the National Museum, Prague.[3]

In Mozart's arrangement of Handel's *Messiah* the use of the timpani in D and A and C and G during the chorus No. 12, 'For unto us' calls for the use of either four drums, or a change of tuning on one pair. Whether Mozart intended four drums, or the timpanist to make the change of tuning during a *tacet* period (for the drums) of eleven bars is uncertain. In modern orchestral parts the timpanist is instructed to

[1] cf. Modern technical approach.

[2] The Viennese composer, Florian Gassman (many of whose works Mozart admired) employed the higher notes of the timpani in the key of D in his opera *L'Issipile* (1758) ♩. A further instance of the early use of the upper register is to be found in a work by the Italian composer Sacchini. In the overture to his opera *Oedipe à Colone* (1786) Sacchini, described by Burney as a 'graceful, elegant and judicious composer', scored for the high and normal B flat, also the high and low F ♩. Here would seem not only the first request for the drums in octaves and the employment of a *piccolo timpano*, but a decidedly novel approach to the use of the tonic and dominant.

Oedipe à Colone   Sacchini

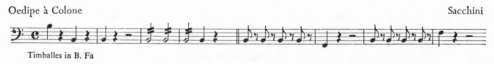

Timballes in B. Fa

[3] The final note for the timpani in the penultimate bar of this work is rarely played.

change D and A to C and G. No such instruction appears in the full score, however. It is unfortunately impossible to refer to the autographed score as the first two parts of the original have been lost (Part 3 is in the National Museum, Prague). The authenticity of the instruction to change pitch, therefore, is doubtful. To effect an accurate change of pitch on two drums (equipped with square-topped tensioning screws) during the course of eleven bars rest, would be no simple matter, as the fitting of the loose key (silently) to at least twelve screws[1] would use up the available *tacet* period and leave no time for a final check. Whether or not the timpanists of Mozart's time were capable of making the change, this procedure did not become common practice until a later date. Nor for that matter did the use of more than one pair of timpani became a common practice.

Though Mozart called for the use of four drums (unless he considered a change of pitch practical), it should be noted that during this *Messiah* chorus in the key of G, he did not employ a drum on D to strengthen certain dominant chords, particularly those in the first half of the final bar. Another instance, maybe, of his unwillingness to use the drums in fifths.

With reference to technical details, Mozart in general made a sparing use of the roll (which he indicated – *tr.* or ⸺). In some cases he treated the timpani as transposing instruments, in each case the notes being written as was usual, on C and G. Only rarely did he give a solo to the drums, as in the *Requiem* (Sanctus), and Symphonies 39 and 41, and in the contrasting texture employed in *Serenata Notturna* (K.239) where the timpani are engaged with strings only in the second orchestra. In *Idomeneo* (1781) and *The Magic Flute* (1791) we find early instances of the term *coperti*. Coperti implies that the drums be muffled by placing a piece of cloth on the membrane. Eisel and Altenburg referred to the procedure of muffling drums on such occasions as funerals. Eisel's alternative of covering the sticks is given by some authorities as applying in later instances to coperti, though this certainly does not apply to-day. It is generally agreed that Mozart's indication referred to the covering of the drumheads. Mozart's muffled drums accompany muted trumpets. In *Idomeneo* (Act III) a quick change to non-coperti (with open trumpets) is indicated. Though the change is practicable (if the drums be played with one hand whilst the other removes the muffling material), it is possible that Mozart may have envisaged additional drums. Cf. Mahler Symphony No. I.

It is in *The Magic Flute* that Mozart scored for the glockenspiel (*Istrumento d'acciaio*) to represent Papageno's chime of magic bells. As with Handel's carillon,

[1] Many drums of this period show a greater number of side screws. Kastner (1845) speaks of six to ten on the small drum, eight to thirteen on the large drum – also of the noisy operation of changing pitch.

opinions are divided as to whether the instrument consisted of metal bars, or was a small adaptation of the carillon. Sachs believes that it was metal slabs, but Berlioz is confident it was a great number of small bells operated by a mechanism of keys.[1] Gevaert is of the opinion that it was a similar instrument to that employed by Handel. He says[2]: 'Now let us cite the Glockenspiel of the *Magic Flute*, which is also a carillon of bells. Like Handel's it goes down to a sounding C3 while its upward compass is a fifth higher. The part is brilliantly executed, the arpeggios, runs and scales make a splendid accompaniment to Papageno's, the happy birdfancier, arias. Mozart wrote it in two staves with the correct clef signs, but an octave lower than the real sounds.' (To-day, quite often a combination of celeste and pianoforte-action glockenspiel is utilised.)

Magic Flute   Mozart

Papageno's 'glockenspiel' suggested a little joke to Mozart. In a letter to his wife (dated October 1791) he referred to a performance of *The Magic Flute*, during which he slipped into the wings and played the offstage glockenspiel in the wrong places, much to the annoyance of Papageno who finally struck the instrument and shouted 'Shut up.' Mozart felt that his prank taught many of the audience for the first time that Papageno does not play the instrument himself.[3]

[1] An instrument of the latter type, consisting of small mushroom bells (like bicycle bells) was left at the Royal Opera House, Covent Garden, by the Italian Opera Company in the early part of the century.

[2] Gevaert, François. ibid. p. 327.

[3] There was the famous baritone playing Papageno, who remarked to an equally famous conductor, that friends had complained of difficulty in hearing the little bells with which he mimed – to which the maestro replied 'Then play them louder.'

The Classical Orchestra

The tambourine is included (with cymbals) in Mozart's *German Dances*, K.571 (1787). (It is signified *tamburino*.) His use of tuned sleigh bells (*Schlitten-schellen*) in the three *German Dances* K.605 remains unique.

German Dances K605   Mozart

The bells occur in the well-known F major trio, which has become known as *The Sleigh Ride*.

As has already been mentioned, Mozart employed the bass drum, cymbals, and triangle in *Il Seraglio*. Here, the instruments are given their Italian names: *Tamburo grande, Piatti, Triangolo*. At this period, the Tamburo grande is usually depicted as a double-headed drum with a deep cylinder, corresponding to the English 'long drum' *q.v.* It is frequently illustrated as being struck in the Oriental fashion, that is, with a stick on one side, and a switch of twigs or a split-rod on the other side, or at times the switch striking the shell of the drum. Mozart indicates this style by the use of 'tails up' and 'tails down' (a method used normally to indicate the combination of bass drum and cymbals). ♩ or ♩ Of this, Julius Reitz in a Breitkopf & Härtel score of 1868, says: 'The double notes on the bass drum are to-day, to many inexplicable. It should therefore be noticed, that this instrument was struck on both sides: on the right side with the drum stick, and on the left side with the switch (Ruthe). The notes which are placed upwards (the quicker strokes) stand for the switch, and the under notes for the stick.' (This interesting effect is evident in the swish of the modern [jazz] wire brushes.)

By the middle of the eighteenth century Europe was under the sway of the Turkish music known as 'Janissary' music, a name taken from the Sultan's life guards. In this music the focus was on percussion, with the emphasis on the 'beat'. According to Schubart, composer and poet of this period[1]: 'No other genre of music requires so firm, decided and overpoweringly predominant a beat. The first beat of each bar is so strongly marked with a new and manly accent that it is virtually impossible to get out of step.'

A full Janissary band could include a number of bass drums, numerous pairs of cymbals, small kettledrums, triangles, tambourines and one or more Turkish crescents (*chapeau chinois*). The latter instrument, called in England 'Jingling Johnnie', was an upright pole with a decorative headpiece of metal in the form of a crescent

[1] Schubart, L. ed. *C. F. D. Schubart's Ideen zu einer Ästhetik der Tonkunst*, Vienna, 1806, pp. 330–1.

and other symbols, from which points were suspended small bells and jingles. Further ornamentation consisted of horse-tail plumes in different colours. Berlioz says the shaking of its 'sonorous locks' adds brilliancy to marching music.[1] These percussion instruments were invariably played by negroes, who were elaborately

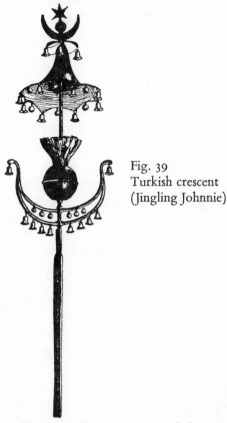

Fig. 39
Turkish crescent
(Jingling Johnnie)

dressed, and indulged in all sorts of contortions whilst playing. Only the more restrained of these gestures survive, the best known being the stick twirling by the bass and tenor drummers. Of the exotic costume only the leopard skin apron, worn by the former, remains.

With the exception of the Turkish crescent,[2] these instruments gained a foothold in serious compositions and to-day, with a host of other percussion instruments, they take their place quite naturally in orchestral scores.[1]

The Janissary music continued popular until the early part of the nineteenth century. Beethoven utilized the combination of bass drum, cymbals and triangle in

[1] A remarkable style of music that was destined to witness a distinct revival in the Early Music Consorts of the present century.

the finale of the Ninth Symphony (1823). In the original score these are given as *gran Tamburo*, *Cinelli* and *Triangolo*. They are given a treble clef signature.[1] An early sketch of this work states: '... end of the Symphony with Turkish music'. Earlier, in *The Ruins of Athens* (1812) in the chorus of dervishes, he wrote that all the noisy instruments possible, castanets, cymbals, etc., were to be employed. In the Turkish March in this work, the score includes bass drum, cymbals and triangle.

Percussion is to the fore in Beethoven's *Wellington's Victory* or *The Battle of Vittoria*, composed in 1813. This work, which Beethoven called *Battle* Symphony (by which name it is generally known), was written in the first place for the Panharmonicon, an automatic musical instrument invented by Maelzel (the inventor of the metronome, and incidentally, the maker of Beethoven's ear trumpet). Due to Maelzel's influence, the work was quickly transferred to the orchestra. The percussion included timpani, side drums, bass drums, and ratchets (cog-rattle). The side drums represent the opposing armies, each camp having its individual rhythm.

(The drum marches, it is said, were composed by Maelzel.) The bass drums suggest the cannons, marked in the score 'Kanonen' and indicated ✗ Eng. ○ Fr.

The ratchets (*ratsche*) again England and France are assigned to a 🎵〰〰 and are obviously intended as an imitation of rifle fire.[2] The timpani, cymbals, triangle and an extra bass drum play a normal part in the orchestra. This work is little remembered today, other than as a curiosity. It is agreed that it contains little of the genius of Beethoven, and that it was written to a great extent as a favour to Maelzel. At the first performance in Vienna on December 8th 1813, however, it was a furore. In the orchestra were many eminent musicians with Spohr among the violins. Beethoven himself conducted, though he said: 'I would just as gladly have taken over the big drum as Herr Hummel did.' Hummel it seems acted in the cannonade, which was directed by Salieri (composer and conductor). Meyerbeer, it is recorded, played the (orchestral) bass drum, and Moscheles the cymbals.[3] A few days later the work was again performed and received with the same enthusiasm.

With the exception of the *Battle* Symphony and the *Ruins of Athens* music, and the part for stage side drum in the music for Goethe's drama *Egmont* (1810),

[1] Most unusual, particularly for the bass drum.

[2] These were probably similar to the large rattle (*matraca*) illustrated in Filippo Bonanni's *Gabinetto Armonico*, 1723.

[3] At a concert given by Moscheles in London in 1832 Mendelssohn played the bass drum in Moscheles' *Fall of Paris*.

Beethoven it seems made no further call on the so-called 'Turkish Music' until 1823 (Ninth Symphony). It is the timpani whose resources were fully exploited and realised in the compositions of this musical giant. Due to Beethoven's enterprise the kettledrum became in every musical sense a solo instrument, and achieved a position of eminence in the orchestra. Forsyth considered Beethoven the great innovator in the drum department. He says[1]: 'With a delicate and truthful perception of its "fundamental" nature he built up its rhythmic-musical sounds into the very substance of his works. It was for this purpose that he enlarged its scope and removed its former restrictions.' This is certainly no overstatement. Hitherto, if we exclude such isolated exceptions as the unusual tuning employed by the Brothers Philidor, the work by Molter, Salieri's use of the major third, and Sacchini's *Oedipe à Colone*, the kettledrums have functioned solely in fourths and fifths, on the tonic and dominant notes of the key. Purcell, Bach, Handel, Haydn and Mozart religiously observed these intervals, Beethoven by no means so. In *Fidelio* he employed (significantly) a diminished fifth 𝄢. Later, in the scherzo of the Seventh Symphony the drums are a minor sixth apart 𝄢, and in the Eighth and Ninth Symphonies they are tuned in octaves 𝄢.

Beethoven was also innovatory in the manner in which he employed the traditional intervals. His use of fourths and fifths is considered unparalleled, and here again we find him highly individual. In the key of B flat he arranged the drums either in fourths or fifths to suit his needs 𝄢 or 𝄢. Tunings of this description point, not only to Beethoven's practical knowledge and invention (possibly after experiment), but to a positive improvement in the instruments themselves. The fact that he used the small drum for the high F in Symphonies Nos. 7, 8 and 9, and for the equally important B flat in No. 4 and the *Missa Solemnis* seems reasonable proof of a range of a fifth with adequate tone both in the high and low register. In the overture to *Fidelio* the large drum is tuned to B natural. In all cases the actual notes are written (never transposed).

In addition to Beethoven's new tunings, such factors as his important solo passages, his remarkable use of the roll, and the effect of his pianissimo (described by Berlioz as marvellous) suggests that he, like Haydn, may have had a personal acquaintance with the instruments. His scrupulous placing of the two notes is best described by Professor Kirby, who says[2]: '. . . Beethoven chooses with con-

[1] Forsyth, Cecil. *Orchestration*, Macmillan, London, 1955, p. 46.
[2] Kirby, P. R. ibid. p. 15.

summate care the particular drum to be used at any given moment, even in "tutti" passages.'

In prescribing only two drums, Beethoven observed an earlier tradition. At times, e.g., when the drums are in octaves, we may feel the occasional lack of the dominant note. In the first movement of the Fourth Symphony (in B flat) in which the drums are tuned to B flat and F, at the end of the exposition occurs a rhythmic tonic and dominant passage in the key of F, in which Beethoven asks only for the lower drum to sound on the tonic chords. In the recapitulation with the passage returning to the original key, the drums play throughout on tonic and dominant. Similar situations occur elsewhere, though to quote P. A. Browne[1]: 'Occasionally the very restrictions under which the older composers laboured have conspired to produce a finer effect than ordinary unrestricted writing would have given.' It seems reasonable to assume that Beethoven was aware that his contemporary and fellow countryman Weber used three drums in the overture to *Peter Schmoll* completed in 1807, and in the overture to *The Ruler of the Spirits* 1811 (generally quoted as the first instances of such treatment). So rather than imply that Beethoven failed to exploit the possibilities of a third drum, it would seem more reasonable to suggest that colouring the orchestra so effectively with only two drums is characteristic of his individuality.

With one exception, the Mass in D (*Missa Solemnis*), and then with ample time to effect the required change of tuning (lower drum A to G), the pitch of the drums is constant throughout Beethoven's movements, though by this period the operation of re-tuning was less laborious and more secure than hitherto. It was an era of experiments with mechanical contrivances to facilitate tuning. It is possible that the timpanists of Beethoven's day had the advantage of T-shaped handles, in place of the square-topped screws requiring a separate handle. (Kastner's[2] chart places this development quite early in the century, other authorities contend the butterfly nut was earlier. He speaks of a similar handle by which the artist can turn the key with a single turn of the hand, very quickly and without noise). In the case of many of Beethoven's compositions this fitment would prove invaluable, for quite often the change of pitch between movements covered virtually the whole range of the drums. On the other hand, the fact that Beethoven never used a three note phrase does not entirely rule out the possibility that individual players may have used a third drum to give easy access to another key, or as an expedient to ensure good

[1] Browne, P. A. 'The Orchestral Treatment of the Timpani,' *Music and Letters*, 1923, vol. IV, January, pp. 334–89.
[2] Kastner, J. G. ibid. p. 18.

notes in solo passages. The best-known examples of solo passages include the octave F's in the scherzo of the Ninth Symphony, the solo to open the Violin Concerto, the remarkable roll covering 25 bars, (continuous for 22), and the solo passage for two drums in the Fourth Symphony, the combination of timpani and soloist in the finale of Piano Concerto No. 5 (*Emperor*), and the transition from the scherzo to the finale of the Fifth Symphony. In the last-named, the soft pulsation of the C timpano throbbing against a background of *arco* strings, is suggestive of a heartbeat. In the Fourth Symphony, the drums (in E flat and B flat) take their turn with other instruments in the melodic structure.

In the coda of the *Emperor* Concerto, a figure which has been heard on all instruments during the movements, is allotted to the drums, and provides a background to the cadenza-style passage of the soloist.[1]

The four solo drum beats (*p*), which open one of Beethoven's most important works, the Violin Concerto, are typical of his confidence in the instrument: in this case to establish a recurrent rhythm and define the keynote. Here Beethoven must surely have desired a fine tone, to 'match' first the orchestral texture and later the soloist.[2] Such a matching tone may have necessitated experiments with covered sticks. Beethoven in his scores specified no particular type of drum stick (an omission which distressed Berlioz); but it is reasonable to suppose that he would not have tolerated a harsh sound from an instrument totally exposed.

If this seemingly simple bar, simple only on paper we hasten to add, gave the early nineteenth-century timpanists (with the instruments at their disposal) as much concern as it does their successors of to-day, they must surely have gone to great lengths to achieve the results Beethoven clearly required. Henry W. Taylor aptly describes the situation as it is to-day[3]: 'Think of that nightmare of perfect tuning and tone colour, the opening of Beethoven's Violin Concerto ... Small wonder that a celebrated conductor once said to me: 'When you can play this, you will be a good timpanist. At that time I thought I was, but I have learned since how right he was!'

[1] It is said that at an early performance of this work in Vienna at which Napoleon was present, the assembled audience, on hearing a roll of drums from without, which announced the Emperor's arrival, was greatly agitated, it being the city's customary mode of fire alarm.

[2] Similarly in the finale of the first movement of the Third Piano Concerto, and the solos in the Fourth Symphony.

[3] Taylor, H. W. *The Art and Science of the Timpani*, John Baker, London, 1964, p. 22.

The drums, again quite solo, are concerned with the solo instrument in Beethoven's arrangement of the Violin Concerto for Piano and Orchestra.

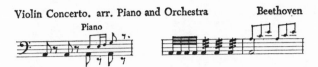

The octave F's in the scherzo of the Ninth Symphony are noteworthy. Here again we find the drums as part of the melodic structure, joining the strings to announce the key of the movement. (Greeted with an ovation at the first performance.)

It used to be said that in the first movement of the Ninth Symphony Beethoven presents the timpanist with an impossibility i.e., maintaining with absolute rigidity the 16 demi-semiquavers in each bar, and passing from drum to drum within what is strictly the space of a demi-semiquaver, as in the following example which is from the present printed score:

Whether or not the passing from drum to drum was Beethoven's initial intention is difficult to say, for in the autographed score (undated) in the *Deutsche Staatsbibliothek*, Berlin, the D is held throughout the bar ( )[1]; whereas in the Royal Philharmonic Society's autographed score of 1823 (in the British Museum) which is in Moscheles' hand, the figure matches the trumpets and is written:

Beethoven's dissatisfaction with incompetent copyists is well known, but it is surprising that a musician of Moscheles' stature should have failed to add the quaver

[1] From Gerassimos Avgerinos, former timpanist of the Berlin Philharmonic Orchestra, who contended the large drum to the right hand ensured a positive final demi-semiquaver.

The Classical Orchestra

tail to the group of four.[1] In the published score dated 1826 (Schott) the passage agrees in principle with Moscheles, though it is written differently (and again incorrectly).

Ninth Symphony
Beethoven

The majority of present editions appear to be taken from the Breitkopf and Härtel edition of 1865, as shown above. The passage, though a difficult one, is not beyond the ability of a competent timpanist. Today (with exceptions), it is certainly played as written, and so no doubt it was by the virtuosi of the past, though in certain printed tutors an alternative is given.

Beethoven's works present many such challenges to the timpanist, as for example the passing from one drum to another in the finale of the First Piano Concerto and the last movement of the Eighth Symphony.[2]

First Piano Concerto Beethoven Eighth Symphony

Here we have a typical kettledrum figure, cross-over beating or Altenburg's double-tonguing. (Similar figures occur in the *Missa Solemnis*.)

It is no easy matter for the player to observe accurately the dynamic variations over which Beethoven was so meticulous; for example:

Seventh Symphony
(Fourth movement) Beethoven

---

[1] In a letter (dated April 1824) to an unknown copyist Beethoven says: 'If all the movements of the symphony are going to be copied as you have copied the first allegro, the whole score will be useless'. *The Letters of Beethoven.* (Letter 1285 p. 1122 vol. 3), edited by Emily Anderson, Macmillan, London, 1961.

[2] It is not improbable that Beethoven, noticing the skill of a particular player of his day, tried out such passages 'on the dog' as it were. Such a procedure is not uncommon at the present time.

He was equally careful in the manner he indicated the true roll: always with the tremolo sign 𝆑——. The numerous occasions on which Beethoven uses 𝄽 (frequently used to-day to define a roll) implies that the demi-semiquavers are to be strictly observed, and not degraded by being played as a roll, as for instance the demi-semiquavers in the above quotation from the Ninth Symphony and those preceding the tremolo in the final bar of the Fifth Symphony, or the hemi-demi-semi quavers 𝅘𝅥𝅲 in the *Missa Solemnis* ('Sanctus'), and in *Fidelio*. (It is now generally accepted that where composers of the classical and romantic period made no use of 𝆑 or —— signs, that unless dotted above, two or more strokes (often according to tempo) indicated a roll. On rare occasions one stroke indicated a roll.[1] Karel Cěrnicky, an eminent Czech timpanist and authority, in his discourse dealing with Smetana's use of the tremolo says[2]: 'Smetana also uses 𝄽 for tremolo sign, also 𝄾 in the finale *Prodana Nevesta*.' Gevaert[3], in discussing the diverse ways in which the roll is indicated, gives a breve five strokes at tempo Largo. Berlioz uses two, three or four strokes. If the bars are tied 𝄽 𝄽 it is reasonably certain that a roll is intended.)

Beethoven's use of the drums in chords has already been mentioned (Bablon and Tedesco anticipating him), though Beethoven's use of this device in such a delicately orchestrated structure as that of the coda in the third movement of the Ninth Symphony, is undeniably original.

Ninth Symphony   Beethoven
in B♭ & F

sempre **pp**   **f**   **pp**

The same could be said of the way in which the drums' rhythmic figure sustains a bass in the Andante of the First Symphony, and the use of the drum, solo and other-wise, in *Prometheus*. Beethoven's influence on subsequent composers is certainly undeniable.

Continuing chronologically, we find Schubert, who, in addition to some fine scoring for the timpani in the Ninth Symphony (*Great* C major) the Mass in

[1] An abbreviation known as *Brillebässe* was used in early scoring for the timpani

[2] Cěrnicky, Karel. *Hudebni Rozhledy* (Musical Views) no. 18, 1962.

[3] Gevaert, François. ibid. p. 324.

A flat and elsewhere, making remarkable use of the upper F sharp on the smaller drum (*Unfinished* Symphony 1822). Like Beethoven, his idol, Schubert used only a pair of drums, but confined their notes to fourths or fifths on the tonic and dominant.

With Schubert, as with Beethoven and earlier composers, the lack of a third drum, and their drummers' inability to re-tune in the course of a movement, undoubtedly led to dissonances. In the first movement of the *Unfinished* Symphony there is a clash so harsh that to-day the part is sometimes modified by changing the B natural drum to C sharp, or alternatively by using an extra drum. In the same movement the drums play on B and F sharp, when a G and D would seem more suitable during a full close in G major. In his Second Symphony Schubert frequently uses B flat in a chord of C major. Whether one should alter the original score in such cases, on the grounds that early composers would have written differently had the full resources of modern technical improvement been at their disposal, is arguable.

Opinions are sharply divided as to the justification of amendments in standard works. That the restrictions under which the older classical composers wrote for the drums resulted in defects is undeniable. P. A. Browne says[1]: 'Every intelligent and conscientious conductor, when he prepares an early classical work for performance, finds himself faced with the problem whether to leave such primitive methods of scoring as he finds them or else to make the most of his composer's musical inspiration and "touch up" the scoring as he feels the composer would have liked it done, had all the modern technical improvements been available for his use.'

There are numerous occasions in the works of Mozart, Beethoven, Schubert, Mendelssohn and Rossini (for example), where there are dissonances which by no means suggest intentional discordances, for here an extra drum, or quick change of tuning would have given the composer access to a more satisfactory note at the point where he obviously desired the additional weight of the drum. With the additional clarity of the modern timpani these dissonances are, to some, intensely disturbing. Many conductors and players are of the opinion that had present-day equipment been available to these early composers, many of these situations would not have occurred, and the timpani parts are altered accordingly, as for instance, the use of the note F in place of the written A in bar 10 of the first movement of Schubert's Third Symphony, or substituting an F for the written G in bars 9, 10, 11 and 12 after letter G in Beethoven's *Coriolan* Overture.[2]

[1] Browne, P. A. ibid. vol. IV, p. 337, January 1923.
[2] Requested from the author by Benjamin Britten.

The Classical Orchestra

In the works of early masters there are also many occasions where the drums are silent, when had it been practical to employ them, there seems little doubt that a part would have been given to them. Many present-day timpanists feel the urge to use a third drum (or a pedal change) to reinforce certain chords in the *Figaro* Overture, or even at times to change the rhythm  to comply with the customary matching with the trumpets. Whether an occasional dressing of this nature is disrespectful is arguable. There are many practising musicians who openly disagree with the purists who consider it sacrilege to tamper with the scores of the great masters. Many eminent musicians have thought fit occasionally to revise.[1] Mengelberg reinforced the horns in the Overture to *Tannhäuser*

Forsyth says[2]: 'According to Strauss, Von Bülow put Beethoven's

on the Mechanical Drums'. Sir Henry Wood's personal score shows this addition to the first movement of the Eighth Symphony, as also

in the Minuet. In Schubert's *Unfinished* Symphony there are interesting additions by Sir Henry, prompted no doubt, as were other examples, by his acquisition of machine drums.[3]

It cannot be denied that the early classical composers were limited in many respects, not only by the mechanical disadvantages inherent in the instruments of their day, but also by the player's reluctance to accept a new feature. In England, as late as 1876, it seems that the improved T handle for instance was not yet accepted.

---

[1] Weingartner, Felix. *On the Performance of Beethoven's Symphonies*, trans. Crosland, Breitkopf and Härtel, London, 1907. Possibly the finest reasoned study of this nature.

[2] Forsyth, Cecil. ibid. p. 51.

[3] The majority of such amendments concern only the timpani, though Stokowski added the xylophone in the second movement of *Scheherazade* and additional percussion to 'Mars' of *The Planets*. Sir Thomas Beecham used a large percussion force in his arrangement of *Messiah*. The author's own temptation (never fufilled) to add a mighty clash of cymbals to announce 'By man came also the resurrection' in *Messiah* may cause certain eyebrows to rise; but he feels it could be defended more easily than the decision of a certain 'bandmaster' to 'cut out' the first bar (the four solo beats on timpani) of the Beethoven Violin Concerto, as 'we know the tempo'!

Victor de Pontigny says[1]: '. . . kettledrums are tuned by means of screws, generally about eight to each, a key being applied successively to each screw. This takes some time, besides causing a slight metallic noise, quite audible if the orchestra is playing softly. Foreign drums have a fixed T-shaped key to each screw, which avoids this, and also saves time. But these fixed keys are in the performer's way in passing from one drum to the other, unless a few of them, at what I may call the tangential point, are made to turn down.[2] Composers should always allow a sufficient number of bars' rest for tuning, and conductors should remember that the drums cannot be ready if there is a change of key between two movements of a symphony, unless they allow sufficient time between those movements.'

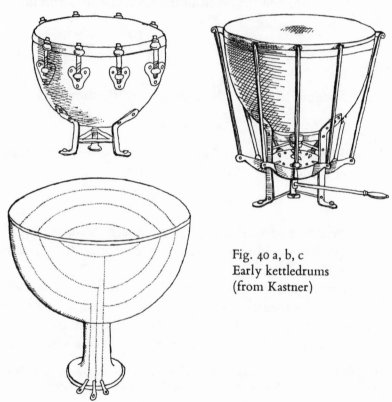

Fig. 40 a, b, c
Early kettledrums
(from Kastner)

The first half of the nineteenth century was a period of constant experiment and progress in the construction of orchestral timpani, particularly in inventions for tuning instantaneously. Innovators in almost every country in Europe made their contribution towards perfecting the mechanically-tuned kettledrum. As early as

[1] Pontigny, Victor de. ibid. p. 51.
[2] Cf. Modern technical approach.

1812, Gerhard Cramer of Munich was responsible for a device whereby the turning of a central screw operated all screws simultaneously, and experiments were made at this period to tune in semitones by a series of pedals. In 1821, J. C. N. Stumpff of Amsterdam applied variable tension by rotating the bowl of the drum (clockwise to tighten).[1] According to Kastner[2] about this time Einlinger in Germany brought forward a system whereby it was possible to perform on a pair of timpani the following passage:

Einlinger's system consisted of a movable hoop just inside the shell, operated by an outer handle. Side screws equalized the tension on the vellum.

In 1827, a French postman named Labbaye was responsible for introducing a mechanically-tuned drum with a regulator system indicating the pressure on the vellum. Labbaye's ingenious instrument did not prove entirely successful. Ten years later, in 1837, an English musical instrument maker, Cornelius Ward of London, patented a cable-tuned kettledrum.[3] (Specification Patents Office, 1837-7505, London.) Here, an endless wire cable passes over pulleys attached to the counter-hoop and shell, and thence to the inside of the drum, where it is connected to threaded brackets working on a long horizontal screw (threaded left and right). The cable is tightened and slackened by means of a single handle on the outside. Ward incorporated a pitch indicator governed by the tension on the cable. Victor de Pontigny says[4]: 'Mr. Ward told me that in the course of his experiments he had found that the note given by a drum under a tension of 37 cwt. was an octave above that given by the same drum with a tension of only 11 cwt.'[5] Ward's instrument, though possessing interesting features, had disadvantages. The stretch on the vellum was uneven, since the tension on the cable was least at the point farthest away from the threaded brackets, resulting in a slight 'flattening' at these points. Also the tone of the drum was somewhat impaired because of the proximity of the internal mechanism to the drumhead.

In addition to this cable-tensioned kettledrum, Ward patented a 'system of tuning by deflecting the head from its horizontal condition'. Here, a rod is passed through a

[1] Retained in the Murbach (Swiss) timpani, and included in the Hinger 'Touch-Tone' Pedal Timpani.

[2] Kastner, J. G. ibid. p. 19.

[3] Ward also patented devices for tensioning side and bass drums.

[4] Pontigny, Victor de. ibid. p. 52.

[5] The musical value of the higher and lower notes of the octave would no doubt be negligible.

hole in the centre of the vellum, with the lower end affixed to the under part of the kettle. The upper end of the rod is threaded to receive a screw nut for applying the pressure. (Later Continental models were tensioned with a central tuning rod.)

1840 saw a single-crew internal mechanism by Boracchi, an Italian (also responsible for a timpanist's manual), drawings of which resemble Ward's model.[1] The latter's system attracted later English makers, including Messrs. Potter and J. Higham the latter designing a modification of Ward's cable-tuned drum, in which the inner rod was replaced by threaded brackets on the exterior of the shell, and the wire tightened and slackened by two (opposite) handles.

In 1843 a German mechanic introduced a pedal-operated machine drum. Here the principle was entirely new. Instead of stretching or releasing the full surface of the skin to alter the pitch, its vibrating area was reduced or enlarged by pressure from three internal steel rings of graduated diameters. The foot pedal working in a series of notches operated each ring independently. Varied pressure on each ring permitted tunings in semitones, indicated by a needle. According to Kastner, these drums were expensive, owing to the complicated mechanism, which, it seems, operated more freely when applying than releasing pressure. Pedal-tuned timpani by Knocke of Munich were operated by turning a wheel with the foot.

Later models included tuning by a hand-operated crank and those involving a series of foot pedals, operating on internal concentric rings – in the case of Darche three pedals, and with Brod, seven pedals. Kettledrums attracted the attention of the indefatigable Adolphe Sax.[2] In 1855 he constructed a species of timbale which he called *trompette-timbale*. In this instrument a vellum was stretched over a long conical resonator, and the pitch changed by adjusting the column of vibrated air by means of foot-pedal operated shutters. According to Pontécoulant,[3] Sax based his theory on the scientific observations of Félix Savart. Sax would doubtless be acquainted with the *tubo timpanite*, the drum with the far-carrying sound suggested in the seventeenth century by Kircher, and illustrated in Bonanni's *Gabinetto Armonico* (1723).

In England in 1856, H. J. Distin patented a drum with rod-tensioning on the exterior of the 'kettle', on the lines of a German model of 1851. In Distin's drum, curved bars connected the upper hoop to a fitment at the bottom of the shell, the bowl being rotated to change the tension (No. 1856–2319). (H. Potter patented a similar method 1884–1695.)

In the following year came Sax's *timbales-chromatiques*, a series of kettledrums

---

[1] British Patent Office, as are subsequent particulars.
[2] Antoine Joseph.
[3] Pontécoulant, Louis Adolphe. 'Organographie'. *Essai sur la facture instrumentale*, Paris, 1861.

without shells, in which the normal bowl was replaced by a flesh hoop and lower hoop supported by cross members. Sax applied this type of framework to the pair of shell-less timpani and other drums he patented in 1862. In these instruments provision is made for the collapsing of the framework to a small compass (see British Patent No. 1862–1657). From the aspect of portability, Sax's inventions obviously had excellent features. Tonally the instruments, particularly the timpani, suffered a loss, due to the non-trapping of the back wave produced by the vibrating membrane (see later chapter).

(The term *timbales–chromatiques* is occasionally applied to the *piano-basque* invented in 1841 by Sormani. In this instrument, a series of thirteen small drums, the vellums are struck with two small sticks actuated by keyboard mechanism.)

A system of tuning on the lines of the earlier model by Einlinger was introduced by Köhler & Sons of London in 1881. In Köhler's instrument a single handle rotated an internal spindle with bevel gearing at each end. The gears operated a series of cams working on a floating inner ring. The head was secured to the bowl in the normal manner by means of a counter hoop, and the pitch raised or lowered by the up or down movement of the internal ring. In theory, this instrument was well engineered, but in practice, as with earlier systems, the proximity of the inner mechanism to the vellum impaired the tone of the drum.

Among the European models, those by Knocke of Munich, Pfundt and C. Hoffmann of Leipzig, Pittrich of Dresden, Stumpff of Amsterdam were the most advanced. Despite the more positive mechanism on these instruments and the constant experiments made elsewhere, the limitations of the machine drums of this period made them of little use to the orchestra. Not the least of the problems confronting these early inventors (and their successors) was the difficulty in maintaining correct tension over the full surface of the vellum. A slight difference of thickness in any part of the head, or a difference in texture due to the irregularities in the membrane would require the tension to be corrected at a particular point in order to obtain equality of pitch. In some models an attempt to rectify this failing was made by the addition of side-screws. Kastner implies that these early inventors concentrated their efforts almost solely upon instantaneous tuning, and that the tone of the drum suffered in consequence. He adds that the manually-tuned drum was, at this period, the generally recognised orchestral instrument. The nineteenth century was however, not only a period of continued experiment in the design of orchestral timpani and other instruments of percussion; what is equally important to progress in this direction, it was also a time of growing demand by composers for general improvements. Berlioz himself made demands so numerous and particular as to constitute a milestone in any history of percussion.

Bibliography: Chapter 12
THE CLASSICAL ORCHESTRA

ANDERSON, E. ed. *The Letters of Beethoven*, Macmillan, London, 1961.

BERLIOZ, Hector. *Instrumentation*, Lemoine, Paris, 1843–4.

BONANNI, F. *Gabinetto Armonico*, Rome, 1722.

BROWNE, P. A. 'The Orchestral Treatment of the Timpani', *Music & Letters*, Hart, London, 1923.

BURNEY, Charles. *An account of the Musical Performance in Westminster Abbey*, Payne, London, 1785.

CARTER, Elizabeth. *Letters*, Rivington, London, 1808.

DART, Thurston. *An Introduction to March & Canzona for Queen Mary's Funeral*, Oxford, London, 1958.

DAVID, H. T. & MENDEL, Arthur. *The Bach Reader*, Dent, London, 1946.

DEAN, Winton. *Handel's Dramatic Oratorios and Masques*, Oxford, London, 1959.

DEUTSCH, O. E. *Handel*, Black, London, 1955.

EISEL, J. P. *Musicus autodidaktos*, Erfurt, 1738.

FARMER, Henry. *Handel's Kettledrums*, Hinrichsen, London, 1950.

FORSYTH, Cecil. *Orchestration*, Macmillan, London, 1955.

GEVAERT, François. *Nouveau Traité d'Instrumentation*, Lemoine, Paris–Bruxelles, 1885.

KASTNER, J. G. *Méthode de timbales*, Schlesinger, Paris, 1845.

KIRBY, P. R. *The Kettle-Drums*, Oxford, London, 1930.

LANDON, H. C. Robbins. *Haydn Symphonies*, B.B.C. Music Guides, London, 1966.

MAJER, Joseph. *Museum musicum*, Schwäb-Hall, 1832; reprint Kassel, 1954.

MALLET, A. M. *Les travaux de Mars*, Thierry, Paris, 1684.

PONTÉCOULANT, L. A. Organographie, *Essai sur la facture instrumentale*, Paris, 1861.

PONTIGNY, Victor de. *On Kettledrums*, Proceedings of the Musical Association, Spottiswoode, London, 1876.

SCHUBART, L. ed. *C. F. D. Schubart's Ideen zu einer Ästhetik der Tonkunst*, Vienna, 1806.

SCOUTEN, A. H. The London Stage 1660-1806, Part 3, 1729-49, Southern Illinois University Press, 1961.

SMART, George. *Leaves from the Journals of Sir George Smart*, ed. Cox & Cox, Longmans, London, 1907.

TAYLOR, H. W. *The Art and Science of the Timpani*, John Baker, London, 1964.

TERRY, C. S. *Bach's Orchestra*, Oxford, London, 1932.

VEJVANOVSKY, P. J. *Musica Antiqua Bohemia*, Statni Hudebni Vydavatelsiui, Artia, Prague, 1961.

WEINGARTNER, F. *On the Performance of Beethoven's Symphonies*, trans. Crosland. Breitkopf and Härtel, London, 1907.

WHITE, Charles. *Drums Through the Ages*, The Sterling Press, Los Angeles, 1960.

ZIMMERMAN, F. B. *Henry Purcell*, Macmillan, London, 1963, St. Martin's Press, New York.

RECOMMENDED READING

CHARLTON, David. 'Salieri's Timpani', *Musical Times*, October, 1971, pp. 961–2.

13

The Romantic Orchestra—I

It is from Berlioz that we gain our most vivid picture of the use of orchestral percussion in his day. The innovatory manner in which he himself employed the instruments already utilised in the works of earlier masters, his responsibility for the introduction of many exciting new devices and his exhaustive literary contributions remain an inspiration.[1]

In his comprehensive study of the resources of the orchestra he investigated the numerous aspects of the use of percussion, both rhythmically and to give orchestral tone colour. Berlioz's regard for 'percussion' is obvious from the manner in which he so ingeniously observed these two factors – rhythm and colour. In the vast orchestra he conceived 'on paper', and was 'curious to try for once', the strength and diversity of the percussion instruments is of unparalleled dimensions. His 'dream' ensemble of 467 instrumentalists included 53 percussion players, divided as follows:

  8 Paires de Timbales (8 pairs of timpani, 10 players)
  6 Tambours (side drums)
  3 Grosses Caisses (bass drums)[2]
  4 Paires de Cymbales (cymbals)
  6 Triangles (triangles)
  6 Jeu de Timbres (sets of bells)
 12 Paires de Cymbales antiques (*en différents tons*) (antique cymbals)
  2 Grandes Cloches très graves (very low great bells)
  2 Tam-tams (gongs)
  4 Pavillons Chinois (Turkish crescents)

[1] Berlioz held that any sonorous body employed by a composer was a musical instrument.

[2] Some trace the French term *caisse* and the Italian *cassa* to Latin *capsa*, others to Arabian *qasa'* (a bowl drum).

(Note that Berlioz makes no mention of the xylophone, neither does he include it in any of his compositions.)

Berlioz considered that[1]: 'from the union of eight pairs of timpani with the six side-drums, and the three bass drums forming a small orchestra of percussion, and almost exclusively rhythmical, would come a menacing accent in all tints. A lugubrious and sinister accent in the *mezzoforte* tint would be provided by a mixture of the two tam-tams, the two large bells, and the three large cymbals with certain chords of trombones. A metallic orchestra of percussion consisting (in addition to 30 pianofortes) of six sets of small bells, twelve pairs of ancient cymbals, six triangles (which might be tuned, like the ancient cymbals, in different keys), and four *pavillon chinois*, would supply joyous and brilliant accents and the mezzoforte tint.'

In his *Instrumentation* Berlioz divides percussion into two groups: the first comprising instruments of fixed sounds and musically appreciable, the second those of less musical product destined to produce special effects or to colour the rhythm. Of all, he considered the kettledrums to be the most valuable. From his remarks it seems that at this period there were still but one pair of timpani in the majority of orchestras. He makes no mention of machine drums, so it is clear that these instruments had so far proved unsuitable for general orchestral use. The pair of drums to which Berlioz refers had, like the orchestral timpani already discussed, a compass of one octave, each drum having a range of a fifth, and allowing a choice of upper or lower dominant in the keys of B flat and F. (These instruments would have similar measurements to the present-day standard pair of drums – 27½ inches, 24½ inches or 28 inches, 25 inches.) Berlioz favoured the quality of tone from a well-tensioned vellum, as he suggests the higher position of the F natural in the keys of B flat and F, though he made considerable use of the lower notes of the timpani, as did many of his predecessors.

Though Berlioz had great respect for the earlier masters, particularly Beethoven, he deplored certain of their practices. He frowned on what he described as 'the vice of transposing the notes for the timpani', saying that it was absurd 'to write movement of a fourth, when a performer had to play movement of a fifth', i.e., in A flat.

 effect . In his own scores he indicates every change of tuning during movements; he appears to be the first composer to be consistent in this matter. On the question of the late arrival of the third drum into the orchestra, he says[2]: 'Composers complained for many years of the vexatious

---

[1] Berlioz. *Traité de l'Instrumentation et d'orchestration modernes*, Schonenberger, Paris, 1843, p. 288.

[2] Berlioz. ibid. pp. 253–4.

necessity in which they found themselves – for want of a third sound from the timpani . . . they never asked themselves whether a single player might not play upon three drums. At length, one fine day, the timpanist at the Paris opera[1] having shown that the thing was easy, they ventured to try the audacious innovation; and since then, composers who write for the opera have at their disposal three notes. It required seventy years to reach this point!'

Here Berlioz was generalizing: it is certain that he was not unaware of the use of three or more drums by certain of his predecessors, as for instance, Molter, Mozart, Weber, Auber and Reicha, the latter a friend of Beethoven. Reicha, in a setting of an ode of Schiller, employed no less than eight drums in four pairs tuned chromatically. Weber (who occasionally transposed) used three drums, tuned to the tonic, dominant and sub-dominant, in *Peter Schmoll* (1803) and *The Ruler of the Spirits* (1811). In 1828 Auber employed three drums in *Masaniello*. Spohr in his oratorio *Calvary* (1833) scored for six timpani.

Reference has already been made to Berlioz's attitude towards the drumsticks, and to his strictures on the negligence of composers who failed to indicate in their scores the type of stick they desired the performer to use. He says that drumsticks with wooden ends produce a harsh sound, those with wooden ends covered with leather a sound less startling, but nevertheless very dry, adding that in numerous orchestras this type of drumstick alone is used, which he says is a great pity. Drumsticks with ends made of sponge he considered the best, as they give to the drum a grave, velvety quality of tone, and moreover, the elasticity of the sponge aids the rebound of the drumstick. He says that in the Beethoven Symphonies in B flat and C minor, the marvellous effect of the pianissimo of the timpani loses much by being played with drumsticks without sponge ends, to which he adds that Beethoven in his scores specified nothing on this point.[2]

In contrast to the lack of directions in early works, we find with Berlioz a complete understanding of the problems confronting the performer. He stresses the difficulty of changing pitch, and suggests that timpanists might be spared this troublesome and difficult task if there were in all orchestras two pairs of kettledrums, and two drummers. Faced no doubt with economic problems similar to those of to-day, he compromised by stating that care should be taken in the first place to give a number of rests proportioned to the importance of the change demanded from him, so that he has time to effect it conveniently. He also reasons that if the drums are in

[1] Possibly M. Poussard, of whom Kastner in his *Instrumentation*, 1837, speaks of having apportioned the octave between three drums.

[2] Isolated instances occur however: Dalayrac's request for *baguettes garnies* in *Lina* (1807) and Spontini's instruction for *bâton de sourdine* in *Fernand Cortez* (1809).

A and E [musical notation] and it is desired to go into the key of B flat, it would be unwise to indicate the new interval as a fourth [musical notation] as this compels lowering the low drum a third and the high drum an augmented fourth, whereas if they are tuned to a fifth the player needs only to raise each drum half a tone. He is mindful of the difficulty of tuning during the performance of a piece full of modulations. Of this he says, as others have said before and since, that the timpanist should be an excellent musician, and endowed with an ear of extreme delicacy.

In his *Grande Messe des Morts* (1837) ('Tuba Mirum'), Berlioz outstripped his predecessor Reicha by demanding sixteen kettledrums operated by ten players – two pairs of drums requiring a player to each drum, with one player on each of the remaining six pairs.

Requiem   Berlioz

The original manuscript specified 16 pairs of timpani, but as Percy Scholes says[1]: '. . . even Berlioz had at times to cut his coat according to his cloth', though if the amount of other percussion (four tam-tams, ten cymbals, large tenor drum and bass drum) employed in the *Requiem* is taken into account, he maintained a tolerably sized 'suit length'! The overwhelming effect of the rumble from the large force of kettledrums, augmented from time to time with rolls on the tenor drum, bass drum, three cymbals and a tam-tam has been sufficiently quoted for us to remark only on the craft of the composer on the deployment of the percussion.[2] In the first place, the disposing of the various intervals on the timpani (all played with sponge-headed sticks) which play in four-part and occasionally in six-part harmony. Secondly, the cunning manner in which he ensures a close roll on these instruments (a technical effect of which he was fond: he refers to delicate rolls, very soft and very close and to the striking effect of very close rolls in his *Instrumentation*). Here, as in other instances e.g., the pianissimo rolls on the four timpani in the *Fantastic* Symphony, Berlioz indicates the roll with four strokes [musical notation]. This procedure he frequently adopts if the tempo is slow. Elsewhere he uses the more usual three strokes [musical notation] and at times only two strokes [musical notation]. In the autographed score of *Beatrice and Benedict*

[1] Scholes, P. *The Oxford Companion to Music*, Oxford, 1938–44, p. 703.

[2] Antony Hopkins, in a B.B.C. talk, described this as 'the most awe-inspring sound I've ever heard in my life . . . I wanted to yell at the top of my voice, to cry out to get the air out of my lungs, I was so filled with the glory of the sound'.

we find allegro ♯ and in a steadier tempo ♯ . As Berlioz used no *tr* ━━━━ sign, such markings are regarded as indicating a roll.[1]

Of the large tenor drum (indicated as in B flat, an unusual request) Berlioz specifies that this be set upright, and the rolls made with two timpani sticks. The bass drum, he says, is to be struck with padded drumsticks alternately on each side (*avec deux tampons*). The cymbals and the tam-tam are also to be struck with soft sticks.

In his *Instrumentation*, Berlioz refers to the gloomy and menacing sound of the bass drum if the instrument be well made and of large size. From contemporary illustrations, (including caricatures) in which the bass drum appears, it is evident that the *grosse caisse* of Berlioz's time was in two forms: the deep cylindrical instrument known as the long drum, and the shallow Turkish drum of larger diameter, both double-headed.[2] In England, at least, the long drum continued popular in both orchestra and military band. (Considering the small diameter of this instrument its tone is surprisingly deep.)

Though Berlioz had little time for economy, particularly in the percussion section,[3] he had strong objections to the way some composers used certain instruments. Of the bass drum he says, they strike senselessly the accented part of each bar, and that used in this style it is scarcely ever unaccompanied by the cymbals (he himself used this combination on occasions as a timekeeper). In some orchestras, he says, bass drum and cymbals are even played by one musician: a situation intolerable to Berlioz who flays this procedure unmercifully, to the extent of advising the conductor to set his face against it. He contends that the resulting sound is trivial in character, deprived of all pomp and brilliance, and – among other things, fit only for making dance music for monkeys! With due respect to Berlioz, and accepting his remarks as true when applied to the symphony orchestra, it would be unfair to deny both the musical quality and the absolute precision obtained from the combined strokes of bass drum and well-matched cymbals when played by a skilled

---

[1] François Gevaert gives the tremolo in his *Nouveau traité d'instrumentation*, p. 324.

[2] Speaking of the Darmstadt opera band in 1825, Sir George Smart in his *Leaves from the Journals of Sir George Smart* (Longman Green, London, 1907, p. 77) writes: 'The long drum was the most effective I ever heard: it is not so large generally but the head was larger than our drums'.

[3] In his *Te Deum* for instance, he requests six side drums (of no definite pitch) and four or five pairs of cymbals.

executant in what is called 'military-band fashion'.[1] What Berlioz would have said of the combination of bass drum, cymbals, and side drum etc., by the so-called 'double-drummer' and 'trap-drummer' of a generation to follow, we hesitate to imagine!

As already stated, Berlioz made every effort to clarify his drum parts, giving constant instructions for the use of soft or hard sticks, not only on the timpani, but on other instruments such as the cymbals and bass drum. In the Fantastic Symphony (Third movement, 'Scène aux Champs') the burst of thunder during the cor anglais solo is carefully marked 'with sponge headed sticks'.[2]

Fantastic Symphony   Berlioz

In 'Marche au Supplice', there are clear instructions for both hard- and soft-ended sticks, muffling the drums (*voilé* – veiled, *coperti* – cover), and precise instructions as to how to perform a given figure, viz:

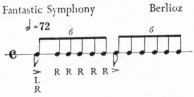

Fantastic Symphony   Berlioz

the first quaver of each half bar with two drumsticks; the other five quavers with the right hand drumstick. Elsewhere he says 'damp the tone with the hand' and so on. Regarding the muffled drum, Berlioz says tambours (side drums) are used muffled

[1] The combining of drum and cymbal by one performer is of Eastern origin and is age-old.
[2] Chords on the timpani are frequent in the work of Berlioz. In the opera *Benvenuto Cellini* he specifies three timbaliers for the three-note chords.

like the timpani, but instead of covering the parchment with a piece of cloth, the players often content themselves with loosening the *cordes* (snares), or with passing a leather strap between them and the lower parchment. (To-day, in addition to covering the head, it is customary to release the snares on the side drum when this instrument is to be muffled, thus relieving the drum of its brightness, and rendering the tone appropriate to compositions of a funereal character. Visually, the draping of drums is a token of mourning. On such occasions as military and state funerals all drums are draped, but in most cases the playing area is uncovered.) In 'Marche Funèbre' (*Hamlet*), Berlioz requests 6 *Tambours-voilés ou sans Timbre*.

Of the two low bells in the finale of his *Fantastic* Symphony, Berlioz says in the score: 'If two bells are not available to produce one of the three C's and one of the three G's as written, it is better to use the pianofortes'. It is clear that Berlioz had in mind 'church bells'. To-day, on occasion (particularly on the Continent) genuine instruments are employed in this work and elsewhere, though all too frequently circumstances are such that tubular bells and metal plates are substituted. (See 'Bells'.)

The orchestral use of bells has already been observed in Bach's *Schlage doch gewünschte Stunde*. It is not until the close of the eighteenth century that bells (real church bells) reappear in orchestral scores; Dalayrac, in his opera *Camille* (1791) and Cherubini in *Elisa* (1794). Rossini calls for a bell in low G 𝄢 to accompany the chorus in the second act of *William Tell* (1829). Gevaert[1] says that in no theatre was the pitch lower than 𝄞, that is three octaves higher than the note written by Rossini. A few years later Meyerbeer scored for low bells 𝄢 in *Les Huguenots* (1836) to give the signal for the massacre. At Meyerbeer's suggestion bells were specially cast for the Paris Opera for this occasion. Gevaert says that rarely does one find in theatres such large bells as those used by the Paris Opera House. Whilst the sound of the great bell in the orchestra is thus not attributed in the first place to Berlioz, the gentle tinkling of the ancient cymbals (*crotales*) most certainly is. In the fairy-like scherzo of his *Romeo and Juliet* (1839), a dramatic symphony (a work containing much excellent writing for the timpani), Berlioz scored for two pairs of ancient cymbals one fifth apart. 𝄞 (Ancient cymbals are required in *The Trojans*, 1865-9). In his *Instrumentation* he gives instructions for sounding these instruments, implying that they should be played 'edge to edge' and not struck 'full face'. He also says that all bell-founders can manufacture

[1] Gevaert, *Nouveau traité d'Instrumentation*, ibid. p. 326.

them. He had the small cymbals manufactured to his instructions[1] (as may have Debussy and Ravel later). When Berlioz conducted the *Dramatic* Symphony in London, no small cymbals were available. With his customary thoroughness he located a manufacturer who supplied the instruments in time for the performance.[2] Berlioz no doubt took these cymbals back with him to Paris as there is no trace of them in London, neither is there a set of tuned cymbals which (according to information supplied verbally, to the author) were included in the equipment of the Crystal Palace Orchestra in the late 1890's. It is possible that these and other instruments with a similar interesting history, such as the large kettledrums 47 inches and 43 inches across, belonging to 'The Sacred Harmonic Society' perished by fire, or found their way to the breaker's-yard possibly during a time of war. Of the Sacred Harmonic Society's drums, Professor Kirby says[3]: 'The difficulty of obtaining suitable heads, however, prevented these mammoth instruments from being seriously considered by musicians'.[4]

Berlioz held a similar opinion regarding kettledrum heads, for he considered that the reason for not obtaining sounds lower than F lay in the difficulty of obtaining parchments to cover a large vessel. He contended that high notes presented no problem. Small drums up to G and A flat could, he said, be used on numerous occasions with the happiest effect. He prescribed a small kettledrum Tarbourka (a drum from North Africa in the shape of a flower pot) in 'Slave Dance' from *The Trojans*. Larger and small drums, however, were a thing of the not-too-distant future, and with carefully prepared vellums came the lower and higher sounds of which Berlioz must often have dreamed. It was, in fact, during Berlioz's life-time that there was built what was for a long time considered to be the world's largest drum.[5] This instrument, a single-headed gong-drum with a diameter of eight feet, was made by Messrs. Distin,[6] a well-known firm of instrument manufacturers, and patented in 1857. It is said that the hide of the champion beast at the Annual Cattle Show provided the original head (other reports say the skin of a buffalo was imported). This

[1] According to Gevaert these were modelled on the lines of those discovered at Pompeii, which Berlioz said he had seen.

[2] Basil Cameron, a conductor with a profound knowledge of the percussion section, had crotales manufactured by Boosey & Hawkes for Debussy's *L'après-midi d'un faune*.

[3] Kirby, Percival. *The Kettle-Drums*, Oxford, 1930, p. 16.

[4] One pair has survived: the large drums (38 inches and 40 inches) in the Rotunda Museum, Woolwich. According to the museum catalogue these were used prior to the French Revolution in Strasbourg Cathedral as an accompaniment to the organ in pieces of military music.

[5] Hardly an innovation if we go back 5,000 years to the large drum depicted on early Mesopotamian monuments.

[6] Responsible for the introduction of the shallow side drum *c.* 1850.

135. Mid nineteenth-century 'Dresden' machine timpani.
By courtesy of L. W. Hunt Drum Co. Ltd., London

136. Late nineteenth-century pedal timpani (property of the late Sir Henry J.
Wood). By courtesy of the Royal Academy of Music, London and the
L. W. Hunt Drum Co. Ltd., London

137. Sir Malcolm Sargent rehearsing a section of the percussionists (author to right of bass drum) in Berlioz's *Grande Messe des Morts* (Prom, Royal Albert Hall, 1961)

138. Long drum, *c.* 1780. By permission of Messrs. H. Potter, London

139. Guard's pattern side drum. By permission of Messrs. H. Potter, London

140. Military tenor drum. By permission of Messrs. H. Potter, London

141
Military bass drum (unbraced).
By permission of Messrs.
H. Potter, London

142. Distin's monster bass drum. By courtesy of Boosey and Hawkes, London

143. *Rheingold* anvils (Vienna Philharmonic Orchestra).
Photograph by permission of Hans Wild

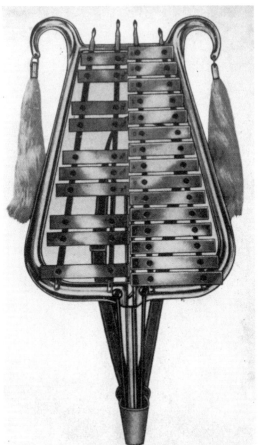

144
'Bell lyra' by
Ludwig Drum Co., U.S.A.

145a, b. Square side drum and sticks (n.d.) By permission of the Museum
of the Conservatoire, Brussels

146. 'Soldiers on the March' *c.* 1828. Turner. By courtesy of the Trustees of the British Museum

148. Cimbalom. By permission of the performer, John Leach

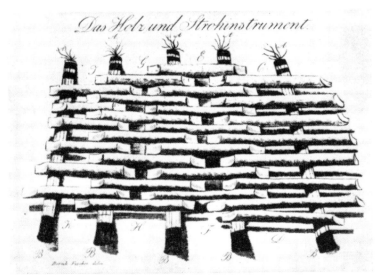

Das Holz und Strohinstrument.

147. Gusikow's xylophone (the player Mendelssohn so admired). By permission of the Austrian National Library, Vienna

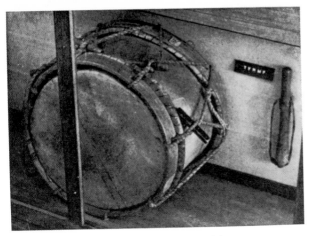

149. *Tumir*, Southern Russia. By courtesy of the Museum of the Leningrad Institute of Music

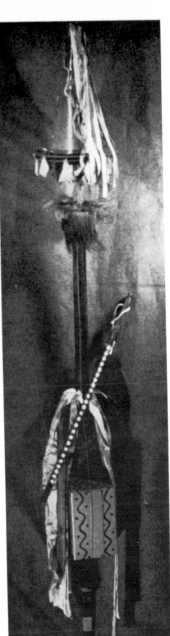

150
Devil's violin. By permission of the Horniman Museum, London

152
Mahir Karayĭlan ('Black Snake') of Kastamonn, performing on the davul.

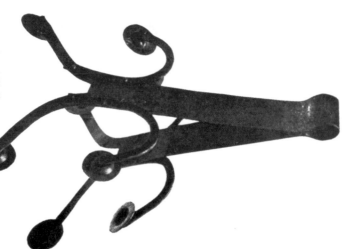

151
Zilia massá. (Thrace). From the Fivos Anoyanakis' (Athens) collection of Greek musical instruments

153. *The Soldier's Tale* ensemble. Newcastle, 1924. First performance in England conducted by the late Edward Clark. From the collection of Mrs. Edward Clark. (Percussionist: William Bradshaw)

154. Stravinsky in his Paris studio (1929). Photograph by Lipnitzki, Paris

155
Hand-screw timpani (modern) by
Boosey & Hawkes, London

156
Modern rotary-tuned timpano by
Murbach, Lucerne

157
Machine timpani (modern) by
Günther Ringer, Berlin. By courtesy
of Messrs. Ringer and Kurt
Goedicke (London)

158. Leedy pedal timpani, *c.* 1935. Pawl system clutch

161. Pedal timpani by Premier Drum Co. Ltd., England. Balanced pedal action and rotary (foot) fine-tuning

159. W. F. Ludwig 'Dresden' model timpani ('sawtooth' clutch)

162. Pedal timpani by Slingerland Drum Co., U.S.A.

160. Modern 'Dresden' timpani by Günther Ringer, Berlin. By courtesy of Messrs. Ringer and Kurt Goedicke (London)

163. Accu-sonic pedal timpani by Rogers Drums, U.S.A. Photograph by courtesy of Boosey & Hawkes, London

164
Tuning gauge for pedal
timpani. (*left*) Ludwig
(*right*) Premier. Photograph
by courtesy of Percussion
Services, London

165. Lapping drumheads (calf). L. W. ('Doc') Hunt, of the L. W. Hunt Drum
     Co. Ltd., London

166. Orchestral gong drum. L. W. Hunt Drum Co. Ltd., London

168. Orchestral side drum. Premier Drum Co. Ltd., England

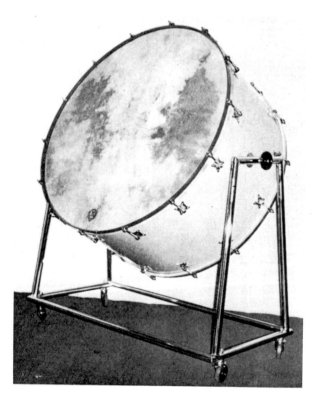

167. Orchestral bass drum (40″ by 20″). L. W. Hunt Drum Co. Ltd., London

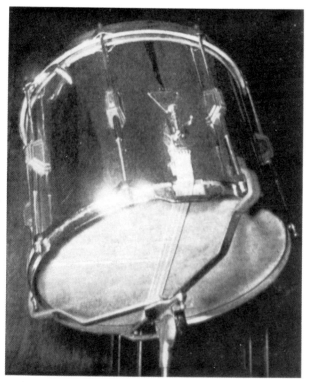

169. Deep orchestral side drum, showing snares. (Author's collection.) Boosey & Hawkes, London. Photograph by permission of the Galpin Society

170. Mounted kettledrummers of the Life Guards and Horse Guards.
Photograph by permission of Media Colour Services, London

171. Draped kettledrums at the State Funeral of Sir Winston Churchill
(30th January, 1965). Drum horse Alexander leading the State trumpeters
of the Household Cavalry. By permission of the *Observer*

172. City of Birmingham Symphony Orchestra recording Bliss's *Meditation on a Theme by John Blow*. Note cymbals on timpani (see text). Timpanist: Howard Bradshaw.
Photograph by permission of *Hi-Fi News* and Hans Wild

173. Rehearsal of *Gurrelieder* (Schoenberg). London Symphony Orchestra, Royal Festival Hall, 8th November, 1963. Chains: Mr. Reginald Flower. Photograph *The Times*

skin lasted until 1957, and was then replaced with the assistance of the Leather Institute.[1] The drum has had its place in London theatrical history. It was, for example, used for thunder effects in the production of *The White Horse Inn*, and *The Whip*. It has been seen on special occasions in the concert hall, notably at the Handel Commemoration Festivals in the Crystal Palace. It is pictured in the *Illustrated London News* of 27th June 1857 (at a preliminary Festival), and again two years later at the 1859 Commemoration Festival. In the *Graphic* of 27th June 1874, it is seen in a sketch headed 'Tuning up the big Kettledrum', the pitch of the latter instrument being adjusted by a man, who is assisting the performer by turning a winch. The Kettledrums in this illustration (machine drums) could well be the artist's impression of the large timpani of The Sacred Harmonic Society, which were probably those made especially for the 1859 Handel Commemoration Festival. Percy Scholes,[2] to whom we are indebted for the information about these illustrations, is of the opinion that these enormous drums may have been made by Distin, the maker of the Monster Bass Drum. Only on one occasion does this latter instrument seem to have been used in the Queen's Hall. In order to get it on to the platform the drum had to be lowered through the roof lights. This proved a hazardous undertaking and was, from all reports, not repeated. (According to the *Guinness Book of Records* (1968) the largest drum in the world is the 'Disneyland Big Bass Drum' built in 1961 by Remo Inc. of Hollywood, U.S.A. The instrument has a diameter of $10\frac{1}{2}$ feet. It is mounted on wheels and towed by tractor.) See authors notes.

Berlioz, who pioneered so effectively and inspired many improvements in the construction of percussion instruments as well as extending their function, like many another prophet, met with opposition. His works were frequently received with little enthusiasm, at times with hostility. It is said that on one occasion he kept watch on the kettledrums throughout the night, as it was rumoured the skins were to be slit.[3] Berlioz could sleep easily if he were here to-day, when both he and his works are accepted as monumental. There can be no better way of leaving this genius than with a reminder of his literary skill – an anecdote from his *Evenings with the Orchestra*.[4] 'Only one member of this orchestra allows himself no sort of diversion. Engrossed in his task, active, tireless, his eyes fixed on his notes, his arm in perpetual motion, he would deem himself dishonoured if he were to miss a quaver or attract censure

[1] This instrument was owned for many years by Messrs Boosey & Hawkes and later by Mr L. W. Hunt of London. (It was recently destroyed due to deterioration.)

[2] Scholes, P. *The Mirror of Music*, volume I, Novello, Oxford, London, 1947.

[3] A satirical engraving shows Berlioz conducting an orchestra in which appears a cannon, a burst bass drum, and timpani played with anvils.

[4] Berlioz, H. *Evenings in the Orchestra*, Peregrine, London, 1963, p. 27.

for the quality of his tone. The close of each act finds him flushed and perspiring, exhausted and breathless; and yet he does not dare take advantage of the few moments afforded him by the lull in the musical hostilities to drink a glass of beer in the nearest bar. The dread of lingering there and so missing the first bars of the next act is enough to rivet him to his post. Touched by his zeal, the manager of the opera-house to which he is attached once sent him six bottles of wine "by way of encouragement". The artist, conscious of his worth, far from accepting this gift gratefully, returned it to the manager with the haughty message, "I do not need encouragement!" It is easy to guess that I am referring to the bass drum player.'

The time of Berlioz was a period of considerable revolution in the orchestra. Bellini made active use of the timpani in his operas, and in 1831 in Meyerbeer's manuscript score of *Robert le Diable* (Act 4) a melody is given to the kettledrums. It is a solo for a single player on four drums tuned to G, C, D and E.[1]

Robert le Diable   Meyerbeer

In the printed score the fourth drum, E, is for some reason omitted, the gaps being filled by the celli and double-basses who play the entire passage. Why he made the alteration which Scholes describes as 'a genuine and attractive tune for kettle-drums', is puzzling, for like Berlioz, Meyerbeer used the kettledrums adventurously. In *Le Prophète* (1849) occurs the famous 'Coronation March' with an important part for three timpani and, incidentally in Act 3 of the same opera, a most effective passage for four drums, (in G, C, D and E) as in the early manuscript of *Robert le Diable*.[2]

Le Prophète   Meyerbeer

In Paris, this was certainly an era of activity in the percussion department of the orchestra, particularly the timpani. In 1845 came G. Kastner's famous *Méthode de timbales*, dedicated to M. Poussard, a reigning virtuoso for whom Kastner obviously had high regard. Kastner's *Méthode*, which includes an informative historical survey of the timpani, contains studies for two, three, four and five kettledrums, in which

---

[1] It is not surprising to find Meyerbeer employing the kettledrums in this novel manner for he was a timpanist.

[2] In this same year (1849) came Nicolai's *Merry Wives of Windsor*, also with excellent scoring for the timpani.

the technical aspect compares favourably with that found in modern tutors. Other instruments of percussion are dealt with in Kastner's *Instrumentation*, 1837, and his *Manuel général de musique militaire* 1848.

It is in the works of the Parisian composers of the first half of the nineteenth century that we find a marked change of colour in the percussion section of the orchestra, resulting from an extension of the use of the now permanent members, and the introduction of further instruments. In 1800 Boieldieu scored for two triangles (high and low) in his opera *Le Calife de Bagdad*. Auber gave the anvil (*enclume*) a place in his score of *Le Maçon* (1825), as also did Halévy in *La Juive* (1835) and Berlioz three years later in *Benvenuto Cellini*. About this time we find the whip (*fouet*) in a composition by G. Kastner (*Les cris de Paris*). Kastner's score also includes an alarm bell (*beffroi*), jingles (*grelots*) and the anvil. The gong occurs in works by Gossec, Spontini, Halévy, Meyerbeer, Cherubini, and, as we have seen, Berlioz. The tambourine was at this time, according to Berlioz, in considerable orchestral use. We find it in Weber's *Preciosa* (1820). Berlioz occasionally calls for two tambourines (two players) and in *Harold in Italy* for three. In his *Instrumentation* he deals, as does Kastner, to some extent with technical details concerning this instrument.[1] Kastner discusses at some length the castanets and mentions a system for the instrument published by Heugel of Paris. Bizet is quoted as the first composer to use the castanets in orchestral music in *Carmen* (1875), concert version and cued in the opera score.[2] Wagner employs them earlier in the Venusberg music in *Tannhäuser* in the revised edition of the opera for performances in Paris in 1861.

The *Tambourin*, an instrument resembling a large tabor (with snare on the upper head) is also known as *Tambourin de Provence*.[3] It occurs in Rameau's *Les Fêtes d'Hébé* (1739), Grétry's *Céphale et Procris* (1775), Berton's opera *Aline* (1803), and later in

---

[1] Steibelt, whose English wife was an expert performer on the tambourine, used the instrument freely and wrote a method for it (*c.* 1800). The popularity of the instrument in England is well described in a document entitled *Instructions for the Tambourine* published *c.* 1800 by J. or T. Preston. The preface to the work reads: 'The Tambourine is an Instrument at this time extremely fashionable; indeed none more so, and from its being sanctioned and performed on, by Persons of the first distinction, there remains little doubt, but it will continue so, – add to this, its beauties have been discovered by the first Composers of the day, as their works can testify; and it is now agreed on, that no Instrument is better calculated to accompany a piece of music, with taste, and expression than the TAMBOURINE.' (By courtesy of Liverpool City Libraries).

[2] The opera score indicates that in No. 17 (Duo) the *castagnettes* may be played in the orchestra or on the stage by Carmen, the latter for preference who may improvise.

The *Carmen Ballet* (Bizet–Shchedrin) is scored for strings and 47 percussion instruments.

[3] In Provence, a long narrow drum, beaten with a single drumstick, and used specially to accompany the *Galoubet* (pipe and tabor).

Auber's *Le Philtre* (1831). The next composer to use it was Bizet (*L'Arlésienne*, Second Suite, 1872). According to Percy Scholes the Paris Opera had a *tambourinaire* attached to it as early as 1750. (Tambourin is at times, not surprisingly, confused with tambourine. In German and Italian, Tambourin is unfortunately used for both Tabor and Tambourine, cf. tambour de basque.) Meyerbeer used the tenor drum (which Berlioz attributed to Gluck) in *Robert le Diable* (1831). Berlioz, as we have seen, followed suit in several of his compositions (and so did Wagner in *Rienzi* and *Lohengrin*). In Rossini's *Chant Funèbre* for men's voices (written at the death of Meyerbeer) a tenor drum (*caisse roulante*) is the sole accompaniment.

Whilst composers were busy experimenting with percussion in the French capital, things were by no means at a standstill elsewhere, particularly in Germany. Mendelssohn wrote magnificently for the timpani, as for example, in his Fourth Symphony (*Italian*) (1833). In the Scherzo from *A Midsummer Night's Dream* (1832) he gave us one of the most delightful solos in the repertoire of the timpani. He wrote for a pair of drums in the high register in the chorus 'Call Him Louder' from *Elijah* (1846). In contrast, there is the roar of the ocean from the lower notes of the drums in the overture *The Hebrides*. Mendelssohn in general employed the drums tuned in fourths or fifths. Exceptions occur in *St. Paul* (F sharp and D) and in *Rondo Brillante*, in each case two small drums being required, tuned in D and E on which notes they remain throughout the Rondo. This tuning is well described in Grove as[1]: '. . . making them available in the keys of B minor and D major as notes of the common chord, and of the dominant seventh, in both keys'. In *St. Paul* (1836) he used three drums, including the upper F sharp.

On occasions the lack of a third drum is noticeable, as in *The Hebrides*, where, in a fanfare in D major, the drum plays on F sharp, as Mendelssohn had only B and F sharp available. As already stated, the temptation to employ a third drum (on D) is strong. In the final E major chord in the overture to *A Midsummer Night's Dream*, the effect of the quiet roll on B natural is befittingly ethereal.

At the time of Mendelssohn's death in 1847, his fellow countryman Wagner had completed *Rienzi*, *The Flying Dutchman* and *Tannhäuser*. Wagner, an ardent admirer of Mendelssohn, displayed an early regard for the drum, for we find one of his earliest works (written when he was 17) entitled *Paukenschlagouvertüre*. In his *Autobiographical Sketches* Wagner refers to the first performance of this work, and to the fact that the audience was puzzled by the persistence of the drum-player who had to

[1] Grove. *Dictionary of Music and Musicians*, Macmillan, London, 1922, p. 730.

give a fortissimo stroke every four bars from beginning to end. The manner in which Wagner used the timpani is interesting. In *The Ring* and *Parsifal* he employs two pairs of drums, a player to each pair. Only on one occasion does he allot to one performer more than one pair of drums – the three note pattern in *Götterdämmerung*

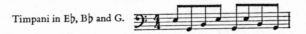

In the 'Funeral March' from the same opera is found an excellent example of Wagner's use of his two players.

Judging from the short length of time given to each player to effect substantial changes, it is clear that by Wagner's day there was a marked improvement in the design of the orchestral kettledrum. By the time of the first performance of these operas (1869 onwards) the machine drum, if not already operated by a completely satisfactory foot pedal device, must have been equipped with a safe system of tuning either by means of a single handle or by rotating the drum. Germany was now the established centre for serious experiments in rapid-tuning mechanism.

There is also evidence in Wagner's works of the availability of a larger-sized drum, for he makes use of the low E in *Götterdämmerung* completed in 1874, and *Parsifal* in 1882.

In *Parsifal*, the four drums support the bell motif:

In certain respects Wagner pushed further ahead with the timpani than did his elder contemporary Berlioz, who, according to Wagner, was 'diabolically clever'. Wagner was fearless in exploiting the kettledrums (which he naturally calls *Pauken*) as solo instruments. In *Parsifal* we find muffled drums (*gedämpft*), and in *Siegfried*, for example, a series of unusual tunings.[1]

In the Prelude to Act II (*Siegfried*) these tunings are given to a rhythmic figure representing the sluggish heart beats of Fafner the dragon. In Scene II the drums typify the final heart throbs of the vanquished creature. The writing for the timpani in this opera, and throughout the cycle, is exemplary in style and attention to detail.

The tremolo Wagner normally indicates *tr*. In *Lohengrin* is found an echo of the scrupulousness of Beethoven, in differentiating between the *tr* and demi-semiquavers, also an effective use of grace notes. (*see facing page*).

[1] See also Siegfried's killing the dragon.

Lohengrin   Wagner

Wagner's use of the other percussion is equally interesting. In general, his use of such instruments was economical, as for instance the triangle part in *The Master-singers* Overture and the single note for this instrument at the end of the 2nd Act of *Siegfried*. One of the finest moments for the cymbals in the repertoire of serious music is their first entry in the overture to *The Mastersingers*. A thrill to the listener undoubtedly, but even more exciting for the performer who waits in eager anticipation of the vital stroke to be delivered on the first beat of the 211th bar. In *The Rhinegold*, Wagner uses the mysterious ringing sound of a single cymbal played with timpani sticks (a roll) to describe the glitter of the precious metal. In *Rienzi*, *Lohengrin*, *The Valkyrie* and *Parsifal*, he calls for the tenor drum (*Rührtrommel*). (The concert arrangement of 'The Ride of the Valkyries' specifies side drum (*kleine Trommel*) in place of the tenor drum). A stroke on the tam-tam typifies the splash of the anchor in the first act of *The Flying Dutchman*.

With the anvil (*Rhinegold*) Wagner calls for no economy – though opera-house managers usually do. In all, eighteen anvils are scored for: six small, six large, and six very large.

The scene in the opera is vividly described by Robert Donington[1]: 'The anvils gradually permeate the orchestra as Wotan and Loge reach the cave of the wretched labouring dwarfs. The orchestra leaves off, and they are heard alone, with strangely moving effect; the orchestra re-enters, and the anvils die away, as the gods pass on: the whole scene being as vivid as if the eye beheld it, although the curtain remains down the while.'

The glockenspiel occurs in a number of Wagner's works: *The Mastersingers* ('The Entry of the Apprentices Waltz-tune', Act III), *The Valkyrie*, ('Fire Music'), *Götter-dämmerung*, ('Siegfried's Rhine Journey'). In 'Forest Murmurs' (*Siegfried*) the glockenspiel, as elsewhere, joins the woodwind. At times its gentle twittering, playing in $\frac{4}{4}$ against $\frac{9}{8}$ in the orchestra, complies with the delightful abandon of the sounds of nature.

Siegfried   Wagner

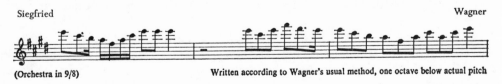

(Orchestra in 9/8)   Written according to Wagner's usual method, one octave below actual pitch

[1] Donington, Robert. *The Instruments of Music*, Methuen, London, 1951, p. 120.

The glockenspiel in Wagner's orchestra would, in all probability, be keyboard-operated. This type of instrument (*jeu de timbres*) was then in general use on the Continent. It is mentioned by Berlioz, and was probably used in *If I were King*, Adam, (1852). In England at this period, in addition to the keyboard-operated instrument, we also find the glockenspiel much as it is to-day, the metal bars arranged in two rows, keyboard fashion, and struck with small hammers.[1] In the German military band, the *lyra-glockenspiel* – a portable form of glockenspiel – was customary. (In England it was less frequent.) This instrument consisted of a row of metal cups (later, steel bars) mounted pyramidally on an upright rod held in one hand of the player, whilst his other held the beater. Later instruments with a compass of two or more octaves arranged in two or more rows, were supported from the shoulder (permitting the use of two beaters). The instrument when fully dressed bore the traditional horse-tail plumes (in some cases red-tipped, emblematic of the battlefield).

The lyra-glockenspiel (bell-lyra) has recently made a return to many marching bands. On the modern instrument the bars are arranged vertically in two rows keyboard style. The earlier full size Continental lyra-glockenspiel was arranged in three rows, the centre row comprising the C and F naturals in each octave, with the remaining 'white' notes to the right, and the 'black' notes to the player's left.[2]

Contemporary with Berlioz and Wagner was Schumann, in each of whose four symphonies, timpani have a prominent part. In the First Symphony in B flat (*Spring*) he uses three drums in B flat, F and G flat ♪. In the following symphonies only a pair of drums are employed, with the normal changes between (and during) movements. The drums have interesting solos in the first movement of the Second Symphony and the last movement of the Third Symphony. In his First Symphony Schumann also makes judicious use of the triangle. (In the first movement of his Piano Concerto in A minor, there is, if played as written, a startling dissonance. The timpani are given A and E during chords of F major. An error in clef is conceded, for a transposition to treble clef avoids the clash.)

In the works of Brahms we find the hand of another master exploiting the possibilities of only two drums (at times in chords) with very sparing use of a third. In the Fourth Symphony for instance, three drums support the tonic, dominant and sub-

---

[1] Grassineau, in his *Musical Dictionary* (1769), refers to an instrument constructed of metal bars with a compass of more than three octaves. The bars were struck with two wooden sticks. This form of glockenspiel to which Grassineau gives the name Cymbal, was known in England as the *Sticcado Pastorale*.

[2] See Cimbalom and Continental four row Xylophone.

dominant in the third movement only. It is in this symphony (No. 4) that Brahms employs the triangle. In the Adagio of the last movement of the First Symphony he indicates a group of 32 hemi-demi-semiquavers by giving a minim four strokes. The minim is preceded by a tremolo and followed by two crotchets, each divided into 12 beats.[1] This figure is doubly interesting inasmuch as all other instruments are sustaining

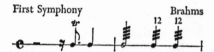

The writing for the timpani in *A German Requiem* (three drums) and *Song of Destiny* is equally interesting.

Brahms and Schumann were in no way extravagant in the use of such percussion as bass drum, cymbals, etc., the focus at all times being on the timpani. So much so that until this period an instrument which figures prominently in modern music had made but brief appearances in orchestral scores: namely the side drum. Gluck is freely quoted as responsible for the earliest orchestral use of the side drum, *Tambour* in *Iphigénie en Tauride*. Berlioz, however, contends that the instrument Gluck specified as Tambour, was a *caisse roulante* (tenor drum). According to M. Lavoix (*Histoire de l'Instrumentation*, Paris, 1878) the side drum was first used by Marais, in the tempest scene of his opera *Alcione* (1706). In Act III tambourin is specified.

If we accept the tambour in Gluck's *Iphigénie en Tauride* as tenor drum, it was Rossini who, after a period of more than a century (Marais 1706), was responsible for re-introducing the side drum into the orchestra. Because of this (or possibly because he elevated the instrument to 'solo rank') he was nicknamed 'Tamburossini'. The introductory solo rolls on the side drums in *La Gazza Ladra* have become a legend, as have the quiet rolls on the smaller of the two kettledrums, giving the impression of distant thunder in the *William Tell* overture. In the autographed manuscript of *La Gazza Ladra* Rossini indicates *Tamburo* 1 and 2 and in the third bar the two drums in unison (no dynamic markings are given). It is possible that Rossini's intention was for a drum at each end of the orchestra.[2] When the overture is played as a concert piece, the second drum is occasionally played 'outside' the orchestra, or where (as is often the case) the part is

---

[1] Like Beethoven, Brahms was meticulous in defining the true roll.

[2] Tom Hammond (Sadler's Wells) is of the opinion that Rossini may have intended the introductory rolls as a convincing announcement to the audience.

played by one player, the first and second bars are performed *f* and *p* respectively.[1] In addition to the side drum, Rossini uses (in the same work) the triangle, bass drum, and timpani in E and B, (given in the original score as Timpani in E – an abbreviation not unusual at this period). In *Stabat Mater* (1832–41) Rossini uses the upper G.

The fact that no cymbals are specifically mentioned does not necessarily mean that he intended these instruments to be silent. In Italy, *Gran Cassa*, or *Cassa*, could signify the combination of bass drum and cymbals, for in many instances (particularly in Verdi) the terms Gran Cassa and *Cassa sola* occur, terms which are generally considered to imply bass drum with cymbals, and bass drum without cymbals.

The lapse in the use of the side drum as an orchestral instrument before its resuscitation by Rossini, and its infrequent appearances for some time to follow, does not mean that it had been idle in other spheres. It remained, however, essentially a military instrument. Structurally, by the mid-nineteenth century the military side drum had a 'new look'. Its diameter (and in some cases the depth) had been reduced, the shell was of brass instead of wood, and from 1837 onwards, due (it is generally conceded) to the inventive genius of the English maker, Cornelius Ward, a method of applying tension by screws was introduced, though the rope-braced drum remained a feature of the regimental band.[2] The snares (at this period a series of gut strings) rested on the lower head.[3]

In general, military drumming continued to be taught by rote. The 'boy' was instructed by the drum major or leading drummer ('leading tipper') by ear, and in the majority of cases assimilated the various drum routines without knowledge of the most elementary principles of music. Many of the exercises for the drum include instructions for the raising and lowering of the arms, to commence and conclude certain beatings, together with other flourishes, such as striking one stick with the other, etc.

Henry Potter says[4]: 'The drums should be slung and properly sloped whilst beating, with the arms brought smartly up, and the knobs of the drumsticks crossed as high as the mouth after each beating, the whole of the drummers lowering their drumsticks to the original position of non-beating together . . . Some regiments, however, still adhere to the practice of raising the sticks after beating, parallel with the eyes'.

In performance the drum was borne on the left thigh at an angle of 45 degrees. It

---

[1] In Britain, in both Theatre and Concert Hall the introductory drum roll is occasionally mistaken for the solo roll preceding the National Anthem.

[2] In recent years rope bracing has been replaced (with an aesthetic loss) by rod tensioning.

[3] The snares to-day are more often of coiled wire or wire-covered silk.

[4] Potter, H. *Drum-Major's Manual*, Potter, London, 1887, p. 23.

was suspended by a leather carriage from the shoulder, as was its forebear the large tabor. The drumsticks were sometimes slightly shorter and stouter than those used to-day. When not in use on the march it was customary for the side drum to be carried on the player's back. The drag-rope, the ornamental cord hanging from beneath the drum, was passed over the head and the slack taken up by it being rolled round the drumsticks until the drum rested firmly on the back, held in position by pressure of the sticks on the chest. In certain cases the sticks were 'housed' in a metal receptacle attached to the carriage straps. (With some regiments a pair of miniature drumsticks were affixed to the Drum-major's uniform.)

In addition to the numerous rudiments, the drummer was obliged to commit to memory a great number of calls, solo, or as an accompaniment to the fife. Here, in addition to its purpose as a timekeeper and an enlivener on the march, lay the real purpose of the military side drum. As already stated, until superseded by the bugle, the drum conveyed the word of command to the troops. In battle, upon the accurate delivery of the calls lay the welfare of the soldiers. As with the earlier drum beatings of Arbeau, these signals were immediately recognisable. Of the numerous calls given by the drum over a period of time, we select for example and comparison the following.[1]

In the anonymous German tutor of 1777 the author gives the side drum beatings for several military duties. He first states that the drum must be tuned to the note D in the bass clef, giving as his reason that the kettledrums sound in the bass clef, and that the note is doubled on many other instruments. Whilst this direction is unusual it is not unique. In a work by J. J. Rousseau (Paris 1788–93) the author, in the section dealing with military music, recommends that the side drums accompanying the fifes, who play in G minor, should be tuned as near as possible in G, and that the

[1] For further drum signals 'French, German, Belgian and Italian' see Kastner *Musique Militaire*. For Scot's Duty, see H. G. Farmer's *Handel's Kettledrums*.

single side drum accompanying the march for wind band should be tuned in D. Whether or not this refinement was observed we cannot say. It certainly has not been handed down. One of the characteristics, and virtues, of the side drum (snared) is that its pitch is indeterminate.

The drum duties given in the German manual include Reveille, Church Parade, Fire Alarm, Tap-room Call, and the Dead March. In the Dead March, instructions are given for *con sordini*, that is, the covering of the drum with a cloth. The five and nine stroke rolls are prominent in the majority of these calls. All rolls are indicated 'w' or 'wirbel', written a series of single beats:

though as directed earlier in the manual, performed with two beats of the drumstick on each written note.

According to the author of the manual the most difficult of these calls to perform (and possibly to obey) was *Zapfen* (Tap-room), where, at the sounding of the drum, the soldier drained his jug and retired immediately to his quarters. (In early nineteenth century English drum manuals we find *taptoo*, from the Dutch *taptoe*. Later came tattoo, a call to quarters, and now connected with a military entertainment.)

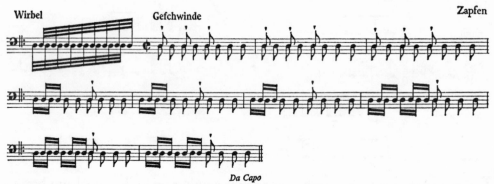

'Dieses Stück ist dem Klange nach, eines der schwersten; fängt mit einem langen Wirbel an und enthält drey Veränderungen, welche hurtig auf einander folgen müssen; wird auch mit grossen Nachdruck gespielet, damit es jedermann höret, auf das baldigste seinen Krug ausleert und sein Quartier zu erreichen sucht.'

By permission of Brussels Conservatoire[1]

Note values are discussed, crotchet, quaver and semiquaver being given as *Tau – Lau – Rau*, and as quarter, eighth and sixteenth notes. The writer states clearly that

[1] The printer, G. L. W. Wiuwe, was responsible for many anonymous publications, including works of his own.

the player should become fully acquainted with these notes and their values. He is also emphatic in the matter of diligent practice, concluding his exposition with the proverb: 'Practice makes perfect'.

Many of these duties and a number of marches, together with various rudiments, including flams, drags, single and double strokes, etc., are given in a mid-eighteenth-century document entitled *Drum Beatings*.[1] The work, which is anonymous, is handwritten. The beatings for the side drum are clearly illustrated, and correspond with many seen in later manuals.

There is also a musical example dealing with the beating of a kettledrum; this it would seem does not apply to a pair of drums. Possibly the author had in mind the small kettledrum employed in the military bands of this period, which was played in much the same way as the present-day tenor drum. The directions for crossing the sticks are interesting. The movements typify the current style.

From an examination of the various manuals, especially the work of Kastner which includes the compositions of the Brothers Philidor and those they assembled, there can be little doubt that in general a high standard of side drumming prevailed in military circles. It seems, however, that excellent as the majority of these players may have been, they did not fit adequately into the orchestra. In England, Chaine in his tutor comments on the picture as he saw it in the mid-nineteenth century. He says:[2] 'Although there are a great number of persons who profess to be Drummers, not one in a hundred could be trusted in an orchestra where good music is played. Some may be good as performers, as they know *certain things*, and perhaps beat the same well "*by ear*", but when in the orchestra they are useless and incapable, simply for this reason, that though beating fairly well, they cannot read even a *simple part*, being entirely ignorant of the Rudiments of Music.'

This state of affairs clearly sprang from the teaching of the drum routines entirely by ear. Having in mind that the duties of the drummer in the Corps of Drums[3] included the memorising of the numerous calls, and that the chief purpose of the instrument was that of a timekeeper and to convey orders, it is not altogether surprising that many of the military drummers of this period experienced some difficulty in complying with orchestral requirements. To-day (and for some time past) matters are very different. Service musicians are given every opportunity to study music, practically and theoretically. Thanks to this, and the assistance of Kneller Hall and the Royal Marine School, for instance, some of our finest orchestral players are men with Service training.

[1] From the library of Sir Samuel Hellier.
[2] Chaine, V. A. *The Drummer's Manual*, Lafleur, London, n.d. p. 4.
[3] A separate body from the drummers in the Regimental Band.

Meanwhile, what of the historical aspect of the military side drum? Throughout the eighteenth century and onwards it continued a constant companion of the fife, a combination as important to the foot regiment as were the trumpets and kettle-drums of the cavalry.[1]

Like the kettledrums, the side drum occupied a place of honour in the regiment in peace or war. It carried the regimental crest and battle honours emblazoned on the shell, a custom which survives. There are numerous references in the Lord Chamberlain's records to the painting and gilding of side drums. The majority of preserved specimens show this custom to be widespread. French drums of the Royal Guard of Louis XV were decorated, as were the drums used during the American Civil War. In Switzerland and Germany a similar practice was followed. In England and Scotland, the tenor and bass drums were emblazoned in the same way as the side drums.

There are examples of the side drum with unusual features. A drum used during the American Civil War is reputed to have had heads of sheet brass.[2] A square drum in the collection of the Brussels Conservatoire is catalogued as: 'A fantastic instrument made by an amateur for some special occasion'. This instrument appears to be unique.

J. A. Kappey[3] mentions a drum with heads of pigskin. This is not unusual, but the circumstances surrounding the instrument are interesting. Kappey speaks of a composer prince, the Landgrave Ludwig IX who, from Kappey's account was so passionately fond of military music that he would daily invite *within* his residence a large band of fifes and drums. Obviously the Prince was extremely fond of noise, for 'it was considered a meritorious accomplishment if a drummer broke his pigskin, because it gave evidence of his having done his duty'.

Whilst on the subject of the military side drum, it would be uncomplimentary to omit a reference to its companions, the tenor and bass drums. The tenor drum is beaten in much the same manner as the side drum, but with felt or soft-headed sticks.[4] It is an essential instrument in a large ensemble, a corps of drums, and with

---

[1] The combination of fife and drum is retained and is responsible for certain duties in barracks. At the changing of the guard, orders in some instances are given on the drum alone.

[2] A British patent issued in 1871 (No. 326) to a Henry Basquit, specifies 'heads' of thin and extremely hard metal, also a 'snare' or 'timbre' consisting of a metal spring which pressed against the inside of the upper head (see internal snares on modern side drum). A few years later (1887) a patent was granted for a drum with the 'batter' (striking) head of wood. A small wooden ring rested on the 'head' and acted as a vibrator. The specification includes a drumstick tipped with rubber.

[3] Kappey, J. A. *Military Music*, Boosey, p. 83–4.

[4] In the orchestra also with side drum sticks.

drums and pipes. The beatings are less involved than those on the side drum, but they none the less demand dexterity. The attendant stick flourishes render the tenor drummer as great a regimental show-piece as the maestro of the big drum. Dr. Farmer says[1]: 'Indeed, there was an unwritten code in the old days that the tenor-drummer had the *piano* passages in which to accomplish his *solo* and the decorative flourishes, whilst the *forte* passages were the property of the big-drummer for his display'.

In form, the tenor drum resembles the large tabor of the fifteenth and sixteenth centuries. It is larger than the military side drum, and due to the absence of snares the tone is in comparison subdued, giving rise to the likening of the two tones to the voices of the sergeant-major and the chaplain.

In France and Germany the tenor drum appears with certainty in the military band from the early nineteenth century. Kastner illustrates rope-tensioned and rod-tensioned tenor drums in his *Manuel général de musique militaire* (1848). (See Inventions and Patents.)

It is not certain when the tenor drum was adopted in the British service, though it is generally considered that it superseded the small kettledrum used by the foot regiments, evidence for which exists as late as the close of the eighteenth century. Samuel Potter makes no reference to the tenor drum in his 'The art of beating the drum' (1815), though Dr. Farmer, in referring to a letter in which a drum without snares is mentioned, makes it clear that the instrument was in use prior to 1834.[2]

The bass drum is the metronome of the regimental band. Henry Potter says[3]: 'As the general credit of a marching regiment depends upon the beating of the bass drummer, he should not only be a good "timist", but incapable of being led away by any melody detrimental to regulation'. In general, in military drumming the bass drummer uses a large-headed stick in the right hand principally to mark the time, and a smaller stick in the left hand for intermediate accompaniment (as the switch was formerly used). As with the tenor drum, the sticks are normally secured to the wrists, a procedure observed with the early cavalry kettledrummers.

The regimental bass drummer is an impressive figure in full dress. This includes the traditional leopard skin or cloth apron. His main task, however, is that of a pacemaker. In conjunction with the side drummers he establishes the tempo of the march with the traditional three- or five-pace preludial rolls,[4] (normally Infantry

---

[1] Farmer, H. G. *Handel's Kettledrums*, Hinrichsen, London, 1960, p. 99.

[2] See *Handel's Kettledrums*, ibid. p. 99.

[3] Potter, Henry. ibid. p. 19.

[4] Approximately 110 to 140 steps per minute according to the Regiment. In 1788, Col. D. Dundas, a writer on military matters, gives Ordinary Slow March 80, Quick March 120, each step to be of 30 inches.

2 three-pace rolls, Foot Guards 1 five-pace). The bass drummer (this time alone) gives the instrumentalists certain cues such as: change of march, or cease playing, by striking a 'double' tap at given points towards the end of the final phrase.

At a march past or similar function, the cue to cease playing may occur at any point. (The equivalent in the orchestra is that the conductor 'taps' lightly for 'second time' or coda.) In the cavalry similar directions are given by the kettle-drummer:

As stated earlier, until well into the nineteenth century the bass drum existed in two forms: as the deep cylindrical long drum, and with a shallow shell of larger diameter, known until the beginning of the nineteenth century as the Turkish drum. The single-skin bass drum, an English product known as the Gong-drum, made an appearance in the middle of the same century (see Distin's Monster Drum).

In addition to its function in military circles the drum had numerous civil duties. In many Continental museums is displayed the 'town drum', used in certain cases by the town crier instead of a hand bell. (This custom still survives in odd corners). In some cases these instruments date back to the sixteenth century, as for example the Basle side drum, 1575. In Scotland, in the Lanark town records of 1598[1]: '... it is ordained that the townsmen be ready night or day quhen the common bell ryngis, or at the straik of the suesch, quhen onye fraye cumis to the toun'. (The *suesch* was the town drum.) From the Lanark records Lyndesay G. Langwill has selected many interesting references to the drum, from which we gather that the town drummer functioned as the town crier, announcing among other items of public interest, the hour of the day. For instance, in May 1581, Watsone was reappointed 'toun menstral', and the curious instruction is given that he 'gang throw the toun with the swys morne and evining, and quhen it is weit, that the swysche may nocht gang, that the said Jhone sall gang himself throw with the pyp morne and evining.' This wise precaution, says Lyndesay Langwill, was made to prevent rain damaging the vellum of the drum-head. Later we find: 'After the middle of the seventeenth century, the expression *straik* (stroke) of the *suesch* (drum) gives place to the phrase "tuck, touck, or tuk of drum",' and it served to announce a quaintly varied series of decisions of the Council.

To the North, at Kirkwall, Orkney, the drum continues to herald the business of a city: a side drum is used by the town crier of this ancient and royal burgh in place of the usual bell.

[1] Langwill, Lyndesay G. 'The Piper, Drummer and Bellman of Lanark in Olden Times', reprinted from *The Hamilton Advertiser* of 21st January, 1939.

A deep side drum in the possession of the Musselburgh (Scotland) town authorities is used in conjunction with the performance (once in every 21 years) of the ancient and traditional ceremony of the Riding of the Marches. (This ceremony is mentioned in the Lanark records). The Musselburgh instrument is possibly 200 years old. Military instruments of a similar vintage are included in an Edinburgh collection (Messrs. Glen's famous bagpipe shop). Here is a long drum made *c.* 1794 for The Edinburgh Royal Highland Volunteer Regiment. There is also a side drum presented on 24th December 1796, at Plymouth, to The 25th Regiment of Foot It is thought that this instrument was used at Waterloo.

It is not surprising to find the drum so highly esteemed in Switzerland and Scotland. The drummers (past and present) of both nations are famous. H. G. Farmer traces the old drum and fife calls of Scottish Regiments back to the early seventeenth century. He also says[1]: 'Possibly the same special martial music was heard from the drummers of those Scottish companies established in France in 1590. . . .' In many respects there is a similarity in style between Basle drumming and that employed in the Scottish Pipe Band.[2] Similar skill was to be found, however, in England and elsewhere: the drummers of the Garde Républicaine, for example, and American drummers of the Civil War period, whose high standard of playing is perpetuated to the present day – N.A.R.D. (National Association of Rudimentary Drummers).[3]

In England, in addition to its military purpose, we find constant references to the use of the drum in civil life, in connection with various forms of musical entertainment and other social activities, particularly that of the showman. Dickens makes several references to the use of a drum, in one instance revealing an interesting custom. In 'Going into Society' from the *Christmas Stories* Magsman, the showman, speaking of Chops the dwarf, his former employee ('gone into society by way of a lottery windfall') says: 'He had a good salary down on the drum every Saturday as the day came round'.[4] This payment of wages, and in some cases the honouring of a debt, seems to be of long standing.

In legends we have the nuisance of 'The Demon Drummer of Tidworth' and the prophetic drumming said to be heard in a well in Northants.

An interesting custom survives in Ireland in the use of the 'Lambeg Drum'. The

[1] Farmer, H.G. ibid. p.34. (The side drum did not join the pipes until c. 1850).

[2] A Guild of drummers still flourishes in Basle.

[3] In Great Britain there is the Guild of Ancient Fifes and Drums.

[4] The author has personal experience of the custom of paying down on the drum in his earliest professional engagement (in a small circus).

Lambeg drum is a large double-headed, rope-tensioned bass drum, played with thin sticks and used in functions connected with the Orange Lodges of Northern Ireland, in particular with the Orange Day March. Lambeg drumming is a singular art. There are no manuals concerning this technique, the craft is, as with the tablā and other notable drums, usually handed down from father to son. Competitions in drumming are held between the various Orange Lodges. In these tests, both skill and endurance are taken into account. One of the chief rhythms played on the Lambeg drum is based on a popular doggerel: 'Are there any public houses on the road to Lambeg – Lambeg – Lambeg?'

To-day, the heads on the Lambeg drum are of calfskin, as it is said that when headed originally with donkey skin (now forbidden) windows were broken during drumming.[1] (In contrast, there is the gentler *bodhrán*, a small frame drum.)

In many of the instruments recently referred to the skill of the drum maker is evident. It is also apparent that there is a marked similarity in instruments of the side, tenor and bass drum family over a large area. Preserved specimens in the U.S.A. resemble those in Europe, including Russia, and so forth. As with the kettledrums, the majority of these preserved specimens are instruments with historical background. The collection of Messrs. Potter of London and Aldershot contains some of the finest examples of the craftsmanship of drum making in existence.

During the latter half of the nineteenth century, we find that not only are composers making demands on an ever-increasing variety of percussion instruments, but that such instruments as the tambourine, triangle, castanets, hitherto regarded primarily as responsible for the introduction of local colour, are becoming an integral part of orchestra structure. Certain instruments have already participated in the melodic structure, bells and glockenspiel, others are about to do so. The xylophone, for instance, though known in Europe from at least the early sixteenth century found no place in orchestral scores until the latter half of the nineteenth century. (Berlioz, it will be remembered, made no reference to the xylophone in his *Instrumentation*.[2])

In the Far East the xylophone had for many centuries been an important melodic instrument. European travellers on their return from Africa had spoken of the

---

[1] Beating such a drum in a narrow street has long been considered dangerous. Similar risks have been connected with other pulsatile instruments. It was reported of the Richardson rock harmonica (q.v.) that the full power was never brought out in a small hall, as the volume of sound and consequent vibrations were too great for the size of the room, and more particularly for the safety of the windows.

[2] Greek: *xulon* – wood, *phone* – sound. Ger: *Xylophon, Strohfiedel* or *Holzharmonika*. It: *Zilafone*. Fr: *Xylophon* or *Claquebois*. These are but some of the names given to the instrument.

pleasant sound and musical quality of the native marimbas. In Europe, a degree of virtuosity sufficient to attract the notice of Mendelssohn had been expressed on a simple instrument made of wooden bars. The player, a Russian Jew named Gusikow, whose performance also drew favourable comment from Chopin and Liszt, made the xylophone known in the musical centres of the Continent from 1830. The instrument had long been associated with his fellow countrymen in Eastern Europe, with the Poles and Tartars, and with the people of Southern Germany. The primitive nature of Gusikow's instrument made a great impression on Mendelssohn and his sister Fanny, who, in a letter to Klingemann dated 12th February 1836[1] wrote: 'I have heard the phenomenon, and without being ecstatic, like most people, must own that the skill of the man beats everything that I could have imagined, for with his wooden sticks resting on straw, his hammers also being of wood, he produces all that is possible with the most perfect instrument. It is a complete riddle to me how the thin sound the thing gives, something like Papageno's flute, can be produced with such materials'. A few days later (18th February), Mendelssohn in a letter to his mother[2] said: 'a real phenomenon, a killing fellow (Mordkerl) who is inferior to no player on earth either in style or execution, and delights me more on his odd instrument than many do on their pianos, just because it is so thankless . . . I have not enjoyed a concert so much for a long time'.

Mendelssohn further expressed his admiration of Gusikow's performance by acting as his accompanist at one or two public concerts. In his regard for the possibilities of the xylophone, Mendelssohn echoed the opinion of Mersenne, who considered that when played to its full effect, the xylophone gave as much pleasure as any other instrument.

Gusikow toured extensively as a soloist, and it was no doubt due to him that the xylophone became a feature in numerous spheres of public entertainment, ranging from the variety show to the concert hall. The instrument that Gusikow made popular was a 'four row' (or four street) xylophone. (These are the names by which the so-called Continental xylophone is known to-day.) An illustration of Gusikow's instrument (in the National Library, Vienna) shows a series of 28 crude wooden bars arranged, semi-tonally, in the form of a trapezoid, the four rows resting on five straw supports.

Subsequent examples of this style of instrument show an extended compass, varying from $2\frac{1}{2}$ to 3 octaves (chromatic) ascending from C, or at times E natural. To effect an economy of space the bars are arranged ladder-wise in four rows

[1] Hensel, Sebastian. *The Mendelssohn Family* 1729–1847, vol. II, Sampson Low, Marston, Searle & Rivington, London, 1881, p. 4.

[2] From Grove's *Dictionary of Music and Musicians*, vol. III, Macmillan, London, 1954, p. 858.

indented into each other, with the diatonic scale of C lying midway in the ladders.[1] The notes C natural, F natural and C sharp are duplicated to the right and left, rendering the instrument, because of the consequent choice of 'fingering', extremely agile. (This style of instrument is occasionally seen to-day in the Continental orchestra.)

Fig. 41. Four-row xylophone

The bars of spruce, maple, rosewood or walnut, were strung together and laid on ropes of straw or, in the case of the more elaborate instrument, suspended in a box-resonator, or resonated individually. The beaters were similar to those still used on the dulcimer. They were spoon-shaped, and cut from spruce or willow wood. In this 'four row' xylophone, and its counterpart in metal, the lyra glockenspiel, is seen an elaboration of the earlier dulcimer with its single ladder of wire strings, and the primitive *strohfiedel* with its single row of wooden bars.

During the nineteenth century the xylophone appeared under various disguises, for instance: the *Triphon* and the *Tryphone*. The former instrument according to Sachs (*Reallexicon*) was a *xylosistron* in the form of an upright wing, invented in 1810

---

[1] Probably influenced by the 'layout' arrangement of the cimbalom, an instrument with which Gusikow would be well acquainted. The keyboard on a seventeenth-century organ in Barcelona Museum suggests a similar influence; it is arranged in three rows of twelve keys each, in the shape of a dulcimer.

by Wiedner of Frankfurt. The Tryphone was the product of a Parisian, Charles de Try. This instrument, which it seems took a slightly different form from that of Gusikow's was introduced about 1870. Like Gusikow, de Try had the reputation of being a vistuoso on his instrument. As this was a period of considerable experiment in keyboard percussion (celesta, etc.), it is possible that the bars of de Try's instrument were arranged in two rows, keyboard-fashion. (The glockenspiel had already arrived in this style). Percy Scholes says[1] 'Perhaps as a result of de Try's demonstration Saint-Saëns rattled the bones of the dead to its music in his *Danse Macabre!*' (1874). Alternatively, he may have been influenced by J.G. Kastner's reference to the xylophone in his *Les danses des morts* (1852). It is generally agreed that it is in Saint-Saëns work that the xylophone first appeared in the standard orchestral repertoire. Consideration must, however, be given to the set of variations attributed to Ferdinand Kauer. In this work, written in 1810, the xylophone is given a challenging and lengthy solo variation. Certain authorities have referred to *strohfiedel* and xylophone in Hans Christian Lumbye's *Traumbildern*. In the British Museum score (1874) reference is made to *steirische (stick) zither,* not xylophone. (see dulcimer p. 308 and pl.90).Danse Macabre   C. Saint-Saëns

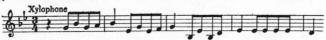

Saint-Saëns employed the xylophone some years later – in 1886, in *The Carnival of Animals* ('Fossiles'). Here the melody is the same as that in *Danse Macabre*, but the metre is two-four as against three-four in the earlier work. In *The Carnival of Animals* 'Aquarium' Saint-Saëns scored for the harmonica. It is considered that he had in mind either the keyboard *glass harmonica* (an instrument resembling the keyboard glockenspiel with which he would have been familiar), or a similar sounding instrument where glass or metal plates are stuck with small mallets. There are preserved specimens of both types of instrument dating from the mid-eighteenth century, at which period the *sticcado pastorale* (a mallet-played instrument with sounding parts of glass) was in vogue.[2] Percussion instruments of this nature would have proved more practical in Saint-Saëns' orchestration than an earlier form of harmonica in which drinking glasses were struck with sticks.[3]

[1] Scholes, Percy. ibid. p. 706.

[2] Dr. Burney refers to the popularity of the *'strofil'* throughout Saxony in his account of a musical tour in Germany and Italy (1770). He says the instrument is made of pieces of glass of different lengths, and played on by sticks like the sticcado.

[3] To-day, the part for the harmonica in Saint-Saëns' work is usually played on the orchestral glockenspiel, though in a certain recording a mouth-harmonica was used, prompting interesting comment in musical circles.

To the modern reader the 'glass harmonica' (Fr. *verrillon*; Ger. *Glasspiel*) may signify an instrument not of percussion, but of friction; musical glasses where the rim is rubbed with a moistened finger.[1] These were extremely popular during the eighteenth century. At first these instruments were tuned (like the *jalatarang* of India) by the addition of a quantity of water, the greater the quantity of liquid the lower the notes, and so forth. Later, the glasses were designed in a manner which rendered the water unnecessary. The instrument attracted the notice of notable composers. Whilst Gluck was in London he performed in 1746 a concerto of his own composition scored for 26 drinking glasses and full orchestral accompaniment.[2]

In 1762 Benjamin Franklin constructed an instrument he first named 'the glossy chord' and later 'the armonica'. Here, the hemispherical-shaped glasses were attached to a treadle-operated spindle, and the moistened finger tips pressed on the revolving glasses; an operation from all accounts subjecting the performer to eventual nervous disorders. Mozart composed in 1791 an Adagio and Rondo for harmonica, flute, oboe, viola, and violoncello and Tomášek a *Fantasie* for Harmonica in 1809. Beethoven included harmonica accompaniment in his incidental music to *Leonora Prohaska* (1814). There is a part for the instrument in Glinka's *Russlan and Ludmilla* (1842).[3]

Experiments with new musical instruments continued throughout the latter part of the nineteenth century. In 1886 the *celesta* was invented by Auguste Mustel. This instrument, strictly speaking a keyboard glockenspiel, consists of a series of small metal bars set in motion by a modified pianoforte keyboard mechanism. Each bar is resonated by an accurately tuned box resonator. This, in combination with the felt covered hammers, is mainly responsible for the dulcet tone of the instrument. It is further equipped with a sustaining pedal, pressure on the pedal lifting a damping action. The original compass was five octaves from C below middle C. Due to the indifferent quality of the lower notes, the bottom octave was abandoned. In recent years, however, with the tone of the lower notes improved, instruments with a five octave range have been re-introduced. The part for the celesta, written on two bracketed staves, as the pianoforte, is written an octave lower than actual pitch.

Tchaikovsky was one of the first composers to use the celesta. Impressed by the tone of the instrument whilst on a visit to Paris, he included it in his *Casse-Noisette*

---

[1] *Glasharmonika* – obviously keyboard action – is requested by Richard Strauss in the finale of his opera *Die Frau ohne Schatten* (1919).

[2] The type of instrument known to Gluck has been revived by the eminent recitalist Bruno Hoffmann.

[3] Musical glasses, to be played with the finger-tips are specified in Carl Orff's stage work *Astutuli* (1945–6). In his first opera *Gisei, das Opfer* (1913) he wrote for glass harmonica.

('Dance of the Sugar-Plum Fairy'), since when it has become an accepted orchestral instrument.

It seems that Mustel's celesta was inspired by an instrument he (or his father Victor) constructed some twenty years earlier, known as the *typophone* (or *dulcitone*). In this instrument the sound-producing agents (keyboard operated) consist of a series of tuning forks, producing a tone similar to that of the celesta, but less powerful. Vincent d'Indy used the dulcitone in *Le Chant de la Cloche*, a composition with which he gained a prize in Paris in 1884 (two years before the invention of the celesta). To-day the dulcitone is rarely used orchestrally.

An instrument similar to the typophone was patented in Leipzig in 1882; this was the four octave *adiophone* of Fischer & Fritz. Both these instruments were anticipated, however, by an English invention in 1788[1] known as Claggett's *aiuton*, or ever-tuned organ. According to its inventor, Charles Claggett,[2] an Irishman living in London, this instrument 'without Pipes, Glasses, Bells, or Strings, produces Tones sweeter than on any other Organ yet invented'. The instrument, which according to Claggett's specification could cover from three to six octaves, was composed of a number of tuning forks, or single prongs or rods of metal, fixed on a board or box by the lower end, and governed or put into vibration by finger keys moving hammers or jacks by means of levers, as in the pianoforte or harpsichord.[3] The aiuton was but one of Claggett's numerous inventions. Interesting as the aiuton appears to have been, we find no record of its subsequent use in compositions, whereas both the celesta and the xylophone have become active members of the orchestra. Certain notable instruments make rare, but nevertheless significant excursions into the standard orchestral repertoire. Foremost among such instruments is surely the *cimbalom*,[4] the dulcimer of the Hungarian orchestra. The dulcimer is the most important of European non-keyboard psalteries – as stated earlier, it is virtually a struck psaltery. It is widely used throughout Eastern Europe, both as an accompany-

---

[1] In principle at least they were preceded by Handel's carillon and Mozart's *istrumento d'acciaio*.

[2] *Musical Phenomena* no. I, 1793, Eyre & Spottiswoode, London, 1856, p. 8.

[3] The pianoforte, whilst undeniably an instrument of percussion, is not to be dealt with in this volume. Like the celesta, it is not included in the percussion section of the orchestra. Strictly speaking, the keyboard instruments differ from those struck with mallets, inasmuch as the sound from the former is produced indirectly through the medium of the keyboard mechanism. The piano-action glockenspiel and keyboard xylophone fall into this class, and it is not usual for them or the celesta to be played by the orchestral percussionist.

[4] Anthony Baines says: '. . . the Hungarian concert *cimbalom* . . . is a telling instrument that merits exploitation in orchestration as the harp is used, for the sake of sonorities and effects obtainable on no other instrument' in *Musical Instruments Through the Ages*, ed. Anthony Baines, Faber, London, 1966, p. 207.

ing and solo instrument. The cimbalom used in the Hungarian orchestra was improved towards the end of the nineteenth century by the addition of foot-pedal damping action, an invention of Schunda of Budapest (who was also responsible for improvement in timpani). On dulcimers without this mechanism the strings are damped by hand, an operation demanding the same high degree of agility and cunnning as does the playing of the instrument itself. The hammers, held one in each hand, are spoon-shaped. They are similar to those used on the four row xylophone. Some of the strings (wire) of the cimbalom are divided by bridges (similar to the Chinese zither *yang-ch'in*) into two or more tuned lengths, giving an overall compass of four chromatic octaves. The lower register has three strings to each note, the middle register four strings, and the higher register four or five strings.

The part for the cimbalom is generally written on two bracketed staves in the treble and bass clefs. Melodic passages, arpeggi and shakes are among its characteristics. Stravinsky introduced this fascinating (and technically formidable) instrument into the orchestra in *Renard* (1917), and a year later in *Ragtime*. (Stravinsky gave instructions for hard and soft beaters, and for the wires to be struck behind the bridge.) Generally better-known is the inclusion of the cimbalom in Kodály's *Háry János* Suite, (1926). The individual tone of the Hungarian cimbalom adds considerably to the character of this delightful work, as it does also to Bartók's First Rhapsody for Violin and Orchestra (1928) – here plucked with the finger-tips. Later works with a part for the cimbalom include *The Midsummer Night's Dream* (Orff), *Carée* (Stockhausen) and *Eclat* (Boulez). The cimbalom has been occasionally used in film scores, such as those by Thomas Rajna. Internationally-known cimbalom soloists include the late Gilbert Webster (principal percussionist B.B.C. Symphony Orchestra), John Leach and Heather Corbett (also a marimba soloist).

In the Magyar band it is the instrument par excellence. It is here that its capacities are to-day most seriously appreciated. In general, it is played from memory or by ear, and with considerable latitude. In gypsy circles, an expert performer on the cimbalom is a man of importance, comparable to the master drummer of Africa, or the leading tablā or mrdanga player of India. Expressively, these instruments have a good deal in common, as much of their significance lies in the art of extemporisation, the drum rhythmically and the cimbalom melodically.

The essence of many folk instruments lies in qualities that are not possible to realise fully in the concert orchestra. This is undoubtedly true of the *doira*, one of the most important membrane percussion instruments of Eastern Europe and Russia. The doira is a hand drum resembling a large tambourine. The jingles, consisting of small rings, or in some cases small bells, are suspended inside the wood shell, the exterior of which is frequently ornamented with mother-of-pearl. The doira accompanies almost every form of folk music. In the hands of an expert, the numerous shades of tone produced by the thumb and fingers on various parts of the skin, combined with complex rhythmic figures, produce as bewildering an effect as that of the percussionist in the Indian chamber ensemble.

The doira is but one of the numerous percussion instruments used in Soviet folk music. Included are small kettledrums with laced heads, joined in pairs in the manner of the Moroccan and other near-Eastern double-drums, and a small kettle-drum with metal bowl, the *daulbaz* (or *chindaul*), originally used for hunting and signalling. Larger kettledrums some with wooden bodies are frequently met. Among these are instruments with crude screw-tensioning, and those with laced heads. One of the latter type has an unusual method of tensioning. The instrument rests on a low stool, and the cords attached to the flesh hoop (a floating head) pass underneath the stool. The only drum we have found with a comparable method of tensioning is the rope-braced drum of Sumatra, where pressure is applied to the head by forcing wedges between the base of the drum and the wooden pedestal to which the instrument is secured (q.v.). Other drums include normal side and bass drums, rope-braced or rod-tensioned. Somewhat unusual is the *tumir*, a rope-tensioned side drum, where pressure is applied by the twisting of wooden dowels which are looped in the rope (cf. Japanese du-daiko).

A further drum of interest is the *tupan*, one of the most notable instruments of Central Europe. The tupan is a double-headed rope-braced drum with heads of goat's hide. In appearance it resembles a large tenor drum. It is played in the manner of the Turkish bass drum, i.e. held vertically and struck on the right side with a stick and the left with a rod or switch, a style utilised by Haydn and subsequent com-posers, and from all accounts a technique dating back several centuries. As with the doira of Russia, the tablā and mrdanga of India, and some of the more important drums of the Far East and Africa, the tupan is no mere timekeeper. It is a solo instrument capable of high expression, and is also the chief accompaniment of the *zurla* (shawm). The technique of the tupanist has been vividly described by Yury Arbatsky.[1]

In Balkan and Turkish folk music one may still hear the *davul*. This is a large drum (double-headed), beaten with a knobbed or hooked stick on one side and a light cane on the other. Occasionally a snare is fitted to one head of the *davul*. (pl. 152.)

A percussion instrument in the form of a 'one man band' is used in the folk music of Russia and Northern Poland. This instrument, known as the Devil's violin, con-sists of a crude violin with three wire strings, a number of small bells, two cymbals,

[1] Arbatsky, Yury. *Beating the Tupan in the Central Balkans*, Newberry Library, Chicago, 1953.

and a drum, the whole mounted on a stout pole from five to six feet in length. A grotesque head, representing the devil with a 'hat' formed by the two cymbals, surmounts the top of the pole. The 'strings' are supported on a bridge resting on the drum, which is secured to the front of the pole, a little below the centre. Bells are fixed to the back of the pole, and hang from the devil's head.[1]

The devil's violin forms the 'rhythm section' of a small group of musicians, consisting normally of two violins, a clarinet, and a devil's violin as leader. The performer on the one-man-band holds the pole in his left hand, and a bow in his right. He uses the bow to rasp the strings (no particular tuning) whilst he taps the pole on the ground, alternating with beats on the drum and cymbals with the tip of the bow, and strokes of various length on the bells performed with the back of the bow, the innumerable sequences being performed with spectacular flourishes.

In addition to this unusual instrument and the equally interesting specimens of membrane drums, there are instruments, particularly in Southern Russia, sufficiently elemental to remind us of past generations. There are stone clappers and others in wood; one species of the latter with its several blades being almost identical with the Chinese p'ai-pan, q.v. Rattles are as diverse and exotic as those found in Africa. Also, over a large area we find castanets in stone, wood and metal, tambourines with jingles, finger cymbals, and sprays of bells in diverse forms. A further percussion instrument (*tornki*) consists of a pair of spoons (in most cases wooden), with small bells attached to the handles – these are used to provide a rhythmic background to singing or dancing.[2] The spoons are either beaten on a hard surface (often a table) or manipulated in pairs as clappers.[3]

A similar instrument (*coutália*) is used among the Greeks of Asia Minor. Here, dancers hold two spoons, which are of box or other hard wood, in each hand. By opening and closing the fingers the spoons are made to strike each other. Other popular Greek idiophonic instruments include the *massá* (cymbals on a clapper), small cymbals in pairs (*zilia*), a triangle (*trigono*), and cowbells of determinate pitch (*coudhoúnia*), all of which serve occasional purpose in religious songs (carols). There is also the *simandron*, a form of wood block used by the priest. Membrane drums include instruments resembling our side and bass drums, tambourines (*dèfi*) and

[1] A similar instrument with a single string, the *Bombas* (or *Bumbas*), is known in Flanders and Germany. There is also the *Violon de Binge* where a notched stick is drawn across a bridge of circular discs of wood and metal.

[2] See *spatula*, a culinary implement used as a timekeeper, etc.

[3] A table is used as a drum by Hungarian gypsies when no other rhythm instrument is available. The complex technique includes friction effects, cf. African drums, Indian tablā, and orchestral tambourine.

single-headed drums with clay bodies. Among the melodic instruments the dulcimer (*sandoúri*) is important.[1]

The tuned percussion instruments of Central Europe include, in addition to the dulcimer, a simple form of xylophone. In many of these instruments, as in folk instruments throughout the universe, there has been little change over a long period of time. It is in those instruments adopted by the orchestra that constant development is observed, due largely to the steadily increasing demands on the percussion department by serious composers. The close of the nineteenth century was an era of exploitation in orchestral tone colour, and in many of these experiments the instruments of percussion played an important part.

[1] See Anoyanakis, Fivos. *Exposition d'Instruments de Musique Populaires Grecs*, Icaros, Société d'Éditions, Athens, 1965.

Bibliography: Chapter 13

THE ROMANTIC ORCHESTRA—I

ANOYANAKIS, Fivos. *Exposition d'Instruments de Musique Populaires Grecs*, Icaros, Société d'Éditions, Athens, 1965.

ARBATSKY, Yury. *Beating the Tupan in the Central Balkans*, Newberry Library, Chicago, 1953.

BAINES, Anthony (ed.). *Musical Instruments Through the Ages*, Faber, London, 1966.

BERLIOZ, Hector. *Traité de l'instrumentation et d'orchestration modernes*, Schonenberger, Paris, 1843.
Evenings in the Orchestra, translated by A. R. Fortescue, Peregrine, London, 1963.

CHAINE, V. A. *The Drummer's Manual*, Lafleur, London, n.d.

DONINGTON, Robert. *The Instruments of Music*, Methuen, London, 1951.

FARMER, Henry. *Handel's Kettledrums*, Hinrichsen, London, 1950, 1960.

FORSYTH, Cecil. *Orchestration*, Macmillan, London, 1955.

GEVAERT, François. *Nouveau traité d'instrumentation*, Lemoine, Paris—Bruxelles, 1885.

GRASSINEAU, James. *A Musical Dictionary*, London, 1740.

GROVE, G. *Dictionary of Music and Musicians*, Macmillan, London, 1954.

Guinness Book of Records (1968), Guinness Superlatives, London.

HENSEL, Sebastian. *The Mendelssohn Family*, 1729–1847, vol. II, Sampson Low, Marston, Searle & Rivington, London, 1881.

KAPPEY, J. A. *Military Music*, Boosey, London, 1894.

KASTNER, Georges. *Méthode de timbales*, Schlesinger, Paris, 1845. *Instrumentation*, Paris, 1837.
Manuel général de musique militaire, Didot frères, Paris, 1848.

KIRBY, P. R. *The Kettle-drums*, Oxford, 1930.

LANGWILL, Lyndesay G. 'The Piper, Drummer and Bellman of Lanark in Olden Times', reprinted from *The Hamilton Advertiser*, 21 January, 1939.

LAVOIX, M. *Histoire de l'instrumentation*, Paris, 1878.

Musical Phenomena, no. I, Eyre & Spottiswoode, London, 1856.

POTTER, Henry. *Drum-Major's Manual*, Potter, London, 1887.

POTTER, Samuel. *The art of beating the drum*, London, 1815.

ROUSSEAU, Jean Jacques. *Les Oeuvres Complétes*, Recueil des oeuvres de Musique de Jean Jacques Rousseau, Tome premier, Nouvelle Edition, Paris, 1788-93.

SACHS, Curt. *The History of Musical Instruments*, Norton, New York, 1940.

SCHOLES, Percy. *The Mirror of Music*, vol. I, Novello, Oxford, 1947.

—*The Oxford Companion to Music*, Oxford, 1938–44.

SMART, George. *Leaves from the Journals of Sir George Smart*, ed. Cox & Cox, Longmans, London, 1907.

14

The Romantic Orchestra—II

From the middle of the nineteenth century we find numerous composers demanding a general extension of the compass of the timpani. Berlioz in his *Instrumentation* hinted at the eventual employment of smaller and larger drums both to comply with the production of notes above and below those in common use in his time, and also to provide an improvement in tone quality. With the exception of Vejvanovsky's, Mozart's and Rossini's occasional use of the high G, and Schubert's and Mendelssohn's employment of the upper F sharp, the classical composers confined their timpani scores to the octave F to F Wagner's use of two pairs of drums called (with occasional exceptions such as the low E in *Götterdämmerung* and *Parsifal*) for nothing above or below F, Berlioz with his numerous demands requested no tunings beyond this compass; so with rare exceptions we can assume the general employment until the middle of the century of drums with diameters in the region of 27½ inches or 28 inches, and 25 inches or 24½ inches. With composers such as Glinka and Rimsky-Korsakov making frequent demands on the upper G, and the later requests by Saint-Saëns and Rimsky-Korsakov for still higher notes, coupled with Mahler's use of the extreme low register, the compass of the drums by 1900 was extended to the compass of two octaves. Glinka employed the high G most effectively in the solo for the timpani in *Russlan and Ludmilla* (1842), as did Rimsky-Korsakov in his *Russian Easter Festival Overture* (1888). Glinka's exciting pattern:

is used in precisely the same rhythm as Rimsky-Korsakov's.

317

There is no doubt that on the Continent the use of three or more drums was common enough well before the turn of the century. In England, however, Victor de Pontigny in a lecture on kettledrums given in 1876[1] refers repeatedly to a pair. The English players were possibly as shy of the third drum as they were of the use of the T-shaped tuning handles. As for the machine drum, it was not until 1905 that pedal tuning timpani found a permanent home in England, due to the personal acquisition of a pair of Dresden drums by Sir Henry J. Wood[2].

During this same period a decided extension in the use of other percussion instruments is apparent. Borodin, in addition to his vital scoring for the timpani, colours his scores characteristically with the side drum, tambourine, cymbals and so forth. In the Polovtsian Dances from *Prince Igor* (completed after his death by Rimsky-Korsakov and Glazounov) the side drum has an impelling part with its repetitive

and later .

The side drum is prominent in many Russian compositions, in some cases as a timekeeper, and in others as a means of colouring. Rimsky-Korsakov employs it delightfully in the third movement of *Scheherazade* where it accompanies (almost

solo) the clarinet. 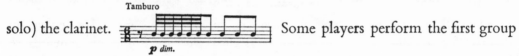 Some players perform the first group

as a seven stroke roll, others hand to hand. Later in the movement the side drum is joined by the timpani, triangle, tambourine and cymbals, resulting in a novel percussion ensemble, as is also the combination of timpani, tambourine and triangle in the fourth movement of his *Capriccio Espagnol*. In the latter work the scene opens with a solo roll on the side drum which is carried through the brass and solo violin cadenzas. The timpani and cymbals then join the side drum in a short solo. In cadenza III a timpani roll accompanies the flute solo. In cadenza IV the clarinet is accompanied by a tremolo (with two soft sticks) on the cymbal, whilst in cadenza V the harp is joined by a *pp* tremolo on the triangle – usually played with a knitting needle to ensure the correct dynamic. In the *Easter Overture* there is a part for the glockenspiel (an instrument seldom used by Rimsky-Korsakov). The sound of the great bell in this work is conjured from the tam-tam *quasi campana granda*. Rimsky-Korsakov also scored for piccolo timpano, having a small kettledrum made to provide the high D flat in *Mlada*. His contemporaries were also adventurous in the

---

[1] Pontigny, Victor de. 'On Kettledrums', *Proceedings of the Musical Association*, vol. II, 1876, Spottiswoode & Co. London.

[2] The redoubtable 'Timber' (as Sir Henry Wood was affectionately known to his players) ensured that his timpanist made full use of them.

use of percussion. In Ippolitov-Ivanov's *Caucasian Sketches* there is a part for small kettledrums (*piccolo timpani orientali*). In Mussorgky's opera *Boris Godunov* there is a 'clash' on four tubular bells (*campani*), the bells being struck simultaneously. In the original score of this opera the upper A flat on the timpani is required. Tchaikovsky's concert-overture *1812* includes in addition to the normal symphonic percussion, a peal of bells and the effect of a cannon. To-day the bell part is normally played on an E flat scale of orchestral tubular bells, to comply with the prevailing key. This was not the composer's intention. In the original score no key signature is

given, there is merely a tremolo sign, thus: Tchaikovsky adds that the

bells should be large, and that the pitch is not important, also that they should give the imitation of a festive occasion. The work was to have been first performed at the consecration in 1882 of the Moscow Cathedral, built to commemorate the liberation of the Russians from the Napoleonic invasion of 1812. The intention was to incorporate into the overture at the prescribed points the bells of the city, together with the firing of cannons. The work, however, was not performed on this occasion, its premiere being given some time later at the Moscow Exhibition, probably with more austere effects. Recently, in gramophone recordings of this overture, measures have been taken to give as faithful a representation as possible of the composer's original plan. Such measures include the superimposing of church bells, in one instance the Laura Spelman Rockefeller Memorial Carillon (Riverside Church, New York), and the use of a French bronze cannon made at Strasbourg, in 1761, said to be of the type used by Napoleon at Borodino.[1] The author recollects a recording of the work by the Decca Company, where several sets of tubular bells were placed at strategic points in the studio (the large hall of the Kingsway Hall, London). For the cannon effects a theatre maroon was exploded in a dustbin in an outer corridor of the hall, resulting in an immediate visit by the police from nearby Bow Street, who feared a safe blowing incident (it was night time). Apart from the shattering of an outside lamp, no damage was caused, and the recording proved completely satisfactory, the arm of the law evincing keen interest in the 'play back'. Earlier and less successful experiments had been undertaken with 6 inch and 8 inch howitzers on Salisbury Plain. What proved more successful than the use of heavy guns was the recording of a shot from a .22 rifle. This was recorded at 30 inches per second and played back at $7\frac{1}{2}$ inches per second.[2]

[1] Similar effects have been used in recording Beethoven's *Wellington's Siege*.

[2] Described to the author by K. E. Wilkinson ('Wilkie'), chief recording engineer of Decca Recording Co., London.

In contrast to the weight of sound in *1812* (*ffff*) Tchaikovsky asks for the gentle flutter of the tambourine in 'Danse Arabe' (*Casse Noisette*) (*mit dem Daumen* – to be played with the thumb). This passage is sometimes played as a thumb roll (produced by rubbing the moistened thumb on the vellum); at other times the demi-semi-quavers are strictly observed by the controlling bounce of the moistened thumb.

(At rehearsal of this work it was customary upon the first entry of the tambourine for one or two members of the orchestra to tap the small change in their pockets). In 'Trepak' (from the same suite) there is a vigorous part for the tambourine, calling for a deft wrist. For this, two tambourines are frequently employed (the player beating the instruments on his knees). At other times, the performer executes the rhythm as shown in the accompanying example, i.e. striking the instrument on his knee to produce the four main quavers, and obtaining the second of the semiquavers in each group with the free hand on the rebound of the instrument.

Tchaikovsky made only sparing use of the glockenspiel. It adds local colour to 'Danse Chinoise' in *Casse Noisette*, and similarly a touch of silver to the waltz in *Sleeping Beauty*. His writing for the timpani is powerful. In the Fourth Symphony there is a fine passage for three drums, of which G. Gordon Cleather says[1]: 'You have to figure that passage out very carefully, and reduce it to a certainty before you can be sure of playing it correctly.'

In the finale of *Romeo and Juliet* occurs the famous 'heart beat' followed by the awesome crescendo roll (solo), one of the most impressive moments in the repertoire of the orchestral timpani.

There is also in this work the frenzy of the duel scene, heightened by the imitative clashing of swords from the syncopation of the cymbals.

[1] Cleather, G. Gordon. *The Timpani*, Lectures to Royal College of Organists, 1908, p. 9.

To deal exhaustively with the whole of the works of Tchaikovsky and those of his fellow-countrymen would require a volume in itself; and so indeed would the works of individual composers elsewhere. In Italy and France, for instance, there was also at this time an extension of the use of orchestral percussion. Verdi made frequent use of three or more timpani in *Othello*, *Don Carlos* and the *Requiem*. On occasions, there is a strong case for the use of a further drum, if only to correct the rather frequent dissonances, such as the first entry of the timpani in the *Requiem*: a sustained A natural throughout a chord of F sharp major.[1] These clashes are puzzling, for elsewhere Verdi was careful in his choice of notes for the timpani, and in dynamic marking. In the autographed score of the *Requiem* he occasionally marks the timpani *pppp*. (The solo for the bass drum in the *Te Deum* is similarly marked.) There are occasions where he employs the bass drum to avoid a change of tuning on the timpani, either because he felt the change too sudden, or because he did not wish to disturb the pitch of the drum (the latter procedure is highly commendable from the timpanist's point of view). Though machine drums were no novelty in Italy at this time, Verdi apparently made no direct demands on them. Of his use of the bass drum much could be said. His employment of this instrument in the *Requiem* ('Dies Irae') has given rise to the term 'The Verdi Gran Cassa'. The largest bass drum possible is associated with this work, though rarely as 'Gran' as the monster bass drum of Distin to which we have already made reference. In the 'Dies Irae' (*Requiem*) Verdi gives instructions for the ropes of the bass drum to be 'well tightened so that this off-beat comes out dry and very loud.' (*Le corde ben tese onde questo contratempo riesca secco e molto forte.*)

Verdi was evidently well served with his timpanists, for among them was a reigning virtuoso Pietro Pieranzovini. Pieranzovini was the author of a famous method for the timpani, and also of a concerto for the instrument. The concerto is in the form of a theme and variations. It is written for a pair of drums accompanied by a quartet of strings. (These works, edited by Luigi Torrebruno, have been re-issued in one volume by Messrs. Ricordi.) A further concerto for timpani was written at this time in the form of a March and Polonaise for six timpani and orchestra, by Julius Tausch (now published by Hinrichsen, London). Professor Percival Kirby, who has made a transcription of this work, *A Concert Piece for Timpani and*

---

[1] Pencilled alterations to orchestral parts (corrections by timpanists) of Verdi's operas are frequently met. Similar alterations can be found in the works of Gounod.

Piano, is of the opinion that it is possible that the eminent conductor Sir Alfred Mann suggested to Tausch 'that he should write such a work for his own timpanist J. A. Smith, whom he, Richter and Liszt are said to have regarded as the best timpanist in Europe'.[1] Professor Kirby considers that the work was written *circa* 1878. The title page of an early score bears the signatures of such famous timpanists as G. Gordon Cleather, Willem Gezink and Samuel W. Geldard. Geldard frequently performed this work at school concerts organised by Sir Hamilton Harty in the early thirties.

Meanwhile, Parisian composers, particularly Saint-Saëns, Delibes and Debussy (and later Ravel) were more than keeping pace with the prevailing development of 'percussion'. In the Bacchanale from *Samson and Delilah* (1877) Saint-Saëns writes extensively for the kettledrums (solo).[2] There is also in this opera a part for the glockenspiel, the writing suggesting an instrument with keyboard action. In his *Algerian Suite*, Saint-Saëns again places the timpanist on his mettle. The recurring

passage 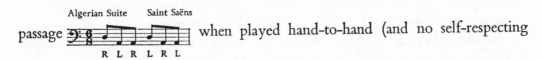 when played hand-to-hand (and no self-respecting

timpanist would play it otherwise) is a study in the technique of cross-beating.[3]

Effective use of the glockenspiel is made by Delibes in *Coppélia* (1870) and *Lakmé* (1883) for example. What more fitting accompaniment could there be to Lakmé's 'Bell Song' than the sound of this delicate instrument? In *Lakmé* ('Airs de danse') the normal timpani and a pair of *Petites Timbales* (sounding an octave higher than the larger drums) are combined. In this same work Delibes employs crotales in A and E. He also scores for *castagnettes de bois – et de fer*; of wood and iron.

---

[1] P. R. Kirby. Preface to *A Concert Piece for Timpani and Piano* (Tausch). Hinrichsen Edition No. 603, London, 1959.

[2] In the original score of his symphonic poem *Phaëton* (Op. 39) Saint-Saëns scored chords for two timpanists.

[3] A similar passage occurs in Stanford's *Irish Rhapsody* no. I (1902). At a rehearsal of this work with the Hallé Orchestra under its conductor Sir Hamilton Harty, the timpanist, to suit a momen-

tary whim, played the passage Sir Hamilton immediately remarked: 'I

observe that Mr. Geldard has a deputy this morning.' Mr. Geldard (Sammy – as this magnificent player was known to the profession) was a pupil of the eminent William Gezink, for many years timpanist of the Hallé Orchestra and for several seasons at Covent Garden. At the orchestra's first concert following Gezink's death (1928) the timpani were draped in memory of this supreme artist. Of Geldard, Gezink had said: 'He has outstripped his master.'

Debussy captures the mystic atmosphere of a dream with the tinkle of the *crotales* in *L'après-midi d'un faune* (1894). Here, the combination of flute and crotales is a

reminder of the aulos and ancient cymbals. The 'cymbales antiques' 🎵 sound

only ten gentle strokes in the work. Their use is similarly restricted in *Six Epigraphes*. This economy in the use of percussion so often proves the master[1]: the use of the crotales – a pair in E flat – in Massenet's *Hérodiade* (1881), the single stroke on the tam-tam in Tchaikovsky's Sixth Symphony (*Pathétique*), the solitary clash of cymbals (*mf*) in Dvořák's *New World*, and the gentle solo on the timpani to open his Slavonic Rhapsody No. 1, or, the rare but extremely effective use of the cymbals by Bruckner. (Bruckner made heavy demands on the timpani, of which the scherzo in his Ninth Symphony is an excellent example.) Debussy too made full use of the more powerful of the percussion forces when occasion demanded.[2] His adroit use of the timpani in *La Mer* and *Images* (in *Images* acciaccaturas are written) is frequently quoted in text book examples, as is also his writing for the glockenspiel in *La Mer* (1905) and that for the side drum in 'Iberia' (*Images* 1912) and 'Fêtes' and 'Nuages' (1899). (The xylophone occurs in 'Iberia' and 'Gigues' (*Images*)). Further text book examples come from Humperdinck, e.g. his writing for the timpani and xylophone in *Hansel and Gretel* (1893) and *Die Königskinder* (1896).

To continue chronologically, as far as this is possible, we arrive at the compositions of Sibelius and Nielsen, and the works of their Austrian contemporary Mahler. Sibelius, in spite of his great demand on percussion instruments, used them 'solo' in only a few instances. Nielsen differed, particularly in his use of the side drum, as can be seen in two of his later works, Fifth Symphony (1922), and the Concerto for clarinet and orchestra (1928). In the last-named, the side drum and the solo instru-

---

[1] Dr. Gordon Jacob in his *Orchestral Technique* (Oxford, London, p. 71) writes: 'Rimsky-Korsakov has said with truth that love of percussion is the besetting sin of the budding orchestrator'. Only a fool would be in complete disagreement with Rimsky-Korsakov and Dr. Jacob, though bearing in mind the prominence given to percussion in such works of the Russian master as *Capriccio Espagnole* and *Scheherazade*, we are of the opinion that had to-day's instruments been available to him, he would have made use of them.

[2] It is said that Debussy was influenced by the timbre of the gamelan cf. Messiaen and Boulez.

ment are skillfully interwoven, whilst in the Symphony, the drum is given the rare privilege (in works of this calibre) of improvising.

Concerto for Clarinet and Orchestra   Nielsen

Tamburo piccolo

By permission of Dan Fog, Copenhagen.

The timpani are prominent in the majority of Nielsen's works. In his First Symphony (1892) a pair are employed in the manner of the classical period. In his opera *Saul and David* (1901) they are used more adventurously. In his Fourth Symphony (*The Inextinguishable* 1914–1916) he employs glissandi. His method was unique, for he utilises two performers playing a passage in minor thirds rising chromatically.[1] The score states that the timpanists should be placed at opposite ends of the orchestra.

Fourth Symphony   Nielsen

By permission of Wilhelm Hansen, Musik-Forlag, Copenhagen.

Credit for the earliest use of the timpani glissandi, however, may well go to Walford Davies in a work composed in 1914, *Conversations* for Pianoforte and Orchestra. John Wilson, nephew of Walford Davies, supplied the author with the following information:

25-2-67

In W.D's "1914" book of MSS, which was bound-up at end of 1914, there are his "sketches" – in 2-piano form – of the Conversations. These show that he was visualising a chromatic tymp in that year, and writing for it.

I enclose 2 passages from the sketches for No. IV, where he has marked "Tym".

[1] Cf. the rise and fall, including glissandi, associated for many centuries with certain Asiatic drums, the Indian *tablā*, for instance.

I also have a *copied* score, with some pencillings by W.D., that was used in performance, and this specifies "Chromatic Tym" on the first page.

I deduce from this that W.D. was interested in the gliss in 1914, though where he had heard it I don't know; and I presume that it was used in the first performance of the Conversations on 14 October 1914 (date given by H. C. Colles in biography).'

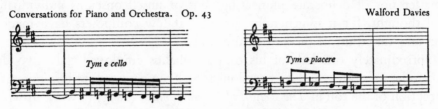

By permission of Novello & Co. Ltd., London.

The writing for the drums in this work is certainly adventurous. In the third movement – 'Intimate Friends' – the following passage is representative.

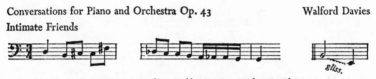

By permission of Novello & Co. Ltd., London.

The revised score (undated) of Walford Davies's G Major Symphony (1911) (dedicated to A. J. Jaeger, one of Elgar's closest friends) requests chromatic timpani. The original score contains no reference to machine drums.

The effect of gradually sliding from one tone to the other has since been considerably exploited, advantageously and otherwise. Walford Davies and Nielsen were possibly influenced to some extent by Vincent D'Indy[1] who employed a chromatic run on the timpani as early as 1905 (*Jour d'été à la montagne*, 2nd movement). D'Indy specifies *timbales chromatiques*, and the passage is of added interest inasmuch as it is solo. No glissando is indicated; there is a clear cut change on each semitone, suggesting that D'Indy may have had in mind A. Sax's *timbales chromatiques*, q.v.

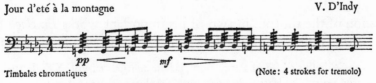

By permission of Durand & Cie, Paris.

[1] D'Indy, it will be remembered, made early use of the dulcitone.

In this same year (1905) Strauss calls for a rising passage in full tones in Salome's 'Dance of the Seven Veils' (*Salome*). It is feasible that Strauss had in mind the use of machine drums, as in many of his works there occur passages which could not be well played by a single performer without the assistance of such mechanism.

Of Sibelius, Ralph W. Wood says:[1] 'His outstanding originality like Beethoven's, is a matter not of deliberate pioneering, but of unselfconscious individuality of musical thought, for it is generally agreed that few composers have made such copious and varied use of the kettledrums as he.'

In approximately one half of his output Sibelius employed only two drums. Elsewhere he uses three, and on occasions four. Solo passages are infrequent. With the exception of the roll in *The Return of Lemminkäinen* (1895) (a work in which he scored freely for timpani), and the arresting figure in the Scherzo of the First Symphony (1899) the drum's solo voice is more confined to quiet rolls and occasional strokes.

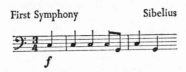

First Symphony   Sibelius

Like Brahms, Sibelius made frequent use of chords on the timpani. In *Swan of Tuonela* (1893) the drums are struck simultaneously in minor thirds, in the Fifth Symphony (1915) in fourths. He made prolific use of the roll (designated *tr* in all cases).

Of Sibelius's diverse manner of employing the timpani, no better examples can be quoted than *Finlandia* (1899), the Sixth Symphony (1923) and *Rakastava* (1913), the last-named a work for string orchestra.

The glockenspiel (Sibelius calls it *campanelli*) occurs in *The Return of Lemminkäinen*. In the finale of the Fourth Symphony (1911) he calls for *glocken*. In some cases the part is given to the tubular bells, in others to the glockenspiel.[2] In *Oceanides* (1914) there is a part for *Stahlstäbe* (steel bars) normally given to the glockenspiel. (Possibly Sibelius had in mind large steel plates.) The xylophone occurs in only one work, *The Tempest* (1926).

The omission of the timpani in two of his important works *En Saga* (1892) and *The Dryad* (1910) is surprising. The fact that the score of *En Saga* contains no part

[1] Wood, Ralph. 'Sibelius's Use of Percussion', *Music and Letters*, vol. XXIII, 1942, p. 16.
[2] Harold Johnson says: 'Finnish conductors, with Sibelius as their authority, insist that the part written for *glocken* should be rendered on the glockenspiel.' Johnson, Harold. *Sibelius*, Faber, London, 1960, p. 128.

for the timpani is, to quote Ralph Wood: '. . . on the face of it one of the outstanding curiosities of music. . .' Here is a work for an orchestra of large dimensions with the kettledrums silent, replaced in fact by the bass drum, for this instrument (played with timpani sticks) figures throughout in a manner expected of the timpani. Whether Sibelius desired the tone of the bass drum for a particular reason, or was hesitant in using the timpani as freely as he would wish in a work so full of modulations, is hard to say. The fact that in other works he considered occasional discrepancies between the timpani and the bass note as immaterial makes his unusual scoring of *En Saga* even more remarkable. Equally puzzling is the omission of the timpani from *The Dryad*. We are in firm agreement, however, with Henry W. Taylor when he says[1]: '. . . this strange and utterly unorthodox writing for the drums is not likely to be copied or equalled . . .'

Mahler was a master in his use of timpani and percussion. In the third movement of his First Symphony (1889) a pair of timpani play almost throughout in fourths, in the keys of D, E flat and a return to D. The opening two bars of the movement are solo for the two drums which are muted (*dämpfer*). From the 29th bar the drums are not muted (*dampfer ab*). It is possible that Mahler visualized the second timpanist assisting the principal player by removing the felt dampers on the drum heads; on the other hand, as the tempo is steady, he may have expected the player to play with one hand at the bar prior to the point at which the drums are to sustain, leaving the other hand free to remove the fabric from the vellum. In the last movement two timpanists are employed, in one instance in quite an unusual manner. At a point during a tremolo the pitch of one of the drums is lowered a semitone. Instructions are given for the second player to effect the change:[2]

By permission of Universal Edition (London) Ltd.

[1] Taylor, H. W. *The Art and Science of the Timpani*, p. 65.
[2] For his Seventh Symphony Mahler said 'very good mechanical pedal drums are necessary'.

F Pauke von einem 2 Musiker herunter nach Fes an stimmen. From this it would seem either that Mahler considered such a change impracticable on machine drums, or that he had no regard for them. Other percussion is prominent in this symphony. Cymbals are clashed in the normal manner by one player, and also combined with the bass drum. Here Mahler specifies *turkische Becken* and *gr Trommel* – one performer. Further colouring comes from use of the suspended cymbal played with soft sticks. Similarly with the timpani, the use of wood sticks (*Holzschlägel*) and the repeated instructions for *gedämpft* ('muffled, muted'). Three timpanists are employed in the Second Symphony (1894) the third player joining the off-stage band. In this work

Mahler scores for low D flat . This is the first occasion (excluding the possibility of Handel's octave basso) on which the timpani may have been heard in this low register. In his Third Symphony (1895) Mahler uses the high G (*kleine Pauke*) and for the low D natural (first timpanist). The low D of the first timpanist is combined with the upper D of the second timpanist – an innovation, as may also have been the use in this work of two glockenspiel players. There are times when the two timpanists play in duet form, and at others in unison. Also in this symphony, Mahler, in addition to signifying that the bass drum and cymbals should be played by one performer, directs that the shell of the bass drum should be struck with the switch (*auf das Holz der grossen Trommel – geschlagen*). Towards the close of the first movement (fig. 54) the side drum is completely solo.

In his Fourth Symphony (1900), Mahler ensures forceful accents by stipulating that two sticks are to be used simultaneously on the same drum, a device of which he was quite fond (see the Eighth Symphony, 1908). He indicates the effect by placing tails up and down on each note – mit 2 Schlägeln.

Fourth Symphony   Mahler

By permission of Ernst Eulenburg Ltd.

The percussion section of Berlioz's 'dream orchestra' is realised to some extent in Mahler's Sixth Symphony (1906) (fourth movement), the requirements being two timpanists, bass drum, side drum, cymbals, tam-tam, triangle, glockenspiel, cowbells (*Heerdenglocken*), large tubular bells, switch (*Rute*), whip (*Holzklapper*) and hammer. Mahler instructs that the Heerdenglocken are to be shaken intermittently to give a true imitation of the actual sound (similarly in the Seventh Symphony). The hammer, he states, must be of wood not metal. It is in the first movement of Mahler's Sixth Symphony that the xylophone makes its first appearance in a symphony.

In his Seventh Symphony (1906) Mahler writes for a peal of deep bells, to be played *ad libitum*. Of this Sir Henry J. Wood's observation (from his personal score) is: 'All the tubular bells beaten without rhyme or reason for six bars' – an effect with which no doubt Mahler would have been delighted. In contrast to the cacophony of the large bells there is the gentler trilling of the glockenspiel (*mit beiden Händen*). The passage clearly indicates a 'keyboard instrument'.

In the finale of this Symphony Mahler writes again for the low D flat on the timpani.[1] The fact that this is marked *fff* suggests the availability of a drum of large dimensions; an instrument less than 30 inches in diameter would give an indifferent note at this dynamic. Mahler was partial to the lower notes of the timpani, though he used on occasions the higher notes (top A flat, Ninth Symphony). He made frequent use of the kettledrums as solo instruments, and was consistent in his instructions respecting tone quality, i.e. the use of hard or soft sticks, drums muted etc. In the finale of the Seventh Symphony there is a solo passage for four timpani.

Seventh Symphony
Rondo Finale

Mahler

By permission of Ernst Eulenburg Ltd.

In the sketches for his Tenth Symphony (which are the basis of Deryck Cooke's recently completed performing edition of the work) Mahler makes unusual use of the timpani (possibly two clusters), to which he adds the bass drum and cymbals. The fourth movement (the second scherzo) ends with a muffled drum-stroke (presumably on a bass drum) and the same drum-stroke is prominent in the introduction to the finale. This feature of Mahler's score had its origins in an incident he witnessed in New York in 1907–8, a fireman's funeral cortège, described by Alma Mahler in her reminiscences of her husband: '. . . the procession halted, and the master of ceremonies stepped forward and gave a short address. . . . There was a brief pause and then a stroke on the muffled drum, followed by a dead silence. . . . The brief drum-stroke impressed [Mahler] so deeply that he used it in the Tenth Symphony'.[2]

[1] It occurs also in the Fifth Symphony, here *p* as in the Second Symphony.

[2] Mahler, Alma. *Gustav Mahler: Memories & Letters*, revised edition, John Murray, London, 1968, p. 135.

The timpani are prominent in works written at this period by the Venetian-born composer Wolf-Ferrari. In *La vita nuova* (1902) he uses seven drums divided between two players.

In England there had been little change in orchestral percussion since Handel's day until the revival in British music towards the end of the nineteenth century. With Elgar and his contemporaries the activity of the past was renewed. It is obvious that percussion fascinated Elgar: rarely extravagant, he made full use of the instruments at his disposal, and created some unique effects, such as the tremolo on the small gong (*tam-tam piccolo*[1]) in E flat in 'Dawn' Part I of *The Apostles* (1903). In this same work as an accompaniment to the singing of the morning psalm, Elgar calls for a tuned cymbal (*cimbale antico*) on the note C Later, there is a part for the keyed glockenspiel, obviously to illustrate the weighing of the thirty pieces of silver. He made equally attractive use of the more usual percussion instruments engaging them frequently to supply local colour, dramatic and otherwise. In the *Wand of Youth* Suite No. 2 (1907) there is the scurry of the wild bears portrayed on the xylophone (and what a scurry! – one of the busiest two bars in the instrument's repertoire). By contrast we have the tremolo on the tambourine in imitation of the chain around the neck of the more patient creature, the tame bear. The glockenspiel typifies the pealing of 'little bells', the effect of small bells being intensified by the use of occasional strokes on a tubular bell. The harness on the horse drawing the cab through London streets is clearly portrayed in *Cockaigne* (1901) by the jingles (*schellen*).

In addition to the majesty of the kettledrums in the *Enigma Variations* (1899) there is the gentle colour of the triangle, with its grace note () depicting the tinkle of the medal on the collar of the great bulldog Dan as he gives himself a shake after his glorious plunge into the Wye (opening of Var. 11). Elgar also knew how to harness his forces on the occasion of a great moment, such as the combination of four kettledrums (played by individual performers if available), bass drum, side drum, cymbals and tam-tam (*fffz* with a wooden beater) at the moment the Lord appears to Gerontius (*The Dream of Gerontius* 1902).

No composer before or since has shown greater care and forethought than Elgar in the assembling of his 'drum parts', especially in preparing the way for the timpanist. With the exception of the use of four drums in *The Dream of Gerontius* Elgar

---

[1] The Eastern instrument with raised central boss. Similar gongs of definite pitch had been used earlier in Massenet's opera *Iris*, based on a Japanese subject.

confines himself to the normal three symphonic timpani. In compass, he employs e.g. the low E flat (*Caractacus* (1898) and *Gerontius*) and the high G (*Enigma Variations* and *Pomp and Circumstance March* No. 4 (1907)). Elgar was most precise in his directions regarding tunings. At the start of every movement the required notes

are indicated, e.g. [musical notation] Every change of pitch is given and ample

time to effect the change (Elgar never asked for machine drums). He was also careful to notify the change at the first convenient moment, allowing the drumhead maximum time to settle. Though earlier composers had given similar directions for tuning, few were as precise over this matter as Elgar. In general, he preferred the full round tone of the timpani produced by the normal felt sticks. His requests for other types were not numerous, the more notable occasions being *The Dream of Gerontius* (*mit dem Griff*), Variation 13 of *Enigma Variations* (with side drum sticks), *The Apostles* (wooden sticks) and *Pomp and Circumstance March* No. 4 (with the stick). In *The Dream of Gerontius* there occurs a smart change from soft to hard ends which Elgar ensures by his use of *mit dem Griff*. Here, the normal felt-headed sticks are used in one bar and reversed for the following bar. (*Mit dem Griff*: 'with the handle' is a rare direction in orchestral scores, though it is frequently adopted by players.)[1]

In Variation 13 of *Enigma* occurs one of the few occasions where Elgar presented the timpanist with a problem, i.e. the execution of a roll with side drum sticks (solo), followed immediately by a rhythmic figure to be played *naturale*. To follow Elgar's instructions would not be impossible. For example, recourse could be had to side drum sticks with heads of felt affixed to the butt ends, and the sticks reversed at the appropriate moment. Even so, the combination of side drum sticks and timpani sticks would have been even less commendable to the timpanists of Elgar's day than to the players of to-day. Elgar's request for side drum sticks for this particular tremolo may have been prompted by a desire for an unusual roll to give the impression of the pulse of ship's engines, the drum's purpose being at this point to illustrate this mechanism. It is well known that this tremolo is rarely played with side drum sticks: instead, two coins are normally used. Of this, Thomas F. Dunhill says[2]: '. . . a mysterious roll on one of the tympani, in the score, to be made by side-drum sticks, but actually played with two coins held tightly between the finger and thumb of each hand by the drummer. This device was invented by that superb tympanist Charles Henderson, who was in Richter's orchestra at the time, and it is

[1] e.g. the change within the bar from *Bacchette da legno* to *Bac. ord.* in 'The Miller's Dance', *The Three-Cornered Hat*, Manuel de Falla (1919).

[2] Dunhill, Thomas F. *Sir Edward Elgar*, Blackie, London, 1938, p. 89.

now generally adopted.'[1] Professor Kirby, in a conversation with the present author, related the circumstances surrounding the first rehearsal of the work, as given to him by the timpanist. Charles Henderson said that after he had played the passage with side drum sticks, Elgar commented that he did not like it. Henderson then used coins, at which Elgar said: 'Good! How is it done?' Henderson replied: 'Sir, if you will give me two gold coins I will show you!' Whether Henderson at this early rehearsal was confronted by the immediate change from side drum sticks to *naturale* is open to question, for the original score in Elgar's hand which was used by Richter who conducted the first public performance of the work, at St. James's Hall, London, 19th June 1899, does not call for a change from side drum sticks to *naturale* as do following editions. In the original score the direction *naturale* occurs only at the end of the movement, preparing the normal timpani sticks for the finale. Possibly the request for the change of tone colour was discussed at rehearsal with Henderson demonstrating to the composer the various possibilities. Unfortunately no reference can be made to the particular score from which current editions are taken, the manuscript having been lost.

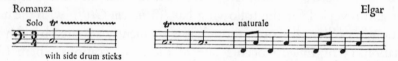

Elgar, in portraying the character of his intimate friends makes cunning use of the timpani in Variation 7 'Troyte'. Here, the stirring pattern on three drums so adroitly arranged as to present no problem in execution, is heightened by the use of contrasting dynamics. The motif typifies in a bantering manner the attempts of Elgar's friend Troyte Griffiths to play the pianoforte.

Much has been written for three (or more) drums since Elgar committed this frolic to paper. Troyte, however, remains an example of superb writing for the timpani.

Both Elgar examples by permission of Novello & Co. Ltd., London.

Fine scoring for the timpani is to be found in the works of such English composers as Ethel Smyth, Delius, Bantock, Walford Davies, Holbrooke, Ireland and Dyson. To Joseph Holbrooke must be given the credit of re-introducing the xylophone into

[1] Many players hold the coins and the timpani sticks. Sir Adrian Boult in a conversation with the writer said that this method is universally adopted.

the full orchestra (*Queen Mab* 1904).[1] There is also a part for the keyed-glockenspiel in this work.

With occasional exceptions, such as Holbrooke's and Mahler's sparing use of the xylophone, and, with other composers, a limited use of the glockenspiel and tubular bells, the attention of most serious composers – until the conclusion of World War I – centred on the timpani. Since it is outside the scope of this volume to give an exhaustive survey of all composers and their use of timpani (and other percussion) we restrict ourselves to some unusual and forward-looking examples. Busoni, a virtuoso pianist and a gifted composer made extensive demands on the timpani. He had a great fancy for the use of four-note patterns and the use of four drums generally. He frequently indicated the notes above C alto, and those below this note basso. In this he would seem to be unique. At times he accommodates the player by setting out the rhythms so that they 'lie well', as is the case of the passage for three drums in *Harlekins Reigen* (Op. 46, 1917).

In the *Indian Fantasy* the approach differs, the passage for four drums involving a good deal of cross-beating, and in a later work *Dr. Faustus* (completed by Philip Jarnach in 1925) the 'fingering' is, to say the least, decidedly tricky.

This example would be played hand-to-hand. Wherever possible an accomplished timpanist avoids a double beat with one hand, this being considered a bad style (cf. Stanford's *Irish Rhapsody*). Later the player is faced with a problem of execution.

With the addition of the C and G drums placed between the drums tuned to the high and low F, the player, in order to perform the whole passage hand-to-hand, will be obliged to cover a distance of at least four feet with each cross-over. A further point to be made clear is that the whole passage is *mf*, rendering the cross-over

[1] The previous appearance of this instrument was in *The Carnival of the Animals*, Saint-Saëns (1886).

doubly difficult on account of impetus adding weight.[1] Faced with such circumstances players may resort to a double beat on the high and low F's.

In *Turandot* (Orchestral Suite 1906)[2] the drums are very much solo and scored in octaves. On one occasion, unless there is an error in copying, the four drums are struck simultaneously by one player.:

In the 'Funeral March', a double stave is used – a line for the first and second timpanist.

All music examples by Busoni are the copyright of Breitkopf & Härtel. Reproduced by permission of British and Continental Music Agencies Ltd.

An unusual approach to the timpani is found in some of the works of the American composer Charles Ives, whose compositions were little played when they first appeared in the early part of the century. To-day, Ives's works are regarded in some circles as masterpieces. To the instrumentalist many of them present a formidable challenge. To the timpanist what often appears at first sight to be straightforward, proves in application to be a mathematical study. A quotation from one work will suffice: the second number 'In the Inn' from *A Set of Pieces* (written in 1906). The following example, though in some aspects a trifle unusual for this period, presents 'on paper' no great problem.

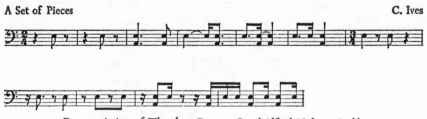

By permission of Theodore Presser Co. (Alfred Kalmus Ltd.).

[1] Composers (innocently maybe) quite often fail to take such factors into consideration (as also the fact that the player is manipulating two sticks and not ten fingers).

[2] The incidental music to the Gozzi play was published in 1911, and the opera (Busoni's own libretto) performed in 1917 and published in 1919.

To fit this with the orchestra, however, is no easy matter, for with the exception of the timpani, the instrumental parts are written in 2/4, 6/8, 7/16, 2/4, 6/16, 9/16, 2/4. Here is a case where the texture of a work, written over half a century ago, presents a similar complexity to certain avant-garde work written in the sixties. The Fourth Symphony is equally complex.

Whilst the majority of such complex structures present an interesting challenge to the player (and possibly the listener), it cannot be denied that the function of the timpani is often more admirably suited to less involved sequences, as for example the effective use of the two-note pattern used by Glinka in *Russlan and Ludmilla*. Russian composers write excellently for the timpani. Prokofiev, who is possibly best known to the timpanist for the exquisite part given to three drums in the *Classical* Symphony (1917) and to the side drummer for his contribution to the final march in *Peter and the Wolf* (1936) was responsible for a virtuoso study for five kettledrums. This work shows a complete knowledge of the instrument, as do the works of Tcherepnine (which include a Sonatina for three (or two) timpani), and the compositions of Rachmaninov, who is well remembered by percussionists for his exquisite use of the bass drum and cymbals (almost solo) pianissimo in his Second Piano Concerto. It is not surprising that the Russians, like the Germans, write well for the kettledrums: both countries have a long tradition of producing first-class timpanists.

The approach of Russian and German composers in recent years to the instruments of percussion is clearly portrayed in the works of Stravinsky and Richard Strauss. In *Elektra* and elsewhere there is excellent employment of machine drums. Of this, Henry W. Taylor says[1]: 'After hearing the operas *Salome* and *Rosenkavalier*, I am convinced that Strauss has reached the limit, in safe and effective scoring for pedal timpani.' Whether or not one agrees entirely with Mr. Taylor it would be impossible to deny the quality of Strauss's writing for the timpani: as in *Symphonia domestica* and *Ein Heldenleben*, and the parts for four drums in *Burleske, München Waltz, Schlagoberswaltzer* and *Till Eulenspiegel*.

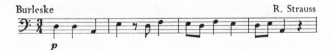

Burleske   R. Strauss

Copyright Steingraber. By permission of Bosworth & Co. Ltd., London.

Such passages certainly require four separate drums just as 'Troyte' in the *Enigma Variations* requires three. Pedal change in such cases would be a technical and

[1] Taylor, H. W. ibid. p. 67.

physical impossibility on the machine drums of the period, and even on the drums of to-day the attendant 'whine' of the glissandi would render the majority of such passages nonsensical. Though Strauss frequently employed the timpani busily and with considerable changing of pitch, he echoed certain of the qualities of his Teutonic forbears in his adroit use of tonic and dominant. His use of the other percussion instruments, orthodox and otherwise, is interesting (e.g. the use of the glockenspiel in *Don Juan* (1888)). In *Elektra* (1908) the crack of the whip in the orchestra adds vividly to the overseer's punishment of the slave, and certain of *Till Eulenspiegel's* (1895) pranks are well portrayed by the skirl of the rattle. The wind machine appears in *Don Quixote* (1897) and again, with the thunder machine, in *An Alpine Symphony* (1915). In *Le Bourgeois Gentilhomme* (1917) the part for the side drum is unusual – the two sticks striking the instrument simultaneously. Side drum (*sehr hoch*) is specified in *Die Frau ohne Schatten*.

By permission of Boosey & Hawkes, Music Publishers Ltd.

The xylophone (repeated notes and scale passages) occurs in *Salome* (1905). In his score Strauss calls the instrument *holz und strohinstrumente* (presumably a four-row xylophone). With Strauss came his younger contemporary Stravinsky.

From the earliest to the most recent of Stravinsky's compositions, the absolute peak of craftsmanship in the employment of percussion is evident. In many cases, particularly in his early works, precise instructions are given regarding these instruments. Commencing with *The Firebird* (1910) we find a direction to the effect that a certain passage is 'to be played with two hands, very rhythmically' – i.e. hand to hand. Stravinsky was fully aware that a double beat in such cases would be less effective.

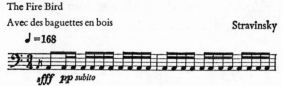

In the same work the exposed re-iterated passage for the xylophone is well known. A part is given to the glockenspiel and to the xylophone in *Petrouchka* (1911).[1] In

[1] Only on rare occasions does Stravinsky use tubular bells or vibraphone. In *Les Noces* and *The Rake's Progress* a single bell is employed. A series of bells is used in *Requiem Canticles* (1966) in conjunction with vibraphone. In this work Stravinsky uses four-note chords on the timpani (2 *esecutori*).

Petrouchka there are recurring solos on the timpani played with hard sticks, joined by side drum without snares and the use of cymbal with metal stick (presumably triangle beater). There is also the combination of bass drum and cymbals to be played by one performer. With due respect to Berlioz, who discountenanced such a practice, the effect of the fair ground would be entirely absent if these two instruments were here played other than as requested by Stravinsky.

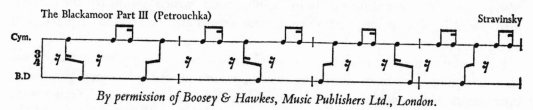

By permission of Boosey & Hawkes, Music Publishers Ltd., London.

Following *Petrouchka* came *The Rite of Spring* (1913) described as 'one of the epoch-marking works of modern times'. In this the percussion comprises: a minimum of five timpani to include one piccolo timpano (B natural – B flat); bass drum; cymbals; tam-tam; triangle; tambourine; antique cymbals (A flat and B flat); and *guero* ('rasp'). (The numbering of the timpani applies to each timpano, not performers.)

By permission of Boosey & Hawkes, Music Publishers Ltd., London.

The Rite of Spring is typical of Stravinsky's 'mathematics' in music, an aspect in which he remains supreme. What is rewarding to the player is that however challenging these situations may be, they all 'work out', as indeed they should, for it is known that Stravinsky made certain that his drum parts were practical by 'trying them out' himself. His studio contained numerous drums of various descriptions. C. F. Ramuz, with whom Stravinsky collaborated (*The Soldier's Tale, Renard, Les Noces*) says[1]: 'We met almost daily in the blue room which dominated the garden, surrounded by side drums, kettle drums, bass drums and every kind of percussion instrument'.

Stravinsky's attention to detail is exemplary. He was an experimenter in sound also, as can be seen from the novel way in which he utilised certain percussion instruments, as for example the uncanny effect produced by scraping the gong with a triangle beater (*glissandi colla bacch. di Triangolo*) in Part II, 'The Sacrifice' (*The Rite of Spring*), and the combination of the antique cymbals with the triangle struck with a wooden stick in the 'Dance of the Adolescents' in the same work. Antique cymbals (*Piatti antichi*) are used in *Le Rossignol* (completed in 1914). There is also a part for two glockenspiels (*Campanelle* I e II).

In *Renard* (1917) Stravinsky makes use of a glissando on the timpani (*gliss pour la Timb a levier*). He makes a heavy demand on machine timpani in a much later work *Introitus* (1965); here, two timpanists are employed.

Stravinsky

Introitus

By permission of Boosey & Hawkes, Music Publishers Ltd., London.

In *Les Noces* there is virtually a percussion orchestra, i.e. four pianos, timpani, xylophone, two crotales, a bell in B 𝄞 two side drums (with and without snares), two tambours (deep side drums) with and without snares, tambourine, bass drum, cymbals and triangle. Stravinsky's partiality for the use of 'double-stopping' on the timpani is apparent in this work. *Oedipus Rex* (1927) could also be quoted, and Concerto for piano and orchestra. In *Les Noces* Stravinsky employs mordents on

---

[1] Ramuz, C. F. *Souvenirs sur Igor Strawinsky*. Nouvelle Revue Française, Paris, 1929, p. 36.

the timpani 𝄢 ♫. ♩ also an unusual interval 𝄢 ♪ . In *Agon* (1957) in addition to the motif of three timpani, a similar rhythm is given to two tom-toms (or high timpani) tuned to B flat and G flat 𝄢 ♭𝅝 ♭𝅝 . The part for the *castagnette* ('tapped lightly with a wooden drumstick') in this ballet ('Bransle Gay' for one female dancer) is a fascinating study in mathematics. The orchestral figuration is 3/8, 7/16, 5/16, 5/16, 7/16, 3/8 and so forth, amounting for the castagnette to a strict 3/8 throughout. The accompanying manuscript is marked as is usual with most players, the crosses indicating the meeting of the figure of 3/8 with the conductor's down beat.

By permission of Boosey & Hawkes, Music Publishers Ltd., London.

Among percussionists it is possible that in all of Stravinsky's repertoire *Histoire du Soldat* remains prime favourite. In this work for seven instrumentalists, Stravinsky makes the utmost demands on the technique of a solo percussionist.[1] He gives the player the arrangement of the percussion instruments at the beginning of the score. The instruments comprise bass drum (*grosse caisse*), large side drum (*caisse claire gr taille*), small side drum (*petite caisse*), a deep military side drum without snare (*tambour sans timbre*), a tambourine, triangle and cymbal (attached to the bass drum). The score contains many detailed directions for the percussionist. These include the exact positioning of certain instruments in a particular movement, the manner of performing a given passage, and the type of drumstick to be used, of which a variety are specified (including those of hard or soft felt or fibre) and a cane stick with fibre head. Stravinsky obtains the maximum of tonal effects from the four drums by a combination of alternating hard and soft tones, which are produced by the use of a drumstick of different quality in the right and left hand, and the striking of the bass drum edge and centre (as in *The Rite of Spring*). In the 'Tango' (the first of

[1] Michael Rosen says: 'In 1918 Igor Stravinsky opened the eyes of composers to the soloistic capabilities of percussion with the composition *L'Histoire du Soldat*'. (Rosen, Michael. 'A Survey of Compositions Written for Percussion Ensemble'. *Percussionist*, Percussive Arts Society, vol. IV, no. 2, January, 1967, p. 106.) See appendix 6.

the three dances) the cymbal, attached to the bass drum, is to be struck lightly at the rim, and with the cane handle of the fibre stick only. The side drum, tambourine and triangle at the start of the last of these dances, 'Ragtime', are approached in a distinctly novel manner. Here it is stated that the three instruments are to be lightly struck with the triangle beater, and the triangle to be held in the performer's left hand, and at his right, very close at hand, facing each other, the tambourine and side drum – conveniently placed in an upright position. The composer gives similar directions regarding the positioning of the two side drums in the 'Devil's Dance'. Here the instruments are placed vertically 'very near one to the other' the drumstick operating between them.[1]

The influence of jazz is noticeable in several cases in *The Soldier's Tale*. The instrumentation closely resembles that of the New Orleans Dixieland Bands.[2] The syncopation of the jazz band drummer (and possibly that of his forbears in remote Africa) is frequently portrayed in this work, particularly the rhythmic pattern for side drums (without snares) at figure 34 in the 'Ragtime'. Here (combined with the solo violin) Stravinsky obtains a veritable 'jazz break' from a combination of 4/8, 5/16, 7/16 and 8/16.

By permission of J. W. Chester Ltd.

The adroit use of accents and *p* and *f* render this passage a model of 'swing'. Re-written, it presents an example of a style of drumming that later was to be claimed in certain circles as innovatory.

The use of the four different toned drums in the finale of this work ('Triumphal March of the Devil'), solo with the violin, as in the 'Tango', is monumental: it is a 'pearl' of percussion writing. (In *Ragtime* written a little later (1918) Stravinsky again uses the jazz idiom. In this work, contrary to his usual procedure at this time, the common time signature is unchanged throughout its 178 bars). Of *The Soldier's Tale*

---

[1] 'To give the utmost precision' the composer said to the author on a certain occasion.

[2] Ansermet had recently given Stravinsky a selection of jazz material from America.

Eric Walter White says[1]: '... The music is unique in the way it combines linear precision with sonorous perspective. The most heterogeneous materials are assembled together in the score; and, by brilliant manipulation, the composer obtains an effect of complete coherence and integration.'

Stravinsky's fellow-countrymen and contemporaries evinced a similar interest in percussion. The barbaric beat of the Russian *litavry*, the small kettledrums of the Russian nobility of the Middle Ages, is echoed in certain of the works of Shostakovich, Prokofiev and Kabalevsky, and so is the rhythm of the Middle East in the works of the Armenian Khachaturian. In the symphonies of Shostakovich and Prokofiev the side drum is prominent: the Seventh (*Leningrad*) and Tenth of Shostakovich, and the Sixth of Prokofiev, for example. All four composers mentioned have much in common in their treatment of percussion. They each make frequent use of the xylophone, which in a number of instances is given quite lengthy statements (at times solo), as opposed to the more general, though unquestionably effective use of the instrument in short passages and interjections to heighten the effect of staccato phrases. Prokofiev combines the glockenspiel with the xylophone in *Alexander Nevsky* (1938) and the *Scythian Suite* (1914). Shostakovich's liking for the timbre of the xylophone is evident from the way he employs it in the ballet *The Golden Age*, Symphonies Nos. 5, 6, 7, 10 and 14, and the Cello Concerto No. 2. In the last-named work exciting solos are given to the timpani, bass drum, whip (*flagello*) and novel percussion ensemble. Khachaturian employs the xylophone freely in *Dance of Young Maidens* and *Sabre Dance* in his *Gayaneh Ballet* (1942), as does Kabalevsky in the overture to his opera *Colas Breugnon* and in 'Comedians' Galop' (*The Comedians*, 1939). The timpani, not surprisingly, are well to the fore in the majority of the works of these four composers. In the last movement of his First Symphony (1926), Shostakovich gives a solo to three drums. The timpani are also prominent in Symphony No. 15.

It is clear from demands of this nature, and from the demands on the timpanist made by Stravinsky, Busoni, Strauss and others, that the symphonic set of three drums had long ceased to cope with the requirements of advanced composers. Not only do we find a steady use of four drums, but also a demand for two or more small drums, and a similar number of large drums, as, for instance, the three drums C, D and E flat in

[1] White, Eric Walter. *Stravinsky*, John Lehmann, London, 1947, p. 81.

Shostakovich's solo in the First Symphony. Similar instances occur earlier in the works of Richard Strauss, e.g. in *Burlesque* (1885) three notes in the upper register are required  and in *An Alpine Symphony* (1915) two drums in the lower register.

Eine Alpensinfonie   R. Strauss

By permission of F. C. E. Leuckart Ltd., Munich. Sole agents Novello & Co. Ltd.

Here it is reasonably certain that Strauss had a pedal change (or single handle) in mind, the six beats rest being insufficient to change the pitch of three drums otherwise. This general expansion in the use of the timpani and the percussion instruments of fixed pitch, such as the xylophone, glockenspiel and chimes, is clearly apparent in the works of other composers.

Composers, anxious for new textures, were turning to the varied aspects and tone colour of the so-called 'kitchen department'. Experiments were made with the timpani. In addition to the chromatic run of D'Indy, the scale-like passages of Richard Strauss, and the glissandi of Walford Davies and Nielsen, Stanford in 'The Middle Watch' from *Songs of the Fleet* (1910) indicates that certain tremolos are to be played with the fingers, an effect befitting the eeriness of the situation. A 'close' roll with side drum sticks is also indicated.

Delius, who before the turn of the century had given the timpani (which he occasionally calls kettledrums) and the tambourine a delightful part in 'La Calinda' (*Koanga*, 1897), (and by way of a compliment maybe, had included the part for the banjo in the percussion parts) gave the xylophone a real 'spotlight' in *Eventyr* (1917). There are numerous solo passages for the timpani in this work. He had previously written for three timpanists in *Song of the High Hills* (1912).[1]

Gustav Holst made use of a full percussion section in *The Planets* (1917), a work with some of the most rewarding writing for these instruments in the repertoire of

Eventyr   Delius
Xylophone

By permission of the copyright owners, Galliard Ltd.

[1] Delius scored for *Stahlolatten* and *kirchenglock* (off stage) in *A Village Romeo and Juliet.*

orchestral music. His scores bristle with telling percussion effects, well calculated, and never overloaded with unnecessary barbarism. Holst rated percussion highly. He insisted that every student at St. Paul's School for Girls (no matter what instrument she had chosen) should study percussion for at least a term, to furnish them, he said, with a good sense of rhythm, and to teach them to count bars rest. His attention to the study of observing rests accurately was indeed a wise precaution, it being so easily overlooked that one of the most difficult of the percussionist's tasks is to do nothing; yet those periods of silence must be calculated to the hundredth part of a second, ensuring a perfect entry at the crucial moment. There are many exciting moments in *The Planets*, as, for instance, the solo for four timpani in 'Uranus' (No. 6), and the use of the two timpanists, each with three drums in 'Saturn' (No. 5).

The Planets (Uranus)   Holst

In addition to the colour of the xylophone in 'Uranus', there is also effective writing for tubular bells (with metal and felt strikers) in 'Saturn'. In *Beni Mora* Suite (1910) Holst employs the timpani melodically in the solo for three drums.

Beni Mora   Holst
Solo. Use sticks with sponge ends

Both the above examples by permission of J. Curwen & Sons Ltd.

In the 'Dance of the Spirits of the Fire' from the ballet *The Perfect Fool* (1923) Holst makes a unique request – the use on the timpani (and bass drum) of one felt stick and one wooden stick.

The Perfect Fool   Holst

* felt stick *ff*
+ wooden stick

By permission of Novello & Co. Ltd.

A full percussion section had by now entered the realm of grand opera. Puccini, in addition to heavy demands on the timpani and the normal percussion such as side drum, bass drum, cymbals and tam-tam, had coloured certain of his opera sequences with the orchestral xylophone and glockenspiel (the latter normally keyboard, and designated *campanelli tasteria*). In *Madam Butterfly* (1904) similar sounding instruments are used on the stage. (Here the instruments are called by Puccini *Campanelli Giappa*). Among the percussion intruments in the Milan collection of Messrs. Ricordi are a number of Eastern gourd bells (small bronze plates, gourd resonated) which have been used at La Scala since the early performances of the opera. This collection, combined with the percussion equipment in La Scala Theatre constitutes one of the most remarkable and interesting collections of instruments in the history of grand opera, including as it does many instruments used at original performances.[1] In contrast to the high-sounding *Campanelli Giappa* used in Madam Butterfly, there is the use of Japanese tam-tams. Here the score specifies *Tam-Tam Giappa*. These are indicated in the bass clef, eleven gongs from .[2] Puccini's original score is interesting concerning these instruments. In Act I it reads *Tam Tam Giappi*

Puccini

The erasure of the treble clef sign and the reference to piccolo tam-tams, suggests that the maestro made the alteration after defining the pitch of the instruments at his disposal, the instruments in the Ricordi collection sounding in the lower register. In *Turandot*, Puccini scores for a series of Chinese gongs (*Gongs Chinesi*). The Ricordi gongs and those used for *Turandot* and *Madam Butterfly* at Covent Garden are identical. These instruments were manufactured by the famous Italian firm of UFIP of Pistoa (also makers of fine tam-tams, bells, etc.). To differentiate between the tuned gongs and the orchestral tam-tam Puccini calls the latter *Tam Tam grave*. In *Turandot*, Puccini captures further Oriental colour with an impression of the gamelan orchestra obtained from the xylophone and bass xylophone (*xilophon Basso*). These instruments are at times combined with the glockenspiel. Tubular bells (*campana tubolare*) are used in the orchestra, and off stage as in *Madam Butterfly* and *Tosca*. In the Third Act of the last-named opera the twelve bells on stage cover an unusual compass

Tosca   Puccini

By permission of G. Ricordi & Co.

[1] In *The Girl of the Golden West* Puccini wrote for a *fonica*: six metal plates in a box struck by handle-generated whirling hammers to produce a continuous rattling.

[2] Gongs with raised boss and of definite pitch.

Puccini uses the tam-tam as orchestral texture and significantly. In *Turandot* (Act I) Calaf strikes a stage tam-tam three times to announce that he will undertake the challenge of the riddles.[1] In *Tosca*, after the heroine has stabbed Scarpia, the tam-tam joins the three typically Puccini chords as Tosca places a candle at each side of the corpse and a cross on his chest. The writing for percussion in *La Bohème* is typical of Puccini's style e.g. the use of the glockenspiel and xylophone (at times combined). (In the third act, the pleasurable chink of wine glasses (*bicchiere e carillon*) is included.)

Of Puccini's writing for the timpani little need be said; it is as fluent as his scoring for other instruments. He had a regard for conventional tunings in fourths and fifths, and was meticulous in indicating changes of tuning and the type of beaters to be used.

The sound of the tuned gongs in *Turandot* excited the interest of Vaughan Williams, who, after a performance of the opera at Covent Garden, discussed the possibilities of such instruments with the performer; hence no doubt their inclusion in his Eighth Symphony.  The score reads 'as used in Puccini's *Turandot*.' It also states: 'The gongs are not absolutely essential, but their inclusion is highly desirable.' The fact that Vaughan Williams 'borrowed' from Puccini, in no way suggests that he was at any time at a loss regarding percussion. Many of his works contain textbook examples: *Job* (1930), Eighth Symphony (1956) and *Sinfonia Antartica* (1947), etc. He made extensive use of all the normal percussion instruments. On examination, his works show a distinct fondness for the glockenspiel and tubular bells (deep and otherwise). To the glockenspiel and xylophone he gave demanding parts. In *Sinfonia Antartica* he conjures an ethereal quality from the xylophone by the use of repetitive bars of tremolo and curling semiquavers played with soft beaters.

Sinfonia Antartica   Vaughan Williams

Xylophone

In the same work he combines the glockenspiel with four-note chords on the vibraphone. In the Eighth Symphony the vibraphone is given frequent three- and four-note chords, solo.

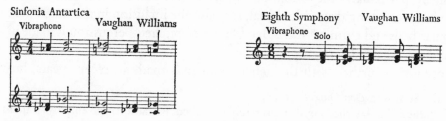

Sinfonia Antartica
Vibraphone   Vaughan Williams

Eighth Symphony   Vaughan Williams
Vibraphone   Solo

[1] Occasionally at a slow tempo, hoping to tire the stage band brass who sustain a chord.

There is an interesting part for the tubular bells in the Eighth Symphony. Frequently two bells are struck simultaneously, and glissandi are employed, to be produced by an upward and downward sweep of the hammer.

The wind machine makes one of its rare appearances in serious compositions, in *Sinfonia Antartica*, to be 'out of sight' says the composer.[1] A further unusual request is the *pp* roll with timpani sticks on the side drum in *A Sea Symphony* (1910).

In the Fourth Symphony Vaughan Williams scores for machine timpani (chromatic drum). He was well aware of the fact that at the time of writing this symphony (1935) many orchestras were not permanently equipped with these instruments, at least in England, for he gives an alternative part with no change of pitch.

All music examples by Vaughan Williams by permission of Oxford University Press, London.

Another British composer with a flair for percussion is Havergal Brian. In his Second Symphony, the *Gothic* (1919–27), a work scored for a large double chorus, a solo quartet and mixed childrens' voices, supported by 176 instrumentalists, the grandeur of the percussion section is a reminder of the ensemble envisaged by Berlioz. Sixteen players are involved (two timpanists and ten percussionists in the orchestra, and a timpanist in each of the four brass bands). The percussion requirements are: twenty-two timpani, two bass drums, long drum, side drum, six pairs of cymbals, gong, tambourine, xylophone, glockenspiel, tubular bells, chimes, thunder machine, chains and bird-scare (ratchet). The scoring points to a firm understanding of each percussion instrument. The timpani have a vital role, as for example, the *ppp* ostinato motif for three drums which opens the scherzo in Part I, and the combination of the eighteen kettledrums and brass in the final section, Part II. The tuned percussion is prominent, particularly the xylophone which is given an extended (and florid) solo. The request for a long drum is unusual, as is also the inclusion in the tuned percussion of tubular bells and chimes.[2] Considerable use of pitched percussion is made in many of Havergal Brian's later symphonies.

Before going further with the general demands made in recent years, however,

[1] As did Strauss in *Don Quixote* (1898).

[2] Cf. Berlioz. To-day the long drum is rarely requested. Richard Arnell employs it in his Piano Concerto (1967).

we need to consider in detail the orchestral percussion family as it has now evolved, the techniques employed by the various players in it, and the scope it offers to the imaginative composer.

Bibliography: Chapter 14

THE ROMANTIC ORCHESTRA—II

CLEATHER, G. Gordon. *The Timpani*, two lectures at The Royal College of Organists, London, 1908.

DUNHILL, Thomas. *Sir Edward Elgar*, Blackie, London, 1938.

JACOB, Gordon. *Orchestral Technique*, Oxford, London, 1931.

JOHNSON, Harold. *Sibelius*, Faber, London, 1960.

KIRBY, P. R. Preface to *A Concert Piece for Timpani and Piano*, (Tausch), Hinrichsen, London, 1959.

MAHLER, Alma. *Gustav Mahler: Memories and Letters,* revised edition, Murray, London, 1968.

PONTIGNY, Victor de. On Kettledrums, *Proceedings of the Musical Association*, vol. II, Spottiswoode, London, 1876.

RAMUZ, C. F. *Souvenirs sur Igor Strawinsky*, Nouvelle Revue Française, Paris, 1929.

TAYLOR, H. W. *The Art and Science of the Timpani*, Baker, London, 1964.

WHITE, Eric Walter. *Stravinsky*, Lehmann, London, 1947.

WOOD, Ralph. 'Sibelius's Use of Percussion', *Music and Letters*, vol. XXIII, 1942.

15

Techniques of Contemporary Percussion

In the large orchestra, the percussion instruments (frequently classified timpani and percussion) are divided into three groups: (i) the timpani, (ii) the instruments of indeterminate pitch: bass drum, cymbals, side drum, etc. (iii) the tuned percussion: xylophone, glockenspiel, etc. Pride of place is given to the timpani.[1]

THE TIMPANI

Though in principle the kettledrum remains a skin stretched over a bowl (usually of copper), there is little similarity between the instrument at the disposal of the modern composer and that used by Lully, Purcell and Bach. In general, from Bach to Weber, as far as history can prove, a pair of drums sufficed. From Weber onwards, three or more drums became usual. The allotment of the various tones embracing higher or lower notes not practical on a pair (or two pairs) resulted in the general adoption of a set of three drums that became known as the 'symphonic set of 3', with diameters 29½ inches, 26 inches and 24 inches, the three drums covering a compass of one and a third octaves.

Their advantage is that in addition to the added voice and the extended range, the tone quality is improved, since the drums operate more frequently in their middle register. With careful planning on the part of the composer, the wide range of a fifth – with the vellum consequently at its tautest or slackest – can be avoided.

[1] Dr. Gordon Jacob says: 'A conductor is always thankful for the presence of a really reliable timpanist. His part in the orchestra is so telling and individual, especially in modern works, that he is looked upon as an important soloist in the orchestra and one who can contribute both rhythmical firmness and dramatic excitement to an interpretation'. *The Elements of Orchestration*, Herbert Jenkins, London, 1962, p. 69.

The Timpani

Forsyth draws attention to this factor in his *Orchestration*, pointing out that the composer with a little tactful arrangement need scarcely go outside the limits of a fourth. In the majority of cases the standard works, until the early part of the century, conformed to the compass mentioned above. Exceptions occurred where two or more large or small drums were necessary, as for instance, Debussy's *Gigues* and Holst's *Beni Mora*.

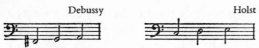

There is no doubt that the players of this period would, where possible, meet such demands by using additional drums of convenient size, a situation judiciously assessed by Professor Kirby who says[1]: 'But for those who desire to produce really artistic results, there is only one solution; more than three drums must be used. Five will be required, measuring in diameter 30, 28, 26, 24 and 22 inches respectively, or thereabouts.'

Whilst the present general use of pedal-tuning timpani has eased certain difficulties encountered in the past, it is clear that practical as these instruments are in the matter of rapid tuning, the production of the best possible sounds throughout the entire compass demands drums with accommodating diameters. Players have long been of the opinion that the ultimate in tone production is surely one drum for each note, with the cubic capacity of each kettle scientifically calculated to form a 'sympathetic' resonator.[2] Theoretically this may be so, but in practice the impossibility of manipulating the sixteen drums required to cover the (normal) range of one and a third octaves is obvious. Arranged keyboard fashion and semi-circularly, the distance between the interval of a fifth for example would be at least six feet.[2]

The 'happy medium' is now the general rule; in the orchestra to-day, it is usual to employ up to five timpani with diameters much as those given by Professor Kirby. To cope with modern requirements a minimum of four pedal-tuning timpani are at times essential. Bearing in mind that the performer can change the pitch on only two of these instruments simultaneously, the composer with an involved timpani part in mind would be well to consider four pedal drums as the maximum. Players find that one ideal arrangement is a pair of pedal-tuning drums with a 'machine drum' tuned by a single handle or rotary movement on each side of the pedal drums, allowing a change on four drums simultaneously in extreme circumstances.

Pedal drums to-day are excellently engineered. Compared with the cumber-

[1] Kirby, P. R. *The Kettle-drums*, Oxford, 1930, p. 35.
[2] Impracticable due to confused resonance.

some machinery of the past, the changing of pitch is effortless. The type of pedal mechanism varies. In the later 'Dresden' models of the several manufacturers (Spenke & Metzl, Dresdner Apparatebau, Dresden; Ringer Apparatebau, Berlin, the custom built drums by Walter Light, timpanist of the Denver Symphony Orchestra, etc.), the original 'sawtooth' clutch, engaged by side-action lever which locks the pedal in any position, is retained. The mechanism is modified, giving swift and silent tuning. These instruments include (as did the earlier models) a master-tuning handle to provide alternative fractional tuning. The foot pedal mechanism of the William F. Ludwig 'Dresden model' timpani is almost identical. Messrs. Ludwig are responsible for the famous balanced-action pedal-mechanism, where spring pressure controls the foot positioning in place of ratchet and clutch. Ball bearing (friction) clutch is incorporated in the latest drums by Premier Drum Co., and in both Messrs. Slingerland and Leedy of the U.S.A.[1] In 'Dresden' models the mechanism leading from the drum head to the foot pedal is placed on the outside of the kettle, which is suspended in a cradle. The 'Dresden' models of Messrs. Ludwig, and their 'Professional Symphonic' drums, the Premier Drum Co. pedal timpani, the drums by Walter Light, and the 'Supreme Timpani' of Messrs. Slingerland operate similarly. In other models by Messrs. Ludwig and Slingerland, the control rods connecting the counter hoop to the pedal mechanism pass through the bowl, as did the mechanism on the early models by Messrs. Leedy, Premier, Parsons and Ludwig.[2] The claim that the outer mechanism ensures unbroken resonance cannot be denied, though at the same time it cannot be disputed that some sterling results were, and continue to be, obtained on drums with inner mechanism, as (in England) the magnificent sounds produced on such instruments by the Brothers James and William Bradshaw have proved.

A tuning gauge, an indicator actuated by the 'travel' or movement of the counter-hoop or the foot pedal is now fitted to the majority of modern timpani. Given favourable atmospheric conditions with a calf vellum, or the use of a plastic head. the results are tolerably accurate.

The recently introduced fibre-glass bowl has proved successful, due to its durability and saving in weight. It is now applied to pedal-tuning and hand-screw drums.[3]

The standard pair of timpani measures 28 inches and 25 inches (diameters), a set of three, $29\frac{1}{2}$ inches, 26 inches, 24 inches with larger drums up to 30 inches and 32 inches

---

[1] Similarly the Rogers Accu-sonic timpani.

[2] These firms, together with, e.g. Messrs Boosey & Hawkes, Weaver & Dickson, Victor Chaine, and Cummings Bros., specialized in the manufacture of hand-screw timpani.

[3] Shallow shells of wood have proved successful in the recent 'Torrebruno-Ludwig' pedal timpani.

diameter, and piccolo timpani from 23 inches to 19 inches.[1] The empirical formula for determining the proportion that two drums a fourth apart should bear to each other has been decided as 2 to 1.732, with which the diameters quoted in the standard pair reasonably comply.

It is in the shape (depth and contour) of the kettle that there has been, and remains, a remarkable divergence in construction. In 1876, Victor de Pontigny[2] said that very little had been done towards investigating the theory and practice of kettledrum making, and that the exact shape and size of the shell seemed to be left rather to the coppersmith than to the scientific musician. 'If the theory of the shell can be properly ascertained', he said, 'it might be easier to decide upon the best shape to be given to it.' According to Pontécoulant[3], Adolphe Sax was of the opinion that the bowl had a harmful effect on the tone, and that the sonority depended only on the quality of the skin, its attachment and its size. He constructed his shell-less kettledrums and *timbales chromatiques* accordingly.

The function of the 'kettle', the tonal effect of its contour, and the vibrations of the membrane is a subject we prefer to approach historically rather than on a basis of a scientific dissertation. Acousticians have, as yet, made scant comment concerning these matters. Chladni (1756) did not pursue on vibrating membranes his experiments determining the modes of vibrations of metal or glass plates, made by scattering sand over the surface. Lord Rayleigh[4], after attempts to analyse the tone of the kettledrum, came to the conclusion that the vibrations are not of the symmetrical class. Sir James Jeans says[5]: 'The drum does not come through in its proper pitch, because the frequencies of its free vibrations do not form a series of natural harmonics (i.e. tones with frequencies in the ratio 1:2:3:4:5: . . .).'

Professor Kirby and Henry Taylor have extended Chladni's tests to the timpani. These experiments have determined, by the agitation of Lycopodium powder on a vibrating drumhead, the points of maximum vibration, and consequently that the correct striking point for musical purpose is approximately from the rim a distance of one eighth of the diameter of the shell. Mr Taylor has also drawn certain conclusions regarding the correct striking position from tracking the path of the sound waves in bowls of varying shape and capacity.[6] As regards the function of the bowl

---

[1] Measurements vary slightly between manufacturers.

[2] Pontigny, Victor de. 'On Kettledrums', *Proceedings of the Musical Association*, Spottiswoode & Co. London, 1876, p. 46.

[3] Pontécoulant, L. A. 'Organographie', *Essai sur la facture instrumentale*, Paris, 1861, p. 530.

[4] Lord Rayleigh. *Philosophical Magazine*, 1879.

[5] Jeans, James. *Science and Music*, Cambridge University Press, 1947, p. 242.

[6] Taylor, H. W. *The Art and Science of the Timpani*, p. 26.

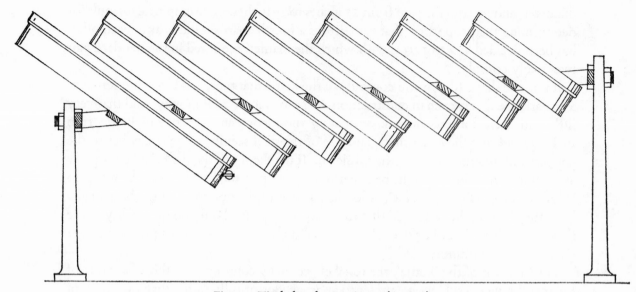

Fig. 42. Timbales chromatiques (A. Sax)

Fig. 43. Shell–less kettledrums (A. Sax)

and the mode of vibrations of the drumhead it may help to consider the matter of musical sound. This, we are told, is a series of regular vibrations which are periodic and of uniform length, in short, controlled vibrations; and a drumhead vibrates from two fixed points, the centre and the edge. To generate a note of musical quality, the head must be even in texture and evenly tensioned over a perfect circle. As little as one sixteenth out of round in the diameter of the circle will result in a flattening of the note at the points where the diameter is the greatest. Similarly, the slightest difference in the thickness or texture of the vellum will result in a difference in pitch at certain points. These inequalities can to some extent be rectified by an adjustment of the tension at necessary points, known to the timpanist as 'trueing up the head'. Therefore, whilst the pitch of the drum is governed by the tension on the drumhead and the diameter of the bowl, the quality of tone depends on the condition of the membrane, the correctness in tensioning and the shape and depth of the 'kettle'. Opinion is fairly unanimous that the bowl of the kettledrum magnifies certain of the overtones in the harmonic series, rendering the note musical (copper, brass, fibre glass and wood shells, hemispherical or near, produce similar results). Professor Kirby[1] says that a shallow bowl tends to clarify the principal note of the drum, a deep shell to increase its resonance. G. Gordon Cleather,[2] who made considerable experiments with kettledrums in the early part of the century, concluded that the shell should be proportionately deeper for low notes, but that the deeper the shell the greater the tendency for the pitch of the note to flatten on impact. H. Taylor considers the 'ideal' drum to be one where the depth of the shell is equal to the distance from the playing spot to the furthermost edge. Modern makers prescribe that the bowl should be as deep as one half of its diameter. Over a period of time we find the bowls semi-circular, parabolic, and with sloping sides.

No final formula for the perfect timpano has yet been evolved, and a wide range of types is still encountered. Tonal differences are compensated for by the performer, who will adjust the striking position to suit the depth of bowl, i.e. reasonably close to the rim in the deeper bowl, and a little nearer the centre if the bowl is shallower.

It is considered by many that the air trapped by the shell resonates in sympathy with the membrane. This is arguable. No appreciable difference in tone is perceptible whether the hole in the bottom of the shell (for the release of the air pressure) is open or plugged.[3] Neither is there any appreciable difference in the volume of sound

[1] Kirby, P. R. ibid. p. 21.

[2] Cleather, G. Gordon. Lectures delivered at The Royal College of Organists, 1908. Printed for The Royal College of Organists, 1908.

[3] A small 'trumpet bell' was fitted inside the bowl of some early continental kettledrums: possibly an attempt to assist the release of the air pressure (and the tone).

at a given point in the register; suggesting that the kettle acts less sympathetically than the xylophone resonator, where the air column corresponds to the frequency of the wooden bar.

Others claim that the chief purpose of the shell is to provide a support for the membrane, and to serve in trapping back the waves produced by the vibrating membrane. They contend that if the back wave was not contained, the front wave would be partially cancelled, resulting in a weak tone, and that the reason for a deep shell adding resonance to the drum, is due to the large volume of air trapped by the shell, determining the amount of restoring force on the membrane. This is in agreement with practical experiments made on a shell-less kettledrum, similar to that patented by Adolphe Sax. (It is only in the case of a closed 'double-skinned' cylindrical drum such as the 'long drum' that the depth of the shell affects the pitch of the drum). Lord Rayleigh's[1] observations respecting the function of the shell are as follows: 'I am not in a position to decide the question as to the function of the shell; but I think it at least doubtful whether it introduces any really advantageous modification into the relations of the component tones. It is possible that its advantage lies rather in obstructing the flow that would otherwise take place round the edge of the membrane. It must be remembered that the sounds due to the various parts of a vibrating membrane interfere greatly. In the case of a membrane simply stretched upon a hoop, and vibrating away from all obstacles, no sound at all would be heard at points in the prolongation of its plane. And even when there is a shell, no sound would be heard at points on the axis of symmetry, at least if the symmetrical vibrations may be left out of account.'

These scientific factors clearly have an important bearing on 'fine' tuning and tone production, the one ultimately associated with the other. Even so, for the performer, the immediate essential factor in 'tuning' is an unerring recognition of the true musical pitch of the drum; a simple statement maybe, but in practice by no means so simple.

With the kettledrum the fundamental note as far as musical purpose is concerned is absent. Professor Kirby says[2]: 'To produce the fundamental, the drumhead would have to be struck perpendicularly in its exact centre, so that it might vibrate as a whole. This cannot be done with an ordinary drumstick, and since kettledrums are not normally struck in this way, we may take it for granted that the tone so produced is not desired for musical performance.'[3]

The nominal (or principal) note of the drum is one octave above the fundamental.

[1] Lord Rayleigh. ibid. p. 161.
[2] Kirby, P. R. ibid. p. 39.
[3] To strengthen the fundamental note would require an extremely deep kettle.

The Timpani

To some, there is a difficulty in appreciating the true pitch of the principal note. In many cases – even to excellent musicians – certain of the numerous upper harmonics tend to register more strongly than the principal note. There is also the danger of confusing pitch with tone, the brighter tone which may be present at some point on the drumhead being mistaken for sharpness in pitch, while the duller sounding places may be thought flat. Given a vellum in good condition, even in texture and correctly tensioned, the fifth above the nominal (the second of the harmonic series from the fundamental) will be strong. The third and fourth of the series (the octave and the tenth) are also audible, and under the most favourable conditions the upper fifth, seventh and double octave are present. These tones, to quote Professor Kirby[1], are the 'constituent tones of a kettle-drum as used in music' and 'therefore in conformity with the harmonic series'. The timpanist utilizes the harmonics when tuning, principally the first harmonic above the nominal note, i.e. the fifth. The procedure is that of humming the nominal and the fifth above (or other harmonics) into the drumhead at the playing spot.[2] To do this, the head is inclined, and the lips placed as near as is possible to the vellum. (This procedure has been responsible for the suggestion that the player is whispering to, or kissing the drumhead.) It is when the drum responds with a singing tone to the humming of these notes, that the timpanist regards the instrument as well-tuned. With a pair of drums tuned in fifths the lower of the two will 'sing' when the higher drum is struck. This phenomenon of sympathetic resonance is used advantageously by the timpanist in the process of tuning – checking the interval of a fifth between the two drums, and so forth.[3] (Elliott Carter uses the ringing background of harmonics in his *Six Pieces for Kettledrums* (1966).) Sympathetic resonance however, has its disadvantages; the 'singing' of the tonic note when the dominant a fifth above is struck, is on occasions disturbing, necessitating a considerable amount of manipulation on the part of the player in the way of 'damping' (the technical term for stilling the vibrations). Cf. Mozart.

The method of applying tension varies. In the hand-tuned drums there are screws, each with its own handle fitted round the counter hoop. (The tuning screw at the playing spot is often square-topped, or in the form of a 'drop handle'.) The counter hoop conveys pressure to the flesh hoop.[4] The screws may be turned one or two at a

---

[1] Kirby, P. R. ibid. p. 43.

[2] The portion of the head from which the finest tone is elicited is chosen as the playing spot and the vellum positioned accordingly. With rotary-tuned drums a fixed playing spot is not possible.

[3] The process of 'pitching' notes into the drums and the response of one drum to another may have added greatly to the influence of the witch doctor, with whom the drum was in many cases an indispensable 'tool of his trade'.

[4] On modern timpani the head is not 'lapped' on the counter hoop as on earlier drums.

time.[1] Machine drums are of three types: pedal-operated; those with rotating bowls; and those fitted with a single master screw. In these three cases the whole counter hoop is lowered or raised in a single operation. In no instance is the tuning positively obtained by a consistent mechanical operation, such as a given number of turns on the handles, or a prescribed 'travel' on the foot pedal. The amount of pressure is variable, and is governed by the condition and thickness of the drumhead and, in the case of calfskins, by atmospheric conditions.

In the initial tuning of a hand-screw drum, some advise that opposite pairs of handles be turned simultaneously, others that the pair of handles nearest the player be first turned and work forward from the playing area. It is usual (particularly if the drum is not equipped with a 'floating head') for the player when lowering the pitch of a drum, to tune slightly below the required note. The head is then 'settled' by firm pressure with the flattened fingers or palm of the hand, followed by the final tensioning. If these precautions are not taken, the pitch of the drum may fall considerably on impact, due to the possibility of the head 'binding' slightly on the shell. Following the initial tuning the head is 'trued' to ensure the absence of a heterogeneous beat. To do this, the player tests the pitch at and between every tuning handle, making the necessary adjustments to correct any inequality due to unequal pressure or variation in texture due to the non-homogeneous nature of the vellum. (He may temporarily eliminate certain overtones by lightly pressing the centre of the head with the finger or thumb.)

The pitch of the drum is tested by 'flipping' the head with the fleshy part of the middle finger, with a light touch of the drumstick, or by the humming process already described; this operation to be audible to none but the executant. To tune two or more drums in the silence of an empty concert hall, or whilst the orchestra is 'tuning up' presents little difficulty to an experienced player. If not possessed with absolute pitch (an asset to the modern timpanist), the preponderance of the A and D in the orchestra's preambles can be utilized, and the required notes pitched relatively. Similarly, to tune the drums to the principal notes (tonic, dominant or subdominant) of the key in which the orchestra is playing presents no great problem. To change the pitch whilst the orchestra is playing in a key foreign to that in which the timpani are to participate is another matter. Here the timpanist is reliant on other factors, mechanical and musical. Given favourable conditions (atmospheric and the 'machinery' in perfect order) the player is conscious of the approximate mechanical operation. Tuning gauges assist, but for reason of atmospheric and mechanical contingencies, these are subject to inconsistency. The musical factors involved may, though rarely do, include the use of a tuning fork. The more usual method is for the

[1] To-day, in professional circles, drums of this type are little used.

356

timpanist to compare the pitch of the drum with an identifiable or cued note in the orchestra, where possible a holding note on the horns or lower brass. The pitch of forthcoming notes is also determined by using already established notes on the drums as reference notes, in which case the player is obliged, as far as possible, to isolate himself from the sound of the orchestra. Even so, there is the problem of recognising the true pitch of the drum's note, for whilst the orchestra is performing in an incongruous key, acoustic phenomena may render this note (produced quietly) difficult to define, even to the most experienced ear.

Wherever possible the player checks the tuning during a quiet passage in the orchestra, or during a few moments of silence. Composers normally give sufficient bars rest for changes of pitch to be effected, and in the majority of cases the change is indicated: 'change to D, A and E' and so forth. (In the bulk of the works of the Classical period, and quite often to-day, *muta* (It: change) is used.) Not the least of the timpanist's problems is that of insufficient time to effect a satisfactory change and, particularly if the drums are 'hand-tuned', making the necessary adjustment whilst keeping an eye on the music (and the conductor) and at the same time counting bars rest.[1] He is also kept busily engaged in maintaining the pitch of his instrument in adverse atmospheric conditions, possibly to a greater extent than that of any other instrumentalist. Of atmospheric variations, the two conditions which most affect the pitch of a kettledrum are temperature and humidity. Both are devastating to a calf vellum, though considerably less so in the case of a plastic head.[2] The animal skin is particularly susceptible to conditions of humidity, a moisture-laden atmosphere causing the membrane to expand and consequently flatten in pitch. At times, as for example in a poorly-heated hall on a damp night, conditions can even render the highest notes in the drums range unobtainable, in which case the player is forced to place the note on a smaller drum where the desired pitch requires less

tension, or in dire circumstances to invert the tuning, i.e.

Conversely, a dry atmosphere tends to shrink a drumhead, causing the note to sharpen. These conditions have led to the use of heating or moisture-carrying units —normally fitted inside the bowl. (The moisture-carrying unit is particularly useful to-day to cope with conditions in centrally-heated concert halls, and film and tele-

---

[1] Of the last-named Saul Goodman in his *Modern Method for Tympani*, Mills Music, New York, 1948, p. 44 says: 'This ability can be developed only by the most careful concentration and closest attention to the rhythmical structure of the music being played. Conductors cannot always give an entrance cue to the tympanist, and for this reason the player must be absolutely certain and sure just when he must "set in".'

[2] See later reference to drumheads.

vision studios). Favourable as conditions may be, there remains the constant checking of pitch. This aspect and the timpanist's task generally has been amusingly described by A. H. Sidgwick[1] 'The man with the drum was top-hole, doing some pretty trick-work with the wrists, and a lot of very quick waggles with both sticks like a bee buzzing. . . . He had a lot of little taps round the side and kept turning them on and off as if he was doing it for a bet against time. Is it to let the air out, or is it simply a game to keep him amused when he hasn't got to chip in? And who arranged his part? Does the composer fix exactly the number of whacks he is to give, or does he simply leave general directions: 'Sit tight for a bit here and turn off the taps, and then let her have ten good ones? I should like to play the drum.'[2] Very amusing for everyone except the 'man with the drum'. Each of those 'ten good ones' may involve a definite technical approach, as for instance the necessity to adjust the tuning according to the volume of tone to be produced. A drumhead at a given tension will not produce precisely the same note over the whole dynamic range. A heavy blow momentarily stretches the membrane and a slightly flatter note is produced than when the instrument is struck lightly. The degree of inconsistency is governed by the pressure on the vellum: the tighter the skin the less the fall in pitch, and so forth. The fact that the head immediately adjusts itself after a heavy blow, and the final after-tone dies away at the same pitch as if the drum had been lightly struck in no way relieves the situation, for the more audible note is that produced on impact. The player compensates for these irregularities in various ways. The notes are placed as advantageously as is possible, i.e. in the upper register of the drums, and consequently a high degree of tension on the heads. In the case of pedal-tuned drums, a fractional move to sharpen or flatten can be made, governed entirely by the time in hand.

In the given example the player would check the slight fall in pitch during the crescendo roll with the foot pedal. Faced with the same example on hand-screw drums, the fact of both hands being engaged with the tremolo would make the minor adjustment impossible.[3] Cf. rotary (foot) fine-tuning, Plate 161.

There are further aspects relating to the matter of fine tuning, such as the 'tempering' of the notes, as essential to good intonation on the timpani as on any other

---

[1] Sidgwick, A. H. *The Promenade Ticket*, Arnold, London, 1928, pp. 16 & 17.

[2] Bringing to mind *Hiawatha* (Coleridge Taylor) with its 122 changes.

[3] Given a moment's respite, e.g. a crotchet rest, a player will give a flick on a handle nearest the playing spot.

instrument. The timpanist's equivalent of the 'lipping' of the wind instruments for example, is a microscopic adjustment of the pitch of his fixed notes which may at times sound the tonic, at others the dominant or mediant, and so forth. Such adjustments can only be achieved through a fine ear and experience, and likewise the ability to be in the middle of the orchestra's pitch at all times. It is by his intonation and tone that an orchestral timpanist is assessed; to quote Dr. Shivas[1]: 'It is by their performance in this department of tympani playing that the great are readily distinguished from the not-so-great.'

Tone quality is dependent on other factors: a definite sense touch is required in timpani playing, since the tone quality of a drum relies to no small degree on the manner in which it is elicited. To produce the best possible tone, the stick must be immediately withdrawn from the drum after the blow has been delivered. The correct stroke can be likened to the spit of a snake's tongue. If the blow is clumsily delivered, loss of resonance and inaccuracy in pitch result from the slight lag and pressure of the drumstick on the vellum. The stick, which is held with the shaft nearly parallel with the drumhead, is firmly gripped between the tip of the thumb and the first joint of the index finger, at a point about three inches from the end of the stick – the exact distance being governed by its length and weight.[2] Both sticks are held identically. In normal rhythmic playing, the third and fourth fingers which are clear of the shaft act as a cushion. In heavy playing, one or both grip the shaft. The little finger remains clear of the shaft at all times. In moderately quiet passages, the movement used in striking the drum takes place at the wrist and fingers.

Fig. 44. Grip of timpani stick

From *forte* upwards, the muscles of the upper arm are brought into play, together with carefully controlled movement from the elbow. This effect is applied in some measure to the roll, which on the timpani consists of a succession of single strokes of equal power. The side drum roll consisting of an alternation of two strokes is rarely applied to the timpani. The rapidity of the strokes, that is, the speed of the roll, is related to the tension on the head, a greater speed being required to keep the head

[1] Shivas, Andrew. *The Art of Tympanist and Drummer*, Dobson, London, 1957, p. 47.

[2] A mid-nineteenth-century German manual illustrates the shaft of a kettledrum stick with a cavity for the thumb. The shafts of this and other types are given as 33 centimetres in length, and 1 centimetre in thickness. A stiff shaft is indicated, as the woods mentioned are cherry, ash and acacia.

vibrating when tensioned to a high note than when tensioned for a low note. If the beating is too rapid on a head when at low tension and consequently vibrating slowly, the vibrations are damped and the tone impaired. Conversely, a head highly-tensioned and vibrating quickly must be 'nursed' with a closer roll.

In the *fp* roll the initial note is struck and allowed to die away to almost the required dynamic level before the roll is commenced, the natural resonance of the drum bridging the gap in beating. If the roll is introduced immediately after the primary blow has been struck, the effect is more that of a diminuendo. In a crescendo roll the player may commence the roll near to the rim of the drum, and with the increase in the rise and fall of the sticks move them towards the 'playing' spot. This procedure is reversed in the case of a diminuendo roll. (Both Speer (1687) and Eisel (1738) preferred this variance in tone. Eisel: 'soft near the rim and booming loudly near the middle'.)

In addition to the technical methods relating to tone production so far described, the timpanist produces substantial degrees of tone quality by the use of 'graded' drumsticks. The modern timpanist's 'stock in trade' would certainly have delighted Berlioz, who, in his *Orchestration*, so firmly recommended the use of three types (wood, leather and sponge ends). Berlioz also recommended handles of whalebone.

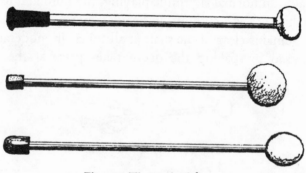

Fig. 45. Timpani sticks

These, and the leather and sponge ends are seldom met with to-day. To meet the demands of modern composers (as well as to satisfy his own particular taste), the timpanist of to-day is equipped with a large variety of sticks, here described briefly. In general, the shaft is of hickory or similar straight-grained wood. The length varies from 13 to $14\frac{1}{2}$ inches, the thickness $\frac{3}{8}$ to $\frac{1}{2}$ inch tapered or otherwise, each factor depending on the player's preference. In some cases the extreme end of the shaft is tipped with a small ferrule. There are eminent performers who prefer a malacca cane handle. Personal research suggests, however, that the stiffer handle is the more popular. The heads of the stick vary in shape, size, weight and texture. In shape they vary from elliptical to pear-shaped, according to the area of contact and tone desired.

Large heads are particularly suitable where the drumhead is tight, i.e. tuned to the middle of its register, or above. If the drum is tuned below the mean of its compass, the consequently slacker vellum would sag under the impact of a large head. Heads that are too large tend to stifle the sound of the drum; in general the diameter ranges from $1\frac{1}{4}$ to 2 inches. The weight of a kettledrum stick varies from $\frac{3}{4}$ to $1\frac{1}{4}$ ounces, according to the content of the head and the thickness of the shaft. 'Hard sticks' (as they are known to the composer and player) have ends consisting of a small ball of wood or hard felt. 'Wooden sticks' are of two types: a small ball of wood fixed to the shaft, or the whole stick fashioned from suitable wood. 'Soft sticks' have an inner core of hard felt, cork or balsa wood, which is covered with either one or two layers of felt (usually soft piano damper felt).

Many professional players make their own timpani sticks, the virtues of which, together with the qualities of drumheads, are as constant a topic of interest as the new bow is in the string section. To-day, percussionists freely discuss the relative qualities of their particular instruments, and their personal approach; there is little of the 'closed shop' of yesterday. (The experience of a lifetime, until recent years so often jealously guarded, is now, as far as this is possible, committed to print or otherwise imparted to the student who, if sufficiently zealous, may gain early entry into the professional orchestra.)

The matter of the overall technical approach to the orchestral timpani continues to be discussed in great detail in literature dealing specifically with this subject, therefore only a few basic points are made here. First, the position of the instruments in relation to the player: it is rightly claimed that a standing position offers considerable freedom of action, but to-day, due to a great extent to the almost general use of pedal timpani, a seated position is the more usual. The height of the drum is such that when playing, the sticks lie horizontally. Normally each drum is tilted towards the player; this reduces the danger of the sticks fouling the rim or tuning handle when passing from one drum to another.

A pair of drums is placed side by side with the playing areas adjacent.

Three drums are placed, approximately on the circumference of a circle, with (excepting the continental style) the small drum to the right.

The placing of the large drum to the right hand is a relic of early cavalry practice, a tradition retained in cavalry regiments and by many orchestral timpanists, German, Russian, Dutch, Austrian and Czech in particular.[1] The arranging of the larger of the

[1] Cavalry drummers contend that the heavier drum to the right assists the horse to wheel to the (normal) right.

361

orchestral timpani to the left (as for example in the U.S.A., Britain, Italy and France) positions the bass notes to correspond to the pianoforte keyboard, as do the bars of the xylophone, etc. The opinions of the two schools of thought are interesting. It is claimed by those who position the small drum to the right hand, that this style of drumming has long existed, as, for instance, the Indian tablā. 'Why play the

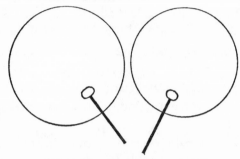

Fig. 46. Placing of drums (pair)

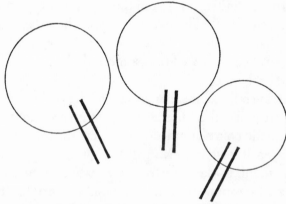

Fig. 47. Placing of drums (three)

timpani in a different manner from the customary keyboard instruments?' they ask. Those who adhere to the bass at the right hand quote the tradition of the kettle-drums, and that this art has been handed down for generations. They contend that the piano cannot tell the drum how to play, and compare their positioning to the style of their masters. There is clearly a strong case to be made for each side, heightened by the expertise of both. See footnotes p. 271 and 361.

In timpani playing alternate beating is the general rule. When passing from one drum to another the player anticipates the change of direction by moving the drum-stick immediately a stroke has been delivered, thus:

The move is similarly anticipated when executing the cross-beat.

In cross-beating it is the rule that the moving hand passes over the other hand. Situations constantly arise where the timpanist is obliged to move rapidly from drum to drum while beating a quick rhythm, involving at times complex passages which unless carefully 'fingered' entail 'hazardous' cross-overs. At a fast speed certain cross-over beats are not practicable: there is the possibility of the drumsticks fouling each other (or the rim) or the danger of the new drum being struck away from the correct playing spot. In the case of a cross-beat at speed between two drums some distance apart (as in the Busoni example, p. 333) the impetus of the movement adds strength to the stroke, which may result in an unintended *sforzando*. It is in such circumstances that the timpanist uses a double beat, often in the form of a paradiddle, the device well-known to side drummers, and probably to the early cavalry kettledrummers. (It is feasible that this beating was originally pou-rou-did-dle, cf. 'Old English March' Randall Holme III etc.). In the paradiddle the first two beats are struck by alternate sticks and the last two by one alone. The principle of the paradiddle and double beats may be extended indefinitely.

Under extreme circumstances recourse may be had to the duplication of a drum.[1]

This expedient and the use of the double beat are used judiciously i.e. where a complicated pattern played otherwise would prove unsafe in performance.

In addition to the contrasting types of tone produced on the timpani by a par-

[1] Rarely. See: Bower, Harry A. *System for the Tympani*, Carl Fischer, New York, 1911.

ticular technique, or the use of a variety of sticks, there are numerous other effects requested by composers, or used at the discretion of the player. In the case of a passage marked staccato, the stick is gripped tightly and lifted from the drumhead at an even greater speed than usual. Given time between each beat, the vibrations are checked by the process known as damping. This process is also adopted to prevent notes ringing on beyond their written value, and where there are *sec* effects. In damping, the drumhead is touched lightly with the flattened second, third and fourth fingers, the stick being held between the thumb and forefinger. The operation must be noiseless, and under no circumstances must pressure be placed on the vellum or a slight sharpening of the note will occur.[1] Where the speed of a series of short notes renders this method of damping impossible, a piece of felt is placed on the drumhead. Likening the drumhead to a clock face with the 'playing spot' at six hours, if the damping cloth is placed at nine hours the pitch remains distinct, and the drum is sufficiently muffled for normal purposes. With the cloth at twelve hours the resonance of the drum is further decreased, and there is a loss of pitch.[2] The effect of damping or muting the kettledrum is frequently met in orchestral scores. It is indicated *timpani coperti*[3] (It.) (cf. Mozart), *timbales couvertes* or *voilé* (Fr.) *dämpfer* (Ger.) (cf. Mahler), etc. The word *naturale* (or *scoperti*) is used when the muted effect is to cease. Composers utilize this muted quality of sound for the purpose of clarifying certain passages, or to obtain a funereal effect. Notable examples include Berlioz, 'March to the Scaffold' from *Symphonie Fantastique*; Liszt's opening of *Hungarian Fantasia*; Mahler's First Symphony (third movement); Stravinsky's *Renard* and Copland's *Statements*. In some cases, though not indicated by the composer, the player will use dampers to obtain a given result. Of this, Percival Kirby says[4]: 'The whole subject is full of exceptions; like the pianoforte pedalling, damping depends almost entirely upon the judgment of the player, which in turn depends upon his experience and knowledge of the score.'

In contrast to the 'shortening' of certain notes, to ensure great sonority two drums may occasionally be tuned to the same note and struck simultaneously, or (ideally) two timpanists in unison as in Mahler's Third Symphony.

Grace notes on the timpani take the form of the side drum ornaments (flams, drags, etc.). As with the paradiddle, the term is onomatopoeic. The 'flam' consists of a light stroke followed by a stronger one ( ). The 'drag' consists of two grace notes played lightly (hand to hand in the case of the timpani), followed by a strong

[1] Pressure with thumb or finger in centre will raise the pitch a semitone, an expedient utilized on occasion to effect a rapid change on a handscrew drum.

[2] The writer made application for a patent for a foot-controlled damping device in 1965.

[3] *Coperto*, singular.　　　　　　　　　　　　　[4] Kirby, P. R. ibid. p. 64.

beat ♫♩ . As with the side drum, though normally written within the bar, the beat coincides with the accent of the music, i.e. [musical notation] In some cases however a grace note precedes a tremolo, in which case it is often played within the bar. In all cases the grace note (or notes) and the following stroke are played from hand to hand. Bruckner, whose fine writing for the timpani in his Ninth Symphony has already been mentioned, makes effective use of grace notes, particularly in his Eighth Symphony (1892). His use of lengthy rolls is equally impressive, e.g. in his Eighth and Ninth Symphonies.

The use of the acciaccatura is rare, as is the striking of the drum with both sticks simultaneously. The latter is indicated ♩ or ♩♩ .

Most composers have employed the kettledrums as solo instruments. To the timpanist the 'solo' is a supreme moment. Many solo passages require special treatment, particularly those at a low dynamic level such as the opening bar in the Beethoven Violin Concerto, and the solo bars in *The Merry Wives of Windsor* (Nicolai 1849). In such cases, for the purpose of matching the sound of each stroke, the passage is usually played with one hand, i.e. the same stick striking the drumhead at precisely the same place, the centre of the playing spot. (Cf. Beethoven Violin Concerto.) It is in such outstanding moments that the quality of the drumhead undergoes its severest test. However evenly-tensioned it may be, the finest player cannot coax a 'dead true' note from a drumhead that is not uniform in texture.

To-day, the timpanist has the choice of calfskin and the recently introduced synthetic head (a form of polethylene terephthalate).[1] Between field and concert hall the quality of the animal skin is affected in a number of ways. In the first place the texture of the skin is determined by the animal's early feeding, and also by its age when slaughtered, usually before it is twelve months old. Thereafter much depends on the care with which the skin is prepared. It is first soaked and then salted on the flesh side to preserve the skin, after which it is placed for about seven days in a pit of lime liquor to loosen the hair. After unhairing (by hand) the skin is strengthened in lime liquor, then washed and stretched on a wooden frame (cf. primitive drumming). It is then scraped by hand with a half-moon shaped knife to the required thickness, with timpani heads from five to six thousandths of an inch, the process of stretching and scraping being a skilled craft. (In some cases to-day the skins are equalized by machinery.) Thin heads are preferable on the large drums, but the inconsistency of the animal skin permits no firm ruling.[2]

[1] See pp. 366–7.
[2] My information came from Mr. Gordon Band of H. Band & Co. Ltd., Brentford, London.

The head is mounted on a flesh hoop by a process known as lapping. The vellum is first soaked in cold water until pliable, then cut to a size, allowing sufficient excess to encircle the flesh hoop, viz.:

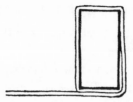

Fig. 48
Lapping vellum to hoop

A lapping tool in the shape of a spoon handle is used for the 'tucking' process.

The lapped head is then placed on the bowl, (the rim having been 'dressed' with paraffin wax to prevent the head from binding), and the counter hoop adjusted to draw the head slightly over the shell, giving a 'collar' to compensate shrinkage in the head as it dries out, thus ensuring the lower notes.

The synthetic head was first applied to the timpani in the middle 1950's. Some few years previously it had been successfully applied to the side drum, and has since been fitted with equal success to the bass drum, tenor drum and bongos, etc. Probably the chief virtue of the plastic head lies in its near imperviousness to varying atmospheric conditions; a situation that has demanded man's attention over a long period of time, for the weatherproofing of drumheads is age-old. The Chinese tanned pig skins for drums as early as 3000 B.C. The varnishing of kettledrum heads, still observed on occasions, is of long standing, whilst from 1863 we find patents granted for solutions for the coating of drumskins, and to the 'All-Weather' head, a varnished fabric (see 'Patents').

The plastic (so-called) timpani head did not receive the approval extended to the synthetic side drum head. The quality of the early material failed to meet the searching demands of players and, in addition, there was the scepticism so frequently levelled at an innovation. By now a marked improvement in manufacture, both in material with its precise thickness throughout (that of a stout calfskin head) and in the method of mounting on the hoop (an involved process of sealing), together with the high degree of tonal consistency under the most trying atmospheric conditions, has resulted in the world-wide, though not unanimous, adoption of the plastic head.

The opinions of the world's most famous players are sharply divided regarding the relative tonal qualities of the calf and plastic head. Players who at one time condemned the plastic head now speak highly of it; others who for some time found the synthetic head acceptable, have reverted to the calfskin. All agree, however, that under extreme weather conditions the synthetic material is a boon. Even the most confirmed adherent of the calfskin will resort to the use of 'plastic' on such occasions as a lengthy tour embracing exceptional changes of climate. As to the diverse opinions regarding the features of the synthetic head, there are players who consider them a great resource for the timpanist, and that they permit perfect intonation and an excellent clarity of sound. Others complain of their lack of perfect harmonics and elasticity. All seem agreed that there is a loss of tone below the mean of the drum's compass. From the point of view of durability, a synthetic head is certainly less prone to the sudden disaster that occasionally overtakes a calf head, usually in the form of the vellum splitting, due to contraction in an abnormally dry or heated atmosphere, or 'going' at the rim when sudden tension is applied in conditions of humidity. (Rarely does a drumhead succumb to a well-delivered blow.)

Nomenclature includes *Kettledrums* (Eng:); *Timpani* (It:); *Timbales* (Fr:); *Pauken* (Ger:).

THE BASS DRUM

The modern orchestral 'symphonic' bass drum would have delighted Berlioz. To-day's instrument (double-headed and rod tensioned) measures up to 40 inches in diameter and 20 inches in width; it is suspended in a frame with swivel attachment for positioning at any angle. The single-headed orchestral gong drum, popular for the best part of a century (particularly in England), is now seen less frequently: despite its admirable resonance it must be admitted that a well-tensioned single-headed drum will unfortunately produce a note of a definite pitch. With a separate-tension double-sided drum the heads are adjusted to produce different tones, rendering the drum's note comparatively indefinable, while the enclosed cylinder increases the depth of sound.[1] The orchestral bass drum is effective over a wide range of dynamics, rhythmic and colouristic. Walter Piston finds that[2]: '... the carrying power of the bass drum is greater than that of any other instrument.'

The bass drummer in a symphony orchestra is equipped with almost as great a variety of sticks as the timpanist, ranging from the large head of lamb's wool to the small beaters of hard felt or wood, the latter used to produce the brittle effects so frequently demanded by modern composers.[3] For general purposes the head of the bass drum is struck mid-way between the centre and the rim, and with a glancing blow.[4] The beater is usually held in the right hand; the left hand, in the case of a

---

[1] Why not a conical shell?

[2] Piston, Walter. *Orchestration*, Norton, New York, 1955, and Gollancz, London. p. 308.

[3] Puccini in *Madam Butterfly* (1914) designates *colla bacchetta di ferro* (iron rod). Stravinsky in *The Rite of Spring* side drum stick, and Britten similarly in *Peter Grimes*, *The Rape of Lucretia* and *Sinfonia da Requiem*, etc.

[4] The heads of the bass drum are of calfskin or plastic.

single-headed drum, controlling the length of the note where required. With a double-headed drum, the fingers of the right hand 'still' the vibrations (if necessary) in a similar manner to the damping of the timpani whilst the left hand controls the reverberations of the opposite head. In a succession of short notes, to minimise the resonance, the drum is struck in the centre. The tremolo, which according to Scholes possibly began with Liszt (*Ce qu'on entend sur la montagne*, 1849) and was used effectively by Wagner, is produced like the roll on the timpani: single beats from hand to hand, and for the purpose of a close roll, on one side of a double-skinned drum. Only on rare occasions does the symphonic bass drummer combine cymbals with bass drum (when a cymbal held in the left hand strikes another fixed to the drum). Here, for *sec* effects the drum is damped as described, and the cymbals muffled simultaneously by drawing the hand cymbal back against the body whilst the body moves forward into the fixed cymbal. (The combining of bass drum and cymbals by one player is as unpopular with symphonic percussionists as it was with Berlioz. For the tremolo on the bass drum, a double-headed beater (formerly tampon) is employed; a rapid oscillating movement of the wrist bringing the heads of the stick into contact with the drumhead. Dukas scores for this effect in *The Sorcerer's Apprentice*, Stravinsky in *The Firebird*, and Britten in *The Burning Fiery Furnace*.)

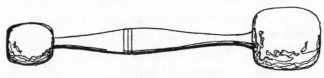

Fig. 49. Bass drum stick

In printed music, the lower space of the stave is normally allotted to the bass drum.[1] The bass clef is generally used, though strictly speaking no clef is necessary for the instruments of indeterminate pitch. In symphonic works a single line is often allotted. Composers usually designate the bass drum with its full title, or abbreviate it: B.D. Its importance as an orchestral instrument is well described by Forsyth who says[2]: 'A single deep booming stroke is sufficient to produce a sense of farawayness, of solemnity, even of hopeless desolation. It is scarcely possible to find an orchestral *Funeral March* which would not illustrate this point.' Composers continue to use the

[1] Unfortunately, as yet no strict rule is observed in this matter. Percussionists are frequently confronted with an instrument placed differently in the stave during the same work. (See later chapter).

[2] Forsyth, Cecil. *Orchestration*, Macmillan, London, 1955, pp. 29–30.

bass drum descriptively, e.g. Tchaikovsky's *1812* and Prokoviev's *Lieutenant Kije*. Nomenclature includes *Gran cassa* (It:); *Grosse caisse* (Fr:); *Grosse Trommel* (Ger:).

THE SIDE DRUM (SNARE DRUM)

The side drum during the course of its 250 years as an instrument of the orchestra has undergone numerous changes in design and purpose, the most radical change in structure occurring in the early part of the nineteenth century, with the advent of rod-tensioning and the shallow shell. Fashions in side drums have changed almost as often as those of the Paris couturier, for the years have seen deep shells, medium shells, shallow shells, metal shells, wood shells and telescopic shells (see Patents) all claimed as the ultimate and the acme of utility.[1] In the symphony orchestra, for normal purposes, the present trend is for a side drum with a depth of five to eight inches, with a deeper model, twelve inches in depth for use as the occasion demands. (These instruments measure fourteen or fifteen inches in diameter.) From time to time composers request a side drum of small dimension, i.e. Schönberg in *Moses and Aaron*, 'high side drum', and Walton in his opera *The Bear* (1967) *cassa chiara*. Vaughan Williams asks for the side drum to be tuned high in his Sixth Symphony in E minor, and Puccini specifies *acuto* in *Madam Butterfly*. Where not specified, the choice of drum is largely a matter of individual preference on the part of the player, or conductor, governed by such factors as the character of the composition, size of orchestra, and sometimes acoustics.

In principle, the side drum is as described in a previous chapter. The cylindrical shell (of wood or metal) is covered at each end with a head of calfskin, or plastic material (sheepskin is now little used). The upper head is still known as the 'batter head', and the lower the 'snare head'. As with the timpani, opinions are divided as to the respective qualities of calf and plastic head. Many players, whilst admitting the hardy nature of the plastic material under adverse conditions, contend that the silky tone of the calf head is preferable for *ppp*. Some players favour a calf batter head and plastic snare head.[2] As a general rule, the lower head on which the snares rest, is thinner and slightly tighter than the upper (playing) head. (On a modern side drum the heads are independently screw-tensioned.) To-day the instrument is usually fitted with an internal damper for controlling the resonance of the playing head. The snares, eight or more in number, are of gut, nylon, wire or wire-covered silk,[3]

---

[1] A few years ago in the lighter field of music, the *pipper*, a side drum two inches in depth was acclaimed. To-day a deeper drum is advocated.

[2] Where the snare head is of calfskin, it is usual to fit a 'slunk' head (from a still-born animal).

[3] Gut snares impart a true military sound.

according to the player's preference.[1] The snares are loosened ('muffled side drum') by means of a lever – the 'snare release'.

The tension of the snares, controlled by screw mechanism (illustrated as early as Praetorius q.v.), is vital to the sound of the drum. They must lie evenly on the vellum and be tensioned to produce a crisp and immediate response from the stroke on the batter head. Snares that are too tight tend to 'choke' the tone. From a scientific angle the action of the snares is well described by Forsyth[2]: 'When the player attacks the batter-head its vibrations set up waves in the air which is contained in the shell. These waves are communicated to the snare-head, and so to the snares themselves. The immediate effect is to alter the character of the air-waves and to double the number of the vibrations. The explanation of this 'doubling' seems to be that the snares continually impinge on the parchment, and so set up a constant series of 'points of nodal contact'. (It is considered that a tight snare head assists vibration.)

In addition to giving the side drum its peculiar quality and brilliance, the snares render the pitch of the instrument less definable. A side drum unsnared and a tenor drum, (which, strictly speaking, is a side drum without snares) though classified artistically as instruments of indefinite pitch, produce readily defined notes, un-musical in comparison with the timpani, but certainly not indeterminate.[3]

Piston says[4]: '. . . the pitch of the drum drops roughly an octave when the snares are loosened'.

To the layman, the sticks used on the side drum may appear to differ little in design. Not so to the side drummer, who is as fastidious in the choice of drumsticks to meet every situation as is the timpanist. Where the timpanist chooses a soft stick for a certain effect, the side drummer may select a stick with a long taper, or else-where – may be for a *ff* – those with a short taper, and possibly a larger acorn (as the tip of the side drum stick is known). Modern manufacturers give the player a wide choice. The more usual woods employed are hickory or lance wood, to which is now added the laminated side drum stick, and those that are nylon-tipped. (The fine-grooved rings on the 'gripped' end of the side drum stick which used to be a feature, ornamental and practical, are no longer in fashion.)

In performance the side drum is positioned at a chosen angle - sloping or horizontal (cf. Changing Styles). Many orchestral players use the sloping angle with the sticks held traditionally - the right hand stick gripped between the tip of the thumb and the

[1] The Premier Drum Company of Great Britain have introduced 'twin snares' – nylon and wire-covered silk.   [2] Forsyth, Cecil. ibid. p. 24.

[3] In the orchestra, on occasions in exposed passages, the pitch of an unsnared side drum can be sufficiently disturbing to necessitate an adjustment of its tension.

[4] Piston, Walter. ibid. p. 304.

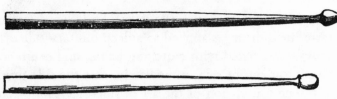

Fig. 50. Side drum sticks

first joint of the index finger, as the timpani sticks (Fig. 44). The left stick is held in the crutch of the thumb and index (first) finger resting on the middle joint of the third finger. The hold of the left stick is known as the 'rabbit grip' so-called from the silhouette of the hand.

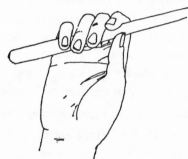

Fig. 51
Method of holding
side drum sticks
Left hand and
right hand

To identify the various types of side drums indicated in scores is problematical. Translation of the differences in meaning of the several languages is often conflicting. The definition by the composer and interpretation by the performer are often at variance.[1] In English we have 'side drum', and/or 'snare drum', an American appellation universally adopted. These terms are applied to the orchestral side drum of medium depth, and also to the deeper model known as the 'military' or 'Guards pattern' side drum. In French, where drum is both *caisse* and *tambour*, there is *caisse claire*, *tambour petit* and *tambour militaire* – the latter equivalent to the English military or 'Guards pattern' side drum. (*Caisse claire* is generally interpreted as a small side drum.) The German *kleine Trommel* is applied to a shallow drum with snares (the deep side drum is not a feature of the German and other Continental military bands, as it is elsewhere). The Italian *tamburo* and *tamburo militare* apply to the normal side drum and the military model. The normal side drum is also called *tamburo piccolo*, and a small shallow drum *tarole*.[2] The latter occurs for example in *Ionisation* (Varèse),

[1] It is generally accepted that a standard classification of the side drum and related instruments is long overdue, e.g. the general adoption of 'snare drum' in place of 'side drum'.

[2] Sometimes *tarolle*. (In Welsh *taro* means to strike, hence Band-taro – Percussion Band.)

Concerto for two pianos and orchestra (Poulenc); and *Signalement* (Peter Schat). The American term 'field drum' is applied to a deep military side drum, an instrument most commonly associated with marching bands, and drum corps.

Technically speaking it can be said immediately, that the side drum is a difficult instrument to play. The foundation of the art of side-drumming remains the roll, together with the numerous fundamental beatings known to the drummer as 'the rudiments', as for example, the paradiddle, and such embellishments as the flam, drag and ruff.

The hallmark of a side drummer is his control of the roll. By this he is judged, as the timpanist is assessed by his tone. Strictly speaking, the roll consists of reiterating beats, free of rhythmical stress and sufficiently close to prohibit analysis. The 'legitimate' roll (so-called) on the side drum is produced by recurring double beats known as Daddy – Mammy.[1] In English and American tutors the lead is given from the left hand – LLRR, etc. In some French, German and Swiss tutors the procedure is reversed – RRLL, etc. To achieve a close and even roll necessitates long and arduous application of the double strokes (produced by wrist action) commencing slowly and accelerating in course of time to a minimum of 32 beats in a bar of common time at ♩= 120 , (virtually the measured tremolo).[2] Tremendous patience is required to produce the double beats clearly, the sticks having a marked tendency to wander, which if not checked in the early stages results in a 'ragged' roll. The author described elsewhere the 'closing' of the roll.[3] 'The effort required to accelerate the beats into a close roll can best be likened to climbing a hill; at a certain point one is conscious of reaching the summit, and the descent on the other side is somewhat easier.'

Mastery of the long roll imparts a degree of versatility which renders the production of certain other rudimentary beats relatively simple. A number of them are in fact rolls of varying length: 5-6-7-8-9-10 and 11, 13 and 15 strokes. In the tutors of the late eighteenth century and onwards the rudiments include the long roll, short rolls from the five stroke (the 'mother of five') to the fifteen stroke and the flam – open and close – the drag, the ruff and the single paradiddle (onomatopaeic terms). In some cases the beatings for the left and right hands are given ♩ ♩ in others

♩ 𝄽 and in some instances the rolls are numbered. ⁶₈ 𝄽 𝄽 7

[1] See 'Changing Styles' for the 'single stroke' roll.

[2] In Arne's masque *Alfred* (1753) (March with a side drum), a series of semiquavers is supplemented with the word 'tremolo' written above the stave. A march with a side drum also occurs in Arne's earlier work *Eliza* (1754).

[3] Blades, James. *Orchestral Percussion Technique*, Oxford, London, 1963, p. 8.

The Side Drum

$\frac{2}{4}$ ♩ ♩. (In the orchestra no strict rule can apply to the latter, as obviously the number of strokes in a roll is governed by the space of time involved). In some manuals the roll is indicated _tr~~~_ or _f_ elsewhere ≋ or ≈. The quaver roll in some cases is shown ♩ in others ♩. To-day the tremolo on the side drum is usually indicated ♩ or _tr~~~_ .[1]

American manuals of the nineteenth century include the paradiddle, diddle, the flamacue and the single, double and triple ratamacue. With minor additions, the beatings given in these early manuals form the basic rudiments in 'up to date' printed tutors.

Unlike the acciaccatura (written similarly) the flam precedes the principal note. Opinions differ regarding the interpretation of the ruff. Many snar drummers contends 'a Drag is a slurred grace note and a Ruff a distinct grace note. ♫♩ ♫♩
RRL RLR

In recent years composers have taken full advantage of the rhythmic resources and the numerous tone colours possible from the side drum. It is no longer an instrument chiefly concerned with the demarcation of rhythm, punctuations, or with strong characterisation, admirable as it still is in such situations. To-day the instrument is

[1] Elliott Carter in his Double Concerto for Harpsichord and Piano with Two Chamber Orchestras (1961) meticulously indicates ♩ as fast as possible – ♩ measured roll (8/32nds). Gunther Schuller specifies exact 64ths – ♩ . Orchestral side drummers welcome such precise instructions. Unfortunately, there remains ambiguity. A sore point with percussionists is the omission on the part of composers to indicate whether or not a roll is to be tied ♩ .
A tie, or comma, as the case requires, would clarify these situations. ♩ .

[2] See 'Paradiddles' by Peter Oslaad Olmquist and Wiksell Laramedel. A B Box 10122 Stockholm.

known to be capable of more subtle effects, and modern composers demand its full range of tone colour. The use of the side drum with snares released is common, as is the striking of the rim, and the use of wire brushes and sticks of various types. On occasions the instrument is further muffled by placing a piece of cloth on the vellum. A less frequent request is 'the striking of the frame', as in Debussy's *Gigues* and the Mussorgsky-Ravel *Pictures from an Exhibition* (*jeu ordinaire sur la caisse*). There is also the *rim shot* in which the rim and head are struck simultaneously with one stick, or alternatively one stick is laid with its tip on the skin and the shaft on the rim, to be struck with the other e.g. Milhaud's *Création du Monde* (1923), Copland's Third Symphony (1946), the overture *Beckus the Dandipratt*, Malcolm Arnold (1948) and Elliott Carter's Variations for Orchestra (1954–5).[1] A fitment was patented in the early '30's by a well-known British drummer, Joe Daniels, which ensured this effect, a feature of jazz drumming. (British Patent No. 463,932). In the original version of *Façade* (1923) Walton asks for the side drum (without snares) to be struck with a timpani stick. There is also the request (possibly original) for the use of wire brushes. Constant Lambert requests a sponge-headed stick in *Rio Grande*, and the American composer, William Russell, asks for felt timpani sticks and medium hard felt sticks in *Fugue for Eight Percussion Instruments q.v.* In Berlioz's *Harold in Italy* instructions are given for two muffled side drums to be placed at some distance from the orchestra. Milhaud in *Choéphores* asks for the side drum to be covered (*tambour voilé*).

Fig. 52. Wire brush

In music the part for the side drum is written on a single line, or given a space in the stave, usually the third space.

Concerning the repertoire of the orchestral side drum, Ravel's treatment of this instrument in his *Bolero* remains unique. Here, the first side drum plays throughout the work (with the exception of the final two bars) the famous two-bar phrase

Bolero   Ravel

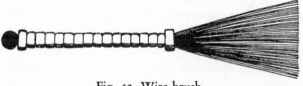

By permission of Durand and Cie, Paris.

[1] In *Canto* (1966) Carter uses a rim shot on the timpani *q.v.*

374

The phrase is played 169 times, a second drum entering at bar 289. For the percussionist, this work, which takes at normal tempo not less than 13 minutes to perform, is a study in dynamic control. Tremendous concentration is required from the opening four bar solo to the final climax to ensure an incessant crescendo. It is usual for the drum to be played at the extreme edge at .the start, and the sticks moved gradually towards the centre as the work progresses. A crescendo roll and similar changing dynamics are performed in the same way.

The side drum has been honoured with one full scale concerto: *Geigy Festival Concerto for Basle Trommel and Orchestra* by Rolf Liebermann (1958). This work, calling for eight timpani played by two performers, embraces for the soloist the formidable technique of the Basle side drum, a subject beyond the scope of this volume.[1] The late Dr. Fritz Berger, a renowned teacher of the method of Basle drumming, performed the work on many occasions (in England at the B.B.C. Festival of Light Music, Royal Albert Hall, 1961). The accompanying example is typical of the side drum part throughout. In his manuals Dr. Berger has given orchestral notation to such Basle trommel routines.

Geigy Festival Concerto for Basle Trommel   Liebermann

By permission of Universal Edition (Alfred A. Kalmus Ltd.).

THE TENOR DRUM

In principle the tenor is one of the most ancient and universal of all drums. Modern composers to whom the instrument is attractive, include Stravinsky, Honegger, Milhaud, Constant Lambert, Copland, Alwyn and Britten; the latter combining it with side drum and bass drum in the percussion solo in the second act of his chamber opera *The Rape of Lucretia* (1946) q.v. William Alwyn gives frequent solo passages to tenor drum combined with side drum in his Second Symphony (1954).

The tenor drum has no snares. Its diameter is larger than its depth – approximate

[1] See *Das Basler Trommeln* (1956) and other literature by Dr. Fritz Berger. (Privately published in Basle)

measurements being 18 inches by 14 inches. Tonally it is midway between the unsnared side drum and the bass drum. It is played with either hard or soft sticks. Its timbre is well described by Forsyth who says[1]: 'The quality of the Tenor-drum, especially when used indoors, is curiously impressive; its flavour sombre and antique.... It might with advantage be more often used in the Concert-Room'.

The French equivalent to the English tenor drum is *caisse roulante*; German: *Rührtrommel*; Italian: *tamburo rullante*. The second space in the bass clef is frequently allotted to this instrument.

THE TABOR

The *tabor*, already discussed, survives in the orchestra in the *tambourin de Provence* (Ger: *Tambourin*). This instrument has a shell longer than its diameter. As with the tenor drum, both ends of the cylinder are covered. A single snare of catgut, silk, or rough hemp passes over the batter head of the tambourin de Provence. The characteristic method of striking this drum in folk music, i.e., with strokes of one time value, or in simply rhythmic sequences, with a single drumstick (originally a short heavy beater, with a head of bone or ivory), is demanded in Bizet's Second *L'Arlésienne* Suite ('Pastoral' and 'Farandole', in the latter ♩♪♪♪♩ etc.). Milhaud uses the instrument similarly in his *Suite Française* (1944) and in *Les Choéphores*. Milhaud says that it is now customary to use two sticks on this instrument. Elgar scores for tabor in *Falstaff* (1913). In *El Salón Mexico* Copland specifies *tambour de Provence*, and Roger Sessions in his Third Symphony (1962) writes for long drum, *tambour Provençal*. (The rarity of the genuine instrument in orchestral circles frequently renders an improvisation necessary, in many instances, regrettably on a drum without snares.)

Other (recent) membrane instruments include chromatic *boobams*, a series of small tunable drums with deep resonators, and *roto-toms*: small drums tuned by rotary motion,[2] and the Sonor pneumatically tuned pedal tom-tom.

(The 'new look' given to many of the percussion instruments in the modern orchestra has been extended to instruments used in the regimental band. Rod-tensioning has in many cases replaced the original rope-bracing on the side, tenor and bass drums. On the side drum, plastic heads and wire snares frequently replace the original calf heads and gut snares. The merits of the plastic head on drums used

[1] Forsyth, Cecil. ibid. p. 30.

[2] Where space is limited, Roto-toms are occasionally used in lieu of timpani - also as practice timpani.

mainly in the open cannot be denied, i.e., their resistence to extreme weather conditions. Whether the instrument has improved tonally, is arguable.

There has been little change in the style of the kettledrums used in the British Mounted Regiments. The silver drums presented to the Blues by George III and those given to the Life Guards by William IV, remain a feature of State occasions. That the fixed interval between the cavalry drums does not fit as accurately to-day as it did a few centuries back when the drums were associated only with the trumpets, cannot be denied. With the changing harmony of a march played by a full instrumental ensemble, constant change of pitch is necessary if the drums are to conform accurately to the musical structure. Of this, J. A. Kappey says[2]: 'Kettledrums look well, yet, if we look at it from a *musical* point of view we must say that it is an anachronism. In olden times when trumpet music could only produce three chords, the timpani tuned in the tonic and dominant gave the real bass notes of the tune. In our time, brass band music modulates into every conceivable progression, still the kettledrums are there beating two notes which mostly have no connection whatever with that which the band plays. Kettledrums should be so constructed, that, while preserving a distinction of two different-sized drums, the sound should have no fixed pitch, but resembling more the side and tenor drum.' Portable timpani (tuned) and bass drums of different pitch are now used in some marching bands.)

CYMBALS

The cymbals (Ger: *Becken*, It: *piatti, cinelli*, etc.), used in the modern orchestra, like the majority of present-day percussion instruments, have experienced marked changes, structurally and otherwise. To-day, the word cymbal is used specifically for a large round metal plate hollowed in the centre. This was not so in the Middle Ages when the term was also applied to small bells. The cymbals of the mediaeval period had a narrow rim and a deep boss. In the course of years the hollow has been lessened and the circumference enlarged. The metal plate is slightly convex, so that only the outer edges touch. A hole is drilled in the centre of the dome to allow for the attachment of a leather strap by which the cymbal is held. The strap is divided at each end and the ends passed through the hole in the dome of the cymbal, and knotted on the inside with a 'sailor's knot'. To shield the fingers a pad of felt covers the outer dome.

The modern Asaph[3] is equipped, as were from all accounts his biblical counter-

---

[1] For a scientific analysis of calfskin and plastic drumheads, see Hardy, H. C. and Ancell, J. E. 'Comparison of the Acoustical Performance of Calfskin and Plastic Drumheads', *The Journal of the Acoustical Society of America*, vol. XXXIII, no. 10, October 1961, pp. 1391–5.

[2] Kappey, J. A. *Military Music*, Boosey, London, 1894, p. 81.

[3] Asaph (the chief) and his brother singers, Heman and Ethan, cymbalists to King David.

parts, with 'loud', 'high sounding' and 'well tuned' cymbals, his instruments ranging from minute crotales to pairs of cymbals measuring 26 inches in diameter.

In most cases cymbals are 'paired' (with a slight difference in pitch) by an expert prior to leaving the factory.[1] The desired qualities are brilliance, resonance, a quick response, a multiplicity of overtones, and lack of a fundamental note. Two or more pairs of cymbals of different size and timbre are necessary in to-day's orchestra, plus a selection of suspended cymbals (and a variety of beaters) to comply with the ever increasing call by modern composers on the varied colour of percussion. (Nono in *La terra a la compagna* (1959) uses eight suspended cymbals of graduated tones; Peter Schat in *Signalement* (1961) writes for twelve suspended cymbals of specified sizes.) In general, the suspended cymbals range from 10 inches to 20 inches in diameter, and the pairs for normal purposes from 15 inches to 18 inches, those of larger dimension being reserved for special occasions.

A cymbal rack to hold one or more pairs of cymbals upright during *tacet* periods is now generally used. The rack is padded, or otherwise insulated, so that the instruments are disposed of silently; no simple matter when effecting a quick change to another instrument. It is usual in large orchestras for the cymbals player to be a specialist. Sam Denov says[2]: 'In most musical organizations, it is now recognized that a well integrated and functioning percussion section is a team of specialists, not the least important of whom is the cymbal player'. He continues: 'The cymbals never become a void in an organization, for whenever they are played they either add to or subtract from the total effort'.

The cymbalist's position in a symphony orchestra is one of great responsibility. He must possess an unerring sense of rhythm, an untiring arm, together with nerves of steel. The sound of his instrument is invariably solo, and quite often after a long period of silence on his part, such as the 210 bars rest in *The Mastersingers* Overture, followed by a mighty clash on the first beat of the ensuing bar. This stroke must be delivered with absolute conviction 'spot on the beat', for a split second's anticipation or lag will shatter the orchestra's performance, here or at any other time. The cymbal part is written either on a single line, or a stave. At times the part is combined with that of the bass drum –

For the ordinary single stroke (the two-plate stroke signified as *cymbals à 2, naturale*, etc.), the cymbals are clashed together, either with a swift up-and-down, or back-and-forth movement, according to the style of the performer. Cymbals are

[1] The tempering process of the metal continues with constant use of the instruments, some time elapsing before they are 'played in'.

[2] Denov, Sam. *The Art of Playing Cymbals*, Adler, New York, 1963, p. 27.

never under normal circumstances played directly face to face. The maximum brilliance is obtained by the almost full circumference of each plate meeting simultaneously. Care must be taken to avoid the plates meeting in such a manner as to produce an air-lock, resulting in a muffled sound (this depressing experience is known to the player as 'catching a crab'). A well-delivered two-plate stroke will cause the cymbals to sound for a considerable time. To obtain the fullest sound the instruments are turned outwards after impact and held at arms' length. This effect is indicated *let ring, laissez vibrer*, etc.[1]

For pianissimo the two cymbals meet as in the full clash, the degree of movements being adjusted to ensure the required dynamic. Only in extreme circumstances are the cymbals played edge to edge to produce a pianissimo effect. In some cases, to produce the minimum of sound or a particular effect, one cymbal is lightly brushed across the other, or the two plates merely pulled apart. To observe note values the vibrations of the cymbals are 'stilled' by drawing the two plates firmly to the chest.[1] Short notes are normally indicated *sec, étouffé, choke*, etc. To indicate in music the desired length of every cymbal note is not always possible. Frequently the decision to dampen or not is left to the player's (and conductor's) experience. The tremolo is indicated in the normal manner. (Applicable to à2 and a suspended cymbal).

A tremolo on a pair of cymbals, a device frequently used in the past, is now less often prescribed. This 'two-plate roll',; as it is known, is produced by agitating the edges of the plates against each other (signified $\cdot$2————), as in Bartók's Violin Concerto No. 2 and his Second Rhapsody for Violin and Orchestra, and Vaughan Williams' *A London Symphony*. The roll is now more generally allotted to the suspended (loose) cymbal.

The use of the suspended cymbal is a modern product compared with the classic use of cymbals in pairs. Berlioz was the first composer to indicate clearly a single cymbal to be struck with drumsticks, though this effect had certainly been used earlier. In his day, the suspended cymbal was one of a pair of hand cymbals; it was held in one hand, the other hand executing the strokes. The tremolo was also produced with one hand (a series of rapid single beats), or the cymbal held whilst another performer executed the tremolo with two sticks, giving rise to the placing of the instrument on a special stand. Of the roll on the suspended cymbal, Forsyth says[2]: '. . . there is no other sound in the orchestra quite so exciting as a long crescendo finely performed with two Kettle-Drum sticks'. Wagner made realistic use of the cymbal roll, two-plate and with drumsticks, thoughout *The Ring*.

[1] Known in the U.S.A. as 'the valuation crash'. In Mendelssohn's 11th string symphony the lengthy rhythmic part given to Becken is possibly a misprint for triangle.

[2] Forsyth, Cecil. ibid. p. 36.

The tremolo on the suspended cymbal is executed as the roll on the timpani, the speed of the strokes being similarly governed by the rate of the instrument's vibrations. To keep the cymbal horizontal during a tremolo, the beaters operate on the opposite edges. The playing spot, unless otherwise requested, is approximately one inch from the edge. Where a single stroke with hard stick is indicated, the cymbal is normally struck on the edge.

In addition to the variety of tones produced by striking the cymbal in the normal manner with beaters of differing texture, composers now specify the plate to be struck on the centre dome and edge.[1] Roberto Gerhard in his *Hymnody* (1963), conjured numerous contrasts in sound from four suspended cymbals struck in different positions, and at varying dynamic levels with hard and soft sticks. In the same work he writes for a tremolo with wire brushes (not unusual) and for the edge of the large suspended cymbal to be scraped with a threaded rod. To ensure the rigid observance of the score at the early performances of the work, the composer supplied the percussionist with the implement specified, thoughtfully made in aluminium. The passing of such an object swiftly across the edge of a cymbal produces a startling crescendo. File, rasp and saw blade have been scored for. A saw blade has a closer association with a cymbal in the case of a 'repair'. The buzzing from a fine crack can be 'doctored' by drilling a small hole at the ends of the fissure to prevent it growing, and the crack opened to the thickness of the saw blade.[2] Damage of any extent is to-day considered irreparable. The repairing of cymbals was evidently a similar problem to the ancients, for in the Talmudian tractate *Arachin* we find (as quoted in Sachs, p. 122): 'In the Temple there was a cymbal of metal having a soft sound. As it was damaged, the sages sent for craftsmen in Alexandria; but after the repair the soft timbre had gone. They restored the previous state, and the sound was soft again'. (Possibly re-cast, as were the damaged Turandot gongs, belonging to the Royal Opera House, Covent Garden).

The use of wire brushes or a steel rod is not unusual. Mahler prescribed the latter in his Third Symphony (1895). Stravinsky makes frequent use of the triangle beater (*Firebird Suite, Les Noces* etc.). In *Façade* (1923) Walton signifies wire brushes on the suspended cymbal (struck and tremolo). A tremolo is frequently produced with one brush, the strands being divided on the upper and lower surfaces of the cymbal.[3]

[1] Gardner Read in his *Thesaurus of Orchestral Devices*, Pitman, London, 1953, p. 158 says: 'It is rather a curious fact that composers have been far more explicit in designating specific stick types for striking the suspended cymbal than for any other percussion instrument, even including the timpani'.

[2] In an emergency a small rent in a drumskin is similarly treated.

[3] By no means innovatory: for centuries the monks of Mount Athos have used a two-pronged beater for striking recurring rhythms on the wooden slab used in religious ritual.

Cymbals

In *Rio Grande* (1929) Constant Lambert asks for the cymbal to be struck with a large triangle beater or wooden hammer. Hindemith in his Symphony in E flat (1940) somewhat anticipated the 'sizzle' cymbal of to-day's rhythmic groups, for he gives instructions that the cymbal be struck with a soft stick whilst a thin rod (knitting needle) is held to vibrate against the edge of the instrument.[1] A similar effect is produced by sliding a coin, or a steel rod, or the finger nail across the striations (tone rings) in the surface of the cymbal; and also, if the edge of one of a pair of cymbals is passed swiftly across the inner face of the other. This, or the brushing of the two

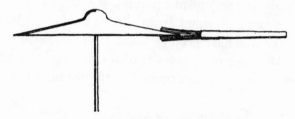

Fig. 53. Brush tremolo on cymbal

faces is requested by Strauss under the term *zischend* in *Ein Heldenleben* (1893). In his *Five Miniatures* Paul White asks for the cymbal to be brushed with a silver coin. Schoenberg writes for a tremolo to be played with a 'cello bow, *Five Pieces for Orchestra* (1909). Given a well-rosined bow and a cymbal of moderate thickness, a resounding screech can be produced by drawing the bow over the edge of the cymbal. Roberto Gerhard employs the sound in his *Concert for 8* (1962). (In an earlier score he had written for a comb to be drawn over the edge of the cymbal).[2] Chinese cymbals (already discussed) are occasionally requested: Varèse in *Ionisation*, Constant Lambert in *Rio Grande*, Maurice Jarré, suspended and clashed, in his film score *Is Paris Burning?* (1966).[3]

Among the variety of 'cymbal effects' requested by modern composers certain remain unique such as Walton's impression of a cow bell from the striking of the suspended cymbal with the triangle in the 'Swiss Yodelling Song', *Façade* (1923), the uncanny effect in *Meditations on a theme by John Blow* (Psalm 23) by Bliss (1958) where the rigour of the 'valley of the shadow' is heightened by the sound of the two cymbals, placed on the heads of a pair of timpani and struck with glockenspiel

[1] To produce a sizzle effect early jazz drummers held a coin or bunch of keys against the lower edge.

[2] The bow has been applied to other percussion instruments – see Patents.

[3] Gerhard, in the preface to the score of his Concerto for Orchestra (1965) says, of cymbals played with a cello bow, 'Harmonics are most successfully produced on 12-inch Chinese cymbals.'

beaters, and Bartók's *ppp* 'with the fingernail, or the blade of a pocketknife on the very edge' (Sonata for Two Pianos and Percussion 1937).

A century has seen a marked change in the utilization of the numerous timbres of cymbals. The products of such famous firms as Zildjian, Paiste, Premier Drum Co. and Zanchi and the present range of cymbals from the Far East give the player of to-day a wide choice. Berlioz would certainly not have said, as he did 100 years ago (on a visit to Germany), that the cymbals were nearly always cracked or chipped, even in the best orchestras.

The ancient cymbals (*crotales*) from the ruins of Pompeii which excited Berlioz, resulting in his recapturing a sound from the past in the 'Queen Mab' scherzo (*Romeo and Juliet*), may well have been identical with the well-tuned cymbals of the Old Testament era. Whether these crotales of the past had the musical compass of the instruments used in the modern orchestra is impossible to say. To-day, a chromatic octave from C to C sounding ⟨music⟩ is usual. The Zildjian models in this range are discs of bronze, machine turned and tuned electronically. In some cases special instruments have been made beyond this compass. Ravel, in *Daphnis et Chloé*, scored for six pairs of antique cymbals, including the lower B. (Where these instruments are not available, the equivalent bars of the glockenspiel are used.)

Daphnis et Chloé Ravel

In recent years many composers have used ancient cymbals; Dallapiccola and Nono have each written for a wide range. On occasions, these delicate instruments are employed melodically, as for instance in much of Christopher Whelen's incidental music for B.B.C. Sound and Television productions, notably that for *The Age of Kings* where six timpani were also employed melodically.

Crotales are employed singly or in pairs. When in pairs (they are connected with a cord, like those of the past), the edge of one cymbal strikes the edge, or the face of the other. Used singly, the disc is struck close to the edge with a small hammer, similar to a glockenspiel or xylophone beater. It is usual to tune the discs a wave apart in pitch, rendering the timbre of a struck pair the more interesting.

THE TAM-TAM[1]

The orchestral tam-tam or gong (synonymous terms in the Western orchestra) is one of the few percussion instruments with an internationally accepted name. Like

[1] Tam-tam is occasionally applied to an African drum.

its Eastern forbear, it is essentially a bronze disc with a narrow rim (the deep-rimmed gong with its non-vibrating edge having little orchestral value). Composers often use the term tam-tam in preference to gong to ensure the use of the large instrument.[1] As with cymbals, the modern composer has a wide choice. To-day, tam-tams of Eastern and European manufacture range from 28 inches to 40 inches for general purposes, whilst for special occasions the firm of Messrs. Paiste are responsible for instruments up to five feet in diameter.

The gong appeared in orchestral scores towards the close of the eighteenth century in Gossec's *Funeral Music for Mirabeau* (1791) and Steibelt's *Romeo and Juliet* (1793). A few years later Lesueur used it in his opera *Les Bardes* (1804) followed by Spontini in *La Vestale* (1807), and subsequently in Bellini's *Norma* (1831), Meyerbeer's *Robert le Diable* of the same year, and Halévy's *La Juive* (1835), from which time it has been in constant use. In general its imposing sound is employed characteristically, or to give an impression of gloom or sadness – as in the Sixth Symphony by Tchaikovsky, and the similarly impressive stroke to signify the death of Gerontius (Elgar), or in contrast to heighten a climax, as with the menacing treble forte stroke (following a tremolo of 39 bars) in 'Mars' from Holst's *The Planets*. Havergal Brian uses the tam-tam uniquely in his Twelfth Symphony (1957), a single stroke concluding the work. Elisabeth Lutyens opens her *Novenaria* (1969) with a single stroke.

The sound of the tam-tam has been described as solemn, dramatic, ominous, evocative, quivering and terrifying. Modern composers take advantage of the whole range of the sounds described, together with others possible through the variety of tones produced by the use of strikers of varying texture, and of the use of instruments of graduated sizes as in Stravinsky's *A Sermon, a Narrative and a Prayer* (1961), and in *Introitus* (1965), two tam-tams (*acuto, basso*) and in the latter work a player to each. Dallapiccola in his opera *The Prisoner* (1947) requires three of different sizes; Peter Schat in his *Signalement* writes for six tam-tams of varying timbre. For normal purposes, the instrument (which normally hangs freely in a frame) is struck with a glancing blow midway between the centre and the edge with a heavy beater, wool covered. Struck in the centre the lower vibrations produce a deep bell-like tone; an effect specifically requested in some compositions.

In an instrument of quality the pitch is indeterminate, due to the multiplicity of overtones, as in a good class cymbal. Bessaraboff says[2]: 'The gong, for instance,

---

[1] Hermann Scherchen in his *Handbook on Conducting* (Oxford, 1956, p. 132) says: 'The tone of the gong does not differ from that of the tam-tam but is definite in pitch. Sometimes, unfortunately, the point is overlooked, and composers prescribed a gong when they obviously mean a tam-tam. Special care should be taken not to use the one or the other indiscriminately'.

[2] Bessaraboff, Nicholas. *Ancient European Musical Instruments*, Harvard, 1941, p. 387.

produces a very complex tone in which many partials are present which do not bear an integral relation to the basic frequency. The vibrations are persistent, requiring from the composer that the intended duration of sound be carefully marked.[1] The sound is dampened with an immediate touch of the beater, or stilled, as in the observance of note values, in a similar way to the control of the bass drum. A tremolo is usually produced with rapid strokes with a single beater, the sustaining quality of the instrument 'filling in the gaps'.

Among the more unusual uses of the orchestral tam-tam occur the following: a tremolo on four tam-tams – *auf dem Theater* – (*Die Frau ohne Schatten*, Strauss); struck with a side drum stick (*Petrouchka*, Stravinsky); timpani sticks (*King David*, Honegger); triangle beater ('Salome's Dance' and *Macbeth*, Strauss); roll with triangle beaters (*Elektra*, Strauss); kept in vibration by friction on the edge (*The Pleasure Dome of Kubla Khan*, Griffes)[2]; vibrated with a bow (*Dimensionen der Zeit und der Stille*, Krzystof Penderecki); laid horizontally, without resonance (*El Retablo de Maese Pedro*, Manuel de Falla); two different sized tam-tams fitted one inside the other, the hollow space filled with pebbles and the instrument revolved (*Ludus de Nato Infante Mirificus*, Orff); and struck with a cymbal (*The Persians*, John Buckland, BBC Third Programme Production). Orff prescribes this effect in the behind-stage music of *Oedipus der Tyrann*. In *Double Music* by John Cage and Lou Harrison, a water gong is specified (lowered and raised in a tub of water after striking).[3] Six muted gongs are required in Arthur Cohn's *Quotations in Percussion*. Antony Hopkins asks for a gong to be struck with a coin in his *A Time for Growing*.

The tremendous power of the tam-tam has already been discussed. The author recalls the occasion of the recording of the incidental music to the B.B.C. Third Programme production *Pontius Pilate*. The composer Elizabeth Poston scored for a tremolo on the tam-tam, *ppp–fff* (she also requested the author's finest instrument). At rehearsal, at the first 'run through' the dynamic marking was observed, to the horror of the balancing engineer, who, halting the proceedings, explained that he had completely lost the orchestra (a sizeable one) and the organ, and that he also feared for the safety of Broadcasting House. Miloslav Kabalac in his *8 Inventions for Percussion Instruments* (1962) writes for eight gongs of specified pitch.

---

[1] A good quality instrument measuring 32 inches or more in diameter will sustain for upwards of 60 seconds. Instruments of this type vibrate quite audibly to strong orchestral chords.

[2] As with certain temple gongs in the Far East which are vibrated with the moistened thumb.

[3] A vibrating gong (or bell) flattens in pitch when lowered into water. After scientific research at the University of Cardiff (G.B.). Professor Charles Taylor considered that a tubular bell swells and thus adds weight when lowered into a vessel of water. Irrespective of the diameter and length of tubing the pitch is lowered in the region of a semitone. A curious 'wow' is produced by swiftly immersing and raising the vibrating tube.

The Tambourine

The tambourine and the castanets are among the few instruments of percussion that have remained practically unchanged over a long period. The tambourine, one of the oldest of instruments, and of world-wide distribution, is to-day exactly as pictured on ancient monuments. It continues to be an important instrument in folk music over a wide area, and in folk performances is often bedecked with coloured ribbons adding a flash of colour to the rhythmic excitement witnessed in our own folk dances (and no less so with the tambourinists of The Salvation Army).

Structurally, the tambourine is a frame drum consisting of a wooden hoop, with a single head of calfskin. In the shallow wood shell are openings to allow the insertion of the small metal discs called jingles; these hang loosely in pairs held in position by a steel pin which passes through the centre of each disc. The jingles are arranged in either one or two rows. The head is usually nailed to the shell, the majority of orchestral players preferring this method of mounting to the rod-tensioned head.[1] Only in rare cases is the present-day orchestral tambourine equipped with any further accoutrement such as small bells. The orchestral tambourine is commonly ten inches in diameter, though the player is usually equipped with larger and smaller instruments to meet various demands.

The numerous ways of playing the tambourine allows the instrument a whole range of possibilities, by no means limited to supplying local colour. The playing technique includes: (a) striking the head with the knuckles, fingertips, palm, closed fist, or striking the instrument on the knee, or back and forth on the knee and hand, producing detached notes and rhythmical groups from the combined sound of vellum and jingles; (b) shaking the instrument, causing only the jingles to sound to produce the sustained note, notated tremolo, trill, or roll; (c) striking the rim with the fingertips of both hands, or with the drumsticks, in which case the instrument is placed on the player's lap, or on a soft-topped stand; the latter method being usually employed to effect a *ppp*, or a series of quickly recurring strokes; (d) by means of friction, i.e., rubbing the vellum with the moistened thumb to produce either the thumb roll, or a given number of recurring strokes. In the latter case the moistened thumb is rubbed along the surface of the vellum near the rim, the speed of the movement controlling the number of 'bounces', these vibrating the jingles. To assist in securing this effect (which at times may elude the most skilful) the vellum, if not mounted with the coarser side exterior, is roughened, or a small quantity of bees' wax or resin applied.[2]

[1] A slack vellum is resuscitated by the application of a dampened cloth – the head tautening in the drying-out process.

[2] As the Indian *bamyà* (cf. *tablā*), or certain African drums, where in some cases the skin is rubbed with ashes or powdered charcoal.

The thumb roll is indicated: 'with the thumb'; *avec la pouce; mit dem Daumen;* etc. Composers make frequent use of this device to ensure a quiet tremolo, or if not marked as such, the player will use his discretion whether to use the shake or friction roll; Stravinsky employs these two methods in *Petrouchka* ('Gypsies and a Rake Vendor') where normal tremolos and thumb rolls occur successively.

By permission of Boosey & Hawkes Ltd.

The more unusual methods include: flicking the jingles (Walton, *Façade*); brushing the jingles (Lambert, *Rio Grande*); on the rim (Khachaturian, *Gayaneh* Ballet Suite); and placed on the side drum or timpani head. It is possible that the most unusual request comes from Stravinsky, who, in *Petrouchka* ('The Scuffle') writes for the instrument to be held close to the floor and dropped.

The notation of the tambourine is on a single line, or more often (to-day) on a stave. It is defined: Tambourine (Eng:); *tambour de Basque* (Fr:); *tamburino* or *tamburello* (It:); *Schellentrommel* or *Tamburin* (Ger:); *Pandero* (Sp:); *Pandeiro* (Port:).[1]

The use (in the orchestra) of a tambourine without jingles is rare (see Stravinsky, *Renard, sans grelots*) and Falla (*El Retablo de Maese Pedro*).

The jingle ring (*Schellenreif*) of the Middle Ages has made an appearance in the modern orchestra. To-day's instrument consists of a hoop surrounded with (tambourine) jingles. Such an instrument is occasionally used in a treble piano passage in place of a tambourine.

CASTANETS

'*Estar uno como unas castañuelas*' – 'Happy, like a pair of castanets'. *Spanish saying.*

The castanets, for many centuries the characteristic instrument of the Spanish peasantry, have, as folk instruments, made little headway outside Spain. The true Spanish castanets (*castañuelas*, the fruit of the chestnut tree) are considered to have been inspired by the ancient finger cymbals, and to have been introduced into Spain by the Moors. (A Japanese belief connects their origin with the invention of music, when the gods beat the measure upon 'the Mother of all', the castanets).

[1] Also (obsolete) travale.

[2] Pandeiro: also applied to a form of jingle ring used in Madeira.

386

Castanets

The castanets used in the orchestra consist of two hollow pieces of hard wood, ebony, rosewood, or some similar wood, or occasionally of a plastic material. They are manipulated in various ways. A few orchestral players have acquainted themselves with the authentic Spanish method, as far as this is possible, for the superb artistry of the Spanish player, like certain notable drum techniques elsewhere, defies imitation. (Glinka, writing of his attempts to perform the Spanish dance, said: 'My feet were all right, but I couldn't manage the castanets'.) In the true Spanish style two pairs of castanets are used, a pair in each hand. A cord passing through holes in the castanets is wound around the thumb and the two plates click together by manipulation of the fingers. The fingers of the left hand normally perform a simple rhythm on a pair known as *macho*, the male, while the right hand plays the full dance rhythm on a higher sounding pair (*hembra* – female). The instruments are played constantly through the dance (by the dancer or instrumentalist), and at prescribed intervals during the song.

In many cases the Spanish method is impracticable in the orchestra, it being so often necessary for the player to make a quick change to another instrument. An alternative is for a pair of shells to be mounted on a central handle (or a pair at each end of the handle). For a tremolo, the implement is shaken in the air as a rattle, the shell beating against the central board. Rhythms are produced by wrist movement, or striking the instrument on the knee or palm, or tapping the shells with the finger-tips. Frequent use is now made of a further device, known as a 'castanet machine'. This convenient arrangement consists of two pairs of castanets, one of each pair fixed to a wooden base, the upper shells secured by elastic. The upper shells are struck with the fingertips or soft-headed drumsticks, permitting greater clarity than with the shaken instrument in the execution of the intricate patterns so frequently allotted to the castanets in orchestral music.[1] This contraption was anticipated to some extent in 1874 by H. Distin (of the family responsible for numerous patents applicable to musical instruments). Distin's device patented as 'an apparatus to produce sound as a substitute for a castanet', consisted of one or more strips of spring steel, operated by finger pressure. Pressure caused the spring to bulge and emit a clicking sound, which was repeated as the pressure was released and the spring returned to normal – Patents No. 1876-762. (A contrivance of this nature consisting of a single strip of spring steel, housed in a small metal box, appeared later in the 'trap drummer's' collection of effects. It was known as the 'Acme clicker', and was used to imitate a grasshopper, etc., as for instance, in Bucalossi's *Grasshopper's Dance*.)

In the standard orchestral repertoire composers, as might be expected, have made

[1] Wood block in leiu of.

extensive use of castanets to colour Spanish dance rhythms, these so frequently in triple time with the central digit sub-divided.

Like the tambourine the use of orchestral castanets is not restricted to local colouring; their individual (and penetrating) clicking sound is utilized for rhythmic and other purposes in compositions very diverse in character, such as the rhythmic structure in Prokoviev's Third Piano Concerto, and the plaintive cry of the night bird in Britten's *Let's Make an Opera*. Milhaud scores for *castagnettes de bois* and *de fer* in *Les Choéphores* (1915).

In orchestral music the castanets are given a place on a single line or on a stave. They are also designated: *castagnettes* (Fr:), *castagnette* (It:), *Kastagnetten* (Ger:). In strict terminology they can be classified as instruments of *concussion*, as are cymbals, claves, etc., being pairs of similar instruments struck together.

THE TRIANGLE

The humble triangle can lay claim to being one of the first purely metal percussion instruments to enter the modern orchestra (Hamburg Opera 1710). Until the end of the eighteenth century, as we have already seen, it was used mainly to give added colour. It became a permanent member of the orchestra during the early part of the following century, and in 1853 was raised to the rank of a symphonic solo instrument by Liszt in his Piano Concerto in E flat, causing, it is said, considerable consternation.

The instrument is a steel bar, bent into the shape of an equilateral (or isosceles) triangle, with one corner open.[1] It is struck with a steel beater (occasionally tapered), or at times with a wooden drumstick. It is an instrument of indefinable pitch, its numerous high dissonant partials obscuring the fundamental note. Its individual timbre is well described by Robert Donington[2]: 'While it is of quite indeterminate

[1] If the corners were closed the pitch of the instrument would be definable.
[2] Donington, Robert. *The Instruments of Music*, Methuen, 1951, p. 119.

pitch when heard alone, it always appears to belong to the prevailing tonality of the orchestra; for this reinforces the appropriate harmonics; while the mind itself tends to pick out from the whole ringing mass, just because they are appropriate.'[1]

The average orchestral triangle measures $6\frac{1}{2}$ to 7 inches on one side (a much larger instrument tends to acquire a distinct note). The modern percussionist avails himself of the number of different sizes and types now freely available (The Avedis Zildjian Co. have now introduced the spindle triangle with tapering sides. The instrument is made from hardened steel. Its construction permits a variety of tone colours.) The triangle is suspended by a thin string, preferably of gut. It is either held in one hand or hung on a support, so as to leave both hands free when necessary for the use of two beaters. A variety of tones can be produced by striking two different parts of the triangle, the general rule being to strike the outer side, the apex or lower end of the closed side being preferred for quiet strokes. Strikers of varying weight are also utilized, including the use of a fine knitting needle (steel). To observe note values, the fingers of the non-playing hand clasp the upper section of the instrument at the appropriate moment. For the tremolo, the beater is placed in either the top or bottom closed corner of the instrument, and the two sides struck in rapid alternation, the crescendo being effected by moving the beater to operate in a larger area. Grieg makes use of the triangle roll to add a touch of silver to the orchestral chord announcing Anitra's Dance (*Peer Gynt*). In contrast dynamically, there are the forceful tremolos in the Overture to *Tannhäuser*.

Though in form a simple instrument, the triangle is by no means a simple instrument to play. Composers do not hesitate to allot it complicated rhythms and grace notes (see Respighi's *Three Botticelli Pictures* ♪ etc.). For rapid figures, as in *Ride of the Valkyries*:

Ride of the Valkyries   Wagner
Vivace

most players prefer to use the inner side of two bars, alternating between the two with a back-and-forth movement. (Two beaters are used only when absolutely necessary). The player must exercise great care in the matter of tone production. Badly manipulated, the triangle will give an impression of a fire bell; in the hands of an artist its sound can enhance the most delicate situation, or reinforce a climax. As Widor says[2]: '. . . when the orchestra would seem to have

[1] The tam-tam also.

[2] Widor, C. *The Technique of the Modern Orchestra*, trans. Edward Suddard, Williams, London, 1946, p. 112.

reached its maximum intensity, it suffices to add the Triangle, in order to convert red-heat into white-heat'.

Many consider that the effect of the triangle is such that it is best used sparingly. No better use of judicious economy surely than the single stroke to be found at the end of the second act of *Siegfried*.

In orchestral scores the instrument in designated 'triangle' (Eng: and Fr:), *triangolo* (It:), *Triangel* (Ger:), and in some cases illustrated: △

The largest existing triangle is possibly the instrument in the American War Cemetery, Epinal. This is equilateral, with sides two feet three inches in length. It was originally situated in a wooded area and used as a means of summoning keepers to a central point in the event of fire. Outsize instruments are still used on the farms and ranches of America as a call to meals.

WOOD BLOCKS

The wood block, from its origin so frequently referred to as the Chinese wood block, is a rectangular block of hard wood with a slotted resonating cavity. (It is also known as 'clog box' or 'tap box'.) Like its forbear the slit drum, the tone of the orchestral wood block is penetrating, and will in consequence surmount the heaviest of orchestral tuttis. Various sizes are used, sounding high or low, according to the size of the block and the fashioning of the cavity.[1] It is struck on the surface, over the slot, usually with side drum sticks or xylophone beaters. Considering its antiquity, it is a late arrival in the western orchestra, being introduced into the standard orchestral repertoire only by twentieth-century composers. Walton uses this simple instrument engagingly in *Façade* ('Popular Song'). It occurs in the Fifth and Sixth Symphonies of Prokofiev, here called *legno*, and in the Second Symphony of Samuel Barber. Copland requests wood blocks, high and low (in addition to temple blocks) in *Music for a Great City* (1965). Tippett scores for *cassa di legno* in his Concerto for Orchestra. In *Amores* John Cage requests seven wood blocks.

In works of a lighter character the wood block has served a variety of purposes, particularly that of colouring an Oriental situation, or typifying a clog dance or patter of horses' hooves, though the latter is quite often suggested by coconut shells, a most realistic use of which (muffled on leather) is to be found in Grofé's *Grand Canyon Suite*.

In contrast to the wood block, which is normally used singly, temple blocks, the

---

[1] An early catalogue of the Ludwig Drum Co. lists a 'tunable tone block' in which the pitch is adjusted by varying the length of the slot.

name by which the traditional 'wooden fish' of the Orient is known in the western orchestra, are used in varying numbers, most frequently in pairs (high and low). The use of these instruments in the modern orchestra (as with the wood block) is probably due to the influence of the jazz of the 1920's, in which both were a feature (cf. Chinese section). Walton, a pioneer in so many aspects of orchestral percussion,[1] scored for a pair of temple blocks as early as 1923 in his *Façade*, ('Old Sir Faulk'). Constant Lambert wrote for a series of six temple blocks in his Piano Concerto (1931); the composer stating two miniature and four others descending in pitch. Britten employs a pair realistically in the 'Coaching Song' (*Let's make an Opera*). Tippett scores for five tuned temple blocks in his opera *The Knot Garden*. q.v.

In incidental music these quaint-sounding instruments are used, possibly too frequently, to suggest the colour of the Orient. As sound effects they are called upon to supply innumerable representations ranging from the popping of a champagne cork (deputising for the 'popgun', in form an open-ended bicycle pump loaded with a cork), to the gurgling of a dripping water tap. Curiously, although the difference in the pitch of the various sizes is clearly definable, their unique timbre is sufficiently accommodating to be undisturbing, tonally. To-day, these instruments have a prominent place in compositions of the avant-garde; in *Signalement* Peter Schat requests seven. In orchestral scores, to differentiate between the normal Chinese wood block, they are quoted as 'Chinese Blocks', 'Temple Blocks', or 'Korean Blocks', and in rare instances as 'skulls'. In performance they are laid on a felt pad or are mounted and struck (ideally) with rubber or hard felt beaters.

SLEIGH BELLS

Mozart's use of tuned sleigh bells remains unique, and more than a century elapsed before these instruments in a simpler form made a firm appearance in orchestral scores: Mahler Fourth Symphony (1900) and Elgar *Cockaigne* (1901). They occur in Ireland's *A London Overture*, Vaughan Williams' *A London Symphony*, Holst's *The Perfect Fool* and Respighi's *Feste Romane*. In some cases the instrument is given as sleigh bells, in others as jingles. In each case it is customary to use a series of small bells of unselected pitch as used on harness. These are attached to a strap, or wire framework, or an upright handle.

Rhythms similar to those used on the tambourine are given to the jingles. The tremolo, produced by shaking the implement is particularly effective when augmenting a brilliantly-coloured tone-scheme. For rhythmic patterns the bells are tapped in the palm of the hand, etc.

[1] As for example the use of wire brushes in *Façade*.

COWBELLS

Cowbells have been used descriptively and otherwise, as in Mahler's Sixth and Seventh Symphonies, and in Strauss's *An Alpine Symphony*, in each case shaken intermittently and in rhythmic structures as in the percussion ensemble accompaniments to the pianoforte cadenza in *Rio Grande*. Here Lambert specifies a small cowbell without clapper. Varèse in *Ionisation* (1931) specifies cowbell (*cencerro*) without clapper, to be struck with a drumstick, and muffled by inserting a handkerchief, or similar piece of material into the bell. Copland in *Music for a Great City* scores for two cowbells of different pitch to be struck simultaneously. Peter Schat in *Signalement* scores for cowbells, $3\frac{1}{2}$ octaves (chromatic) F to C, and Messiaen for an even larger number in *Et exspecto Resurrectionem Mortuorum*.[1]

EXOTICS

Among the lesser-used purely metal instruments are: anvil (*enclume* (Fr:), *Amboss* (Ger:), *incudine* (It:)), chains, bell plate and flexatone. The fact that Praetorius illustrates the anvil and that it is included in other inventories, is sufficient evidence that this implement has been connected with instruments of music over a long period. In the modern orchestra the genuine implement is employed when possible. If inconvenient, an 'anvil effect' is substituted, consisting of (i) a rectangular steel 'box' – the shorter side producing a higher note than the longer side (normally at least a fifth higher) (ii) two substantial steel bars of different length and pitch, mounted on a frame (iii) resonant metal bars, e.g. a short length of railway line. These improvisations are perfectly adequate, for in concert performance the traditional instrument rarely sounds as brilliant as in its natural haunt (it possibly misses the solidarity of the floor of the smithy, and the attendant glow of the forge).[2]

   The anvil has a modest repertoire, serving certain operatic sequences (*Il Trovatore* and others already discussed), and heightening situations on a few other occasions (Gounod in *Philémon et Baucis*, 1860, Bizet's *Fair Maid of Perth*, 1867, and Goldmark's *Queen of Sheba*, 1875). Walton employs the anvil significantly to supplement the orchestral texture (male voices and brass) typifying the iron god in *Belshazzar's Feast*, 'Praise Ye the God of Iron'. It occurs in works by Varèse: *Hyperprism* (1923) for

[1] Bliss asks for sheep bells ('small, silvery, to be quietly shaken') in his *Meditations on a Theme by John Blow* (1955).

[2] Sir Henry Wood owned a full size smithy anvil, sledge hammer and various substitutes. On one occasion, as guest conductor, on hearing at rehearsal the anvil stroke at the conclusion of *Rheingold*, he shouted: 'Hi, that's mine.' He insisted on the implement (a substantial portion of railway line) being upturned to prove his point (to reveal his initials). 'Get it in a cab and send it to my house after the performance,' he growled

small orchestra and percussion, and *Ionisation* (1931) (*enclumes* – high and low), and in Copland's Third Symphony.

Chains have a limited repertoire, notably Schoenberg *Gurrelieder* (1911) – 'some big iron chains'; Varèse, *Intégrales* (1920), and Benjamin Frankel, Second Symphony (1962). To render the chains audible, they are usually rattled against, or lowered into, a metal receptacle. In Frankel's symphony, to ensure a novel sound, instructions are given that the chains be dropped on a bass drum or a wooden box.

The bell plate is a plaque of sonorous metal. It is occasionally found in light orchestral scores and incidental music to describe the clang of an alarm bell, or the small bell associated with the ship, fire engine, or Western express.

The flexatone consists of a flexible sheet of metal suspended in a wire frame. A wooden knob mounted on a shaft of spring steel lies on each side of the metal sheet. The player bends the metal sheet to alter the pitch, at the same time shaking the instrument with a trembling movement. This then causes the beaters to strike the sides of the metal sheet and thus produce a tremolo. An invention for a flexatone occurs in the British Patent Office records of 1922 (203,208) and 1923 (205,444) (W. Bartholomae). An instrument called the 'Flex-a-tone' was patented in the U.S.A. in 1924 by the Playertone Company of New York. It was introduced as a new instrument, making 'jazz jazzier' and announced as combining the tone effect of musical saw, orchestra bells, and song whistle.[1]

As a novelty, the flexatone in this period of lavish experiment had an immediate, though brief, success, sufficient however to attract the interest of Honegger and Schoenberg. Honegger employed it in *Antigone* (1927), and Schoenberg in *Variations for Orchestra* (1928), *Von heute auf morgen* (1929), (in which there is a part for an electric bell), and in *Moses and Aaron* (1951). In Khachaturian's Piano Concerto (1946) the flexatone is solo in the second movement. Other composers to score for the flexatone include Henze (*Elegy for Young Lovers*, 1961); Penderecki (*De Natura Sonoris*, 1966) and Vladimir Vogel (*Sinfonia Fugato*).

The musical saw, though usually played with a bow, is also played as a percussion instrument. Milhaud in his book *Études* (1927) describes the sounding of this instrument with blows from a drumstick. The tremulous tones of both the flexatone and the musical saw have been employed occasionally in incidental music for films, etc., to heighten eerie situations.

---

[1] The song whistle was also known as the 'Swannee Whistle' or 'Lotus Flute'. The pitch of this instrument was adjusted by the movement of a sliding plunger. The above reference to a musical saw gives an earlier date to this instrument than that given by Percy Scholes, who says in *The Mirror of Music* vol. II, p. 827, that the date of the introduction of the 'Singing Saw' can possibly be placed from a 1927 advertisement in an American journal.

Other instruments which make brief excursions into the symphonic repertoire include the *ratchet, whip* (slapstick), *switch* and the *wind* and *thunder machine*; the latter a modification of the *bronteron*, (q.v.) in the form of a revolving drum partly filled with balls of hard material, or more often a thunder sheet, consisting of a large metal sheet which is suspended and shaken, in which form it occurs in works

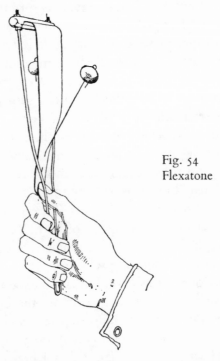

Fig. 54
Flexatone

by Carl Orff.[1] There is also the *thunder stick*, a descendant of the primitive bull roarer, a flat pointed piece of wood, one end of which is attached to a cord. When swung, the implement produces a whirring sound, the speed of the movement governing the volume and pitch. In Germany this instrument is called *Schwirrholz*, in France *Planchette ronflante*, and amongst the Navajo Indians the 'groaning stick' cf. *Waldteufel*. The Australian composer John Antill included the bull roarer in his *Corroboree*, a descriptive work about an aboriginal ritual ceremony. Henry Cowell produced an Ensemble for two violins, viola, two celli and two thunder sticks.

The wind machine (*aeoliphone*) is certainly not a percussion instrument, but it is normally included in the percussion section. The more usual wind machine would

[1] John Cage requests five graduated thunder sheets in *First Construction in Metal* (1962). A thundersheet (tonitruone) is requested in Paderewski's Symphony in B minor (1907). Vide Michael Rosen P.A.S. Percussive Notes, vol. 3, no 2 (1991). See App.6.

well be classified as a friction instrument, for it consists of a barrel framework covered with coarse canvas or silk which is in friction against the slats as the cylinder is rotated. The rise and fall in volume and pitch is gained by a variation in the speed at which the barrel is rotated. Other means of reproducing the sound of wind include a modification of an electirc fan in which the blades are replaced by lengths of cane, or similar whirring machinery electrically operated. In addition to the composers already mentioned (Richard Strauss and Vaughan Williams), the wind machine is included in scores by Ravel, *Daphnis and Chloé*, Milhaud, *Les Choéphores*, Grofé, *Grand Canyon Suite*, Manuel de Falla, *Atlantida* and Schoenberg, *Jacob's Ladder*.

The ratchet (a mechanical form of stridulator), an instrument that has served a religious and secular purpose over a long period is, in principle, little changed. It consists of a cogwheel which is revolved against one or more stout tongues of wood or metal. The ratchet has long been used as an alarm signal and as a bird scarer.[1] In a considerably quieter form, it is used by bird watchers. This instrument (*Ricciane*, part of an Italian collection of bird call imitations) has a single tongue and small wheel, the latter being operated with the thumb. The gentle click emitted when the grooved wheel springs over the wooden tongue is a realistic imitation of the tweet or tap of certain birds. The instrument used in the orchestra is rarely whirled like the traditional watchman's pattern. In most cases the cogwheel is wound by means of a handle. Its use in the works of various composers has already been mentioned. Respighi employs it unusually: in a rhythmic pattern in *The Pines of Rome*.

By permission of G. Ricordi & Co.

Like the ratchet, the whip has been connected with musical activity for many centuries. Engel speaking of an Assyrian bas-relief from Nimrud (British Museum) says[2]: 'One of the dancers is carrying a whip in his right hand, which he used, perhaps, to produce a rhythmical accompaniment to the music of the tamboura. Similar customs exist at the present time in European countries.' In comparison to the flexible whip, the instrument used in the modern orchestra is, strictly speaking, a whip effect. It consists of two wooden slabs hinged at the base, or within a few inches of the end to form a handle. It is occasionally referred to as a *slapstick*, possibly a better definition of the implement, as is also *Holzklapper* (German) as given in

[1] A bird-scare is requested in Havergal Brian's Second Symphony (*Gothic*).
[2] Engel, Carl. *The Music of the Most Ancient Nations*, p. 98.

Mahler's Sixth Symphony. Milhaud uses it in several of his works, as do Britten, Copland and Ravel: the latter (as *frusta*) to open his Piano Concerto in G. The sound of this instrument is surprisingly penetrating. It is particularly effective when employed to open or conclude a statement, or to announce with a startling surprise a change of mood. Britten employs it to add 'weight' to Mrs. Noah's hand as she slaps the face of Mr. Noah (*Noyes Fludde*), and in contrast, to give an impression of the gentle flap of the sails in the breeze at the start of the storm in the same work. The whip (and jingles) occur in Adam's *Le Postillon de Longjumeau*, 1836.)

Fig. 55
Pu-ili,
Polynesia

The switch (*rute*, etc.), as known to Haydn and Mozart, and later to Mahler and Strauss, is still used on occasions in its original form, a bundle of twigs, or a split rod. In modern compositions it is more usual for the wire brush (a spray of fine steel wires, also in nylon) to be prescribed. The request by Varèse in *Intégrales* for a *verges et fouet* (switch whip) is unusual. It is possible that this adventurous composer had in mind a split rod, or the clapper used by the Franciscan monks as an alarm, a piece of wood cut into many strips. It is illustrated in Bonanni's *Gabinetto Armonico*.[1] A similar instrument of bamboo (the *pu-ili*) is used by Polynesian dancers and in the hula orchestra. Occasional use is now made of the Japanese *binsasara*, a number of small boards which collide consecutively when the instrument is shaken.

In addition to the sounds so far described, composers have enlisted many others,

[1] See *The Showcase of Musical Instruments*, Harrison and Rimmer, Dover, New York, 1964.

not all strictly percussive. As their manipulation is the percussionist's responsibility, they are here included. The hammer (wooden hammer on a plank) occurs, in addition to its use by Mahler, in works by Milhaud *Les Choéphores*, Respighi *Feste Romane* (tavolette), and Berg *Three Pieces for Orchestra*. Like the majority of the remaining 'effects' to be discussed, the hammer is self-explanatory.[1] Another implement more often connected with the carpenter's bench is the sandpaper block, reminiscent of the soft shoe dance, and an integral part of the trap drummer's outfit before the wire brushes became general.[2] Copland writes for sandpaper blocks in *Music for a Great City*.

Implements connected with the home have found a place in notable musical compositions, e.g., Britten's use of slung mugs (struck with wooden spoons) typifying the raindrops heralding and ending the storm in *Noyes Fludde* (q.v.), and Ibert's unique use of scissors in *Clown's Dance*. Henze requests a wine glass – *ein Cocktail-glas*, to be shattered in *Das Ende einer Welt* (1953). Carl Orff writes for a small glass or china bell in *A Midsummer Night's Dream* (1952), and for musical glasses in *Der Mond* (1937/8), *Astutuli* (1945/6), and *Ludus de Nato Infante Mirificus* (1960). A *rape à fromage* is requested in Ravel's *L'Enfant et les sortilèges*.

The *Bouteillophone* (a series of tuned bottles) occurs in Honegger's *Le Dit des Jeux du Monde* and Satie's *Parade*. In the latter work Satie scores also for a typewriter, a water splash, and sirens. In *L'Heure Espagnole* Ravel scores for three metronomes at different speeds. The siren has most attracted serious writers: Hindemith, Chamber Symphony, last movement (1922); Lidholm, high and low sirens in *Riter*; Varèse in *Ionisation* writes for *Sirene claire* and *Sirene grave*, and states (as he did in *Hyperprism*) that the instrument must be operated by hand with a button for instantaneous stopping. He adds that mouth sirens must not be used. Malcolm Arnold requests Scout whistle, Guard's whistle, bird whistle and cuckoo in his *Toy* Symphony. A 'Swannee Whistle' (Lotus Flute) is requested in Ravel's *L'Enfant et les sortilèges*.

Tuned motor horns (bulb, klaxon, etc.) appear frequently: Poulenc, Gershwin and Torch, for example. Two of the compositions of Johann Strauss, *Freikugeln* and *Auf der Jagd* include a part for rifle, and in *Die Fledermaus* and *Gypsy Baron* the jingling of spurs (*sporen*) is called for. Hindemith in *Kammermusik* No. 1 writes for a tin box filled with sand – an effect used in the theatre and studio to create the impression of marching feet. This effect is produced realistically from a conical gourd rattle in Britten's parable opera *The Prodigal Son* (1968).[2]

[1] A similar effect is produced from the Spierholzplatte, a form of tom tom with a single head of plywood (e.g. Stockhausen's *Kontakte für Klavier, Schlagzeug und elektronische Klänge*), cf. Tamb di legno-pelle, Luigi Nono.

[2] Also called feathers; Flyswatter: Whisk, Iazz stacks.

Techniques of Contemporary Percussion

Messiane in *Des Canyons avec Étoiles* (1974) scores for geophone, a revolving drum partly filled with lead shot to produce the effect of tidal waves.

To the above, which is but a tolerable representation of the instruments authentic and otherwise employed in twentieth-century compositions, could be added the glass-breaking machine, bursting balloons and similar bizarre devices. (For a comprehensive survey see: Read's *Thesaurus*).

THE TUNED PERCUSSION (MELODIC PERCUSSION)

The tuned percussion section of the orchestral percussion comprises the glockenspiel, xylophone, marimba, vibraphone and tubular bells, with the occasional inclusion of the cimbalom and tubaphone. In the standard repertoire the glockenspiel is the most frequently encountered of these. Forsyth says:[1] 'Its main use is to "brighten the edges" of a figure or fragment of melody in conjunction with the upper octaves of the orchestra.'

THE GLOCKENSPIEL

The orchestral glockenspiel comprises a series of steel bars (on rare occasions an alloy) of graduated length, arranged in two rows chromatically. It is usual for the 'back row' to be raised. To obtain the maximum resonance the bars are supported on felt or similar insulation, or suspended at the nodal points. These positions may be determined (as with the bars of the xylophone and allied instruments) by Chladni's method. Metal filings or a similar substance strewn on the bar will, when the bar is vibrating, transversely form two ridges where it is to be supported.[2]

The glockenspiel is seen in two forms: the open type played as a dulcimer (with which it has occasionally been confused); and the instrument with keyboard mechanism, little used to-day, the tone of the mallet-played instrument being superior. The two standard patterns have a respective range of $2\frac{1}{2}$ and 3 octaves, sounding two octaves higher than here written:

The smaller instrument is the more general. As yet, no firm ruling has been applied to the tuned percussion instruments regarding compass, and a practical 'lay out'. For example, the width of the bar varies from 1 inch to $1\frac{3}{8}$ inches in different glockenspiels. Many players prefer the larger bars, the 'span' being nearer to that of the

[1] Forsyth, Cecil, ibid. p. 62.
[2] In certain instruments the supporting points are adjustable to slightly reduce resonance.

normal xylophone. The glockenspiel is rarely resonated.[1] The hammers, held like timpani sticks, are varied to comply with the scoring. The heads, mounted on flexible cane shafts, are of several kinds, including wood, bone, plastic, rubber and even metal. In general, composers have in mind the bright bell-like tone of the glockenspiel produced with hard, or moderately hard beaters. In rapid figures the sounds tend to overlap, but this characteristic of the instrument is rarely detrimental. Though seen on occasional instruments, damping mechanism has to date not been considered essential, the performer where necessary using a finger-damping technique, e.g. *Pantglas, Idyll for violin, glockenspiel and pianoforte* by Ian Parrott.

Composers have naturally employed the glockenspiel imitatively, ranging from the carillon in *Les Cloches de Corneville* (Planquette) to the gentle tinkle of a musical box in Liadov's *Musical Snuff Box*. The better-known examples of the use of the glockenspiel in the orchestral repertoire, in addition to those already described, include Strauss's *Don Juan*, Liszt's *Second Hungarian Rhapsody*, and Ponchielli's 'Dance of the Hours' from *La Gioconda* (1876).

In certain works the part for the glockenspiel was obviously written for an instrument with pianoforte action, as with Papageno's little bells (*Magic Flute*). Respighi writes similarly pianistically in *The Pines of Rome* and elsewhere, Honegger also in his Fourth Symphony, and Ravel in *Daphnis and Chloé*. The florid writing in *The Sorcerer's Apprentice* (Dukas) was at one time generally considered to be 'a job for the keyboard'. The glockenspiel part in Järnefelt's *Praeludium*, though less complex, carries a footnote to the effect that it is only practicable on an instrument *mit Klaviatur*. To-day the mallet specialist takes such examples in his stride.[2]

Carl Orff in *Oedipus der Tyrann* (1957/8) writes for three glockenspiels, specifying one with keys. Three glockenspiels are requested in Orff's *Carmina Burana*.

The music for the glockenspiel is written in the treble clef, normally two octaves lower than sounding. Nomenclature includes *Glockenspiel* (Ger:) (frequently

---

[1] An instrument called the 'harpaphone' was introduced in the late twenties. The sounding position was one octave lower than the glockenspiel. The instrument was fully resonated. Its mellow sound had qualifications, but the instrument lost place to the vibraphone as did the *aluminophone*: a metallophone with bars of aluminium formerly used during recording sessions in place of the more resounding xylophone.

[2] Whilst in no way denying the skill of performers in the past, the approach to the tuned percussion instruments, particularly in sight-reading, has made great strides in recent years. In a sizeable orchestra there is now at least one 'mallet man', though it is necessary that all the percussionists be conversant with the tuned percussion. The prevailing high standard of percussion playing is due in no small way to excellent tutorial facilities. Young aspirants now have the opportunity of studying under players of repute, of gaining percussion diplomas, and acquiring experience in youth orchestras. See Appendix 4.

abbreviated *glock*); *campanelli* (It:); *jeu de timbres* (Fr:); and in America 'Bells' – a term now universally recognized, though in the past confused with tubular bells.[1]

The glockenspiel family includes the *tubaphone*. It occurs in Khachaturian's 'Dance of Young Maidens' from *Gayaneh Ballet*.[2] The tubaphone is more closely associated with the concert repertoire of the military band, where until recent years it was as popular a solo feature as the xylophone. The tubaphone consists of a series of small metal tubes arranged as the bars of the glockenspiel and sounding similarly.

A further instrument in the glockenspiel family is the (modern) *sistro* (Italian), consisting of a series of small mushroom-shaped bells arranged in a pyramid.

Other instruments similar in tone to the glockenspiel appeared in occasional scores, as for example, in certain works of Percy Grainger. In *Molly on the Shore* (1911) Grainger specifies *resonaphone* – a title applied to a series of gourd-resonated metal plates. The composer gives as an alternative *marimbaphone* or bells, in this case a series of resonated metal plates or wooden bars (see Patents). Grainger was explicit in his requirements from the percussion, as were certain of his contemporaries in the field of light classical music: Percy Fletcher and Eric Coates for example. In *Molly on the Shore* Grainger states: 'the player should be armed with a pair of combination wood and leathern top beaters – so that the quick changes from 'wooden' to 'leathern' merely means turning the handles of the beaters round in the hand.' In *Shepherd's Hey* he refers to the xylophone as 'Hammer-wood'. There is also (in the arrangement for small orchestra) a request for a stamping effect.

THE BELLS

The sound of the bell, the most universal of instruments, continues to attract the attention of composers. In the course of centuries the form of the bell has been modified from broad basin-like proportions to a graceful cuniform shape. The invention of the large bell in pendulous shape is generally attributed to Paulinus, Bishop of Nola (A.D. 400), a town in Campania, Italy, where it is said, large bells were first used in the Latin Church (hence the name *campana*). Tulip-shaped bells were, however, known in the Far East considerably earlier.

Bells have been associated with religious ritual, secular life, and musical offering over a long peorid of time. They entered orchestral music, to the best of our knowledge, with Bach. Later composers of the eithteenth century scored for bells in general their use

---

[1] The Sun Life Centenary Carillon (The Voice of Expo 1967) constitutes the largest glockenspiel existent. This instrument consists of 671 small bars of bell metal electronically amplified. The lowest tone is equivalent to that produced by a 22 ton cast bell.

[2] Khachaturian suggested the vibraphone as an alternative.

174. Thunder sheet (Vienna Philharmonic Orchestra). Photograph by
permission of Hans Wild

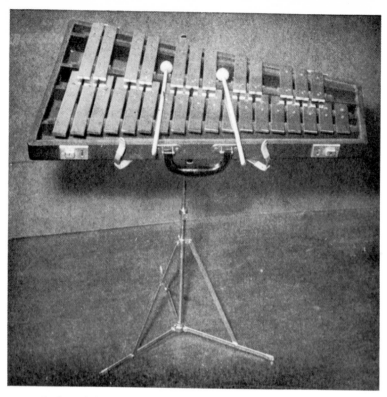

175. Orchestral glockenspiel (J. C. Deagan Inc., U.S.A.), author's collection. Photograph by permission of the Galpin Society

176. Tubular bells (Orchestral Chimes). Premier Drum Co. Ltd., England

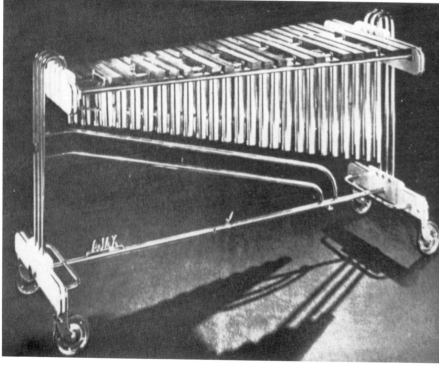

177. Orchestral xylophone by Boosey and Hawkes, London

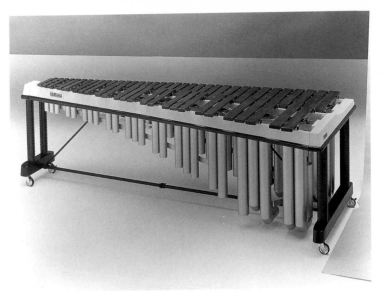

178
Yamaha YM-6000
Marimba

179
Vibraphone (with arched
'dummy' resonators). Tuned
Percussion, London

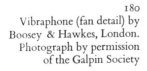

180
Vibraphone (fan detail) by
Boosey & Hawkes, London.
Photograph by permission
of the Galpin Society

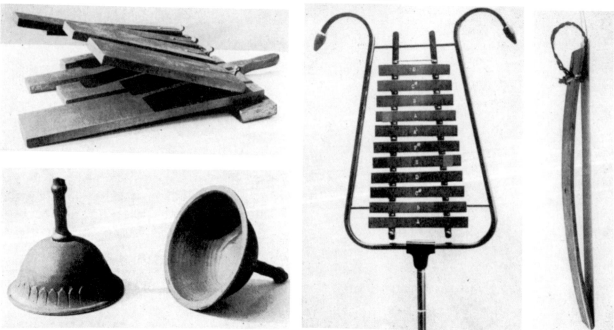

181
Benjamin Britten discusses a
point with the author. Record-
ing of *Albert Herring*, 1964
(Jubilee Hall, Aldeburgh).
Photograph by courtesy of the
Decca Record Company
Limited

182. Percussion instruments designed for Britten's church parable *The Burning Fiery Furnace*. (*above, left*) Multiple
whip. (*below, left*) Small cymbals, used in the procession. (*centre*) Lyra glockenspiel, used in the procession.
(*right*) Anvil. The anvil is a car suspension spring (Rolls Royce)

183. City of Coventry Drum Corps (1967). Photograph by permission of
Caters News Agency Ltd., Birmingham

184. Nuns' Drum Corps at Marymont College, Salina, Kansas. U.S.A.
Photograph by courtesy of the *Ludwig Drummer*

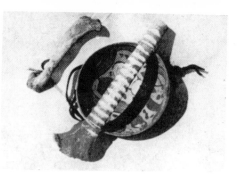

186. Bone scraper (resonated) *omichi-cahuaztli*. Collection Dr. and Mrs. F. Ll. Harrison

185. Rattles (American Indian) from *Historie of Virginia*, Capt. John Smith (1624). By courtesy of the Trustees of the British Museum

187. Eskimo frame drum with wooden beater. By courtesy of the Royal Scottish Museum, Edinburgh

188. Cree Indian Healing Ceremony (V. M. Bramley, 1876). By courtesy of the Trustees of the British Museum

189. 'Trap' drummer, 1921. (Jack Humphries, London Coliseum.) Photograph
by courtesy of L. W. Hunt Drum Co. Ltd., London

190. Modern 'kit'. Premier Percussion Leicester England.

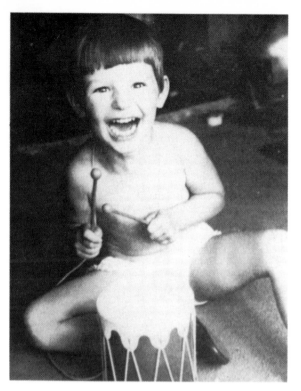

191. 'Youth takes over' Subject, Miriam Harriott.
Photograph by permission of Sheila Nelson

192. Cornelius Ward's cable-tensioned bass drum with foot
pedal, *c.* 1840 (with Richardson Rock Harmonica).
By permission of the Fitz Park Museum Trustees,
Keswick

193. University of Wruzburg Percussion Ensemble. Conductor Siegfied Fink.

being dramatic and realistic. In modern orchestration, in addition to serving such purposes, the timbre of the bell is employed to give contrasting tone colour according to the composer's inspiration.

The use of church bells, or their near equivalent, is connected more with the theatre than the concert hall; the stage equipment of many major opera houses includes real church bells.[1]

Substitutes for real church bells, in addition to producing their harmonic effect with orchestral colour, as did Manuel de Falla in *El Amor Brujo* ('Minuet des Sortilèges'), include tubular bells, bell plates, mushroom bells and electrically amplified metal bars, piano wires and clock gongs. Experiments with the latter which reproduce the inharmonic partials characteristic of bells, have been made at Bayreuth and Covent Garden. At Covent Garden clock gongs are supported by lower strings of the pianoforte. Of the experiment at Bayreuth (Mottl's bell machine) Percy Scholes says[2]: 'Wagner's use (of bells) in *Parsifal* is notable; he provided a problem, however, that proved difficult to solve, for such deep tones as he requires call for very heavy and large bells, the hum notes and harmonics of which would clash disturbingly with the rest of the orchestra; at one time Bayreuth used very long thick piano wires stretched on a resonator and musically supported by gongs (orchestral) and the bass tuba' (these are still used).

Mushroom bells and large bronze plates, such as those used in La Scala, Milan, and the Covent Garden mushroom bells, have proved effective substitutes for church bells. With rare exceptions, however, such as the series of metal plates owned by the Concertgebouw Orchestra of Amsterdam, and the moderate sized church bells used by The French National Radio Orchestra for such works as Berlioz's *Symphonie Fantastique*, tubular bells are used in the concert hall. According to Galpin tubular bells were introduced by John Hampton of Coventry in 1885. There is a record of their use in The Leeds Festival in 1886, for the peal of four bells in Sullivan's *Golden Legend*.

The Golden Legend   Sullivan

In 1890, tubular bells appeared with a keyboard (the *codophone*) in the Paris Opera House.

Tubular bells consist of a series of brass or steel tubes ranging in diameter from one to two inches ($1\frac{1}{2}$ inches diameter is the more usual, as is also brass tubing).

---

[1] Almost every theatre of note in Russia possesses genuine church bells – The Bolshoi Theatre has a series of 38.

[2] Scholes, Percy. *Oxford Companion to Music*, Oxford, p. 90.

The standard set of orchestral tubular bells consists of 18 tubes with a compass of

1½ octaves (chromatic) sounding. Bells above or below this

register are occasionally prescribed. For notes in the high register, one inch diameter tubing is preferable. Larger tubing, not less than two inches in diameter, is generally used for low-sounding bells.

The compass in special cases extends to one octave below the above, the tubes reaching a length of ten or more feet, governed by the diameter of the tubing. The tubes hang in a frame, mounted in two rows keyboard fashion. A diatonic or chromatic octave, normally in E flat, is generally mounted in a single row. (See Tchaikovsky, *1812*). (Messrs. H. Harms of Hamburg have recently introduced a chromatic scale of 25 bells, in steel tubing, descending to F above middle C, also a series of bronze plates for bell effects).[1]

The tubular bell is struck at the top edge, which is capped, or reinforced with an inner metal disc or pin. For general purposes a raw-hide mallet is employed, one side being covered with leather or felt for a contrast in tone. Hand or foot damping mechanism is usual.

The deep notes on metal tubing are not always satisfactory owing to the problem of eliminating the hum note. There is also the difficulty of determining the true pitch of such a bell owing to its peculiar acoustic properties. To produce notes in this low register with church bells would indeed be a problem in both theatre and concert hall. Forsyth says[2]: 'Such a bell, even if it is to produce a note no lower than middle C would have to be over twenty tons in weight'.[3] Gevaert contends that bells are not made to function as musical instruments.[4] 'Not only is the use of bells at the pitch indicated by composers actually impracticable because of the expensive price, it is equally inadmissable on purely artistic grounds. This immense voice, destined to be heard from the top of a cathedral tower or belfry by a whole town, would quench any other sound.'

Genuine church bells have however been employed effectively in recorded works (*1812 Overture* for example), and in film scores. Benjamin Frankel used three large

[1] The Wingfield Music Club of London (for the physically handicapped) possesses a set of glass tubular chimes, two and a half octaves. These were made by Ernest Lawes of London in 1913.

[2] Forsyth, Cecil. ibid. p. 52.

[3] The author recalls his feeling of apprehension on a Russian tour with The English Opera Group when observing Benjamin Britten's interest in the Tsar Bell in Moscow, some 193 tons in weight. (Big Ben weighs 13 tons, 11 cwts. See: *Bells of all Nations*, Ernest Morris, Robert Hale London, 1951. *Carillon*, Frank Percival Price, Oxford, 1933).

[4] Gevaert, F. A. *Traité d'instrumentation*, 1885.

church bells in the title music to his film score for *The Years Between* (1946). The bells were upturned and struck at the inner clapper point, the performer (the author) being mounted on a movable trolley.

Adequate as tubular bells have proved in the orchestra, opinion is agreed that there is here room for experiment.[1] A possible improvement might be tubes graduated in diameter according to their length. For the composer there is also ample scope for experiment, with little worry about repetition. To absorb the possibilities of twelve bells, as in the mathematical permutations in campanology, requires, in Maximus, 479,001,600 changes, and, it is calculated, would take 37 years, 355 days to complete.

Outstanding bell writing in the orchestral repertoire occurs for example in Messiaen's *Turangalîla* (1947), in Peter Racine Fricker's *A Vision of Judgment* (1957) and Britten's chamber opera *The Turn of the Screw*. Here Britten employs a chromatic set of bells

To-day the part for the orchestral chimes is usually written in the treble clef, notated an oct. lower. Earlier composers frequently wrote in the bass clef. It is doubtful whether they were always favoured with the instruments at the pitch written.

Nomenclature includes Bells or Chimes (Eng:); *cloches* (Fr:); *Campane* (or *Campanelle*) (It:) and *Glocken* or *Röhrenglocken* (Ger:).

THE XYLOPHONE

The xylophone (from the Greek *xylon* – 'wood', *phone* – 'voice') was one of the first known melodic percussion instruments. Though in principle a series of wooden bars, the modern instrument is elaborately and scientifically constructed. The bars are of the finest rosewood (or material of similar resonant and durable quality), carefully seasoned and precisely tuned. (The Musser Division of Ludwig Industries have introduced a new bar material of great durability – *Kelon*: a pultrusion silicate. Messrs Deagan have also developed a new bar material: *Klyperon* – prepared from synthetic reinforced resins.) The tuning process involves considerably more than the shortening of the bar to sharpen, and shallowing the underside (arch fashion) to flatten. The bars are treated on the underside to ensure that the overtones are in harmonic relationship to the fundamental. The overall range is tuned (by ear, or electronically Strobo-tuned) to equal temperament.[2] Each bar is suspended over a tube resonator in which the air column frequency matches the pitch

---

[1] On occasions composers supplement a tubular bell with a gong (or tam-tam) as for example Britten in *Peter Grimes*.

[2] Applied also to the tuning of the glockenspiel, marimba and vibraphone.

of the bar.[1] The bars either rest on a cushion of felt, or are drilled at the nodal point for cord suspension. Large modern instruments are often fitted with dummy resonators, arranged in the form of an arch.

The compass of the two standard instruments in general use is:

  (i) four octaves ascending from middle C.
  (ii) three and a half octaves ascending from F or G above middle C.

To meet the demands of modern composers, the larger instrument is preferable, both from a point of view of compass and timbre. In many cases octave transposition is necessary on a smaller instrument. The larger instrument, in addition to the extended range, makes possible the effective use of soft beaters in the lower register. The normal beaters for the xylophone are similar to those used on the glockenspiel, with the addition of a variety of softer beaters of felt, rubber, etc. The beaters are held in the same manner as when playing the glockenspiel. In the majority of orchestral xylophones the back row of bars is raised (the 'black' notes of the piano), as in the glockenspiel, though unlike the latter instrument where the bars are invariabily struck in the centre, the forward ends of the notes on the back row of the xylophone are employed in rapid passages. Some players prefer the two rows of bars to be level-mounted to facilitate four-hammer-playing. Here, the span of the beaters, held two in each hand, is adjusted to the required intervals by a scissor action of the shafts, obtained by pressure of the forefinger and thumb, or, twisting the wrist.

Technically, wherever practical, alternate beating from hand to hand is employed. To avoid a long jump, the xylophonist may, like the timpanist, employ a double beat with the right or left hand as in the accompanying example.[2]

The tremolo on the xylophone and similar mallet instruments is played as the roll on the timpani (recurring single beats).

[1] In *Danse Macabre* (Saint-Saëns) the clatter of the skeletons is best imitated by the removal of the resonating tubes. Speaking of modern xylophones Percival Kirby says: 'But in their new dress they completely stultify the effect intended by nineteenth century composers who wrote for the non-resonated instrument such as Saint-Saëns in his *Danse Macabre*'. (Kirby, P.R. 'The Indonesian Origin of Certain African Musical Instruments'. *African Studies*, vol. XXV, no. 1, 1966. Witwatersrand University Press, Johannesburg, pp. 12–13).

[2] A rare instance of the composer giving the 'fingering' for the xylophone is found in Messiaen's *Chronochromie*.

The Xylophone

The part for the xylophone is written (in the treble clef) at its true pitch, or, to avoid the use of extensive leger lines, an octave lower than sounding. If no precise directions are given regarding *8va* or otherwise, the player will place the part in the most convenient position on the instrument.[1] Normally only one stave is employed. Rare exceptions (two staves) include *Mother Goose* ('Laideronette') by Ravel.

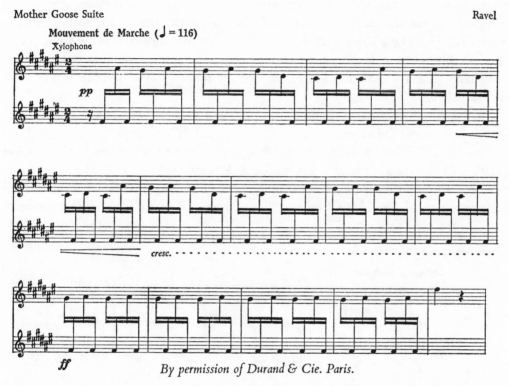

Mother Goose Suite   Ravel

Mouvement de Marche (♩ = 116)

By permission of Durand & Cie. Paris.

Gordon Jacob[2] describes the xylophone as 'a very agile instrument'. Dr. Jacob's apt adjective could also be fittingly applied to the modern xylophonist. In recent years the ever-increasing complexity of writing has revolutionised the use of this instrument as compared with the demands of earlier composers, who, with occasional exceptions, such as Stravinsky in *Les Noces*, asked only for short passages, repeated notes etc., (often memorised). The demands on the modern xylophonist are heavy, as a glance at Boulez's *Le marteau sans maître* and *Pli selon pli*, certain works of Messiaen, Tippett's Concerto for Orchestra and his Piano Concerto, Lutoslawski's Concerto for Orchestra and John Addison's *Carte Blanche* will show. Other notable examples in the standard orchestral repertoire include Hindemith, *Kammermusik*

[1] Rubbra, e.g. in his Seventh Symphony (1957) states 'true pitch'.
[2] Jacob, Gordon. *Orchestral Technique*, Oxford, London, 1940, p. 79.

No. 1; Rawsthorne, First Piano Concerto and *Street Corner Overture*; Walton, *Sinfonia Concertante*; and Britten's *Young Persons Guide to the Orchestra*. Tomasi uses the instrument freely in his *Concerto Asiatic*.

The orchestral xylophone and allied percussion instruments are challenging instruments, particularly with regard to sightreading. Stephen Whittaker, an internationally known xylophone virtuoso, says[1]: 'It is a most difficult instrument to sight read, for the player's eyes need to be on the conductor, the music and the instrument, more or less simultaneously'. In no other instrument does the kinaesthetic sense require greater development. So reliant is the player on this judgment of movement that a standardization of the size of mallet-played instruments is long overdue.

The keyboard xylophone[2] is used on only the rarest of occasions. Bartók writes for this instrument (*xilophono a tasteria*) in *Bluebeard's Castle* (1911).

Thomas B. Pitfield uses the xylophone uniquely in his Concertino for Percussion and Full Orchestra (1962) and Sonata for xylophone solo (1967). Here the composer has arranged the part to suit four beaters, held two in each hand, at a fixed distance of a third. David Bedford specifies a 'cluster of sticks' for the vibraphone in his *Piece for Mo* (1965).

Reel from Sonata for Xylophone   T. Pitfield

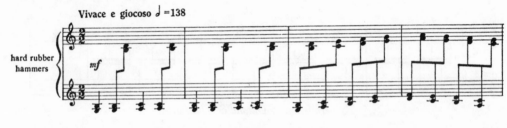

By permission of Peters C. F. Inc., New York.

Nomenclature includes: 'xylophone' – (Eng: and Fr:); *Xylophon* – (Ger:); *xilofono* – (It:). The German *Strohfiedel* and *Holzharmonika* as well as the French *Claquebois* occur in isolated cases. (*Hölzernes Gelächter*, obsolete S.Ger. and Austrian.)

[1] *Drums and Drumming To-day*, Boosey & Hawkes, London, 1964.
[2] No innovation according to Kircher, 1650.

The Marimba

(In 1931 America laid claim to the world's super-xylophone. The instrument, the property of a famous xylophone artist Clair Omar Musser, later concerned with the manufacture of the famous Musser mallet-played instruments, was reputed to have cost $5,000. The length of this giant instrument, made by Messrs. Deagan of Chicago, was 10½ feet, and its weight 12½ hundredweight. It consisted of a five octave marimba-xylophone combined with a two octave vibraphone. The tone of the lower register of the marimba was amplified by microphonic 'pickups' emitted through two large horns. Foot pedal mechanism controlled the volume. The instrument was finished in fourteen carat gold and chromium plate, and further enhanced by three rows of 'dummy' resonators. Musser toured America with this instrument. His repertoire included *Mignon* Overture (Thomas), *Polonaise Brilliante* (Weber-Liszt) and (Chopin's) *Fantasie Impromptu*).[1]

THE MARIMBA

The orchestral marimba (the name it is universally known by) may be described as a deep-toned (resonated) xylophone. The wooden bars are shallower than those used on the orchestral xylophone. The compass of the normal marimba is 3 or 3½ octaves. In general, the lowest note is one octave lower than that on the four octave xylophone which ascends from middle C. The Musser Concert Grand Marimba has a compass of 4⅓ octaves ascending from 𝄢. In the orchestra (to date) deeper sounding instruments such as those used in the African and Mexican marimba bands are rare. The bass marimba owned by Don Henry of New York descends to C, two octaves below middle C. This instrument was manufactured by Messrs. Deagan (U.S.A.) for use in a marimba band.[2] The *Marimba a Basse* built by Frank K. MacCallum of El Paso, Texas, (a marimba soloist) descends to A two octaves and a third below middle C. (According to MacCallum it is not the bars of a marimba that give the sound we hear (except in the high treble where they are naturally loud): it is the pulsating air column in the resonators).[3]

The instrument with extended compass (4½ octaves or more) has been frequently referred to as *xylorimba, xylophone-marimba,* or *marimba-xylophone.*[4] e.g. Berg, *Three Pieces for Orchestra*; Stravinsky, *The Flood*; Dallapiccola, *Parole di San Paulo*; Roberto Gerhard, *Hymnody*; the latter using two players on one instrument.

---

[1] A name synonymous with the xylophone as an instrument of entertainment was that of Teddy Brown, a supreme artist. (See vintage 70's. Appendix 6).

[2] Cf. *nabimba,* etc., (Inventions and Patents).

[3] From *The Book of the Marimba* by Frank K. MacCallum, Carlton Press, New York, 1968.

[4] In the 'thirties, the marimba-xylophone (compass five octaves) was popular as a solo instrument.

Technically the approach to the marimba is similar to that used on the xylophone. Hard beaters are rarely used on the slender bars. These would in any case rob the instrument of its characteristic mellow sound.[1] The marimba is being increasingly used in the large orchestra, as for instance in Malcolm Arnold's Fourth Symphony; Richard Rodney Bennett's First Symphony; Wilfred Joseph's Second Symphony, and Aaron Copland's Film Suite for Orchestra, *The Red Pony* (1948). Among the various concertos written by Milhaud is one for marimba and vibraphone (1947). Recent compositions include: *Concertino for Marimba*, Paul Creston; *Concerto for Marimba and Orchestra*, Robert Kurka; *Concerto for Marimba and Orchestra*, James Basta; and the Icelandic composer Axtell Masson's *Concerto for Marimba and Orchestra*. A prominent part is given to the marimba in Denis ApIvor's *Crystals* (Concert Miniscule) (1951).[2]

The part for the marimba is written (usually at actual pitch) in either the treble or bass clef, or at times on a double stave, as for the pianoforte.

A development of the mirimba was the *Vibra-Rimba*, a product of the firm of Tuned Percussion of London. In this instrument the open end of each resonatiang tube was alternately closed and opened by means of a revolving disc (see Vibraphone).

The *Octa-rimba* was a pre-war product of the Leedy Drum Co. of U.S.A. (1930). In this instrument, two narrow bars an octave apart in pitch are arranged side by side. The octaves are struck simultaneously with forked beaters. The compass of the octa-rimba is $3\frac{1}{2}$ octaves, ascending from one octave below middle C. Only a few of these instruments were manufactured. The Vibra-Rimba and the Octa-Rimba are discontinued.

THE VIBRAPHONE

The vibraphone is the most recent addition of note to the orchestral percussion section. Vaudeville it seems was responsible for the introduction of the vibraphone. In this field of entertainment, the xylophone, marimba and numerous novel percussion instruments were popular features. There was, not unnaturally, constant experiment to provide the extraordinary. Bar-percussion provided a useful medium. In 1916 Hermann Winterhoff of the enterprising Leedy Drum Co. applied a mechanical vibrato to a 'steel marimba', where a *vox humana* effect was produced by lowering and raising the resonating chambers by means of a motor driven apparatus. In 1921 a development of the original principle was applied, whereby the vibrato was obtained by alternately opening and closing the upper (open) ends of the

[1] In *The Vision of St. Augustine* (1965) Tippett requires the contrasting tones of marimba and xylophone in the same register.

[2] Holst's early employment of the marimba (*Capriccio*, 1932) is exemplary.

resonators by means of revolving discs. This principle is retained in the present-day vibraphone. The discs are attached to s spindle, one to each of the two rows of resonators. The spindles are driven by motor mechanism, electric, or in some cases clockwork. The repeated breaking-up of the sound causes it to emerge in a series of pulsations, the speed of which is governed by adjusting the revolutions of the spindle. This principle was later applied to a saxophone F. S. Brasor, U.S.A. Patent 1,554,782.

Winterhoff's instrument was christened 'vibraphone' by George H. Way of the Leedy Drum Co., both names synonymous with 'drumming' and drum making. The term 'vibraharp' was introduced by Messrs. Deagan. By the middle 'twenties, the vibraphone was an integral part of the dance orchestra. In 1934 Berg gave it a place in his opera *Lulu*, though some years elapsed before it was frequently employed in serious compositions. Britten employed it so in his *Spring Symphony* (1949), and later in his opera *A Midsummer Night's Dream*. It adds to the impression of the sacring bell in 'Sanctus' from his *War Requiem*, here 'without fans' (discs stationary), and similarly in the Cello Symphony – in this case to give the colour of the metallophone (q.v. Asiatic section). The vibraphone occurs in Walton's Cello Concerto and *Partita*, and in works by Malcolm Arnold. Intricate parts are given to the vibraphone in many chamber works, such as Boulez' *Le marteau san maitre* (1954). It is an important instrument in modern jazz (q.v.) and Siegfried Fink's Concertino for vibraphone, string Orchestra or Piano (1967).

The compass varies from $2\frac{1}{2}$ octaves [musical notation] to four octaves [musical notation]

[musical notation] The instrument known as the 'Concert Model' has a range of three

octaves [musical notation]. The part for the vibraphone is usually written at actual

pitch.

Technically the approach to the vibraphone is similar to that employed on the marimba and xylophone. (The 'keyed' vibraphone, such as a model by Mustel, is rare). The bars (an alloy) are invariably level-mounted to facilitate the use of three or more beaters. (For certain chords three beaters are held in one hand, the inner pair adjusted as in four-hammer playing). Beaters of varying texture are employed to comply with composers' requests, or the player's conception. Soft hammers are

[1] In the now discontinued Deagan *Electra Vibe* no tube resonantors were used, each bar was individually fitted with a pick-up transducer. The Ludwig Drum Co. have introduced electronic amplification, with tone, tremolo and 'reverb' controls, in their (patented) *Electro-Vibe Pickup*.

considered normal and are used unless otherwise specified. These consist of a wool- or yarn-covered rubber core, the texture (in general) being defined by a colour code.

The instrument is equipped with a foot-controlled sustaining device, operating similarly to the pianoforte sustaining pedal. (In early models, pressure on the pedal 'damped' the tone.) Occasionally instructions are given for the instrument to be played with no resonance (pedal off). In the First Symphony (1951) of Ernst Toch: vibraphon *ohne vibrato* is given as a substitute for marimba. More unusual requests include 'with a steadily accelerating (or retarding) vibrato,' and the demand by A. Paccagnini in *Musica da Camera* (1961) for the bars to be struck with the hand open and with the fingers, cf. Milhaud, Concerto for Marimba and Vibraphone. Possibly unique is William Kraft's request in his *Configurations* (1968) to 'set discs so that "whites" are open (vertical): "blacks" are closed (horizontal)'.

The instruments described in this chapter form (with minor rare additions) the percussion section of the modern orchestra. It is this section of the orchestra that has been the subject of the greatest experiments in recent years, so that our final chapter is concerned with its use as a family in the works of composers from the beginning of the century to the present day.

Bibliography: Chapter 15

TECHNIQUES OF CONTEMPORARY PERCUSSION

AVGERINOS, Gerassimos. *Handbuch der Schlag-und Effekt-instruments*, Verlag Das Musikinstrument, Frankfurt am Main, 1967.

BERGER, Fritz. *Das Basler Trommeln*, 1956. (Privately published in Basle).

BASSARABOFF, Nicholas. *Ancient European Musical Instruments*, Harvard University Press, 1941, 1965.

BLADES, James. *Orchestral Percussion Technique*, Oxford, London, 1973.

BOWER, H. A. *System for the Tympani*, Fischer, New York, 1911.

DENOV, Sam. *The Art of Playing Cymbals*, Adler, New York, 1963.

DONINGTON, Robert. *The Instruments of Music*, Methuen, London, 1949, 1951.

ENGEL, Cecil. *The Music of the Most Ancient Nations*, Reeves, London, 1864.

FORSYTH, Cecil. Orchestration, Macmillan, London, 1955.

GEVAERT, Francois. *Nouveau traité d 'instrumentation*, Lemoine, Paris-Bruxelles, 1885.

GOODMAN, Saul. *Modern Method for Tympani*, Mills Music, New York, 1948.

Bibliography

HARDY, H. C. & ANCELL, J. E. 'Comparison of the Acoustical Performance of Calfskin and Plastic Drumheads'. *The Journal of the Acoustical Society of America,* vol. XXXIII, no. 10, October 1961.

HARRISON, F. L. and RIMMER, Joan. *The Showcase of Musical Instruments, Dover,* New York, 1964.

JACOB, Gordon. *The Elements of Orchestration,* Jenkins, London, 1962.

Orchestral Technique, Oxford, London, 1940.

JEANS, James. *Sience and Music,* Cambridge, 1947.

KAPPEY, J. A. *Military Music,* Boosey, London, 1894

KIRBY, P. R. *The Kettle-drums,* Oxford, 1930.

'The Indonesian Origin of Certain African Musical Instruments', *African Studies,* vol. XXV, no. I, Witwatersrand University Press, Johannesburg, 1966.

MACCALLUM, Frank. *The Book of the Marimba,* Carlton Press, New York, 1968.

PISTON, Walter. *Orchestration,* Norton, New York, 1955. Gollancz, London, 1965.

PONTÉCOULANT, L. A. Organographie, Essai sur la facture instrumentale, Paris, 1965.

PONTIGNY, Victor de. 'On Kettledrums,' *Proceedings of the Musical Association,* Spottiswoode, London, 1876.

RAYLEIGH, Lord. *Philosophical Magazine,* 1879.

READ, Gardner. *Thesaurus of Orchestral Devices,* Pitman, New York and London, 1953.

SACHS, Curt. *The History of Musical Instruments,* Norton, New York, 1940.

SCHERCHEN, Hermann. *Handbook of Conducting,* Oxford, London, 1956

SCHOLES, Percy. *The Oxford Companion to Music,* Oxford London, 1938.

The Mirror of Music, vol. II, Novello and Oxford, London, 1947.

SHIVAS, Andrew. *The Art of Tympanist and Drummer,* Ediburgh University Press, 1986.

SIDGWICK, A. H. *The Promenade Ticket,* Arnold, London, 1928.

TAYLOR, H. W. *The Art and Science of the Timpani,* Baker, London, 1964.

WIDOR, Charles. The Technique of the Modern Orchestra, translated, E. Suddard, Williams, London, 1946.

RECOMMENDED READING

BRINDLE, Reginald Smith, *Contemporary Percussion,* Oxford, 1991

GROVES, V & VI, Macmillan Publishers Ltd., London, 1980.

16

Composers' Use of Modern Percussion

Twentieth-century orchestration has demanded a dominant role from the instruments of percussion. Succeeding years have witnessed an ever-increasing use of the normal percussion instruments, together with a desire on the part of composers to exploit the possibilities of unusual devices and novel instruments. The combination of these facets has exercised considerable influence on creative orchestration, to the extent that with many modern composers the majority of percussion instruments are often indispensable ingredients to the tone palette of their orchestrations. That colourful orchestration does not depend on the employment of unusual devices, percussion or otherwise, is undeniable. Nevertheless, few twentieth-century composers have spurned the additional colour from instruments now at their disposal, orthodox or otherwise. Of the former, the timpani, the cymbals, and the side drum have been the subject of considerable experiment.

Though in many cases the side drum remains chiefly an instrument concerned with the demarcation of rhythm, the exploitation of its tonal and other possibilities has been greatly extended, especially by such composers as Debussy, Stravinsky, Ravel and Bartók.

Rimsky-Korsakov's earlier employment of the side drum in *Capriccio Espagnole* and *Schéhérazade* may have been in no small degree responsible for the general acceptance of this instrument in delicate orchestral textures. Outstanding examples include *Nocturnes* and *Images* of Debussy, numerous works of Ravel, including *Alborada del gracioso*, his arrangement of Mussorgsky's *Pictures from an Exhibition*, and of course his *Bolero*, and many of the works of Bartók.

Bartók (particularly in his later works) made greater use of the contrasting tones from the edge and the centre of the side drum head, and the instrument snared and unsnared, than any other composer. Examples can be found in his *Cantata Profana* (1930) where he also makes frequent use of glissandi on the timpani, at times rising and falling – an effect of which he was extremely fond.

By permission of Universal Edition (London) Ltd.

Though other composers such as Walford Davies, Nielsen and Stravinsky, made use of timpani glissandi before Bartók, he exploited this effect to a greater extent than either his predecessors or his contemporaries. Even so he was discreet in its employment. In the third movement of his *Music for Strings, Percussion and Celesta* (1937) the glissandi are with and without tremolo. They are, as in his other works, well within the register of the drums. This is a detail not always strictly observed; some over-energetic composers stretching the compass, and the drumhead, or placing the interval in the mean of a drum's register and ascending or descending to a point beyond its compass.

Bartók was meticulous in every respect regarding his percussion. His parts are perfect examples of careful arrangement and familiarity with the instruments involved. His piano and violin concertos and Concerto for Orchestra contain challenging material. In the latter work the second movement opens with a solo on the side drum without snares. There is also in this work the use of chords on the timpani, and instructions that the drums be played with side drum sticks. Three timpani are struck simultaneously in the second movement of his First Suite for

Orchestra. [1]

In his First Piano Concerto (1926) Bartók writes for four suspended cymbals of different size, and specifies by reference numbers the type of beater intended, and where the cymbal is to be struck (dome or otherwise). Instructions are also given for a 'sizzle' effect. Here Bartók anticipated the fitment used by the modern drummer in which a series of thin metal strips are suspended to rest lightly on the cymbal. Bartók says the hanging cymbal is to be struck on the rim with the handle of one side drum stick, while the other is fastened to the leather hanger of the cymbal so that the point of the drumstick touches the cymbal. Two small side drums are required in this work, one unsnared and tuned low – the other with snares, tuned

[1] In *Trionfo di Afrodite* Orff uses

413

high. The sign ∧ indicates to commence at the rim and work to the centre, and back to the rim.

In Bartók's Sonata for Two Pianos and Percussion (1937), his use of the machine timpani and other percussion is exemplary, and has unquestionably been a source of inspiration to subsequent composers.[1] In the second movement the combination of cymbals, struck on the edge and dome with a thin wooden stick and a soft stick, the snared and unsnared side drums ('c.c.' – *con corde* and 's.c.' – *senza corde*), struck on the extreme edge and centre, the tam-tam, the xylophone, and the timpani with their exciting groups of five notes echoing the pianos, makes this movement one of the gems of the chamber repertoire. In the finale, instructions are given that the cymbal be struck with the fingernail, or the blade of a pocketknife, on the very edge (*pppp*). The side drum closes the work; 'played with two very light and thin sticks' (quite often played with knitting needles). In contrast to these delicate sounds, the cymbal stroke (struck on the dome with the heavy end of the side drum stick) in the intro-duction of the first movement is the more startling, following as it does the fragile texture of the *pp* timpani and piano entries.

With the two side drums Bartók gives the second percussionist a tremolo on the bass drum, to be played with a double-headed stick. The tremolo is produced by an oscillating movement of the beater (see combination of bass drum and cymbals). Bartók specifies the beaters required for the triangle: '(a) with the usual metal beater; (b) with a thin wooden stick; (c) with a short, but rather heavy, metal beater'. He also states that 'the snares of the side drum should be released when the instrument is not in use, to prevent vibration'.[2] The writing for the xylophone in this sonata is typical of Bartók, as is the effect of accelerando and rallentando, to open the third movement for his *Music for Strings, Percussion and Celesta*. Here, as always, Bartók writes for the xylophone at actual pitch (*see facing page*).

Full use is made of the melodic percussion in *Bluebeard's Castle* (1911), *The Wooden Prince* (1916–18) and *The Miraculous Mandarin* (1919). In *The Wooden Prince* Bartók uses the glockenspiel, though in general he prefers to obtain his 'bell sounds' (percussive) from the celesta.

It is possible that Bartók's enthusiasm for percussion was inspired by the employ-ment of these instruments by his Central European predecessors, e.g., the fine writing of Dvořák, and also by the predominance of rhythm in folk music of the Balkans.

Contemporary with Bartók we have his fellow-countrymen Kodály, Dohnányi, and his near-neighbours Janáček and Weinberger. *Háry János* provides typical

[1] A plan indicating the grouping of the entire instrumentation is included in the introductory notes.

[2] To prevent 'snare buzz' – particularly distressing with modern snares.

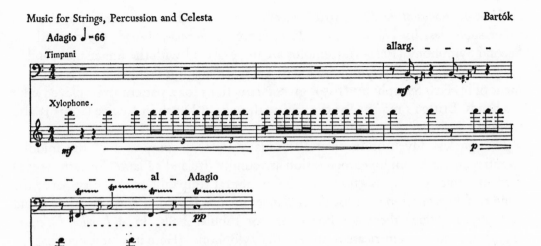

By permission of Universal Edition (London) Ltd.

examples of Kodály's use of percussion. Janáček made heavy demands on the timpani, and his employment of them was individual because of his consistent use of an unusually large number of drums in the upper register. Piccolo timpani are prominent throughout such works as his operas *Kátyá Kabanová* (1922), *The Makropulos Affair, From the House of the Dead* (1928), and his Sinfonietta (1925). In each case, particularly in the latter opera and his earlier *Jenufa* (1904), the timpanist's score calls for a highly skilled performer. Similarly with Weinberger's opera *Schwanda the Bagpiper* (1927).

In Dohnányi's *Variations on a Nursery Song* two timpanists are needed, also a glockenspiel and 'glocken' (bells). The latter is often given to tubular bells, or the vibraphone. Deep-sounding tubular bells however could be contrary to the composer's intention, for according to a footnote the tone of the 'glocken' should be pure and sweet though contrasting with the higher-sounding glockenspiel.

With composers of all nationalities orchestral percussion proved a rich field for experiment during the 1920's and '30's. Further possibilities regarding varying tones on the timpani and the tuned percussion were exploited, and the indefinitely pitched instruments, in addition to their function as carriers of accents and rhythms, constantly gained ground in the colouring of orchestral texture.

The use of chords on the timpani was by now quite common. This device, for which Beethoven was responsible, and which Berlioz and Busoni extended, obviously intrigued Arnold Bax, for he uses it in his First Symphony (1922), Fifth Symphony (1931–2), and in *Tintagel* (1917). Stanford's use of the tremolo with finger-tips (*Songs of the Fleet*, 1910) may have suggested to Bax the use of this and other subtleties. In *The Garden of Fand* (1916), *November Woods* (1917), and the Second Symphony (1924–5), tremolos are to be played with the finger-nails, and in the Second and Fourth Symphonies with coins. (Benjamin Frankel in the last movement of his First Symphony (1959) gives instructions for a pattern to be played with the hands. Britten's request for timpani with *ruthe* in Death in Venice (1973) is also unusual.)

Though less adventurous than Bax, many notable composers of the middle-twenties onwards employed percussion arrestingly. Ireland's Piano Concerto (1930) is an example of what is known to the orchestral timpanist as a 'meaty part'; the same could certainly be said of *These Things shall be* (1936), a work for chorus and orchestra, in which there is a florid part for tubular bells. In *A London Overture* (1937), Ireland gives intricate figures to the xylophone. (Here it is indicated that the instrument is to sound as written.)

Compositions from the twenties onwards show not only that composers were becoming increasingly demanding in quantity, but that what might hitherto have been considered a fastidious or highly specialized use of percussion was fast becoming common practice, as for example, the request by Falla in *El Retablo de Maese Pedro* (a work with a large percussion force) not only for the gong to be played with a wooden stick, but that the instrument be laid horizontally to reduce the resonance. Berg, a composer with forward ideas regarding percussion (he was responsible for introducing the vibraphone into the major orchestra, *q.v.*), used a large percussion section (with accent on timpani and xylophone) in his opera *Wozzeck* (1921–5).

Paris, not surprisingly, had produced its school of adventurous spirits, as had also the U.S.A. From France, there came with that prince of orchestrators Ravel, such names as Varèse, Koechlin, Satie, Milhaud, Poulenc and Auric. In Milhaud's *Concerto pour batterie et petit orchestre* (1929–30), the soloist is engaged on four timpani in addition to a full complement of unpitched percussion, including the combination of *caisse claire*, *caisse roulante* and *tambourin provençal* – a favourite one with Milhaud. This work necessitates no small amount of athleticism, not the least being the management of the foot pedal operated bass drum and cymbal.[1] Milhaud gives (as did Stravinsky and Bartók) a detailed diagram of the arrangement of the percussion instruments. He suggests double-headed drumsticks (felt and wood), to provide additional tone colours. In contrast to the activity of the soloist in his concerto, Milhaud divided the percussion instruments in his *Choéphores* (1915–16) and *Christopher Columbus* (1929) between a large group of performers. In both these works the percussion ensemble is frequently the sole accompaniment to the speech.

[1] See 'Changing Styles in Light Music'.

In *Les Choéphores* Milhaud makes novel use of two bass drums – one to be played with the normal beater, and the other with timpani sticks. (On occasions a *pp* marking is identified *frolé* – lightly touched.)[1] In his music to the ballet *La Création du Monde* (1923) Milhaud scores for piccolo timpani in the treble register 🎼 (as did Ravel in *L'Enfant et les sortilèges* – a *petite timbale en re* 🎼). For notes in this high register, drums not more than sixteen inches in diameter are necessary.

A later work by Milhaud, his Concerto for Marimba and Vibraphone (transcribed in 1947 from his Suite for Piano and Orchestra) is still considered one of the most elaborate works for these instruments.[2] Milhaud specifies in detail the various types of mallets required (linen thread, yarn, medium and hard rubber) and asks that the back ends of the mallet should be used. He also asks for the bars to be struck with the hands. (Milhaud used the vibraphone as early as 1933 in *L'Annonce faite à Marie*.)

Other composers utilizing a large percussion force (solo or otherwise) include Varèse (*Hyperprism*, (1926), *Intégrales*, (1926) and *Ionisation*, (1931)), and the American composer William Russell. In his Fugue for Eight Percussion Instruments, written in 1933, for piano, timpani, bass drum, side drum, cymbals, triangle(s), xylophone and glockenspiel, Russell's requirements are certainly unusual; they include: 'placing handkerchief over the head of a side drum, placing a piece of paper over the drum head, and scratching strings (snares) lengthwise along winding, with a coin held like a banjo pick', The numerous effects required from the timpani include: 'sweeping of wire brush across the head near the rim, and the metal rim and the copper kettle of the small timpano to be struck with a triangle beater.' Russell asks for muffled triangles and specifies three separate instruments to measure four, six and ten inches respectively. A suspended Chinese crash cymbal, and a fourteen inch Turkish cymbal are required in addition to two pairs of cymbals to be sixteen and eighteen inches in diameter. There are also instructions for a wire brush to be held against a vibrating cymbal, that the cymbals on occasions be held together after striking, and that the bass drum be played with side drum sticks and with the finger-tips; high notes near the rim, low notes near the centre. The timbre of the primitive friction drum is conjured from the bass drum: 'rubbed with a rosined glove or cloth over a snare drum stick with tip of the stick pressed against the centre of drum head'. Russell is equally demanding in his *Three Dance Movements*. In this work he specifies that the triangle should be struck with a hammer, an anvil or steel pipe with a heavy

[1] This work caused great consternation in Paris, Milhaud encountering (as had Berlioz) the violent opposition of the city's conservative element.

[2] For a later work see *Liaisons* – Mobile for Vibraphone and Marimba by Roman Haubenstock – Ramati.

hammer, a saw-blade to be drawn across the cymbal, and that the cymbal be struck with a wood stick with rubber bands across one end. A small dinner bell is prescribed, and the striking of a ginger-ale bottle with a triangle beater, also the breaking of a bottle.[1] There is a request for the drawing of a bow across the edge of a xylophone bar, (cf., 'Patents') and for the effect of a glissando by sweeping the beater across the resonating tubes. Certain of Russell's devices remain unique, though whether the subjecting of orthodox instruments of percussion to such unusual treatment has enhanced their purpose is questionable.

Bloch, Ravel, Honegger, Tcherepnin, Hindemith, Schoenberg and Webern, each made exemplary use of percussion. A typical example of Bloch's approach is to be found in one of his early works, *Schelomo* (1915–16). The sequences for the timpani are florid, and interesting ornaments are applied to the side drum.[2] Ravel's imaginative scoring for percussion ensemble in *Daphnis et Chloé* is historic. Honegger's employment of a percussion ensemble in *Pacific 231* is well known. The Russian-born Alexander Tcherepnin uses a percussion ensemble uniquely in his Second Symphony (1927). Here, the second movement is given entirely to a percussion ensemble (bass drum, two side drums – snared and without snares – cymbals, tam-tam, triangle and castanets), coupled with the strings tapping the bodies of their instruments with the reverse bow.

An outstanding example of the use of embellishments (on four small drums) is found in Hindemith's *Kammermusik* No. 5 (1929). A lengthy statement for the xylophone occurs in *Kammermusik* No. 1 (1922). In *Neues von Tage* (1929) Hindemith asks for an Indian drum, an instrument requested by only a few composers (Charles Ives, *The Indians*; Inghelbrecht, *La Métamorphose d'Eve*; Silvestre Revueltas, *Sensemaya*; Hanns Eisler, *Nonette* No. 2). Hindemith, who is described by Read as 'one of the creative giants of the twentieth century and an orchestrator without peer'[3] employs a solo percussion ensemble in *Symphonic Metamorphoses* (1943).

Schoenberg made unique demands of the percussion, as for example the semitone shake on the timpani in his *Five Pieces for Orchestra* (1909), requiring, as Professor Kirby says, exact tuning and flawless execution.[4] Reference has already been made to Schoenberg's use of heavy chains in *Gurrelieder*, the cello bow on the

---

[1] The American composer H. Davidson in his *Auto Accident* asks for glass to be smashed with a mallet and emptied on a hard surface. He also requests musical tumblers, water tuned.

[2] An earlier instance of the deft use of grace notes on the side drum occurs in the opera *Louise* (1900) by Gustave Charpentier. The marches of Sousa are also typical of the effective employment of embellishments. In his book *The Trumpet and Drum*, Sousa acknowledges the assistance of a famous drum instructor, his close friend F. W. Lusby of the United States Marines.

[3] Read, Gardner, *Thesaurus of Orchestral Devices*, Pitman, New York and London, 1953, p. 10.

[4] Kirby, P. R. *The Kettle-drums*, Oxford, London, 1930, p. 19.

cymbal in *Five Pieces for Orchestra*, and the flexatone in *Variations for Orchestra*, and the operas *Von Heute auf Morgen* and *Moses and Aaron*. In *Moses and Aaron*, Schoenberg's last work, two side drums, high and low in pitch are required. In this work Schoenberg writes for two timpanists, also for two xylophonists, suggesting that he felt that the dividing of the part would be more secure than a single player manipulating three beaters, a device of which he would surely be aware (see 'Orchestral xylophone').

Schoenberg's distinguished pupils include Berg (*q.v.*), Skalkottas and Webern. A typical example of Webern's approach to percussion is seen in his *Sechs Stücke für Orchester*, a work requiring three timpanists, the normal static percussion, glockenspiel and large bells. The style of Skalkottas is represented in *Andante Sostenuto* for piano solo, ten wind instruments and timpani (1954).

Meanwhile, the writing for percussion by notable British composers was no less resourceful, e.g. works by Walton, Bliss and Lambert. Walton makes novel use of a simple force (side drum, suspended cymbal, tambourine, castanets, wood block and triangle) in *Façade* (1923). In this work, in addition to his original use of wire brushes on side drum and cymbal, there is the unique effect from the cymbal struck with triangle. (In the later orchestral suites from *Façade*, Walton added timpani and other percussion, including xylophone). *Belshazzar's Feast* written in 1931, has been described as 'a feast for percussion'. In this work, each god is invoked by appropriate orchestral tone colour, in which the percussion plays an integral part, *viz*, the silver god: glockenspiel and triangle; the iron god: anvil; the wood god: xylophone; and the stone god: slapstick. The drums, cymbals and gong accompany the baritone, assisting the tense description of the writing on the wall. Walton's partiality for a motif on three timpani is evident in his First Symphony (1935). In the finale of this work, two timpanists, each with three drums, play in duet. His film scores bristle with percussion, *Henry V* and *Hamlet* for example. Though such film scores were sometimes published, sequences essentially for use 'on the floor' were omitted. Many of these sequences involved unusual percussion effects. Bliss in the musical accompaniment to the workshop scene in *The Shape of Things to Come* included an anvil effect played on two huge girders suspended from the studio roof. This was combined with a rhythmic pattern played slapstick on the lower notes of the xylophone.[1] To the orchestral timpanist, Bliss is probably best known for his Piano

[1] Slapstick, a popular feature on the xylophone and marimba, was played with large leather-topped beaters which were pressed on the bars.

Concerto, and the extensive part given to the drums in his *Pastoral* ('Lie strewn the white flocks') and his opera *The Olympians*.

Constant Lambert was a composer whose works show a passion for rhythm and the influence of jazz. It is no surprise to find Lambert's percussion scores entertaining, for he manipulated percussion instruments expertly.[1] The scores of *The Rio Grande* and his Piano Concerto describe his style admirably. In *The Rio Grande* the composer's notes include that the side drum player be provided 'with a wire-brush as used in Jazz bands', and that the instructions concerning the method of playing the percussion instruments 'should be meticulously followed'. These instructions include a tremolo with finger-nails on the timpani (combined with a tremolo on the suspended cymbal with wire brush), the striking of the tambourine on the rim, and the cymbal with a large triangle beater or wooden hammer. He uses the octave on the timpani, and the xylophone colourfully and significantly ('Loud is the marimba's note'). A percussion ensemble accompanies the piano cadenzas. His film scores include *Anna Karenina*, in which (to represent the bells of St. Petersburg) he commissioned the author of this book to experiment with metal tubes of gigantic length.

The influence of jazz is expressed in works by Mátyás Seiber. Seiber was a creative genius with a varying style. Like his master Kodály he was a renowned teacher. His flair for the jazz idiom is particularly evident in *Jazzolettes* (1928) a work for chamber orchestra, and *Improvisations for Jazz Band and Symphony Orchestra* (Seiber and Dankworth), and in such film scores as *Animal Farm*. In the latter he used an extensive tuned percussion section. In *Jazzolettes* the current fashion of the jazz drummer complete with slap hand cymbals ('sock' cymbals) and slapsticks is faithfully imitated. In his serious compositions *Ulysses* (1949) and 'Three Fragments' from *A Portrait of an Artist* (1956–7), especially the timpani are prominent. Many of his scores for film and radio contain text book examples in the use of percussion generally.

Film and incidental music for radio has attracted many notable composers, and interesting examples in percussion writing lie hidden in this material. Quite early in his career film music attracted the attention of a composer whose inventions in the use of percussion seem inexhaustible – Benjamin Britten. In his works for full orchestra, and in his compositions for a smaller ensemble, Britten captures the essence of each percussion instrument. The dramatic element of the timpani is aptly expressed

---

[1] It is said that, at a convivial gathering in London, he performed *solo* the greater part of the percussion score of *The Rio Grande* – written for five players. Among the eminent composers of the past who had practical experience of percussion playing were Haydn, Meyerbeer, Massenet and Adolphe Charles Adam.

in his opera *Billy Budd* (1951), particularly in the funeral march where he uses three timpanists. The writing for the timpani is similarly expressive in his first opera *Peter Grimes* (1945), and in such later works as *War Requiem* (1961) and Cello Symphony (1964). In *The Prince of the Pagodas* (1956) the tuned percussion is used extensively. Here, as in his later opera *Death in Venice*, the orchestration unquestionably captures the timbre of the gender and saron of the gamelan orchestra.

The variation for percussion in *The Young Person's Guide to the Orchestra* (1947) is considered to be one of the most delightful show-pieces in the orchestral repertoire; Britten's individual use of percussion is equally expressed in his chamber operas. Though demanding, he never presents the performer with an impossibility. On the contrary, like Holst, Stravinsky and Bartók, his scoring indicates obvious calculation, and an acquaintance with percussion generally. That he has long been attracted by the potentialities of pedal-tuning timpani is clear from his early scores. In *The Rape of Lucretia* (1946) occurs a recurring scale passage featuring the timpani melodically. There is also a solo passage for bass drum, tenor drum, side drum and cymbal.

Rape of Lucretia   Britten

In the operas *Albert Herring* (1947) and *The Beggar's Opera* (1948) pedal-tuning drums are used extensively. The combination of bass, tenor drum and side drum (a favourite one with Britten as with Milhaud) is included. In variation four 'Tom, Tom the Piper's Son' from *The Turn of the Screw* (1954), the timpani are added to the combination of bass drum, tenor drum and side drum. (*see following page*).

In *The Turn of the Screw* the writing for the tubular bells is such that it would be difficult to find a work where the scoring for orchestral chimes has been more fully explored. With the use of such effects as grace notes, a three-note clash produced so: (*see Fig. 56 on page 423*) the use of the damping mechanism to clarify

Fourth Variation : Tom, Tom the Piper's Son   Britten

rapid passages, and the unique employment of glissandi (played with the handle of
the bell hammer), Britten brings the belfry to the opera house. The solo for the four
timpani in the introduction to Act I, and in the orchestral variation to open Act II,
also the motif on six timpani in the finale are representative of the writing throughout, and render this work, like Stravinsky's *The Soldier's Tale*, a 'pearl' among
percussion scores.

422

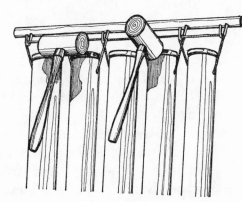

Fig. 56
Chimes
(three-note clash)

The obbligato for timpani in Britten's *Nocturne for Tenor Solo, Seven Obbligato Instruments and String Orchestra* (1958), is an ideal example of the possibilities of the modern machine drum. In this work the timpani obbligato starts with a sinister motif on four drums of fixed pitch which is followed by the solo movement for pedal timpani. The ascending and descending passages are chromatic in all cases, and are carefully planned so that each drum recommences on the note on which it has previously been halted, allowing the player full concentration on one drum at a time.

The above three examples by Benjamin Britten are by permission of Boosey & Hawkes, Music Publishers Ltd., London.

Machine drums are used significantly to portray Bottom's snore in *A Midsummer Night's Dream* (1960). A small drum (*tamburo*) in F sharp is used in this opera as an accompaniment to the solo trumpet.

A well recognized aspect of Britten's ingenuity is his gift for employing unusual

423

instruments.[1] In *Noyes Fludde* (1958) the patter of raindrops is culled from a series of slung mugs struck with wooden spoons (the result of experiments with kitchen utensils in Imogen Holst's Aldeburgh home). There is also the ethereal sound from handbells (played traditionally by a group of ringers).

Britten scores for a series of handbells in *Curlew River* (1964). Here the bells are suspended and played with xylophone beaters. The percussion in this work is in the hands of a soloist (the instrumental ensemble comprises only seven players, virtually members of the cast). The percussion instrumentation is simple – five small untuned drums, a bell or gong in C[2] and the series of small bells already mentioned. The several effects from the drums include the use of thimbles, fingers, flat of the hand, soft and hard sticks, and the many tones obtainable from the edge and centre of the drums. At the start and the close of the work Britten uses the slowly accelerating tremolo used on the Japanese taiko – indicated (⬥ıllllll). By contrast, in *The Burning Fiery Furnace* (1966) the tremolo commences as a 'close roll' and loses speed (|||||llı)·. In this opera the percussion requirements are five small untuned drums,[3] anvil, two tuned wood blocks, to sound 𝄞, a lyra glockenspiel (used in the procession), a pair of small cymbals, a multiple whip (four tones) typifying the crackling flames, and a Babylonian drum (to sound 𝄢).[4] Here is no fastidious request for bizarre effects. On the contrary, Britten has represented visually and aurally, as far as is possible, instruments known in Old Testament Babylon.

In latter years composers have made effective use of the more simple instruments of percussion in symphonic works. Except in Mahler, such instruments were rarely heard in large scale orchestral compositions. To-day, they fall into place quite naturally in major works. Outstanding examples of the combined use of modest instruments of indefinite pitch, and such tuned percussion as the marimba and vibraphone (with the timpani, etc.), are found in the symphonic works by Copland, Arnold and Tippett. Copland's Third Symphony and *Music for a Great City* are representative of his style.

Thirty years ago, the inclusion in a symphonic work of an anvil, slapstick, wood block, ratchet, claves and rim-shot, would have been surprising. Not so to-day:

[1] Some of which he has created.

[2] For this, the author experimented (with the help of the Mitcham Foundry) with bronze plates.

[3] For the original productions five graduated Chinese drums (as illustrated) were used.

[4] Produced from the author's private collection, or manufactured with the assistance of patient friends, to the composer's requirements. (See plate 182.)

Copland used them all effectively in his Third Symphony (1946), which also contains imaginative use of the xylophone and glockenspiel.[1] In the finale, full advantage is taken of the range of the modern cluster of timpani, i.e. [musical notation]. In *Music for a Great City* (1964), *El Salón Mexico* (1939) and *Rodeo* (1946), Copland again employs a full percussion section, strengthening the indigenous American and Latin-American element in these works. In *Appalachian Spring* (1945) an important part is given to the xylophone, an instrument Copland uses frequently. It occurs in his *Dance Symphony* for large orchestra (1931), here alternating with a wood block.

Appalachian Spring   Copland

By permission of Boosey & Hawkes, Music Publishers Ltd., London.

Reference to the xylophone calls to mind the style of writing for this instrument in such works as Tippett's Concerto for Orchestra (1963) and *Vision of St. Augustine* (1965), Addison's *Carte Blanche* (1956), William Bardwell's *Little Serenade* (1953), and *Fantasy on Japanese Wood Prints* by Alan Hovhaness (1965). It is a great credit to the modern player that composers should entrust such exacting parts to the xylophone and other melodic percussion. In *Vision of St. Augustine* Tippett writes for marimba; at times in the same register as the xylophone. Here he wishes two distinct instruments to be used, to ensure the resulting contrast in tone quality in a similar register. In his Second Piano Concerto Henze writes for the xylophone as formidably.[2]

Tippett's writing for the timpani is equally challenging, as a glance at the scores of the First Symphony (1945), *King Priam* (1962), Concerto for Orchestra, and his most recent opera *The Knot Garden* (1967) will show. In the last-named work he asks for a series of five tuned temple blocks [musical notation].

Bardwell's *Little Serenade* for piccolo, xylophone and mandolin (typically Eastern in style) shows the possibilities of the xylophone as a chamber instrument. Xylophonists are unanimous in their appreciation of Bardwell's use of this instrument in such delicate structure. They are equally agreed about Addison's use of the xylophone as a solo instrument in his *Carte Blanche*. This work was a favourite with Sir Thomas Beecham.

[1] See also his First Symphony (1931).

[2] The technically formidable part in Henze's Piano Concerto No. 2 (1967) was resolved by an eminent xylophonist assembling, in a single row, the required notes from three xylophones (nicknamed *Henzephone*).

Composers' Use of Modern Percussion

In Malcolm Arnold's scoring for percussion, his practical knowledge of the manipulation to its best advantage of the percussion team is evident.[1] An influence of jazz, and a liking for the rhythm and the instruments of the Latin-American orchestra is also clear, particularly in the Fourth Symphony (1960) where the marimba, maracas, bongos and tom toms are prominent in a vivid orchestration. He writes floridly for the timpani, though at all times with an awareness of the kettledrummer's craft, and of the numerous subtleties of the instrument. He is partial to a three-note pattern with the drums tuned in fourths (which surely remains their most arresting interval). The figure occurs in the true Arnold manner, in the finale of the First Symphony (1952), the Second Symphony (1953) and *Four Scottish Dances* (1957).

Many of the percussion instruments of Latin-America now have a permanent place in serious compositions. In some cases, certain of these age-old instruments colour modern orchestration in a novel manner. In Bernstein's *Jeremiah* Symphony, the timpani are beaten with maracas. Farberman employs this effect in his Concerto for Timpani and Orchestra (1962).[2] Bernstein's stylish use of percussion is portrayed in *The Age of Anxiety* and *West Side Story*. Further composers with a definite place in the history of percussion are Samuel Barber and Menotti. To the timpanist Samuel Barber is best known for his timpani accompaniment to the voices in *A Stopwatch and an Ordnance Map* (1942). Of the works of Menotti (who incidentally wrote the libretto for Barber's opera *Vanessa*), *The Medium* and *The Consul* are indicative of his use of percussion.

Such examples as the foregoing works and those of Bartók and Britten, and for further examples Richard Arnell's Fourth Symphony (1947), Andrzej Panufnik's *Sinfonia Sacra* (1966) (a work with an extensive part for pedal timpani and percussion), and Symphony No. 7 (1968) by Egon Wellesz, are representative of the general expansion in the use of timpani by modern composers. In addition to exploiting the numerous possibilities of tone colour and unique effects, in recent years there has been an increased use of the extreme upper and lower registers of the timpani. Milhaud's exceptionally high tuning 𝄞 is no longer unique, the use of the high C and D is now fairly common, and notes above this register are not infrequent. An outstanding example of the use of piccolo timpani is to be found in a work by Philip Lambro, *Two Pictures* for solo percussion and orchestra (1966).

Low D and D flat (cf. Mahler) occur frequently to-day. In rare cases timpani basso

---

[1] He was for some time principal trumpet of the London Philharmonic Orchestra.
[2] The Rumanian-born composer Marius Constant writes similarly for maracas in his ballet *Paradis Perdu* (1967) similarly Prokofiev in *Romeo and Juliet,* (1935).

Fourth Symphony ... Richard Arnell

Andante

Composer's note to timpanist "Please play all of this symphony as a solo part"   *By permission of Hinrichsen Ltd., London.*

are requested: Stokowski in his arrangement of Bach's *Komm Süsser Tod* writes for the low C. Harsanyi in his *Suite pour Orchestre* requests the low B 𝄢. (A single low C, possibly a slip of the pen, occurs in the Dead March in *Caractacus* by an unknown composer c. 1795 – BM vol.: G227).

To-day there is no lack of the instruments necessary to comply with these requests. Piccolo timpani to cope with the high C and beyond are fairly common, as are drums measuring thirty inches or more in diameter, necessary for good results in the lower register. Some players prefer to use large drums for notes in the middle register. Whether this is advisable on special occasions is a matter of opinion. H. C. Robbins Landon says[1]: 'It has become the fashion to employ very large and highly resonant timpani in modern orchestras. For the execution of eighteenth-century music this is a mistake: Haydn's brass and drum parts should be able to be played forte without drowning the other instruments, and as far as the latter are concerned this is only possible on the small kettledrums employed during the period, on which the drummer can play loudly without causing the unpleasant deep reverberations caused by large timpani.'

The manufacturers of musical instruments have responded admirably to the continual expansion of ideas on the part of the composer, and the constant demand of performers for the ultimate. Messrs. Zildjian, together with their wide range or cymbals and gongs have made available a large range of crotales, (instruments used so advantageously by Petrassi, Nono, Dallapiccola, Richard Rodney Bennett, Peter Schat and others). Similarly Messrs. Paiste have delved successfully into the production of tam-tams and gongs. Reference has been made to the several manufacturers who are responsible for to-day's efficient machine timpani. The modern side drum has made possible numerous subtle effects. With the tuned percussion there is now available to the composer the colour of the vibraphone – with or without vibrato. The xylophone gives numerous tone shades; also the marimba with its organ-like quality in the lower register and unique sound in the higher octaves. To these can be added the introduction in recent years (due in many cases to collaboration between composer, player and maker) of unique instruments, or the expansion of existing types, factors which have played no small part in modern compositions.

[1] Landon, H. C. Robbins. *The Symphonies of Joseph Haydn*, London, 1955, p. 126.

Composers' Use of Modern Percussion

Among those composers associated with the 'new look' are Messiaen, Francis Chagrin, Humphrey Searle, Bruno Maderna and Elisabeth Lutyens. Olivier Messiaen has given us remarkable examples of the use of modern percussion, such as those to be found in *Trois petites liturgies de la Présence Divine* (1944), and in such later works as *Turangalîla* (1947), *Chronochromie* (1963), *Et exspecto resurrectionem mortuorum* (1964) and *7 Haikai* (1962). In *Chronochromie* there is an exacting part for xylophone, marimba, glockenspiel (piano-action) and tubular bells (*cloches* – two chromatic octaves). The composer states that the parts for these instruments are difficult, and demand excellent instrumentalists.

In *Et exspecto resurrectionem mortuorum* and *7 Haikai*, Messiaen writes for a fantastic array of percussion instruments. The emphasis is on the timbre of the Far Eastern gamelan, conjured from a combination of glockenspiel, vibraphone, tubular bells, celeste, numerous gongs and cymbals and similar instruments of an exotic character. Three sets of cowbells are required in *Et exspecto resurrectionem mortuorum*:

Francis Chagrin's Prelude and Fugue (1947) and Suite No. 1 for Orchestra (1957) contain excellent examples of the use of the modern percussion section. In addition to his activity in forward composition, Chagrin was prominent among those connected with the promotion of new music, being the founder of the Society for the Promotion of New Music in 1943.

In Searle's opera *The Diary of a Madman* (1958) the timpani and melodic percussion are prominent. The cascades of sound from the glockenspiel, xylophone and vibraphone are typical of Searle's style. In his Second Symphony (1959) there is a 'solo' duet for *tambours militaires*.

Maderna's Serenata No. 2 for eleven instruments (1957) is an interesting example of the use of the glockenspiel, xylophone and vibraphone, as is Divertimento for Orchestra (Berio-Maderna) in the employment of a large percussion force.

Elisabeth Lutyens' earliest scores show the use of the contrasting colours of tam-tams, gongs and cymbals, together with a wide use of timpani and tuned percussion. Percussion is prominent in her later works, e.g. *Catena* (1960), *Symphonies* (1961) and *Time Off? Not a ghost of a chance!* (1972).[1]

Among composers who have written extensively for orchestral percussion during

---

[1] The fact that many women composers have made such active use of percussion instruments is not surprising if we consider that for centuries instruments of music, excluding the martial drums, were their prerogative. Works by Dame Ethel Smyth, Priaulx Rainier, Elizabeth Poston, Elizabeth Maconchy, Phyllis Tate, Ruth Gipps and Thea Musgrave could be quoted as examples.

recent years are Henze, Hartmann, Elliott Carter, Gunther Schuller, Orff, Boulez and Stockhausen.

Their works are illustrative of the trend in latter years. Hartmann's Seventh Symphony (1960) and Henze's opera *Elegy for Young Lovers* (1961) and his Fifth Symphony, could be quoted as examples of what is expected of the modern timpanist. In his Seventh Symphony Hartmann employs two timpanists, and gives them virtuoso solo passages to be played in chamber style. In the Eighth Symphony (1963) the tuned percussion is prominent. Here are cadenzas for two marimbas, two vibraphones, xylophone and glockenspiel.

Henze's writing for the percussion family is well illustrated in *Antifone* (1960), a work which opens with a jet of sound culled from the contrasting timbres of 22 percussion instruments. Commencing with the depth of a bass tam-tam, the pitch steadily rises through a series of smaller tom-toms, gongs, cymbals and various drums, and approaches its peak by way of four crotales, followed by four triangles of different sizes and terminating with a single glockenspiel note in the highest register. This combination of instruments is used later in the work in a solo cadenza.

Examples of the elaborate use of percussion are found in Gunther Schuller's Music for Violin, Piano and Percussion (1957), *Seven Studies on Themes of Paul Klee* (1959), and *Contours* (1960); also in Elliott Carter's Double Concerto for Harpsichord and Piano (1961), and his Concerto for Orchestra (1969). Schuller writes extensively for timpani and vibraphone in the *Seven Studies*. The request in this work for the bass drum to be tuned to low C is unusual.[1] Carter's earlier work which calls for 45 percussion instruments is without timpani, or (excluding crotales), melodic percussion. Four percussionists are involved. Carter gives precise instructions to each. The details regarding the various types of mallets necessary are supplemented with readily-recognisable diagrams, both at the beginning of the work and throughout (a fairly common procedure to-day). The fact that this work contains no part for the timpani does not signify any lack of interest on Carter's part for these instruments; on the contrary, that he values them highly is obvious from his Six Pieces for Kettledrums (1960). In *Canto* and *Adagio* (1966), also for unaccompanied kettledrums, he makes extensive use of pedal timpani. In *Recitative* and *Improvisation* (Six Pieces for Kettledrums) he uses chords and specifies controlled resonance (*see following page*).

Works for unaccompanied timpani, such as those of Carter's are rare. Daniel Jones' Sonata for Three Unaccompanied Kettledrums (1953) is a commendable addition to this limited repertoire, as is Alan Boustead's Sonata for Timpani (1960), Sonatina for Timpani (1967) by Alan Ridout. (Daniel Jones' Sonata is recorded by

[1] In the revised editions of *The Rite of Spring* (1947 and '67) at fig. 128 Stravinsky asks for the bass drum to be played at the edge with wooden sticks and to sound in the region of B flat.

Recitative and Improvisation for Four Kettledrums (one player) Elliott Carter

Notes with ✕ heads indicate the moment at which each drum is to be damped

Tristan Fry on EMI CFP 40207). The mid-seventeenth-century March for Two Pairs of Kettledrums by the Brothers Philidor has recently been revived as a concert item. Occasional works for unaccompanied kettledrums have existed in unpublished manuscript form. G. Gordon Cleather played, as a concert item, a work of his own composition for thirteen timpani. He also used the timpani with the church organ. In a lecture delivered at the Royal College of Organists in February 1908, he said[1]: 'Timpani add a solemnity and grandeur to the musical service of the Church which I have found recognised and appreciated wherever I have played. I played twice every Sunday for fifteen years at the Church where I first introduced them.' In recent years the timpani and organ are combined only occasionally: outstanding examples in Britain are Sir Malcolm Sargent's combination of organ and timpani with the voices of the Royal Choral Society on the occasions of the Society's annual carol concerts, and that of Frederick Haggis with the Goldsmith's Choral Union.

Poulenc's scoring for the timpani in his Concerto in G minor for organ, strings and timpani (1939) is unique. Similarly the combination of timpani and organ by the Dutch composer Henk Badings in his *Passacaglia* (1958). Alan Ridout gives the

[1] Cleather, G. Gordon. *The Timpani, with special reference to their use with the Organ*, printed for the Royal College of Organists, 1908, p. 29.

430

kettledrums an outstanding part in his *L'Orgue Concrète* ('*Il combattimento d'organo e Batteria*') (1966). Elizabeth Poston combines timpani and chimes with the organ in a choral work: *Superest Plebs Pessima* (1961). (The combination of voices, organ and chimes has proved a most satisfactory ensemble, as has the combination of brass and chimes.)[1]

The timpani concerto is a recent development in the field of music. Until Tcherepnine's delightful Sonatina for two (or three) timpani written in 1940 (revised 1951), the repertoire of the timpani as a solo instrument has been modest, consisting (in published form) only of such works as the late nineteenth century compositions by Pieranzovini and Tausch (q.v.). In latter years a number of concerti have been added to the constantly increasing mass of percussion literature. The contemporary composer in exploiting new possibilities of sonority, has been influenced by the flexibility of modern percussion instruments and the co-operation and skill of the performer. The potentialities of modern machine timpani, melodically and tonally, are extensively realized in Concerto for Timpani and Orchestra by Werner Thärichen (1954); Concerto for Five Kettledrums and Orchestra by Robert Parris (1955); and Concerto for Timpani and Orchestra by Harold Farberman (1962). (All eminent timpanists). Prokofiev wrote a Virtuoso Study for 5 timpani, published 1948 in a Russian tutor by State Publishing Co. Moscow. (Highly recommended tutor, as are those for side drum, etc.).

Other concertos for timpani and orchestra include *Mytho Logica* by Karl Heinz Köper, *Capricietto* for Timpani and String Orchestra by Ottmar Gerster, Concerto for Five Timpani and Orchestra by Jorge Sarmientos, and Theme and Variations and Introduction and Allegro for timpani by Saul Goodman (timpanist of the New York Philharmonic Orchestra for nearly half a century, and described by Pierre Boulez as 'a legend on his instrument').

The use of the timpani as an integral part of the ensemble is well represented in such works as Martinů's Concerto for Two String Orchestras, Piano and Timpani (1939), Kenneth Leighton's Viola Concerto (with harp, strings and kettledrums) (1952), Donatoni's Concerto for Strings, Timpani and Percussion (1950), Frank Martin's Concerto for Seven Wind Instruments and Timpani (1950), and Graham Whettam's *Sinfonietta Stravagante* (1964).

The percussion ensemble has attracted many composers: Stravinsky (*Les Noces*), Milhaud (*Les Choéphores* and *Christopher Columbus*), Carl Orff, Luigi Nono and Alexander Goehr.

[1] The combination of timpani and piano and percussion and piano is effectively used by Britten in *Timpani Piece for Jimmy* (the author) and Arnold in *Concert Piece for Percussion and Piano*. For Malcolm Arnold, see App. 6.

Composers' Use of Modern Percussion

Andreas Liess says[1]: 'Orff has created in the percussion orchestra an individual instrument for the expression of rhythm as a symbol of magic. Even in his earliest work, his preference for percussion and for the piano as a percussion instrument was evident.' In three of his works for the stage (*Catulli Carmina, Astutuli* and *Ludus de Nato Infante Mirificus*) Orff uses an ensemble composed entirely of percussion instruments. In all cases the writing is that of a composer with the gift of producing rhythmic and tonal intensity without complexity. In *Comoedia de Christi Resurrectione* the orchestra, with the exception of the harp and double basses, is comprised of percussion, and elsewhere where the full orchestra is employed, he frequently accompanies dialogue with percussion only. Orff's requirements are lavish, and in some cases unique in modern literature, as for instance, his revival of the *steinspiel*, his use of musical glasses (struck and played with the finger-tips), the *waldteufel*, and in the melodic percussion the inclusion of metallophones and trough xylophones (soprano, tenor and bass). The latter instruments are to his own design and are a feature in his *Schulwerk*.[2] It is not surprising that Orff employs percussion so actively. His ambition at school was to study the timpani. The fact that this was never realized resulted in no loss in his regard for the instrument. His style (predominately rhythmic and frequently capturing the sound of the Far Eastern gamelan) is well portrayed in *Catulli Carmina, Antigonae* and *Astutuli*. In *Antigonae* he writes for ten to fifteen percussionists in addition to the timpanist. The requirements are timpani (seven to eight drums), xylophones, trough xylophones, wood blocks, bells, glockenspiels, ten pairs of cymbals, anvil, three triangles, two bass drums, six tambourines, six pairs of castanets, a soprano steinspiel, ten Javanese gongs and six grand pianos (played directly with drum sticks).[3]

Further examples of the use of a percussion ensemble as an accompaniment to voices are to be found in Luigi Nono's *Cori di Didone for Chorus and percussion* (1958) and in *Virtutes* for chorus, piano duet and percussion (1963/4) by Alexander Goehr.[4] Goehr's aptitude for producing attractive sounds echoes the originality of his eminent father Walter Goehr, a pioneer in composition and arrangement.

Interesting examples of the use of a percussion ensemble to support a solo instrument, and as an integral part of a chamber ensemble are, *Favola* for B flat clarinet and *Batteria grande* (Sven-Erik Báck), *The Burning House* Overture for flute and percussion (Alan Hovhaness), Lou Harrison's Concerto for Violin and Percussion, and Karl-Birger Blomdahl's *Concert du Camera* for piano, woodwind and percussion.

[1] Liess, Andreas. *Carl Orff*, Calder and Boyars, London, 1966, p. 45.
[2] The vibraphone seems not to interest him.
[3] This effect and others of a similar nature occur frequently in avant-garde composition.
[4] Nono also used a vast percussion force in Intelleranzo(1962).

Other examples include Music for Cembalo and Percussion and *Triofolium*, Karl Schöfer; Sonatine, Peter Benary; Divertimento, Jurg Baur (all edited by Franzpeter Goebels); Fantasy for piano and percussion, Ian Parrott; Duo for Timpani, Vibraphone and Piano, David Harries; *Four Études* (Percussion and Chamber Orchestra), Marius Constant; *Sonata da Camera*, Don Banks; *Improvisation Seven* (for Grilly), Franco Donatoni; *Meditations* for Soprano, Organ and Percussion (thirteen executants) by the Polish composer Augustine Bloch; *Available Forms* by Earle Brown; *Suite Ancienne* by Maurice Jarre; and *Chant après chant* for voice, piano and six percussion players by Jean Barraqué.

The percussion ensemble is no innovation if we consider the Asiatic gamelan, and the drum and xylophone ensembles of Africa and Latin-America. As we know it to-day, the percussion ensemble originated in all probability with compositions by Russolo, Antheil, Varèse and Ardēval. In *Ionisation* (1931) Varèse divides 34 percussion instruments between 13 executants. The instrumentation, which includes bongos, maracas, anvils (high and low) and sirens of different tones, is well known.[1] Equally well known is Chávez' Toccata for percussion instruments, written twenty years later. These works are monumental in the history of the percussion ensemble, as are William Russell's *Fugue for Eight Percussion Instruments* and Henry Cowell's *Ostinato Pianissimo*. A comparison of the instrumentation of the modern percussion ensemble with that of the works of Varèse and Chávez is interesting. What may have appeared in the past to be prodigious, is in many instances dwarfed by present-day requirements, (which includes in many cases two or more distinct groups of percussion). As an illustration of modern requirements we quote Peter Schat's *Signalement*, written in 1961 for the Percussion Group of Strasbourg.[2] The requirements are as follows: xylorimbas (two), marimba, vibraphone, chimes and glockenspiel, two sets of crotales (each, one chromatic octave), and two sets of tuned

cowbells ♪ timpani (to cover a compass of nearly two octaves)

♪ twelve suspended cymbals and two pairs of cymbals, six tam-

8va

tams, eleven tom-toms, two conga drums, two pairs of bongos, two African drums, three side drums and two bass drums, seven temple blocks, two whips, three cowbells of no particular pitch, claves, maracas and a piano. To-day, an ensemble of this description is not unusual, e.g., Miloslav Kabelac's *Eight Inventions for instruments of percussion*, *Reaktionen* for four percussionists by Bo Nilsson, the ballet *Diadalos* by

---

[1] Varèse had already used a sizeable and unusual percussion force in *Hyperprism* and *Intégrales*.
[2] *Les Percussions de Strasbourg*.

Hans Otte, which is accompanied by a percussion group of six players, the opera *Amerika* by Roman Haubenstock-Ramati (four percussion groups) and his *Mobile für sechs Schlagzeuggruppen, Parallels for two percussion players* by Tim Souster, and *Rhapsody Fantasy* for percussion soloist and small orchestra by Michael Colgrass, In Diario Polacco' 58 Luigi Nono writes for sixteen percussionists. The instruments are divided into four groups and include four slit drums, four *Tamb di legno-pelle* (double-headed drums - wood and vellum, both utilized) and four thin metal sheets.

There is no lack of written material for the modern percussion ensemble. Composers (and players) are constantly adding to the already sizeable repertoie. The following could be quoted as representative: Concerto for Percussion and Orchestra, Henry Cowell; Suite for Percussion, William Kraft; *Salmigondis* for Timbales, percussion instruments and piano, Pierre-Petit; *How the Stars were made*, Peter Sculthorpe; *Sambas for six Percussionists*, Jacques Charpentier; *Auriga* for four percussionists, Reginald Smith Brindle; *Three Brothers*, Michael Colgrass; Études *Choreographiques*, Maurice Ohana; *Designs for Percussion Instruments*, Leonard Salzedo; Symphony for Drums and Wind Orchestra, Warren Benson; *Quotations in Percussion*, Arthor Cohn; *October Mountain* for percussion sextet, Alan Hovhaness; *Cantata per America Magica* for fifty-three percussion instruments and dramatic soparano, Alberto Ginastera; *Double Music for Percussion Quartet*, John Cage and Lou Harrison; Concerto for Percussion, Saul Goodman; *Variations on a Lyrical Theme*, Robert Lombardo; *First Construction in Metal* and *She is asleep*, John Cage and the various works by Morris Goldenberg, William Schinstine, Charles L. White, Harold Farberman, Vic Firth, *Festive Drumming*, Yiu-Kwong Chung; Peter Tanner and Dick Schory (Schory's name is synonymous with percussion, and the development of the modern percussion ensemble).[1] An attractive addition to the repertoire for percussion ensemble is John Mayer's concerto for tabla, mrdanga, tambura and western percussion.

The combination of brass and percussion has proved attractive to Gunther Schuller, Symphony for Brass and Percussion; William Alwyn, *Fanfare for a Joyous Occasion* for Brass and Percussion, (dedicated to the author); the Israeli composer Noam Sheriff, *Destination Five for Brass and Percussion;* Chou Wen-Chung, *Soliloquy of Bhiksuni* for Trumpet and Brass with Percussion Ensemble; Donald Erl, *Diversion for Two* for trumpet and percussion; Edward Miller, *Le Mi le Sol* for percussion and brass quartet; William Sydeman, Duo for Trumpet and Percussion; and Yiu-Kwong Chung, *Chariots Ballad.*

[1]See current literature e.g. the Journals of The Percussive Arts Society, *Percussive Notes* and *Percussionist*. Also the catalogues of the International Percussion Reference Library (Arizona State University), and *Solo Literature for Percussion*, 1972, (University of Tennessee), see Appendix 6.

Composers' Use of Modern Percussion

The modern percussion ensemble flourishes universally. It has for example, taken firm root in Japan, a land steeped in the tradition of drumming, e.g., Tokyo Percussion Ensemble. In Britain there is the Percussion Ensemble of London (formed by James Holland, principal percussionist of the B.B.C Symphony Orchestra). *Les Percussions de Strasbourg* is representative of Continental combinations, and in the U.S.A. there is (among others) the famous Dick Schory Percussion Ensemble.

To-day, particularly in the U.S.A., percussion is a feature in the life of the university, college and school. Almost every institution has its percussion ensemble (many of the world's major orchestras also). The drum corps is also a dominant factor in school life. Here is a medium in which young people the world over freely express their rhythmic instinct in a well-disciplined manner. There is surely no better example of the drum corps than those found in Switzerland, sponsored by the late Dr. Fritz Berger, q.v. As an example of the interest in corps drumming in Britain could be given 'The Coventry School of Music Corps of Drums' founded 1945, winners of numerous competitive awards.[1]

The corps of drums in some form or other is centuries old; there seems little doubt of its activity in future years. But what of the prevailing focus on the percussion ensemble and the use of the percussion force in the orchestra? Once again we find opinions sharply divided. There are those who contend that only the surface of the possibilities of percussion has been skimmed. Others are of the opinion that their potentialities have been almost fully exploited, and that the time is not far distant when composers will seek a fresh medium of expression. One factor however is unquestionable, and that is the enthusiasm of the present-day percussionist. These factors have never been more necessary. Only a zealot can do justice to the demands of Boulez and Stockhausen.

The name of Pierre Boulez (a pupil of Messiaen as was Stockhausen) is synonymous with percussion instruments. Boulez, in *Le marteau sans maître* (1954-7), a chamber work for alto voice and six instruments, flute, viola, guitar and three percussionists, launched a new phase in the use of percussion instruments, particularly in his scoring for the xylophone and vibraphone. The weaving of these instruments in the fragmented texture employs the players in a challenging manner. No less so the third percussionist, to whom Boulez gives the most precise instructions regarding the manipulation of side drum, bongos, maracas, double cowbell, tam-tam (*aigu*), tam-tam (*très profond*), gong (*grave*), cymbal (*grande*), and two cymbalettes and triangle; the latter instrument for instance to be struck on both sides alternately, and

[1] Drums, xylophones, 'dulcimers', handbells, and fairy bells were a feature of Dr. Barnardo's bands as far back as the latter part of the last century. (From *The National Waifs Magazine*, December, 1902).

Le marteau sans maître

Pierre Boulez

the sound dampened with the third and fourth fingers. That Boulez is deeply influenced by African and Eastern music is manifest in his writing for percussion. The sound of the Far East is heard in *Le marteau sans maître*, and even more so in a later work *Pli selon pli*, where a gamelan-like array of high-pitched percussion instruments is added to a full section of normal symphonic percussion – a force that has been described as a celestial kitchen. The melodic percussion includes two five-octave xylorimbas, two vibraphones, glockenspiel, a series of large cowbells, two octaves of tubular bells, and two octaves of bell plates (the bell plates being made to the composers' specification).

No. 9, *Zyklus* (1960) by Stockhausen is a work for solo percussionist. It demands not only a high degree of skill from the performer, but also his creative ability. As a detailed description of Stockhausen's work is only possible by quoting the whole of the score and the multitude of instruments, a summary is submitted. Graphic illustrations are given of each instrument, and of the type of beaters required. In the place of traditional notation, time values are indicated with symbols; similarly speed, intensity, etc. Symbols are also given to indicate the exchangeability of groups and periods and performance selectivity; also for strict measures. Freedom is given to the performer to begin at any point in the score[1] (*see following page*).

Stockhausen's orchestral style is clearly seen in No. 6. *Gruppen für drei Orchester* (1958). The percussion forces are large in each case. In *Mikrophonie I* (1960) a work for large tam-tam (two players) two microphones, two filters and controls, Stockhausen's use of the tam-tam is unique.

Further composers to exploit the possibilities of modern percussion include Luciano Berio and Siegfried Fink. In *Circles* (1960), a composition for female voice, harp and two percussion players, Berio requests among a gigantic array of percussion: Indian tablā, wood chimes, glass chimes and *lujon* (a metal plate – box-resonated). The singer plays claves, finger cymbals, wood chimes and glass chimes. (These instruments are in addition to those in the percussion section). Fink's *Ritmo* (1971) for Percussion Ensemble – 7 players is fully scored for Latin-American instruments.

The Polish composer Wlodzimierz Kotoński's *Trio per Flauto, Chitarra e Percussione* (1962) is another example of the use of the modern percussion section, also of

[1] At the turn of the nineteenth century (1802), Sir George Smart, whilst in Paris with friends, wrote: 'all five went underground to another coffee-room to hear a concert and a man play upon five drums, triangle and small bells at once . . .' (From *Leaves from the Journals of Sir George Smart*, Longman Green, London, 1907, p. 20). If Sir George was impressed by that feat, it would be interesting to hear his reactions to the executant in *Zyklus*, or to the percussion recitals of the Japanese virtuoso, Stomu Yamash'ta. (The player described by Sir George Smart was no doubt the French drummer who is reported to have earned his livelihood by attending different coffee-rooms and playing a concerto.)

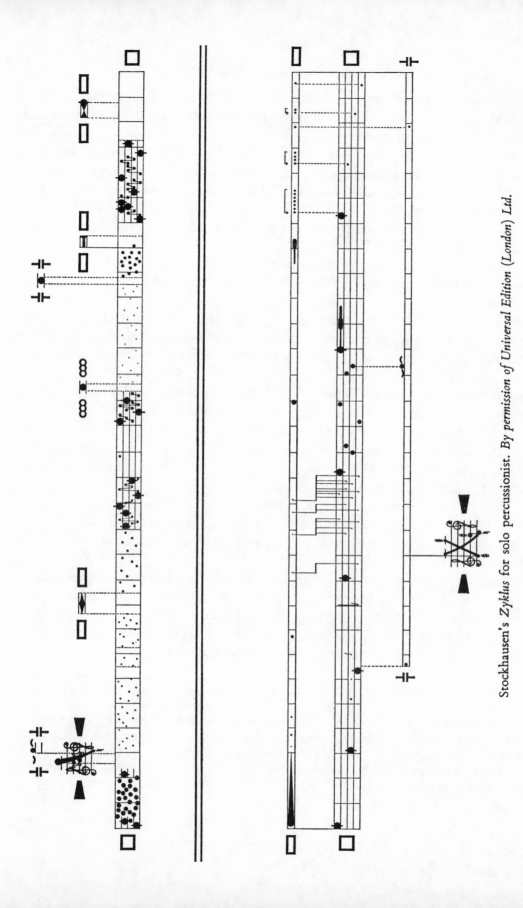

Stockhausen's *Zyklus* for solo percussionist. By permission of Universal Edition (London) Ltd.

the manner in which composers allocate the percussion instruments in an extended stave.

To-day the normal stave is in many cases quite inadequate. The use of a percussion score, such as Varèse, Milhaud and subsequent composers employ for a percussion ensemble, is also quite often impracticable for a solo performer. Percussionists are unanimous in that there is need for improvement in notating their instruments, particularly where multiple percussion is concerned, also that a strict percussion clef is long overdue. It is surely not unreasonable to submit, they say, that a more careful use should also be made of the normal stave. With minor exceptions, an immutable allocation of such instruments as bass drum, tenor drum, side drum, cymbals and triangle, could certainly be observed. Such examples as the following (unfortunately no exaggeration) are quite inexcusable

The consideration given to the percussionist's problems by many modern composers is a forward step. Easily recognisable shapes (similar to those already discussed) are given defining the instruments, beaters and method of use, e.g. ⌒ a suspended cymbal struck with soft stick, ( ) cymbals clashed, ⊙ tambourine and so forth (an illustration of the triangle △ has been used for many years). All concerned with preparing the percussionist's score would do well to study Professor Luigi Torrebruno's[1] *Notazione per Strumenti a Percussione*. Here, each instrument of indefinite pitch is unmistakably defined (the timpani and tuned percussion are relatively trouble free). Brought into general use, this document would solve many problems. Similarly, the signs used by percussionists could be generally adopted, (such as the marking of an important cymbal stroke in red), for, at the present rate of expansion, a complete colour scheme is not inconceivable.

Luigi Torrebruno

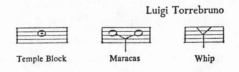

Temple Block   Maracas   Whip

Of late, in many avant-garde works, there has evolved, in addition to a new style of percussion clef, a new manner of notating time values. These are indicated

[1] Former timpanist of the Orchestra of La Scala, and Professor of Percussion, Verdi Conservatoire, Milan. (See also Siegfried Fink's *Tabulatur 72*, EE2826. Simrock, Hamburg and London.)

in various ways, chronometrically or proportionally by means of squares and rectangles: etc. Considerable freedom is given regarding the distribution of the various tones, and the expression of rhythmic sequences within the limits of the prescribed time factors. The scores of such works as *Actions for Six* (1965) by Bernard Rands, *Zyklus* by Stockhausen, and *Das Fleisch des Kreuges* (1964 by Ladislau Kupavic and *Aria pour timbales et quelques instruments,* Guiseppe G. Englert (1965) are representative of these styles of notation, which in comparison with the traditional stave is indeed a new language *(see facing page).*

In latter years, as well as their prominence in the repertoire of the orchestra, percussion has been used importantly in such experiments as machine-music, *musique concrete,* and is today a feature of the highly scientific electronic music. Opinions are divided concerning the values and the future of Electronic Percussion and whether such remarkable 'machinery' as the Midi synthesizer will be further developed as a part of contemporary percussion, and ultimately present a serious challenge to 'live' music.

Many are convinced that nothing will ever replace the skills of a great artist and his rapport with his instrument. Norman Weinberg (Electronics editor of The Percussive Arts of America) and Assistant Professor of Music, Del Mar College, Corpus Christi, Texas, U.S.A. is of the opinion that the talents of great players are not going to lose too many 'gigs' to a synthesizer or a computer, 'but for a dog food commercial or a TV soundtrack or a film score it's becoming obvious that electronics will do just fine.' The late, highly esteemed Buddy Rich however, on being asked his opinion of electronic percussion replied succinctly 'Is it necessary?' (For an up-to-date and complete survey of Electronic Percussion see Norman Weinberg's 'The Electronic Drummer', *Modern Drummer,* (1989), 87, Pompton Avenue, Cedar Grove, New Jersey, 07009, U.S.A.).

Music, like the rest of the arts has had its patrons and its critics. Some have criticised the manner in which modern orchestral percussion has at times been used, hinting at the possibility of complexity disguising a lack of imagination. There have been instances of avant-garde compositions receiving abuse at their first performances; but this is no modern reaction. The compositions of many notable composers of the past were severely chastised, as for example, the ridicule hurled at works by Berlioz who frequently suffered the indignity of being caricatured, in one instance among, a *batterie* of grotesque instruments. In an article in the *Musical Times* (August 1879), the editor, H.C. Lunn, in speaking of Saint-Saens' use of the xylophone in *Danse Macabre* says: 'Whether the instrument expressly used for this purpose, which we understand is called the 'Xylophone', will ever occupy a permanent place in our

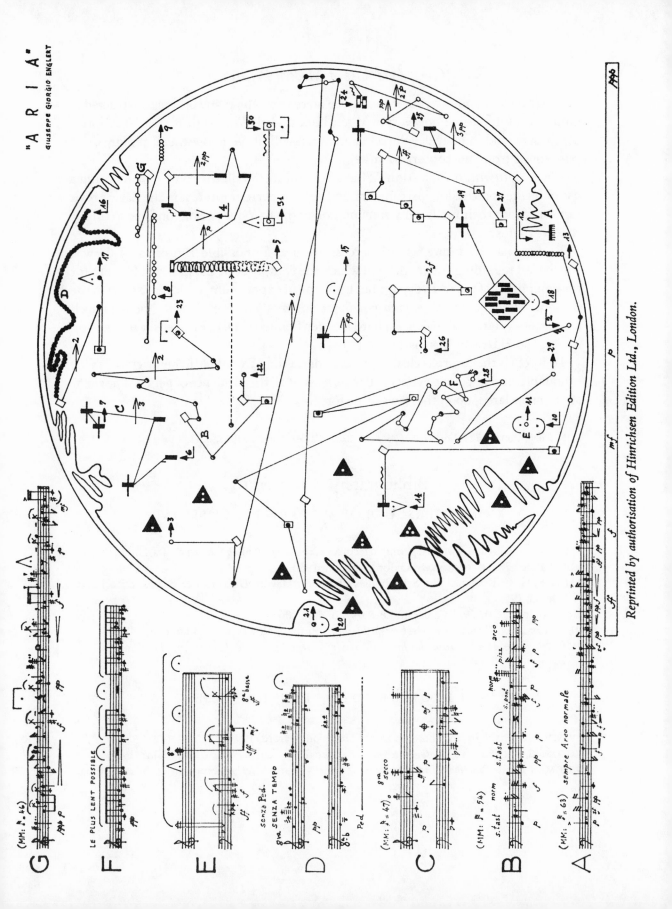

orchestras we cannot say; but if so , we see no reason why many others constructed to emit equally repulsive noises should not be included. The truth is that 'descriptive composers' and 'higher developed executants' will, if we allow them, rapidly drive pure music from our concert rooms...'

We are left with the question 'What of the future?' Will the coming years bring a use of further percussion instruments, and will the current interest in the Early Music Consorts, with their modest instrumentation of the Baroque period continue to fill our concert rooms?

To forecast the future use of percussion is as impossible a task as to draw a conclusion regarding the manner in which the composer of the past would score for the equipment of today. Every age has been one of experiment, none more so than the present. What new timbres and permutations may emerge from the pens of such composers as Iannis Xanakis, Richard Rodney Bennett, Marta Ptaszynska, Heinz von Moicy, and Harrison Birtwistle?

To forecast the future is clearly a rash undertaking. Donald Mitchell writes [1]: 'One cannot predict the course events will take, least of all the influence of genius, known or as yet undeclared, upon the 'laws of history.'

[1]Mitchell, Donald. *The Language of Modern Music,* Farber, London, 1963, p. 133.

Bibliography: Chapter 16

COMPOSERS' USE OF MODERN PERCUSSION

CLEATHER, G. Gordon. *The Timpani,*two lectures at the Royal College of Organists, London, 1908.
KIRBY, P. R. *The Kettle-drums,* Oxford, London, 1930
LANDON, H. C. Robbins. The Symphonies of Joseph Haydn, Universal & Barrie & Rocklieff, London, 1955
LIESS, Andreas. *Carl Orff,* Calder and Boyars, London, 1066.
READ, Gardner. *Thesaurus of Orchestral Devices,* Pitman, New York and London, 1953.
SMART, George. *Leaves from the Journals of Sir George Smart,* ed. Cox & Cox, London, 1907

RECOMMENDED LITERATURE

BRINDLE, Reginald Smith, Contemporary Percussion, Oxford, 1991.
KOTOŃSKI, Wlodzimierz, *Schlaginstrumente in modernen Orchester,* Schott, Mainz, 1968.
WILDMAN, Louis, *Practical Understanding of the Percussion Section,* Humphries, Boxton, 1964.

Appendix 1
The Americas

The wheel is turning full circle. In the present-day Latin-American dance orchestra the focus is on instruments of percussion which have shown little change over a long period of time. The majority of them can be traced back to the beginning of musical sound, and certainly to the music of the earliest residents of the western hemisphere. These instruments continue to be an essential ingredient of the rhythm section of the Latin-American dance music, and in recent years their attractive timbre has been utilized by many serious composers.

There is ample evidence of the use of percussion far back in history by the Aztecs, the Mayans, the Incas, and other early inhabitants of the Americas. Clay objects excavated in Costa Rica point to the use of rattles and drums in pre-historic times. Sachs says that it is from this period that the Peruvians inherited gourd and strung rattles, metal jingles filled with pebbles, and clapperless metal bells. There is also evidence of the ancient double-skinned Peruvian drum, the skeleton of which is preserved in Munich Museum; this is a shallow drum. Other specimens confirm the existence of cylindrical drums.

In speaking of the Mound Builders of the Mayan Civilization and the Olmec of southern Veracruz and western Tabasco (said to have flourished some 2500 to 2800 years ago) H. G. Stafford says[1]: 'The Olmecas . . . were known by other tribes as "the Rubber People" because they were experts in the use of rubber, which they use for various purposes. Among the uses were the tipping of drumsticks . . .' (a very early example of the covered stick).

It is known that Columbus found the Indians with drums, large and small, some decorated with paintings of tribal symbols. In 1519, according to W. H. Prescott[2],

[1] Stafford, H. G. *The Early Inhabitants of the Americas*, Vintage Press, New York, 1959, p. 34.
[2] Prescott, W. H. *History of the Conquest of Mexico*, Bohn Edition, Bell, London, 1901, vol. II, p. 141.

Cortés observed at the Great Temple in Mexico: '... the huge cylindrical drum made of serpents' skins, and struck only on extraordinary occasions, when it sent forth a melancholy sound that might be heard for miles – a sound of woe in after-times to the Spaniards'.

Continuing chronologically we find the evidence of Captain John Smith who, in his *Historie of Virginia* (1624) in addition to his reference to membrane drums, speaks also of rattles made of gourds or pumeone shells which sounded 'Base, Tenor, Countertenor, Meane and Treble'. He said that the sound of twenty or thirty of these, mingled with the sound of voices, would rather affright than delight any man. Here we are reminded of the ancient Brazilian ceremony tupinamba in which rattles are combined with the body slap.

There are early records relating to the use of slit drums, in particular to the teponaztli (already described). This instrument is reported in numerous sizes, varying from a few inches to several feet in length, the sound of the large drums carrying a distance of two miles. H. H. Bancroft says[1]: 'The teponaztli produced a melancholy sound which is considered by Brasseur de Bourbourg to have been a symbol of the hollow warning noise preceding the annihilation of the Earth, which was symbolized by the instrument itself'. The teponaztli is still used in Mexico.

An equally important drum in Mexico is a membrane drum, *huehuetl*, meaning 'old, old'. The huehuetl is a footed drum with a single membrane braced with rope. It is played in a vertical position, and in general with the hands and fingers. A description of a pre-Columbian orchestra includes, with wind instruments and the musical bow, the teponaztli, the huehuetl, scrapers and rattles. Like the teponaztli, the huehuetl continues in use.[2]

As in Africa and elsewhere, a profusion of styles have existed, including the covering of the drums with the human hide of slain enemies. There are numerous other percussion instruments. Travellers report in addition to slit drums and membrane drums (the latter including the tambourine and friction drum) the use of rattles, sistra, small bells, scrapers (bamboo, and in some cases tuned to different notes), also bone scrapers, (including those made of the thigh bones of vanquished foes), stamping tubes and dancing sticks. Other primitive percussion includes the pounding of a plank, and the use of an upturned canoe as a drum, the striking of a skin stretched over stakes driven into the ground (as the African ingqongqo) and, even more rudimentary, the hide folded into a bundle as used by the Indians of New

[1] Bancroft, H. H. *The Native Races of the Pacific States of North America*, Appleton, New York, 1876, vol. II, p. 293.

[2] Chávez writes for the *huehuetl* in *Xochipilly*, a work originally written for a group of primitive Indian instruments. The present score calls for hawks bells and clay rattles.

Mexico. G. Thompson speaking of the latter in an account of a Piñon dance, says[1]: 'This was laid flat upon the ground, and was pounded with a club some three feet long with all the force and regularity of a trap-drummer, at the rate of nearly one hundred strokes to the minute. This was the rude drum we had heard three miles away at sunrise.'

Ingenuity was displayed in the scraping (with a stag's antler) of a turtle shell – the *ayotl* – in the use, in Mexico, of a shield as a gong, and the *Jicara de agua*, the Mexican water drum an inverted gourd half submerged in a basin of water, and played with sticks. Metal discs discovered in Peruvian tombs are considered to be gongs, prototypes quite possibly of the copper gong, the *tetzilacatl*. (Sachs considers that a civilization familiar with metal work would have used cymbals.) A further link with antiquity is found in the recent discovery of a stone chime left by an archaic race in Peru.

The age-old quest to improve the sound, or to increase the volume of simple instruments by means of resonance, is apparent in certain of the musical instruments of the North American Indians as, for instance, the connecting of a scraper to a gourd or pottery dish; while the sheet of metal used by the Ute Indians in the Bear dance, and vibrated with a notched stick (*morache*), is placed over a trench for amplification.

Adding the effect of a snare to a drum was also achieved by the inclusion inside the shell of a cord knotted with wooden pegs or small pieces of quill which rattle on the vellum. There is also the keg-shaped drum which is partially filled with water to keep the skin moist and adjust its pitch. (Cf. bambus.)

With the exception of whistles of various kinds, including a combination of pipe and drum, many tribes possessed no instruments of music other than those of percussion: the bearskin or sealskin skin-covered frame drum of the Eskimo (and the Laplanders generally) was the only accompaniment to the dance. Equally rudimentary is the drum of Alaska, with a covering of skin from the stomach of a walrus, and the basket drum of Navajo Indians. The latter instrument is important in the ritual of the medicine lodge. It is made from the twigs of a sacred shrub. The choice of material and construction of the drumstick is also important. This is made (anew for each ceremony) with considerable ritual from carefully chosen leaves of *yucca baccato*. Symbolic grains of corn are enclosed in the tip of the stick. The ritual attending the destruction of the stick at the conclusion of the lodge proceedings is as intense as that employed in its preparation, or in the making of the drum. Dr. W. Matthews says[2]: 'The most important use of the basket is as a drum. In none

---

[1] Thompson, Gilbert. 'An Indian Dance at Jemezi, New Mexico', *American Anthropologist*, October, 1889, vol. II, p. 356.

[2] Matthews, Washington. The Basket Drum, *American Anthropologist*, vol. VII, pp. 202–7.

of the ancient Navajo rites is a regular drum or tom-toms employed.[1] The inverted basket serves the purpose of one, and the way in which it is used for this simple object is rendered devious and difficult by ceremonious observances'.

As elsewhere, we find the percussion instruments of the American steeped in tradition and symbolism. In war, the drum has been all-powerful as a means of encouragement, and a system of telegraph. In peace, it has been a means of communication and of serving all great events of family and communal life, being also concerned with recreation and in the serious business of ritual. Legends concerning the magical powers of certain instruments in the healing of the sick, and their power in other circumstances (particularly concerning religion) are numerous. Some of these instruments were objects of worship, particularly the rattle and the drum. (The rattle was also concerned with the ancient Aztec ceremony at which a young woman, impersonating the Goddess of the Maize, was sacrified). With many North American Indian tribes these instruments had the power to appease the malignant spirits responsible for the storm, and to bring good weather, or rain in a period of drought.

The presentation of a drum ensured permanent peace between two tribes (a custom observed universally over a long period of time). The power of the drum was also involved to strengthen faith and a sense of justice. In some cases the belief was held that the beat of the drum conjured back the spirits of the ancestors. In speaking of the Drum religion of the American Indians, Frances Densmore says[2]: 'Certain specified men may sing the Songs of the drum, but only one may speak to it, and he is the chief who keeps the instrument'. With some North American Indians, beads or other movable objects were placed on the drum head at night, and guidance taken from the patterns described in the morning. (In the case of the drum used by the Lappish shaman, symbols were painted on the skin-head. A metal object which rested on the vellum moved in different directions as the drum was beaten. When the drumming ceased the future was divined from the position of the object. Similarly in trances the diviner positioned the movable piece as the unseen powers directed.)

Many nineteenth-century writers describe the belief in the healing powers of the drum and rattle. In one dance, to the sound of a drum, those who were afflicted with ailments of any kind placed their hands upon the affected part and made gestures of casting off the disease. There is also recorded the belief held by the Ojibwa Indians of Minnesota, that two great spirits gave to Menabosho, the first man, two presents:

[1] The description tom-tom is applied to certain Indian and Hindu drums, not to the drums of Africa. In England, it is loosely applied to many unsnared drums.

[2] Densmore, Frances. 'Chippewa Music', *Bureau of American Ethnology Bulletin* 53, 1910, p. 142.

one a sacred drum which was to be used at the side of the sick, the other a sacred rattle to prolong the life of a patient. (This belief in the healing power of certain percussion instruments such as cymbals is age-old).

With the American Indians the instruments of the shaman had the power of magic. The shaman, the medicine man, was as dominant a figure as the African witch doctor, and possessed similar tools of trade – the power of song and skill in the use of the drum and rattle. The drum, normally a single skin frame drum, was used to accompany verses and also to modify the sound of the voice by movement in front of the mouth. Sometimes the frame of the drum was square, sometimes double-headed with stones inside forming a rattle. Unquestionably the shaman was a great artist, as were no doubt many of the 'drummers' (always men) outside the field of medicine. James Mooney, who refers to the use of the drum in the Cherokee Ball-Play Dance, speaks of the ability of the drummer as a singer and his power of improvising appropriately to the subject of the dance.[1] 'As this requires a ready wit in addition to ability as a singer, the election of drummer is a matter of considerable importance, and that functionary is held in corresponding estimation'. At times, as in the singing of the ceremonial songs of the North American Indians, a drum will be played by as many as twelve men, who sit round the instrument. Singers surround the drum, and dancers circle about them.

Opinions differ as to whether the North American Indians have shown an acute sense of rhythm, or a general high standard of musicianship. Some writers speak of the dancing and singing being in perfect unison with the musicians. Others speak of irregularity. To the south, there is the Mexican belief in a supernatural origin for music, and that drums crossed the bridge of turtles built by the God Tezlatipana in sending music from the sun. Here we find nothing to dispute the contention that a strong sense of rhythm has existed for centuries; no doubt fostered by the contact of Negro culture.

In Guatemala and Mexico one of the most favoured percussion instruments was the marimba. According to Schaeffner the marimba was taken to the South Americans by Negro slaves, and the Guatemalans made it their national instrument. Structurally, the instrument retains features common to the African xylophone. The wooden bars are gourd or tube-resonated. In most cases the resonators are equipped with buzzers formed of membrane, which further strengthen the tone (the 'charleo'), cf. African xylophone. In contrast to the African instrument which is so frequently placed on the ground and played with the performer seated, the Mexican marimba is mounted on a raised frame and the players stand to perform. Two or more marimbas

[1] Mooney, James. 'The Cherokee Ball-Play', *American Anthropologist*, vol. III, April, 1890, p. 132.

are often combined musically. In some cases two or more players perform on one instrument. From observers' descriptions, in earlier instruments the bars were arranged diatonically in a single row. To-day, the bars are arranged chromatically, in some cases the compass extending to six and a half octaves.

H. H. Bancroft[1] in an 1876 reference to Guatemalan music refers to a fork-shaped beater used to strike two plates at once, also to a coating of wax being used on the 'keyplates' to regulate their pitch. Schaeffner says that the players who supply the harmony generally use three sticks each. The fork-shaped beater we have observed in Africa and the Far East, also the tuning of certain Asiatic gongs and xylophones (and Hindu drums) by weighting with wax, supporting in some measure the contention of an early contact between the various cultures. Some of the percussion instruments of Central and South American tribes certainly reflect an influence of Negro culture. In the Caribbean Islands the Haitian voodoo drums are identical with many African 'pegged' drums. Voodoo drums are always three in number, differing in size. Like many of their African counterparts, newly-made drums are consecrated, at which ceremony they are given presents and personal names, in addition to *maman*, *papa* and *boula* (mama, papa and baby – large, medium and small).

Of the modern Latin-American dance orchestra Edmundo Ros says[2]: 'To obtain some idea of the backgrounds of Latin-American music we must go back into history. Before the discovery and conquest of South America in the sixteenth century there were two large and highly-developed civilizations where Brazil, Mexico and the neighbouring countries now lie. These civilizations, the Aztec and the Mayan had languages, customs and religions completely different from any known by the Old World, and had highly developed many of the arts. The culture, customs and manners of the Spanish and the Portuguese conquerors were imposed upon the conquered peoples, yet the native culture was not without its influences, and these can be detected in Latin-American music to this day. What we know now as Latin-American music contains much that is used in Spain and Portugal superimposed upon something that is quite different – the music of the early South American peoples, together with subsequent Negro influence.'

[1] Bancroft, H. H. ibid. vol. II, p. 705.
[2] Ros, Edmundo. *The Latin-American Way*, Rose, Morris, London, 1949, p. 2.

Bibliography: Appendix 1

THE AMERICAS

BANCROFT, H. H. *The Native Races of the Pacific States of North America*, vol. II, Appleton, New York, 1876.

DENSMORE, Frances. 'Chippewa Music', *Bureau of American Ethnology Bulletin* 53, 1910.

MATTHEWS, Washington. 'The Basket Drum', *American Anthropologist*, vol. VII, 1894.

MOONEY, James. 'The Cherokee Ball-Play', *American Anthropoligst*, vol. III, April, 1890.

PRESCOTT, W. H. *History of the Conquest of Mexico*, Bohn Edition, Bell, London, 1901.

ROS, Edmundo. *The Latin-American Way*, Rose, Morris, London, 1949.

SMITH, John. *Historie of Virginia*, London, 1624.

STAFFORD, H. G. *The Early Inhabitants of the Americas*, Vintage Press, New York, 1959.

THOMPSON, Gilbert. 'An Indian Dance at Jemezi, New Mexico', *American Anthropologist*, vol. II, October, 1889.

RECOMMENDED READING

CHASE, Gilbert. *A Guide to the Music of Latin-America*, Pan American Union and The Library of Congress, Washington, 1962.

HOWARD, Joseph. *Drums in the Americas*, Oak Publications, New York, N.Y., 1964.

IZIKOWITZ, K. G. *Musical and Other Sound Instruments of the South American Indians*, Göteborg, 1934, S. R. Publishers Ltd., Wakefield, 1970.

SCHAEFFNER, A. *Origine des Instruments de Musique*, Pagot, Paris, 1936.

SLONIMSKY, N. *Music of Latin-America*, Crowell, New York, 1946.

Appendix 2

The Latin-American Orchestra

The percussion instruments comprising the rhythm section of the conventional Latin-American dance orchestra recall the earliest musical activity. In the maracas (gourd rattles), the cabaça or *afochê*, (a gourd with an outer mesh of beads) and the *chocalho*, (a metal cylinder containing lead shot or beads) we have in form what is considered to be one of the earliest musical instruments – the rattle. The claves recall the early concussion and dancing sticks, the güiro the significant scraper. Antique origins are also evident in the bongos and timbales: the first a pair of small single-headed drums (of flesh or plastic) reminiscent of the nakers, and the second – a pair of larger open-ended drums evocative of many African drums.

Other percussion instruments involved include the tambourine; triangle; cowbells; the conga drum, *tumbadora*, a deep barrel drum with a single skin; the *cuíca*, a friction drum; the *paila*, a metal instrument in the form of a bucket; the *quijada*, an asses' or zebra's jawbone. Small bells are frequently added to the *quijada*, augmenting the loose teeth as rattling pieces. The body of the instrument is struck with the butt of the palm. (The *quijada* is occasionally replaced by the *vibra-slap*, in which the striking of a sprung handle vibrates rattling pieces inside a small box). Further instruments include a jingle-rattle reminiscent of the sistrum; *cincerri*, cowbells; the *gongue*, similar to the African gong-gong; the *adufé* or *tamborin*, a square frame with a single skin played with a drumstick; a wood block; the two halves of the shell of a coconut; the normal orchestral side drum, *caixa*, played with sticks and wire brushes; a bass drum, *bombo* or *caxambu*, foot-pedal operated; and occasionally a *tumba*, one of a family of Afro-Cuban drums resembling the conga and played similarly. In some cases the cabaça is replaced by the *LP Cabasa*, in which the natural gourd is ingeniously substituted. (As with the majority of native instruments, there are numerous spellings.)[1]

[1] Villa-Lobos uses many Latin-American percussion instruments and their native names in *Amazonas* (1917) and *Bachianas Brasileiras No. 2* (1930).

450

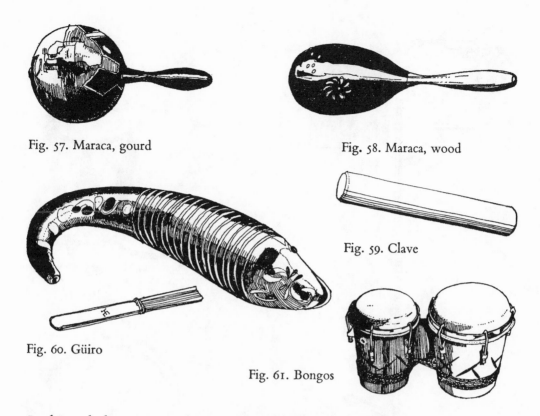

Fig. 57. Maraca, gourd

Fig. 58. Maraca, wood

Fig. 59. Clave

Fig. 60. Güiro

Fig. 61. Bongos

In the melodic structure the marimba is frequently employed.

When the rhythm of the rumba swept the dance halls of Europe and elsewhere in the late 1920's, the dancing world was swayed by a novel and exciting rhythmic ostinato. The original rumba with its ♩♩♩♩♩♩♩♩ coloured by the sound of traditional instruments, brought a breath of exotic Latin-America, and an influx of 'pukka' native orchestras. The power of the rumba and the numerous dances which followed lay in the apparent simplicity of the rhythm: in the rumba, for instance, the relentless click of the claves: ♩. ♪♩♩♩♩♩. These instruments – concussion sticks – consist of two pieces of hard resonant wood, about one inch in diameter and eight inches in length. Held correctly, one resting lightly on the finger-tips with the cupped palm of the hand acting as a resonator, the other (the striker) held between the thumb and the first two fingers, the sound they produce is sufficiently powerful to dominate the largest ensemble, as indeed it must, for the claves player is a leader. Edmundo Ros says[1]: 'To the uninitiated the Claves

[1] Ros, Edmundo. ibid. p. 8.

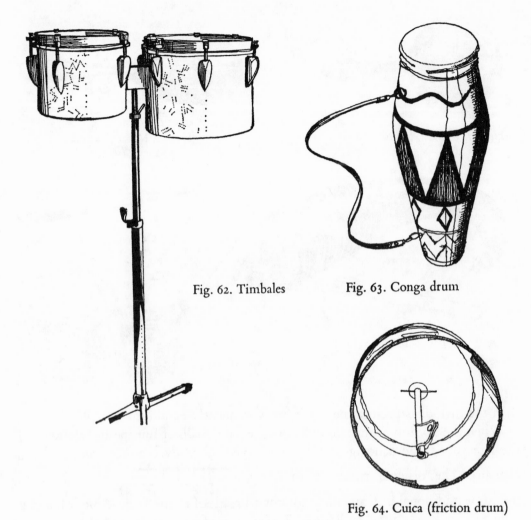

Fig. 62. Timbales

Fig. 63. Conga drum

Fig. 64. Cuica (friction drum)

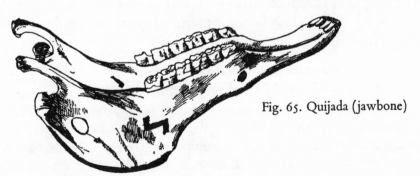

Fig. 65. Quijada (jawbone)

would appear to be the most simple of the Latin-American instruments, yet their player is beyond all question the most important man in the band. On him the perfection of the performance depends: his timing must be perfect and the tone produced must be sharp, clear and penetrating, audible above the rest of the combination'.

Whilst the rhythm of the claves never varies[1] the other percussion instruments – which may include maracas, bongos, timbales, conga drum, etc., – are permitted some latitude, though the rhythmic form remains unbroken. The maracas (a pair) play basically ♩ ♫ ♩ ♫ . The rhythm is normally performed ♩ ♫ ♩ ♫ the right hand maraca being the 'master' and used to mark

R R L R R L

the accented beats. The bongos are permitted a similar liberty of improvization to that of the maracas remaining, however, a decoration of the main beats of the maracas and claves. Bongos are tensioned to clear high-sounding notes at least a fourth apart. They are played with the fingers, which strike the vellum like drumsticks, the tone being varied by use of the finger-tips, flat fingers, and other 'tricks of the trade', including varying the pitch by pressure on the vellum. An effective feature in bongo playing is the use of an extremely close tremolo, known as the 'nerve-roll'. This tremolo, like that on the orchestral timpani, is produced by reiterating single beats from hand-to-hand.[2]

The timbales[3] are, strictly speaking, a pair of large bongos, played with thin sticks, or at times with sticks tipped with small rattles. They are tuned (like the bongos) a distance apart for differentiation. The player improvises on a basic beat: in the rumba

The timbales, bongos and the congas, are played with the large drum to the right; not an uncommon procedure in the history of drumming, as we have seen in the

[1] To play this unchanging two-bar rhythm for some hours may seem a monotonous occupation. Not so with the Latin-American claves player of a famous London night club, who, in reply to the author's question on this matter, said: 'No, no, I think of every bar to make it good.'

[2] Many composers have included bongos in their scores, e.g. Varèse *Ionisation*, Blomdahl, *Concerto da Camera*, and Malcolm Williamson in his operas, *The English Eccentrics* and *Julius Caesar Jones*. Orff writes for bongos, timbales and conga drums in *Oedipus der Tyrann* and *Ludus de Nato Infante Mirificus*. Bliss scores for conga drum in *Miracle in the Gorbals*.

[3] Not to be confused with Fr. *Timbales* (Timpani) as did the London organization, who, when supplying an orchestra for a visiting French ballet company, arranged – to the horror of the conductor – a Latin-American timbalist instead of the customary timpanist. (Perhaps *timbalettes* would be a safer name than timbales.)

cavalry kettledrums and their forbears the nacaires. In many cases two cowbells are secured to the timbales. These also differ in pitch, allowing the player the combination of four tones. In a large rhythm section the cowbells are given to a separate performer, as is also the *paila* (bucket). In a small combination the timbales player obtains the effect of the paila by striking a piece of metal fixed to the shell of the drum (if of wood), or the shell itself (if of metal). Striking the shell of the drum is by no means uncommon, particularly in Africa. In the West Indies, the player of the *ku*, a single-skinned barrel drum, beats the open end of the shell with two sticks, whilst another player, seated astride the drum, strikes the vellum with his hands, at the same time regulating the pitch of the drum with heel pressure on the skin. The latter technique is applied (but using the arm instead of the heel) to the conga drums in the Latin-American orchestra. These, reminiscent in form of the tubular drums of Africa, are used in pairs, or at times, singly. On the conga drum, the change of pitch (including glissandi) is obtained by elbow pressure, a style also applied to the timbales, bongos, the side drum (without snares) and tom toms.[1]

A number of different dance forms have sprung from the basic rhythm of the Cuban rumba; for example, the *son*, the *mambo*, and the *beguine*. In South America and the West Indies the focus is on the *calypso*. In Brazil the national dance is the *samba*, with such off-shoots as the *baião*, the *batuque* and the *maxine*. Each dance has its essential instrument such as the tambourine in the *samba*, the triangle in the *baião*, and the side drum and bass drum in the *maxine*. As in the Cuban dances, additional percussion is used at will, with occasional variation in instrumentation generally, to suit a particular occasion.

In the samba, the basic rhythm is played on the tambourine, popularly known as *samba-tam*. The instrument is held upright, and a steady movement of the wrist produces a series of semiquavers from the jingles, whilst the thumb and fingers of the free hand strike the vellum. Varying degrees of tone are produced by pressure on the inner side of the vellum, effected by movements of the fingers of the hand holding the instrument. The rhythms are given variously, and include:

The shakers (chocalhos, cabaça and maracas) play similarly on an eight quaver rhythm. The scraper too has the eight quaver rhythm, varied by ♩ ♪ ♫ ♪ ♫ or ♩ ♪ ♪ ♪ ♪. The scraping implement – a piece of cane or forked bamboo is not lifted from the body of the scraper: a stem of bamboo (*reso-reso* or *reco-reco*),

[1] The increasing use of tom toms is exemplified in John Cage's *She is Asleep*, scored for twelve tom toms.

or a gourd (güiro) serrated to form a series of notches. The implement passes back and forth over the notches, producing a continuous sound in the rhythms described. In the baiáo, an eight quaver rhythm is given to the triangle, which in this case is held by the thumb and forefinger. The beater is held inside the triangle and strikes on two angles alternately, whilst a muffled and ringing tone is cleverly produced by varying pressure on the instrument by the tree fingers of the other hand, thus:

Recently another sound has entered the music of Latin-America – that of the Steel Band. The Steel Band had its origin in Trinidad, considered the most cosmopolitan of the Caribbean Islands. Here the drum is a dominant feature of a music influenced by that of East India and Africa, two of the principal groups from which the Trinidadians have sprung. The major influences on the development of the modern Steel Band are the music of the East Indian Hosian Festival, the *tamboo-bamboo* drum, and the *bottle and spoon*. Tamboo-bamboo was the music of the ordinary creole people. The instruments, strictly speaking, were stamping tubes. Variation in tone was produced by the use of tubes of different length, making possible accompaniment to a chant in addition to the stamping of various rhythms (a primitive form of music observed in other territories). Tamboo-bamboo took the place of the normal African drums, which were banned by the authorities in the early history of the island, after rioting at festivals, and for fear that these instruments would encourage rebellion or provide an illicit means of communication.[1] Eventually (in the 'twenties) the use of bamboo was prohibited, for in addition to providing a cheap and exciting musical accompaniment to Carnival, these bamboo tubes were all too frequently used as weapons during disturbances. Bamboo was succeeded by the bottle and spoon, and later, iron bars and metal tubes, which in their turn led to tumult, resulting in a legal ban on this form of music. There remained the East Indian Hosian Festival. Here, elaborate temples of bamboo and paper were paraded through the streets to the accompaniment of drums – barrel drums resembling the Indian dolak (played with the hands), small kettledrums (played with sticks), and tambourines. These instruments are said to have inspired the steel drummers to make use of the large oil drums as a substitute for the instruments denied them (though other theories will also be met).

Constant experiment over a period of time has produced from an oil drum a complete musical instrument. There are now four basic types of pans (as the drums are

---

[1] This forcible destruction of drums and other instruments to suppress indigenous music is reported as early as 1614.

known) – bass, tenor, alto and treble. The deep tone pan is called *boom*, the tenor – *cellopan*, the alto – *guitar pan*, and the treble – *ping pong*. The construction of these instruments is a skilful undertaking, and the craftsmen are as respected as their counterparts in drum-making elsewhere. Briefly the construction of a pan is as follows. First, the bung end of the container is cut off, to leave a vessel of the required depth. The flat surface of this portion is then hammered into a concave surface. On this surface the notes are reamed by grooving with a cold chisel. In some cases, the areas are also clearly outlined with paint. Grooving is an important and delicate process, as the depth of the channel removes excessive overtones. The number of notes of a pan varies from two to four on a boom, to as many as thirty-two on a ping pong. The instrument is then heated and tempered – by a process usually regarded as a secret to be jealously guarded. Finally, the intricate business of forming the 'notes' by hammering the areas into an upward curvature from the underside, the degree of curvature (with the area of the domed surface) governing the pitch. The arrangement of the 'notes' in most cases conforms to a general standard, though the lay-out is not immutable and may vary for convenience. The pans (often gaily painted) are played with rubber-ended beaters. In tone, the instrument resembles the mellow sound of a marimba. A large steel band may number up to one hundred performers, with two or more pans at times played by a single performer. The repertoire of this novel orchestra (rarely less than four performers) is extensive, ranging from the simplest of folk tunes to arrangements of serious compositions.

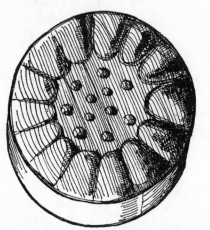

Fig. 66
Steel drum

Outstanding compositions for the steel band include *Theme and Variations* and *Concerto for Piano and Steel Orchestra* by Vernon Evans. A steel drum is requested by R. Haubenstock-Ramati in his *Vermutungen über ein dunkles Haus* (1964).

Bibliography: Appendix 2

THE LATIN-AMERICAN ORCHESTRA

BLADES, J. & DEAN, J., *How to Play Drums,* Elm Tree, Hamish Hamilton, London, 1985.

MORALES, H. *Latin-American Rhythm Instruments and How to Play Them,* Kar-ral Publishing Corporation, New York.

ROS, E. *The Latin-American Way,* Rose Morris, London, 1949.

RECOMMENDED LITERATURE

BECK, J. Latin Fantasy, Columbia Pictures, Miami, FL.

CHARLES, D. Conga, Bongo and Timbales Technique, Marimba Productions, New York.

CHRISTIAN, B. Basic Latin Rhythms, Malcolm Publishers, Illinois.

DEAN, J. *Latin New Wave,* Chappell's Music, London, 1981.

SEEGER, P. *Steel Drums. How to play them and make them,* Oak Publications, New York, 1964.

Appendix 3

Changing Styles in Light Music

In no section of the orchestra has there been a greater change in the design of instruments than in the realm of percussion. The advances in symphonic percussion have already been discussed; but there have also been numerous changes in the percussion instruments involved in the less serious forms of music. A comparison, for example, between the equipment of that prince of entertainers, the 'one-man band' with his drum, cymbals, and cunningly-controlled gadgets, the trap-drummer of the early part of the century, and that of the percussionist in the present-day world of swing is interesting. The trap-drummer was connected with various forms of light entertainment, including the dance hall, the travelling show, the circus and the theatre pit. In the dance hall he and the banjo constituted the rhythm section of the ragtime and early jazz bands, the piano and double bass coming later. His equipment was simple: Bass drum, side drum, Chinese cymbal and one or two Chinese tom-toms. In the pit of the theatre and elsewhere he was both orchestral player and effects man. His 'kit' (traps) consisted of a bass drum with cymbal attached, side drum, a 'crash' cymbal, a wood block, and a few luxuries (effects), such as a triangle, tambourine, castanets, slapstick and a few whistles, a pair of sandpaper blocks, and later the wire brushes.[1] In the early years after World War I the 'pukka' jazz drummer added a number of tin cans, washboard, saucepan lids, and similar noise makers to the normal trap-drum outfit. Despite such atrocities, and the frugal nature of the early equipment, the majority of these players were extremely skilful. The trap-drummer was not only the metronome of the band: his purpose was to colour it with every sound possible from the instruments at his disposal, and to give the combination style with his *ad lib* syncopation (*see facing page*).

'The drum part' (if any) was, in most cases, taken merely as a guide. The drummer

---

[1] Leonard Feather says: 'The date of the wire brushes is in doubt, though white musicians certainly used them during World War I'. *The Book of Jazz*, Arthur Barker, London, 1959, p. 125.

was expected to extemporise, and a good 'busker' was usually the man for the job (such a 'busker' being in no way a 'faker', or musical illiterate). W. F. Ludwig, jnr, says[1]: 'In the ragtime era of roughly 1910 to 1920, this freedom of expression was given even greater reign. Ragtime was new and exciting. The tempo was fast and the syncopation catchy. Many drummers, particularly the older set, refused to recognize this form of rhythmic freedom and branded ragtime drummers as "fakers". These progressive drummers were far from "fakers". Though they frequently did play without printed parts, they could read, understand musical moods, and, most important, perform with great showmanship thus bringing the drummer definitely into the lime-light.'

With these players the bass drum was operated by a foot pedal. There were 'die-hards' who retained the technique of double-drumming,[2] where the side drum and bass drum were played simultaneously by hand. (In double-drumming the bass drum was to the right of the player, and the side drum, angled at about 45 degrees, to the immediate left of the bass drum.) A pair of cymbals (on a hinged foot board) was usually played with the left foot, though the other foot was by no means idle, being engaged if the situation demanded with a 'foot triangle', motor horn (bulb), or klaxon motor horn, etc. The side drum and bass drum were struck simultaneously or alternately. Grace notes were rarely omitted, and the roll on the side drum suffered no break when the bass drum was struck. Double-drumming survived well into the 'twenties', experts in this particular style scorning the use of the foot pedal as 'an easy way out'.[3] The following examples are typical of what was to the competent double-drummer 'all in a day's work' (*see following page*).

To-day in the world of jazz the foot pedal operated bass drum is a necessity for the drum routines featured in the many aspects of this style of music. Like jazz, 'pop' music has experienced many vicissitudes; the former its era of pots and pans, and the latter the over-insistence of the 'beat' in early 'rock' and 'skiffle'. To-day, whilst basically simple in structure, pop drumming demands a good technique (and in the best circles musicianly restraint). It is no simple matter to play the following, which are based on the 'eight feel' style, combining bass drum accents (foot pedal)

[1] Ludwig, William F. jnr. *Modern Jazz Drumming*, Ludwig Drum Co. 1959, p. 2.
[2] Not to be confused with the term 'double drums' used during the classical period (and after) to denote a pair of timpani.
[3] The pedal timpani and other innovations have met similar opposition.

and in most cases a steady 'off-beat' on the foot-operated hi-hat cymbals, cf. Patents.

Opinions remain divided regarding the merits of this phase of entertainment, despite its commercial success. Rarely, however, is opinion divided regarding the quality of drumming in the modern jazz group, its excellence is matched by the quality of the equipment used. A modern 'kit' will include bass drum, side drum, two or more suspended cymbals (including a 'ride' or 'bounce' cymbal, and a 'sizzle' cymbal[1]), the hi-hat pedal-operated cymbals, two or more tom-toms (cylindrical drums, single or double-skinned) and a similar array of bongos, played as the situation demands with sticks or with brushes.[2] The modern jazz drummer leaves little to chance where his 'tools' are concerned. In general, he is as particular about the quality and appearance of his instruments as of his standard of performance.

It is generally agreed that the pioneer of modern drumming was Gene Krupa. This remarkable player evolved a style of drumming, which, in the years following World War II, revolutionised 'swing drumming'. The course of years has seen a change of style, but the stamp of Krupa's creative genius remains. He combined the spontaneous enthusiasm of rhythmic drumming with a thorough knowledge of the instrument, gained to a great extent through his knowledge and command of the

[1] A 'sizzle' cymbal is one that is drilled to receive a number of loose rivets, or alternatively, fitted with an overhead attachment to provide a 'sizzling' effect. In the middle 'twenties a similar effect was obtained from a cymbal studded with tambourine jingles. Recent additions to the 'cymbal set-up' include the 'flat' cymbal (non-building on repetitive rhythms) and Chinese type cymbals.

[2] In the mid 'thirties Chauncey Moorhouse (drummer with the Red Norvo Quartet) used a chromatic scale of tunable tom-toms. Cf. boobames, etc.

rudiments (paradiddles, etc.). The various 'stroke rolls', the customary grace notes, and in particular the paradiddle, formed the basis of his innumerable and interesting drum rhythms. So with his successors; the long-standing rudiments given a new dress, include the additional paradiddles (triple etc.), the single stroke roll, the crush roll (where a slight pressure is used), and the augmenting of the traditional wrist control with finger control. In the latter, the fingers control the rebound of the stick, and make possible a series of rapid beats with one hand, as opposed to the strictly rudimentary wrist-controlled single and double beatings. Many modern players use the 'single stroke roll' on the side drum, performed like the roll on the timpani, though at a greater speed. The side drum sticks are quite often held like timpani sticks, known as the 'matched' grip.[1] The side drum is usually played in a near-horizontal position to give speedy access to cymbals and tom-toms. (The advantage of positioning the drum in this manner cannot be denied. There would seem no reason, when this instrument is not concerned with marching, why the technique of the timpani or xylophone should not be applied to it.)[2]

In addition to the changes in technical approach, there has also been in recent years a marked change in style, including a frequent application of counter rhythms.

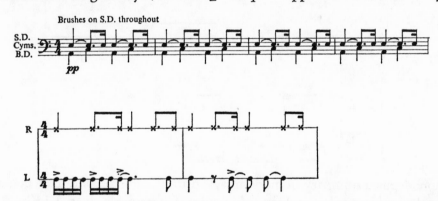

In to-day's 'modern style', this disconnected action is known as 'independence' (a new term for a musical device long known to the 'serious' composer). Speaking of counter-rhythmic execution in Western music, J. Chapin says[3]: 'This preoccupation

[1] The traditional double-beat roll on the side drum, however, has suffered no loss of face. The possession of this 'king of rudiments', and the practice to attain and retain it, remains a sheet anchor in all circles of drumming, as does the original 'rabbit grip' of the left hand stick, (also called the 'unmatched grip').

[2] A number of notable players in the symphonic world play the side drum in a horizontal position.

[3] Chapin, Jim. *Advanced Techniques for the Modern Drummer*, Chapin, New York, 1948–58, vol. I, p. 1.

with counter-rhythmic effects on other instruments emphasizes how slowly, in some respects, the drumming of "civilized peoples" has progressed.'

In applying co-ordinated independence to the drum, the modern player (jazz and be-bop) embellishes the beat with numerous counter rhythms whilst retaining the rhythmic structure. The hands operate independently, and the feet (on bass drum and hi-hat cymbals) likewise. Additional variety in tone colour is produced by pressure with one hand, or the elbow, on the drumhead,[1] whilst the other hand strikes it in various positions, and with subtle accents (including the striking of the rim and head simultaneously – known as the rim-shot). Frequently the left hand is the busier member. Whilst the right hand maintains a steady beat on the 'ride' cymbal, the left hand performs a counter rhythm, e.g., on the side drum. The speed in the left hand is achieved with the combination of wrist and finger control. With the 'top' exponents this is developed to a remarkable degree, and is admired and envied by many a symphonic player.[2] The accompanying examples are typical of the 'modern style' effects.

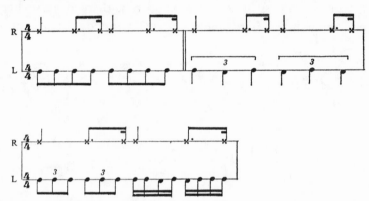

A more detailed summary of modern style drumming is beyond the scope of this volume. The subject of jazz is discussed in current literature such as: *Jazz* by Robert Goffin, Musicians' Press, London, 1946; *The Book of Jazz* by Leonard Feather, Arthur Barker, London, 1959, Horizon Press, New York, rev. ed., 1965; *The Story of Jazz* by Marshall Winslow Stearns, New American Library of World Literature, New York, 1958; *The Literature of Jazz* by R. G. Reisner, New York Public Library, New York, 1959; and *Toward Jazz* by André Hodier, Grove Press, New York, 1962.

In addition to the percussion already described, the vibraphone ('vibes') has an

---

[1] An echo of the craft of the Indian tablā player and the African drummer.

[2] This appreciation is reciprocated. There is to-day a deep understanding of the relative arts expressed in the different idioms (a happier state of affairs than the author recollects in the 20's when straight and jazz players often despised each other).

important place in the modern group, and is usually in the hands of a specialist. Like the drum, this instrument has experienced a series of phases, progressing from the so-called 'hot vibraphone' (extemporizing around the chords with plenty of added sixths), to the superb artistry of the star performers of to-day. Modern style percussion playing demands specialists no less than the symphony orchestra. Though many players remain extremely versatile, there is to-day less call for the 'Jack of all trades' of the 20's.

If ever there was a busy percussionist it was the drummer in the silent cinema, or variety theatre. Here, the player was obliged to cope with the orchestral drum parts and, at the same time, provide the innumerable sound effects required for stage and screen.

Monday morning rehearsal in the variety theatre brought its nightmare of fourteen acts with band parts in varying stages of decomposition, plus a host of effects sheets, or, 'Drummer, see me after rehearsal for the rolls and crashes'. These verbal instructions may well have included, 'Catch my steps as I walk on, ratchet when I raise my hand to the conductor, crash when I bring down my arm, and motor horn as I bend down.' Jugglers and gymnasts spelt a crop of side drum rolls, cymbal crashes and so forth. Most knockabout comedians required bumps and bangs calling for varying degrees of musical skill, intermingled with the inevitable siren or motor horn (and if a cue was missed, and the act proved a 'flop', the drummer got the blame!).

While the effects work for the stage was important, the musical director wanted his 'pound of flesh' from the drum part.[1] This was often marked and re-marked almost to the point of obliteration. 1–1, 2–1, 3–2 over a period of time became

1–1, 2–2, signified 1st verse 1 coro, 2nd verse 2 coro, and so forth, and woe betide the newcomer who played 2–2 as 2 verses 2 choruses (no less a crime than making the repeats on D.C. in the minuet of a classical symphony).

In the silent cinema the percussionist was equally pressed, with at least half a dozen themes and a batch of music ranging from jazz to classics. (Snippets of this, snatches of that, the first 24 bars of *Coriolan* Overture, but ready for love theme, etc. For wherever the orchestra may have been in an item, it was necessary to jump

[1] All for £2. 15. 0. per week, and provide your own drumheads and 'dicky' (shirt front).

directly into such themes as were required, directed in some cases by a flashing light cue – blue for love theme, red for dramatic theme, etc.).

To cope with orchestral demands, the minimum percussion equipment required was timpani, side drum, bass drum, cymbals, gong, etc. glockenspiel, xylophone and tubular bells. In addition, the numerous effects required for the screen demanded such equipment as: wind machine, rain machine, thunder sheet,[1] a tray of broken glass, dog bark, a bull roar, an electric 'rolling' machine for attachment to side drum, bass drum or timpani, a cylinder of compressed air for the imitation of rushing water, etc., and the blowing of tug boat whistles and fog horns (the last two sounds being effected by means of a 'reducer' on the nozzle of the cylinder), plus a host of other effects too numerous to be mentioned.

A variety of imitations were produced from the regular percussion instruments: a roll on a Chinese cymbal for a rough sea or, combined with a ratchet, for a forest fire; rifle fire from the side drum; a rim shot[2] for the crack of the sheriff's revolver. A substitute for the rain machine (a metal cylinder containing lead shot) was effected by placing a length of fine chain on the timpani head, and playing a close tremolo with side drum sticks. Horses galloping over the prairie involved 'timpani coperti', or side drum without snares. This, combined with a tattoo on the bass drum (fast pedal-operated) served for a stampede. Coconut shells suggested a horse trotting on the cobblestones, with the addition of a loop of sleigh bells affixed to the wrist if the effect of harness was required.[3]

Besides satisfying the management with the screen effects, the conductor expected at least the important features of the drum part. Playing with one hand the timpani part of an excerpt from a symphony, and winding a ratchet, rolling on a cymbal, or catching a pistol shot with the other was no mean feat. Like some of their counterparts in the variety theatre, many of these players possessed an independent technique, comparable to that of the 'maestro' in the 'modern group', and an inventive flair worthy of perpetuity.

With the advent of the talkies the silent cinema orchestras were disbanded, resulting in considerable hardship and a complete change of life for many fine

[1] The thunder sheet consists of a large sheet of metal. It is suspended and shaken. In the past in some theatres a device known as the *bronteron* was used for thunder behind the scenes. In this, pebbles were poured into a large metal vessel, or alternatively, bags filled with stones flung against a metal surface, or lead balls dropped on a sheet of leather. A further effective imitation was produced by rolling a heavy stone or ball of lead down a slatted ramp (to-day recorded sound effects are used).

[2] See drum technique.

[3] The author's collection includes a pair of coconut shells, one of which is equipped with a small metal plate, loosely fixed. The shells were used to imitate a horse with a loose shoe.

orchestral players. In recorded music for the new medium percussion instruments (orchestral and as special effects) played an important part. It is possible that there has been no finer example of artistry in their general use than in the memorable Disney cartoons.

Bibliography: Appendix 3

CHANGING STYLES IN LIGHT MUSIC

CHAPIN, Jim. *Advanced Techniques for the Modern Drummer*, vols. I and II, Chapin, New York, 1948-58, 1971.

FEATHER, Leonard. *The Book of Jazz*, Barker, Lòndon, 1957, 1959.

LUDWIG, W. F. jnr. *Modern Jazz Drumming*, Ludwig Drum Company, Chicago, 1959.

RECOMMENDED LITERATURE

ABRAMS, M. *Modern Techniques for the Progressive Drummer*, Premier Drum Company Ltd., London, 1966.

BROWN, T. D. *A History and Analysis of Jazz Drumming to 1942*, (Volumes I & II). The University of Michigan, 1984.

GROSSMAN, N. *Book of Today's Drumming*, Amsco Music Publishing Co., Ltd., 1972.

GROVE, *The New Dictionary of Jazz*, Macmillan, London and New York 1988.

NAPIER, Frank. *Noises Off*. Frederick Muller Ltd., London, 1936-45.

SCHULLER, Gunther, *Early Jazz*, O.U.P. New York, 1986.

Appendix 4

Use of Percussion in Education

The composer, after careful calculation, adds the drum part to his score: the performer studies it and gives of his best in performance. The African drummer performs feats of skill and endurance in the transmitting of signals, and complies with a host of ritual duties. The Asiatic, and his counterparts elsewhere, drums for rain, or to quell it. The maestro in the world of swing strives constantly for a more staggering drum sequence. The child drums for fun, rattling and banging are his pleasure, not his problem. In so doing, he explores the properties of vibrations and becomes conscious of the difference between noise and a pleasant sound. To some, however, music-making is a difficult business, and it is here that a simple percussion instrument often 'opens the door', and leads to participation in what proves to be jolly good fun, and is at the same time a lesson. Yvonne Adair says[1]: 'The percussion band is definitely a favourite activity on the school time-table. It is a medium of expression that instantly captures the interest of the child. The instruments are comparatively easy to play, and it is possible for children to take part in 'music-making' with little or no technique to be acquired. At the same time, it must be clearly kept in mind that the percussion band is but a medium and not an end in itself. The end must be – music.'

In recent years there has been a tremendous growth in the junior orchestra. The percussion band has played no small part in stimulating the young in this branch of making music, and the study given to this subject by such specialists as Ann Driver and Stephen Moore has proved invaluable.

Composers too have played their part. The Carl Orff *Schulwerk* has inspired young people the world over to make music. Of this work Andreas Liess says[2]: 'Even the instrumentation centres on the child. The primitive, rhythmic instruments, notably the xylophone, metallophone and glockenspiel built especially for this purpose, are

[1] Adair, Yvonne. *Music through the Percussion Band*, Boosey, London, 1952, p. 3.
[2] Liess, Andreas. *Carl Orff*, Calder and Boyers, London, 1966, p. 59.

more suited to the child's direct music-making than the piano and violin, with their burdensome traditions and techniques'. Benjamin Britten's *Noyes Fludde* is an excellent example of a composition in which the young love to do it themselves. Among a mass of recorder players and budding virtuosi on violins and cellos, some of the latter executants somewhat smaller than their instruments, is the *pièce de résistance*, the *batterie* aided and abetted by the bugles. The 'percussion' includes slung mugs, handbells, side drum, tenor drum, bass drum, tam-tam, cymbals, triangle, tambourine, Chinese wood blocks, sand paper blocks and a whip, presided over by a squad of young people who have given a good many of their after-school hours (as have their instructors and the rest of the orchestra) to do something well.[1] Young people have been similarly inspired to make music by such works as *A Time for Growing* by Antony Hopkins, *The Midnight Thief* by Richard Rodney Bennett, *Meet My Folks* by Gordon Crosse, and works by Harold Farberman, Greta Tomlins, Anne Mendoza, Joan Rimmer, Thomas B. Pitfield, Gordon Jacob, and David Stone.

The making of simple instruments is also a means of inspiring their use, and what better medium than the instruments of percussion? In fashioning a maraca from a coconut shell, a scraper from a strip of bamboo, claves from a piece of broom handle, a drum from an empty tin and a portion of car inner tube, or a xylophone from a few pieces of wood, the child is delving innocently and adventurously into the pre-historic past. Their home-made instruments may be simple, and their musical offerings may be considered modest, but they are participants, benefiting from an interest in age-old activity, as has indeed many a mite (and a grown-up for that matter) with physical or mental limitation where so often only a simple percussion instrument is manageable.

'School percussion' is no innovation for we find that over a century ago a percussion instrument was offered a place in schools' curriculum. This was Thomas Croger's 'New Patent Educational Transposing Metallic Harmonicon'. This instrument was in fact a glockenspiel played with small mallets. The metal bars were arranged keyboard fashion, and were movable to allow for transposition. The inventor claimed that the instrument was 'not only amusing, but very instructive; many of the rudiments of music (as Transposition, etc.), are conveyed at once to the mind; for schools, etc., where singing, etc., is being studied they are really valuable'.[2] Mr. Croger also recommended 'Merchants, Shippers, Captains, and

---

[1] Britten's Ballad for children's voices and orchestra (*Children's Crusade*, 1969) is scored for a large band of percussion, including the effect of a dog's bark from an amplified scraper (cf. morache).

[2] In principle, one of the most important aspects in many of the tuned percussion instruments used in schools to-day. (There are now few schools without percussion instruments.)

Emmigrants... to procure the instrument, it being very excellent for a Sea Voyage, or for Exportation, because the notes are not all affected by the variation of climate, always remain perfectly in tune and cannot be broken or destroyed.'[1] From our investigation it seems that Mr. Croger's instrument did not sail the high seas to any extent, nor take an immediate active part in the field of education. His efforts, nevertheless, have not been entirely unrewarded. To quote Percy Scholes [2] ..'toys of this kind have seen our day, and as Croger held a patent possibly he was the inventor of the whole type.'

The subject of music in present-day education is fully dealt with in specialized literature, The activity of the percussion band has led to the School and Youth Orchestra. In the latter, due to the experience of their dedicated teachers and the endeavour of these young players, quite challenging works are taken in their stride. Given further training at a School of Music, College of Academy, those who reach professional standard and so desire may be auditioned and if successful become orchestral players, soloists or qualified teachers.

[1] Scholes, Percy. *Mirror of Music*, vol. II, Novello, Oxford, 1947, p. 825.
[2] Scholes, Percy. ibid. p. 825.

Bibliography: Appendix 4

USE OF PERCUSSION IN EDUCATION

ADAIR, Yvonne. *Music Through the Percussion Band,* Boosey, London, 1952.
LIESS, Andreas. Carl Orff, Calder and Boyers, London, 1966
SCHOLES, Percy. *Mirror of Music,* vol. II, Novello, Oxford, 1947.

RECOMMENDED LITERATURE

BAVIN, Charles. The Percussion Band from A to Z, Evans, London, 1936, 1962
BLADES, J. & Skinner, M. Playing Tuned Percussion, Faber Music, London, 1981.
COOK, G. D. Teaching Percussion, Schirmer, London & New York 1989.
DRIVER, Ann. *Music and Movement,* Oxford, 1036.
MANDELL, Muriel and WOOD, Robert E. *Make Your Own Musical Instruments,* Sterling Publishing Co., Inc., New York, and Oak Tree Press, London, 1957, 1959.
ORFF, Carl. *Schulwerk,* Schott, Mainz, 1950, *et seq.*
ROBERTS, Ronand. *Musical Instruments made to be played,* Dryad Press, Leicester, 1965 & 1967.
SELF, George. *New Sounds in Class Teaching,* Universal Edition, London, 1968.
WHALEY, Garwood. *Percussion Education:* A Source Book of Concepts and Information, P.A.S. Publications, ibid, 1990.

Appendix 5
Inventions and Patents

Musical instruments have long attracted man's ingenuity, and in many cases he has sought the means of safe-guarding his discoveries. Over a period of years considerable time and money have been spent on patenting the multifarious ideas of fertile minds. During the last 150 years the instruments of percussion have been no exception. Certain archetypes have stood the test of time, or have been developed to good purpose. The remainder, as with many other subjects, though often ingenious in perception, remain but a record of curiosity, and indeed in some instances, as an absurdity.

The majority of the early inventions concerning kettledrums have been discussed. Though, as we have seen, the first attempts at rapid tuning proved unsuccessful in the orchestra, they were nevertheless the inspiration for the more secure drums which followed, which included the pedal timpani of the latter half of the nineteenth century by Pfundt-Hoffmann of Leipzig, Quiesser and Pittrich of Dresden, and later those by Jahnke and Boruvka, also of Dresden. These highly successful instruments were equipped with outside mechanism, foot pedal, with ratchet clutch engaged by side action, a master tuning handle operating independently of the foot pedal, and a tuning gauge.

In 1897 Franz Lyon took out a patent for an instantaneous tuning device where a pair of rings clasped the vellum from above and below. The rings were of various diameters designed to control the area necessary to sound the required note. Two years later I. H. Sapp and W. T. Stuart devised a system of tensioning a vellum by pneumatic means, in which the expansion of a tube forced the membrane upwards.

The first pedal timpani to be patented in America were those built by W. F. Ludwig and R. C. Danely in 1911. In these the tuning was effected by means of a fluid-controlled pressure pump, acting on an expandible tension ring. In a later model (1918) foot-operated cable tensioning was introduced by Messrs. Ludwig, followed in 1921 by a spring balanced pedal mechanism, which is retained in the majority of this firm's current models.

In the early 'twenties, the Leedy Manufacturing Company of U.S.A. came forward with a pedal mechanism where, in contrast to the foot plate action on the 'Dresden' and Ludwig models, a foot-operated lever with ratchet clutch was utilized. The Premier Drum Co., and Messrs. Parsons & Sons of England, followed with timpani of this description, which, with the Leedy drums, were highly regarded by the profession. In these and the Ludwig drums, (similarly esteemed) tuning by means of the 'T' handle was retained, rendering the instrument hand screw or pedal action.

An excellent piece of engineering on this principle came from A. F. Wiedoeft of Los Angeles in 1922. Here, the 'T' handles were operated by a system of worm wheels and shafts acting in bevel gearing, the whole being rotated by a pedal wheel. (See British Patent 1922 – 184,698).[1] It is possible that the weight and cost of this system was the reason for its not being generally adopted.

The post-war years brought a modification of the ratchet–clutch–lever principle, the Leedy Drum Company and the Slingerland Drum Company of U.S.A. and the Premier Drum Company of England, adopting a pedal lever with a friction clutch.

A good deal of attention has also been focussed over the years on improvements in the systems of 'hand tuning'. In 1898 J. Ball and A. Smith introduced a cable-tensioned kettledrum on a rocking lever, whereby one handle placed tension on the rim in two positions (1898. No. 11746). Messrs. Parsons incorporated this principle in a cable-tensioned drum with outer mechanism, in one model using four handles which placed tension on four further brackets.

Messrs. Ludwig and certain well-known Continental firms continue to produce a most satisfactory rod-tensioned machine drum tuned by a single handle. In the Continental models – as with the Dresden style pedal timpani – certain features observed in drums as far back as 1850 are retained. 1952 saw an ingenious system of instantaneous hand-tuning by one of the world's most eminent timpanists, Saul Goodman of the New York Philharmonic Orchestra. Mr. Goodman has replaced the 'T' shaped handle at the top of each threaded bolt with a cog wheel, and inter-connected the whole for simultaneous operation with a link chain. Each cog has two holes into which a 'T' handle (or two if desired) is plugged. By temporarily lifting off the chain to a jockey wheel, the head may be 'trued' by adjustment to any tensioning rod (see timpani tuning). In 1959, Henry W. Taylor, for many years professor at the Royal College of Music, London, and timpanist of the London Symphony Orchestra, was granted a patent for a similar device (1959 – 812,297). In Mr. Taylor's drum, a locking nut renders each tensioning rod either a fixed or free

[1] Identification numbers are British Patent Office.

element. (In recent models by F. D. Hinger and the Anheier cable drums, a cable connects all tuning handles.)

Saving space in transport was effected by the introduction (date uncertain) of sliding feet, and economy in weight by the recent use of the fibre-glass shell. Here should be included an invention by Miessner where, to produce the tone of a conventional timpani, thirteen gut strings are stretched over a rectangular frame and tuned in semitones. The strings, which are electrically amplified, are struck with kettle-drum sticks.[1] A recent extension of this system is found in the *monici* by André Monici.

Among the less practical ideas applied to the timpani, many, in theory, were interesting. An 1895 specification (Reicher & Friedberg, 1895–4523) shows a kettle-drum tensioned by means of an iron weight. Rods connect a flesh hoop to a lower ring, forming a framework over a kettle. The pressure on the vellum is governed by the position of the weight on a lever operating on the lower ring. A detrimental factor here is that no provision is made for adjusting the tension on the head at any particular point.[2]

In 1927 (291,050) a patent by T. N. Mirfield deals with a system whereby the pitch of a drum is indicated by communicating forced vibrations from the instrument to a set of tuned reeds. The reeds carry mirrors from which beams of light are reflected to a translucent drumhead on which a scale is painted. In this invention, which is also applicable to the double bass and cello, the reeds may be tuned to harmonics or other components instead of to fundamental notes.[3]

Numerous patents have been applied to the side drum. In 1837 came Ward's system of rod tensioning, and a modification of the normal method of rope tensioning by the employment of a cable system similar to that applied to his kettledrum.[4] In 1854 H. Distin introduced a shallow side drum, and a leg-rest in the form of a crescent-shaped leather-covered wire frame to fit into the thigh and hold the drum in a fixed position.[5] Five years later, Rose & Carte were responsible for a telescopic side drum. In 1862 came Sax's shell-less side and big drums. A year later this indefatigable inventor of the saxophone, etc., conceived the notion of coating the skins of drums with a solution of collodion or similar mixture containing india-rubber, etc., rendering them less liable to be influenced by variation in the humid conditions

---

[1] Cf. *Tambourin de Béarn*.

[2] To date, most attempts at rapid tuning have been centred on various means of stretching a vellum over a bowl of given size. Is it unreasonable to assume that in course of time a system will be advanced in which the size of a kettle is diminished or extended, and the tension on the vellum constant – on the lines of Darche's invention?

[3] Is press-button or air-pressure tuning inconceivable?

[4] A similar system was applied to early-nineteenth-century Continental side drums.

[5] See Distin's 'substitute for a castanet' (orchestral castanets).

of the atmosphere (an annoying inconvenience says Sax). A patent was granted to a 1903 inventor for a similar idea, and again in 1935 to the inventor of a specially prepared drumhead designed to combat adverse weather conditions. (Later types were known as 'all weather heads'.)

In 1871 we find a drum with metal heads, and in 1903 a side drum with a single skin. Over a period of years various means of tensioning drum skins are recorded, including internal mechanism, tensioning by fluid pressure, and in 1892 a system of separate tensioning. This latter system of tensioning the heads individually is applied advantageously to the majority of modern side and bass drums. In the event of one head 'going' the tension on the opposite head is retained, whereas in a single tensioned drum the tension on both heads is lost.

In 1954 L. W. Hunt added screw mechanism to a rope-tensioned drum, retaining the military appearance of the instrument (1954 – 745,789). A side drum with a framework shell has recently been invented by Saul Goodman.

Among the numerous patents concerning snares, the majority deal with methods of tensioning and 'quick release'. A fitment (dated 1886) consists of a screw-operated snare strainer, though this means of adjustment was undoubtedly much earlier. Berlioz refers to loosening the cords, and further back, if we are not mistaken, there is the threaded fitting on Arbeau's diagram. The instantaneous snare release is a product of the early part of the present century. This accoutrement has proved a boon to the modern percussionist, permitting a rapid change of tone colour (improvisation of tenor drum, tom-tom, etc.) and, equally important, rendering the instrument harmless during a period of *tacet* by obviating the disturbing snare 'buzz' (with snares on) caused by sympathetic vibration from certain wind instruments, or the impact of the timpani or bass drum. The releasing of the snares by foot-pedal action was granted a patent, as was a similar attachment incorporated in a pedal cymbal beater.

Snares under the batter head are listed as early as 1871. These consist of a metal spring, resting on the metal head previously mentioned. Later patents (1930) concerning this fitment, show side drums equipped with snares under the upper and lower head. The various materials used in the specifications of snares include gut, wire, or wire-covered silk. The even straining of the snares has also received a good deal of attention from inventors, in some cases to the extent of each snare being individually adjusted by means of a threaded unit.

There are numerous records in the files of the Patent Office (and elsewhere) concerning improvements and adjustments to the bass drum. When Cornelius Ward applied rod tensioning to the side drum (1837), it is clear that this method was soon applied to the bass drum. In Kastner's *Musique Militaire* (1848) there is an illustration of a *grosse caisse: nouveau modèle* with fifteen tensioning rods, two of which are fashioned to avoid pressure on the player's body when on the march. A music stand is attached to the shell of the drum. Side and tenor drums, and a tambourine with rod tensioning are also illustrated in Kastner's work.

The bass drum also received the attention of the enterprising Cornelius Ward, for he applied his cable system of tuning a kettledrum and a side drum to this instrument, an example of which is included in the accoutrements connected with the Richardson Rock Harmonica in the Keswick Museum. A foot pedal beater for the bass drum is also included, in which the similarity of the rope and pulleys suggests Ward's handiwork.

Later inventions concerning the bass drum apply mainly to attachments (internal and external) for 'damping' the tone. The 'collapsible' bass drum by Boyle (1927 – 291,610) has proved a boon to the 'gig drummer'. In models elsewhere, a further modification to assist in transportation included a large trap door, or the shell designed in two pieces, to make possible the inclusion of the side drum and other paraphernalia, not forgetting the small trap door for the reception of an electric-light bulb to give added lustre to the halcyon 'twenties.

Foot pedal beaters for the bass drum have interested manufacturers and players alike. The apparatus used by the Richardson Brothers before 1850 was unusual. There is no record of the use of a pedal-operated bass drum in the orchestra at this period. (It is reasonably certain that had this appliance been known to Berlioz, he would have frowned as heavily on its use as he did on the combination of the bass drum and cymbals). The trap drummer of the 1890's was, to the best of our knowledge, the first to make regular use of the bass drum foot pedal. The mechanical apparatus used to operate percussion instruments in organs and pianos may have suggested this appliance, unless it was inspired by the 'one man band', where the bass drum and a cymbal were operated (among other methods) by a cord fixed to the performer's foot. The trap drummer's foot pedal combined a cymbal with the bass drum. According to W. F. Ludwig Sr.,[1] who speaks of using this type of pedal (a heel pedal) as early as 1894, it was crude, but nevertheless effective. Improvement, however, was sought, and in 1909 according to the records of the firm of Messrs. Ludwig, W. F. Ludwig invented the floor toe pedal in which a short beater rod was mounted on an elevated post – 'and thereby founded the modern drum manufacturing business'.

From 1909 to the present moment, the foot pedal beater has occupied the mind of the inventor, as has the combination of bass drum and cymbals. The early idea,

[1] See '67 Years of Drum Pedals' in *The Ludwig Drummer*, Spring 1962, The Ludwig Drum Co., Chicago. (W. F. L. Ludwig, Sr., 1879-1973.)

which involved an attachment to the pedal beater for striking a cymbal affixed to the bass drum, was improved and the cymbal beater hinged, allowing, by a flick of the drumstick, an 'off' and 'on' position. (1st Coro *p*, 2nd Coro *f*, etc.).[1] Further systems using twin foot plates (or similar mechanism) made possible the combination of bass drum and cymbal, or bass drum and a pair of cymbals.

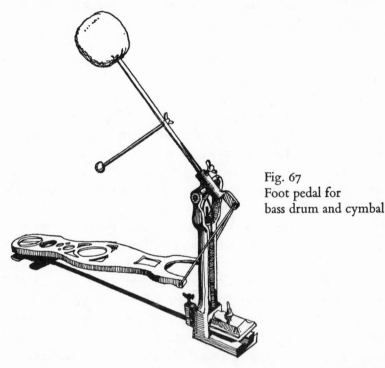

Fig. 67
Foot pedal for
bass drum and cymbal

(Two ideas whereby the tone of the drum is 'damped' as the pedal beater leaves the drum head are recorded. Equally interesting is the deep cylindrical drum (played in an upright position) where the upper head is foot tuned, and the lower head struck with an 'up beat stroke' pedal beater.)

As with so many of man's brainwaves, extremely simple things followed the more involved: for instance, the beater with half the surface of hard felt, and the remainder of softer material.

Combining a pair of cymbals on a hinged foot clapper is no novelty. Apart from an elaboration of the mechanism and raising from floor level, little change is seen in the general principle.[2] The exceptions are: (i) the striking of two pairs of cymbals

[1] Milhaud specified this attachment in his Concerto for Percussion and Small Orchestra (1929–30).

[2] Floor-level foot cymbals were known as the 'snow-shoe'.

simultaneously, (ii) a mechanism for beating a pair of cymbals, which also comprises an independently operable mechanism which strikes the lower cymbal with a stick, and (iii) the hi-hat cymbal pedal (originally known as the Charleston cymbal pedal). In the latter the cymbals are raised to allow free playing with the drumsticks. This unit remains one of the most important items in the modern drummer's 'kit' - hence kit drummer.

The combination of bass drum and cymbals did not escape the vigilance of Mr. Cornelius Ward. In 1853 he invented 'The Cymbal Drum' (1853–141) to ensure, he says: 'precision in effect in orchestra and band music of the drum and cymbals'. Ward's specification refers to the placing of the cymbals in the interior of the drum, and sounding them simultaneously with one blow of the drumstick. To receive the cymbals he proposes a large aperture in the centre of the vellum. This aperture, he claims, also serves the purpose of equalizing the vibrations of the head. (He stresses this point in an earlier reference to timpani, reasoning that when the skin is drawn to a high degree of tension the note produced from the centre is considerably higher than that near the outer surface. 'I have discovered,' he says, 'by having an opening in the centre, the whole remaining surface will give off an equal tone.')[1] In addition to the aperture in the centre of the bass drum head, Ward proposes holes in the shell to allow free vibration of air inside, equalizing elasticity on both sides of the head. The extent to which Mr. Ward's 'cymbal drum' was employed in orchestra and band music is uncertain. We find no further reference to this invention, literary or pictorial. Its principle, however, may have inspired subsequent inventors, for among later references there is a beater for striking simultaneously the bass drum, cymbals and triangle. There are, not surprisingly, a great number of patents appertaining to drumsticks. These include sticks with hard and soft ends, others with the head divided into two textures, a combined wire brush and drumstick, and recently (from H. W. Thompson, percussionist of the Boston Symphony Orchestra and Boston Pops Orchestra) a patent bass drum stick allowing the player the use of four impact points, each producing a different quality of sound.

In 1914, an inventor sought to assist those who found it difficult to produce a roll with drumsticks, by submitting an apparatus consisting of a serrated implement, which, when drawn over a cranked rod, 'trembled' the rod on the drumhead. The ends of the rod, the specification says, can be fitted with hard or soft ends (1914 – 14957). A later apparatus consists of a beater for the glockenspiel or xylophone, powered by an electric battery to produce a tremolo. (1958 – 846,826).

---

[1] The hole in the centre of the head most certainly eliminates many of the overtones, though in general, timpanists are not prepared to risk a good head to obtain this minor difference in tone quality.

Appendix 5

An 1861 invention by a James Waddell (1861 – 9855) claims that if the head of a drum is connected to metal bars, the sound emitted is about an octave lower than a similar drum constructed with the head mounted on a barrel. In the same year J. Azěmar (1861 – 2135) brought forward 'an instrument to facilitate the practice of the drum'. He says of his patent: 'the beating of the drum may be practised without noise, the effect of the strokes being conveyed through the medium of feeling mostly, instead of through the ear'. Azěmar's instrument is scientifically constructed. It consists of two round plates of wood, between which is an insulator of rubber. The plates are screwed together, the degree of pressure on the two plates governing the resonance and consequent volume of tone. The sheet of rubber, of sufficient thickness to give the proper recoil of a drum, is fixed to the top plate. Attachments enable the instrument to be fixed to the player's leg, or to the drum. In some respects Azěmar's is an advance on the present-day practice pad.

1861 was certainly a year of experiments in percussion instruments. Specifications of 1861 (and 1876) deal with the making of gongs and bells from carbon steel. George Potter of the famous Aldershot firm of instrument makers was granted a provisional protection in 1874 for an invention concerning an alloy sufficiently ductile or malleable to cope with the manufacture of gongs and cymbals. In his specification, Mr. Potter says: '. . . the manufacture of these instruments cannot be carried on in this country for want of the means of rendering the metal sufficiently malleable to admit of its being wrought by the hammer to the form desired'.[1] This is a reminder of the craft of the original gong and cymbal manufacturers.

The above are only a few of the numerous patents, improvements and modifications applied to instruments of percussion, particularly drums. Numerous as they are, it is interesting to note that there seems no endeavour to strengthen the sound of a drum in the manner Kircher conceived in his drum with a long resonating tube (tubo timpanite q.v.). Many patents have been applied to instruments of the xylophone and glockenspiel class, the majority of the earlier by the firm of Messrs. J. C. Deagan of Chicago. The firm's founder (J. C. Deagan) was a universally recognized authority on acoustics, and an untiring worker in establishing recognition of A440 as standard pitch. He was personally responsible for many improvements in orchestral glockenspiels, xylophones and marimbas.

Messrs. Deagan's earliest instrument, the result of a series of experiments with metals as tone-producing mediums, was a glockenspiel, designated 'Deagan Orchestra Bells'.[2] Shortly after came the 'Deagan Parsifal Bells' (the Orchestra Bells

---

[1] Gongs and bells supplied to military authorities and others by the present firm (Henry Potter & Co.) are manufactured in England to the firm's own specification.

[2] Possibly the reason for the general adaptation in the U.S.A. of the term 'bells' for glockenspiel.

resonated), and a resonated xylophone, claimed by the manufacturers as the first orchestral xylophone to be thus equipped. Later, various patents were applied to the orchestral marimba, including tunable resonators where the length of the resonating chamber (a tube) could be adjusted to suit the slight variation in pitch (due to changing climatic conditions) of the wooden bars. A Deagan catalogue of the early 'twenties shows a six octave marimba-xylophone descending to F one and a half octaves below middle C (the lower resonators curled to render the instrument normal height), a lower sounding nabimba in which the resonators were equipped with buzzers,[1] steel marimbas sounding two octaves lower than the Parsifal Bells,[2] and marimbaphones with bars of either steel or wood. The marimbaphones were designed to be played with mallets or bows. To receive the bow, the end of each bar was shaped thus

Fig. 68. Marimbaphone bar, shaped for bow

and the two rows of bars raised to a vertical position for convenience in playing. Instruments of this type were used as solo instruments by stage artists, and in marimba bands.

Messrs. Deagan were also responsible for the introduction of percussion novelties, again designed primarily as instruments of entertainment. These included the 'Aluminium Harp', 'Organ Chimes', 'The Tapaphone', etc. The 'Aluminium Harp' consisted of a series of aluminium tubes played with resined gloves.[3] In this instrument a tremolo effect was obtained by moving the finger over the upper end of the tube. (Here could have been the inspiration for the vibraphone). The instrument, given as 'Organ Chimes' (U.S.A. Patent 1900 – 644,817), consisted of a number of metal tubes each with an internal clapper. The tubes were shaken, as in the Javanese angkleong. In the 'Tapaphone', a series of metal bars were arranged an octave apart in pitch. The bars were struck by a hinged two-pronged hammer operated by the finger. (See 'Octa-rimba').

Other novelties were resonated handbells, single or in clusters of two or four, the latter allowing one performer a range of eight notes; staff bells – 'handbells' or mushroom-shaped bells mounted on a framework and struck with beaters; arch-

[1] Used occasionally by Percy Grainger, e.g. in the suite *In a nutshell* (1908-1916).
[2] The earliest vibraphone was a modification of the steel marimba.
[3] Extended in the interesting French instrument *Les Structures Sonores*.

bells – where the internal clapper was operated by pulling a cord, and tap-bells – sounded by tapping a disc extending through the top of the bell.[1] There were also musical sleigh bells, musical cow and sheep bells, musical rattles (two chromatic octaves) and a set of musical coins played by spinning on a marble top table. An era of novelties indeed, but at least a cog in structural development.

[1] Swiss Staff Bells are requested in Grainger's *In a nutshell*. He was also intrigued by the Deagan marimbaphones, etc. In *Tribute to Foster* (1931) a work in which he specifies musical glasses and bowls rubbed with the finger-tips, he scored for bowed metal marimba which he says 'is especially useful in providing volume in the lowest notes'. Grainger's personal collection of instruments included Swiss Staff Bells, xylophones, marimbas, metallophones, etc., on which his wife Ella frequently performed. They are preserved (with others) at Grainger's old home in White Plain, New York, and the Grainger Centre, Melbourne, Australia.

Bibliography: Appendix 5

INVENTIONS AND PATENTS

LUDWIG, William F. Senr. '67 Years of Drum Pedals', *The Ludwig Drummer*, Spring 1962, The Ludwig Drum Co. Chicago, 1962.

RECOMMENDED TECHNICAL AND RECITAL LITERATURE
(*Recital work)

ABE, Keiko. *Works for Marimba,* European and American Music, Valley Forge, CA USA.

ABEL, A. *20th Century Studies for Orchestral Percussion,* Schirmer, New York and London.

ARNOLD, M. *Concert Piece for Percussion and Piano,* * Faber, London and Boston.

BECK, J. *Advanced Studies for Snare Drum,* Kendor Music, Delevan, New York; *Three Movements for Five Timpani,* * Meredith Music, FL, USA.

BENNETT, R. R. *Marimba Concerto,* * Novello, London and New York; *Concerto for Percussion and Chamber Orchestra,* Novello, London and New York

BELLSON, L. *Modern Text Reading* (s.d.)Belwin Mills, New York.

BURTON, G. *Jazz Vibes,* Ludwig Drums Co., Chicago, USA.

CARTER, Elliott. *Eight Pieces for Timpani,* * (See Discography).

CIRONE, A. *Portraits in Rhythm* (Timpani), Belwin Inc., New York.

CHRISTIAN, B. *Oddities in Rhythm.* Also Original Music at all levels (s.d.) P.O. Box 2090, Oak Park, Illinois, USA.

CUMBERLAND, A. *The Cumberland Recital Series,* (Timpani)* A. Cumberland, Box 25, North Quay, Queensland, Australia.

DAVIES, Sir Peter Maxwell. *Three Studies for Percussion,* Chester, London and New York.

DELACLUSE, J. *Twelve Studies for Snare Drum,* Leduc, Paris; *Twenty Etudes for Timpani,* Leduc, Paris.

DYSON, L. *Orchestral Extracts for Timpani,* 69, Botley Rd., Park Gate, Southampton, England. SO3 7AZ

EYLES, E. *The Golden Age of the Xylophon* (G.H. Green), Meredith Music, FL, USA.

FINK, S. *Plaisanterie for Percussion Sextette,* Wrede D. Wiesbaden; *Batu Ferringhi for Marimba Solo*, Trommel Suite, Concertino for Vibraphon and String Orchestra,* Zimmermann, Frankfurt (or R. Schauer, Belsize Park, London).

GREEN, G. H. *A Complete Course of 50 Lessons for Xylophone,* Meredith, FL, USA.

GRIEDER, A. *Basler Trommel Musik,* Hug, Basle.

GROSSMAN, N. *Complete Book of Modsern Drumming,* Wise, New York.

HAMPTON, L. *Method for Vibraharp, Xylophone and Marimba,* Robbins, New York.

HATHAWAY, *Orchestral Excerpts,* Woodsmoor Press, London.

HOCHRAINER, R. *Etuden fur Pauken,* i. 2, 3. Doblinger, Munich.

HOUGHTON, S. and WARRINGTON, T. *Essential Styles for Drummer and Bassist,* Alfred Music, Van Nuys, CA, USA.

JONES, D. *Sonata for Three Unaccompanied Kettledrums,* * Hinrichsen Ed. No. 271, New York & Frankfurt.

KRUPA, J. *The Science of Drumming,* Robbins, New York and London.

LANG, Michael. *Suite for vibraphone solo,* * Southern Music, San Antonio, Texas.

LARRICK, G. *Twentieth Century Percussionists,* Greenwood Press, Westport, CT 06881, USA.

LEONARD, S. *Timpani Techniques,* Ludwig Music, USA.

LYLLOFF, B. *Etudes for Percussion,* 1-8, W. Hansel, Copenhagen.

MACLEOD, J. *Concert Percussion and Orchestra,* Griffin Music, UK.

MASSON, A. *Konzert Stuk for Snare Drum and Orchestra,* Iceland Music Information Centre; *Prim* (s.d.)* and Fyrir Litla Trommoug; *Concertö for Marimba and Orchestra,* * Iceland Music Information Centre.

NOVELLO, J. *New Directions in Rhythm,* (s.d.), Ludwig Music, Chicago, USA.

MULDOWNEY, D. *Figure in Landscape,* (Concerto for Percussion), Faber, London and New York.

PITFIELD, T. *Concertina for Xylophone,** Edition Peters, New York.

PINKSTERBOER, H. *The Cymbal Book,* Hal Leonard Inc. , Milwaukee, Wis. USA.

RICHARDS, E. *Advanced Techniques for Vibraphone,* pp. 2100, Canyon Drive, CA, USA; *Studio Techniques,* pp. 2100, Canyon Drive, CA, USA.

RIDOUT, A. *Sonatina for Timpani,** Boosey & Hawkes, London.

SCHISTINE, W. *26 Mallet Studies,* Southern Music, San Antonio, Texas, USA; *The Developing Timpanist,* Southern Music, San Antonio, Texas, USA.

SKINNER, M. *Roll Review,* (s.d.) pp M. Skinner, The Orchestra, Royal Opera House, London.

STEVENS, L. H. *Method and Movement for Marimba,* Marimba Productions, New York.

STOUT G. *Etudes for Marimba 3-6,** Macmillans, New York.

TCHEREPNINE, A. *Sonatina for 2 or 3 Timpani and Piano,** Boosey & Hawkes, London.

WARING, R. *Concerto for Vibraphone and Chamber Ensemble,* Norwegian Music Information Centre.

WHETTAM, G. *Lento and Fugue for Marimba,** Meridan Music, Ingatestone, Essex, UK; *Andromeda for Percussion Quartet,* Meridan Music, Ingatestone, Essex, UK; *Suite for Timpani,** Meridan Music, Ingatestone, Essex, UK.

Consult dealers for availability of literature and discography.

Discography

ABE, Keikio. *Works for Marimba,* European and American Music, Valley Forge, CA, USA.

ARSENAULT, F. *The 26 Standard American Rudiments,* Ludwig Drum Co., USA.

BREUER, H. Percussion Vaudeville, Audio Fidelity DFM - 3001 - B; Mallet Magic. . . AFSD 5825 and Mallet Mischief . . .AFSD 5882; Mallet Magic. Five New Ragtime Solos. No 011, Lang Percussion Co., New York, NY.

BROWN, Teddy. *Poet and Peasant,* Overture and *Light Cavalry,* Overture, Imperial 1718, (Vintage 78).

CARTER, Elliott. *Eight Pieces for Timpani,* (Timpani: Morris Lang) Odyssey, New York.

ERSKINE, P. *Timekeeping* (video), DC1, Art of the Americas, New York.

FARBERMAN, H. All Star Percussion Ensemble, H SPA (90) 190148.

FINK, S. *Impulse,* Thorofon, CT #2063; *Concertino für Vibraphon,* Accordata, 1P 7979; *Art of Percussion,* Thorofon CTH 2085. C.D.

GLENNIE, Evelyn, *Light in Darkness,* RCA RD 60557; *Dancin',* RD 60870.

GREEN, G. H. *Choice from Repertoire,* Meredith, FL, USA.

HARRISON, L. *Lakora Sutro,* New Albion Inc. San Francisco, CA, USA.

HASS, J. *18th Century Concertos,* (timpani), Qualiton, New York.

KRAFT, W. *Percussion,* Crystal, S104.

KRUMATA, Percussion Ensemble (with Keiko Abe, marimba), Gramofon, AB DIS, Qualiton, New York.

LANG, M. A., See: Carter, Elliott. *Eight Pieces for Timpani.*

MASSON, A. See Recommended Recital Literature.

MEZA, F. A. *Percussion Discography,* Greeenwood Press, Westpoint, CT, USA.

NEXUS, *Nexus Now* (W. Gahn, 8740, Wesley Road, Halcomb, New York, 14469); *The Best of Nexus,* #10251; *The Music of G. H. Green,* #10273.

NORVO, Red. Commodore Town Hall Concert vol. I. London, HMC 5001; *High Five,* RLA Victor, RD 27013.

PALMER, C. *Atlantic,* col. I, WEA. K80009; *Percussion Discography,* Greenwood Press, Westport, CT 06881, USA.

RICHARDS, E. *The Essence of Playing Mallets* (video), Interworld Music, San Francisco, CA, USA.

RITCHIE, G. and REMATO, A. *New Music for Percussion and Organ,* Titanic Records, Somerville, MA, USA. C.D.

SHAUGHNESSY, E. *Drum Clinic,* E. S. Enterprises, CA, USA.

SIMARD, Marie, *Le Productions, Inc.* Montreal.

STARITA, R. *Dancing Tambourine,* Columbia 4622 (vintage 78); *Hit the Deck Medley,* Columbia 4622 (vintage 78).

THIGPEN, E. *The Essence of Brushes,* (video), Interworld Music, San Francisco, CA, USA.

UDOW, M. *Four Chamber Percussion Works,* The University of Michigan School of Music, Ann Arbor, Michigan, USA.

VINTAGE DRUMS (video) Cook's Music, PO Box 6 Alma, Michigan USA

Footnote: In view of the constant issuing of further percussion literature, it is suggested that reference is made to the current catalogues of international publishers and dealers; for example, The Steve Weiss Catalogue of Percussion Material (reputedly over 5,000 references); the comprehensive (membership issued) pariodicals of The Percussive Arts Society of America, Box 25, Lawton OK 73502 USA, and catalogue of Drums Unlimited Inc. 4928 Saint Elmo Avenue, Bethesda, Maryland 20814 USA.

Glossary of Principal Terms

English	Italian	French	German	Russian Transliteration
Antique cymbals	Crotali	Crotales	Antiken Zimbeln	Drévnie Tarélki
Anvil	Incudine	Enclume	Amboss	Nakovál 'nya
At the edge	sul bordo	au bord	am Rand	U óbrucha
Bass drum	Gran cassa	Grosse caisse	Grosse Trommel	Bol 'shói barabán
Bells – tubular (Chimes)	Campane Campanelle	Cloches	Glocken	Trúbchatye kolokolá
Bongos	Bongos	Bongos	Bongos	Bóngos
Brush (wire)	Spazzola Scovolo di fil di ferro	Brosse en fil de métal Balai métallique	Stahlbürste Drahtbürste	Metëlochka
Castanets	Castagnette Nacchere	Castagnettes	Kastagnetten	Kastan'éty
Chains	Catene	Chaînes	Ketten	Tsépi
Claves	Claves	Claves	Claves	Kláves
Covered (muffled)	Coperto Coperti (plural)	Couvert (e) Couvertes (plur.) (Voilé)	Bedeckt Gedämpft	S surdínoi
Cowbell	Cencerro (Campanaccio)	Sonnaille Cloche à vache	Almenglocke Kuhglocke (Schelle) Heerdenglocke	Bubénchik koróv
Cymbals	Piatti Cinelli	Cymbales	Becken Tellern	Tarélki
Cymbal (suspended)	Piatto sospeso	Cymbale suspendue	Becken hängend	Podvéshennaya tarélka
Dampen (short)	Secco	Étouffé Sec	Dämpfen	Súkho
Drum	Tamburo	Tambour	Trommel	Barabán
Glockenspiel	Campanelli	Jeu de timbres (Timbres)	Glockenspiel	Kolokól 'chiki
Gong	Gong	Gong	Gong	Gong
Jingles	Sonagli	Grelots	Schellen	Bubentsý
Kettledrums	Timpani	Timbales	Pauken Kesselpauken	Litávry

Appendix 6

English	Italian	French	German	Russian Transliteration
Let ring	Lasciare vibrare	Laissez vibrer	Klingen lassen	Ostávit' zvuchát'
Maracas	Maracas	Maracas	Maracas	Marákas
Marimba	Marimba	Marimba	Marimba (phon)	Marímba
Military side drum	Tamburo militare	Tambour militaire	Militärtrommel	Voénnyi Barabán
Percussion	Percussione	Percussion	Schlagwerk	Udárnye instruménty
Ratchet	Raganella	Crécelle	Ratsche, Knarre	Treschotka
Rattle	Nacchere (pl.)	Cliquet, Hochet	Rassel, Schnarre	Pogremúshka
Side drum	Tamburo	Caisse claire	Kleine Trommel	Mályi Barabán
Snare drum	„	„	„	„
Stick	Bacchetta	Baguette Mailloche	Schlagel Stock	Pálka, Pálochka
Strike (beat)	Colpite	Frappez (Blouser – to beat)	Schlage	Udárit'
Switch	Verga	Verge	Rute (Ruthe)	Metlá
Tabor	Tamburo di Provenza	Tambourin de Provence	Tambourin	Provansál'skii barabán
Tambourine	Tamburino Tamburo basco Tamburello	Tambour de Basque	Tamburin Schellentrommel	Tamburín
Tam-tam	Tam-tam	Tam-tam	Tam-tam	Tam-tam
Tenor drum	Tamburo rullante	Caisse roulante	Rührtrommel Wirbeltrommel	Tsilindrícheskii barabán
Tom tom	Tom tom	Tom tom	Tom tom	Tom tom
Triangle	Triangolo	Triangle	Triangel	Treugol'nik
Vibraphone	Vibrafono	Vibraphone	Vibraphon	Vibrafón
Whip	Frusta Flagello	Fouet	Holzklapper Peitsche	Knut
Wood block	Cassa di legno	Bloc de bois	Holztrommel	Derevyánnaya Koróbochka
Xylophone	Silofono	Xylophone	Xylophon	Ksilofón

General Index

(See glossary for general foreign names of instruments)

Aburukuwa, 61
Acetabulum, -a, 174, 180
Acme clicker, 387
Adapu, 159
Adiophone, 311
Adufé, 450
Aeoliphone, 394
Afochê, 450
African drumming techniques, 66–8
Aghāti, 134
Aiuton, 311
Alal, 159
Alarm bell in score, 291
Al'ud, 190
Aluminium harp, 477
Aluminophone, 399 n. 1
Ambira, 52, 72, 85 n. 2
Amboss, 392
Anglice, 256
Angkloeng, 104–6, 477
Angklung, 105
Anvil, -s, 189, 291, 392, 424, 432–3; composers and works using, 392–3; Henry Wood's personal, 392 n. 2; score for eighteen, 295; substitutes, 392
Apentemma, 61
Armonica (revolving glasses), 310
Ass, jawbone of, 450

Atabal, 186
Atambor, 175, 185, 205
Atari-gane, 129
Atumpan, 52, 61
Aulos, 323
Avanaddha vādyas, 135
Avant-garde compositions, abuse greets, 440
Ayotl, 445

Bacchette da legno, 331; di triangolo, 338; ord, 331; di ferro, 367
Bagpipes, 190, 224, 305
Bacchette, Baguettes, etc., *see glossary*
Baguettes en bois, 336; garnies, 283 n. 2
Balag, 159
Balloon, bursting, 398
Bamboo, primitive instruments from, 43, 54, 106; resonators, 102
Bambus, 64–5, 445
Bāmyā, 137, 385 n. 2
Banjo, 342, 458
Basle drumming, 210–11, 305, 375
Bass drum, 55, 62 n. 3, 84, 190, 197, 205, 260–261, 265, 267, 281–2, 284–5, 298, 302–4, 306, 314, 321, 330, 337, 367–9, 421, 432, 454; cymbals and, 368; foot-pedal operated, 416, 473; modern, 367–9; patents, 473; range of sticks for, 367; tampon, tremolo, 368

Index of Names and Works

Index of Names and Works

Index of Names and Works

Index of Names and Works

FINIS

OTHER MUSIC TITLES AVAILABLE FROM THE BOLD STRUMMER LTD.

GUITAR

THE AMP BOOK: A Guitarist's Inroductory Guide to Tube Amplifiers *by Donald Brosnac.*

ANIMAL MAGNETISM FOR MUSICIANS: Making a Bass Guitar and Pickup from Scratch *by Erno Zwaan.*

ANTHOLOGY OF FLAMENCO FALSETAS *collected by Ray Mitchell.*

ANTONIO DE TORRES: Guitar Maker — His Life and Work *by José Romanillos. Fwd. by Julian Bream.*

THE ART OF FLAMENCO *by D. E. Pohren.*

THE ART OF PRACTICING *by Alice Arzt.*

CLASSIC GUITAR CONSTRUCTION *by Irving Sloane.*

THE DEVELOPMENT OF THE MODERN GUITAR *by John Huber.*

THE FENDER GUITAR *by Ken Achard.*

THE GIBSON GUITAR FROM 1950 *by Ian C. Bishop. 2 vols.*

THE GUITAR: From the Renaissance to the Present Day, REISSUE *by Harvey Turnbull.*

GUITAR HISTORY: Volume 1 — Guitars Made by the Fender Company *by Donald Brosnac.*

GUITAR HISTORY: Volume 2 — Gibson SGs *by John Bulli.*

GUITAR HISTORY: Volume 3 — Gibson Catalogs of the Sixties *edited by Richard Hetrick.*

GUITAR HISTORY: Volume 4 — The Vox Story *by David Peters & Dick Denney.*

GUITAR REPAIR: A Manual of Repair for Guitars and Fretted Instruments *by Irving Sloane.*

GUITAR TRADER' VINTAGE GUITAR BULLETIN. 6 vols.

THE HISTORY AND DEVELOPMENT OF THE AMERICAN GUITAR *by Ken Achard.*

AN INTRODUCTION TO SCIENTIFIC GUITAR DESIGN *by Donald Brosnac.*

LEFT HANDED GUITAR *by Nicholas Clarke.*

LIVES AND LEGENDS OF FLAMENCO, 2ND EDITION *by D. E. Pohren.*

MANUAL OF GUITAR TECHNOLOGY: The History and Technology of Plucked String Instruments *by Franz Jahnel. English vers. by Dr. J. C. Harvey*

MAKING MUSIC SERIES: THE GURU'S GUITAR GUIDE *by Tony Bacon & Paul Day.* MAKING 4-TRACK MUSIC *by John Peel.* WHAT BASS, 2ND EDITION *by Tony Bacon & Laurence Canty.* WHAT DRUM, 2ND EDITION *by Geoff Nicholls & Andy Duncan.* WHAT GUITAR: The Making Music Guide to Buying Your Electric Six String, 3RD EDITION. WHAT'S MIDI, 2ND EDITION *by Andy Honeybone et al.*

THE NATURAL CLASSICAL GUITAR, REISSUE *by Lee F. Ryan.*

PACO DE LUCÍA AND FAMILY: The Master Plan *by D. E. Pohren.*

THE RIOPLATENSE GUITAR *by Rick Pinnell.*

THE SEGOVIA TECHNIQUE, REISSUE *by Vladimir Bobri.*

THE SOUND OF ROCK: A History of Marshall Valve Guitar Amplifiers *by Mike Doyle.*

THE STEEL STRING GUITAR: Construction and Repair, UPDATED EDITION *by David Russell Young.*

STEEL STRING GUITAR CONSTRUCTION *by Irving Sloane.*

A WAY OF LIFE, REISSUE *by D. E. Pohren.*

THE WELL-TEMPERED GUITAR, ENLARGED ED. *by Nicholas Clarke.*

OTHER MUSIC TITLES AVAILABLE FROM THE BOLD STRUMMER LTD.

OTHER MUSIC TITLES AVAILABLE FROM THE BOLD STRUMMER LTD.

FLUTE, REISSUE *by James Galway*

GOGOLIAN INTERLUDES; Gogol's Story "Christmas Eve" as the Subject of the Operas by Tchaikovsky and Rimsky-Korsakov *by Philip Taylor.*

THE MUSICAL INSTRUMENT COLLECTOR, REVISED EDITION *by J. Robert Willcutt & Kenneth R. Ball.*

A MUSICIAN'S GUIDE TO COPYRIGHT AND PUBLISHING, ENL. EDITION *by Willis Wager.*

MUSICOLOGY IN PRACTICE: Collected Essays by Denis Stevens *edited by Thomas P. Lewis.* Vol. 1: 1948-1970. Vol. 2: 1971-1990.

MY VIOLA AND I, REISSUE *by Lionel Tertis.*

THE NUTLEY PAPERS: A Fresh Look at the Titans of Music (humor) *by James Billings.*

PEACE SONGS *compiled & edited by John Jordan.*

PERCUSSION INSTRUMENTS AND THEIR HISTORY, REV. EDITION *by James Blades.*

THE PRO/AM BOOK OF MUSIC AND MYTHOLOGY *compiled, edited & with commentaries by Thomas P. Lewis.* 3 vols.

THE PRO/AM GUIDE TO U. S. BOOKS ABOUT MUSIC: Annotated Guide to Current & Backlist Titles *edited by Thomas P. Lewis.* 2 vols.

SKETCHES FROM MY LIFE *by Natalia Sats.*

VIOLIN AND VIOLA, REISSUE *by Yehudi Menuhin & William Primrose, with Denis Stevens.*

PERFORMANCE PRACTICE / "HOW-TO" INSTRUCTIONAL

GUIDE TO THE PRACTICAL STUDY OF HARMONY *by Peter Il'ich Tchaikovsky.*

HOW TO SELECT A BOW FOR VIOLIN FAMILY INSTRUMENTS *by Balthasar Planta.*

IMAGINATIONS: Tuneful Fun and Recital Pieces to Expand Early Grade Harp Skills *by Doris Davidson.*

THE JOY OF ORNAMENTATION: Being Giovanni Luca Conforto's *Treatise on Ornamentation* (Rome, 1593) *with a Preface by Sir Yehudi Menuhin and an Introduction by Denis Stevens.*

MAKING MUSICAL INSTRUMENTS *by Irving Sloane.*

THE MUSICIAN'S GUIDE TO MAPPING: A New Way to Learn Music *by Rebecca P. Shockley.*

THE MUSICIANS' THEORY BOOK: Reference to Fundamentals, Harmony, Counterpoint, Fugue and Form *by Asger Hamerik.*

ON BEYOND C *(Davidson):* see PIANO, below.

THE STUDENT'S DICTIONARY OF MUSICAL TERMS.

TENSIONS IN THE PERFORMANCE OF MUSIC: A Symposium, REVISED & EXTENDED EDITION *edited by Carola Grindea. Fwd. by Yehudi Menuhin.*

THE VIOLIN: Precepts and Observations *by Sourene Arakelian.*

OTHER MUSIC TITLES AVAILABLE FROM THE BOLD STRUMMER LTD.

PIANO/HARPSICHORD

THE ANATOMY OF A NEW YORK DEBUT RECITAL *by Carol Montparker.*

AT THE PIANO WITH FAURÉ, REISSUE *by Marguerite Long.*

EUROPEAN PIANO ATLAS *by H. K. Herzog.*

FRENCH PIANISM: An Historical Perspective *by Charles Timbrell.*

GLOSSARY OF HARPSICHORD TERMS *by Susanne Costa.*

KENTNER: A Symposium *edited by Harold Taylor. Fwd. by Yehudi Menuhin.*

LIPATTI *by Dragos Tanasescu & Grigore Bargauanu.*

ON BEYOND C: Tuneful Fun in Many Keys to Expand Early Grade Piano Skills *by Doris Davidson.*

A PIANIST'S GUIDE TO PRACTISING *by Zelda Bock.*

THE PIANIST'S TALENT *by Harold Taylor. Fwd. by John Ogdon.*

PIANO, REISSUE *by Louis Kentner.*

THE PIANO AND HOW TO CARE FOR IT *by Otto Funke.*

THE PIANO HAMMER *by Walter Pfeifer.*

PIANO NOMENCLATURE, 2ND EDITION *by Nikolaus Schimmel & H. K. Herzog.*

RAVEL ACCORDING TO RAVEL *by Vlado Perlemuter & Hélène Jouran-Morhange.*

SCHUBERT'S MUSIC FOR PIANO FOUR-HANDS *by Dallas Weekly & Nancy Arganbright.*

TECHNIQUE OF PIANO PLAYING, 5TH EDITION *by József Gát.*

THE TUNING OF MY HARPSICHORD *by Herbert Anton Kellner.*

See also above: ALKAN *(Smith)* — LISZT AND HIS COUNTRY *(Legnány)* — PERCY GRAINGER *(Dorum)* — PERCY GRAINGER *(Simon)* — RONALD STEVENSON *(MacDonald)* — SOURCE GUIDE TO THE MUSIC OF PERCY GRAINGER *(Lewis)* — TENSIONS IN THE PERFORMANCE OF MUSIC *(Grindea)*